The field of Christian counseling continues to grow and expand at a rapid pace. Every day we look for insights and tools to help expand our work with lost, confused, broken, wounded, or exploited people. This is a real gift to the profession. Each chapter in *Counseling Techniques* translates theory into practice through effective and practical discussion of strategies, intervention, and techniques that are grounded in and supported by theory and research. The twenty-eight chapters are also jam-packed with conceptual, clinical, theoretical, and theological resources. Be sure to add this book to your library!

Tim Clinton, EdD, LPC, LMFT, BCPCC, President,
American Association of Christian Counselors

Counseling Techniques is a comprehensive resource that will be of great benefit to students and practitioners alike. Christian clinicians and those who train them will be indebted to John Thomas and the array of contributors who have offered us such a wealth of knowledge and practical direction.

Mark A. Yarhouse, PsyD, Professor of Psychology and
Rosemarie S. Hughes Endowed Chair, Regent University

Counseling Techniques is a valuable resource for all Christian counselors and psychotherapists. The chapters are authored by the leading experts in the field, and Dr. Thomas brings the volume together well with a winsome and wise introduction where he situates strategies, interventions, and techniques in the broader context of effective counseling.

Mark R. McMinn, PhD, ABPP, Professor of Psychology,
George Fox University

All practitioners are better with some tools than others. This book prepares students and newer counselors with an enlarged toolkit and provides wisdom on how to use the tools you they may not be as familiar with. The range of strategies, interventions, and techniques is impressive, as are the counseling professionals presenting them.

Marshall Shelley, Director of the Doctor of
Ministry program, Denver Seminary

Counseling Techniques, edited by John C. Thomas, is an excellent and very useful compendium of clinical strategies, interventions, and techniques for Christian counselors in helping a wide variety of clients. There are eleven chapters on theory-based strategies, four on population-based strategies, and twelve on clinical issue-based strategies. I highly recommend this practical resource as must reading for Christian counselors and others involved in people-helping.

Rev. Siang-Yang Tan, PhD, Professor of Psychology, Fuller
Theological Seminary; Senior Pastor, First Evangelical Church Glendale;
author, *Counseling and Psychotherapy: A Christian Perspective*

I found *Counseling Techniques* to be erudite, comprehensive, practical and innovative. I expect the text to become an invaluable resource to clinicians, supervisors, and counselor educators. It will take its place among the truly outstanding books in the realms of clinical training, supervision, and practice. It is a book that will be kept within arm's reach both literally and figuratively. It may be placed on a shelf, but it will not collect dust.

James Trozer, PhD, Professor, Senior Lecturer, Granite State College; retired psychologist and marriage and family counselor

With ever-changing cultural trends and more updated research in the field, the need for a counseling-techniques book that marries the data with the truth of Scripture cannot be understated. Dr. John Thomas carefully selects the most respected practitioners in the field to provide a comprehensive yet-easy-to-read manual for today's counseling student. I know this because I personally sat under Dr. Thomas and many of the authors in this book as a student myself. You can rest assured that not only are you getting the best of scholarly wisdom, you're getting experts who genuinely care for the human condition. This is a must-have book for every Christian counselor and counseling student in the twenty-first century.

Joshua Straub, PhD, Marriage and Family Strategist, LifeWay Christian Resources; author, *Safe House: How Emotional Safety is the Key to Raising Kids Who Live, Love, and Lead Well*

Counseling Techniques provides novice and advanced students as well as practicing psychotherapists with detailed information on clinical techniques stemming from a diversity of counseling theories. Leading Christian experts in collaboration with Dr. John Thomas skillfully integrate theory, research, practice, and Christian thought in a resourceful text for the counseling community.

John J. S. Harrichand, PhD, Assistant Professor of Counselor Education, The College of Brockport, State University of New York

Counseling Techniques blends theological perspective, counseling strategies, and learned wisdom from numerous seasoned practitioners. Accessible to counselors at all skill levels, the contributors deliver practical insight as well as consolidate useful techniques into a valuable reference resource.

Matthew K. Elliott, PhD candidate, Southern Baptist Theological Seminary, and church counselor

Counseling
Techniques

ALSO BY JOHN C. THOMAS

Therapeutic Expidition: Equipping the Christian Counselor
for the Journey (John C. Thomas and Lisa Sosin)

What's Good about Feeling Bad? Finding Purpose and a Path
through Your Pain (John C. Thomas and Gary Habermas)

Enduring Your Season of Suffering
(John C. Thomas and Gary Habermas)

Counseling Techniques

A Comprehensive Resource
for Christian Counselors

John C. Thomas, PhD,
PhD, General Editor

ZONDERVAN®

ZONDERVAN

Counseling Techniques
Copyright © 2018 by John C. Thomas

This title is also available as a Zondervan ebook.

Requests for information should be addressed to:
Zondervan, *3900 Sparks Dr. SE, Grand Rapids, Michigan 49546*

ISBN 978-0-310-52944-6

In memory of my parents,
who, in spite of their brokenness,
did more for me than I will ever know.
Thank you both
for leaving fingerprints of grace
and love on me.

Contents

PART 3: CLINICAL ISSUE–BASED STRATEGIES

Acknowledgments

This book is the culmination of dreams and ideas to put forth a practical, conversational, and professional book that presents strategies, interventions, and techniques that work with a multitude of clinical issues. The creation of this book is the result of the work of many dedicated and encouraging individuals. Having my name on the cover is humbling and is a privilege when so many others have contributed to its completion in various ways.

First and foremost, I want to express my gratitude to Zondervan for taking a risk on me and providing me a platform to voice my say. Zondervan has been a delight to work with in the editing, designing, and marketing of this book. My editor, Madison Trammel, has especially been a joy to work with and a fountain of feedback and stimulation, without which this project would have been impossible. He has been extraordinarily patient with me, tolerating all the inconveniences the completion of this book has caused. I was also blessed similarly by the assistance of Bob Hudson of Zondervan, who carried the project through to completion. Finally, Zondervan blessed me with an incredible copy editor, Laura Weller, whose attention to detail is extraordinary.

I owe a debt of gratitude for the assistance of those whose contributions helped me achieve this milestone. Tim Sosin, thank you for volunteering to be my assistant. You worked tirelessly in coordinating the project, communicating with contributors, and keeping me from insanity. Chelsea Breiholz, your willing and humble spirit coupled with invaluable comments and suggestions not only blessed me but will also bless those who use this book. Nils Juarez Palma, your contributions to this project have been meaningful to me. And Dr. David Jenkins, I am very appreciative of your providing me with insightful thoughts.

A special friendship has developed out of this project. I have personally been enriched by Dr. Fred DiBlasio. Fred, your goodwill, amicable spirit, and calming presence provided enjoyment and encouragement. I look forward to our new relationship growing.

Where would any of us be without prayer support? This project would have been unbearable without the pledges of a cadre of praying brothers and sisters in Christ. They provided both shade from the oppressive heat of this project and sunshine to move forward. Among those people are my LifeGroup, Live with Purpose, and family members whose prayers girded me through obstacles and frustrations.

A host of students and friends provided invaluable help with the indexing of this enormous manuscript. I wish to acknowledge each of them for rising to the occasion to bear my burden: Krista Clifton, Mary Katie Blevins, Nils Juarez Palma, Kay Griffith, Donna Fitch, Katie Thomas, Kelly Carapezza, Yatpor Lau, Dr. Sally Goh, Eric Kananen, Linda Kananen, Cayli Snipes, Patrice Parkinson, Bradleigh Thomassian, Yulia Gray, Kevin King, Dr. Patricia Kimball, Katie Thomas, and Denise Thomas.

I would not have embarked on this venture without the wholehearted support of my wife, Denise. Throughout our marriage she has never wavered in encouraging me to pursue my aims. I've also benefited by the warm presence of my three dogs: Eli, Buster, and Nellie. Their companionship, snuggling, and playfulness furnished enjoyable respite during writing blocks and wearisome editing.

A final expression of heartfelt gratitude goes to my Lord and Savior, Jesus Christ. He provides a firm foundation and sustenance for my life. He has blessed me beyond my ability and, I know, will use this work to further the kingdom and continue his mission of binding the brokenhearted and setting the captives free.

Truly, I am among all men most richly blessed.

John C. Thomas
Lynchburg, Virginia
February 19, 2018

CHAPTER 1

Laying the Groundwork

JOHN C. THOMAS, PHD, PHD

The Spirit of the Lord is upon me; he has appointed me
to preach Good News to the poor; he has sent me to heal
the brokenhearted and to announce that captives shall
be released and the blind shall see, that the downtrodden
shall be freed from their oppressors, and that God is
ready to give blessings to all who come to him.

LUKE 4:18–19 TLB

As a counselor educator and clinical supervisor, I've heard a recurring request from students and supervisees: "How do I _____?" Novice counselors want a how-to description to apply a strategy, intervention, or technique (SIT) to therapeutic situations. Experienced counselors who attend clinical workshops want to see SITs taught and enacted. As Bandura's (1977) research affirmed, we learn by observing those we consider models of clinical prowess.

As the field of counseling continues to grow and develop, the diversity and complexity of SITs also progresses. Concomitantly, innovative and effective SITs have been developed to leverage the process of change and promote soul transformation. While many of these SITs are easy to implement, others require a sufficient knowledge of the theory to effectively employ.

The pursuit of a graduate degree launches us into a new frontier of providing professional services to clients. Though supervised throughout the residency requirements of our states, we can collect only a selective sampling of SITs during that time. This book seeks to address that space between training and practice and to prepare students with a wider range of ideas prior to the start of their professional career. Furthermore, this book provides the experienced clinician with opportunities to learn and grow. It is a useful resource for the novice and seasoned counselor.

Consider the scenario wherein numerous leading Christian mental health clinicians agree to provide their expert supervision or consultation to develop your counseling prowess. Through this improbable gift, you are afforded the opportunity to learn how they interact with particular clientele and client issues. You are able to digest the intricacies of their counseling theory, conceptualization, and use of SITs. Most importantly, you gain understanding of how they integrate the Christian worldview into their clinical work both explicitly and tacitly. Imagine what you could take away from that privilege and incorporate into your own work to enhance your therapeutic outcomes.

Thanks to the graciousness of these seasoned Christian counselors, you gain the opportunity to ingest their knowledge, skill, and experience. The chapters in this volume bring together wisdom and insight from hundreds of years of clinical experience. Throughout the book you will absorb theoretical and relevant underpinnings for specific classes of SITs, learn about effective SITs used with their clients, read how their knowledge and SITs apply to relevant case studies, and even peer through the office door to discover clinical dialogue. Skilled in their areas of expertise, these contributors offer a treasure chest of understanding and tools.

Because counseling is a complex enterprise with seemingly infinite nuances, every therapist can grow—and needs to grow—in their work. For this book to be useful, you must apprehend their concepts, be receptive to them, and believe that you can discover new ways of conducting therapy. No matter where you are on your professional journey, the experiences of colleagues and experts in the field can benefit you. This notion has been articulated by Jeffrey Kottler (2012): "These [counselors] are constantly questioning what they do and why, being brutally honest with themselves about their work and its outcomes. . . . They are always soliciting feedback from their clients and colleagues, begging for the most frank assessments about what is working and what is not. Most of all, they are often so humble that they don't seek attention or the limelight but just quietly go about their extraordinary commitment to helping others" (as cited in Shallcross, 2012).

Over the course of my editing, I've incorporated a number of SITs into my own clinical practice. I told one of the contributors that I am the first to have profited from this project. As they say in Alcoholics Anonymous, people must be "humble, open, and willing" (HOW) to change.

Moreover, mastering particular SITs requires repetition and quality feedback through clinical supervision or consultation. While supervision is a vital method for learning how to apply or improve clinical skill, it isn't always practical or affordable. Nevertheless, the knowledge and expertise of accomplished clinicians in this volume provide a treasure chest of ideas and strategies to skillfully address sundry clinical presentations.

THE TECHNIQUE CONTROVERSY

Most counselors advocate for the judicious use of interventions and techniques, believing that they are vital to therapeutic effectiveness (e.g., J. S. Beck, 2011; Burns, 2008; Conte, 2009; Corey, 2005; Ellis & MacLaren, 2005; Leahy, 2003, 2015; Satir, 1987; Thompson, 2003). Conte (2009), for instance, captures both the benefits and beauty of using SITs: "If theoretical orientations constitute the canvases of therapy, then techniques are the brushes that paint counselors' work into something memorable for clients" (p. 1). When the art (SITs and skills) and science (theories) of counseling are merged in a masterful way, clients experience the transforming impact of the work. While many of these clinical necessities are taught in graduate programs, others are acquired and developed through clinical practice experiences. Once a competence has developed, practitioners can naturally exhibit basic counseling skills, establish goals, construct treatment plans, and focus a session. Such therapists have self-awareness, monitor potential countertransference while using it therapeutically, and are in tune with God's leading.

However, the use of interventions and techniques in counseling is not without dispute. Other theorists and clinicians oppose or caution the use of SITs (e.g., Elkins, 2007, 2009; Mahrer, 2004; Mozdzierz & Greenblatt, 1994; Orlinsky, 2010; Schneider & Krug, 2010). Unsurprisingly, existential psychotherapist Yalom (2003) asserts that counseling is a relationally driven enterprise rather than theory or technique driven. For instance, Yalom believes that the healing strategy is entering into a close relationship with clients. Consistent with existential thought, it might be fair to say that Buber (2010) would consider counseling to be an "I-Thou" experience, while an "I-it" experience is more closely aligned with SITs.

A newer train of thought is that of determining the best approach based on practice-based evidence (Miller, Duncan, & Hubble, 2004). Advocates are neither for nor against the use of SITs. Evidence-based practice is unpacked in chapter 2. Regardless of one's viewpoint on SITs, fostering a therapeutic relationship always requires the use of a SIT. Focusing on the therapeutic relationship as the vehicle of client change and healing is using a SIT. Being authentic, though it springs from the person of the therapist's own growth, is at its core a strategy in counseling practice. I contend that the use of SITs is critical to produce true and lasting change in clients. When a therapist is attuned with the client in such a way that the client feels cared for and accepted, the freedom to choose the most effective and appropriate SITs for addressing relevant client issues is apparent.

TECHNIQUES AND TARGETS

SITs and counseling skills are arrows used to hit an identified target (Thomas & Sosin, 2011). If you are aiming at the wrong target, it doesn't matter how well you choose and employ a SIT; it will be misguided and ineffective. Even if you have identified the right target but poorly align the arrow, the outcome is a miss. What are some identifiable targets?

SITs often target problematic emotional processes. Barlow and colleagues (Barlow et al., 2011) have identified eight protocols for treating emotional disorders that span the entire mental health system: (1) motivational enhancement, (2) understanding emotions and monitoring and tracking emotional responses, (3) emotional awareness, (4) cognitive appraisal and reappraisal, (5) emotional avoidance, (6) emotionally driven behavior, (7) awareness and tolerance of physical sensations, and (8) interoceptive and simultaneous emotional exposure. These protocols, or targets if you will, can have an array of SITs to address them.

An additional target is the spiritual dimension. Hook, Worthington, Aten, and Johnson (2013) proposed that mental health practitioners, specifically Christian counselors, should be able to use various techniques "to facilitate deep-level sanctifying transformation in clients' relationships with God, others, and themselves" (p. 123). While Christian counselors often work with non-Christians, an integrative approach can be expressed in how you exemplify Christ-incarnate with the client—for example, being present and counseling in such a way that the client witnesses the adorable attributes (e.g., love, gentleness, longsuffering) of God as evidenced in the person of Jesus Christ embodied in you and your clinical work (Thomas & Sosin, 2011). The heart of a Christian counselor is to see transformation at all levels in their clients—not just in psychological outcomes but in God-centric outcomes as well.

The bottom line is that the measuring stick for counseling efficacy is client outcome, which is defined *ultimately* by the client (Thomas & Sosin, 2011). Client outcome can include whether the client feels less distressed, feels more in control, has improved relationships, possesses a better sense of self, and is no longer impaired, deviant, dangerous, or dysfunctional. Thus, skill development aids in implementing strategies and employing techniques and processes that facilitate effective change in the lives of clients.

STRATEGIES, INTERVENTIONS, AND TECHNIQUES

Most people do not differentiate between the terms *technique*, *strategy*, and *intervention*. Though the terms are often used interchangeably without violating the therapeutic "gospel," they do represent different aspects of clinical work. Strategies are "modi operandi," or plans of action customized to meet a particular goal. In essence, they are a procedural plan to get from point A to point B (Cormier & Cormier, 1985); they represent the overall target, or the forest instead of the trees. Interventions, on the other hand, refer to a clinician's aim at disrupting and/or alleviating client problems. To further our analogy, interventions represent the trees within the forest or a specific arrow to fire at the chosen target. I consider techniques as the branches on the tree or aiming for the bull's-eye. In sum, Thompson (2003) offers a slightly different perspective of the terms: "Fundamentally, a counseling technique is presented as a strategy. A strategy is an intervention. An intervention is a counselor or therapist's intention to eliminate or illuminate a self-defeating behavior" (p. xi).

The starting place is to formulate a path forward that addresses the client's concerns and issues. Then the counselor can customize the strategies based on the assessment data and the desired outcomes or targets. Interventions are best understood as functions of goals and outcomes. In other words, an intervention is determined for each concern or issue in the treatment plan that is aimed at the client's targets. Though techniques can be linked to theory, they are the actual therapeutic action that corresponds to an intervention and strategy.

Figure 1.1 illustrates the differences between strategy, technique, and intervention. Other strategies would include motivational interviewing, systemic work, behavior modification, self-awareness, sobriety, normalizing, referral for psychiatric evaluation, reducing frequency of maladaptive behaviors, taking a sexual history, and even spiritual growth. After settling on the strategy, the basis is set for selecting an intervention, such as addressing core beliefs. Others could include considering evidence for a belief, assigning homework, putting a filter on one's computer, and learning self-enhancement training. Finally, examples of techniques include learning about distorted beliefs, using the cognitive downward arrow, or using the antecedent-belief-consequence model (ABC). Other techniques that are associated with various strategies and interventions could

include systematic desensitization, self-monitoring, reframing, cognitive restructuring, relaxation training, response prevention, sculpting, enactment, the empty chair, genogram, sensate focus, and a host of others.

A prerequisite of an effective intervention or technique is timing. Cormier and Cormier (1985) suggested five criteria to consider prior to implementing SITs: (1) the therapeutic relationship is established, (2) the problem has been thoroughly assessed, (3) goals have been mutually agreed upon, (4) the client is ready and committed to change, and (5) baseline measures have been created. For example, if a client is uncertain of whether to deal with a problem, a therapeutic strategy might be to address client readiness. The intervention might be to address a discrepancy between the client's future desires and current behavior, and the technique might be to side with the negative (explore motivational interviewing for deeper understanding of these concepts).

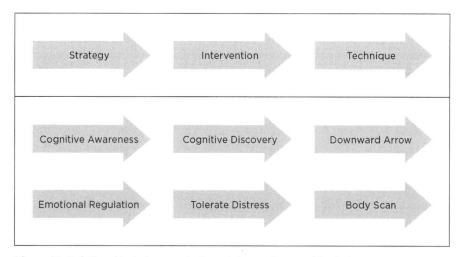

Figure 1.1. Relationship between strategy, intervention, and technique

Because client problems are multi-dimensional, are controlled by diverse variables, and are the targets of change, treatment is often implemented in combination. Recall the famous question by Paul (1967): "Which treatment strategy or combination of strategies will be most effective for the client with these desired outcomes?" (p. 111). In sum, it is necessary to select and sequence a variety of strategies, interventions, and techniques to address the complexity and range of problems presented by a single client.

TECHNIQUES AND THE PERSON OF THE COUNSELOR

In this profession, the person of the counselor is the instrument and the tool by which therapy happens (Thomas & Sosin, 2011). Corey (2005) contends that the person of the counselor is the main technique of counseling. When it is used, everything about the therapist is dynamically present in everything that occurs in the session. Famed family therapist Virginia Satir (1987) said, "Therapy is a deeply intimate and vulnerable experience, requiring sensitivity to one's own state of being as well as to that of the other. It is the meeting of the deepest self of the therapist with the deepest self of the patient" (p. 17). Raines (1996) asserts that when we meet people who have suffered "malignant deprivations and losses . . . only the provision of an authentic person will suffice" (p. 373).

While the counseling profession does attract healthy individuals, it also has a notorious reputation of being a magnet for the impaired and unhealthy (Thomas & Sosin, 2011). Diane Langberg eloquently articulated this truth:

> If it is true that those who seek us out are broken, needy, and vulnerable, and if it is true that you and I are called by God to shepherd such people, then we must learn how to shepherd fitly. Furthermore, if it is true that such a task is so serious and awesome because of its potential impact for good or evil in the lives of others, and if it is also true that shepherding selfishly and unfitly grieves the God who has called us, then we had better learn to counsel according to the Master's own heart. (as cited in Clinton & Oschlager, 2002, p. 75)

Because of this fact, many counselors harm rather than help. Whereas general ethical codes hold that the foundation of the code is to do no harm, as Christians our foundational ethic is to love as Christ loves. That mandate necessitates careful monitoring of our own hearts.

The effectiveness of counseling hinges on the person of the counselor (Wampold, 2001) and his or her ability to draw from God. The apostle Paul scribed in his letter to the Corinthian congregation: "Our conscience testifies that we have conducted ourselves . . . in our relations with you, with integrity and godly sincerity" (2 Cor. 1:12). Wisdom, compassion, and integrity cannot be taught in a classroom, seminar, or book. Openness and curiosity are essential to cultivate self-awareness.

Therapeutic skill is important, but the person of the therapist subsumes any ability, theory, or technique (Thomas & Sosin, 2011). If honoring God through your work is your desire, then you will not become complacent where you are; rather, you will continue to press toward excellence (cf. Phil. 3:13–14; Col. 3:23). Be committed to a life of spiritual and psychological growth. The past is the blueprint for a person's present and future life. It will dictate one's life unless that person intentionally chooses to do something about it. Just as we advocate for clients in their struggles, we must choose to face our own issues (Thomas & Sosin, 2011). If lack of spiritual vigor characterizes your heart, seek renewal.

One indication that the person of the counselor is not being sufficiently emphasized is when the therapist fails to communicate his or her values. Therapist values will be manifest in and through the work of and approach toward counseling. Seasoned therapists creatively use strategies, interventions, and techniques that are consistent with their value system, personality, theory, and the client's issues (Thomas & Sosin, 2011). Giving novice counselors a how-to list that covers every scenario is simply not possible. But if I had to try, the person of the counselor would be at the top. Crabb (1977) aptly described it this way: "Counselors who value technique above conviction and theory above character will not adequately shepherd their clients" (p. 15). Because we are the tool with which God engages our clients, we must be well-maintained three-dimensionally—body, soul, and spirit. A dull machete cuts very little.

STRATEGIES, INTERVENTIONS, TECHNIQUES, THEORY, AND SCHOOLISM

Even though techniques emerged out of particular schools of counseling (e.g., Gestalt, Adlerian, Jungian, classical behaviorism), most are applicable to clinical situations regardless of the school. Colleague Dr. Gary Sibcy (personal communication, October 14, 2016) says that schoolism is dead. He coined the term *schoolism* to denote the idea that one theoretical system is correct and all other systems are incorrect, inferior, and/or irrelevant. Sibcy says that trans-theoretical integration and metatheory as well as various forms of eclecticism have replaced schoolism. Presently the view that different modalities provide a separate level of analysis or lens into human functioning is a preferred framework. This shift is toward understanding how disorders/spectrums of problems develop and maintain across various levels of functioning (cognitive, behavioral, emotional, interpersonal/social, and even spiritual).

Consequently, several meta-theories such as developmental psychopathology and interpersonal neurobiology have been created. The evidence-based treatment (EBT) movement has developed out of and parallel to this evolution of theory, promoted by experts such as Barlow, Linehan, and McCullough. Clinicians are to consider the spectrum of emotional disorders and, based on the current "science" about those disorders, develop unified treatment protocols or treatment packages that target specific processes that underlie the broad range of emotional disorders that play a role in the maintenance of the problematic emotions. Treatment packages draw from a variety of treatment approaches (e.g., cognitive, behavioral, emotional, relational) or theoretical perspectives (e.g., emotional-focused therapy, cognitive behavioral therapy, Adlerian, Gestalt). The common factors movement has also linked into this evolution. This movement looks at various components involved in all or most of the effective treatments and incorporates these into the treatment packages. Research has found nonspecific factors and core competences, or common factors that are foundational to counseling and span all theories and schools of psychotherapy (cf. Drisko, 2004; Russell, Jones, & Miller, 2007; Stuart, Levy, & Katzenstein, 2006).

As a result, therapists have come to classify themselves as eclectic. This is typically code for their practice of borrowing SITs from many schools of psychotherapy. Gladding (2006) associates techniques with specific theories, such as the empty chair technique with Gestalt theory. Without consideration of the purpose and function of the SITs in these schools of therapy, eclectic therapists fall into the trap of using what they think might work for the problem at hand. Yontef (1993b), for example, challenges the notion of separating techniques from their theoretical schools of thought. His rationale is that each technique functions to accomplish a clearly relevant outcome; for example, the empty chair technique is a means to the client resolving unfinished business, a key point in Gestalt. As an existential-

ly based theory, the empty chair moves a client from dialogue about a person or issue toward the present moment experience in a fuller and more holistic form. It allows clients to "get in touch" with their felt experiences. This technique would be unhelpful, therefore, for emotional and dramatic clients who are overly connected with an emotional part of self.

This doesn't mean, however, that non-Gestalt therapists can't still use techniques associated with this school of clinical thought. For example, a counselor might consider himself a cognitive behavioral therapist but employ the empty chair since it is appropriate to the strategy and intervention. If the cognitive behavioral counselor believes that a client needs to connect with the whole of self and express latent emotions (strategies), he can incorporate it into his stated approach. If the later strategy is the focus, the intervention might be to express feelings associated with particular beliefs, and the technique the empty chair.

The conclusion is that "techniques can be responsibly or effectively used without considerations of relationship and overall methodology and philosophy" (Yontef, 1993a, p. 84). For example, a counselor might consider himself a cognitive behavioral therapist but employ the empty chair since it is appropriate to the intervention and strategy. Yet the empty chair technique arose out of an existential theory, specifically Gestalt. The empty chair was a means of working through unfinished business, such as integrating disowned parts of self and promoting catharsis.

BENEFITS OF THERAPEUTIC STRATEGIES, INTERVENTIONS, AND TECHNIQUES

A number of writers have proposed a rationale for the use of techniques in counseling (Conte, 2009; Jacobs, 1992; Rosenthal, 1998; Sobell & Sobell, 2008). They agree that the use of counseling techniques can improve therapeutic outcomes. For example, Conte (2009) says that techniques help therapists to construct effective communication with clients. Using techniques can increase client understanding of self, the world, God, and how he or she interacts with others. In addition, Rosenthal (1998) offers six benefits of using techniques: (1) they allow the client to surmount an impasse or sticking point; (2) they can renew the client's interest in therapy; (3) they offer an escape from the humdrum experience of doing the same thing session after session by adding variation and creativity; (4) they can be used as an adjunct to any brand or modality of therapy; (5) they are often what clients insist are responsible for their improvement; and (6) they can be highly efficacious when applied to a given symptom, difficulty, or disorder.

Likewise, Jacobs (1992) offers seven benefits of techniques: (1) they make concepts more concrete; (2) they heighten awareness; (3) they dramatize a point; (4) they speed up the counseling process; (5) they enhance learning because people are visual learners; (6) they enhance learning because people learn through experience; and (7) they give focus to the session.

MULTICULTURALISM AND STRATEGIES, INTERVENTIONS, AND TECHNIQUES

Cultural competence is a staple of any counselor's toolbox. The uniqueness of the individual as well as his or her cultural group membership needs to be respected at all times. The counselor needs to be knowledgeable regarding culturally competent psychological evaluations and other types of assessment and regarding treatment planning and choosing and implementing SITs. This volume does not specifically discuss how to adapt SITs for specific cultures nor which ones might be contraindicative for a specific culture. Though I have decided not to detail the cultural issues of a specific SIT that is discussed, that does not mean, however, that multicultural discussion of it is unimportant. I defer to your cultural competency in making prudent decisions concerning each SITs cultural appropriateness.

THE LIMITATIONS OF STRATEGIES, INTERVENTIONS, AND TECHNIQUES

Over the course of my lifetime, I've heard thousands of sermons, each having a different level of impact. Some were exceptional and inspirational. Others were challenging, nourishing, and illuminating. Sadly, I've heard messages that were scripturally unsound, heretical, and shaming. In spite of the fact that a sampling of the ministers had constructed a homiletic masterpiece, their messages had as much positive spiritual impact as a pew.

As part of my undergraduate degree, I enrolled in a homiletics class. I preached a semester of assigned sermons and learned the central factor in a good sermon. But after my first message, I was taken aback by my low grade. While the message was technically sound, it lacked impact. Though I adhered to all the guidelines for writing a quality message and my hard work led to a well-crafted sermon, I failed to pray and commit the process to the work of the Spirit. In my case, I consulted the commentaries without consulting the Holy Spirit. With prayer, even a sermon that does not adhere to homiletical guidelines can have a positive spiritual impact far beyond these deficits.

While the use of techniques is woven into the fabric of counseling, reducing counseling to a collection of techniques is misguided. Leitner (2007) articulated this point well, saying that counseling is not about assembling a bag of tricks or incorporating a formula. A counselor who has acquired many techniques is merely a technician skilled in a "gimmick." According to Thompson (2003), "The counseling experience is much more than the counselor's use of technique; the human dimension of the relationship as well as the readiness and responsiveness of the counselee are also very important" (p. xii; as cited in Thomas & Sosin, 2011, p. 92). As Thomas and Sosin (2011) remind us, "Helping someone is not a procedure but a healing relationship. It is through the interaction of the counselor and counselee, with the work of the Holy Spirit that produces real change" (p. 64).

DISTINCTIVENESS OF SPIRIT-INFUSED COUNSELING

A unique feature of Christian counseling is that the therapist and client(s) are never the only presences in the office. Indwelling within believers in Christ and operative within the office walls is the powerful Holy Spirit. The apostle John recorded Jesus's words that he would ask the Father to give us the Holy Spirit as our advocate. He said, "You know him, for he lives with you and will be in you" (John 14:17; see also 6:13; 1 Cor. 3:9, 16–17; 6:17, 19; 1 John 2:27). Since the Holy Spirit is already within us, we are responsible to connect with and draw awareness and discernment from him. As we share our hearts with the Holy Spirit, we engage in dialogue; we speak to him and he speaks to us. As we linger in his presence, he will abide with us during therapy. He not only transforms the therapist personally but also supernaturally empowers the counseling. This process is not limited to therapy with clients who consider themselves Christians, but can be used with anyone. Spirit-infused counseling can take place even if no faith issue is ever discussed.

A counselor who seeks to work distinctively from his or her Christian center must be sensitive to the Holy Spirit's leading. He is our sixth sense, the most important sense that we can have since he is the Spirit of truth. We must grow in grace and truth ourselves, holding tightly to the Word of God. Employing a psychotherapy theory or SIT without it being well formed in you is impossible. The theory and therapy must be formed well in your mind to be effectively used. Knowing a Bible verse and having it well formed in your mind and heart are quite different.

The clinician's cleverness in choosing SITs or prowess in employing them will not promote true transformation in the client. Rather, transformation will come from the counselor's willingness and ability to be fully present with the client and fully engaged with the Spirit of God. SITs are simply tools that can help us as we are already spiritually present and engaged.

GENERAL GUIDELINES FOR EMPLOYING SITS

The collection of SITs in this book are not meant to be a "cookbook" approach to clinical work. The intent is to provide you with a sampling of effective means of addressing particular problems, issues, or populations. It is not expected that all of the SITs will work for every client. The selection of them, however, should be purposeful (Mozdzierz, Peluso, & Lisiecki, 2011). While EBTs are considered to displace the need for schools of psychotherapy (e.g., Barlow, 2011; Luborsky et al., 1999; Nathan & Gorman, 2002), it is still important to have a theoretical orientation that encompasses how humans function and come to dysfunction, and what it takes to move the maladaptive patterns, improvised life themes, distressful emotions, problematic cognitions, spiritual impairment, and pathological disorders to healthy functioning. Always remember, however, that SITs are founded on an accurate and thorough assessment of the client(s), client motivation and readiness,

the quality of the relationship, the therapist's experience, and the whisper of wisdom from the Holy Spirit into the therapist's mind. Following are seven guidelines to keep in mind when selecting and implementing SITs.

GUIDELINES

First, determine whether the SITs are consistent with a Christian worldview. As I noted in *Therapeutic Expeditions: Equipping the Christian Counselor for the Journey* (Thomas & Sosin, 2011), "A skill is a skill; the philosophy upon which counseling is built matters greatly. For this reason we contend that a biblical worldview aptly anchors the counseling techniques and skills in God" (p. x). Christian counselors consider whether the SITs can and should be used given their philosophical underpinnings and their targets.

For example, mindfulness is used to assist clients with slowing down their stress-filled, hurried pace of life that feeds rumination and anxiety (Garzon & Ford, 2016). When mindfulness is conceptualized from its roots in Buddhism, it involves an emptying of the mind. Mindful meditations, however, focus attention. The "work" of mindfulness is not working; it is a kind of surrender. From a Christian standpoint, clients are to maintain a nonjudgmental and present acceptance of awareness based on divine grace. Garzon and Ford (2016) view mindfulness from the biblical idea of a conscious connection with a present and relational Godhead. Garzon and Ford advance such adaptations as using meditation to support self-acceptance and self-compassion by focusing on God's grace and goodness. Additionally, mindfulness can be explained by likening it to being "watchful" of unruly thoughts and feelings in the present moment through the peace of the Spirit (Gal. 5:22). It is a way to lasso those wayward thoughts and feelings that enter the mind, no matter how godly an individual lives. The mindful Christian observes what is happening, maintains distance by avoiding those thoughts, collects them, and then corrals them, while resting in Christ.

Since the foundation and scaffolding of a Christian worldview is truth, wise counselors choose and employ SITs that are also based in truth. Standard of care requires the use of EBTs (Thomason, 2010; Worthington & Johnson, 2013), though its prudence is questioned (Mozdzierz et al., 2011): "When mainstream counselors seek to build their approach upon evidence-based treatments they are advocating that counselors employ strategies that are based on 'truth.' . . . Christians committed to honoring God's Word realize that while evidence-based treatments are worthy of being utilized, the philosophical underpinnings of one's entire approach should also be 'evidence-based'; that is, based on truth" (Thomas & Sosin, 2011, p. 21).

Garfield and Bergin (1986) stated that progress in developing new and more effective techniques of psychotherapy has obscured "the fact that subjective value decisions underlie the choice of techniques, the goals of change, and the assessment of what is a 'good outcome'" (p. 16).

Often the use of SITs does not pose an issue for a Christian therapist. For example,

while the empty chair technique has existential and humanistic origins, it is based on the Gestalt notion of internal polarization, which makes it easily adaptable to use in Christian counseling, given that Christians have their own reasons to appreciate the internal complexity of human beings, since we are made in God's image. "The purpose behind using the technique is generally far more critical than the technique itself" (Thomas & Sosin, 2011, p. 23). In sum, a Christian worldview doesn't mean that we have to throw the technique out with the humanism bathwater.

The second guideline is to ensure that the SITs are consistent with you, the therapist. The more naturally a SIT can be carried out, the more authentic and poignant it will be. Any SIT that makes you uncomfortable or is discordant with your person needs to be avoided. Allow what is inside you to flow into the client. Part of what emanates from you, as well as being infused in you, should be the Holy Spirit (John 14:26; 16:12–13) and his bestowed fruit (Eph. 5:22–23). More importantly, "just as God actively enters the world, the counselor enters into the world of the counselee. The counselor exists outside of her work and outside of the therapeutic helping relationship" (Thomas & Sosin, 2011, p. 23). Be aware of your beliefs, attitudes, values, and feelings.

Third, ensure that the SITs are germane to how you conceptualize healthy and problematic functioning. While schoolism might be dead, as counselors we still need to have a robust and coherent understanding of human behavior in order to make sense of client behavior. Additionally, clients also have reactions to our derived SITs based on our conceptualization. Some clients will outright reject an intervention or technique that they believe is not going to help them, violates their values, or will make them uncomfortable. Other clients may passively go along with it but will likely not return, citing that the therapist was a poor match. For very disturbed clients, it is best to avoid using any interventions and techniques that might be viewed as contrived, rote, repetitive, or impersonal. Many may feel humiliated by the suggestion or will be unable to engage with the intervention or technique. The best strategy is offering them a strong and stable safe haven so they can face their issues and behavior with a clear sense of warmth and acceptance.

The fourth guideline is consideration of client welfare. Most SITs pose no risk for clients, especially when context, demographics, timing, and skill level are accounted for in the decision making. A selective few SITs, however, may pose a risk for certain clients. Clearly any SIT that the client feels uneasy about should be explored and an acceptable alternative used instead. Certain SITs might be unwarranted and harmful based on the nature of the client's disorder or issue, or due to the phase of treatment. Consider an individual who has been traumatized and is susceptible to abreactions. Employing a technique with such an individual is contraindicated if there is concern for decompensation. If uncertainty exists that the client might not weather a SIT due to inadequate ego strength and coping skills, don't use it. Additionally, exposure techniques are effective with anxiety disorders,

but the client might not be able to tolerate them. Examples are those clients who have co-occurring disorders that mitigate standard techniques or those who are too fragile for a technique such as flooding. Paradoxical techniques are very effective but pose the risk of confusing clients, shutting them down, or making them feel attacked.

Fifth, the SIT should be suitable for the issue. Rather than thinking about particular interventions or techniques, begin with knowing what it is you want to accomplish. This is "counselor intentionality." By knowing what you want to do or need to do, you can have a clearer sense of how the session should proceed and how to accomplish what is necessary to bring change.

Sixth, be flexible. Because of the diversity of populations that counselors serve, "one size does not fit all" (Thomas & Sosin, 2011, p. 63). A seasoned counselor knows how to adapt and apply a particular SIT to a particular client. Additionally, speak the client's language. Though SITs will be expressed through each therapist in a unique way, skilled clinicians have the ability to adapt them to each client.

Finally, when choosing to implement a particular SIT, first explain its purpose. Consistent with informed consent is the client's understanding and willingness to experience the course of action. Connect the SIT with a sound rationale for using it. To do so is not only ethical but demonstrates respect for the client's freedom and autonomy. Becoming proficient at the use of SITs takes time, but it begins with understanding their nature and purpose and learning to effectively communicate this to your clients.

THE HEART OF THIS BOOK

This book is designed to be a clinical resource in your educational training and practice. It contains an impressive roster of accomplished and skilled contributors. The volume is composed of well-known authors, speakers, and faithful workers who desire to love and minister to others in the name of Christ. Other contributors will be introduced to you, and although they may not have established a platform to have name recognition, they, too, bring a wealth of knowledge and extensive experience. We all are fortunate to be able to learn from the expertise of these esteemed colleagues. I am both honored and pleased to be able to share and disseminate their clinical wisdom. This book is a testament to the quality and depth of the field of Christian counseling.

The chapters in this book are designed to include particular features: an introduction; a theology and psychology of the topic; at least one case study; and then exemplary strategies, interventions, and techniques. Every contributor also provided a recommended reading list to deepen your knowledge, abilities, and skills on that given topic.

Every attempt is made by the contributors and myself to create a conversational volume that will benefit advanced graduate students with relevant conceptual and practical clinical information to enrich their counseling. The main purpose of the informational section of each chapter is to provide a foundational platform and conceptual bridge to wisely applying the therapeutic tools of clinical work. Contributors were asked to share their thoughts and experiences in their own manner, following the broader chapter guidelines.

In the twenty-seven chapters that follow, the contributors and myself address a wide range of practical strategies, interventions, and techniques that can augment more effective counseling. Arguably, one volume cannot adequately address all the factors that comprise the complex and holistic aspects of helping all clients and addressing every clinical presentation. We have, however, attempted to provide you with a broad perspective based on various theoretical strategies and a range of clinical issues with which therapists are presented. I pray that these chapters will renew your interest in learning and growing in your clinical expertise and/or build on your interest to further develop and mature your knowledge and skills. Readers with more extensive knowledge of some of these strategies, interventions, and techniques can expect to broaden their understanding and obtain additional knowledge and tools to augment their practice.

As you work with the wounded, broken, lost, and exploited, take with you the words of psychologist, philosopher, and physician William James, "Act as if what you do makes a difference. It does."

CONCLUSION

The debate over the value of SITs will likely never be settled. The effectiveness of using them, however, cannot be dismissed as invaluable. All would agree that counseling is an interpersonal process, meaning that it is the active engagement of two or more participants. As providers of clinical service, counselors who walk in the Spirit are often prone to avoid a technical approach. Interventions and techniques are only a vehicle to accomplish the objective of change. The nature of counseling lends itself to equifinality; many paths can be taken to reach the desired destination. Seasoned therapists have knowledge of numerous passages and believe they are competent to negotiate them. This book is one means of learning the tools to guide and help others achieve their aim.

The armamentarium of available and viable SITs is far beyond the scope of this book. Including even the lion's share suitable for every client issue or from a particular theoretical model is impossible. If a reader finds his or her favorite SIT not discussed, it is likely due to space limitations. I am delighted to be a part of this volume with gifted contributors who provide outstanding insights into clinical presentation.

I end this introduction with the Prayer of St. Francis, a prayer that captures the heart of counseling:

Lord, make me an instrument of your
*   peace;*
where there is hatred, let me sow love;
where there is injury, pardon;
where there is doubt, faith;
where there is despair, hope;
where there is darkness, light;
where there is sadness, joy.
O divine Master, grant that I may not
*   so much seek*
to be consoled as to console,
to be understood as to understand,
to be loved as to love.
For it is in giving that we receive,
it is in pardoning that we are pardoned,
and it is in dying that we are born to
*   eternal life.*
Amen.

RECOMMENDED READING

Barlow, D. H., Farchione, T. J., Fairholme, C. P., Ellard, K. K., Boisseau, C. L., Allen, L. B., & Ehrenreich-May, J. T. (2011). *Unified protocol for transdiagnostic treatment of emotional disorders: Therapist guide* (1st ed.). New York, NY: Oxford University Press.

Garzon, F. (2013). Christian devotional meditation for anxiety. In E. L. Worthington Jr., E. L. Johnson, J. N. Hook, & J. D. Aten (Eds.), *Evidence-based practices for Christian counseling and psychotherapy* (pp. 59–78). Downers Grove, IL: IVP Academic.

Satir, V. (1987). The therapist story. *Journal of Psychotherapy and the Family, 3*(1), 17–25.

Shallcross, L. (2012). The recipe for truly great counseling. *Counseling Today.* Retrieved from http://ct.counseling.org/2012/12/the-recipe-for-truly-great-counseling/

PART 1

Theory-Based Strategies

CHAPTER 2

Evidence-Based Counseling

David Lawson, PsyD

Dear children, let us not love with words or
speech but with actions and in truth.

1 JOHN 3:18

Most of the time I struggle with chapters that address evidence-based therapies (EBTs), and I have been known to skim or skip the chapter altogether. For me, EBT chapters just do not have the glamour of other chapters that discuss theories, skills, and pathologies. For many, the idea of another chapter that addresses numbers, statistics, and research can feel unnecessary in a field dominated by relationships. Who wants to read another chapter highlighting cognitive or behavioral approaches as the two clear victors in the "Who has the most effective therapy? game" when working with clients? I believe this mentality has slighted the field at a time when other theoretical approaches are becoming more prominent in studying strengths through the evidence-based approach.

Another difficulty is the connection of EBTs to insurance companies and reimbursements. Many of my students, when I lecture on the topic of EBTs, interpret the attempts by insurance companies to contain costs as attempts by companies who have little to no heart for the client or profession to mandate behaviors and therapeutic modalities. Although the bottom line of any business plays a role in the development of limits and directives, one positive feature of EBTs is that they continue to refine and define the profession, helping us make adjustments in certain areas, changing the emphasis in others, and honing the skills of our practice and trade. And so, despite the challenges of working with institutions like insurance companies, EBTs have provided valuable evidence to balance the overemphasis on business and expediency in finishing therapy.

Add into the mix the weakness of the classes on research and statistics that are generally offered in master's level counselor training programs, and you have a setup for disaster. Most of the graduate classes at my university and others are designed to help counselors be critical consumers of research. Although this is good for the many who struggle with math and numbers, a lack of critical understanding of research has weakened our ability to effectively understand and apply, and thus benefit from, EBTs. So although EBTs have significantly gained influence in the counseling and therapy cultures, many practitioners are incapable of reaping their benefits because of a lack of training. And many are dependent on others to interpret the significant movements of EBT.

Moreover, much of our mental health curriculum highlights ways in which research done well can further the knowledge base. Yet a poor understanding of research can cause problems for counselors and guide them to incorrect answers. We often teach students to be highly critical consumers without reminding them to balance the weaknesses with the strengths found in the research being criticized. I fear we have created more doubt in the value and strength of our students' research. This weakness in our training programs sets up many consumers of research to marginalize what is being accomplished in EBT versus informing or getting counselors excited about the field and its research.

Finally, this chapter benefits the reader in multiple ways, even if your therapy of choice is not the prescribed EBT found in the literature. First, EBTs not only give insight into what therapeutic modalities work but also provide guidance for use of what techniques might work with specific populations. So, even if you are not a supporter of a specific therapeutic modality, any therapist can benefit from integrating techniques that work with the given problem. Second, EBTs are a constant reminder of the changing field that we work within. Therapists can easily become complacent about their work, comfortably repeating the same styles and techniques even if better and more effective techniques are available. By staying connected to the research and EBTs, we not only stay current but provide the best services to our clients who desperately need the best from us.

Although some readers may hope this chapter provides reading lists of therapies that work with specific populations or pathologies, I, however, focus on the concept of EBTs and provide a summary of their strengths and weaknesses. Many other great books connect diagnosis to the specific EBT. For readers who would like more formulaic approaches, *Practitioner's Guide to Evidence-Based Psychotherapy*, edited by Fisher and O'Donohue (2006), is an exhaustive volume, covering the field of EBT and the approaches that work based on research. Also, the series Treatments That Work, edited by David Barlow and colleagues, takes a more specific approach to EBTs, highlighting therapeutic choices and techniques for specific cases, such as anxiety, depression, and other emotional disorders. Many books and articles provide these resources, and it is beyond the scope of this chapter to unpack the therapies that work and why. We will begin by understanding how and why EBT began, then the benefits and hopes of EBTs. Finally, I will conclude by addressing the weakness found within EBT.

HISTORICAL FOUNDATIONS OF EBTS

Although the current iteration of EBTs sounds very new or novel, for many authors the foundation of EBTs began in the 1970s and continued through the 1990s with the advent of health management organizations (HMOs). In one sense, however, EBTs are as old as the profession itself. From the moment Sigmund Freud began working with "patients," other professionals and the culture in general doubted that his work had meaning (Masson, 1984). Freud worked diligently to create an intrapsychic framework to model counseling after the acceptable EBTs of the time, which were structures in medicine, that is, the body. Freud therefore created a map of the intrapsychic "body," and developed a theory around how that system functioned, how it became "sick," and how to move that body to health. Thus, Freud's emphasis on the id, ego, and superego, as well as his drive theory were all attempts at constructing a model that was consistent with the knowledge and understanding of his time; he medicalized the inner world to fit the medical (EBT) needs. Freud's emphasis on making therapy fit the accepted medical models of the time was simply his way of creating an EBT. Without this extensive theory building, others in the professional community would have rejected his work outright, and the field would have died.

Although many modern counselors, particularly those who research EBTs, struggle with Freud's ideas today, we cannot ignore the fact that Freud not only created the process for modern therapy but also started the process through which we study it and, in the case of EBTs, how we currently evaluate the field. And while the field of therapy continued to grow and develop, it wasn't until Freud's death that therapy branched out into the various theories we have today.

Throughout therapy's brief history as a profession, we have needed to constantly defend ourselves from naysayers who argue that therapy is ineffective (e.g., Eysenck, 1992; Maloney, 2013). Although small pockets of cynics existed in both the medical and psychological communities, it wasn't until the 1960s that a true attack on therapy began from the very system we are now discussing—research. One such researcher, Hans Eysenck, is one of the most quoted psychological researchers in the twentieth century. His interests ranged from the nature of intelligence, pathologies and the effectiveness of therapy, to the eccentric, parapsychology and astrology. He is best known for his psychological tests that are still in print today; however, one of the grandest claims he made during his life was that therapy was a fraud and ineffective. He researched people going to therapy for problems and compared them to a control group who were not in therapy and discovered that the therapy group didn't get better, and shockingly to him, many got worse (Eysenck, 1992). This only confirmed his belief in the "falseness" of therapy, and like Nietzsche before him declaring that God is dead, he declared that the therapy field was dead. Although nearly everything about his research was discredited, his work was cited for years as the critical study proving/debunking the myth of therapy. When I took Introduction to Psychology in the 1980s, his works were still being presented as having validity despite the criticisms of his research.

From the 1960s to the 1980s, the number of therapeutic styles and theories ballooned. Many of these "newer" modalities stretched the boundaries of what was acceptable and even socially accepted. From nude encounter groups to scream therapy, the field exploded into a myriad of ideas and techniques. During this time, costs for therapy also skyrocketed, with many clinicians charging hundreds of dollars to insurance companies for an hour of therapy. And, since insurance companies began researching cost comparisons of all medical services around the United States, they decided to evaluate the cost of mental health services. Consequently, the field began to move toward HMOs, and given the various and sometimes extreme variance of costs and charges around the country, the development of cost controls began to even the playing field among multiple and at times extreme variance in payments.

As insurance companies were evaluating costs, they also realized that many health professionals were using various and at times conflicting forms of therapies to help their patients and clients. It is from this awareness that insurance companies, as well as many researchers, began asking the question about what actually works. Although it may seem like there has been an inordinate amount of emphasis on counseling and psychotherapy, in truth the whole medical profession has gone through an evaluation of what works and what does not. EBT is a key component of how nearly every medical community currently evaluates what they do and why.

EVIDENCE-BASED PRACTICE DEFINED

Defining EBTs has been a difficult and at times polarizing process. Many continue to struggle with how and why we define EBT, and as the field grew, so did the challenges. Although there are many who disagree on an exact definition, most agree on one key principle. The following quote accurately summarizes the principle behind EBT and gives us a starting place for defining it: "The unknown is unacceptable; evidence is a human safety net" (Smith, James, Lorentzon, & Pope, 2004, as cited in Ross, 2012, p. 5). One of the great difficulties confronted in medicine and even in the mental health community is the common reliance on lore and tradition over evidence from our field. Although often benign, therapies without valid evidence did at times both weaken the trust of our communities in their providers and deeply harmed clients to the point of death (Josefson, 2001). Thus, one of the challenges confronting our field is to validate the practices used in therapy to protect our clients and serve them in their healing.

Sackett, Rosenburg, Muir-Gray, Haynes, and Richardson (1996) define EBT as the conscientious, explicit, and judicious use of current best evidence in making decisions about the care of the individual patient. It means integrating individual clinical expertise with the best available external clinical evidence from systematic research. Simply put, EBT is the best way for therapists to research what works in therapy and what does not. In his definition of EBT, Sackett has identified three key components of the decision process for therapy with clients.

First, the clinical expertise of the clinician is key. One of the great challenges when working with a client is the general level of complexity. Not every depressed client who walks into a room expresses depression in the same way. Therefore, one of the more central functions of the counselor is to gain enough training and to have enough practice to know the various ways a problem can manifest itself. Culture, family styles, religious traditions, as well as various other factors impact expression of an issue. Thus, a clinician needs to know about an issue and its various expressions. Humbly placing yourself in supervision with other clinical experts or entering a supportive training group where you can collaboratively learn to diagnose and case conceptualize is key to developing your skills. Entering personal counseling as a method to understand yourself, your biases, and your blind spots is another effective way to grow that skill.

Second, clinicians must evaluate what evidence is available in best practice and treatments. Evidence does exist in nearly every area of medicine and mental health for which practices are effective. Constantly reading literature in your area is a key component to staying abreast of current trends, theories, and practices in the field. Taking advantage of continuing education classes in a specific area as well as supervision, consultation, or therapeutic groups in which you can share your ideas and your knowledge is also beneficial.

Finally, every client is unique and requires a uniquely different way of engage-ment and relational process. Even if you have studied and developed the requisite skills necessary to diagnose and treat a client, and even if you are current on the most effective therapies available, if you do not account for the individuality of the client and his or her style of engaging, the best therapies will be rendered ineffective due to a lack of social, cultural, and relational awareness. Counselors have been taught for years that every client is a unique cultural experience, and this is exceptionally true when utilizing EBTs with clients. Effective therapists learn to balance themselves and their training with the most effective EBTs alongside the uniqueness of the client. This exceptionally complex process may explain why many clinicians struggle to engage in EBTs after they graduate and might help us identify ways of moving forward to help encourage young clinicians to keep developing, growing, reading, and utilizing the best practices for clients.

BENEFITS OF EBT

Using EBTs has many benefits. Probably the greatest benefit within the EBT framework is the greater care provided to clients. Best practices are not just a process of following rules and regulations. The real benefit of developing best practices occurs in the healing and potential as our clients get better. Often therapists may help their clients, and although research indicates that being present with clients can cause change, by utilizing EBTs, the hope of greater success in therapy exists, as well as quicker alleviation of symptoms. This is particularly relevant with clients who are overwhelmed or nonfunctional because of their pain. By integrating EBTs into practice, a professional knows she is providing the best treatment available. And if the client is nonresponsive to the treatment, the counselor can still feel confident that she provided the best of her profession to the client.

The second benefit of prescribing EBTs is the movement away from eclecticism and toward a more cogent theoretical framework. The last few decades have seen an increase in atheoretical approaches to treatment (Duncan, 2010). This increase has grown as more technique-focused or technique-driven approaches dominate graduate programs versus developing and utilizing a grounded theory from which to use EBTs. Although theory is not the panacea to any problem, therapists who use techniques without a clear understanding of the theories behind them run the risk of using techniques inappropriately or ineffectively. The adage holds true that when you discover the benefits of using a hammer, everything looks like a nail. Further, the integration of EBT forces mental health providers back into a theory's development and integration, particularly when therapy is not going well. Problems or complications in a client or with a disorder must be dealt with through the grounded theory, not by hammering harder.

Furthermore, EBT creates a greater emphasis on diagnosis. Diagnostic ability is the key to developing an effective plan and an effective technique. As therapists become better diagnosticians, they become more capable of utilizing the correct therapy necessary for healing. One of the challenges among many current therapists is the disregard for diagnosing while treating. This causes many to become "mushy" in their therapy and in the development of goals for the client. Without a clear goal, a counselor is not likely to hit the target, the problem the client is dealing with. Or if he does hit a target, it could be the wrong one.

Although much has been discussed about the limits of time and resources placed on therapists using EBTs, it must be noted that research can also create opportunities to request more time and resources. This is especially true when counselors are using prescribed treatments, and their clients don't seem to be improving. This model is much more effective for requesting and receiving additional resources, especially when the alternative could be keeping clients for an indefinite amount of time. If prescriptive models haven't been working for a client, then we know that whatever the client is struggling with is more intransigent.

One of the most challenging parts of therapy is preventing the development of unhealthy relationships with clients and/ or their unhealthy dependence on the therapist. I have heard numerous stories from students conducting therapy who continued scheduling sessions even though the client was seeing no progress. A friendship may develop between client and counselor, thus diminishing any therapeutic dynamic in therapy. Our job is to help the client get better and grow, not create paid friendships. And sadly, therapists often lose sight of the therapeutic goals with clients as their personal needs are met and their egos stroked as clients like spending more time with them.

THE HOPE OF EBT'S FUTURE IN THE COUNSELING PROFESSION

Hope has grown in the EBT community that practicing EBT will constantly keep therapists returning to the literature and staying updated (Duncan, 2010). Many counselors leave school overwhelmed and in debt, often decrying the volumes of reading they have done. This can lead to an antagonistic/hostile relationship with training and research, and in turn lead therapists away from the very things that helped frame the academic process. For others the frenetic need to get every certification leads them down a path of wide but shallow levels of training. As the EBT field continues to expand and additional research and new techniques are evaluated, it is imperative that therapists continue their journey of learning and growing. The hope of EBT proponents has been to instill a sense of curiosity and interest in what works, hoping to keep therapists reading and training after they graduate. This ongoing challenge is made more difficult by the unique state requirements for continuing education and training.

Practitioners hope that EBTs can help with one of the challenges impacting modern society and the therapeutic community specifically—the lack of overall prevention used both medically and psychologically. Although great volumes of data exist on self-care, the vast majority of Americans rarely utilize it. Moreover, if

they do, they actually use what ultimately isn't self-care. I have talked to many students who explain to me how they are utilizing self-care for themselves, only to discover that their choices have put them deeper in debt or made their lives busier, or that they have simply numbed themselves through weekend binging on Netflix or movies. Because so few budding therapists are reading about self-care, or at least not applying it, they will ultimately not guide clients into their own self-care/prevention. Reading about and employing prevention techniques are not only essential for therapists in this crazy world we live in but also desperately needed by clients. The hope is that as EBTs become a greater part of the landscape, counselors will be more likely to consume research and utilize it with their clients.

Additionally, there is hope that EBT will positively impact psychotherapy's challenge of inconsistency and the often-extreme variance found between therapists. As clients have become savvier, and as more materials are published on therapy and what works, we are becoming more aware of how radically different each therapist functions. Although each client is unique and our job is to connect and adapt to the client's style and culture, use of some uniform process, particularly when research supports the use of specific interventions, becomes more imperative. This is especially true as clients move or need to change therapists. Often clients who need to begin with new therapists discover that nothing their previous therapists did was like the new therapists' work. Therefore, many clients become confused about the process of therapy and struggle to gain traction moving forward if new or old therapists aren't following similar or prescribed treatments. Although many of our students who enter therapy discover that the previous therapist's work was "good" and productive, it failed to lead to growth or healing in the areas most needed.

Finally, it is with confidence that we in the field can say that therapy works. Research supports this idea, and in many cases therapy is as effective, or even more effective than, medications given to treat clients. Given our history, the challenges to our profession, and the concerns many in the public have about counseling, this is certainly a reason to cheer.

Although therapy is successful and there is reason to believe that most of what people practice is helpful, it must be noted that not all therapies are equal, and in some cases, therapeutic techniques can be harmful and even deadly if they are not validated through EBT (Josefson, 2001). For example, the rebirthing technique became popular with some therapists working with clients to help them process through birth trauma. The idea sounded like another experiential technique that could be used to help clients confront their intense pain. Yet concerns arose about using the technique after the death of a client who suffocated going through the rebirthing process. Only then was action taken to limit or ban it. Whether or not one believes the technique had merit, there was no research indicating its effectiveness, and given the threat of harming the very clients therapists were trying to help, should have been challenged before the death of a client. EBT gives us the ability to validate therapeutic techniques so that we can assure both therapists and clients that the prescribed therapy or technique is useful and has been evaluated to assess for risk and for success.

CHALLENGES TO EBTS

The challenges for EBTs are great and have been growing during the past few years. From general lack of training and understanding of research and statistics, which is a huge weakness in most training programs, to doubt about the value of research in general, the idea of developing a prescriptive process for dealing with problems remains. And some of the original critiques against "old school" therapy, stuck in its unilateral adherence to analysis, can now be claimed with the original critiques by cognitive and behavioral therapists. Currently much of their work and materials sound as religionistic as the very groups they initially confronted.

We are all too human in our ability to evaluate and critique our own biases. So, whether we are discussing therapists who use emotion-focused therapy (EFT), Adlerian therapy, relational therapy, cognitive behavioral therapy (CBT), or any other theoretical process, we are all likely to see the world from that framework and deny or attack any other model that challenges its ideas (confirmation and selection bias). We appear to be trapped by our self-understanding and limited by it. Therefore, as we approach the challenges of EBTs, we must humbly hold that we cannot, do not, and will not understand all there is to know about humanity, change, and the therapeutic relationship. The great teacher-trainer Jeffrey Kottler (2017) says, "I have never really trusted anyone who claims to understand how therapy works. I think it is far too complex. What the client brings to us in a session is so overwhelming and so full of content that we can't hold it all. So we have to find ways to live with that—to live with all of this uncertainty, all this mystery, all this ambiguity" (p. 14).

To honor the idea proposed by Dr. Kottler, I will challenge EBTs in three ways.

Challenge One

Therapy is an extremely thorny human endeavor. The relational dynamics are difficult, and the communication process is often loaded, with every word having complex meanings and symbolic representation. Therapists' own worlds and their own understandings of meaning also play roles in the dynamic dance between themselves and their clients, thus making the process even more complex. Therefore, taking this active, dynamic process and trying to force it into a research study, whether quantitative or not, is tantamount to pushing a tomato through a small hole. The tomato can certainly be pushed through the hole, but something will be lost in the process. To effectively control for and balance out the impact of chance in any research design is definitely possible but risky given the very complex nature of the therapeutic relationship. Therapy and the therapeutic process can be studied and evaluated but often at a cost. Sometimes the cost is controlling specifically how the therapy process is managed, and some-

times it is controlling whether the client has more than one diagnosis. Either way the cost impacts how effective we are in understanding research and then applying it to the real world.

With this in mind, every limit placed on the natural process and rhythm of therapy to appease the need to do the research effectively weakens the applicability of the study in real life—think internal and external validity. Living near Disney World, I have had the opportunity to visit numerous times. One thing that has fascinated me is a fully ripened watermelon, in the exact shape of Mickey Mouse, with a head and two small ears. I initially thought the watermelon was fake, or that small pieces had been glued together to make the ears. However, I was assured by an employee that they grew this way. Years later I saw how the Imagineers had created plastic shells in the shape of Mickey Mouse, ears and all. Then I saw the watermelon mature through its stages and grow into the shape. We can create structures that force objects or results to fit the shapes we have created. Studying therapy through the research process creates certain types of results, but do these results actually work in real life with real people under normal circumstances?

There will always be tension in doing research on a human relational process, particularly given that the more prescribed or controlled the research is, the more concern that its results are applicable beyond the experiment that framed it. This dynamic has certainly impacted clinical practice in various fields. During the teaching revolutions of the 1960s through the 1980s, researchers were quick to apply current methods of pedagogy that were effective in their research studies to the classroom. And every two to three years, new research highlighted significant shifts that teachers needed to make to be more effective. Unfortunately, this time period was filled with constant transition, and many teaching styles that were embraced were just as quickly abandoned when it became clear that the research did not apply to the "real world." When utilizing EBTs we must understand their strengths but recognize their unique limits.

Challenge Two

Part of what makes evaluating problems or pathology unique for the mental health field, as compared to the medical field, is that we do not see or evaluate primary data. What I mean by this is that our field still struggles to understand what depression, anxiety, or any pathology actually is (i.e., chemical, relational, emotional, or all of the above). By this, I am not saying that our clients don't know depression or anxiety. Because we don't evaluate the primary data, our ways of measuring these pathologies are actually secondary ways, descriptive data, and/or tests created to evaluate the diagnosis. Though the scores have gone down, we have no idea whether they truly represent the most accurate data on the problem.

For example, if I come into therapy with a Beck Depression score of 16 and then leave therapy with a score of 8, I cannot be assured that the reduction is as accurate as measuring the amount of virus or bacteria found in my body. This further complicates the evaluation of both our diagnosis and the change in reported experience. We can never be completely certain what factors actually led to the score being reduced by the client. Understand that secondary data is not meaningless, but that it needs to be held with caution.

In response to this concern, many therapists moved over to using consumer response questionnaires to evaluate what the client thought and felt about therapy. Not so shockingly, the consumer reports indicate that most therapeutic modalities and many of the therapists who had been practicing them were highly effective, and the clients thought therapy had been successful. This led to what is referred to as the dodo bird effect, harkening back to Alice in Wonderland's famous phrase "Everyone's a winner." Although this form of research does not carry the empirical weight of EBT, it does provide evidence through client responses that therapy is effective, and that most therapists are engaging in successful practice.

Challenge Three

Finally, one significant variable has developed over the last couple of years impacting the power that EBT research has had in evaluating treatment and outcome, and that is regression to the mean. Although scores on a test or values in research be high or low, if tested and retested over time, all numbers tend to return to a point of balance—the mean. So one might predict that although earlier research found greater change in clients, over time the differences become more centralized and therefore less significant.

When efficacy studies began in earnest in the late 1980s into the 1990s, cognitive and behavioral therapies immediately raced to the front, highlighting their effectiveness in treating various diagnostic issues. The early National Institute of Mental Health research by Elkin and colleagues (1989) has been used as the genesis of the modern EBT movement for explaining the benefits of CBT with depressed clients. However, upon closer review and as the research was followed later, there were little to no effect sizes carried by CBT. But by the time this information had been broadly disseminated, the race to prove that CBTs were more effective was on.

By the early 2000s, a tidal wave of change spread throughout the mental health field. New programs renovated their departments around this data. Some European countries decided to drop every other theory but ones supported through researched EBTs. Not long after this, the traditional CBTs started showing less powerful effects over competing therapies. What was once the unstoppable juggernaut in the research community seemed less significantly powerful (Shedler, 2015). To use an analogy, when CBTs first dominated research over other modalities, they were like runners who in a sprint beat their opponents by ten seconds or more. But over time the differences between the runners have narrowed. They may still be winning but only by two to three seconds. This change has shocked many in the research community who have pushed for cognitive and behavioral methods. However, this data seems to make sense when further evaluated.

More recently other theoretical approaches have become more capable and competent in aligning their styles and theory to be researched. Over the last twenty years, most therapeutic modalities created better and more effective processes for careful examination and scrutiny, and currently do a much better job of adapting the theory to research models. Another more benign possibility is that much of what is done in the cognitive and behavioral models can be read about and implemented by anyone. As the popularity of self-help books has increased and the integration of the techniques used within cognitive and behavioral therapies has occurred, there simply may be a greater saturation of the knowledge within the general public. This could be viewed from a negative viewpoint, particularly from more rigorous researchers who may find it a confounding variable for research. However, if this is the case, I am thankful that people are integrating healing techniques into their daily lives.

Finally, whether the criticisms of EBTs remain, the concepts will remain as long as insurance companies, as well as questionable therapies, are created. I believe the emphasis on research-based evidence has benefited the field and will continue to help us grow and mature as a profession. However, two issues have developed that may impact future research, and the future of EBTs.

FUTURE TRENDS WITH EBT

First, evidence-based techniques (EBTs), another acronym with the letters EBT, has become a topic of conversation and is particularly supported among researchers. The idea that a technique itself might be the key to helping the profession, although not new, has become a proposition made among researchers who believe that the human element, namely, the therapist, is really the problem in doing therapy and in conducting quality research. Thus, many of the proponents of this form of EBT highlight the fact that often effective therapies have specific techniques that are more effective than other techniques within the modality. Some researchers who espouse this position have gone so far as to say that theory itself might be the more problematic issue with therapy (Chambless & Hollom, 1998). The complications with this concept, including the attempt to create an atheoretical approach, are beyond the scope of this chapter. In addition, many have argued that this concept does not take into account the research indicating how many of the benefits of research occur through the relational construct itself. Others have argued that the idea would take the cookbook approach to evidence-based therapy and create a robotic process of utilizing techniques to engage clients. I believe this research will continue and will be something worth watching.

The second area of interest that has developed of late is the idea of evidence-based therapists (EBT)—my acronym. This form of EBT and its continued research began when researchers noticed that great amounts of variance existed among therapists using evidence-based therapies. They decided after much review that the variance could not be accounted for by the clients or by the therapeutic training. Therefore, it must occur from within the therapists themselves. Since this revelation, a plethora of research has been conducted on the qualities of evidence-based therapists (Anderson, Ogles, Patterson, Lambert, & Vermeersch, 2009; Wampold, 2006). Although various lists of what makes for an effective therapist exist, the American Psychological Association, through the Education Directorate, has identified fourteen constructs that help therapists be more effective with their clients. The qualities range from verbal ability to awareness of themselves, to the therapist's interaction with the client's unique cultural and familial characteristics, to empathy, adaptability, development of trust, and a working alliance with the client. Each of these factors should come as no surprise given the research on the impact of the relational process (Norcross, 2011).

CONCLUSION

Maybe what we are looking for in evidence-based therapy is a combination of all of the above research approaches and perspectives sprinkled with a significant amount of humility and a dash of curiosity. My hope is that as we move forward in the field, we don't lose the sense of wonder and awe that this field exists and "works." The fact that two or more people can enter into a relationship and something happens that changes another's life is miraculous, even as we study and understand more about the process of therapy. In the end, therapy will be what we as the therapists make of ourselves, and what the clients ultimately want to do with the relationship and the treatments brought into the sessions. My hope is that readers walk away wanting to study and learn more about this complex but fascinating practice called therapy and the EBTs we use when working with clients.

RECOMMENDED READING

Barlow, D. H., Farchione, T. J., Fairholme, C. P., Ellard, K. K., Boisseau, C. L., Allen, L. B., & Ehrenreich-May, J. T. (2011). *Unified protocol for transdiagnostic treatment of emotional disorders: Therapist guide* (Treatments That Work). New York, NY: Oxford University Press.

Duncan, B. L. (2010). *On becoming a better therapist.* Washington, DC: American Psychological Association.

Duncan, B. L., Miller, S. D., Wampold, B. E., & Hubble, M. A. (Eds.). (2010). *The heart and soul of change: Delivering what works in therapy* (2nd ed.). Washington, DC: American Psychological Association. doi:10.1037/12075–000

Fisher, J. E., & O'Donohue, W. T. (2006). *Practitioner's guide to evidence-based psychotherapy.* New York, NY: Springer.

Lambert, M. J. (2013). *Bergin and Garfield's handbook of psychotherapy and behavior change* (6th ed.). New York, NY: Wiley.

Norcross, J. C. (Ed.). (2011). *Psychotherapy relationships that work* (2nd ed.). New York, NY: Oxford University Press.

Thomas, G., & Pring, R. (Eds.). (2004). *Evidence-based practice in education.* New York, NY: Open University Press.

Wampold, B. E. (2006). What should be validated? The psychotherapist. In J. C. Norcross, L. E. Beutler, & R. F. Levant (Eds.), *Evidence-based practices in mental health: Debate and dialogue on the fundamental questions* (pp. 200–208). Washington, DC: American Psychological Association.

Wampold, B. E. (2010). *The basics of psychotherapy: An introduction to theory and practice.* Washington, DC: American Psychological Association.

CHAPTER 3

Cognitive-Based Strategies

Gary Sibcy, PhD
John C. Thomas, PhD, PhD

As [a man] thinketh in his heart, so is he.

PROVERBS 23:7 KJV

If behavior is the overt side of our personality, both cognitions and emotions are the covert side, though they do find expression through behavior. In the broadest sense of the term, cognitions refer to events that occur inside of us that help us make sense of the world (Leahy, 2017). Cognition includes a host of phenomena, including perception, imaging, attention, thinking, reasoning, judging, problem solving, values, philosophies, beliefs, standards, rules, expectations, labeling, coding, categorization of stimuli, memory and retrieval, and conditional linkages between stimuli in memory and conscious awareness (Granvold, 1994).

Yalom and Leszcz (2005) spoke of the salience of cognitions when they wrote, "Often automatic and flying beneath the radar of one's awareness, one's thoughts initiate alterations in mood and behavior" (p. 513). In both the psychological and Christian literature on counseling, more attention and effort have been directed toward understanding cognitions and developing strategies, interventions, and techniques (SITs). At the core of cognitive behavioral therapy (CBT) is the fundamental assumption that emotional, behavioral, and relational problems largely result from maladaptive patterns of thinking. As thinking patterns are codified and become increasingly flexible, coherent, and realistic, those suffering from emotional, behavioral, and relational challenges are likely to experience psychological, emotional, behavioral, and spiritual growth. While cognitive SITs tend to come under the broad umbrella of CBT (cf. Backus & Chapian, 2000; Beck, 1976; Burns, 1999; Leahy, 2017; Meichenbaum, 1985), many theories such as Adlerian employ them.

Since research has demonstrated that identifying and altering dysfunctional cognitions is significantly related to positive outcome, it is incumbent upon each clinician to know them and be skillful in using them (Dobson & Dobson, 2009, 2017). To this end, this chapter will lay out a basic framework of understanding cognitive therapy (CT) from a Christian point of view. We will address a theology and psychological overview of cognition and the core components of CT. The greater part and thrust of the chapter is to describe effective SITs to provide effective CT.

THEOLOGY AND PSYCHOLOGY OF COGNITION

Sometimes our cognitive processing and subsequent behavioral responses are maladaptive because of misperceptions, misinterpretations, and dysfunctional appraisals of situations. The many cognitive phenomena within the human psyche don't simply respond to the stimuli that confront them directly. Rather, each person perceives and constructs an idiosyncratic interpretation of each stimulus event, which might be flawed. Put another way, we do not respond directly to a stimulus, but to our interpretation of that stimulus. For example, a wife recently reported feeling depressed when her husband brought her flowers. How could such a seemingly benign event lead to depressed feelings? Once we looked at how she interpreted this situation it became more obvious: she thought that his buying flowers was an admission of guilt for doing something untrustworthy. Though objective reality exists, no one person completely possesses it. Everything we perceive and receive from the environment is filtered through a complex network of cognitive processes, and our cognitive processes impact the environment in which they exist. We are active "meaning makers" in this world, and

each person's interpretation of life events both facilitates and hinders functioning.

The foundation of the cognitive scaffolding is schemas, also known as core beliefs. They are "mental templates derived from prior experience and knowledge and are used to evaluate events and inform future expectations" (Stallard & Rayner, 2005, p. 217). Schemas are formed in early life based on repetitive and emotionally charged experiences with significant figures in the family of origin and world around us. Schemas root themselves in the limbic or emotional center of the brain and subsequently operate on an implicit level typically outside a person's level of awareness. Though schemas can lie dormant for years, they are activated by emotionally stressful events. Since schemas are designed to protect the self, they are therefore difficult to change. They are self-sustaining and self-perpetuating and seek to maintain their own homeostasis. Practically speaking, this means that schemas determine a person's attention to a stimulus, how that is interpreted, and what the brain retrieves from memory.

Various lists of schemas exist, but the most widely used are those by Young (1998), who has identified eighteen schemas:

    abandonment/instability
    mistrust/abuse
    emotional deprivation
    defectiveness/shame
    social isolation/alienation
    dependence/incompetence
    vulnerability to harm or illness
    enmeshment/undeveloped self

failure to achieve
entitlement/grandiosity
insufficient self-control/self-discipline
subjugation
self-sacrifice
approval-seeking/recognition-seeking
negativity/pessimism
emotional inhibition
unrelenting standards/hypercriticalness
and punitiveness

These schemas are linked to emotions, such as "showing sadness is a sign of weakness" or "expressing anger is sinful." For example, consider a client whom we'll call "Ben," whose schema involves approval and recognition seeking; in other words, he believes that he is undeserving of respect. Based on Ben's schema, he developed a cognitive rule to prevent the schema from being activated and to protect the vulnerability produced by the schema. He develops a cognitive rule that says, "I will present myself in ways to get respect from others." Ironically, cognitive rules often reinforce the schemas, ultimately augmenting the dysfunction.

Cognitive rules require compensatory strategies to stay operative. Compensatory strategies arise out of the schemas and subsequent rules. These strategies are behavioral and cognitive maneuvers that serve as coping strategies aimed at alleviating emotional distress. The goal is to prevent the schema from being activated, which to Ben would serve to prove his worse fear. As Job said, "What I always feared has happened to me. What I dreaded has come true" (Job 3:25–26 NLT). For Ben, one compensatory strategy is not to reveal

anything that might provoke a person to have "cause" to disrespect him. He also acts out his rage through passive aggressive behavior toward others. The bottom line is that people tend to behave in ways and attend to information consistent with their schema.

If the previous cognitive processes represent the greater part of an iceberg that lies beneath the surface of the water, conscious or automatic thoughts or automatic appraisals are the tip. Clients are very conscious of these thoughts. When Ben perceives and concludes that a person is dismissing him, the automatic appraisal is "he is obviously disrespecting me." Such an appraisal can then activate the underlying schema.

Theology of Cognition

Many aspects of CT are easily integrated into a Christian worldview for many of the key assumptions made in most approaches to cognitive therapy are consistent with Christian theology and biblical anthropology. CT makes assumptions about human nature, with an emphasis on the importance of truth, and the process of "renewing the mind" by testing beliefs against reality and aligning behaviors with new beliefs. What is unique about Christian CT is that it also uses Scripture as a key source of evidence and truth against which beliefs are examined and restructured.

Cognitions are one aspect of what it means to be fashioned in the image of God. However, our cognition—like all of humanity—is fallen, unreliable, and imprecise in determining truth. A Christian view of cognition recognizes that Christlikeness is not based solely on healthy or rational thinking. Yet Scripture clearly places the content of our thinking in the spotlight (cf. 2 Cor. 10:5; Phil. 4:8). Though our cognitive world is in the spotlight, the Bible places our heart at center stage.*

Sinful behavior can corrupt the mind. We can rationalize, minimize, and distort objective truth because of the way we act. Moreover, we are prone to internalizing lies. It becomes apparent, then, that no one has complete rational or functional thinking; each person's cognitive processes and skills are flawed by the effects of sin and the flesh. A theologically sound perspective on cognition anchors what is "rational," "healthy," and "functional" in the absolute truth of Scripture, God's revealed standard (cf. Tan, 1987). Jones and Butman (2011) point out that in modern uses of cognitive counseling, a client's cognitions are judged based on their utility, not on their truthfulness. Backus and Chapian (2000) write, "When we inject the truth into our every thought, taking a therapeutic broom and sweeping away the lies and misbeliefs which have enslaved us, we find our lives radically changed for the happier and better" (p. 10).

The inclusion of Christ into the "psychology of cognitions" is more than additive; it is transformational. Thankfully, God has provided a means of redeeming cognitions. Redemption of cognitions begins at the process of conversion, and redressing faulty cognitions is the spiritual work of sanctification and formation. Because Christian theology provides a philosophy of living, it targets both the schematic and core belief layers of our cognitive structure. As a result, Christian conversion and sanctification transform thinking from the foundation—literally, from the bottom up

CASE STUDY

Cindy, a thirty-five-year-old Caucasian woman, was quite depressed and had episodes of panic. She reported several salient life events, including her husband's new job, which required him to travel a great deal. This meant that she now carried the primary responsibility of caring for her eight-year-old son, Brian, who had notable academic issues but failed to qualify for special needs. This also impacted her job demands. Cindy, an elementary school teacher, believed her job might be in jeopardy due to decreased performance.

Cindy reported feeling guilt and numerous depressive symptoms, including fatigue, regret, sadness, bouts of crying, apathy, amotivation, haplessness, helplessness, and hopelessness about life. She reported regular and significant verbal fights when her husband returned from his business trips. Clinically relevant were a patterned series of events that involved Cindy coming home from work. Though she wanted to cook her son dinner, have dinner with him, and then help him with his homework, she typically made him a microwave dinner and retreated to her bedroom to sleep. Cindy's primary goal was to elevate her feelings of depression and helplessness.

---

* Cf. Pss. 9:1; 24:3–4; 26:2; 32:3–7; 37:27–31; 44:20–21; 51:5; 139:23–24; Prov. 3:3–5; 4:23; Jer. 17:9; Matt. 12:31–35; Luke 6:45; Gal. 5:16–23; Phil. 4:7–8; Col. 3:15–16; 2 Tim 2:22.

COGNITIVE-BASED STRATEGIES, INTERVENTIONS, AND TECHNIQUES

Techniques aimed at cognitions are directed primarily at correcting biases, errors, and distortions in information processing; modifying problematic core beliefs and schemata; and building cognitive regulation skills. Cognitive SITs can be broadly categorized into two kinds: traditional and third-wave techniques. Traditional refers to the first two of three waves of CT. Wave one is primarily of the behavioral tradition while the second is similar to Ellis's (Ellis & Grieger, 1977) logical disputation SITs and A. T. Beck's (1976) emphasis on cognitive distortions, collaborative empiricism, and cognitive restructuring. Ellis's approach is largely philosophical in that he examines the client's logic, whereas Beck's tendency is toward empirical evidence. What these two strategies have in common is that they are focused on the content of a person's thinking. Ellis targets the demands people make about the way life "should be," "ought to be," and "must be" in order to be happy. Regarding Ben, whose schemas we introduced earlier, Ellis would very likely target his demand to be respected all the time by everyone in order to be happy. Beck, on the other hand, tends to focus on how people systematically distort experiences. He might, for example, target Ben's tendency to "mind read" negative thoughts and intentions into other people's behaviors. Eventually Beck's approach helps people identify and modify underlying schemas.

The third wave of CT is less concerned about the content of how a client thinks. It focuses on the relationship the client has with his or her thinking. Mindfulness and acceptance commitment SITs, for example, do not challenge the content of a client's thinking but how the client interacts with that content. The river metaphor (described on page 60), for example, teaches clients how to observe thoughts, feelings, images, and sensations without attaching themselves to these experiences. Additionally, the third-wave approach examines the functionality of thoughts. In the cognitive behavioral analysis system of psychotherapy (CBASP; McCullough, 2006), another third-wave CT, clients are asked about the relevance of their thinking in relation to the desired outcome. "Does that thought help you get your desired outcome?" "If you want to speak up and tell your wife how her behavior is affecting you, what kind of thought would you need to tell yourself?" These encompass the methods of CT that can be categorized as one of the following: discovery, deconstruction/deactivation, or development.

Discovery SITs

Discovery involves activities aimed at gathering cognitive data from clients. Cognitive discovery techniques assist with the task of identifying and labeling faulty cognitions. Understanding clients' cognitive content is vital to alleviating their distress. Limited discovery SITs are described below.

Assessment tools. One means of evaluating a client is by using inventories. Numerous cognitive scales exist to assess such capacities as cognitive flexibility (Martin & Rubin, 1995), cognitive errors (Leitenberg,

Yorst, & Carroll-Wilson, 1986), cognitive competencies (Strunk, Hollars, Adler, Goldstein, & Braun, 2014), negative attributions (Ronan, Kendall, & Rowe, 1994), cognitive fusion, (Herzberg et al., 2012), and automatic thoughts (Schniering & Rapee, 2002). One we like is the Young (1998) schema questionnaire that assesses the maladaptive schemas he identified. A children's version has also been developed (Stallard & Rayner, 2005).

Socratic questioning. One technique highly useful for teasing out what a client has learned from life experiences by becoming clearer about their cognitive processes is Socratic questioning. The goal was to move Cindy from her concrete to abstract thinking so she could find newer information that would reevaluate her previous conclusions or construct new ideas about herself (Padesky, 1993).

Goal setting. Although goal setting is a staple of all therapies, in both cognitive and behavior therapies it plays a vital role. Setting goals may seem deceptively easy, but skill is needed in directing the process to specific, realistic, and measurable goals. Goal setting sets the stage for the choice of SITs. Thus, if goal setting is not done well, the best SITs will be ineffective. Goals are identified and set collaboratively, and client motivation and commitment are essential for treatment to be successful. Goals are also linked with agenda setting, which will be discussed later (see pages 50–51).

Daily mood log. The mood log is a strategy for recognizing automatic thoughts, improving problem solving, and developing emotional regulation skills (Burns, 1999). It raises client awareness

about the reciprocal relationship between cognition, emotion, and behavior.

The log works best with a prepared form that consists of columns in which the client records details of upsetting situations, automatic thoughts, emotions related to the thoughts, and evidence for and against those thoughts. A targeted event is recorded along with the emotions and automatic thoughts. Many variations of mood logs can be found on the internet and generally request similar information.

The first step requires that the client describe a distressful event in detail and then record the negative affect associated with the event. Since many clients struggle to accurately label a feeling, a feeling wheel or feeling list is virtually essential. Once the feeling is recorded, the client identifies the intensity of that feeling on a subjective units of distress (SUD) scale (e.g., 0 = the least intense to 100 = the most intense). Additionally, Cindy was asked to report any thoughts, feelings, and behaviors that occurred while she was driving home, entering home, and seeing her son. We ask our clients to close their eyes and replay their events as they unfolded in time.

Clients next explore the negative thoughts associated with the identified afflicted feelings. Burns (1999) encourages clients to tune in to their internal dialogue, to ask what they are saying to themselves. As thoughts are identified, they are recorded in the "automatic thoughts" column of the log. Afterward the client estimates how much he or she believes each of the thoughts using the SUD scale (typically 1–10). The task now is to find the distortions or lies. We use a cognitive distortions list and the Bible to aid in the recognition process. Discerning the cognitive distortions is a crucial step in assisting clients to move forward. Satan is the father of lies. To not confront them empowers the Evil One's malevolent intentions to destroy people.

Collaboratively, new beliefs and truth for each faulty cognition are identified. The process is like the affect and automatic thoughts columns, where the client estimates the strength of the belief using the SUD scale. The client then rerates the current strength of original automatic thoughts. For example, Cindy originally believed the thought that she was a failure as a mother at 98 percent. Cindy now crossed out the 98 percent score and wrote in 15 percent. Finally, Cindy recorded the feelings she now felt in the outcome section of the log.

Agenda setting. One of the most important cognitive strategies is agenda setting. It is used in the discovery, deactivation, and development phases of CT. Burns (1999) uses the acrostic I STOP to identify the steps in setting an agenda with clients.

1. *Invitation.* Even though a client states that he wants help with a particular issue, do not assume that he is ready or truly wants to change. Clients need to be held accountable to change, which fosters more investment in the outcome. As clinicians, we might ask, "Cindy, you want to work on becoming attentive to your son's needs. Would this be a good time to work on that problem?" We are also inviting clients to the work of monitoring their symptoms, being willing to tolerate feeling anxiety to feel better.

2. *Specificity.* Too often counselors allow clients to get away with vague examples. Thus, it is critical to specify the issue as clearly as possible. Inquire about a particular situation that stands out for the client. In Cindy's case, we would want to look at a specific example of a time where she felt like she was unable to be as attentive as she felt she should have been to her son's needs after she got home from work. Instead of talking about what usually happens, specificity digs down into the specifics using the situation analysis / mood monitoring sheet that looks at: the situation, thoughts, feelings, behaviors, and consequences.

3. *Troubleshooting.* **Here the counselor attempts to determine the nature of the problem.**

4. *Openness.* **Openness refers to determining the client's willingness and readiness to address the problem. It represents how motivated the client is to change. You might ask, "Is this a problem you want help with, or did you simply want to talk about your feelings?** A client's motivation is linked to the level of resistance toward change. Clients can oppose change on two different levels: process resistance and outcome resistance. Process resistance refers to the fact that clients may not be motivated or willing to do the work required to get better. For example, a client may not complete homework, expose herself to situations that will initially make her feel more anxious, actively examine thoughts, or be willing to revise her thinking. For Cindy, the process resistance was for her to learn how to interrupt her "emotional thinking,"

in which she assumed that not to feel motivated meant that she didn't value something. In other words, because she didn't feel motivated to spend time with her son, that must mean she didn't love him. She needed help to see that love is not defined as feeling good and motivated all the time but as doing what is in the best interest of another person despite how you feel.

Another aspect of lack of openness is referred to as outcome resistance, that is, fear of the outcome the client says he wants. Getting better regardless of how much work needs to be done has a perceived untoward outcome. If a client suffers with panic disorder, getting well may mean needing to learn how to tell other people no or needing to make some life choices that he has been avoiding. Alice, an agoraphobic client, told her counselor that if she was well, she would need to move out of her parents' home and start dating again. She had experienced numerous painful breakups in her early twenties and had moved back home and lived with her parents for the last seven years. For that reason, we tell clients that we don't want to help them change something they think they should experience, or eliminate a feeling that they believe they should feel. One technique that is useful with outcome resistance is the magic button (see below).

5. *Plan*. **The plan depends on your conceptualization of the client.**

Conceptualization is really the main tool of the entire system. After examining a specific situation, a client's specific problem can be conceptualized as fitting into one of four categories: a mood or anxiety problem, an unwanted habit or addiction, a relationship problem, or no problem since the client's emotional reaction is normal. The type of problem sets the basis for developing the treatment road map and directing the choice of SITs. In Cindy's case the situation analysis revealed that when she got home she started telling herself that she didn't have the energy or the determination to spend time with her son. She felt guilty because she thought that if she really did love him, she would be motivated and energized. Based on this information, we could see that these thoughts directly interfered with her taking the time to spend with her son. And when she went to bed instead of spending time with him, her guilt was exacerbated.

Magic button technique. The magic button, also called paradoxical cost-benefit analysis, is very useful for getting at outcome resistance. In addressing Alice's panic, the magic button proved very helpful.

Counselor: Alice, imagine a magic button in front of you. If you press the button, your symptoms will be gone. You no longer have panic. In fact, you are not even afraid of panic symptoms. You can do the things you did in the past. Would you hit the button?

Alice: Of course I would!

Counselor: Okay. I'm glad you said that, but let's dig into it more. Let's consider the advantages and disadvantages for changing. What are some of the advantages?

Alice: I would get my old life back. [*Press for specificity.*]

Counselor: What do you mean you get your old life back?

Alice: I would get to do some of the things I used to do.

Counselor: Like what?

Alice: I love to help people do stuff. They have things they need me to help them with . . . like cleaning or helping them with some project. I would also be able to go back to being an accountant. I like being an accountant.

Counselor: You like being useful.

Alice: Yeah, I do.

Counselor: [Continue to press for specificity.] Alice, what are some of the disadvantages to this? Keep in mind that anything that is an advantage can be a disadvantage. What might be those things that you cannot tolerate? What is it that stops you?

Around 90 percent of the time, clients don't see any disadvantages. This requires you to exercise your knowledge and understanding of human behavior so that you can help the client consider disadvantages to changing. Not in a critical way, but in a gentle and understanding way, suggest possibilities.

Counselor: You know, Alice, what strikes me is the Walmart episode you described to me. If you get back to your old self, you are going to get out and about. People might ask you to do things, to help them with stuff. Before you know it, you might find yourself overcommitted and overwhelmed with responsibilities. You might become spread too thin. It is very hard for you to say no.

Alice: You're right. I don't like to tell people no.

Counselor: If you did say no to them, what do you think might happen?

Alice: I don't like to upset people. I don't like to get them angry.

Counselor: Alice, this is a very important point. One of the things that anxious people tend to have in common is they don't like to say no. They are very, very nice people. You are right that sometimes saying no can disappointment people. So one of the good reasons not to hit the magic button is that you would have to learn to say no. After all, people are used to you helping them with things. You see, I would like to help you with your panic attacks, but to do so would mean you would have to face the possibility that they might be upset with you.

At this point, Alice must decide if it's worth overcoming her panic anxiety if she will ultimately need to learn how to say no to demanding people. In many instances, the client makes the case for why she needs to overcome her fear of saying no and dealing with the possibility of disappointing someone. This technique is a powerful way to overcome resistance because the client is now trying to convince you why she needs to learn this new skill.

A similar phenomenon also occurs with clients who have happy phobia. Elizabeth, who was feeling good at the end of the session, went home and cut herself—a behavior that had plagued her very chaotic past. She described an incident with her mother, whose mental health problems led to frequent hospitalization as much as thirty days at a time. Elizabeth said that her mom was discharged from the hospital and was doing well. One day she arrived home from school and found that the house was pristine with the pleasant smell of dinner cooking—both firsts in Elizabeth's life. Pleased with this foreign experience, she went to her room, which was also immaculate. While changing into her play clothes, Elizabeth remembered thinking, *Maybe things are really going to turn around here.* At that very moment, Elizabeth heard a *ka-thump* downstairs. She shot down the stairs and found her mother lying on the kitchen floor, passed out from a drug overdose. Though not the first time her mother tried to commit suicide, this time she died. Elizabeth had previously shared that her mom had died from suicide, but she had not offered this specific information. "Elizabeth, it seems that your mom was trying to make everything perfect for you. As a result of this traumatic experience, you concluded that happiness is a harbinger that bad is coming. Everything is going down from here. Deep down you feel scared to death to feel happy, because if you do, something awful will happen." This is outcome resistance. Elizabeth had developed a framework that led to her covertly choosing to stay down because it hurt too much to feel good. Thus, Elizabeth sabotaged her mood.

Counselor: So, I understand, Elizabeth, why you are not interested in hitting the button.

Elizabeth: Of course I am! Why do you think I'm coming?

Counselor: Are you sure? Because it is going to be very scary for you. Remem-

ber after the last session when you felt so good you were going to go to Starbucks and get your favorite coffee? On your way over, you started feeling guilty. *I don't deserve this. My life sucks. My life doesn't matter. We don't have the money to get it. I'll just get water when I get home.* Thoughts like this are going to keep coming. Are you willing to work at resisting these internal directives?

Since Elizabeth was willing to risk facing these irrational directives, we could get down to work. Outcome resisters might be afraid of feeling good, of autonomy, of abandonment, of disapproval, or of finding self (e.g., of what they like or don't like). For resisters, it comes down to their choices.

Cognitive restructuring. A traditional technique is cognitive restructuring, which helps clients discover their flawed cognitions, deactivate them, and develop alternative cognitions based in truth. The focus in this section is on the discovery and deactivation tasks. The technique is not difficult to understand but does take skill in applying. One means of cognitive restructuring involves two broad steps.

Educate. The first step is to educate the client. We begin with teaching clients that emotions and behaviors are the by-products of cognitions, and this provides a framework for discovering and challenging beliefs and schemata. We also educate clients that their reactions are the effects of flawed beliefs. Reactions can be cognitive, emotional, physical, and behavioral, and can impact the client's individual, social, and spiritual life. Strong and disproportionate emotions and behavior to a stimulus event are clear evidence of maladaptive schemas.

Cognitive distortion checklist. The introduction of sin into a perfect creation has distorted God's original design. Since that time, humanity has succumbed to believing lies and allowing emotions to subsume the logical thought process. As an attempt to identify the distortions and lies, several cognitive theorists have developed a list of cognitive distortions (Beck, 1967a; Burns, 1999). Scriptural truth, of course, is another means by which lies and distortions can be disputed. The list of distortions can be given to clients to evaluate the accuracy and truthfulness of their cognitions.

Awareness. Clients must also learn to recognize the faulty cognitions. One means of accomplishing this task is through discrimination training. Clients are made aware of what they are telling themselves before, during, and after a targeted stimulus event. Then the work is to determine the validity of the identified cognitions using such techniques as the downward arrow and the experimental technique.

Downward arrow/vertical arrow technique. To identify the chain of cognitions that underlie the client's automatic thoughts, you may choose to use the downward arrow (Beck, Rush, Shaw, & Emery, 1979; Burns, 1999; Leahy, 2017). Rather than challenging the original thought, operate on the basis that the thought *might* be true. No matter what the client says, the responses are always accepted at face value.

The inference of the client's statements is examined until it reaches a conclusion. The underlying cognition typically takes the form of "if . . . then" statements or conditional beliefs.

Begin by clearly identifying the automatic thought the client wants to address. From this point forward, keeping asking, "Suppose that [what the client says] was true, what would that mean to you? Why would that be upsetting to you?" (Burns, 1999). Judith Beck (1995) distinguishes between asking what the thought means *to* the client, which elicits an intermediate belief, and asking what it means *about* the client, which usually uncovers the core belief. The questioning and the redefinition of each of the connections can be a therapeutic end. Beck and associates (Beck, Steer, Beck, & Newman, 1993) write, "Many patients are unable to articulate these underlying beliefs until they have been asked to consider the personal meaning that their more manifest thoughts have for them. Therefore, when patients exhibit strong negative emotions that seem to be far more intense than their automatic thoughts alone would cause, therapists can ask patients to probe a bit deeper by asking successive variations of the question 'What does that mean to you?'" (p. 140).

Continue asking the same question to each elicited cognition until you notice a shift in your client's affect or when the belief repeats itself in the same or similar words (J. S. Beck, 1995). At that point, you have arrived at the core belief or schema. Consider the example below that illustrates the technique with Cindy.

Counselor: Let's use a special technique to see if we can get to the bottom of this thought. How does that sound?

Cindy: That sounds like a good idea, but I don't know how to get to the bottom of it.

Counselor: No problem. We'll take a stab at it. You mentioned that whenever you begin to prepare for an exam you wonder whether you can actually pass it or not. Suppose that you are preparing for an upcoming exam and you start obsessing over whether you can pass it or not. What would that mean?

Cindy: It would mean that I am a failure at something I want to be good at. A complete failure?

Counselor: Yes. Suppose that you were a complete failure, that your worse fear was true. What would that mean to you? Why would that be upsetting to you?

Cindy: It would mean that I would let down God and my family.

Counselor: If you let down both God and your family, what would be so bad about that?

Cindy: You cannot let God down, and my parents are paying for school.

Counselor: So what does that mean about you, letting down both God and your parents, who are paying for your education?

Cindy: It would prove that I will never amount to anything and that something is totally wrong with me.

Counselor: So it sounds like you are drastically afraid of wasting your life and being unredeemable to God. If that were true, what would it mean about you? Why would it be upsetting to you?

Cindy: It would mean that I'm worthless.

Counselor: So deep down in your heart of hearts, you fear that you are not enough, that you have absolutely no value.

Continue following your client's cognitive chain until you reach the foundational schema. At this point, you could begin work to deactivate it and introduce a new core belief rooted in truth.

The experimental technique. The client is asked to conduct an experiment to determine whether a seemingly dysfunctional belief is true (Burns, 1999). The technique also can be used for discovery and for developing new cognitions.

First, explain the technique and the benefits of testing the validity of each thought. Next, collaboratively develop an experiment to test the truth of the thought. In Cindy's case, she thought that because she was unmotivated and fatigued she couldn't possibly spend any quality time with her son in the evening. She also believed that because she had these feelings, she would be unable to show loving, caring behavior toward her son. So we set up an experiment where we could test these thoughts. We first asked her to predict how hard it would be for her to spend twenty minutes with her son after eating dinner. She said that on a scale of 0 to 100, where 100 is the most difficult anything could possibly be, it would be a 90. We then described what she might do during that twenty-minute time frame that her son might find enjoyable. We then picked a specific day she would carry out the experiment. Cindy's job was to see if in fact she could do it and to rate how difficult it was to do after the fact. She was also to rate how much enjoyment and satisfaction she received from doing it. Finally, we wanted her to rate how guilty she felt after the fact. This was important, because Cindy said that she felt very guilty when she went to bed. Now we wanted to see how guilty she felt after spending some quality time with her son.

After carrying out an experiment like this, we often have our clients email us the results so that we can reinforce their efforts for carrying out such an experiment. In Cindy's case, she found that once she made the decision that she was going to do this no matter what, it was much easier to do (only a 20 instead of a 90). She also could tell that her son was really enjoying the time, which made her feel good about herself as a mother, and she reported feeling virtually no guilt after the fact.

At times it is necessary to discern the interrelationships between one thought and another. Ferreting out the faulty cognitions can take a couple of sessions, so be patient. Negative and faulty thoughts need to be replaced with truth-based counters, thoughts that are incompatible with the self-defeating thoughts. If the thought is not confirmed, the goal is to develop a new reality-based belief and then investigate whether evidence exists that the alternative cognition is reality based (e.g., biblical, logical). Cindy learned to override her motivational perfectionism with a more realistic thought: *I don't have to be perfectly motivated to do something. I just need to start doing it, and then the motivation will come.*

You must assist the client in making the new thoughts a habit; thus, continual practice is required. The aim is the client internalizing these new thoughts. Collaboratively identify ways to reinforce the new cognitions. In session you might consider using role play or covert imaginary rehearsal. The rehearsal may take the form of a dialogue or a script and may be read aloud by the client, put on index cards, and/or audio-recorded. McMullin (1986) found that it takes about six weeks of practice for the alternative thoughts to replace the problematic thoughts.

Cognitive behavioral analysis system of psychotherapy (CBASP). One way to gain insight into clients' cognitive and emotional worlds is through a detailed analysis of the situations that trigger negative reactions (McCullough, 2000, 2006). Known as CBASP, the analysis is a counseling model that seeks to modify cognitive, emotional, behavioral, and interpersonal problems. It is recognized as the only evidence-based treatment for chronic depression.

While more than an intervention, strategy, and technique, the model is highly useful in helping clients walk through many mood issues. Unlike classic CBT, less attention is given to cognitions. The primary focus is directly on "behavioral social problem-solving" (Swan et al., 2013, p. 269). The cognitive behavioral analysis system of psychotherapy uses contemporary learning theory, so clients learn new ways of interacting to achieve desired outcomes through relationships by examining old maladaptive ways of relating and cultivating interpersonal strategies (Sayegh et al., 2012). Rather than specifically addressing cognitions, the social component of CBASP is especially tailored to the interpersonal hostility and preoperational thought that is often seen in chronically depressed clients (McCullough, Lord, Conley, & Martin, 2010).

One CBASP technique is situational analysis (SA). SA teaches clients about their roles in relationships and how to change their long-standing maladaptive interpersonal behaviors. SA is a systematic way of examining situations that the client experienced and describing the situation, the client's interpretation of the situation, the client's action while the situation was taking place, the result of the situation, and the desired outcome of the situation, including whether the desired result was attained. The process can be completed with a number of different experiences over a period of time as a way to teach the chronically depressed patient how to adapt their social behaviors to achieve desired outcomes. Once this initial phase of SA is completed, the client and therapist begin the second phase of SA and discuss why or why not the desired outcome was accomplished.

The first step involves discovering the range of antecedents or situations that are deemed as triggers to problematic thinking and feeling. The situation is described in detail, as if the client were playing a movie of what happened. Then the client's thoughts and feelings are elicited. Clients typically frame their reactions as causal (e.g., "He made me mad," "She hurt my feelings," "The situation really upset me"). What clients often edit out is what they said and did in response to the situation to justify their reactions. It is helpful to have the client write her reactions on paper or on a whiteboard. You work with the client to help her examine whether her thoughts in that particular situation were helpful in obtaining the desired outcomes. If her thoughts were not helpful, they can be revised and replaced with more relevant and useful thoughts.

Deconstruction and Deactivation SITs

Deconstruction techniques are one means by which clients are assisted in diminishing the strength of their cognitions. The goal is to make faulty cognitions inoperative. Because the mind can be viewed as a giant computer, nothing is ever deleted from the memory. All cognitions are stored in our hard drive whether we put them into the trash bin or not. Cognitive viruses are malicious codes or programs that when activated are designed to serve as destructive viruses that corrupt our minds.

Double-standard technique. In this powerful technique, the therapist asks the client if he or she would use the same negative, perfectionistic, black-and-white patterns of thinking to relate to a dear friend. The idea is that in many cases people are much more difficult on themselves than they would be on someone they love and value. If we should treat others with sensitivity and warmth, we should do the same to ourselves.

Counselor: What would you say to a friend who is in the exact same situation as you?

Cindy: Well, gee, I don't know.

Counselor: Well, would you tell her, "You are a total failure"?

Cindy: Oh no.

Counselor: Would you not say it because you don't believe it, don't want to hurt her feelings, or because you really believe it is true that she is a total failure but just don't want to say it?

Cindy: Oh, no. I won't think that. I'd never think that.

[Let's suppose Cindy would reply]: Well, I may think it is true, but I wouldn't say it to her.

Counselor: Why wouldn't you say it to her?

Cindy: Because it would make her feel horrible.

Counselor: Okay. Why wouldn't you want her to feel horrible?

Cindy: Well, that would be a horrible thing to do.

Counselor: Yeah, but why? Would you think that making her feel horrible would make her feel better? Perhaps motivate her to improve.

Cindy: Of course not. No!

Counselor: Well, then, why do you do the same thing to yourself?

One of the things we are trying to build in CT is a sense of self that relates to the self, talks to itself. We want the internal self to be a good and healthy internal leader. We'll often ask, "What are characteristics of a good leader?" and kick that around for a while. A good leader is kind, loving, sensitive, and realistic. Realistic means that they see things with flexibility, they are not black-and-white or all-or-nothing thinkers. Keep in mind that being self-destructive

comes easiest for human nature. Of course, as Christians we call this the "sin nature" or the "flesh." Living in the flesh is inherently destructive, and sin will eventually destroy those who serve the flesh. Some of this internal bent toward destruction is in human DNA. Diseases are part of sin. Thus, depression, for example, is in part a disease that affects how people think about themselves. Any issue is the externalization of the problem. People buy into the lie. Then, with the hook set, they berate themselves. It isn't that they love doing so. They simply accept the lie as fact.

Our ultimate desire is to help clients assimilate the mind of Christ into the sense of self. We encouraged Cindy toward this end. Just as she would relate kindly to a friend who said the negative things to herself that Cindy was telling herself, Christ would relate to Cindy with matchless compassion and grace. Just as you wouldn't put down a good friend, you don't put down yourself. Just as Christ doesn't shame us, we don't shame ourselves. We're not saying that this doesn't mean that you don't point out your own shortcomings and sin. The bottom line is that through CT, we help clients learn to treat themselves the way Christ treats them. It is more than helping them see what is unhealthy and unrealistic and more than deconstructing them. It is challenging them to replace those thoughts by developing healthier ones. To being kind and realistic with themselves. It is helping clients follow the Golden Rule with themselves.

Counselor: Cindy, rather than telling yourself that you are a total failure, what could or would you say to yourself that is both kind and realistic? [*Of course, this is not just cognition. The way you decide to talk to yourself is behavior.*]

Cindy: I'm not sure.

Counselor: Okay. So think about it this way. You didn't like the outcome that you had before. Right? So what outcome would you rather have instead?

Cindy: Well, I wouldn't want to tell myself I'm crap.

Counselor: If we rewound this, after you eat dinner with your son, what would you do differently?

Cindy: I wanted to make dinner, eat dinner with him, and help him with his homework or maybe just play a game with him.

Counselor: If you wanted to do that, what would you have to say to yourself?

Cindy: I don't know?

Counselor: Well, if I wanted to pick this pen up off this desk, what would I have to do?

Cindy: Tell myself to pick it up? [*both of us laughing*] [*It is interesting how many clients say they have no idea; so, you might have to answer for them.*]

Counselor: Yes. That isn't rocket science. [*This is what is known as self-directed behavior.*] So, if you wanted to go home and make dinner, eat with your son, and help him with his homework or play a game, what would you have to say to yourself?

Cindy: Tell myself to do it.

Counselor: Did telling yourself that you were a piece of crap help? Or did telling yourself that you were a terrible mom help? Calling yourself a failure—did that help you?

Cindy: No.

Counselor: So then what would you have to say?

Cindy: When I get home I need to do those things.

Counselor: Say, "Even though I'm tired, even though I'm feeling bad, I want to do this."

Cindy: I see what you mean.

Counselor: Good. Cindy, can you see yourself doing that? Telling yourself, "I'm not going to be negative or let it control me. I already know that what I've been telling myself isn't true and works in opposition to what I want." You don't have to become your own internal cheerleader. You just need to know that when these thoughts come into your head, they are wrong. Then you need to create new ones.

Sibcy river technique. We are different from our thoughts (T), feelings (F), images (I), and sensations (S), which we abbreviate as TFIS. In short, we are not our thoughts. They are of us, but they are not us. If you have a thought, it doesn't make it true. Also, if you have a thought, it doesn't mean that you believe it. This is known as "thought-behavior fusion" or "thought affect fusion." It is important for people to realize that just because they have a thought that does not mean they have to act on it or believe it. The fusions are correlated with many forms of psychopathology.

The river (see figure 3.1) is a powerful metaphor that illustrates those truths. Moreover, the river makes the idea of mindfulness digestible for clients. It is especially useful for those who have unpleasant, intrusive TFIS they judge to be bad or dangerous. It is also useful when people are lost in their daydreams, that is, their internal dialogue.

The following represents the content of what was shared with Cindy. Psychologically, consciousness can be considered a stream that is constantly flowing in our mind. TFIS are released by the brain and float down the river. These represent the content of the river. Though TFIS may come individually, they typically come in packages, and one of the contents can trigger others in succession. For example, an image can trigger feelings, and then feelings can activate thoughts, and so forth. Additionally, we explained to Cindy that having an image of herself engaging in some behavior was equivalent to doing that behavior. The brain simply doesn't recognize the difference.

Distinguishing between the mind and the self is also important. The self resides on the bank. It can step back from the content floating down the river and just observe the different TFIS as they come floating downstream. To observe means that the self can direct its attention. The arrow from the self is the person directing his attention. The brain will attend to things that it finds important, and can do so automatically. The self, though, can override the brain. The self can redirect focus on any content in the river, grouping, or package. This is called "focal" attention; it is intentional and volitional. People typically can attend to it for four to seven seconds before it begins to drift, requiring that the person grab their attention and bring it back.

If, then, we are not our TFIS, where do they come from? They originate in and proceed from the brain. Just as we are not our TFIS, we are also not our brains. The brain is an organ that God gave to our bodies, just like any other organ. An analogy we use is that people do not consider themselves responsible for what their gut does, nor do they confuse themselves with their stomachs. People also don't confuse themselves with the content or activity of their stomachs.

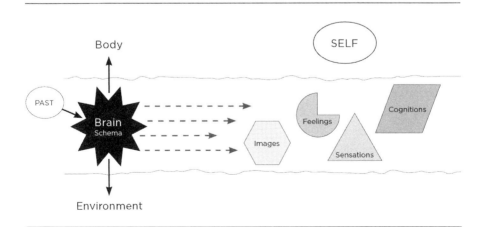

Figure 3.1. Sibcy river metaphor

For example, if someone burps, we know that the burp was not intentionally produced. People don't think, *Why did I do that? What's wrong with me? I'm such an acidic person!* People don't do burp because they want to; the gut simply works that way.

Interestingly, all the chemistry that resides in your brain also resides in your gut. Your gut sometimes is viewed as a second brain. You may feel things emotionally occur in your gut—they are felt at the gut level. Likewise, the brain has contents that result in outcomes as well. For example, the brain has developed contents such as schema (based on life experiences). It constantly and automatically processes information coming in from the environment and up from the body. The result is schemas that are born and established. Based on these processes, the brain burps TFIS into the river of consciousness. Literally, about 90 percent of what the brain does is automatic, including the autonomic nervous system, limbic system, and so on. Realizing this is important because many people think they generate their thoughts. We can, however, override what our brains do 90 percent of the time.

When Alice's brain threw out the thought *I can't handle this anxiety*, she was able to use her sense of self and override what she was experiencing. She was able to say to herself, *This is just anxiety; it can't hurt me. It is uncomfortable but bearable. It also likely occurred because of something that triggered it in my environment.* Her brain made an evaluation that things were hopeless. Because she allowed that thought to roll on from her conscious-

ness, her body lost energy and vitality. She wanted to sleep. She then felt like she was a failure, accompanied by feelings of sadness and worthlessness. She had images of past failures and images of future ones. She lost herself in the river. We don't want people like Alice to get swept away and lost in the river. We want to help them to stay on the bank to observe.

We also want people to build a bridge over the river where the environment is; that is, to be in the real world as it is happening in the now. Even though Cindy had the thought of being a worthless mom in her head and the physical sensation of tiredness in her body, the river metaphor allowed her just to observe these as experiences in the stream of consciousness. Instead of getting lost in the river, we helped her build a bridge into the real world where she focused her attention on making dinner for her son, eating with him, helping him with his homework, and playing a game with him. By focusing her attention on the real world, the other thoughts and feelings just drifted away from her awareness, and before she knew it, they were replaced with feelings of value and self-worth.

In a study of five thousand participants, Killingsworth and Gilbert (2010) sought to determine a difference between happy people and depressed people. The participants received an app that allowed them to get a random daily text message asking several questions: (1) On a scale of 0 to 10, how happy would you rate yourself? (2) What were you doing just before you got this text? (3) Did you want to be doing it? (4) Was your mind wandering?

Were you inside your head being swept away by whatever internal content was in there, or was the self anchored into what you were doing?

Here is the interesting finding: How happy people felt was not directly tied to what participants were doing or whether they wanted to do it or not. For example, you might be doing something you don't want to be doing, such as yardwork. However, if you focus on the task without allowing your mind to wander, you can still be okay despite the unpleasant task. Conversely, you might be doing something you enjoy, such as going to a movie, but if you allow your mind to wander about what you think you should be doing, you will not feel very happy. The study found that being focused on the activity at hand, that is, staying present, improved mood.

A slice of time technique. To move beyond a client's global, transitional description to an actual place and an actual time frame, consider the slice of time technique. Identifying a slice of time provides a beginning, middle, and end to an event. It is considered a discovery and deconstruction task. Consider Cindy's narrative about her husband. "My husband doesn't appreciate me. Nothing I do interests him. He cares more about his video games than me. He has always had an addictive personality—he absorbs himself in everything but me. I guess it's just me. If I try to tell him how I feel, he'll just go off again and start putting me down. It's useless for me to say anything to him about my feelings. I don't matter to him." After working with Cindy, we developed an alternative narrative that represented a slice of time. "The other

evening I decided to tell my husband my feelings about him spending so much time playing a video game. I told him that I felt he was addicted to the game and even told him there is research on how these games work like addictions. I also told him that it was like he had a mistress, and that I couldn't stand it anymore. He told me I was overreacting and that I blow everything out of proportion. I told him I was just trying to tell him my feelings. He told me I needed to get a life and walked off."

Cost-benefit analysis technique. A. T. Beck (1995) employed the cost-benefit analysis technique as a straightforward approach to examining problematic cognitions. While it is like "examine the evidence technique" (Leahy, 2017), it elicits and examines the costs (e.g., losses, disadvantages) and benefits (e.g., advantages, secondary gains) of a particular belief.

The value of this strategy is that it is a logical and sensible approach to problematic thinking, is user-friendly, and puts the weight of evidence on the option that makes sense to the client. As Christians, however, we must remember that at times God does call us to choose options that violate human logic or human comfort. Consider Abraham's illegal and preposterous decision to obey God and sacrifice Isaac. Never get so locked into a technique that you ignore the work of God in the situation.

First, brainstorm the costs and then benefits of a belief. Ask the client: (a) "What would change if you believed this less?" and (b) "What would change if you believed it more?" Once the costs and benefits have been established, ask the client to determine the split between the costs and benefits. Leahy (2017) offers a few questions to consider in evaluating the split: "(a) If you had to apportion 100% between the costs and the benefits, would it be a 50/50 split?; (b) if not, what is the split?; (c) how would you apportion the 100% between those costs and benefits?; (d) considering an alternative belief, what are the costs and benefits of that thought?; and (e) how does the cost-benefit analysis compare with analysis of the current belief?" (p. 41).

The last step is to test the chosen or alternative belief according to the costs and benefits.

Survey technique. The survey method is used to determine if other people agree with a client's cognition (Burns, 1999), that is, to find collateral evidence of whether the belief is common. If the technique seems appropriate, the client seeks out key people who can provide their opinion on the belief. For example, if a client believes that she is not genuinely spiritual unless she prays and reads her Bible for hours each day, she can survey "godly" people to obtain their opinion on the legitimacy of that belief. A man who becomes extraordinarily anxious when he speaks in public can ask public speakers if they ever feel anxious when they speak and, if so, how much.

The reattribution technique. Attribution theory undertakes to detail the processes by which we attempt to determine and label causation of events. It is our way of making meaning and explaining the world. The reattribution technique *challenges* people's natural tendency to introject blame; it is well suited for those who engage in the cognitive distortions of personalization or self-blame (Burns, 1999). Reattribution encourages people to focus on solving a problem instead of using up all their energy in self-reproach. Responsibility needs to be accepted where it is legitimate to do so. Our tendency toward hindsight bias, however, makes assigning causation problematic. The point is, once the outcome is known, we can attribute causation (e.g., gutsy decision or poor decision) based on what happens. When people make decisions, they do so without knowledge of the outcome, without seeing all the factors that could influence the result.

As with many of these cognitive techniques, using the reattribution method is uncomplicated. Encourage the client to consider what other factors might have contributed to the problem. Together you and the client make a list of the possibilities. We often use a whiteboard in our office to write them down, but the technique can be assigned as a homework project or the list kept on a sheet of paper. Burns (1999) shares the illustration of a man whose wife had lost interest in sex. The man's automatic thoughts were along the lines of feeling rejected, undesirable, unloved, and unworthy, and they contained several distortions, including personalization, mind reading, and all-or-nothing thinking. He was encouraged to generate a list of possible reasons for the wife's loss of interest in sex. His list included the possibility that it was physically painful for her to engage in sex, that it was her means of communicating anger over some issue, that she was depressed, and that she was dissatisfied with his lovemaking. Whereas being undesirable and unworthy were difficult problems to address, the reasons on his list offered a great deal of hope.

Define terms technique. This technique is based on the idea of "What is in a name?" All of us have had the experience of labeling ourselves in the midst or on the heels of an event. Cindy called herself a "lousy" mother. By doing so, she was labeling herself without consideration of the full meaning of the term. The define terms technique asks the client to give the definition of the term (Burns, 1999; Leahy, 2003).

Leahy (2003) introduces this technique with the following: "For us to examine and challenge your thoughts, we have to know what you are talking about." Burns (1999) encourages asking, "How are you defining your terms?" or "What do you mean by this?" A client who is shaming herself for giving a poor speech in class might say something like, "I am so stupid . . . a real loser!" Your task is to help your client consider what those words actually mean. For example, "You say that you are stupid and a real loser. What is the definition of *stupid* and *loser*?" A dictionary will ultimately show that the terms apply to everyone; we are all stupid at times and we all lose at times. Leahy (2003) asks clients to imagine that they are scientists conducting research. If someone said, "Bill is stupid," and you wanted to determine if the statement was an accurate perception of Bill, the first step would be to define the term. Put another way, "How would you know whether someone else was stupid?"

Burns (1999) writes, "Labels like 'fool,' 'loser,' 'winner,' 'jerk,' or 'inferior person' are useless abstractions. It is far more productive to focus on what you do and what you can do to learn and grow than on what you are" (p. 109). God, too, knows the power of a label. We are called God's friends (John 15:15), "God's holy people (Rom. 1:7), sons and daughters of God (2 Cor. 6:18), God's treasured possessions (Deut. 14:2; 26:18), and the beloved children of God (Eph. 5:1), and we are given a new name representing our new identity (Rev. 2:17). Labeling ourselves according to God's terminology rather than our own distortions and lie-based abstractions changes our perception of and relationship to ourselves.

The semantic method technique. The purpose of the semantic method, according to Burns (1999), is to help clients stop scolding themselves. This technique is based on the idea of using language to create meaning. When a client uses more intense, emotionally laden, or extreme language, he can be asked to provide more reasonable words. Burns (1999) categorizes client semantic problems into "self-focused" and "other-focused." Self-focused cognitions typically produce such feelings as guilt, shame, anxiety, or depression. For instance, self-focused semantic problems noted in someone who says, "I can't," might be rephrased with the words "I don't want to." "I must" can be converted to "It would be a wise decision to. . . ." Clients often say, "I should . . ." or "I shouldn't . . . ," which creates an experience of feeling controlled or manipulated. Use the semantic method to rephrase the client's expression to "It would be wise . . ." or "It would be nice . . . ," or "there would be some advantages to. . . ."

Other-focused (e.g., people, organizations, objects, God) cognitions generate problems because they are outside of a client's control. "He should have thought about that before he did it"; "The smartest thing she could do is tell that person what for"; "God is punishing me"; and "My wife should be more thoughtful" are examples of other-focused cognitions. Intense feelings such as frustration and anger are noted in those who have other-focused expectations. When clients hear themselves and consider the ramifications of their words, they may become aware and motivated to change.

Role reversal technique. One easy technique that helps clients both challenge their thoughts and develop new thoughts is role reversal (Leahy, 2003). Role reversal provides a means of helping the client examine the world from another person's point of view. We have structured the technique into four steps. First, after obtaining consent to use the strategy, assign the problematic role, such as being a failure, to the client, and you play the opposite, in this case not being a failure.

Ask the client to work as hard as possible to shut down your positive comments using their negative ones. Your task is to use sound logic to combat the client's negativity. One of the most important requirements in using this technique is your ability to articulate a sound disputation. You can use Scripture, common sense, rationalism, and so forth to form your arguments. The main point is that you must be convincing.

Finally, once the dialogue has reached a clear conclusion and it is evident that your logical responses are stronger and more based in reality than the client's negative ones, exchange roles. In this role you must work hard to challenge the client to give up; of course, you are externalizing the client's negative self-statements. At times you will need to stop to encourage the client or suggest ideas before reengaging in the disputation.

Developing Healthy and Truth-Based SITs

In Ephesians 4:22–24 and Colossians 3:1–14, the apostle Paul encourages us to "put off" poor thoughts and behavior and to "put on" Christlike thoughts and behavior. Deconstructing or deactivating cognitions necessitates replacing them with more rational, functional, and reality-based cognitions. A fundamental principle of CT is SITs geared toward breaking down automatic maladaptive cognitions and replacing them with more realistic, adaptive cognitions. Cognitive development techniques facilitate growth of new, more adaptive, and reality-based cognitions. Several development SITs are described below.

Healthy cognitive thinking can be achieved using cognitive restructuring, experimental technique, situational analysis, role reversal, and others. One additional cognitive development technique we will provide is problem solving.

Externalization of voices technique. Burns (1999) considers this strategy one of the most "powerful and entertaining cognitive therapy techniques" (p. 122).

It is a role-play exercise whereby you verbalize the client's dysfunctional thoughts as accurately as possible while the client attempts to counter your verbalizations with healthier and more adaptive responses (Burns, 1993). It is important to remember that you are not talking to the client. Rather, you are speaking for her in such a manner that an alternative dialogue is moved from the client's head to open conversation. As Cindy spoke her internal dialogue, her verbalizations were countered by the counselor. The idea is that you are another voice inside your client's head. You speak the voice of the Spirit, if you will. The strategy ends with processing the dialogue that took place. By making the internal voices external, it is easier to recognize the messages, to hear them in a clearer manner, and to address them. Externalization of voices helps clients learn adaptive responses and rallies their motivation to dispute maladaptive responses.

Problem-solving technique. Counseling can sometimes be simplified to a problem-solving enterprise (Dixon & Glover, 1984). Frequently, a problem calls for action. Consider these typical types of problems: (1) What do I do about a demanding and demeaning workplace supervisor? (2) Should I consider taking a better job that would require a move? (3) Should I move out from my parents' home? (4) Should I get a divorce? Each problem is comprised of cognitive and emotional concomitants that usually impact the client and his or her significant others.

One approach to decision making is a problem-solving method that uses discrete steps that can be taught to address immediate and future problems. Using such an approach is intuitive, logical, and not cumbersome. Nevertheless, you must know when and how to tackle problems using this approach. The question of when to use a problem-solving approach is not an easy one. Clearly it is well suited for short-term, time-limited counseling. A client might not wish to explore the past, examine present relationships, or enlist help on issues deemed irrelevant to the problem at hand.

First, define the problem clearly and as the client views it. Next, determine how the client has already tried to solve the problem. At times, people's decisional impasses are because the current decision has been contaminated by previous "solutions" to the problem.

Once you have identified the client's perspective of the problem and previous attempts at resolving it, you need to evaluate the real problem and frame it in a solvable way. Take, for example, a client who believes that his problem is his supervisor's inequitable treatment of workers. The client might believe that he is treated unfairly and as a result has slacked off in his performance. The supervisor's employee treatment is not directly solvable, though action can be taken to address it. The real problem is the client's response to the situation and what needs to be done.

The next step is to brainstorm and create a list of all possible options to address the problem (Osborn, 1963). Several guidelines are necessary for a successful brainstorming session: (1) Freewheeling is encouraged to generate as many ideas as possible—the more unusual or bizarre the ideas the better. (2) Judgment on the feasibility or rightness of each idea is deferred until as many ideas have been generated as possible so that ideas can emerge without fear of criticism. (3) The client is encouraged to think up as many ideas as possible—the more the better. (4) Previous ideas can be improved on or expanded. This activity can be done in session, assigned as homework, or completed as a combination of both. If the problem is defined as the client coping with his supervisor's behavior, a list of possible coping responses can be developed to handle the situation better. If the problem is determined to be the place the client is working, options can be generated about how to get out of the department or find another job.

Once completed, fairly investigate all the options. The client might be encouraged to search the Scriptures for principles that help evaluate the options. The cost-benefit analysis technique might help to evaluate choices. The client should be encouraged to pray about his situation, perhaps discuss the issues with his spouse or significant other, and take time to adequately weigh all options.

Once the options have been weighed, the client must choose his option regardless of how poor you might believe that choice to be. The client must also fully commit to it without agonizing over whether it was the right or best decision as he attempts to make it work. A halfhearted attempt is no attempt. Jesus said that no one should look back once he puts his hand to the plow (Luke 9:62). Second-guessing will only contaminate the implementation of the decision, cause misery, and lead to a lack of peace.

After the choice is implemented, you and the client will evaluate the quality and effectiveness of the decision. This is another place to consider the morality of the chosen course of action. If the decision turned out less than desirable, and if possible, revisit the previous steps in the problem-solving method to arrive at a new decision.

As with all techniques, problem solving must be used within the context of multicultural sensitivity and with sensitivity to the environmental forces that have impacted the client's growth and development. It is but one technique to use in conjunction with other procedures to address the unique needs of the client.

CONCLUSION

Cognitions are a highly-esteemed component of human functioning by secular counseling theorists and Christian counseling theorists alike. Addressing problematic cognitions is a staple of all types of counseling, though some theoretical orientations are more explicit about it and more concerned with it.

Although many cognitive SITs exist, we discussed agenda setting, the downward arrow, the double-standard technique, Sibcy's river, the magic button, cognitive restructuring, Socratic questioning, the daily mood log, situational analysis, pros and cons, cost-benefit analysis, role reversal, the survey and experiment technique, and several others. The value of using cognitive techniques is that they are evidence based and thus effective in promoting client change.

We also discussed that cognitions are a central component of being image bearers of God and, unsurprisingly the Bible has much to say about them. Faulty cognitions are more than dysfunctional or unhealthy—they are often lies rooted in the Evil One's character. As Christian counselors, we seek to replace such lies with biblically based truth that can produce significant emotional, behavioral, physical, and cognitive changes eliminating emotional and behavioral problems. The major tasks of cognitive work require discovering problematic cognitions, deconstructing them, and developing alternative healthy and truth-based cognitions. Remember that all helping strategies should be based on a clear conceptualization of the client and fit into an overall treatment plan aimed at reaching therapeutic goals.

RECOMMENDED READING

Backus, W., & Chapian, M. (2000). *Telling yourself the truth*. Bloomington, MN: Bethany House.

Burns, D. D. (1999). *The feeling good handbook*. New York, NY: Penguin.

Leahy, R. L. (2017). *Cognitive therapy techniques: A practitioner's guide* (2nd ed.). New York, NY: Guilford Press.

McCullough, J. P. (2000). *Treatment for chronic depression: Cognitive Behavioral Analysis System of Psychotherapy (CBASP)*. New York, NY: Guilford Press.

McMullin, R. E. (1986). *Handbook of cognitive therapy techniques*. New York, NY: W. W. Norton.

CHAPTER 4

Emotion-Oriented Strategies

Todd Bowman, PhD

A time to weep, and a time to laugh;
a time to mourn, and a time to dance.

ECCLESIASTES 3:4 ESV

Perhaps no single dynamic contained within the human experience possesses the same power to shape our development as the experience of emotion. Emotion propels us toward a loving embrace of a mother, a father, and other family members and caregivers. It enhances the moment of joy shared between two siblings who laugh until it hurts. It repels us from the objects that elicit intrinsic fears deep in our mind. In fact, the Latin root for the word *emotion* literally means "to move." From the heights of ecstasy to the deep trenches of despondency, the currents of emotion ebb and flow, molding our minds and shaping our relationships as we move forward in the developmental progression of life.

While the power of emotion enables us to overcome significant obstacles or accomplish incredible feats, it can also render us paralyzed, a bundle of nerves facing our most terrifying reality, or a puddle of tears at the loss of a beloved family member or pet. The quality of movement that emotion facilitates, then, operates in direct correlation to our ability to attune to it in such a way that fosters productivity, connection, and meaning in our lives.

It is evident in the story of God that he is comfortable with feeling and expressing emotion. In many respects, our emotional makeup is in part a reflection of *imago Dei*, the image of God in us. Throughout Scripture we see the reality of emotion played out before us; some examples point us to adaptive strategies for regulating emotion, such as Christ reaching out to his disciples in the dark, stressful hours of Gethsemane (Matt. 26:36–46; Luke 22:39–46), whereas others demonstrate maladaptive approaches, such as Adam and Eve covering themselves and hiding from God in their shame in the garden (Gen. 3). In God's image, we are created to feel the full range of emotions and to manage them in such a way that we become more connected to God, others, and ourselves.

THEOLOGY AND PSYCHOLOGY OF EMOTION

No scientific or theological model of emotion would be complete without returning to the developmental origins of this essential aspect of the human experience. Emotion lies at the heart of attachment, and attachment is the driving force inherent within our most important human relationships (Lougheed, Koval, & Hollenstein, 2016). When Bowlby began studying the human attachment system, he stumbled upon a rich tapestry of interpersonal concepts, all with one common denominator: emotion. For instance, the safety of the safe haven calms the distress created by separation, and the power of proximity minimizes fear and activates the exploratory system. The truths regarding human connection that Bowlby discovered all point us to the inherent design for connection that God embedded in creation. Consider this: In Genesis God surveys creation and determines that it is "not good for the man to be alone" (2:18). While this passage tends to be used in wedding ceremonies to speak to the covenant of marriage, which is celebratory in its own right, a larger universal reality about God's design is sometimes missed. It is not good for mankind to be alone because we are created in the image of a trinitarian God who exists eternally in relationship. Ultimately we are created for connection beyond marriage.

Because of the relationship between secure attachment and emotional processing, it seems necessary to investigate the relevant applications of attachment in the process of spiritual growth and development in the Christian life. We must begin with the understanding that the biblical narrative is first and foremost an attachment narrative as it intentionally details the covenantal relationship between God and his people. God continually pursues, beckons, and responds to the people of Israel in spite of their continual struggle with collective shortcomings and outright sin. How God moves in relationship to Israel throughout the Old Testament speaks to this dance of attachment between God and his people. He serves as a consistent presence, going before Israel in their journey to the promised land, providing safety and security in the presence of their enemies, acceptance and grace in the face of their Baal-related shame and guilt, and comfort in the pain of consequential living following the breaking of covenant with him (repeatedly). He hears their cries, responds to their needs, and provides for their well-being. In this process, God embodies the fullness of secure attachment, offering the people of Israel a secure base from which to explore the blessings he provides for them. At the same time, he allows the natural consequences for these deviations from his word to run their course. These essential dynamics in the narrative of God's relationship with his people suggests that secure attachment is a critical component of healthy relationship with self, God, and others; the Scriptures were given to promote secure attachment with God, so long as we interpret them through the appropriate lens. And this story is not just the story of Israel thousands of years ago; it is the narrative that we are invited to participate in through the shed blood of Jesus Christ.

As God reveals himself to the people of Israel throughout time and space, he is understood through a variety of names that describe his unchanging nature and character. At the heart of these names, we find the essential tenets of secure attachment. Specifically, God is understood by Israel as Jehovah-Shammah, the Lord who is present (Ezek. 48:35); Jehovah-Shalom, the Lord is peace (Judg. 6:24); Jehovah-Rohi, the Lord my shepherd (Ps. 23:1); and El-Roi, the Strong One who sees (Gen. 16:13). He is known to Christians in the person of Christ as Immanuel, God with us (Isa. 7:14), and in the Holy Spirit as the Comforter (John 14:26). In God we experience presence amid our sorrow, peace in the midst of life's storms, and protection in the face of life's threats. There is no pain he cannot comfort. In him we are seen clearly in our shame and brokenness yet loved unconditionally and invited back into wholeness through Christ. These names by which we understand God fully help us to understand secure attachment, mutuality, and reciprocity within the Trinity; these concepts are also evidenced in a variety of relationships depicted in the biblical narrative (see David and Jonathan in 1 and 2 Samuel). Understanding this truth enhances our capacity to love God with the fullness of our being and, subsequently, our neighbor as ourselves (Matt. 22:37–39; Mark 12:30–31). Likewise, our ability to navigate the wide range of emotions contained within the human experience is shaped by the quality of our connection to God and to our primary attachment figures.

The Relational Dimensions of Emotional Experiencing

In his groundbreaking work, Harvard psychologist Ed Tronick led a team of researchers (Tronick, Als, Adamson, Wise, & Brazelton, 1978) who explored the role of parental engagement in the emotional processing of infants. In the famous "still face experiment," mothers and infants are placed in a room together, interacting with natural, connective behaviors known as *synchrony*. The synchrony evidenced between parent and child in the study is easily distinguished by the eye-to-eye contact that the two share; the verbal interactions between the two are exchanged with comfortable *prosody*, or intonation, rhythm, and stress of speech; and the shared exploration of the environment occurs with the child pointing and gesturing and the mother's eyes tracking to the object that has captured the child's interest. The infant expresses her curiosity with her vocalizations and gestures, with the mother mirroring the experience the infant is having with her own tone and gestures. This process is reflective of secure attachment between infant and caregiver.

Then, in an effort to demonstrate the emotional upheaval of emotional unavailability or psychological disconnection, the mother is instructed to blunt her affect and "still" her face. She no longer responds with curiosity or interest to the infant's exploratory behavior. She does not smile, nor does she communicate any emotion nonverbally to the infant. She simply sits in front of the child, unresponsive to the attempts at connection the infant exhibits. As the mother becomes unresponsive, the child's emotional experience changes. With the primary caregiver emotionally inaccessible to her, the infant quickly becomes emotionally activated, and she moves through a series of protests to communicate her emotional distress. First, she points to things in the room in an effort to share an experience with the mother. Next, she uses her language, mostly cooing and making single syllable sounds, because she is accustomed to the mother responding to these. Then she becomes more visibly upset and stretches her arms out toward the mother and makes a high-pitched screeching sound, determined to gain the mother's attention. Finally, this interaction reaches crescendo with the infant's eventual loss of volitional movement and the subsequent turning away from the mother, back arched, tears falling with eyes diverted and her face covered by an arm. As we see in the "covering and hiding" evidenced in the garden as God calls to Adam and Eve, shame, by its very nature, threatens vulnerability in relationship. The power of shame disconnects the mother and infant, distorting the connection they were created to share. In each instance, a core truth is highlighted: it is not good for mankind to be alone.

The brief exchange between the infant and the caregiver in Tronick's experiment sheds tremendous insight into a more relationally oriented understanding of emotion. In particular we see the birth of shame manifest in the experience of becoming psychologically cut off from one's primary attachment figure, leading to a sense of deficiency and inherent lack of worth (Lopez et al., 1997). For many individuals who struggle with process addictions, such as sexual addiction and gambling, chemical addictions, and other indicators of ongoing emotion dysregulation, this experience of isolation serves as the launching pad for the intensification of their psychological symptoms. If idle hands are the devil's plaything, a lonely mind is the devil's amusement park. When disconnected from our primary attachment figures and the sense of belonging that is rooted in community, our fears have a tendency to balloon, our sadness has a tendency to overwhelm, our pain is susceptible to intensify too, until it becomes unbearable, and our shame has a proclivity to consume us from the inside out. Alone, we are overcome by the intensity of our affective experiences and come to be defined by the behaviors we use to soothe these emotional states; in meaningful, connected relationship, we are able to integrate our emotional experiences into a healthy self-concept and dwell richly in community with God and others.

The relationship between psychological disconnection and unhealthy behaviors is rooted in the need to regulate these dysphoric experiences of emotion. We are not created to persist in shame, to wallow in sadness, or to tremble in fear; we are created to connect in positive affect, such as joy, calmness, and security. Psychological connection is a necessary condition for these positive affective states to be experienced. The inaccessibility of primary attachment figures leaves the individual reaching to *self-soothing* activities or turning to external mood-altering behaviors to regulate their emotional experience.

In her work on affective neuroscience, Katehakis (2009) writes, "For infants to attain a healthy self-regulating system, they must first have the early experience of interactive regulation" (p. 7). Our neurobiology is designed to prioritize natural rewards over synthetic ones, so variables with high primitiveness and high potential for novelty become remarkably powerful mechanisms for escaping undesirable emotional states, even if only for a few minutes. Sex, food, high sucrose beverages, alcohol, drugs, social media, video games, and other stimuli all serve as agents of self-soothing that tend to disconnect us from our emotional experiences. Emotional regulation will be examined in more detail in the following chapter.

While these neurological processes and associated chemicals have a profound influence on our development and behavior, we have been blessed with a more powerful stimulus to overcome the snaring influence of maladaptive self-soothing: human connection. In John 19:26–27 we see Christ on the cross providing instruction for how his loved ones should carry on: "When Jesus saw his mother there, and the disciple whom he loved standing nearby, he said to her, 'Woman, here is your son,' and to the disciple, 'Here is your mother.' From that time on, this disciple took her into his home."

One could surmise from these words of Jesus from the cross his emphasis on relating with greater familiarity, trust, connection, and compassion. In the depth of their individual pain, the overwhelming sadness of losing a son and the unbearable grief at the loss of a friend and mentor,

Christ directs his mother and his beloved disciple to connect with one another, to grieve with one another, to entrust themselves to one another as a mother and son would. Christ's words redirect us toward one another in a way that stretches us beyond our relational comfort zone in much of Western culture.

In this model of relating that Christ points us to, we are identified as more than objects to consume, more than strangers and random passersby. We are invited to become more fully known. The invitation to engage fully in the lives of those we live alongside is in and of itself an invitation to delve more deeply into the footsteps and mind-set of Christ himself. By attuning more intentionally to our emotional experiences, as well as the emotions of others, and in both communicating with and responding to those needs in healthy ways, we activate a process of *relational soothing* in which shame is replaced with acceptance, fear is exchanged for a deep sense of safety, sadness is lifted through the gift of presence, and pain is soothed away by the outstretched arms of comfort. It is here where we become regulated, balanced in both mind and spirit, and we have the capacity, as Paul described in 1 Corinthians 2:16, to embody the mind of Christ. It is into this space of suffering that we enter as therapists, seeking to foster a corrective connection in the lives of those who entrust themselves to our care (Gal. 6:2). The work to which we are called is truly sacred.

Ultimately what Tronick found in his studies emulates this profound scriptural principle. Consider this: when the mother softens her face, expresses her affect, and becomes attuned to the child's felt experience, the infant's affect begins to change, mirroring the mother's facial and vocal expressions, she returns to a state of physiological and psychological homeostasis, and her face expresses the joy of feeling felt, connected, and affirmed. In almost every way, we are no different than the infant. We are created for connection and live most completely into the design that God has for us when we live richly in the caring community that is the body of Christ. In Christian counseling the therapeutic relationship serves as a microcosm where the therapist assists in the exploration of the client's internal world, elicits emotion, deepens self-awareness, provides emotional responsiveness and regulation, and offers relational space for the client to foster a new sense of identity in Christ. After all, we are created for connection.

Defining Emotion

The study of emotion is extremely complicated. Throughout the course of the twentieth century alone, more than ninety definitions were used for this concept, of which Plutchik (2001) writes, "The empirical study of a psychological phenomenon so complex and so elaborately cloaked cannot help but present a special challenge" (p. 344). It is in this uncertain terrain of understanding and defining emotion that the therapist begins the journey of discovering the unique constellation of affect within the client's psychosocial makeup. Contained within this journey of emotional discovery are the raw materials by which the individual will move toward a more psychologically,

socially, and spiritually healthy version of himself. The art of therapy, then, is to assist the client in transforming these raw goods into a finely polished style for acknowledging, identifying, experiencing, and expressing his emotional world.

In spite of the difficulty in operationalizing a construct as multifaceted as the human experience of emotion, some clarity can be gleaned from Plutchik (2001), when he writes, "An emotion is not simply a feeling state. Emotion is a complex chain of loosely connected events that begins with a stimulus and includes feelings, psychological changes, impulses to action and specific, goal-directed behavior" (p. 345). This definition, incorporating the Latin root mentioned previously in the chapter, can be read as "the psychological experience of being moved by a feeling toward something the individual deems important." For instance, jumping away from a shape on the ground that appears to be a snake moves us toward something important, namely, safety or survival. That which we deem important might be connection, escape, pleasure, or any number of additional biopsychosocial motivations. Depending on what we deem important, some emotions move us more powerfully than others.

Primary and Secondary Emotional Experiences

Plutchik's 1958 model of emotion classifies emotions as primary and secondary (table 4.1). He proposes four pairs of primary emotional experience: joy versus sorrow, anger versus fear, acceptance versus disgust, and surprise versus expectancy.

These eight emotions serve as the core or primary emotions that drive the human experience, with the idea that they will vary in intensity depending on the circumstances under which they are elicited. Plutchik's model suggests that fear can range in intensity from timidity to terror. For example, think back to the infants who participated in Tronick's still-face experiment. The emotions they experienced during that window of time when their mothers were unresponsive did not flood them all at once; rather, the provocation of their affective states slowly crescendoed with continued inaccessibility on the part of their caregivers. This aspect of emotion is critical for the therapist to understand since strategies for emotion regulation depend on *specificity*, or identifying the emotion accurately, as well as *sensitivity*, or feeling the emotion to a degree that is appropriate for the context from which it originates within.

In some psychological conditions or diagnoses there is disruption, and potentially impairment, in the individual's ability to accurately identify her emotion, as well as difficulty with feeling a degree of emotion appropriate to the situation. Recognizing such deficits can help with assessing the individual's psychosocial functioning, discerning the most appropriate diagnostic code, and developing the most beneficial treatment plan.

In the therapeutic process, there are certain diagnostic categories wherein clients may demonstrate, to varying degrees, a more pronounced lack of emotional awareness and expression. These disorders are shaped in part by the lack of emotional

sensitivity or specificity the client is capable of displaying. For example, children who are diagnosed with autism spectrum disorder may have mild to severe difficulty in reciprocating emotional experiences, facial expressions, and the like, depending on the severity level of their diagnosis. Similarly, individuals diagnosed with schizophrenia spectrum and other psychotic disorders may present with blunted affect and other negative symptoms that impair their emotional awareness and expression. Additionally, in the context of bipolar illnesses, major depressive disorder, and some anxiety disorders, the intensity of emotion, which can also present as numbness or anhedonia, can incapacitate the experience of subtler ones. Lastly, one of the criteria for determining a diagnosis of a personality disorder is affectivity, when "the range, intensity, lability, and appropriateness of emotional response" deviates significantly from the individual's cultural expectations (American Psychiatric Association, 2013, p. 646).

A proper framework for understanding the nature and function of emotion would include the interaction of primary emotions in the creation of secondary emotions (e.g., simultaneous disgust and anger create contempt—see table 4.1). Secondary emotions, then, become more familiar to us in their colloquial expression, as well as in their behavioral indicators. For instance, some individuals tend to feel more comfortable expressing love than expressing trust or joy. However, when we say we love (*phileo*) someone, we are making an expression of joy shared in relationship with them, as well as the degree to which we entrust ourselves to them. Similarly, other individuals are more inclined to express disapproval than to communicate surprise or sadness.

While these secondary emotions provide rich detail into the affective experiences that we share in our humanness, they are oftentimes used as methods for avoiding the deeper, more intense experiences and expressions of emotion. In the clinical environment, this softening of affect deflects the vulnerability that is intended in the therapeutic alliance. Thus, clinical skills, such as reflections of feeling (e.g., "I hear you saying that you are afraid that things will not work out with him"), immediacy (e.g., "I can see in the tears in your eyes the depth of sadness you are feeling as you share this with me"), and even empathic conjectures (e.g., "It seems to me that there would be some disgust at what those behaviors have done to destroy the relationship") become important strategies for accessing the primary emotional experiences that clients have. In fact, emotional awareness is a valuable variable in accessing adaptive emotion-regulation strategies and is comprised of two features: attention to emotion, or how much attention one gives

their affective state, and emotional clarity, or the "extent to which one understands his or her emotional experiences" (Boden & Thompson, 2015, p. 399).

Recent research from Germany found that "low emotional awareness may strengthen the relationship between maladaptive emotion-regulation strategies and negative affectivity" (Subic-Wrana et al., 2014, p. 9). When we are not aware of the emotional experiences we are having, we use less-developed coping tools and tend to have an overall more negative mood state. Therefore, emotional attunement, including how much one recognizes his emotion and the intensity with which those emotions are experienced and expressed, is an essential part of healthy personal living and serves as the foundation for relational well-being. This could be extended into the spiritual realm as well.

Noticeably absent from Plutchik's model is the emotion of shame. In many ways, shame is not only a primary emotion, but could be considered, along with fear, as a gatekeeper emotion, meaning its presence has the potential to overshadow other, less primitive emotional states.

Table 4.1. Plutchik's primary and secondary emotions

Primary Emotion	Combination	Secondary Emotion
Joy	Trust	Love
Trust	Fear	Submission
Fear	Surprise	Awe
Surprise	Sadness	Disapproval
Sadness	Disgust	Remorse
Disgust	Anger	Contempt
Anger	Anticipation	Aggressiveness
Anticipation	Joy	Optimism

In defining shame, Lopez and associates (Lopez et al., 1997) write: "Shame refers to the phenomenological experience of sudden and unexpected exposure, one that renders the self diminished or defective in some way. Pointing to the 'quintessentially' social nature of shame, Lewis proposed that 'shame involves the failure of the central attachment bond', whereas Kaufman relates shame to the experience of being emotionally and psychologically cut-off from one's significant attachments" (p. 188).

In this way, shame, along with fear and joy, becomes one of the earliest emotional experiences that manifests within the human developmental process because of our very relational nature. We are created in the image of an inherently relational God, after all! In their work differentiating the psychosocial aspects of shame and guilt, Parker and Thomas (2009) cite that Erik Erikson's theory of development introduces shame prior to guilt in the preverbal state of development, suggesting that shame is a more embodied, preverbal affective experience. This preverbal, embodied aspect of shame makes it very powerful in the individual psychological experience, as well as difficult to regulate because it likely operates outside the individual's conscious awareness. Therefore, shame and fear pervade the clinical landscape, and shame has even been shown to impact the experience of depressive features (Matos & Pinto-Gouveia, 2011).

In the therapeutic process, differentiating shame from guilt can be tedious, especially given the colloquial use of these terms among the general population.

While the terms are often used synonymously, Parker and Thomas (2009) denote the myriad differences that exist in the respective psychosocial functions of these two affective states, including cognitive, affective, and motivational differences. Regarding the cognitive aspects of shame, Parker and Thomas (2009) write, "With guilt, the self was pronouncing judgment on its *activity*; with shame, the self pronounced a more summary judgment on the inadequacy of the *self* itself" (p. 215). In addition, worthlessness and powerlessness were greater in individuals experiencing shame, with a greater degree of blaming others (Parker & Thomas, 2009). Likewise, these authors identify anger, aggression, and a lack of empathy as affective dimensions of shame, as well as movement away from others, rather than toward them, as motivational differences between shame and guilt.

From a biblical perspective, these concepts can be made sense of from two familiar passages, the first in Genesis 3, and the second in 2 Samuel. With regard to shame, the quintessential moment when shame is introduced into human history occurs after Adam and Eve have tasted the fruit of the Tree of the Knowledge of Good and Evil. Scripture tells us, as God came walking in the garden looking for the pair, they had covered themselves with fig leaves and were hiding among the trees. These avoidant behaviors point directly to the experience of shame, as defined by the sense of powerlessness, self-consciousness, and personal deficiency identified by Parker and Thomas (2009). Because shame impairs vulnerability and diminishes our capacity for connection, it interferes with our ability to remain attuned to God and others. In many ways, this experience of shame reveals the inherent corruption of the human person.

Conversely, when the prophet Nathan confronts a psychologically fragile King David, we see a very different story unfold. Having tried to cover up his shameful misdeeds, David listens to a simple story Nathan tells about a rich man, a poor man, a traveler, and a lamb. David is incensed by the rich man's behavior, demanding the man be killed. The brilliance of Nathan using a story that would connect with David's inner shepherd and evoke the powerful emotion that would move David to anger should not go unnoticed here. Stories are significant containers of our emotional experiences. And what we see next is beautiful. Rather than Nathan challenging his emotionally distraught king, which is perhaps informed more by our "Rambo" masculinity, which can pollute our reading of Scripture more than anything else, the simplicity of his statement "You are the man!" (2 Sam. 12:7) is even more powerful when delivered with a disarmingly introspective certitude.

In appealing to a previous self-state, Nathan helps David move away from shame toward a healthy experience of guilt. Parker and Thomas (2009) note, "Guilt produced a sense of tension and regret borne of empathy, which often led to reparative action, such as confession, apology or making amends" (p. 217). David's response of reconciliation with both God and the people of Israel speaks to the power of connection in creating self-awareness and deepening emotional processing. In isolation David was stuck in his shame, but through healthy confrontation he experiences the healing power of emotion and is able to be restored to healthy functioning socially, psychologically, and spiritually. In this account, David's humility is a key ingredient in moving him toward reconciliation; a spirit of pride would likely have led to a different conclusion.

Emotions and Affective Neuroscience

While entire volumes have been written on the role of emotional processing in the human brain, Jaak Panksepp provides a model for understanding neural circuitry and its predisposition for emotional processing, namely, through seven distinct yet interrelated systems. These seven systems include seeking, fear, rage, lust, care, panic (separation distress), and play (as cited in Fosha et al., 2009). These systems stand at the intersection of neurological processing and physiological expression and offer a frame of reference for identifying and managing affective states in each individual person. Contrary to "top-down" models of emotional experiencing, which prioritize conscious appraisal and interpretation of affect, Panksepp offers a model that is driven more by "instinctual" neurophysiological processes. This "bottom-up" model emphasizes deeper regions of the brain, such as the limbic system and brain stem, suggesting that our propensity for emotional processing is as fundamental to our existence and survival as eating and reproducing. In fact, emotional experiencing might be even more important than these drives, as these behaviors exist as responses to the emotional priming contained within Panksepp's seven systems (Fosha et al., 2009).

From a developmental perspective, the first system related to emotional processing would be care/nurturance. In utero the mother's body provides the safety and nurturance the infant requires to grow and develop, and the connection between the mother and child is symbiotic. The mother's body prioritizes the care/nurturance system by fostering significant hormonal changes, including "increasing estrogen, prolactin, and oxytocin along with diminished progesterone [which] help prepare the mother for the arrival of the infant, sensitizing her brain to help assure that interaction with the newborn is a special delight" (Fosha et al., 2009, p. 13). Both mother and child benefit from this experience of nurturance, and the infant's neurodevelopment is primed for care long before he expresses his first cry.

Perhaps the most primitive dysphoric affective experience, the fear/anxiety system serves the function of bypassing other affective states to ensure that the individual is keenly aware of the potential for threat in the environment. While as adults we possess more capacity for reframing our fears through activating left-brain cognitive activity, infants experience fear first and foremost as a means of maintaining proximity to their primary caregivers. Being cold, tired, hungry, or dirty can serve as a cue for fear, which elicits a cry, which activates the corresponding response from a caregiver. The infant is changed, fed, swaddled, and rocked to sleep, all of which

validate the function of the fear/anxiety system and reinforce the soothing influence of the care/nurturance system.

As the consistency of the caregiver's response shapes the infant's care/nurturance system, the fear system is sedated to the point that exploration of the environment can happen. Beginning with simple eye movements, the infant, when calm and connected, is able to begin taking in the world around her. The awe expressed in the eyes of a small child looking up at a mobile hanging above her in her crib is a quintessential example of this exploratory intuition. Panksepp (2009) calls this system the seeking/desire system and suggests it "energizes the many engagements with the world as individuals seek goods from the environment as well as meaning from the everyday occurrences of life" (p. 9). As children age into toddlerhood, they are able to use caregivers as a secure base from which to actively explore and interact with their environment with increasing degrees of autonomy. For example, introduce a loud sound or a new person into the child's environment and the fear system fires, which activates the care system, which brings the child back to the caregiver for nurturance.

In some instances, the departure of the caregiver activates the panic or grief/distress system, which Panksepp would call "psychic pain" (2009, p. 13). Rather than suggesting panic and grief as distinct ends on a single continuum, Panksepp (2009) suggests, "Ultimately it is the pain of social loss, whether the loss of mommy when one is young or social status when one is older, that opens the gateway to depression"

(p. 15). This system is more intrinsically related to the care/nurturance system, and the intensification of panic over simple fear speaks to the significance of the experience of distress in the face of disconnection between the infant and the caregiver.

With continued development and appropriate engagement from caregivers, the play system is activated. It is through the play system that the child comes to internalize the many roles and responsibilities of his social world. Boundaries are established, then tested, then renegotiated. The seeking system assists the play system by introducing novelty into the equation, ensuring that play does not become robotic or predictable, therefore diminishing its significance. This curious exploration of the self in the social context of play is a critical dynamic that helps to drive the therapeutic process.

Intricately linked to the fear and seek systems, rage/anger is a system that "is aroused by restraint and frustration, particularly when organisms do not get what they SEEK and want" and "is often intertwined with the FEAR system, with which it probably interacts in reciprocating ways during agonistic social encounters" (Panksepp, 2009, p. 11, emphasis in original). The primary function of the rage/anger system is often one of egocentric orientation, specifically creating a distinct boundary between self and other, such as in moments when the play system is activated and an intrusion occurs (e.g., a toy is taken, a child is pushed down, a boundary is provided, etc.). It can also serve a self-protective function given its association with dominance (Fosha et al., 2009).

Lastly, the lust/sexual system evidences the reality of the drive for pleasure through endogenous opiates. The propensity for the lust system to link up with the dopamine/excitatory aspect of the seeking system suggests that sex can provide a powerful appetitive and consummatory experience of pleasure. While not fully activated until puberty, the lust system is influenced by gender specific differences, specifically the relationship between testosterone and vasopressin in males and estrogen and oxytocin in females (Fosha et al., 2009).

I would be remiss to reduce the totality of emotional processing to the underlying neurophysiology and neurochemistry identified in Panksepp's seven systems. Created in God's image, we are far more than physical beings who have emotional experiences. However, these structures, chemicals, and their functions play a significant part in the experience and expression of emotion across the lifespan. While the manifestations of these systems might look different at eighteen months than at eighteen years of age, these systems each play a vital role in the emotional life of the human person.

CASE STUDIES

Case One

Chelsea is a forty-nine-year-old female from Great Britain who is currently married to her fourth husband, and the couple resides in a large metropolitan area. She has no children from these relationships, and she moved to the United States from London at the age of twenty-six after completing a graduate degree in fashion design. Chelsea describes her marriages as "overwhelmingly burdensome, given that I am the only one contributing anything of real value. It is probably why I cheated in my first three." She reports a history of volatile interpersonal relationships at work, having been labeled "petulant, labile, shallow, and grandiose." When asked about the validity of these descriptors, Chelsea smiled smugly but offered no response. Chelsea indicates she was referred to therapy for demonstrating a "significant lack of empathy" for a coworker who had a heart attack at the design studio where she is employed. She recounts "sitting at my desk as she clawed her way across the floor clutching her chest; other people were already helping her, and I have more important things to do than deal with that mess." When asked about goals for treatment, Chelsea responded, "I am here because they all know I am the best designer around and everyone else is threatened by me. I will run the fashion industry in this town. This mandated therapy is just their way of trying to hold me back." Chelsea is the only child born to her parents, both of whom own businesses in London.

Case Two

Leroy is a fifty-seven-year-old African American man who was born and raised in Atlanta, Georgia. He lives with his wife in a small rural community, and his four adult children all live nearby. He is currently employed as the principal of the local middle school, where he has worked since obtaining his bachelor's degree in education. Leroy reports that his stress "really increased back when I went from

being a teacher at the school to the assistant principal about fifteen years ago." Leroy describes his experiences of stress as "I just get real irritable, can't seem to shake it off. And I don't get much joy from my hobbies or family; seems like I am always nervous about something. I start thinking, *I can't handle this*, and everything just goes to 'blah.'" Leroy indicates that his church community is a strong social support that has been helpful in the past.

STRATEGIES, INTERVENTIONS, AND TECHNIQUES FOR EMOTIONS

In their book, *The Whole-Brain Child*, Siegel and Payne Bryson (2011) begin the process of developing emotional awareness in children with a number of strategies that center on helping the brain become more integrated. They focus on vertical integration, including the connection between higher-order brain processes, limbic system processing and body states, as well as horizontal integration, including the different kinds of processing that characterize the right and left hemispheres of the cortex, to increase attunement to one's internal world. Several of the skills mentioned below are appropriate for therapists to have in mind while helping their clients deepen a sense of emotional awareness and experiencing.

Connect and Redirect

The first element in Siegel and Payne Bryson's (2011) model emphasizes the importance of connection in identifying and eventually managing our emotional experiences. They suggest that by connecting through right-brain experiencing and "nonverbal signals like physical touch, empathic facial expressions, a nurturing tone of voice, and nonjudgmental listening," it is easier to provide redirection, such as exploring a range of potential options for responding to a given circumstance in a relationship or at work (p. 24). In other words, "feeling felt" helps the individual to tune in to their underlying emotional experience, increase the specificity of what they are feeling (e.g., primary versus secondary emotion), and choose a different option for navigating their circumstances. This is a central concept of human attachment and corresponding neurological development. Schore and Schore (2008) state, "Attachment experiences shape the early organization of the right brain, the neurobiological core of the human unconscious . . . .Thus, emotion is initially regulated by others, but over the course of infancy it becomes increasingly self-regulated as a result of neurophysiological development. These adaptive capacities are central to self-regulation, i.e., the ability to flexibly regulate psychobiological states of emotions through interactions with other humans, interactive regulation in interconnected contexts, and without other humans, autoregulation in autonomous contexts" (pp. 10–11).

In the case of Leroy, we see that his primary affective experience is comprised of irritability, nervousness in his body, negative thoughts, and feeling blah. Noting that he identifies his transition from teaching to administration as the period of time when he first noticed the symptoms that continue to plague him is important. Experiencing a degree of disconnection from peers is common for individuals who experience a job transition, so Leroy should find examining changes he experienced in his relationships with coworkers as a result of taking this new position beneficial. Moreover, an unaddressed depressive element inherent in the cluster of symptoms that Leroy communicates merits the attention of the therapist. While using an empirically supported treatment to address Leroy's symptoms is a must, the quality of effectiveness for any intervention, including cognitive behavioral therapy, will be tied to the quality of the therapeutic relationship that is established. Treatment outcome, or redirection if we use Siegel and Payne Bryson's model, is most significantly impacted by the quality of the relationship between client and therapist, or connection. Thus, the degree of interpersonal responsiveness and feeling felt that the therapist provides for Leroy will actively contribute to the positive outcomes that are being worked toward in the counseling process. If we use the notion of "social loss" identified in Panksepp's model from earlier in the chapter, it would make sense that these symptoms originate in moving into a new space of responsibility and the loss of collegiality; and having a social space, namely, the therapeutic relationship, to make sense of this loss will be cathartic for Leroy.

Name It to Tame It

A second intervention from Siegel and Payne Bryson (2011) that provides a significant contribution to the increase of affective awareness in the therapeutic process is known as "name it to tame it" and involves the processing of emotion through story to better understand one's emotional experiences (p. 27). Just as connect and redirect seeks to integrate the right and left hemispheres to provide language and logic to the experience of emotion, "one of the best ways to promote this type of integration is to help retell the story of the frightening or painful experience" (p. 27). Because of the contributions from the right and left brain in the process of storytelling, the individual's experience of telling the story helps him to process the associated emotions, as well as gain new perspective on his experience.

As you have likely guessed, this is exactly what the therapeutic process is intended to facilitate. Through examining the individual's stories, both his past experiences and his more present appraisal of his life, he has the chance to tune in to his current emotional experiences and gain new perspective through insights, summarizations, reflections of feeling, and other appropriately timed counseling techniques.

With regard to Chelsea, there is a significant disconnect between her cognitive appraisal and her affective functioning. This is quite common in individuals who present with characterological deficits and personality disorders, which certainly applies to Chelsea. While it might seem that the story to process has to do with her colleague's heart attack, the real stories to process occurred many, many years before, during her more formative years. Schore (2001) states, "Because attachment bonds are vitally important for the infant's continuing neurobiological devel-

opment, these dyadically regulated events [repairing ruptured attachment bonds] scaffold an expansion of the child's coping capacities, and therefore, adaptive infant and later adult mental health" (p. 205). The absence of healthy coping strategies evidenced in Chelsea's response to her coworker's heart attack, paired with her failed marriages, suggests that the best use of therapeutic time would focus on her early experiences where the self was being shaped by interactions with her primary caregivers. In this process the therapist has the opportunity to provide a corrective experience in the context of the client sharing her story. Specifically, the therapist has the chance to awaken the realization of pain, fear, rejection, disappointment, and other dysphoric emotion that Chelsea's current presentation denies, minimizes, or altogether compensates for through grandiosity.

The SIFT Model

Perhaps the most basic, and simultaneously most impactful, model for increasing emotional self-awareness can be found in neuroscientist Dan Siegel's SIFT model (Siegel & Payne Bryson, 2011). The acronym SIFT stands for sensations, images, feelings, and thoughts. The primary function is to assist individuals to use a variety of avenues for identifying their emotional experiences. Similar to the mindfulness technique of body scanning, looking for latent emotion housed in the body, SIFTing involves looking to the bodily sensations for emotions that might be housed there. Examples might include fear manifesting as uneasiness in the gut or stress showing up as tension or pain in the neck or shoulders. SIFT-ing also involves looking to other bodily systems to accurately identify an emotional experience that exists outside of the conscious awareness of the individual. The goal is to increase the sensitivity and specificity of the emotion being experienced. In this model, images can be understood as the visual representations or snapshot memories associated with a previous event that contained a similar memory. These images may be acute recollections from actual events or may be fabricated based on the individual's perception of the event (Siegel & Payne Bryson, 2011).

In addition to sensations and images as containers of emotional experiences, Siegel's model also looks to feelings and thoughts to better understand one's affective experience. Regarding feelings, it can be helpful to provide a list or a chart for clients to recall the full range of their emotional experiences rather than more simplistic emotions, such as "mad, bad, or glad." In the case of thoughts, core beliefs, self-talk, and evaluations of the self often contain big emotions; calling these into the present in the therapeutic process can prime the experience of affect and deepen the client's awareness of their emotional experience. It is in the immediacy of feeling in response to these thoughts that the specificity and sensitivity of emotion can be better discerned.

Perhaps the most striking feature found in the vignette of Chelsea is her startling lack of self-awareness. Her inability to empathize with a coworker who was experiencing a medical emergency, or her previous husbands, all of whom she cheated on, is indicative of her deficit to feel *with* others. Authentic empathy, as compared to sympathy, or feeling *for* others, is dependent on the ability to attune to the emotions evoked within the self, which are then used to connect with the other who is in a state of emotional activation. We feel the pain of loss with others when we tune in to the reality that the death of a loved one might create, or we draw back on the previous reality of pain of a sustained loss. Chelsea's lack of capacity for empathy suggests that she has very limited capacity for emotional awareness in herself as well as in others.

An excellent tool for increasing Chelsea's emotional awareness would be having her SIFT through the moment she looked up from her desk and saw her coworker on the floor. In this space, having Chelsea examine her body for sensations that were in her body as she envisions herself back in the moment can provide clues for her emotional experience. Additionally, having her describe the images she can recall from that moment provide a framework that the therapist can help interpret. For example, if Chelsea can describe the look of pain on her colleague's face or the position of her body crawling across the floor, the therapist can model empathy for Chelsea in an effort to foster greater emotional awareness. An empathic statement, such as "That sounds like such a terrifying moment from the details that you have been able to recall," models empathy and provides emotional language for the client to better make sense of her felt experience of her coworker's medical emergency.

Regarding Leroy's experience of depression, feelings and thoughts from the SIFT model may be additive in increasing his degrees of sensitivity and specificity of emotional experiencing. He has endorsed a number of symptoms that fit nicely into this framework, namely, irritability, anhedonia, nervousness in his stomach, and thoughts of *I can't handle this*. These raw materials are excellent fodder for the SIFTing process, explicitly as a starting point for Leroy to begin connecting the dots of his cognitive, affective, and bodily experiences to come to a more accurate understanding of his emotional experience. Communicating this constellation of symptoms as depression allows the therapist to provide Leroy a framework for understanding these previously unrelated variables.

CONCLUSION

Emotion is at the very heart of the human experience. It serves as a primary motivator in nearly every aspect of the human experience and is intended to move us toward one another in our attempts to live out the image of God within us: to entrust ourselves completely. In fact, God himself displays a great deal of emotion throughout the biblical narrative, and attachment provides perhaps the best frame of reference for understanding how God is orienting himself to the people of Israel in the Old Testament and to the whole of humanity through the person of Christ in the New Testament. While we cannot reduce the totality of emotional processing or the human experience to the underlying neurobiology, the fact is that we have been created with a variety of systems, as Panksepp describes, which serve as evidence for the importance of emotion. The brain does not waste space for nonessential functions!

Additionally, this chapter has examined the notion of primary and secondary emotions, which shed light on the diversity of emotional experiences and expressions that arise from these underlying neurological systems. It has also emphasized the importance of increasing the specificity and sensitivity of one's emotional experience, and the role of the therapeutic relationship and specific interventions in facilitating this increase in self-awareness. Key to fostering this development are therapeutic experiences that promote an increase in right-brain to left-brain integration, namely, connecting and redirecting, naming and taming emotion through storytelling, and the process of SIFT-ing.

RECOMMENDED READING

Fosha, D., Siegel, D., & Solomon, M. (Eds.). (2009). *The healing power of emotion: Affective neuroscience, development and clinical practice*. New York, NY: W. W. Norton.

Siegel, D., & Payne Bryson, T. (2011). *The whole-brain child: 12 revolutionary strategies to nurture your child's developing mind*. New York, NY: Delacorte.

van der Kolk, B. (2015). *The body keeps the score: Brain, mind, and body in the healing of trauma*. New York, NY: Penguin.

CHAPTER 5

Emotional Dysregulation Strategies

Todd Bowman, PhD

Let the peace of Christ rule in your hearts, to which
indeed you were called in one body. And be thankful.

COLOSSIANS 3:15 ESV

Since the 1990s, the topic of emotional regulation has garnered clinical and research attention. Research strongly associates emotion regulation with mental health. Deficits in emotional regulation significantly contribute to both the development and maintenance of a wide range of disorders (Berking & Whitley, 2014). Many clients feel out of control or fear losing control over highly distressful, acute, and chronic emotions. Unsurprisingly, a therapeutic task is helping clients recognize, label, contain, process, express, and reduce afflicted emotions. Toward that end, this chapter builds on the previous chapter on emotions. My purpose here is to focus on regulatory skills that help clients steward their emotional experiences.

Given the complexity of emotion experiencing, noting that each individual utilizes a wide array of emotional coping resources is important. These resources tend to get utilized throughout the day,

often on an implicit level, to negotiate the mosaic of stimuli that awaken an emotional response. If we had to engage in this process consciously, we would find ourselves capable of little more than just feeling affect and expending high amounts of cognitive energy simply managing those feelings. For example, individuals who have experienced a trauma during their childhood fashion developmental narratives around neglect or abandonment, or for those who find themselves having a bout of depression, paralyzed by panic attacks, or constantly worrying due to the presence of intense stressors in their lives, the process of regulating emotion can overwhelm existing coping mechanisms. It is in this space that therapists provide both a therapeutic relationship and a set of intentionally developed emotional regulation strategies, equipping individuals to manage their affective experience with a greater degree of effectiveness. While each individual will gravitate toward a different constellation of techniques based on the nature of their unique circumstances, the process of developing emotional regulation strategies is fundamental to the process of counseling. Given the holistic nature of the human person, this chapter will explore physical, emotional, cognitive, and spiritual strategies for enhancing the emotional regulation skills of the clients we serve.

THEOLOGY AND PSYCHOLOGY OF EMOTIONAL REGULATION

Emotions are complex to psychologists and theologians alike. Christians root emotions in the trinitarian God who poured aspects of his image into the creation of humankind. A God who feels endowed human beings with emotions. Thus, emotions are a gift of God to enjoy and experience life. Due to original sin, however, emotions can destroy the one emoting and others who experience those emotions. Inherent in the gift of emotions is the need to steward them. It is surprising to know that many passages urge us to control them in healthy ways. For example, we are to regulate anger (Prov. 12:16; 14:29; 16:32; 19:11; 29:11; Eph. 4:26–27; Col. 3:8; James 1:19), anxiety and fear (Ex. 14:13; Phil. 4:6–7), and passion (1 Cor. 7:9). All of us need to know how to control all emotions to live life in a godly way.

Stewarding emotions requires a biopsychosocial-spiritual understanding and skills that facilitate emotional regulation. While we tend to think of emotion regulation as a response to the sudden, unexpected experience of a significant emotion, Nives Sala, Testa, Pons, and Molina (2015) provide a more holistic framework for understanding this phenomenon: "Emotion regulation is described as a family of emotion regulation strategies that may be differentiated into antecedent-focused, when the strategy intervenes before emotional responses are displayed, or response-focused, when the strategy intervenes after emotional response patterns have appeared" (p. 440).

Inherent within this framework of emotion regulation is the variable of timing in relationship to the emotional stimulus. In many ways, this definition echoes Viktor Frankl's words: "Between stimulus and response there is a space. In that space is our power to choose our response. In our response lies our growth and our freedom" (quoted in Pattakos, 2010, p. vi). Whether in anticipation of an event or in response to a stimulus that has been introduced, emotion regulation is comprised of the strategies that are used to fill the aforementioned space in an effort to move the individual toward the things that are deemed important in that moment. Personal growth and freedom exist in direct correlation to one's ability to fill these spaces in life with adaptive coping strategies.

One's capacity to regulate one's emotional experiences well is directly tied to one's neurobiology. In fact, it is impossible to understand emotion-regulation techniques apart from the underlying neurobiology of emotion. Considerable scientific literature regarding the role of the human brain and its role in this process is summarized by Ginot:

> The right brain is responsible for regulating the hypothalamic-pituitary axis, which construes the interface between the body and emotions and is the center for perceiving and processing both internally generated as well as interpersonally induced emotions. In this way it is essential to the mediation of the visceral aspects as well as the subjective experience of feelings. It is very adept at recognizing and appreciating the meaning of facial expressions, vocal intonations, and gestures, all primary communication venues from early on. In addition to being essential to the visceral awareness of the body's state of arousal, its orbitofrontal cortex is involved in regulating these sensations and their accompanying affects. (Joseph, 1992; McGilchrist, 2009; Schore, 2003c, 2005, as cited in Ginot, 2012, p. 62)

The core of emotional processing is rooted in these right-brain experiences, which suggests a more intentional investigation of the interpersonal attachment experiences that foster growth in this region of the brain. Matos and Pinto-Gouveia write, "There is now strong empirical support for the significant impact that early interactions with attachment figures have on expression of genes, brain maturation, autonomic, neuroendocrine and immune function, affect regulation and development of a whole range of cognitive competencies" (2014, p. 218). Schore states that the right hemisphere is "dominant in preverbal infants," including throughout their first three years of life, and is the brain region shaped by early social experiences (2000, p. 32).

Externalizing Behaviors

In examining adaptive and maladaptive strategies for emotion regulation, one element to consider is the issue of *externalizing behaviors*. Whereas alexithymia is a challenge to emotion regulation due to a lack of emotional awareness or inability to verbalize affective experiences, externalizing behaviors poses a challenge to emotion regulation due to their negative impact on the individual's physical and emotional functioning. While externalizing behaviors tend to be studied among children, focusing on disruptive, hyperactive, or aggressive behaviors (Liu, 2004), the function of externalizing behaviors can be defined as "the use of external stimuli to escape one's current unpleasant emotional state." Inherent within this definition for externalizing behavior is the notion that the emotion is not properly regulated but rather repressed and replaced with a powerful, albeit short-term, escape from the dysphoric emotion. Some examples of adult externalizing behaviors include the use of drugs and alcohol, sexual behavior (e.g., viewing pornography, masturbation, hooking up), cutting and other nonsuicidal self-injury, disordered eating (i.e., restricting, binging), and video game/social media/internet addiction, among others. These strategies for emotion regulation are largely maladaptive over the long term in spite of their short-term effectiveness.

In examining the relationship between coping strategies and attachment styles, Dawson and colleagues (Dawson, Allen, Martson, Hafen, & Schad, 2014) indicate, "Coping strategies may, therefore, be viewed as one manifestation of the attachment system" (p. 464). The authors demonstrate the link as follows: healthier attachment styles lead to increased coping and emotion-regulation strategies, which in turn reduce externalizing behaviors. Specifically, the authors write, "Literature on the relationship between coping strategies and externalizing problems links the more adaptive coping strategies to fewer externalizing problems in adults" (Dawson et al., 2014, p. 464). The stronger our attachment relationships, the less inclined we are to use maladaptive regulation strategies to soothe our unwanted emotional states (e.g., disappointment, boredom, sadness). This points us back to the central truth we noted earlier in this chapter: we are created for connection.

Such thinking fits well with biblical admonitions to steward and manage behavior and emotions (Prov. 25:28; Gal. 5:22–23). A heart for God can transform problematic behavior to behavior that is consistent with godly righteousness. For example, Noah did all that God commanded him (Gen. 6:22), and Peter challenges his readers to maintain excellent behavior (1 Peter 2:12). Problematic behavior often receives negative feedback, generating affective distress and creating a feedback loop with the heart, which is the origin of our live issues (Matt. 15:18–19).

In short, we are created for connection, and the quality of one's neurobiological and interpersonal functioning operates in direct relationship to the health of the attachment bonds they are provided in early childhood especially and throughout the course of one's life (Moutsiana et al., 2014). These high-quality interactive experiences are the foundation for healthy emotional regulation later in life. Emotion regulation, then, can best be defined as "all of the processes, intrinsic and extrinsic, through which individuals manage their emotions to accomplish their goals" (Thompson, 1994, as cited in Nives Sala et al., 2014, p. 440).

CASE STUDIES

Case One

Cal is a thirty-seven-year-old male of mixed Caucasian and Native American descent who reports frequent participation in sexual fantasy and masturbation, as well as losing hours of sleep and productivity at work due to social media consumption and online gaming. In addition to the healthy sexual intimacy Cal shares with his wife approximately two to three occasions per week, Cal indicates that he cannot go "more than a day or two" without "succumbing to temptation." He reports no past or present participation in other sexual behaviors, such as viewing pornography, visiting strip clubs, engaging in anonymous sex, or hiring prostitutes. Cal was sexually abused by a female babysitter from the age of seven until the age of eleven, when the family moved from that community. This abuse occurred, on average, one to two times per month. From the age of twelve to eighteen he was repeatedly molested by a male member of the church his father was pastoring. The frequency of these experiences ranged from "every week" at its height to "every few months" at its low. While attending a small Christian college, Cal reports that he engaged in same-sex acting out "off and on for two or three years" until he met his wife and the two began dating. He has not disclosed his experiences of abuse to anyone except the therapist and has no intention of ever sharing his past with his wife. Cal is currently married with four children, two daughters and two sons. He indicates that he has struggled with periods of depression "since [he] was younger," as well as constant anxiety. He is currently underemployed in a stressful job with little opportunity for advancement after eight years of working as a youth pastor. He has few social relationships outside of his family, although he attends church regularly.

Case Two

Maria is a twenty-five-year-old female of Hispanic descent who is currently single and has no children. She was raised by Spanish-speaking parents in a small farming community and is the youngest of six children born to her parents. After graduating from high school at the age of eighteen, she left home and moved to a large metropolitan area to live with her boyfriend, whom she met online. The relationship lasted two years before she broke it off due to his substance abuse, which repeatedly ended in Maria experiencing emotional and verbal abuse. Since leaving the relationship, she has bounced from house to house, living with friends over the past five years, working odd jobs

when she can find them. In that time, she developed the habit of using recreational drugs, mostly marijuana and cocaine, approximately five to six times per month. While she does not currently meet the diagnostic criteria for a substance use disorder, she reports at a session that "using coke or weed is just my way of escaping it all, you know." She denied symptoms of anxiety or depression, instead suggesting, "I just feel numb all of the time." She has had limited social contact with her family since she moved to the city nearly seven years ago, suggesting that they were "too traditional" for her liking. When asked, she indicated, "My father was distant and my mother was overbearing; I was raised by my two older sisters and watching cartoons."

STRATEGIES, INTERVENTIONS, AND TECHNIQUES FOR EMOTIONAL REGULATION

No single effective strategy, intervention, or technique (SIT) exists for regulating one's emotions. As I noted in chapter 4, much like Plutchik's definition, there is so much complexity and nuance to the experience of emotion that a "one-size-fits-all" approach to emotion regulation would be ridiculous even to propose. This becomes even more evident when one begins to factor in variables such as temperament, life experiences, and the varying situations where an emotion might be evoked. Rather, what is needed to successfully navigate the sea of emotions that comprise the human experience is a robust set of skills for experiencing and expressing emotions that increase one's sense of intrapsychic and interpersonal coherence.

Preliminary Considerations

Examining the notion of timing as it pertains to the various emotion regulation strategies employed by the individual is imperative. Gross and John (2003) describe *antecedent-focused* and *response-focused* approaches to emotional regulation (a distinction already noted). Antecedent-focused approaches refer to the "things we do before the emotional response tendencies have become fully activated and have changed our behavior and peripheral physiological responding," whereas response-focused strategies can be defined as the "things we do once an emotion is already underway" (p. 348). Inherent in this dichotomy of emotional regulation responses is that a diversity of tools is necessary for managing the breadth of affective experiences contained in the human experience.

Rather than thinking of emotion regulation in terms of "all or nothing," thinking of strategies for regulating emotion in terms of "effective/ineffective" and "adaptive/maladaptive" might be helpful. Specifically, effective strategies are appropriate for the situation and adequately regulate the intensity, whereas ineffective strategies do little to modify the individual's current mood state. Likewise, adaptive strategies contribute to the overall health or functionality of the individual, whereas maladaptive strategies leave the individual more prone to further dysregulation at best or more vulnerable to emotional disorders at worst. Ideally the process of implementing emotion-regulation strate-

gies in the context of therapy focuses on identifying, practicing, and eventually mastering those techniques that are both effective and adaptive. Many clients seek therapy because their best attempts at emotion regulation can be considered ineffective, maladaptive, or both. This chapter seeks to examine those strategies that have a high degree of clinical utility due to their simultaneous adaptive and effective quality.

When it comes to strategies for emotion regulation, noting that some differences by age and by gender exist is important. Specifically, older adults have a greater tendency to use acceptance as a strategy for managing emotional situations than young adults, who are more prone to using maladaptive strategies (Schirda, Valentine, Aldao, & Shaurya Prakash, 2016). In a study examining differences in coping strategies between male and female students, Pascual and colleagues (Pascual, Conejero, & Etxebarria, 2016) found that teen boys scored statistically significantly higher in the use of positive thinking, cognitive restructuring, and acceptance, whereas teen girls scored higher on problem-solving strategies, emotional expression, and rumination. These differences in emotion-regulation strategies by age and gender suggest that exploring strategies for emotion regulation in the therapeutic process must take into account the client's characteristics.

Externalizing behaviors are present in each of the two clinical examples provided in this chapter. Specifically, Cal spends hours of time engaged in social media use, online gaming, and masturbation.

Likewise, Maria indicates that she uses recreational drugs in an effort to "escape." Alongside Cal's depression and Maria's numbness, there is an underlying loneliness and subsequent inability, or unwillingness, to move toward healthy auto-regulation or relational coping strategies to manage this dysphoric affect. Together with this need for effective emotion-regulation strategies is a need for greater attunement to others and a greater overall sense of secure attachment.

Alexithymia

Prior to examining these strategies, however, we must address the reality that some individuals undergo interference in the communication between their emotional experience and their cognitive appraisal of said emotions. This concern poses a significant challenge to emotion regulation and is known as *alexithymia*. According to Bermond and colleagues (Bermond, Clayton, Luminet, & Wicherts, 2007), alexithymia is defined by five prominent features, including: (1) reduced ability to *identify emotions* or differentiate between emotions, (2) diminished *fantasy life*, (3) difficulty *verbalizing* emotional experiences, (4) *emotionalizing*, or the reduced ability to determine the origins of an emotional experience (e.g., internal or external stimuli), and (5) the reduced capacity for *analyzing* emotions or reflecting on emotional experiences. Bermond and colleagues suggest that alexithymia can be placed onto two dimensions, an "affective factor," characterized by emotionalizing and diminished fantasy, and a "cognitive factor," characterized by difficulty iden-

tifying and verbalizing emotions (2007, p. 1127). The reduced capacity to analyze and reflect on emotional experiences is evidenced in each of these two types of alexithymia (Bermond et al., 2007).

While a number of experiences, such as emotional trauma, neglect, concussions, and brain injuries, or diagnosed mental illness, may increase the presence of one or more of these domains of alexithymia, the best understanding for alexithymia is that it is informed by a combination of genetic and environmental influences (Jorgensen, Zachariae, Skytthe, & Kyvik, 2007). Vanhuele and colleagues (Vanhuele, Verhaeghe, & Desmet, 2011) specify a three-step strategic process that is practiced in the therapeutic environment and later generalized to the client's personal world outside of the therapeutic context. These three steps include: "(1) putting into words the chain of events that makes up the distressing situation, (2) making the patient's appraisal of the difficult situation explicit, and (3) addressing affective responses and discussing the patient's way of dealing with the difficult situation" (p. 84). Psychoeducation about the scope of emotion, the varying levels of emotional intensity, and the modeling of emotional expression and emotion-regulation strategies are requirements for working with clients who present with alexithymia.

In Maria's case, a few elements of alexithymia may be present. First, she does not use typical emotional language to express herself, nor does she endorse symptoms of anxiety (fear) or depression (shame, sadness) during the session. Additionally, she has experienced emotional abuse in a previous relationship and has indicated the potential for neglect during her childhood years. These factors, paired with long-term drug abuse, are all indicators that increase the probability that Maria is experiencing some degree of alexithymia.

In working with Maria, one starting point would be for her to begin developing an emotional vocabulary (e.g., *mad, glad, sad, bad*), and then broadening that vocabulary by degrees (e.g., *annoyed, irritated, angry, fuming, irate*). Upon obtaining a working vocabulary, it would be important for Maria to begin associating these varying emotions with situation-specific moments. This process can be started vicariously, such as by working through past scenarios in her life (e.g., processing a memory of her family) or through role plays in the therapeutic process. Helping Maria identify the physiological cues in her body (e.g., upset stomach, racing heart) and connecting those to her emotions (e.g., fear) will be important for her treatment as well. Then the therapeutic process will focus on replacing Maria's maladaptive coping skills (i.e., avoidance and illegal drug use) with new skills that might be helpful in regulating her emotions. By the end of her treatment, Maria should be able to describe the situation that is evoking emotion, as well as name it and identify it in her body, articulate it to another person, and select an appropriate coping strategy for managing her experience of the emotion.

Techniques for Auto-Regulation

Contrasted against externalizing behaviors and other forms of unhealthy emotional regulation, which can be considered maladaptive self-soothing, auto-regulation can be conceptualized as the organismic experience of adaptively and effectively regulating emotion by drawing on the collectivity of internal resources, including resiliency, strengths, and internal representations of primary attachment figures. The following section will examine a variety of SITs that promote healthy auto-regulation.

Spiritual exercises. In examining attachment to God, Homan (2012), citing work done by Kilpatrick (1992), states, "In many ways, perceived relationships with God show the characteristics of human attachment relationships, and thus, should provide similar psychological benefits" (p. 324). Spiritual exercises, then, can be seen as the behaviors that increase the individual's perception of closeness in relationship with God and serve to enhance their internal representation of him. This idea of an internal representation is of critical importance in the process of auto-regulation. Schore (2001) writes, "Because attachment bonds are vitally important for the infant's continuing neurobiological development, these dyadically regulated events [repairing ruptured attachment bonds] scaffold an expansion of the child's coping capacities, and therefore, adaptive infant and later adult mental health" (p. 205). Think back for a moment to Dr. Tronick's still face experiment, which was discussed in chapter 4. The repair of the rupture that the child experienced was a relationally regulated event in that the mother "returned" and the infant was able to calm down effectively. It is in this process of internalizing the mother that the child will develop the capacity to auto-regulate in healthy ways, rather than regulate through externalizing behaviors and maladaptive self-soothing strategies.

Secure attachment with God is illustrated in the Bible through the story of Hagar, an Egyptian slave who was taken from her homeland. She lost everything, finding herself with a new family and exposed to a new faith. Disconnected from her previous life, she was taken into the home of Abram and Sarai. Sometime after the birth of her son Ishmael, Sarah caused Hagar to be evicted from their home. Abandoned by her family, she likely felt all alone and unsure of what to do. In her journey, the angel of the Lord found her (Gen. 16:7). In Genesis 16:13 she exclaimed, "You are the God who sees me ... I have now seen the One who sees me." Meeting God was so profound that Hagar attributed a new name to God, "El Roi," that is, "the God who sees." God never meets us with a still face, disconnected with our needs. He is the God who sees and responds with attentive compassion and soothing.

Prayer. At its very core, prayer stands as the primary vehicle by which people communicate with God. While it is evident that prayer is a tool used by many people to manage their emotional experiences and is a foundation of the faith, scholars still know little about how individuals use prayer to navigate dysphoric emotions such as sadness, fear, and the like (Bade & Cook, 2008; Sharp, 2010). One dynamic proposed by Sharp is that prayer is an "imaginary, yet legitimate, social interaction" that provides individuals with:

1. an other to whom one can express and vent anger;
2. positive reflected appraisals that help increase self-esteem and lessen sadness;
3. reinterpretive cognitions that make situations seem less threatening and thus less fearful;
4. an other with whom one can interact to "zone out" negative emotion-inducing stimuli; and
5. an emotion management model to imitate to mitigate feelings. (2010, p. 418)

Inherent in these five dynamics is the regulation of dysphoric emotion by way of connecting with God through prayer. In fact, the language used in this short passage suggests that prayer is both an effective and adaptive strategy for processing emotions such as anger, sadness, fear, and threatening stimuli that might elicit a negative emotion. In borrowing language from chapter 4, prayer is the primary mechanism by which we spiritually connect to emotionally redirect.

In a review of the function that prayer serves for Christian believers, Bade and Cook found that individuals responded with items such as "express thoughts and emotions," "calms me down," "pray for God's peace," and "seek comfort," all of which indicate the use of prayer as a mechanism for emotion regulation (2008, pp. 126–127). Of the four most frequently endorsed items in the study, Bade and Cook found that respondents endorsed "ask God to help me through difficult times" and "pray for strength to handle difficulties" as the first and third most frequent, respectively (pp. 126–127). It is partly through these interactions, both directly and indirectly, that the individual's internal representation of God is shaped and refined over time. As stated previously, when there is a healthy internal representation that can be drawn on in times of stress, we are more inclined to manage our distress adaptively and effectively rather than falling prey to externalizing, self-soothing strategies that create more harm than they provide relief.

In Cal's case, he has a long-standing history of being raised in the church and later working in the church, as well as attendance at a small Christian university. While Cal is actively attending a church on a regular basis, he does not endorse prayer as a strategy for (a) deepening his sense of connection to God, (b) coping with stress in his life, or (c) reducing his sexual acting-out behaviors. One aspect of Cal's treatment process will be to examine the role of prayer in his spiritual life. Specifically, one aspect of Cal's treatment will be to replace his sexual acting out with behaviors that have the same ability to help him manage his emotions. Because of the mood-altering aspects of sexual acting out, such as viewing pornography or masturbating, replacing the behavior with a coping strategy that also addresses the underlying mood is essential. Given the stress and depression indicated in his life, prayer will become an important tool for managing Cal's mood; however, it will be only one part of his treatment process and not an exclusive strategy for managing his emotions.

With regard to Cal's situation, the framework for using prayer as an emotion-regulation strategy, proposed by Sharp (2010), could be beneficial. Specifically,

Cal exhibits symptoms of depression and anxiety, and prayer could help with lessening depression through "positive reflected appraisals that help increase self-esteem"; his anxiety may be moderated by prayer through "reinterpretive cognitions that make situations seem less threatening and thus less fearful" (2010, p. 418). Additionally, the traumatic past that Cal reports could result in a degree of latent anger or periods of unhealthy dissociation. Given the dynamics of prayer that Sharp discusses, it could be used as a healthy process for venting anger or "zoning out" (p. 418).

Scripture. Along with connecting to God through prayer, reading and memorizing Scripture is a common practice through which Christian believers commune with God. The Bible is full of passages that speak to emotion regulation and entrusting oneself to God in the midst of difficult times. As we have seen throughout this chapter, the process of deepening relationship with God has a positive impact on emotional functioning. It should come as no surprise, then, that spending time in God's Word would contribute to this sense of personal wellness for those who believe. Following are a few common passages that relate to managing dysphoric emotion:

Fear—"Do not be anxious about anything, but in every situation, by prayer and petition, with thanksgiving, present your requests to God" (Phil. 4:6).
Sadness—"Why, my soul, are you downcast? Why so disturbed within me? Put your hope in God, for I will yet

praise him, my Savior and my God" (Ps. 42:5).

Pain/suffering—"Therefore we do not lose heart. Though outwardly we are wasting away, yet inwardly we are being renewed day by day. For our light and momentary troubles are achieving for us an eternal glory that far outweighs them all. So we fix our eyes not on what is seen, but on what is unseen, since what is seen is temporary, but what is unseen is eternal" (2 Cor. 4:16–18).

Anger—"'In your anger do not sin': Do not let the sun go down while you are still angry" (Eph. 4:26).

The process of memorizing these or other meaningful passages can help create a script by which the individual is able to redirect the intensity and direction of her emotional response. Scripture offers the individual an opportunity to make different meaning of her experience of emotion and to frame her response in a different way. In this process, drawing on an internal representation of Christ and using the will to direct responses, one can partner with the Holy Spirit in practicing healthier regulation strategies (Phil. 2:12–13; Gal. 5:22–23). By striving to embody Christ, Scripture helps us to ride the waves of emotional upheaval and to gain insight into how and why we regulate our emotions the way we do.

Scripture may be a very useful tool for helping Maria foster a new experience of connection with God. In particular, Maria indicated that her father was distant and her mother was overbearing. Given the tendency for individuals to project their early attachment relationships onto their understanding of God (Clinton & Straub, 2010), it would make sense that Maria's perception of God is as uninvolved, overbearing, or some toxic combination of the two. Introducing Scripture as a tool for managing her emotion, with the goal of helping her cut down her drug use and create a healthier God image in her life, could be an aspect of the overall treatment plan for Maria. A very useful resource to equip you to improve your work on God-image issues is *The God Image Handbook for Spiritual Counseling and Psychotherapy: Research, Theory, and Practice* by Glendon Moriarty and Louis Hoffman (2013).

Cognitive and Mindfulness-Based Exercises

Perhaps the most far-reaching and widely researched bundle of strategies for emotion regulation emerge from the cognitive and mindfulness-based models within the psychological literature. One major reason for both the level of interest in these strategies and the level of effectiveness they provide can be found in the shared underlying neurobiology. Specifically, Opialla and colleagues (Opialla et al., 2015) write, "Both strategies recruited overlapping brain regions known to be involved in emotional regulation. This result suggests that common neural circuits are involved in the emotion regulation by mindfulness-based and cognitive reappraisal strategies" (p. 45). Given their effectiveness and shared neurological foundation, these concepts will be examined in more detail in the following section of this chapter.

Cognitive Reappraisal

In examining cognitive reappraisal as an emotion-regulation strategy, Hermann and colleagues (Hermann, Beiber, Keck, Vaitl, & Stark, 2014) cite Gross and John (2003) in defining the phenomenon as "interpreting a potentially emotion-eliciting situation in a way that changes its emotional impact" (p. 1435). This approach has been found to increase interpersonal functioning, emotional well-being, and mood (Hermann et al., 2014). One of the most powerful depictions of a cognitive reappraisal is found in the film *Good Will Hunting* (Bender & Van Sant, 1997). Will, a young man from the rough side of the tracks in South Boston and a mathematical genius, is befriended by Sean McGuire, a psychologist, who is working to help him find direction in life. Through their relationship, Will discloses an experience of abuse that is responsible for the hard exterior shell that he uses to protect himself (e.g., frequently getting into fights, being underemployed, etc.). In a beautiful depiction of the impact of the therapeutic relationship, Sean repeats to Will, "It's not your fault. It is not your fault." At first Will suppresses his emotion, shrugging smugly and saying, "I know." Subsequently, he lashes out verbally as Sean continues to repeat himself, "It's not your fault." The scene ends with Will experiencing an emotional breakthrough that evidences his ability to reappraise the emotions he has carried in response to the abuse he experienced. While not all therapeutic moments contain quite the same intensity, there are numerous moments where introducing a cognitive reappraisal can induce a breakthrough for the clients we serve.

Converse to cognitive reappraisal is *excessive suppression*, which can be defined as "a form of response modulation that involves inhibiting ongoing emotion-expressive behavior" (Gross & John, 2003, p. 345). The best example of this strategy is the "poker face," in which any behavioral indication of emotion is extinguished. In the clip from *Good Will Hunting* cited in the paragraph above, Will uses a variety of strategies to suppress his emotion. Initially he minimizes the significance of what Sean is suggesting. When Sean continues to repeat himself and the weight of his words begins to sink in, a much more primitive form of suppression emerges: displacement. He becomes angry at Sean in an effort to stop the vulnerability he is feeling in his pain and fear from the abuse. It should come as no surprise to the reader that this approach has been demonstrated to decrease individual well-being, although it may have utility under certain conditions (Hermann et al., 2014). In reflecting on the externalizing behaviors that were indicated previously in the chapter, the function of these behaviors could be conceptualized as suppressive in the fact that they provide regulation only through hijacking the neurobiology of pleasure or pain, rather than addressing the individual's primary emotional experience. Suppressed emotion is simply avoided and will inevitably reemerge; regulated emotion is healthily expressed and put away.

With regard to Maria, her self-report of feeling "numb," rather than expressing more specific emotional experiences in the past two years, may indicate a number of features covered to this point in the chapter.

First, it is possible that she is presenting with some degree of alexithymia, and is having difficulty giving words to her emotional experiences. Second, she may have underreported the scope of her substance abuse, which has left her feeling numb. Given the nature of the relationship she reported previously, it is also possible that her numbness and difficulty feeling emotion is a symptom of post-traumatic stress disorder (PTSD). Regardless of the dynamic that is creating it, Maria presents with a style of emotional regulation that appears excessively suppressive.

With regard to implementing cognitive reappraisal with Maria, one direction the counseling process could go would be to examine her relationships with her parents, siblings, and boyfriend through the lens of the emotions she felt when she was with them. In exploring these memories from her relational world, the likelihood of a primary emotion being uncovered is quite high. In the immediacy of the therapeutic relationship, the counselor could begin to (a) provide emotional language for Maria based on the details of the story (e.g., "Wow, that sounds very sad to feel left alone to fend for yourself," etc.); (b) connect the dots for Maria between the emotion in her story and the present moment (e.g., "I can sense the sadness in you as you sit slumped in the chair you are sitting in"; "I can see the loneliness in your eyes right now as you share that story with me"); and (c) implement cognitive reappraisal for managing this primary emotion (e.g., "So when you feel nervous or lonely you tend to leave others before they can leave you. How do the stories you have shared from your past influence the relationships you have in the present?").

Guided Therapeutic Imagery/Visualization

Another cognitive approach to emotion regulation is guided imagery/visualization techniques. In his work on the impact of guided imagery/visualization on immune system functioning, Trakhtenberg (2008) writes, "[It] is popularly conceptualized as the language used by the mind to communicate and make sense of inner and outer experiences" (p. 840). Essentially, guided therapeutic imagery is a mind-body exercise whereby the counselor directs the client to concentrate on particular images that generate relaxation. At the heart of this concept is the communication between the mind, senses, and the body. The primary goal of guided imagery/visualization as an emotional regulation strategy is to induce a state of deep relaxation in both the body and the mind, toward the end of helping the client develop the ability to effectively manage their thoughts and emotions. While this technique can be used as a response-focused tool for managing emotion, regular use of guided imagery can maximize its effectiveness as an antecedent-focused strategy.

When considering doing guided-imagery work, there are a number of important considerations. Hall, Hall, Stradling, and Young (2006) recommend that the therapist take into account five primary dynamics:

1. managing client expectations and assumptions;
2. clients' preparedness and readiness for the activity;

3. timing and time implications for generating and working with guided imagery;
4. the physical setting of the counselling room; and
5. additional equipment, e.g. paper, drawing equipment, clay, and so on. (p. 20)

Some clients feel particularly vulnerable sitting in the counseling environment with their eyes closed, so giving clients explicit permission to stop the exercise at any given point in time is an essential aspect of informed consent for this intervention.

The following is an example of a guided imagery exercise for use in clinical work:

With your feet flat on the floor and your hands resting gently on your knees, I would like you to sit back in your chair and take a long, slow, deep breath. As you breathe in, see in your mind a lush green forest spreading out in front of you. You can hear the sounds of birds chirping, see the mosaic of light breaking through the tapestry of branches, and feel the warmth of the breeze on your face as you walk down the dirt path that lies before you. As you walk, you can hear the crunching of leaves and twigs under your feet. You take in the sights and sounds of the forest around you. Squirrels frolic to your right, and you sense their playfulness; a smile finds its way to your lips as you feel more and more relaxed in the serenity of the forest around you. As you continue to walk, you notice a break in the trees and are greeted by the warmth of sunshine on your face. Billowing clouds dance across the background of a perfect blue sky. As you take in the wonder of creation, you notice a sense of gratitude spreading throughout your body. You are reminded that you are loved by a God who would send his beloved Son to this beautiful earth on your behalf. Refocusing on the path ahead, you enter into a small meadow with a bubbling brook running through it. As you take a long, slow, deep breath, notice how heavy your body has become. Relaxed, you rest for a moment in the soft, emerald-green grass next to the babbling stream. As the song of the running water washes over you, you image your stresses and concerns being carried downstream. As the water splashes down a small waterfall, the thoughts and feelings you carried into the forest dissipate into small bubbles of foam and are carried into the distance as the stream dips and twists out of sight. Refreshed, you stand up from the nest of grass you have been resting in and begin to walk slowly back to the path. The sound of running water fades as you retrace your steps through the forest. Your slow, methodical breathing indicates that you are feeling a deep sense of peace. As you return to the present moment, you leave the forest feeling much lighter, having left behind the stress and concerns that you carried in with you. As you continue to notice the newfound sense of warmth and relaxation, you feel an overwhelming sense of God's love enveloping you. Rest in the safety of his arms. Lean into the grace he is offering. Believe the words he is speaking: "You are my beloved son/daughter." Continue to take slow, deep breaths, and whenever you are ready, open your eyes.

While this is just one example of a guided imagery exercise, you can see that the language used has created a visual picture intended to initiate a state of relaxation. The rich use of colors, sounds, and sensations is purposefully intended to foster a total body experience of calming, with the goal of releasing whatever sense of distress, anxiety, or any other unpleasant emotion the client might be experiencing. A small degree of Christian imagery is included in the present example, which can be tailored specifically to the preference of the client and therapist.

With her desire to "escape it all" through regular substance abuse, Maria could benefit from guided imagery. Her intermittent use of marijuana and cocaine indicates that there are times when she is looking to *up-regulate*, or move from conservation-withdrawal (feeling low) to a more balanced affective state, such as in the context of alleviating depression, boredom, or general anhedonia. Caffeine, cocaine, and other stimulants serve this function, and this need for up-regulation is a typical narrative in individuals who abuse these substances. At other times, she reports using substances to *down-regulate*, or move from ergotropic arousal (feeling keyed up) to a more balanced affective state, such as the experience of calming anxious symptomology. Depressants such as marijuana, alcohol, and opiates tend to serve this function.

With Cal, sexual addiction and other process addictions (e.g., video games, internet surfing, spending, etc.) can serve as either an up-regulating or down-regulating stimulus, depending on his affective state

and the intent behind the behavior. In his story, both anxiety and depression are present, which suggests that his sexual behavior has provided both types of regulation at different points in time. One of the primary goals of substance use or process addiction treatment is to replace the function of the substance/process with a tool that serves an identical function yet is more adaptive. If Cal is able to manage his experience of anxiety and depression more effectively through antecedent-focused (i.e., preventative) coping strategies, he will have less of a need to move into self-soothing with a sexual, mood-altering behavior.

Breathing Exercises

Diaphragmatic breathing. Perhaps the most foundational exercise that one can participate in to regulate one's emotional state is diaphragmatic breathing. While this often conjures up images of overwhelmed clients breathing into a paper bag to ward off the full impact of a panic attack, the clinical application of this principle is much less dramatic, albeit identically beneficial. Specifically, this exercise is intended to pull oxygen deep into the lungs and expel carbon dioxide. One primary piece of feedback that the brain uses to determine stress level or emotional reactivity is oxygen content in the blood. Under prolonged stress, chronic hyperventilation can occur, during which the individual is breathing through the upper third of her lungs, rather than pulling oxygen deep into the bottom half of her lungs. Diaphragmatic breathing, then, is an exercise in intentionally slowing down one's breathing in an effort to induce a state of deep relaxation.

As a caveat, with diaphragmatic breathing the folks who have not slowed their breathing over a long period of time might find that this increase in oxygen leaves them light-headed or dizzy. This discomfort provides testimony to how their bodies have tried to adapt to an unhealthy way of being, namely, chronic hyperventilation. Therefore, helping clients understand what is happening in their bodies and why mindful awareness of their breaths and purposeful slowing of their breathing can increase their sense of emotional regulation is important.

The following script is an example of a diaphragmatic breathing exercise that can be used as an adaptive and effective tool for emotional regulation:

To begin, sit with your feet flat on the floor, and let your hands rest comfortably in your lap. Gently let your eyes close as you remain aware of your surroundings.

Let yourself sink comfortably into the chair, and begin to notice the breaths coming in and out of your lungs.

Slowly move your left hand to your breastplate, and place your right hand just above your belly button so that your palms are resting toward your body.

Begin to notice which hand moves more while you are breathing.

For the next minute, begin to count the number of breaths you are taking.

Begin . . . [one minute elapses] . . . and end.

Notice how many breaths you took.

People with chronic hyperventilation tend to take more breaths per minute because they are breathing more shallowly. If you took more than seven breaths in a minute, you are at risk for chronic hyperventilation and will feel more nervous, tense, and worried throughout your day.

Now, as you breathe in, pull your breath deep into your lungs, down to your bottom hand resting right above your belly button.

Feel your hand rise and fall, while your upper hand remains relatively still.

You may begin to feel somewhat light as you continue to draw in slow, deep breaths.

Let's continue this new way of breathing for the next few minutes.

[Two to three minutes elapse.]

Notice how your body feels with the influx of oxygen. You might feel warm, heavy, relaxed, or even fatigued as your body's resting state changes.

Continue breathing slowly and deeply.

Now, whenever you are ready, open your eyes.

In examining the cases of Cal and Maria, both are using external coping mechanisms that are maladaptive in their attempts to manage their biopsychosocial experience. Specifically, drugs and sex tend to have a profound impact on our neurobiology and create a temporary sense of physical release or relief. The problematic dynamic with these strategies for managing emotion is found in the process of *resensitization*, the return of the original dysphoric mood state. In my neuroaffective model of sexual addiction, it is this process of resensitization that initiates an experience of regret, remorse, and subsequent experience of shame. This process tends to drive clients to a state of internal conflict, in which they detach from others and end in a state of loneliness and disconnection. If we are created for connection, it is this process that takes us away from connection that serves as a powerful driver in the etiology of addiction. In an attempt to soothe big emotion in a maladaptive way, the client is rewiring his or her neurobiology for a struggle with addiction.

For Maria and Cal, diaphragmatic breathing could be a helpful source of calming their physiology without the ingestion of drugs or alcohol, or moving toward process addiction behaviors (e.g., porn and masturbation, internet surfing, gaming), respectively. This simple changing of how breaths are being taken has a profound physiological impact for our bodies. To be precise, it activates our *parasympathetic nervous system*, or the part of our autonomic nervous system that calms us down and enables us to connect with others, while simultaneously quieting our *sympathetic nervous system*, or the part of our autonomic nervous system that gets us ready for fighting, fleeing, or in certain situations, freezing. In short, it helps us tap the brakes, rather than driving through life with our foot on the gas pedal.

Autogenic phrases. Another form of cognitive relaxation/stress-management strategy is called autogenic phrases. Autogenic phrases involve a series of phrases that have a degree of suggestibility, with the goal of helping the client reach a state of deep relaxation by adhering to the directions indicated in each progressive phrase. Often entailed in this process of

guiding the client into a state of relaxation is emphasizing warmth and heaviness in a variety of body regions. As with guided imagery, the client places his feet flat on the floor, puts his hands in his lap, and sits back in his chair. One important dynamic with autogenic phrases is to have a quiet environment that is free from distractions. Another detail of importance is the tone of voice and rhythm with which the phrases are delivered. With this exercise, there is no rush, and the phrases should be delivered slowly and deliberately. The following is an example of a set of autogenic phrases that could be used to help clients increase their capacity to regulate their emotions:

As you sit with your eyes closed, feet flat on the floor, and your hands resting in your lap, take a long, slow, deep breath.

As you breathe in slowly and deeply, notice the feeling of oxygen entering your body as your chest expands and contracts.

As you exhale, notice the warmth of the air and feel the tension leaving your body.

Your hands are beginning to get warm. Your body is becoming heavy and relaxed.

Feel yourself relax into the chair you are in as your body slowly calms.

Notice the flow of blood in your hands. They are becoming warm and relaxed.

As your body becomes heavy, notice any tension in your body, and simply release it.

Your arms feel warm and heavy.

Feel your feet on the floor, supporting you as you become more and more relaxed.

Continue to breathe slowly and deeply, letting the tension slowly flow from your back and shoulders.

Feel the coolness of the air as you breathe in and the warmth of your breath as you exhale.

Notice your heartbeat, and feel your heart thump in your chest and in your body.

You are feeling warm, heavy, and relaxed.

If you have any distracting thoughts, simply acknowledge them and let them float away.

Continue breathing in slowly and deeply.

Your head is feeling heavy and relaxed.

Warmth is spreading up from your hands into your arms.

You are now in a state of deep relaxation.

As you prepare to transition out of this exercise, notice the feeling of your body sitting in the chair, your feet on the floor, and your hands resting in your lap.

Notice the sounds in the room and the environment around you.

Whenever you are ready, open your eyes.

As you can imagine just by reading these phrases, they have a powerful impact in slowing down the body and inducing a state of relaxation. With regard to emotion regulation, the purpose of relaxation exercises, such as autogenic phrases, is to provide a greater degree of self-awareness. They also serve to increase blood flow to the prefrontal cortex, which is the seat of executive functions, including body regulation, emotional regulation, empathy, and morality. Chronic decreases in neural functioning in the prefrontal cortex lead to what Wilson (2014) labels as *hypofrontality*. The process of slowing down

our bodies through the use of autogenic phrases increases blood flow to the prefrontal cortices and enhances our capacity to move toward and maintain "the mind of Christ" (1 Cor. 2:16).

Cal indicates that he is struggling with impulsive masturbation and "succumbs to temptation" multiple times per week. In addition to this hypersexual presentation (intercourse two to three times per week, as well as frequent masturbation), Cal presents with high amounts of time dedicated to online gaming and social media. Unknowingly, Cal has developed a collection of strategies that are effective in the moment yet maladaptive in the long run. Wilson (2014) suggests that brain-related changes to these activities include "alterations in the prefrontal regions' grey matter and white matter correlated with reduced impulse control and the weakened ability to foresee consequences" (p. 98). Van der Kolk (2003) suggests that this struggle with emotional self-regulation is one of the more prominent features of chronically traumatized children. Cal's struggle with these behaviors makes sense given his personal narrative. The development of adaptive and effective emotional regulation techniques is the driving factor in Cal's therapeutic process. Autogenic phrases can serve as a tool for helping him reduce the power of his impulses and increase his sense of emotional well-being. Cal was very open to these interventions once he understood how the mind-body connection worked in light of God's design.

Progressive muscle relaxation. Similar to autogenic phrases, progressive muscle relaxation seeks to modify the internal state of the client from distressed or anxious to calm and connected. Progressive muscle relaxation borrows from the notion that the human body stores emotion, and these physiological cues tend to be the primary source the brain uses to determine level of stress or emotion. The function of progressive muscle relaxation, then, is to systematically and intentionally scan the body for points of tension and allow for the release of any tension that is being held there. For example, many clients carry their stress in the neck, shoulder, face, and back. The tension in these areas is interpreted by the brain as a signal that there is something to be stressed about. Consequently, more cortisol is released in an attempt to fight off or flee from the stressor that is creating the tension. However, in our twenty-first-century environment, many of the stressors we feel are perceived rather than real. Progressive muscle relaxation helps foster a state of vertical neurological integration by allowing the mind to calm down by modifying the signals received by the brain stem that are interpreted as the stress signal.

The following is an example of a progressive muscle relaxation exercise that could be used to help clients increase their capacity to regulate their emotions.

Sit with your feet flat on the floor and begin to take in long, slow, deep breaths.

As you breath in, slowly and deeply, begin to notice your body . . . the feeling of your back against the chair . . . the feeling of your feet on the floor.

As you notice your body, begin to feel any place where you feel pressure or tension in your muscles.

Begin with your feet. Notice any tension you feel in your toes . . . your arches . . . your heels. Slowly curl your toes down and in, feeling the pull of your muscles. Squeeze tightly, and then let them relax. Now extend them upward, as far as you can go without injuring yourself. And now let them relax. Feel the flow of blood to your feet as your muscles begin to relax.

Now notice your calves and lower legs. Gently raise your heels off the floor as you flex your calf muscles, digging your toes into the floor. And now let them relax. Next, leave your heels on the floor and move your feet toward the ceiling, feeling the strain in your calves as you do so. Now let them relax. Feel the flow of blood to your calves and lower legs as your muscles continue to relax.

Now notice your thighs and upper legs. Gently tense your quadriceps and upper legs. Feel the tension in them as you flex. Now let them relax. Feel the flow of blood to your thighs as your muscles relax more and more.

Next, flex your torso, including your abdominals and lower back. Notice any points of tension you feel there as you flex these muscle groups. As you relax, take a long, slow, deep breath and feel the flow of blood as your torso muscles begin to relax.

Now squeeze your elbows to your sides, and flex your upper back and shoulder muscles. This is where many people carry their stress. Feel your shoulders and upper arms contract. Now let them relax. Notice where you felt tension while you were flexing, and let the blood flow there as the tension melts away.

Squeeze your hands into a tight fist,

pulling your curled fingers deep into your palms. Sometimes your arms may bounce because of the flexing in your forearms. As you let your tightened fist relax, notice the tension you have carried in your hands, and let it slowly disappear.

Your body is feeling heavy and relaxed as you let go of the tension it has carried.

Now focus on your neck, flexing your neck muscles by squeezing your chin downward. Now slowly lift your chin and feel the muscles in the back of your neck and upper shoulders contract. Feel how much tension you carry there. Continue squeezing . . . and now relax them, letting your shoulders slump to your sides.

Last, squeeze the muscles in your jaw and face by furrowing your brow. Many people do not realize how much stress they carry in their jaws and forehead. Feel the tension there, and now . . . relax. Feel the warmth of blood flowing to your now relaxed muscles.

Do one last scan of your body. Notice any remaining points of tension. If you identify an area, simply repeat the tensing and then releasing of the muscle group.

Now take one long, slow, deep breath, and when you are ready, open your eyes.

Emotional Expression Exercises

Another tool that can be a beneficial form of emotional regulation is expressive writing. When speaking of expressive writing, the name that inevitably comes up is James Pennebaker. Rather than journaling about a specific topic, such as in a diary, when we do expressive writing, we seek to access the more creative attributes housed in the right brain. In this process, little emphasis is given to accuracy of spelling, proper grammar, or appropriate punctuation; rather, expressive writing is an endeavor to allow language to express oneself in an effort to let go of dysphoric emotions and increase a general sense of well-being.

Pennebaker and Beall (1986) first studied expressive writing with a group of undergraduate students. They asked participants in the experimental group to write about their most upsetting or traumatic experiences for four days in a row, fifteen minutes per day. At the follow-up four months later, those in the experimental group had significantly higher levels of emotional and physical well-being than participants in the control group (Kallay, 2015).

For expressive writing exercises, the prompts can be customized to the current circumstances of the client, but typically these prompts center around having the writer examine their responses to some life event that was profoundly impactful, even to the point of traumatic. Dan Siegel provides a helpful framework for helping clients tune in to their internal world, and this framework can be used by clients who engage in expressive writing. The acronym that Siegel uses is SIFT, which stands for *sensations*, *images*, *thoughts*, and *feelings* (Siegel & Payne Bryson, 2011). In the context of expressive writing, the writer is encouraged to reflect on the event that emerges in response to the prompt and then SIFT through his internal world, expressing whatever sensations, images, feelings, and thoughts he experiences. In addition to being a helpful tool for expressive writing, it can be used in the moment by clients who are trying to better understand and regulate big emotion.

Given the family of origin dynamics evidenced in Maria's life story, and the overt traumatic elements of Cal's story, expressive writing would be a helpful intervention to help them better understand the full range and depth of their emotional experiences. One added benefit of expressive writing, beyond the increase in physical and emotional well-being, is that the client brings information into the therapeutic process to further unpack with the therapist. Thematic elements can be of particular importance to deepening the therapeutic process, and the images and sensations clients provide in their writing become rich veins of content for the counselor to mine.

Exploring Relational Regulation

Relational regulation is at the heart of the human experience and is the most powerful form of managing emotions. After all, the guiding concept for this chapter is the fact that we are created for connection in the image of an inherently relational God. One story makes this point with special poignancy.

My second son, Graham, was born via Cesarean section. The process went as smoothly as one could expect. I can distinctly recall seeing his little head pop out of my wife's abdomen and how similar he looked to his older brother. Within a few short seconds, the nurses received him from the doctor and began their work of caring for him in his first few moments of life. As they were whisking him away

to a neonatal care room, one of the nurses looked over her shoulder and beckoned me, saying, "Come on, Dad." Thrilled, I followed, uncertain of what awaited me in the adjacent exam room.

As I entered the room, three nurses were busy checking Graham for fingers, toes, and more importantly, signs of life: breathing and a pulse. He was alert and attentive as they found his pulse but had yet to cry. It was but a few seconds later when they gave him a shot of Vitamin K that he announced his arrival into the world. As he cried out in this new world where he was cold and naked, and now in pain, he screamed reflexively, instinctively, trusting that the voices he heard so frequently in utero would be there to hold him. I was standing against a row of cabinets about eight feet away from him as he screamed, and in the moment the words that came from my mouth were quite simple: "It is going to be okay, baby Graham. Daddy is right here." I was not prepared for what happened next. At just a few minutes old, my son immediately ceased his screaming and turned his head toward the sound of my voice.

There was a profound beauty to this moment, and I must admit that I was not fully aware of its significance at the time. Newborn infants can see only about twelve to fifteen inches away from their faces, about the distance from the mother's breast to her eyes. I was about eight feet away, and yet his little eyes strained into the uncertainty of the chasm that separated us in that moment, determined to perceive me amid the blurriness in his eyes. In faith he attuned himself to the sound of my voice, trusting that my presence was real, and in that trust he was comforted. Quickly the nurses swaddled him and handed him to me. As our eyes met, his belief in my presence was further reinforced by our mutual gaze. We looked at one another with a sense of profound wonder, soaking in the awe of this first shared experience. I then walked him back into the surgery room where my wife was being tended to by the physician, and her joy was made complete by sharing in this special moment of gazing on him and looking into his deep blue newborn eyes. In that space, we created a holding environment for him to begin the process of bonding, and that holding process continues to this very day, though the swaddling and diapers have been exchanged for knee-torn jeans and worn-out sneakers.

I have replayed that moment from my life again and again in my head, and the poignancy of the memory does not escape me. In fact, it has only intensified as Graham has gotten older. I cannot help but recall that moment with a tender fondness because of the analogy it provides for the faith to which we are called. Like Graham, I sometimes lose the ability to see the Lord's presence, but that does not mean he is not there. Instead, I am reminded to strain into the uncertainty, in faith, believing that his voice is real and entrusting myself to it. The words of the writer of Hebrews echo through the millennia: "Now faith is confidence in what we hope for and assurance about what we do not see" (Heb. 11:1). We are created to respond to the sound of the Father's voice because we are created for a deep and profound connection with him, with others, and with ourselves. The joy of our hope is that one day we will be greeted by the opportunity to gaze mutually into the Father's eyes and experience the full measure of belovedness as he says, "Well done, my good servant!" (Luke 19:17).

The beauty of this story extends beyond the beauty of God's design for parents and children; it points us straight to the role of the therapeutic relationship in that we create a holding environment for our clients in the midst of their fear, confusion, sadness, shame, and distress. As they look into our eyes, reeling from whatever life circumstances they are negotiating at the time, they are looking for a glimpse of the Father, straining to see him in the midst of the blurriness that their circumstances entail. The sacredness of our counseling profession is found in this intimate space. In our clients' vulnerability, we hold them with our words, we speak truth from the Father, and we give them an experience of feeling felt, heard, and understood. In doing so, we invite them into a process of relational regulation that is an experience of emotional regulation that draws on the connection they share with us.

This principle extends far beyond the story of my son's birth and into the clinical realm in which we work as counselors. In their article on relational emotional regulation, Ben-Naim and colleagues (Ben-Naim, Hirschberger, Ein-Dor, & Mikulincer, 2013) discuss how suppression of emotional responses has a negative impact on one's romantic partner. This is especially true for individuals with high degrees of attachment anxiety or attachment avoidance

(Ben-Naim et al., 2013). This study, then, validates, first, that we are created for connection in that our responses to emotion extend beyond the individual and impact interpersonal relationships; and second, that how we relate via attachment style impacts the degree to which these emotional responses interfere with healthy functioning. Marganska and colleagues (Marganska, Gallagher, & Miranda, 2013) extend this study more specifically by researching attachment style and certain anxiety disorders, with the results remaining identical. Connection, especially comforting, nonsexual touch, and a gentle tone of voice paired with affirming words, is a powerful source of emotion regulation.

Client-Therapist Dyad as Emotional Regulating Resource

If connection plays a significant role in the regulation of emotions, then it is possible that the connection shared between the therapist and the client can play a similar role. In many respects, the client-therapist relationship will begin to be a microcosm of the client's larger social and relational world, including attachment style. The goal of relational regulation in the therapeutic relationship, then, is to identify the client's existing attachment style and move her toward a securer style, thereby increasing a sense of regulation through connection. Katehakis (2009), citing Ginot (2007), states, "Indeed, this 'earned secure attachment' is one of the most powerful forces helping patients learn to regulate their nervous systems" (p. 14).

Regarding Cal and Maria, one of the most pronounced dynamics in each of their clinical narratives is the sense of disconnection they experience in their close relationships with others. Given the inherent anxious and ambivalent features they manifest in their strategies for emotional regulation, including a high degree of emotional suppression and subsequent externalizing behaviors, such as compulsive behaviors and substance abuse, the therapeutic relationship is a powerful interpersonal experience of feeling felt, heard, and understood in a different way. One tool that would be beneficial for Cal and Maria, as well as the therapist, is the Experience in Close Relationships questionnaire (ECR; Fraley, Waller, & Brennan, 2000). The ECR, a thirty-six-item questionnaire, has two scales that measure avoidance and anxious attachment. By more specifically determining each individual attachment style, the therapist can determine how to manage the therapeutic relationship with respect to emotional regulation. For more specific details on an example of a specific intervention for affective regulation in the therapeutic relationship, see Katehakis's 2009 article "Affective neuroscience and the treatment of sexual addiction."

In working with Cal and Maria, the therapeutic relationship must center on consistency of responsiveness and heightened attunement to the nonverbal dynamics present in the room. Frequent use of empathic immediacy, or the therapist naming the experience he is having in the moment with the client, will be of utmost importance to give Cal and Maria the opportunity to experience themselves through another's eyes. This expression of empathy forces the client to experience herself, which is essential for clients who, like Cal and Maria, regularly participate in coping strategies that disconnect them from their internal world of thoughts and emotions.

CONCLUSION

Emotions are a powerful piece of the human experience and are the driving force in our experiences of connection. Inevitably, the experience of disconnection leaves us prone to their influence and in need of tools for regulating our minds and bodies. Therefore, learning adaptive and effective strategies for managing these intense feelings is a critical piece of healthy individual and relational living.

A number of individual strategies can be implemented in the therapeutic process to increase the client's capacity for effective, adaptive emotional regulation. Specifically, tools such as diaphragmatic breathing, autogenic phrases, and progressive muscle relaxation use the low-road of the brain to manage emotion in the body from the bottom up. Additionally, cognitive strategies such as guided imagery/visualization and expressive writing empower the high-road of the brain to quiet big emotion from the top down. Lastly, interpersonal connection can be used as a tool for regulating emotion. Modeling secure attachment and responding to the needs of the client within the therapeutic environment plays a significant role in this process.

RECOMMENDED READING

Berking, M., & Whitley, B. (2014). *Affect regulation training: A practitioners' manual*. New York, NY: Springer.

Leahy, R., Tirch, D., & Napolitano, L. (2011). *Emotion regulation in psychotherapy: A practitioner's guide*. New York, NY: Guilford Press.

Moriarty, G., & Hoffman, L. (Eds.). (2013). *The God image handbook for spiritual counseling and psychotherapy: Research, theory, and practice*. New York, NY: Routledge.

Pattakos, A. (2010). *Prisoners of our thoughts: Viktor Frankl's principles for discovering meaning in life and work* (2nd ed.). Oakland, CA: Berret-Koehler.

Schore, A. (1994). *Affective regulation and the origins of the self*. Hillsdale, NJ: Lawrence Erlbaum.

Schore, A. (2003a). *Affective dysregulation and disorders of the self*. New York, NY: W. W. Norton.

Schore, A. (2003b). *Affective regulation and the repair of the self*. New York, NY: W. W. Norton.

CHAPTER 6

Behavioral Strategies

John C. Thomas, PhD, PhD

> Speak to the people of Israel and say to them, I am the Lord
> your God. You shall not do as they do in the land of Egypt,
> where you lived, and you shall not do as they do in the land
> of Canaan, to which I am bringing you. You shall not walk in
> their statutes. You shall follow my rules and keep my statutes
> and walk in them. . . . You shall therefore keep my statutes
> and my rules; if a person does them, he shall live by them.

LEVITICUS 18:1–5 ESV

In contrast to other psychotherapies, behavioral therapy works from the outside in, rather than from the inside out. The foundation of behavioral therapy most closely traces to the psychology laboratory and empirical research. Another term often used as a generic term for behavior therapy is behavior modification, which refers to any procedure that modifies behaviors.

Whereas early theorists maintained the exclusive role of treating behavior, since the 1980s behavior therapies have been commonly coupled with cognitive therapy to understand and challenge beliefs that activate behavior. Yet behavioral therapy contains viable and effective strategies, interventions, and techniques (SITs) for a wide range of clinical presentations.

In addition to treating mental disorders, the principles and procedures of behavior therapy have been harnessed for a variety of purposes, such as preventing and treating physical and psychological effects of medical disorders, improving daily functioning (e.g., work productivity, parenting), addressing societal problems (e.g., safety hazards, recycling, violence, injustice), and enhancing athletic and academic performance.

This chapter provides an overview of behavioral psychology and a biblical perspective on its philosophical assumptions and practical implementation. I discuss and describe selective behavioral strategies, interventions, and techniques (SITs) and connect them to one or more of six case studies.

THEOLOGY AND PSYCHOLOGY OF BEHAVIOR

Because behavior is the only observable part of human activities (Thorpe & Olson, 1997) it has become the primary or sole focus of many (e.g., Skinner, 1953, 1972; Wolpe, 1982) who view humans as animals or machines that can be controlled by providing certain conditions and removing others. The rationale is to help clients act in a healthier manner or more effectively. Jones and Butman (2011) frame the orientation this way: "Behavioral understandings of the person are generally that the person is a bundle of behavior patterns, reflexes, perceptions, and impressions" (p. 148).

From a counseling perspective, problematic behaviors are evident in two primary forms: *behavioral deficits/excesses* (Ramnerö & Törneke, 2008) and *behavioral regulation* (Aldwin, Skinner, Zimmer-Gembeck, & Taylor, 2010). Behavioral deficits describe behaviors or skills that are underdeveloped in terms of frequency, duration, intensity, or effectiveness. You are helping clients with behavioral deficits when you address poor prosocial behaviors, inadequate emotional intelligence, poor hygiene, and sexual avoidance or low sexual desire, to name only a few. Deficits in individuals can occur from numerous sources, such as developmental impairments, addictions, and psychopathology. In comparison to having too little of a behavioral skill, excesses exist when the behavior occurs too frequently, such as the intake of too much alcohol or food, oversleeping, impulsivity,

compulsivity, being agitated and angry, and relational neediness.

Typically a normative standard is used to determine what is too little or too much of any given behavior. Various standards, such as statistical prevalence (the commonness of the behavior), clinical criteria, societal expectations, or conceptualization of particular behaviors by individuals or groups (e.g., a church contending that any alcohol use is excessive) may be operative in the decision making.

Theology of Behavior: The Bible Places Emphasis on Our Actions

Bufford (1981) notes that many biblical directives, such as putting on and off certain behaviors, equate with behavioral principles. For example, we are directed to remove sexual immorality, impurity, obscene talk, lying, slander, and much more (Col. 3:5–9). In contrast, Scriptures challenge us to augment particular behaviors that are deficient or need strengthening. We are to serve (e.g., Gal. 5:13; Heb. 6:10), be doers of the Word (James 1:22; 2:17, 26), share the Gospel (Acts 1:8), imitate God (Eph. 5:1–2), and encourage others (1 Thess. 5:11; Heb. 10:24–25), to name a few.

Theology of Behavior: We Are More Than Behaviors

Clearly, behavior is important to God, and therefore it ought to be important to us. Yet an honoring of biblical truth requires viewing humans as living souls. Though behavior is a significant part of being human, we are far more than behavior. Here are a few reasons.

We are made in the image of God (Gen. 1:27). We are more than machines and responders to our environment. We are image bearers of the Creator who has fashioned us to interact with the environment and shape it more than it shapes us. Solely focusing on behavior mitigates the integrity of personhood; it disregards the reality that we are much more than our behavior. The fundamental truth is that we act and we behave because it is an expression of God who acts.

We are interconnected with the environment around us. God designed us to respond and be influenced by contexts around us. Accordingly, Clouse (1985) said, "God created us as beings who respond to reinforcers and punishers in our environment" (p. 194). My colleague Dr. David Jenkins likes to say that "God is the ultimate behaviorist" because he is the "great rewarder" (personal communication, July 7, 2012). In other words, learning theory and behavior modification play a role in human development, and using them is compatible with biblical truth. God placed us in a social context with environmental influences that shape and influence behavior. This occurs in part through classical and operant conditioning, and respondent behavior. Free will and quality of our psychological and spiritual health are integral in how we are influenced and respond to the world around us.

We were created with moral freedom and personal agency. Another reason we are more than behaviors is that God's human blueprint included moral freedom and free will. Jones and Butman (2011) expound on this point (see Martin & Sugarman, 2003). They note that while Chris-

tians hold to freedom and moral agency, that does not mean that certain behaviors are not learned, or that choice and free agency are not shaped by constitutional or environmental factors.

We were created with great complexity. Like all aspects of our humanity, behavior is complex. Yet it is only one of the many dimensions of humanity that are also complex in their own way. God created us to be complex, perhaps because he is complex. One aspect of that complexity is that we are part of all creation. Though we were the capstone of God's creation, we were part of the process. This complexity means that our relationship with the environment is interconnected and dynamic. This is partially what is meant by "We are holistic beings" (Mackewn, 1997, p. 159). The complexity even extends to descriptions of our personhood. The great apologist Francis Schaeffer (1968) captured the complexity of being a living soul. He remarked, "As God is a person, he thinks, acts and feels; so I am a person, who thinks, acts and feels. But that person is a unit. I can think of my parts in various ways: as body and spirit; or as my physical parts and my spiritual parts. I can quite correctly think of myself as intellect, will, and emotion" (p. 140).

Behavior is soul language. Jesus said, "By their fruits you will know them" (Matt. 7:20 NKJV). Based on the consistency of behavior over time, people perceive patterns of behavior and attribute characteristics about them. Yet, since behavior is the only observable aspect of the inner-outer connection, accurately determining what a person's behavior means is impossible. For instance, while it might seem that someone is treating you "nicely" due to their engaging behavior, that person could actually be setting you up. That is why we must reflect on what is happening inside a person and consider the context. Jesus's teachings inform us that behavior is a reflection of a person's heart (Mark 7:20–23; Luke 6:45). The heart is associated with the activities of the mind and the will, as well as feelings and affections. While we can project behaviors that do not reflect the true nature of our heart, we cannot free ourselves from the inescapable reality that we ultimately express who we are through our behavior (Johnson, 2009). Biblically speaking, behavior is soul language. At the same time, behavioral change can also influence modifications in cognitive and emotional change. Alcoholics Anonymous says, "Fake it till you make it," and Adler (Carlson, Watts, & Maniacci, 2006) proposed that change can come from acting as if you are what you desire to become.

Behavior reflects our inner life. Viewing humans as holistically constituted is essential. Biblical descriptions of us communicate that we are created beings with certain psychological, physical, and spiritual laws that continually interact and influence one another. We are holistic systems in which our whole beings are greater than the sum of our parts. As living souls we are integrated. From a biblical perspective, we are more than observable behavior. Our internal life and external life are interconnected (cf. Gen. 2:7; Hos. 4:2–3, 13). The outer part corresponds to that which is visible, or behavior. The apostle Paul used the term "inner being" (cf. Rom. 7:22–23; 2 Cor. 4:16; Eph. 3:16)

to describe our souls, including the spiritual dimension of a person. Whatever the caliber of a person's inner person, it is lived out through behavior (cf. Rom. 6–7).

The Bible puts our heart as the hub of human personhood, the center of the inner person. Biblically, many behaviors are linked with our hearts (see Prov. 4:23; Jer. 18:12; Rom. 2:5; Heb. 3:8). In fact, Samuel informs us that our tendency is to consider outward appearance and behavior over the heart (1 Sam. 16:7). When we conceive sin in our hearts, we invite wrongly motivated, misguided, or sinful behavior. For example, Pharaoh's hard heart caused his stubbornness, anger, and the actions he took to exterminate Israel (Ex. 4:21; 7:3–14; 8:15–32; 14:8); Israel's heard hearts caused their grumbling and defiance in the wilderness (Ex. 16:2; Num. 14:2); Jonah's sinful heart motivated him to flee to avoid preaching to people he detested; and King Nebuchadnezzar's narcissism led to his command to build a statue in his honor (Dan. 3; 5:20–21). Further, Jesus connected the action of divorce to hard-heartedness (Matt. 19:8). While the Bible recognizes the place of habits and behavioral patterns in our lives—both good and bad—actions work as a correlative of the entire soul.

Behavior reflects our fallenness. I will not belabor this point, since it is so fundamental to the gospel. Original Sin encapsulated every aspect of humanity and our environment. Sin deformed everything. Whereas humanity's fall from innocence is the Sin from which we need to be saved, little *s* sins are the output. Whether the expression of Sin is in attitude or behavior, every aspect of our human experience is fallen. Behavior, then, is more than a by-product of classical or operant conditioning, learning theory, or any other principle of behavioral psychology. We cannot do behavioral work without a sure footing on a biblically grounded anthropology.

Behavior can be deceptive. A person might exhibit charming behavior to you but internally simply want to get what he desires. The result is exploitation. Behavior in such cases deceives, yet it reflects the inner world of the person's true intent. Peter penned the reality that "in their greed they will exploit you with false words. Their condemnation from long ago is not idle, and their destruction is not asleep" (2 Peter 2:3 ESV; cf. Ps. 119:61).

Theology of Behavior: We Can Control Behavior

Scriptures also teach us that our behavior can be controlled and regulated (cf. Matt. 4:3–11). First, having the ability to regulate our actions is rooted in the character of God, whose image we bear (cf. Ex. 34:6). Johnson (2009) views Christian counseling as having a significant role to play in helping clients develop the ability to regulate their behavior. He says that counselors can help clients by "promoting awareness of triggers of inappropriate or sinful behavior and increases in arousal, reflecting on the counselee's explicit and implicit goals (including secondary gains), talking through future scenarios and appropriate action options, role playing and then discussing the internal dynamics that the counselee was experiencing, and the assigning of homework, including rehearsal of actions in vivo and journaling afterward

that promotes reflection on action regulation issues" (pp. 528–529).

In sum, behavior is worthy of clinical attention by Christians. Behavioral SITs have merit in the fact that we learn from interacting with our environment. Behavioral counseling models are based on the premise that specific, observable, maladaptive, badly adjusted, or self-destructive behaviors can be modified by learning new, more appropriate behaviors to replace them. Strategies, interventions, and techniques are devised that target the interaction of specific behaviors, the person's environment, and outcomes, both pleasurable and painful. Major concepts of behavioral counseling, such as operant and classical conditioning, are woven into an unpacking of the strategies and techniques described below. Behavioral SITs are effective with a wide range of disorders, including substance use disorders, sexual addiction, sexual problems, eating disorders, anger management, post-traumatic stress disorder, attention-deficit/hyperactivity disorder, obsessive-compulsive disorder, and pervasive developmental disorders, among others.

CASE STUDIES

In lieu of lengthy case descriptions to set the stage for discussing the SITs for behavioral issues, six succinct cases are presented.

Case One

Adriana is a fifty-year-old Hispanic female who reports experiencing nightmares every night for about seven months. Generally the nightmares involve being chased down alleys of a city until she is finally caught, and then she wakes up in a cold sweat and hyperventilating. At least once a week the dream continues and involves torture and death. Upon waking, Adriana gets out of bed trembling and paces around her room.

Case Two

Tyreek is a thirty-year-old African American male who fears asking women out to the point of never having had one date (i.e., behavioral deficit). His anxiety and avoidance began when he was thirteen following a few incidents of being cruelly mistreated and rejected. While in college, roommates coerced Tyreek into online dating sites, but he evaded any communication with others online. Tyreek believes he will be single the rest of his life and has begun avoiding social situations where even female friends are present.

Case Three

Chung-Ho is a twelve-year-old Asian male who is bullied in school. He has a learning disability yet still does well in school. He is an accomplished pianist, which seems to be a trigger for more bullying. Chung-Ho's parents brought him to counseling because he was refusing to go to school.

Case Four

Kristen is an eight-year-old Caucasian female who consistently fights in school (i.e., behavioral excess). She has exhibited aggression since she was six years old. The school, parents, and district superintendent are all working collaboratively to address the issue. If Kristen cannot regu-

late her behavior, she will be placed in an alternative school. In spite of everyone's efforts, Kristen seems apathetic about dealing with her problem.

Case Five

Bryant, a twenty-three-year-old Caucasian, is a Christian graduate student in a large eastern city who had developed obsessive-compulsive disorder (i.e., behavioral excess) related to contamination and an excessive fear of birds, especially pigeons. He had previously suffered from panic disorder, extreme nightmares, and substance use of cannabis. To avoid "toxins," Bryant takes circuitous paths around birds and wears latex gloves when not at home.

Case Six

Bob and Carol are the parents of three children. The middle child, Clint (age ten), has been difficult to manage since infancy. Though fairly compliant in school and church, Clint has marked temper tantrums around homework, dinner, and bedtime, when he throws things at walls, yells obscenities, and rolls on the floor kicking his feet (i.e., behavioral excess). The tantrums occur daily and have gone from brief outbursts to now lasting as long as fifteen minutes. Bob and Carol are at their "wits' end" on how to "handle this child"!

BEHAVIORAL STRATEGIES, INTERVENTIONS, AND TECHNIQUES

The strategies below are useful for a wide range of child, adolescent, and adult problems. For our purposes here, strategies are categorized in terms of those that teach new behaviors and those that alter behaviors.

Learning New Behaviors

An important counselor task is helping clients learn particular life skills. Many SITs are available, but because of space constrictions, I will discuss only a few: modeling, self-monitoring, shaping, chaining, overlearning, acting "as if," role playing, and behavioral rehearsal. (See Recommended Reading at the end of this chapter for a list of resources.)

Learning new behaviors begins with determining what behavior/skill is deficient and what prerequisite skills (e.g., attitudes, social skills, feelings, knowledge) are needed to lay the groundwork. Before selecting a strategy, ask yourself the following: (1) What specific behavior is problematic? (2) Under what specific conditions does this behavior occur? (3) What antecedent, consequent, or event tends to occur in conjunction with the behavior? (4) What perpetuates the behavior? (5) What strategies best address the need?

Modeling. Based on social learning theory, modeling is a highly complex yet universal form of learning via observation (Bandura, 1967). The main purpose of modeling is skill acquisition through imitation, though it can also inhibit behavior already learned. The rationale is based on the assumption that if unhealthy behavior can be learned through the process of observation and imitation, then healthy behavior can be learned through the same process. Obviously, to use modeling there must be a *model* and client agreement to

learn from or imitate the model. The greater the similarities between the model and client, the greater the likelihood that the client will imitate.

Two broad types of models are available. First, you—the counselor—will hopefully model healthy behavior throughout the counseling process. It makes sense to capitalize on your position to teach skills through your comportment, not just verbally. Second, connect the client to a particular model. Ask the client to identify an individual who can serve as a model, or instruct the client to observe and imitate models in their natural environment (e.g., teachers, peers, coworkers, godly individuals). In other words, connect the client to anyone who is believed to appropriately exhibit the targeted behavior. Tyreek, for example, was connected with an older gentleman in his sphere of social contacts who modeled relating to women as image bearers of God— desensitizing the perceived threat women posed. Chung-Ho benefited from seeing me model assertive skills at times when he needed to be challenged. Role play can also be used.

Modeling has been categorized into covert (imagine a model performing the behavior), in vivo, symbolic (virtual video, audio), and participant (client involved in the process). For example, covert modeling was used with Tyreek, who imagined a man confidently asking a woman for a date, and participant modeling was used with Chung-Ho, who was instructed to watch other teens effectively responding to bullies as well as learning prosocial skills to develop stronger relationships with cooperative peers. Chung-Ho also used a behavioral form to track what he was learning, which is a method of self-monitoring.

Self-monitoring. Self-monitoring involves two steps. First, it includes systematic observation of one's own covert or overt behavior. Second, it involves recording it using such methods as written diaries, monitoring forms, timing devices, and mechanical counters (Foster, Laverty-Finch, Gizzo, & Osantowski, 1999). In today's technological world, devices such as smartphones and tablets enhance the process. And of course, an app is available to use in tracking behavior. A constructive and valuable application is assessing behavior with self-monitoring throughout the entire counseling process.

The usefulness of self-monitoring depends on the client's ability and willingness to make careful and candid recordings. For those who comply, self-monitoring benefits include (1) gaining awareness of the frequency and nature of a particular behavior (adults often learn better through self-discovery) that is the baseline level of the target; (2) monitoring low frequency events, which would be difficult to observe independently; (3) decreasing or increasing a targeted behavior through enhanced awareness of the behavior; (4) becoming aware of internal experiences, such as cravings or dysfunctional thoughts; and (5) measuring change over time, including tracking the use and effects of a specific strategy. Self-monitoring is applicable to such behaviors as self-harm, substance usage, classroom participation, eating and purging episodes, depression, panic, and angry outbursts, to name a few (cf. Craske

& Tsao, 1999; Korotitsch & Nelson-Gray, 1999; Wilson & Vitousek, 1999).

To incorporate self-monitoring, first assess the client's motivation and cognitive ability to monitor the behavior, and determine whether the client possesses sufficient insight to recognize the targeted behavior and its contextual features. Then discuss its use, rationale, and the specific behavior that is being monitored. In case four, eight-year-old Kristen is resistant to addressing her issues and changing. Thus, it is necessary to build good rapport and enlist her cooperation. To collect information on the nature and extent of his behaviors, Tyreek recorded the frequency, antecedents, and events surrounding his avoidance of females. Chung-Ho noted antecedents and the nature of the bullying. Kristen tracked antecedents and consequences of being aggressive, and Bryant monitored frequency and consequences of hand washing.

Next, adequately train the client in the procedures. Determine the frequency of recording, such as prescribed times throughout the day, at the end of the day, or at each episode. Also, discuss the method of recording. Chung-Ho was instructed to daily note behaviors using a smartphone. Adriana, Bryant, and Bob and Carol journaled to more descriptively document through narratives. In each of these cases, the following session began with reviewing their tasks and exploring what insights and themes were gleaned from the activity.

Though self-monitoring is a straightforward and useful technique to employ, drawbacks include inaccuracy, noncompliance, increased discomfort, and the impact of self-monitoring on the targeted behavior. Also, in and of itself, the technique is limited on changing the person. It is the behavioral equivalent of "insight," necessary but insufficient for the attainment of self-control (Korotitsch & Nelson-Gray, 1999).

Shaping. Most behaviors are not easy to master because they involve complex units and sequences. A common-sense approach to mastering complicated behavior, then, is to break it down into smaller parts that can be learned by taking "baby steps" (Miltenberger, 2012). Two behavioral strategies are used for this purpose: *successive approximation*, or *shaping*, and *chaining*. Whereas shaping is appropriate for learning simple behaviors, complex behaviors require chaining. Often the two are used toward helping someone learn a behavior (chaining) by reducing the behavior to many simpler tasks (shaping). Obviously, learning complex behaviors and skills requires time, effort, and practice. This holds true for behaviors and skills such as social skills, assertiveness, anger management, breaking addictive rituals, or becoming more patient; we baby-step toward mastery. This is time consuming because many approximations are typically necessary before the target behavior is achieved.

Be aware that shaping can be combined with other established behavior strategies (e.g., chaining, modeling, self-monitoring, role play) and cognitive strategies (e.g., mental rehearsal). First, as in all behavioral techniques, carefully define the targeted outcome behavior (Sulzer-Azaroff & Mayer, 1991). For example, the target outcome

for Tyreek was to ask a woman out on a date. Next, using operant conditioning principles, Tyreek and I created a variable ratio schedule of reinforcement, where behaviors that moved him toward that target were reinforced according to a predetermined random pattern. Be aware that it is unwise to overreinforce or underreinforce. Developing that balance and finding the sweet spot is probably the hardest aspect of shaping. Begin by reinforcing after the first occurrence of the behavior. Tyreek chose to reward asking a woman for a date by splurging on NBA tickets. Subsequently, Tyreek and I developed a variable-ratio schedule with fishing after three and then five invitations. (I was praying he would get a yes after the first invite, but it took about seven times. We also had to work on his delivery.) Of course, this step also requires choosing the best reinforcement. Those reinforcements should be available, immediately presented following the desired behavior, able to be used repeatedly, and not time consuming or expensive (Poling, Schlinger, Starin, & Blakely, 2013).

Third, in collaboration with Tyreek, we developed a written list of successive approximations. This is known as *task analysis*. To do this, construct a staircase outlining the situations that can lead to skill development, and rank the items to move from least complex to greater complexity (also referred to as a *behavioral hierarchy*). Each step serves as a cue to the next step. By linking steps together in sequential successive approximations, a process is established. The components must be easy enough that they can be learned without great difficulty but not so elementary that they fail to provide sufficient incentive. Importantly, the components must be taught in the proper sequence to avoid poor stimulus control. Be mindful of the client's skill level, age, communication and processing abilities, motivation, and experience in attempting the target.

I have found it useful to teach relaxation skills to ground the client to a baseline calm setting. Next, after identifying and ordering the components, begin with the identified easiest one, and if possible, one closest to the one the client possesses. To enhance success, raise each criterion in small increments. To avoid confusion, don't try to shape two criteria simultaneously. Prior to using the operant method described in the previous paragraph, Tyreek and I developed the following behavioral hierarchy of Tyreek's task analysis shown below.

1. You say hi to women as you pass them on the side walk.
2. You are in a bus and sit near an unknown female, making no effort to connect.
3. You respond to one "poke" from a woman on the online dating site.
4. You sit next to a woman on a bus, and if she says something to you, make small talk ("Are you having a nice day?").
5. You respond to a total of three women on the dating site.
6. You "poke" a woman on the online dating site.
7. You reply if she responds to your "poke" and attempt to create a dialogue.
8. You "poke" three women on an online dating site.
9. You reply if anyone responds to your "pokes" and attempt to create a dialogue.
10. You have a meaningful, but not deep, conversation with a female coworker whom you have not known for long.

The process continues through all of the approximations toward the outcome. End each session on a positive note, because a failure or stressful situation could reduce the client's sense of efficacy. Also, debrief each session. I keep in mind that I want the client to be functioning and feeling as well as when the session began. This is also part of the learning process. Clients come to understand that feelings are fickle and can change rapidly and in intensity.

You will need to adapt if one shaping procedure is not eliciting progress. If the behavior deteriorates, return to the beginning. Quickly review the whole shaping process with a series of easily earned reinforcers. It is possible that the client is bored or inattentive because the steps are too easy or too small, or because you might be proceeding too fast. The client may also be experiencing too much emotional or physiological intensity. As steps are mastered, change reinforcers and use them on an intermittent basis. Finally, it is best to finish a session with a success rather than a failure. Be encouraging and edifying throughout the process. Focus on what was done right.

Chaining. If you understand the process of shaping, you will easily understand chaining. Think of shaping in terms of behavioral units (links) and chaining in terms of sequences of behavioral units (chains). In chaining, new complex behavior patterns are broken down into smaller specific behaviors. The client learns the behaviors through a series of links (specific behaviors) that are joined together for reinforcement until an entire chain of behavior is established (Cooper, Heron, & Heward, 2007). A behavioral chain is a specific sequence of discrete responses, each associated with a particular stimulus condition. Each response and stimulus serves as an individual link in the chain (Cooper et al., 2007). Linked together, all of the stimuli and responses create the desired behavior. Remember the saying that a chain is only as strong as the weakest link. Thus, the use of reinforcements must generate a strong enough response to make the chain secure. As progress occurs, behavioral chains rather than links can be reinforced, adding efficiency to the change process described below.

First, conduct a task analysis of the various components that comprise the targeted behavior. In the case of Tyreek, task analysis is breaking up the behaviors necessary to ask someone out on a date into small tasks. Follow the task analysis with a fading procedure whereby the client performs some of the steps in the sequence. To understand fading, you also need to know about prompting. Prompting is encouraging a behavior to occur. Conversely, fading is a process by which the prompt is gradually removed. In other words, the behavior is no longer reinforced. A systematic approach to fading allows Tyreek to progress toward the target behavior so that it will eventually be part of the repertoire of his behavior. Explaining this behavioral

learning process to clients is quite simple. I tell them that this is a user-friendly way to learn something new.

First, model the desired behavior so the client can see the entire process, or chain. Then role-play (discussed later) the first link of the chain to correct potential errors or provide instruction. Use ample immediate reinforcement early in the training. As the trials continue, these reinforcements should gradually decrease so that the chain is maintained by the single reinforcer at the end of the chain and the client internalizes the behavior.

Next, make sure the client performs all components learned up to that point. Each time new behavior is learned, all preceding components are reviewed. While I wouldn't suggest that you and your spouse have a double date with Tyreek and his date, a double date for Tyreek and his date with another safe couple would make for an important approximation as the goal behavior is neared.

Overlearning. Overlearning or overkill is based on learning theory. The aim of the technique is to foster competency and mastery of a particular behavior or set of behaviors. In essence, it encompasses the axiom that "practice makes perfect." In truth, it is not practice that makes perfect, but perfect practice that makes perfect. How well clients learn behavior and skills prior to implementing them is of critical importance to success (Ramnerö & Törneke, 2008).

Each behavior or skill has its own unique learning curve, which refers to the average rate required to learn. To name but a few factors, a person's learning curve is affected by prior knowledge, intellectual capacity, complexity of the skill to be learned, quality of instruction, and how much effort is directed to learning (Ramnerö & Törneke, 2008). Overlearning occurs by taking a repetitive and multifaceted approach to mastering a new behavior. For example, a client who is anxious about a public speech might benefit from overlearning. Chung-Ho would benefit from repetitive practice standing up to "bullies," whereas Kristen would benefit in overlearning pro-social behavior. There is nothing complicated about using this technique. It simply requires repetition via client practice outside of the session. Through practice (operant conditioning), the client's anxiety lessens (classical conditioning).

The act "as if" technique. Also known as "reflecting as if" (RAI), this technique has its roots in Adlerian psychology (Dinkmeyer, Dinkmeyer, & Sperry, 1987), not behaviorism. Still, it involves learning new behavior by considering the behavior a reality and anticipating it as expected. I often refer to it as "acting the new behavior into existence." In Alcoholics Anonymous parlance, "faking it till you make it" encourages addicts to maintain and sustain a healthy behavior even if it seems unnatural and ineffective.

People often act in ways that are inconsistent with the way they want to be. Accordingly, the client is instructed to pretend and enact a future event, belief, or desired behavior as if it were occurring naturally (Carich, 1989), one that is consistent with the target. Eventually, if continually acted out, the behavior will be more

natural and subsequently more effective. Carich (1989) describes variations and applications of acting as if, including incorporating it in role play, imagery, metaphor, reframing, and paradoxical prescription.

One application of the act as if technique is to describe a client's behavior as acting as if he is _____. For example, I told Tyreek, "You seem to act as if you are inadequate when around women, especially potential dates." In Chung-Ho's issue, "You seem to act as if you are small and weak when you see and are around those bullies." To Kristen, "You seem to act as if you need to prove something about yourself, as if you are afraid and need to show yourself and others that you aren't." Another application is promoting functional and/or godly behavior. In fact, this technique can help you bridge from inability to perform a particular behavior to achieving a desired state of being or the target outcome. Tyreek was encouraged to "act as if you have desirable traits that a woman would be attracted to," Chung-Ho to "act as if you can hold your ground against a bully," and Kristen to "act as if you are caring to others, especially the ones that hurt you." Of course, all these states of being need to be operationalized.

Tyreek's paralyzing anxiety about inadequacy in relating to women was inconsistent with his belief of having an identity in Christ; nor was he acting in ways that reflect a sense of "rest" and "peace." Next Tyreek was challenged with the following: "What would happen if you acted as if you were fully confident in Christ and what he has for you? And what if you related to women not as potential intimate partners but as image bearers who can give you more awareness of your masculinity?" The open-ended question points to another possibility and frames the target to resting in Christ and removing the potential of dating from his opposite-sex interactions. In essence, Tyreek takes on the dreaded task to act as if he is confident in Christ in order to relate to women's sexuality as image bearers.

The final step in the act as if technique is to obtain the client's agreement to try out the new behavior. Ask the client to describe what he would be doing if he was experiencing rest or a sense of peace (similar to solution-focused questions). Anticipate and process possible obstacles to implementation. With adequate preparation, the acting as if behavior becomes the new comportment.

Role playing and behavioral rehearsal. These techniques involve practicing a behavior in a contrived situation with the counselor being in an auxiliary or observer role. People often use the terms *role playing* and *behavioral rehearsal* interchangeably, though they are different. Role playing involves portraying scenes from a client's life experience to work through problems, whereas behavioral rehearsal emphasizes learning new behavior (Cooper et al., 2007). In a way, the distinction is similar to that of shaping (small units) and chaining (sequences). Role playing is a broader concept, including assessment, catharsis, changing of attitude, and provision of insight. Behavioral rehearsal is primarily focused on specific skill development.

Additionally, role playing can address discrepancies between role behaviors and the expectations held by others (Poling et al., 2013). It helps clients prepare for situations that they are or will be facing. It is applicable to learning assertiveness, social skills, and conflict resolution skills, and to dealing with a difficult person. Role playing and behavioral rehearsal would be effective with Tyreek (fears women) and Chung-Ho (bullied), and for Kristen to end intimidating behavior and develop prosocial skills.

The technique involves five stages: (1) informed consent and client motivation, (2) choice of scenario and identification of the goal, (3) determination of roles—at times the counselor may model the appropriate responses or play the antagonist, (4) enactment of the role play, and (5) evaluation and feedback (cf. Spiegler & Guevremont, 2010). As counselor, you are the director who guides and advises the client to get into the role with actions and gestures that align with the role. Reinforce the client with encouragement and regulate the pace of the learning so that it is neither too fast nor too slow.

Following informed consent and client motivation, collaboratively create scenarios as accurate and vivid as possible so that the scenes will elicit the desirable targeted behaviors. Effectiveness is linked to the scenes representing the client's real-life situation. For example, in one scenario Kristen shared an experience where she saw someone vulnerable. Rather than helping, she used it as an opportunity to bully (a behavior I refer to as "terrorism"). When all the scenes have been developed and agreed upon, assign roles that each will play. Typically these roles will change throughout the process. As part of the assessment, Kristen played herself and I played the victim. If possible, videotape the role play so that the client can learn from watching the interaction. Play your role in the scene as accurately as possible, which means fleshing out how the victim acts. Most importantly, I helped Kristen to stay in role. After the role play, we evaluated the performance. If you videotape the role play, review it. If role play is being used for learning purposes rather than assessment, provide positive feedback on the client's effort and performance. Initially, however, reserve comments for more salient issues.

Once the need to develop a new behavior has been established, whether by role play or by another means, it is time to learn. The implementation of behavioral rehearsal is very similar to role play. You do not need to use the term to describe the technique; simply say:

> Kristen, when learning a new skill, it is helpful to practice. Just as you learned to play softball, the need for repetition and feedback on performance is essential. Likewise, Kristen, what will help you learn [target skill] is practicing how to act a new way when in [particular situations]. What thoughts do you have about creating opportunities in the safety of this office to learn how to [target skill]?

Each hierarchy will be unique to the client, even if the presenting concerns are similar. Use a subjective units of distress scale (SUD) in which you create a 1 to 10 (or whatever number you want to use, such as 100) to evaluate each situation by asking the client to rate a particular behavior. Be sure that the level of behavioral complexity increases as the client climbs the staircase. In our example of Tyreek, asking a young lady out for a date is far more complex than sitting down next to a young female student and making small talk.

In the case of fighting eight-year-old Kristen, she began by learning to ignore a provocative situation and to think of what she could first say or do to deescalate the situation. Once the task analysis or behavioral hierarchy had been constructed of Kristen's internal and external anxiety-generating cues, the next step was to engage in the behavioral rehearsal. Starting with the least anxiety-provoking behavior, each scene was acted out.

To promote prosocial skills in a client like Kristen, pay attention not just to the words but also to the delivery, which includes the tone of voice, pace of speech, gestures, eye contact, and posture. It is wise to focus on only one, no more than two, of these components at one time (Sulzer-Azaroff & Mayer, 1991). As with role play, record the session if appropriate. Reinforce client efforts, and provide verbal feedback regarding the execution of the skill. Afterward, recycle back to the beginning, and continue on.

Finally, encourage the client to practice the new behavior outside of the office. Recommend that the client involve a trusted person to practice the skills. It is prudent to explore potential adverse outcomes and remind clients that new behavior has repercussions. When one person in a relationship changes the pattern of interaction, it directly impacts others. Not everyone in the client's circle of relationship will take to the new behavior; in fact, some people might even become enraged at the change (Spiegler & Guevremont, 2010). It is also true that the client might notice positive benefits from engaging in the new behavior and receive positive feedback as well.

Imaginal rehearsal. Imaginal rehearsal is a cognitive behavioral technique often referred to as covert sensitization (Cautela, 1967) or covert behavioral rehearsal. The technique is used either to link aversive consequences associated with the target or to perform target behaviors through imagining them occurring (Poling et al., 2013). For instance, Tyreek imagined the loneliness he feels because he avoids women; Kristen imagined the adverse consequences of her aggressive behavior. Alternatively, Bryant imagined himself sitting around pigeons, and Chung-Ho imagined standing up to a bully. Imaginal rehearsal is also a common technique for sleep problems such as nightmares, particularly those associated with post-traumatic stress disorder (PTSD).

In the case of Adriana who suffered from nightmares, the aim was to help her change the narrative of her distressing dreams. After learning relaxation skills, Adriana recalled a nightmare and then journaled about it with as much detail as possible. I chose to begin with the least frightening nightmare in order not to overwhelm her. Next I assisted her in changing the theme, story line, and ending of the nightmare to make it positive. You ought not to prescribe the changes that

need to be made, but encourage the client to produce and propose the changes. Once the new script was completed, Adriana rehearsed it via imagery. We continued the focus on mentalizing the altered version. In time the noxious dream would be replaced with the newer one.

Altering Behaviors

Moving on from learning behaviors, we will now pivot to altering behaviors. These SITs include counterconditioning, exposure and response prevention (ERP), and behavioral contingencies that facilitate changes in behavior. Modeling, self-monitoring, positive and negative reinforcement, role playing, and covert rehearsal can also be used to alter behavior.

Counterconditioning. An individual might respond to a given stimulus, such as an unwelcome situation or feared people, objects, or images with habitual marked anxiety, disgust, or avoidance. In such cases the goal is to use an effective emotional reduction procedure to diminish the distressful feeling(s). This can be accomplished by substituting a new response (unconditioned response) for the previous response (conditioned response). Helping a client lessen anxiety by relating to a stimulus of anxiety differently is known as "counterconditioning." It is a useful technique with disgust-based emotional responses because such reactions are reduced by gradually replacing them with a more beneficial response (Engelhard, Leer, Lange, & Olatunji, 2014). To be effective, you must pair a strong positive unconditional stimulus (US) to counter the conditioned response or stimulus (CS)

(Kerkhof, Vansteenwegen, Baeyens, & Hermans, 2011). For example, providing small amounts of money as the US by pairing it with the aversive stimulus will likely be insufficient to alter the conditioned response (CR).

In the case of Adriana, the fifty-year-old Hispanic woman who had nightmares, counterconditioning was used by pairing positive emotional imagery to produce relaxation. Fearing another night of horrifying dreams inhibited Adriana's sleep onset, yet despite her best efforts, she would fall asleep having another nightmare. Sleeping and anxiety had become associated, forming a conditioned stimulus. The result is that Adriana would become anxious (CR) when nearing bedtime, fearing another night of terror. Brief, graduated exposure counters this conditioning by associating anxiety-evoking sleeping with relaxation.

Exposure and response prevention (ERP) techniques. Exposure involves repeatedly facing one's fear until it subsides via the process of habituation. Response prevention, on the other hand, involves inhibiting the typical avoidance or escape behaviors when in the presence of the negative stimulus. While exposure and response prevention can be employed separately, they are often incorporated.

The purpose of exposure response prevention. Exposure response prevention, which is an evidence-based intervention (Myerbroker & Emmelkamp, 2010) for obsessive-compulsive disorder, panic disorder, agoraphobia, phobias, eating disorders, post-traumatic stress disorder, and any marked anxiety associated with an object or situation, works by diminishing the distressful and foreboding responses (Abramowitz, Deacon, & Whiteside, 2012). The therapeutic goal of ERP is for the client to maintain contact with the feared or detestable stimulus without the client engaging in his typical ritual or escape behaviors (Foa, Yadin, & Lichner, 2012; Henslee & Coffey, 2010; Shoenfelt & Weston, 2007).

How to use exposure response prevention. ERP is a formidable threat to clients because it requires them to face their most terrifying fears, urges, impulses, and affect. Keeping the client's emotional welfare in mind is a consideration in the method and manner used. The first consideration is whether the client's contact with the feared stimulus will be gradual or engulfing. Gradual exposure is deliberate, slow, and piecemeal, and progressively brings the client in contact with the stimulus as in the use of shaping. At the other end of the spectrum, exposure can occur in the form of flooding, in which the client is totally immersed in the feared stimulus for a period of time believed to sufficiently desensitize the client—like "being thrown into the deep end of the pool." Because most clients are resistant to being flooded with their feared stimulus, shaping (graduated) might be an effective alternative.

Pre-decisions. Several issues demand consideration prior to moving into using EPR. First, you must decide on the manner in which contact with the stimulus can occur, depending on access to the feared object or situation. When the trigger is accessible, the preferred method is in vivo (face-to-face with the stimulus); otherwise, imaginal or virtual exposure is the method of choice (Myerbroker & Emmelkamp, 2010).

Shaping is typically slow and often unwieldy, especially when being applied to situations where it is difficult or impossible to gain access to the feared stimulus, such as a concert venue, restaurant, or church. Whereas exposure forces the client to face the anxiety, response prevention (RP) inhibits the client's choice to act on thoughts or obsessions before, during, and after exposure. Bryant, for example, agreed to face his perilous trigger of becoming contaminated by touching doorknobs without ritualistically using gloves or excessive washing. The objective was to learn that abstaining from his compulsive behaviors does not result in sickness.

Next, discuss with the client the nature of ERP. Beyond the typical informed consent, EPR requires more time than the "therapeutic hour," thus, planning extended session time is wise (Abramowitz et al., 2012). The client must be financially and logistically able to adhere to that schedule.

It is imperative that you garner the client's willingness and commitment to soldier through these dreaded experiences—in other words, informed consent. If the client agrees, be very patient. Remember that these techniques require clients to forebear and wrestle a marked disgust and its concomitant peril. Understandably, reluctance and resistance are expected along with a marked increase in his anxiety (Abramowitz et al., 2012). Commonly, a step might be taken forward only to find that the client steps back again and again.

Exposure response prevention steps. With the previous decision made and pri-

or to using ERP, you help the client decide on a safe place that generates peace and relaxation to dissipate the anticipated anxiety prior to and during the activity. For Christians, weaving in Christ-based imagery is a powerful grounding and calming place. Bryant constructed imagery of sitting on a lake dock with the Lord. If you have established rapport, you, too, are a safe place or haven for the client to find support.

Next, teach the client deep muscle relaxation to begin at a low baseline level of anxiety. Relaxation is a physiological counter to anxiety because it is impossible for one's body to be simultaneously anxious and in a state of relaxation. Bryant and I spent an entire session on relaxation, with the instruction to practice it twice a day between sessions. In the following session, Bryant began with the relaxation exercise without guidance to assess his comfort and competency with the technique.

For Bryant, gradual exposure to the stimulus was the chosen manner to do the EPR intervention. Imagery was used to prepare for the eventual in vivo exposure. Bryant needed to concretely imagine each scene in sufficient detail with all available senses—touch, sound, sight, and smell (Abramowitz et al., 2012). Moreover, Bryant was instructed to imagine the scenes as a participant rather than an observer. He was to hold a scene in his mind's eye without drifting off, changing it, or shutting down. Note that these are likely responses with ERP, especially at the initial stages and when presented with the most anxiety-provoking scenes (Abramowitz et al., 2012).

Stimulus	Consequences	Rituals	Avoidance
Birds	Contamination and sickness	Wear gloves, cover head, excessively wash hands	Avoid hangouts of birds by taking different routes

Figure 6.1. Bryant's functional analysis of OCD response to contamination

Next I educated Bryant about anxiety, arousal, avoidance, and cognitive distortions so that he would have a clear understanding of how these experiences work together to create heightened anxiety (Abramowitz et al., 2012). Collaboratively, we identified as specific as possible the nature of the stimulus(i), including the threats it posed and the triggers, cues, feared consequences, and avoidance rituals for Bryant (figure 6.1). This step is often referred to as "functional analysis." The basic idea is to identify clinically relevant behaviors, including cognitive, emotional, physiological, physiological, spiritual, and behavioral variables (figure 6.2). Likely, you will need to construct multiple hierarchies in a way that would ensure each one is "pure" on its given dimension (Brady & Raines, 2009). For Bryant, this was what contamination by pigeons meant and represented to him. Bryant used self-monitoring, in which he intentionally attended to what was happening with him cognitively, emotionally, physiologically, and spiritually.

The next step was to establish or map a hierarchy of Bryant's anxiety intensity related to contamination. It is similar to the staircase-of-change approach used in behavioral rehearsal. The hierarchical situations may or may not have been experienced but would likely occur if he were exposed to the stimulus (Abramowitz et al., 2012). It took time to construct the list of stimulus situations to which Bryant reacted with graded amounts of anxiety. Included in this step was the use of a SUD scale to rate his average level of anxiety (either 1 to 10 or 1 to 100) for each one of the items in the hierarchy; I refer to the SUD scale as an "Anxiety Thermometer." Bryant began with the mildest stimulus, progressively preceding to more anxiety-provoking ones via the ratings of the SUD scale.

Event	Cognitive	Emotional	Physiological	Spiritual	Behavioral
Pigeons on sidewalk	• Overestimation of threat • Perfectionism • Intrusive thoughts	• Marked anxiety • Marked anticipatory anxiety • Panic attacks • Disgust	• Vigilance • Diminished physiologic flexibility • Increased heart rate • Tensing of muscles • Sweating • Nausea	• Fear-focused relationship with God • Disconnection from God's person	• Avoidance

Figure 6.2. Functional analysis of Bryant's anxiety of pigeon contamination (maladaptive)

Once it was clear what Bryant was afraid of, the number and rating of stimuli that comprised it, and the themes and purpose of his feared scenarios, we began the work.

The actual ERT phase of treatment begins when the client seems able to adequately manage the exposure. Setting the table for the exposure by ensuring that it will work is very important to set, thereby reinforcing the client's buy-in. Success breeds success. One approach I used for the imagined-exposure technique was Cromier and Cromier's (1985) RHA method—method R (remove), method H (hold), and method A (adaptive alternative). Method R involved Bryant visualizing a picture of a pigeon until he felt anxious and then rating the experience. Bryant decided not to exceed a SUD rating of 5 in the initial phases of the treatment. Once at that level, Bryant was instructed to stop or remove the anxiety-provoking image (method R), then to relax as an alternative coping strategy that is within his control. We settled on Bryant using an alternative coping strategy (method A) by repeating, "Stay calm; be at peace. Thank you, Jesus, for being present with me; with you nothing is impossible. Through you, I can handle this fear," while concomitantly using deep, relaxed breathing.

In real-life situations, the client may not be able to remove or stop the stimulus situation from occurring. This was true for Bryant, who was going to encounter pigeons. Next, using method H required that Bryant hold the relaxing image when he felt anxious. The length of exposure for each item on the list varies person to person but is typically based on how long it takes to reduce the client's distress by 50 percent (from the SUD number reported at the start). ERP requires repeating the items until each is subsequently desensitized.

The final phase of treatment involves relapse prevention and maintenance of the new responses to the stimuli. Instruct the client to repeatedly practice the new skills and behavior between sessions. With sufficient practice the imagined or real event loses its anxiety-provoking power. When Bryant was confronted by contamination stimulus, the new coping response gradually became natural and automatic. Booster sessions, the first one typically six weeks following the end of treatment, were scheduled to reinforce the change (Abramowitz et al., 2012). Of note is the fact that others have furthered ERP by incorporating cognitive-focused interventions such as danger ideation reduction therapy (DIRT; Jones & Menzies, 1997, 1998).

Event	Cognitive	Emotional	Physiological	Spiritual	Behavioral
Pigeons on sidewalk	• Cognitive regulation skills • Reality Orientation	• Emotional regulation skills • Enjoyment of God's creation	• Breathing management • Muscular calmness	• Communion with God and others • Practicing God's presence • At rest	• Limited interference • Nonavoidance

Figure 6.3. Adaptive response to Bryant's pigeon contamination

Behavioral contingencies. *Contingency management* is the name given to the use of operant conditioning when employed as an intervention or strategy (Cipani & Schock, 2008). It is a behavioral contract between you and the client who wishes behavioral change or needs to be changed. Most commonly behavioral interventions are used with children and adolescents, though there are many applications for adults (Cipani & Schock, 2008). Remember that in contingency management the therapist rewards desired behaviors while punishing the undesirable ones (Higgins & Petry, 1990).

Using rewards. One use of rewards is called *token economy* (Ayllon & Azrin, 1968), which rewards clients when they display desired behavior. The token (e.g., poker chips, coins, tickets) is awarded immediately after the behavior is exhibited. Later, exchange the tokens for a more tangible benefit, such as food, passes from a unit, free time, or special time with a parent. A child who needs to get ready for school in the morning in a timely manner could be rewarded with fewer chores.

In the case of Kristen, a contingency contract specified a plan of action in which she received a card with a smiley face on it at different times each day: in the morning, midmorning, at lunch, midafternoon, and at the end of the school day.

The teacher assigned the card, not based on Kristen avoiding fighting, but rather on Kristen engaging in cooperative play with other children. The cards accumulated toward a payout (also specified in the contract) of more computer time (tangible reward). Additionally, her parents provided encouragement,[*] a nontangible reward (generally the ones who need encouragement the most get it the least), and extra rewards, such as staying up later if Kristen had continued successes. Kristen's parents posted the card in a conspicuous place as a reminder of Kristen's new behavior. Prior to the contract, Kristen averaged four to five fights weekly; after three to four weeks of initiating the contract, fights dwindled to one to two per month. Continued use of the contract eventually led to elimination of the behavior. A penalty clause can also be used in a contract, whereby an undesirable behavior costs the client something; this is known as *response cost*.

Using negative reinforcement. Negative reinforcement occurs when a behavior or response is strengthened by removing, stopping, or avoiding an aversive stimulus or unpleasant outcome (Poling et al., 2013). Negative outcomes typically involve physical or psychological discomfort of some sort. Consider pigeons in a laboratory who are subjected to a very loud noise. Pecking at a disk turns off the noise

---

[*] I'm using an Adlerian concept of encouragement rather than praise. Whereas praise is judgmental, extrinsic, and connects deeds to the doer, encouragement is positive feedback focused on effort and improvement rather than outcomes. It is recognizing and conveying faith in a child for his or her existence and image bearing. It acknowledges the child's worth. Whereas praise is given only if one receives good results, encouragement can be given anytime—even when the child is doing poorly. I contend that God is far more a giver of encouragement (as well as challenge) than praise. Our role is to praise God, rather than for God the Father to praise us. For more information, read about Adler's concept of encouragement. Adler Graduate School. (n.d.). *Alfred Adler: Theory and application*. Retrieved from http://www.alfredadler.edu/about/theory.

for thirty seconds. If the pigeon increases its pecking, then reinforcement is taking place. The pigeon experiences negative reinforcement because pecking increases in frequency when the noise is removed. Bob and Carol used a response cost system with Clint, taking away an allowance and using other punishments every time he threw a tantrum. This was a highly successful intervention.

In the case of Chung-Ho's harassment by bullies, negative reinforcement was one intervention that was used. When the stimulus of bullying was presented to Chung-Ho, he inadvertently reinforced the bullies' behavior with his nonassertiveness. By failing to stand up for himself, he became even more desirable prey to his bullies. While Chung-Ho had attempted ignoring the bullies' comments (acting as if he didn't hear), he was negatively reinforcing the bullying. I chose to try a negative reinforcement approach to see if a particular intervention would dissuade the bullies from acting. In addition to other interventions, such as avoidance as an adaptive strategy and using humor, our major approach was to establish a bully defense team. Chung-Ho culled together others to participate in the bully defense team, which they called The Misfit Incredibles (TMI). They even had T-shirts made (though they forgot to give me one). The behavioral conceptualization was removing his (and others') feared stimulus that was reinforcing the bullies' behavior, Chung-Ho and his friends would negatively reinforce their behavior by withdrawing their feared response. I worked with the team, combining role play and behavioral

rehearsal, and eventually used in vivo by bringing in a few "bullies" to crush TMI. Of course, it is expected that at first bullies would increase their efforts to obtain their desired reaction (Cipani & Schock, 2008). To prepare the team, we worked on numerous adaptive coping responses to shore up their anxiety over something not working (Poling et al., 2013). Over the course of a month, the bullying behavior substantially decreased, only showing up when one of the "misfits" was separated from his team members.

Parenting issues hold many applications of negative reinforcement, as in the case of Bob and Carol, who sought help with their ten-year-old son, Clint. Recall that Clint had temper tantrums when told to do his homework, come to dinner, go to bed, or any other directive. Helping Bob and Carol learn and use negative reinforcement for Clint was quite dramatic in effect. The first step was for Bob and Carol to monitor their reactions to Clint's behavior, and in particular to note any unpleasant experiences that Clint was able to avoid through his abreactions. One negative reinforcement intervention was meeting Clint's dinner tantrums with no dinner and no other food afterward. Another one was that he could leave the dinner table when he ate four bites of broccoli.

Negative reinforcement has been successfully used with sexual deviance, heavy alcohol use, and overeating, to name a few behaviors.

Using punishment and penalty. Commonly, many equate negative reinforcement with punishment. Whereas negative reinforcement involves removing, avoiding, or escaping an unpleasant or undesirable event in order to strengthen a particular behavior, punishment occurs when the consequences (called a *punisher*) of a behavior decrease the likelihood that the behavior is repeated; that is, it weakens the behavior (Spiegler & Guevremont, 2010). A penalty is the removal of a positive. Whereas punishment applies pain and unpleasantness, penalty applies loss of comfort. Such interventions are a form of operant conditioning in which a noxious stimulus is paired with an undesirable behavior, and this is referred to as *aversion therapy.*

Penalty, and particularly punishment, have an unfavorable public image, and many counselors shy away from them, viewing them as ineffective and abusive. A few applications, however, have a place. For example, time-out is considered a form of penalty because positive reinforcers have been removed for a specified period of time. Charging a "no show" fee to clients who fail to attend a scheduled appointment is also a type of punishment known as *response cost.* Each implemented consequence or penalty is a "cost" for an undesirable response. This technique is generally more effective if the punishment and penalty immediately follow the targeted behavior.

In the case of Clint's externalizing behavior, Bob and Carol could effectively punish his outbursts via an undesirable consequence, such as taking a significant item or privilege for each outburst. This could include establishing a cost, such as losing an allowance or other privileges when he acts out. Punishment would

be appropriate strategy for Kristen, who bullies, including being assigned difficult tasks, such as cleaning walls, or more poignant consequences, such as taking back a cell phone or another type of technology. A penalty might be removal of time with friends or the removal of technology such as her cell phone (considered a traumatic event by most children and adolescents). The key is customizing the cost (punisher or penalty) for each client. Of course, prevention and peer intervention are most desirable with the social malady of bullying.

You might choose to use a form of punishment when you are attempting to shape behavior. A form of *aversive therapy*, *covert sensitization*, requires that clients imagine scenes that pair the undesired behavior with a highly unpleasant consequence (Cautela & Kearney, 1986). Lead the client through a guided imagery experience, supplying lavish detailed and lurid descriptions of the consequences of engaging in the behavior. For instance, an unpleasant fantasy could be imagined by Kristen (being put in a detention center) as an unconditioned stimulus, which leads to an objectionable and repulsive experience (e.g., fear, shame, loss of freedom) that forms the unconditional response (classical conditioning). The idea is to turn the stimulus that previously encouraged the behavior into a conditioned stimulus for an unpleasant response. Thus, Kristen's aim was to mistreat and dominate others to elicit unpalatable responses. Specifically, Kristen would imagine seeing a victim and then feel the sensation of bullying. At this point, imagery is introduced to create an aversive situation. Kristen is instructed to see herself being arrested and taken to juvenile detention, and then being the subject of ridicule by others. The scene experience is repeatedly imagined by the client as homework.

Using extinction. In operant learning, all behaviors are maintained by reinforcement. When the reinforcers maintaining a behavior are no longer present, the behavior stops, disconnecting the reinforcement diminishing the behavior. With correct implementation of extinction, frequency of the response eventually decreases because the response no longer serves the function of obtaining the reinforcement (Kazdin, 1982). Bob and Carol responded to Clint's whining and tantrums by ignoring them. Conversely, when they failed to respond positively to Clint's compliance, the probability of the compliance decreased, augmenting future deference. It is for that reason the slogan "Catch them behaving well" is wise.

A number of experts have repudiated extinction as an intervention for severe maladaptive behavior due to the length of time required to extinguish behavior, the intensity of side effects, and difficulties in carrying it out (e.g., Duker & Seys, 1983; LaVigna & Donnellan, 1986; Rolider & Van Houten, 1984). Moreover, since Christian therapists believe that every person is made in the image of God, the idea of ignoring someone in distress seems inhumane. While a skilled clinician might do extinction well, unresourceful parents might implement it in a cold and demeaning way. Still, extinction may have a place in a counselor's toolbox.

To properly use extinction, you first must understand the function of the behavior. Second, determine the most prudent type of reinforcement based on how you wish to schedule it. For example, when a client has been reinforced every time (continuous reinforcement), the reinforcement often rapidly extinguishes with removal of the reinforcer. Conversely, when behavior has been periodically reinforced (intermittent), it extinguishes slowly. Unless the client can identify a new means of deriving reinforcement, she is more likely to continue the same behavior, no matter how maladaptive or unreinforcing. In such cases, the target behavior will diminish slowly; many unreinforced responses will occur before reduction in the behavior occurs (Kazdin, 1982). In fact, initially an increase in the behavior is not uncommon, a side effect known as an *extinction burst* (Salend & Meddaugh, 1985).

Actually, extinction is more effective when combined with other techniques that stimulate and simultaneously reinforce alternative appropriate actions such as positive reinforcement. For Kristen, the contingency contract involved the teacher ignoring her behavior (assuming that reprimanding had not worked) while still considering injury to a classmate. Instead of focusing on Kristen, the teacher responded to the victim, redirecting the victim to an alternative activity away from Kristen.

Another form of extinction is spontaneous recovery from any issue, a process by which the behavior dissipates over time without intervention (Poling et al., 2013). It is also consistent with classical conditioning principles. In the case of Clint, his parents reported that his swearing had stopped altogether without therapy addressing that aspect of his tantrums at all. As much as counselors would like to take credit for the transformation, we had nothing to do with it. For all of the cases, spontaneous recovery would be considered a welcomed miracle.

CONCLUSION

Targeting behavior can be an effective means of increasing desirable behavior, reducing problematic behavior, and learning new behavior. Behavioral interventions, however, are not an exclusive enterprise. They work best when joined with ones that target other aspects of human functioning. Moreover, the fact that techniques are useful or practical does not always mean that they are the best choice. Sin is a pathology that plagues us. Simply choosing not to focus on sin does not negate the possibility of its culpability. Yet we can become strength oriented without losing focus on the reality that we all have a sin problem.

Behavior is a God-given component of our *imago Dei*. Human behavior is, in many ways, a vehicle through which the heart moves. As with all aspects of human functioning, our behavior is fallen because our hearts are fallen. Through salvation and sanctification, God can redeem and transform behavior so that it is consistent with loving God and loving others. Behavior is transformed through the indwelling of the Holy Spirit, who renovates the heart and produces fruit through behavior (Gal. 5:22–23).

RECOMMENDED READING

Abramowitz, J. S., Deacon, B. J., & Whiteside, S. P. H. (2012). *Exposure therapy for anxiety: Principles and practices*. New York, NY: Guilford Press.

Bufford, R. K. (1981). *The human reflex: Behavioral psychology in biblical perspective*. San Francisco, CA: Harper & Row.

Cipani, E., & Schock, K. M. (2008). *Functional behavioral assessment, diagnosis, and treatment: A complete system for education and mental health settings* (2nd ed.). New York, NY: Springer.

Jones, S. L., & Butman, R. E. (2011). *Modern psychotherapies: A comprehensive Christian appraisal* (2nd ed.). Downers Grove, IL: InterVarsity.

Masters, J. C., Burish, T. G., Hollon, S. D., & Rimm, D. C. (1987). *Behavior therapy: Techniques and empirical findings* (3rd ed.). Fort Worth, TX: Harcourt College.

Ramnerö, J., & Törneke, N. (2008). *The ABCs of human behavior: Behavioral principles for the practicing clinician*. Oakland, CA: New Harbinger.

CHAPTER 7

Behavioral Dysfunction Strategies

Stephen P. Greggo, PsyD

A man without self-control is as defenseless
as a city with broken-down walls.

PROVERBS 25:28 TLB

Strategic skills and relational openness are indispensable essentials for every helping professional to assist clients to make behavioral changes (Dobson & Dobson, 2009; Miller & Rollnick, 2014). A client's unique reason for requesting services will guide counseling conversations into profound searches to locate hope, identity, wholeness, restoration, or relational stability. These themes reflect the inspirational narrative-crafting and meaning-making aspects of counseling. Nevertheless, growth in nearly every area of life is likely to demand reform in down-to-earth behavior patterns. Undesirable habits, dead-end routines, or automatic toxic responses can be carried forward across a lifetime from early modeling and ongoing rehearsal. Reversing everyday patterns is non-glamorous change. Yet there is no more necessary set of helping strategies than those that provide prudent assistance to modify, manage, or eliminate dysfunctional behaviors.

Vince Lombardi, legendary coach of the Green Bay Packers during the 1960s, is often tagged as the most outstanding head coach in the game of football. Lombardi had an unrelenting obsession that his players master fundamentals, which became profoundly evident during training camp in the summer of 1961 (Maraniss, 1999). At the close of the previous season, the Packers had come within minutes of earning the championship in a heart-wrenching defeat. When Lombardi's veteran players came back to camp, they were eager to take their near championship prowess to new levels. Instead of rehearsing their accomplishments, Lombardi began what would become one of his most famous speeches with the phrase, "Gentlemen, this is a football," with the pigskin in hand. Practice thereafter became a relentless persistence to master the fundamentals of blocking, tackling, and running basic plays. For an experienced team, this tactic bordered on being insulting. But from that point forward, Lombardi won three straight championships—five total. Lombardi's strategy and the resulting victories explain why the famous Super Bowl trophy now carries his name.

Mastering fundamentals is as critical in the game of people helping as it is in moving the ball forward in competitive sports. This chapter aims at helping therapists foster change in deep-seated and troublesome habits. The strategies surveyed here are straightforward. In fact, most of this material ordinary folks would call common sense. Be forewarned. The principles to formulate a realistic change plan are easily within reach of novice or lay counselors. The challenge is that genuine and sustained change requires fortitude, flexibility, and a deep heart of empathy. The analogy of moving the ball forward against a rugged defense on a football field is not random, because behavior change and football both require a strategic plan and serious effort.

THEOLOGY AND PSYCHOLOGY OF BEHAVIORAL DEFICITS AND EXCESSES

Turning to common biblical terminology, the strategies described here are advantageous to implement a rewarding path to exhibit self-control. "Like a city whose walls are broken through is a person who lacks self-control" (Prov. 25:28). In the ancient Near East, settlements were intentionally constructed on elevated, rugged ground. This was so that they could readily be defended by high stone walls with watchtow-ers to detect approaching threats. A city without intact fortification was utterly defenseless. Imagine a bustling, vibrant city with no protection from wandering armies or roving bandits. The unfortunate inhabitants would be constantly under threat and vulnerable to violation. In the same way, a counselee overwhelmed with a pervasive but unwanted behavior pattern cannot experience the beauty of safety or maintain a satisfying state of well-being.

Self-control takes a central position in Peter's description of progressive movement toward a mature walk with Jesus Christ: "For this very reason, make every effort to add to your faith goodness; and to goodness, knowledge; and to knowledge, self-control; and to self-control, perseverance; and to perseverance, godliness; and to godliness, mutual affection; and to mutual affection, love" (2 Peter 1: 5–7).

According to Peter, self-control is the critical link that ties the starter elements of faith, goodness, and knowledge to the spiritual maturity of perseverance, godliness, and love. We recall this is the same Peter who boldly professed his love and devotion by exclaiming, "Lord, I am ready to go with you to prison and to death" (Luke 22:33). During that last supper, Jesus even gave Peter the foreknowledge that his faith would be put to the test. Nevertheless, Peter later acted out along his customary, dysfunctional, impulsive style and blatantly lied about his association with Jesus of Nazareth—and this behavior happened three times, as Jesus predicted. Peter became personally aware that self-control is central to behavior management *and* spiritual growth.

Self-control in Scripture is identified as a fruit of the Spirit (Gal. 5:22–23). Counselors need to keep in view the reality that fruit is the by-product of a long and steady maturation-reproductive process. For clarification, self-control is *not* a high-level internal regulator switch that governs willpower and determination. Nor is it a power pack of fortitude held in reserve. Rather, self-control is a series of small, nearly involuntary, rapid-fire, life-affirming decisions. Joined together these active movements contribute to eventual mastery over external conditions magnified in their power by internal temptations, impulses, and passions. Basic methods to alter these behavior, cognitive, and affective chains are available and can be practically identified.

Counselors in this scenario become personal trainers for change who coach clients to exercise self-control-enhancing behaviors where these once appeared impossible. This is the "competitive," soul-shaping preparation to win the crown that will last forever (1 Cor. 9:25). Self-control activates the change potential to move the ball down the field (Gal. 5:22–23). Christian counselors, as divine representatives, come alongside to partner with those who struggle with dysfunctional behaviors to jointly pursue a righteous and healthy way of living.

What exactly is referenced by the term *dysfunctional behavior*? This broad and messy classification captures any pesky, disagreeable, or unproductive behavioral pattern. From overindulging to underperforming, the term *dysfunctional behavior* depicts the sequences that result in em-

barrassing or self-destructive exploits. Put simply, behavioral dysfunction is an action outcome that is unwanted, destructive, or disruptive, or the absence of a behavior that would be healthy, environmentally advantageous, or worthwhile. For clarity, when clinicians use the term *behavior*, they mean observable, overt action as well as covert happenings, that is, internal activity (Fishman, Rego, & Muller, 2011). Covert behavior includes the cognitive processing and emotional stirring inside a person. Mental activities that are reactions to one's surroundings are also events. Thus, in contemporary models, inner cognitive and affective responses are included as behavioral patterns.

One benefit of the adoption of generic behavioral language is that the helping strategies can be applied nicely across the full developmental lifespan. In addition, the general classification of behavioral excesses or deficits can be captured theologically in a description of sin as either performances of commission (destructive action perpetrated) or omission (loving service withheld) (Cross & Livingstone, 2005).

The category behavioral dysregulation encompasses an extremely wide assortment of behaviors. For instance, it is entirely feasible to survey the current *Diagnostic and Statistical Manual* (DSM-5; American Psychiatric Association, 2013). Behavioral syndromes could be identified, such as attention-deficit/hyperactivity disorder, obsessive-compulsive disorder; binge eating, substance-related disorders, addictions, or insomnia. This is not a complete list. It is a mere sampling of mental health malfunctions with core self-defeating behaviors that require modification (American Psychiatric Association, 2013). In addition, most of the criteria for DSM categories include problematic, behaviorally oriented items.

As an alternative descriptive scheme, one could draw directly from the Christian faith tradition the framework of the seven deadly sins (i.e., pride, covetousness, lust, envy, gluttony, anger, and sloth). This grouping captures behavioral excesses and deficits that Scripture repeatedly identifies as harmful. The theological language here may appear harsh according to contemporary customs. However, when the impact on self, others, and one's relationship with the Lord of these behavior patterns is calculated, the no-nonsense, traditional language seems appropriate. Scripture also contains comprehensive lists of actions that believers are to put off and put on (e.g., Eph. 4:21–32; Col. 3:5–11).

Christian theological tradition, however, may consider noxious behavior patterns not only as foolishness or evil human irregularities, but as an outright rejection of the limits and parameters contained within the gift of human life bestowed by our Creator. As a result, behavioral excesses or deficits that do not reflect a love of God, neighbor, or self are cataloged as sinful transgressions. These actions display rebellion against the One who deserves to be honored by faithful living. This overview is not the opportunity to explore the overlap, similarities, and conflicts between psychiatric descriptions of psychopathology and a Christian depiction of sin, shalom, and salvation (where sin is a falling short of biblical ethical standards, and soteriology is the investigation of the means of salvation; see Johnson, 2017; Yarhouse, Butman, & McRay, 2005). In short, the Bible addresses many behavioral patterns using its unique language.

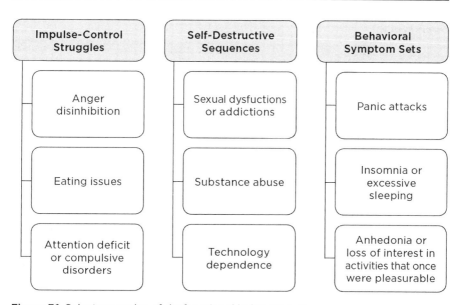

Figure 7.1. Select examples of dysfunctional behavior patterns

These are portrayed as signs of spiritual brokenness and a fatal disposition toward sin. It calls for a repentance that involves turning away from ways of relating or behaving that do not honor our Lord and turning toward patterns that demonstrate love for him. Repentance can be described using the phrase "changing direction" or "behavioral reversal." Behavioral excesses are addressed here with strategies to manage these occurrences. Behavioral deficits become opportunities to demonstrate new actions that bring blessing or well-being, or exemplify love toward others.

The strategies offered below have been selected for two reasons. First, these can be applied in accordance with these biblical parameters even if the language of repentance (turning away from sin and toward God) is not utilized. This is practical for settings and/or clients where an explicit Christian approach would not be welcome (Greggo, 2016). Second, these techniques serve as basic building blocks that typically appear in the evidence-based treatment options. For dysfunctional behavioral patterns that have been explicitly addressed in the literature, clinicians should use strategies that have a reasonable or promising level of research support (Worthington, Johnson, Hook, & Aten, 2013; Perkinson, Jongsma, & Bruce, 2009). Often such behavioral and cognitive strategies are grounded on the premise of increasing behavioral/cognitive deficits or limiting excesses. The emerging field of behavioral medicine involves the collaboration between health care professionals so the relevant biomedical, psychological, cultural, social, and behavioral knowledge can as-sist patients in preventing, treating, and recovering from disease (Dekker, Stauder, & Penedo, 2016). In this effort, psychoeducational and direct treatment protocols are developed to increase compliance with health-affirming practices. These behavioral medicine models are constructed by incorporating principles from the very strategies that are about to be explored.

CASE STUDY

Alex (fifty-six) and Bernice (fifty-three) are desperate to rescue their troubled marriage. Both identify themselves as Christians and report being highly active in a cozy country church. Their pastor referred them because he no longer views himself as competent to address the serious threat to the viability of the marriage. Alex told the pastor that Bernice should move out. Alex and Bernice are both civil service employees. Bernice is a clerical worker doing data processing. Alex is in technical support with responsibilities for installing and repairing computers. They travel forty minutes together each way to an office complex at the county seat. Their schedules are similar. In the initial interview, Alex offers the dry comment that the only thing they can agree on is when to leave work. The couple listen to Christian radio in the car to avoid fighting. They both actually believe that God has the power to heal each of them and their marriage, but he hasn't been interested enough to do this yet. This couple has read books, attended marriage conferences, prayed with their pastor, and taken in advice from Christian celebrities on the radio or through books.

This is a second marriage for both. The couple met at a divorce recovery ministry seminar and have been married for thirteen years. Both became believers when their early marriages shattered. Both families of origin were rampant with brokenness. They view their coming together as a miracle from God. Each brought teenage children into the marriage. Alex's two boys are married and have moved out of the area. Visits are rare. They do not like their stepmom and are never shy about saying so. Bernice's two sons live nearby with girlfriends. Her one daughter is pregnant and newly married. Each of her adult children has financial struggles due to one major crisis after another. Bailing them out financially is a significant source of disagreement for Alex and Bernice.

Alex explains at the outset that they spoke with a psychologist a few months back. Her recommendation was to separate and then try individual therapy. She had reflected on a serious buildup of hurt, mistrust, and resentment, and deep patterns of dysfunctional relating, stating, "That may be the way to go, but our pastor wants us to speak with a Christian counselor before we throw in the towel."

Bernice picks up to share more about why they have come. She openly admits that they have always had really bad arguments, saying, "We brought heavy baggage in and still throw it at each other." But now Alex hints at leaving and ending the nightmare. He retreats to spend hours on his laptop, no longer interacting much with Bernice or her family members. Bernice reports, "He has just given up." Bernice does not hide or deny that she gets

angry, yells, and unleashes uncontrollable rage. The couple lives in the home of Alex's mother, a Polish immigrant who tirelessly labored with her deceased husband to achieve a good life in America. Alex is her only son. Bernice reports that her mother-in-law complains that she can't take the constant bickering. Alex's mother depends on their assistance but would prefer that Bernice move out.

Marital conflict is constant. Typical fights are over money. They also argue about dinner, social schedules, the kids, or nearly any subject. Bernice acknowledges she worries a good deal about her kids, health, the future, national news, and everything in between. When she explodes, she uses foul language and throws objects around the room. There is no reported physical violence between them.

Alex defers to Bernice to continue the saga. She asserts that Alex is constantly bitter, sullen, and angry. His downcast mood is nothing new. He has always been a deep thinker who gets discouraged and has dark moods. Bernice claims that he became far worse when he experienced three years of unemployment. He was let go from a high-level executive position and could find no similar position. He finally accepted this lower-status position with its steady government paycheck. During Alex's years of unemployment, the couple lost their modest home and had to move in with his mother.

Alex stays quiet during this introduction. His eyes seem to burn as he slumps in his chair. You ask him to contribute; he holds back. When he finally speaks, Alex blurts out a few concise, seemingly rehearsed sentences that carry a helpless tone:

"I am an alcoholic with twenty years of sobriety. The Lord brought me out of being a drunk, so maybe he has another miracle for this marriage. I attend an AA meeting every week. When we were married, we did not know how to handle our children. We fought in the beginning and continue to fight the same fights even though the kids do not live with us. Our finances are terribly tight. Money goes to others, mostly to Bernice's sons, and we take care of my mother. We do not have funds to separate. My wife is constantly fretful and agitated. She controls everything. The anger she spews is poison. Our pastor instructed us to speak with you. Neither of us sees a way to deal with this mess. We have little confidence that counseling can fix our problems."

STRATEGIES, INTERVENTIONS, AND TECHNIQUES FOR BEHAVIORAL CONCERNS

The pressing need is to salvage what is left in this marriage and nurture its future. Alex and Bernice are curious readers who have done their homework. They have worked the self-help angle as best as they were able. They have an image of what a Christian marriage should be but no longer see themselves as capable of bringing this into reality. Marital treatment could follow an evidence-based approach, such as hope-focused marriage therapy (Worthington, 2005) or attachment interventions associated with emotionally focused couple therapy (Johnson, 2004).

There are possible aspects of their conflict that the counselor could focus on (e.g., financial bailouts for adult children; the expressed viewpoint of Alex's mother; the indirect communication between Alex and his pastor that Bernice should leave). However, taking the bait on such particulars early on would only stoke further conflict, thus discouraging the couple. Instead, we will address the broader dysfunctional behavioral patterns and by that means build hope.

Admittedly, neither Bernice nor Alex has requested help to curb a personal behavioral problem. Bernice would like Alex to be engaged, helpful, supportive, and full of life. Alex wants Bernice to halt her fussing and raging. At this juncture, the tension is high, the expectations for success are low, and the sheer deadlock around communication is intolerable. Nevertheless, there are indications of prominent anger and emotional dysregulation both on the side of excesses (Bernice) and in deficits such as passivity and noncommunication (Alex). Further, the lack of self-efficacy and spiritual perseverance to alter the hollowness of their marriage may stem (in part) from individual mental health concerns. Alex may be exhibiting symptoms associated with a form of depression. His expressions of happiness or a hope for the future are seriously blunted. In fact, questions about potential suicidal ideation are warranted. Bernice's symptoms may suggest the presence of a generalized anxiety disorder. Her heightened insecurity and weakened ability to regulate her emotions could stem from the adversarial nature of her immediate context. In light of these observations, three fundamental techniques will be used to promote behavior change: motivational dialogue, assessment, and reciprocal inhibition.

Motivational Dialogue

Partners in a change conspiracy. Counselor training programs help to develop interpersonal skills. The technique of active listening, using skills such as accurate empathy, immediacy, probing, self-disclosure, and confrontation, are all helpful when challenging engrained behavior patterns (Egan, 2014). Clients are to be engaged in a mutually endorsed, conspiracy-to-achieve-change agreement. The relational dynamics between client and counselor are supposed to promote candid contact.

Mentioning the well-known person-centered, necessary, and sufficient conditions voiced by Rogers (1992) may seem ironic, since the focus here is on behaviorally targeted techniques. Nonetheless, all Christian therapists must take seriously the experience of the counselee to promote the formation of change-invested partnership. Rogers argued that a genuine, honest, and authentic interpersonal connection between client and counselor promotes motivation and opens the way for therapeutic movement. The experience of unconditional positive regard (the Christian analogue here is called "grace") creates confidence and awakens hope that change is feasible. This is the basic axiom. Finally, clients, including those in acute psychological distress, resist taking risks to change until they experience empathy and understanding. New information about the benefits of change or the dangers of denial is not apt to motivate. Instead, humans need a reasonable partner with whom to take on novel change.

William Miller and Stephen Rollnick (2014) developed Rogers's approach more systematically in "motivational interviewing" (MI). They describe MI as a style of conversation that allows people to talk themselves into change. The method relies on stirring up the person's own values, interests, and unique circumstances. Rather than the "expert" counselor providing reasons to change, motivational fires are located within the narrative and cultural commitments of a client. The counselor locates the inner ember, fans it into flame, and tends the fire to keep it burning (Isa. 42:3). Motivational interviewing is applicable to many types of dysfunctional behavior, and a series of excellent works on various kinds of problems is readily available (Arkowitz, Miller, & Rollnick, 2015; Westra, 2012; Naar-King & Suarez, 2010). Motivational interviewing guides—never manipulates or bullies—others to alter rigid behavior routines or addictions. The helper works with the client's motivations and strives via dialogue to rally inner resources. The intent is to reach the tipping point that will allow for a sensitive exploration of the pushes and pulls regarding new routines, choices, or lifestyles.

Traditional pastoral counseling might attempt to present evidence intended to push clients to revise behavior from a biblical, medical, or psychological angle. The tendency is to use the authority of the ministry or office of the pastor to convince the client that change is in their best interest. Clergy may be successful in leveraging positional power on occasion. An authority-anchored counseling style may have merit with select client populations. It is rarely the best move for helping professionals, since it fails to access the heart of the most powerful resource, which is in this instance the center of the client's passions. Clients are caught in a serious struggle between an inner voice that desires to venture into new behavioral practices and competing social, physical, and developmental forces that almost violently compel them to hold on to the status quo. Imagine two competitive football teams positioned to fight for yardage over the scrimmage line. The contest will be intense. It is best to take stock of how the field conditions appear to the person who is going to take the ball. Experienced helpers recognize that venturing into the client's own ambivalence (stubborn indecision and ongoing doubt) is the optimal place to begin. Further exposure and actual practice with the material found in MI approaches is recommended (Miller & Rollnick, 2014). The candid flow of MI is likely to expand out from approximations of direct questions, such as the following:

1. "What is awakening in you to want to make this change at this point in your life?"
2. "How might you get started and follow a plan to be successful?"
3. "Tell me the top three reasons for you to change these persistent patterns."
4. "Exactly how important is it for you to make this change and why?"
5. "So, with this information out in the open, what do you think you'll do?"

The essential tactic is to form a "change partnership." This is accomplished by locating and surfacing what the client currently values, desires, and is ready to do. The intent is to generate realistic, mutual dialogue that fosters constructive change. Respect for the client, without any hint of condemnation, is forthrightly communicated. Rather than undercutting a client's sense of self, experienced therapists develop effective ways to empathetically share what they see in clients as a means to align with the voice within that is calling for change (Wachtel, 2011).

Consider Alex and Bernice. Can such an open, nonjudgmental stance be adopted by a Christian helper when there is such a pungent odor of divorce in the air? Can the counselor come across as gracious when anger is being expressed in sinful ways and marital oneness is being squandered? Real tension exists in this case over matters that are plain in Scripture. In their defense, remember that these folks are seeking help. They are doing so even after being told by a competent expert that separation would be the kindest and most realistic way to deescalate the multiple crises in their lives. They determined to ignore that direction and speak with a Christian counselor. Thus, counselor compassion, honor, and heartfelt concern are aided by the recognition of how far Bernice and Alex have come and how steady they have been in pursuing their faith. Plainly, their story displays poor decisions, unkind talk, and failed boundaries. Openly labeling their sinful choices, words, or actions at this juncture may not hold much advantage. These folks are already deep into shame.

Both are attending church, speaking with their pastor, and showing up for counsel. This allows you to step into the very role the profession has trained you to perform, that is, as a catalyst for change.

The best way to spark hope would be to openly exhibit the hospitality the Great Comforter would have you to convey. You will have ample opportunities ahead to address themes of forgiveness and mutual grace. Aiding these clients to name those ordinary behavioral outcomes that perpetuate conflict is imperative. Wondering out loud with them regarding the priorities they cherish and pondering who they wish to become (or who the Holy Spirit is directing them to be) would be helpful. Other kinds of pressures, those for or against change, can be unraveled. This means that dialogue would embark on unpacking their ambivalence regarding change. This approach could create a thirst for wisdom and stimulate ongoing counseling conversations.

Putting on new behaviors. The New Testament reminds those who are in Jesus Christ that we are to "walk in the way of love" (Eph. 5:2). Taking each step to live out the will and mind of Christ is done because of the love he demonstrated on the cross. Scripture uses "walking" in the figurative sense to promote living out a pattern of life that faithfully honors the Lord (Fitzsimmonds, 1996). This entails putting aside any action that detracts from displaying goodness, righteousness, and truth (Eph. 5:8–9), or that flows out of anger, malice, crassness, foolishness, impurity, greed, or selfishness. Our walk, on the positive side, is to display forgive-ness, kindness, compassion, and the fruit of the Spirit.

A nonbeliever is not likely to speak of making change due to the influence of the Holy Spirit. Nevertheless, human motivation is present. Family loyalties, cultural virtues, or social pressures may create an urgency to put aside behaviors that are destructive to self and others. The language of change can turn on simple terms and be furthered by keeping a focus on who the client is seeking to please in making behavioral adjustments. Motivational interviewing encourages counselors to highlight what the client expresses in his own change talk by capturing anything close to commitment, activation, or taking steps (CATs). As clients speak of what they want to do, need to do, and expect to start, they expose a commitment to walk a different path. As partners with the client, a counselor will draw attention to examples of the client doing something that is moving her in the right direction. For those who follow Jesus Christ, counseling also fosters hope of sanctification and growing toward spiritual maturity.

When counseling Bernice and Alex, it might be useful to approach each one privately. This would reduce conflict potential momentarily and allow for an opportunity to tap into what the Holy Spirit may be prompting each to do. Are there behaviors, attitudes, or practices that each would prefer to put off and put on? What words or phrases emerge in the awakening of change? Motivational interviewing "evokes" such language. This is the MI term that represents talk about the wishes, abilities, and small action steps a client is prepared to take. Motivational interviewing launches productive dialogue about the client's personal and perhaps Spirit-directed change goals.

The power of social support. When addressing dysfunctional behavior, it is wise not to take on the change journey as a solo adventure. Three types of social support are typically described when facilitating change: (1) Informational support is guidance from others about resources, perspectives, or practical opportunities. (2) Emotional support is the earnest flow of compassion, care, and encouragement. (3) Instrumental support describes how the involvement of others increases coping skills, endurance, or the momentum to push forward (Greggo, 2008). You can provide any combination of these. Yet when the behavior pattern is long-standing or the habits run deep, as in an actual addiction, locating fellow sojourners to forge a united force in establishing a new walk can be useful.

In a nutshell, social support is finding help from others to boost change dialogue, sustain the courage to stay the course, and join with teammates who know what it is like to turn one's walk in a different direction. Group options can assist clients to take on the challenge of change. Counselees can join a support group, a self-help group in the community, or a therapeutic group in a clinic. Step groups similar to Alcoholics Anonymous exist for other addictions (e.g., gambling, internet addiction, smoking), eating disorders, and compulsive behaviors (e.g., hoarding, sexual acting out, self-mutilation). Alex, even after twenty years of sobriety, reports that

he continues to attend AA. This is not a sign of weakness. Rather, it is a signal that he understands what it takes to persist in holding on to a life pattern that runs against entrenched biological, psychological, historical, and social pressures. Celebrate Recovery (CR), a well-known ministry birthed at Saddleback Church nearly three decades ago, provides an extensive network of step groups built on Christian principles with a design to assist people in overcoming hurts, habits, and hang-ups (http://www.celebraterecovery.com/). CR is an ideal forum for believers to locate fellow Christians who are also working to realize change in areas where it does not come easily.

In working with Alex and Bernice, select change behaviors would need to be identified, such as breaking the rage habit, letting go of bitterness and hurt, and implementing short, positive conversation. Imagine if Bernice and Alex were to find others to collaborate with on their change journey. What if Alex spoke weekly with other men who are likewise working on their marriages or anger management? This is a routine he has applied to maintain his sobriety; might it help him to behave differently with his wife? This couple is already familiar with seeking the advice of experts. Joining with peers to cultivate a mutually supportive team may now be beneficial. Professional therapy can assist marital communication, reduce family conflicts, and foster the marriage bond itself, but a support group can keep the underlying behavior change strategies.

When it comes to a struggle with impulse control, curbing self-destructive behavior, or facing behaviors embedded in a mental health concern, multiple methods can be used to keep motivational dialogue vibrant, real, and supported. Thus, support groups are an ideal resource, not only to follow or supplement individual therapy, but perhaps to serve as a key resource to break long-term, detrimental behavioral chains.

Assessment as Intervention

Behavioral assessment for awareness, intervention, and prevention. The process of increasing self-control moves from creating the motivation base to training clients to identify the intricate and detailed interactions contained within complex behavioral chains (Gross, 1985). A target behavior is selected as the focus. Clients then become familiar with the progression of how external events interact with inner states to build toward a critical point when the destructive action seems nearly inevitable.

Behavioral theory has long advocated an A-B-C assessment technique, that is, identifying antecedents (A), behavior (B), and consequences (C). The before, during, and after is systematically examined by conducting a detailed behavioral analysis. This unpacks interactions to increase understanding and invites new strategies for engagement. Early applications of this model narrowly focused on examining rewards and reinforcements (just consequences). Today's applications are more continuous and comprehensive (Dobson & Dobson, 2009). This is like looking at a behavior using time-lapse photography to discern how each phase blends into the

next. Counselors investigate with clients all of the notable conditions, inside and out, that precede acting out or shutting down (e.g., rejection of a request, boredom, a social embarrassment, emotional turmoil over hearing a harsh word, feeling ignored). The tie between external events and arousal of one's internal state could be termed triggers, cues, or stressors.

Clients use this type of behavioral assessment to become acquainted in very concrete terms with what happens before, during, and after a dysfunctional episode. A deliberate effort is also made to notice exceptions or breaks in the ordinary unwanted behavioral chain. This allows one to discover strategies already in place that could aid in change. Advanced awareness of the total behavioral chain permits clients to learn how to work toward the desired outcome before the default option becomes entirely predictable. As a primer for this activity, spending a week or two observing the conditions when the undesirable behavior occurs is useful. Patterns will emerge regarding the influential people, timing, places, and things. From here assessment increases recognition of the interactive chain of events/responses that eventually proceeds to the unwanted outcome.

Bernice does not hide that she becomes explosive and full of rage, though she is filled with regret. The pattern is so familiar; its aspects appear rooted and fixed. She needs help distinguishing how her tension, anxiety, and inner state begin to build via behavioral interactions. The upsurge in arousal tends to persist until she snaps and begins to rage (tantrum). She uses anger to dispel the perceived threat. Such behavioral dysregulation requires management. An extensive interplay occurs between external cues and her internal emotional state. She can, with the Holy Spirit's presence, learn to recognize her bodily responses early, anticipate her emotions, and predict the direction of the behavioral chain.

In many therapeutic circles, becoming aware of fluctuating inner states so that a more deliberate course of action can be taken is known as mindfulness (Swales & Heard, 2009). This requires breaking down what has become an automatic chain of events into its smaller component pieces to allow for oversight, choice, and the introduction of a meaning-enhancing narrative. Alertness to cues and states brings the possibility of a deliberate, aware, and mindful response. Another useful term, from acceptance and commitment therapy (ACT), is willingness (Batten, 2011; Waltz & Hayes, 2010). This entails accepting and letting inner states, even drastically uncomfortable ones, occur instead of avoiding them in various ways. Frantic impulses to head off those churning emotional states are rarely successful. The better plan is to willingly accept the coming turmoil but commit to perform a response that is consistent with one's goals and intentions. There are many variations to this general A-B-C assessment procedure. All involve counselors partnering with clients to increase comprehension of how a series of events can progress, from external conditions, the activation of inner states, to the eventual elimination of unwanted behavior.

Preparing for gradients of change.
A second assessment technique marks de-sired progress. It entails collecting information on the frequency (number of occurrences), severity (distress/intensity level), and duration (length of acting out) of a behavioral event (i.e., Frequency, Severity, Duration [FSD]). Procuring a detailed look at dysfunctional behavior three-dimensionally allows for improvement on more than one level. It is particularly useful to get an accurate picture of these elements at the outset of care. Clients can carry around a simple index card with an FSD matrix for a week to record counts and ratings in targeted areas. Further, clients can locate available behavior tracking options for their favorite device at an app store. For this data to be practical, discussion is needed to scale details of acting out into a ranking system that readily codes the event severity (i.e., extreme, moderate, or low). Once an FSD baseline is established, benchmarks can be determined to gauge progress.

For example, Alex is prone to becoming agitated and angry. Instead of acting out or drinking, his present tendency is to withdraw into a solitary place where he takes a technological escape. The details of what he does during this screen time are not yet known. On a continuum, this may indeed be a healthier substitute than using alcohol. Eventually Alex may elect to address this as a dysfunctional pattern since there may be even more relationally and personally preferable responses. He may not change the frequency of his isolating behavior over the short term. However, he may experience gains in the form of going through fewer severe dark moods or fewer minutes/hours in isolation. Grasping the FSD dimensions can allow Alex to continue to use withdrawal when conflict becomes unbearable, since he can still improve by cutting back on the length of his absence or replacing his persistent use of technology with a relaxation or prayer protocol. This procedure identifies improvement in the dimensions of both severity and duration, and so alters his walk in Christ.

Rapid assessment instruments (RAIs). Besides using informal assessment models via interview (i.e., Antecedenent, Behavior, Consequences [ABC] or FSD), an extensive range of semi-standardized measures known as rapid assessment instruments (RAIs) (Corcoran & Fischer, 2013; Greggo & Lawrence, 2012) can be used. These are brief measures, established in the research literature, available for clinical practice, that contribute information for diagnosis, problem identification, and outcome evaluation. One distinction between an RAI and a fully standardized measure is that norming populations are often limited. An RAI in therapeutic settings can survey a behavior pattern and experience *within* a client (criterion referenced) as opposed to making a comparison *between* the client and general population (norm referenced). For convenience, consider the emerging measures listed in section 3 of DSM-5 (American Psychiatric Association, 2013). These are readily available for reference and clinical use (https://www.psychiatry.org/psychiatrists/practice/dsm/educational-resources/assessment-measures).

The Level 1 Cross-Cutting Symptom Measure–Adult (CCSM-A) would be ideal to apply with both Bernice and Alex.

This is a short, twenty-three-item behavioral questionnaire that touches on clinical diagnostic conditions across the full spectrum of psychiatric disorders. Alex would likely endorse moderate to severe scores on at least the first three items, which tap into depression and anger (i.e., little interest in doing things; feeling down, depressed, or hopeless; feeling grouchier, angrier, or more irritated than usual). Or the Severity Measure for Depression–Adult presents nine items to identify features of depression. The results would provide a quick, tangible way to measure potential depression as well as target behaviors that are eroding the stability of Alex's happiness as well as his marriage (Dimidjian, Martell, Herman-Dunn, & Hubley, 2014).

Applying the level 2 tool for Emotional Distress (Anger) in Adults with Alex would also make sense. This tool has only five items on the short form (i.e., irritation, felt anger, readiness to explode, being grouchy and/or annoyed). The results could ascertain if Alex is ready to acknowledge mild, moderate, or severe distress in this area. This baseline would allow for tracking change over time. The severity level would assist targeting behavior chains that result in his most uncomfortable states. Anger and frustration may not only be eating away at him; his inner state may be unknowingly fueling his wife's insecurity and thus could be undermining the kind of marriage he so clearly would like to enjoy.

For Bernice, the items in section 4 (items 6–8) of the cross-cutting measure gauge anxiety (i.e., feeling nervous, anxious, frightened, worried, or on edge;

feeling panic or being frightened; avoiding situations that cause anxiety). The seven-item, level 2 form for Anxiety in Adults would follow. As an alternative, the Severity Measure for Generalized Anxiety Disorder–Adult (GAD-A) presents ten behavioral experience items for Bernice to assist her in recognizing the cycle that may be disabling her. Again, this would create a common understanding between all parties about the level of anxiety that Bernice experiences. Further, her battle for control (Alex's description) could be shifted from pushing others away to accessing her strength to regulate her emotional state. Such basic investigation can be pursued before marital work gets fully under way. This would give Bernice ample material to discuss in a self-help group such as Celebrate Recovery, where healing from past hurts and handling present stressors are regular goals. Further, should the result of more comprehensive assessment point to a diagnosis of GAD, other evidence-based treatment techniques would be useful (Roemer & Orsillo, 2014).

Using assessment techniques when partnering to address impulse control issues, addictions, or behavioral symptoms does provide a productive pathway to guide change (Greggo, 2017). Interestingly, using easy-to-grasp assessment methods can encourage clients to mentally gauge their state using these criteria as they move through their week. A language-based, self-rating procedure can become automatic. Self-monitoring is both a method to create momentum toward change and an intervention strategy to break dysfunctional behavior chains.

Reciprocal Inhibition

Identifying competing behaviors.

The principle of reciprocal inhibition is central to behavior management. This phrase is carried over from the first wave of behavior therapy where it denoted two contradictory or incompatible physiological responses. The classic example is anxiety/tension and relaxation. It is not possible for muscles to be tight and at ease at the same time. One state is plainly incompatible with the other. As behavioral approaches expanded to address other life concerns, the notion of reciprocal inhibition shifted to capture the concept of "competing behaviors." It is impossible to be simultaneously attentive and distracted (on task/off task), at peace and agitated, active and passive, moving and sitting still. The treatment principle that follows is that it is feasible to decrease undesired behavior by increasing a competing one. Reciprocal inhibition is a simple gift with multiple applications across the spectrum of behavior concerns mentioned in this chapter. Let's apply this principle to the constant conflict dilemma faced by Bernice and Alex.

To assist Bernice and Alex with reducing the heat and disruption in their marital communication, it might be worthwhile to do a session or two of elementary work on assertiveness training. This technique is often applied to address matters related to passivity and anxiety. Parallels are found in techniques that foster anger management. When anxious or upset, Bernice defaults to an aggressive verbal tactic that disrupts the flow of the communication. This may bring the conflict to a hasty halt, but it never fosters being heard or understood. A simple way of explaining aggressive communication is to define it as forcefully demanding one's rights or perspective without expressed regard for the rights, concerns, or feelings of the other (self over others). Passive communication is giving in to the demands of others. There is little awareness or acceptance that this deficient response pushes aside one's own needs, wishes, or hopes (others over self). Assertive communication is the charmed middle ground. Assertiveness entails speaking up for one's own desires or requests while steadily demonstrating empathy and concern for the person on the receiving end (self and others).

Alex withdraws, adopts a hostile silence, or resorts to sarcasm and humor that bites. This is aggressive communication masked as softness or understatement, thus this pattern can be termed *passive-aggressive*. In counseling this couple, these communication patterns could be rehearsed, role-played, or otherwise illustrated so that both persons come to easily recognize each category. Moving them to increase assertive communication over the other options (e.g., reciprocal inhibition) is alone not going to save the marriage. Nevertheless, it could make constructive dialogue possible, and this could prepare them for successful rounds of marital therapy.

Based on the principle of reciprocal inhibition, assertiveness is introducing a competing communication style to passive, aggressive, or passive-aggressive communication. The emphasis is on protecting the rights and wishes of both parties. Without expanding on the application in detail, Bernice and Alex could be challenged to increase the use of assertive com-

munication (Prov. 15:1). For Alex, making respectful requests for change to his wife and adult children could reduce his sullen silence (e.g., move from passive-aggressive to assertive). For Bernice, increasing mindfulness of how her impulsive behavior is self/other destructive could assist her in substituting strategic communication for her present repetitive ranting (e.g., move from aggressive to assertive and from passive to assertive). This would take practice, but it would inevitably cut back on the destructive patterns that have become so dominant in their relationship with each other. It would only take a few successful experiments to light a flame of hope. This would give them a tangible way to step back and recognize how poor communication habits formed over a lifetime are inconsistent with the scriptural command to love our neighbors as we love ourselves.

Systematic desensitization. The technique of systematic desensitization has had wide application when it comes to managing behaviors, phobias, and unwanted distress (Wolpe, 1985). A client is given training to relax his muscles on cue, thereby producing a physiological state of rest. This skill of bringing oneself into a deliberate quiet state is gradually applied to imaginary or actual situations that previously provoked fear, distress, or panic. Mere awareness that one can achieve calmness with intentionality reduces the power of the fear-provoking stimulus. It is no surprise that anger management treatment protocols also make use of systematic desensitization, because anger is often accompanied by a physiological state of arousal. Turning one's involuntary state of tension or anger back to a more reasonable place of composure is the skill of self-soothing. This permits a person to bring behavioral reactions under the guidance of her desires, commitments, and values. For those who want to intimidate or pressure others to conform to their wishes, this will not impact behavior. It is applicable only for those who would like to proceed in a more deliberate and character-enhancing manner when circumstances or words have stirred up their emotional state.

Raising awareness of how to appropriately express anger, frustration, and unhappiness would be a core component of any treatment plan for Bernice and Alex. Anger is prominent in their interactions, but it presently offers no redeeming benefit. Systematic desensitization may be useful to slow down the conflict cycle and promote longer opportunities for constructive communication.

Skill and performance deficits. Dysfunctional behaviors persist for more than one reason. Some clients do not have the requisite social or self-management skills to govern their choices. This is where psychoeducational approaches are extremely useful. Psychoeducation provides informational support and instrumental training to empower clients to deal with the intrapersonal and interpersonal concerns they face. Any time information regarding behavior cycles, developmental phenomena, or emotional responses can be supplied to increase a client's behavioral options, a skill deficit is addressed.

On some occasions the skill is already in the client's repertoire, but for one reason or another, it is not put to use with partic-ular persons or in certain contexts. This signals a performance deficit. Discerning the likely cause of a deficit is useful for counselors. Education and training are not likely to alter these performance deficits. The solution with this type of underperformance issue is best approached through motivational dialogue followed by assessment and reciprocal inhibition.

Both Alex and Bernice hold responsible and respected employment positions. Not long ago Alex held a position he highly valued because it was associated with leadership and status. Exploring how each tends to manage conflict, negotiate interpersonal differences, and solve problems in the workplace would be useful. The behavioral excesses and deficits that occur in their family conversations may not be as prevalent in other settings. Are there ways to transfer available relational or problem-solving skills that are available in other social settings (e.g., workplace, church, AA meetings) back into their home? Interpersonal skills and/or self-control tactics that are available in one environment may be imported to more troubled interpersonal relationships and circumstances. There may be more hope for this marriage than Bernice and Alex realize. The Lord may help them to experience his grace in ways they have not yet anticipated.

CONCLUSION

Behavioral dysfunction includes a wide range of people problems, such as impulse-control struggles, addiction or self-destructive tendencies, and symptom sets common to many mental health issues.

Solid counseling skills and techniques are necessary to come alongside another person to form a partnership for change. Putting brakes on one's temper, turning away from an addiction, or letting go of compulsive routines is never easy. Counselors strive to affirm and fortify a client's *own* recognition and motivation that change is possible.

Behavioral dysfunction is an action outcome that shows up as an unwanted excessive behavior or as a failure to perform an advantageous one. Christian theology has long recognized that the failure to act in a way that honors our Creator can show up as sins of commission (doing, speaking, and thinking) or as an omission (failure to act in a loving manner). Scripture speaks about putting on behavior as one would dress and undress, that is, putting on and putting off (Eph. 4:21–32; Col. 3:5–11). This fits well with a definition of dysfunctional behavior as excesses and deficits, since competing behaviors can be applied to replace those that need to be rejected.

Building a firm and robust motivational framework to pursue change is a must. The counselor-client partnership should invest in drawing out a client's language, values, priorities, and self-narrative to lay the groundwork for the hard work of walking differently. A community of supporters is needed to keep a person motivated to make serious change. Care groups in which a team comes around the person striving to change are highly recommended.

The principle of reciprocal inhibition assumes that two mutually exclusive activities or states cannot occur in the same moment. So bringing out the desirable one is an ideal way to reduce the other. Behavioral analysis looks at the before (antecedents), during (behavior), and after (consequences). Detailed exploration will search out needed information about cues, provocative circumstances, triggers, and so on so that an alternate pathway can be intentionally chosen. Further, describing problem behaviors in terms of how often (frequency), how bad (severity), and how long (duration) will shed light on three dimensions of a behavior. This gives multiple possibilities for improvement. Rapid assessment instruments are useful to deepen understanding of experience and develop strategies to accomplish change. Counselors learn by experience to recognize when to train clients to remediate a skill deficit or when to look for what might be inhibiting performance of an acquired skill with a particular person or setting.

No instant fix is available to interrupt entrenched behavior. Rather, self-control is a character quality that must be developed. This can be done by growing in our understanding of all of the common events and little decisions that push us toward acting in predictable ways. Self-control is fostered by seeking wisdom to know how to use behavioral principles, unrecognized opportunities, and supportive partners to make constructive changes in our behavior. Fortunately for those who follow Jesus Christ, the Great Comforter is already in place to awaken our minds, stir our hearts, and direct our walk in ways that allow us to become more like Jesus Christ.

Coach Lombardi had it right. Fundamentals matter. We grow the fruit of self-control through the fundamentals of motivation, untangling behavior chains, and managing competing behaviors.

RECOMMENDED READING

Batten, S. V. (2011). *Essentials of acceptance and commitment therapy.* Thousand Oaks, CA: Sage.

Greggo, S. P. (2008). *Trekking toward wholeness: A resource for care group leaders.* Downers Grove, IL: InterVarsity.

Miller, W. R., & Rollnick, S. (2014). *Applications of motivational interviewing: Motivational interviewing, helping people change* (3rd ed.). New York, NY: Guilford Press.

CHAPTER 8

Experiential Strategies

John C. Thomas, PhD, PhD

Rejoice with those who rejoice; mourn with those who mourn.

ROMANS 12:15

Experiential strategies, interventions, and techniques (SITs) involve using novel approaches to the therapeutic process (Bradley, Whiting, Hendricks, Parr, & Jones, 2008; Rosen & Atkins, 2014). This collection of techniques is variously described as "experiential," "creative," "nontraditional," "unconventional," and "provocational." Regardless of the name, the thrust of this collection of SITs is to create experiences that connect clients to both deep emotions and unresolved issues, and promote self-awareness. Experiential therapy can help you move clients through internal blocks to their pain. Such is the case with the late Dr. Rafiki's brilliant clinical work, which provides keen insight into the use of experiential strategies.

Having set up his practice in an ancient, giant baobab tree in a metropolis known as the Pride Lands, Dr. Rafiki, a mandrill, rose to fame as a clinician by playing a vital role in serving his government. His prowess is chronicled in the work known as *The Lion King* (Hahn, Allers, & Minkoff, 1994). For "The Case of the Lost Lion," Dr. Rafiki traveled to meet with his client Simba without invite. Rafiki knew Simba needed help to process the traumatic death of his father, Mufasa, who had been king of the Pride Lands. Mufasa's brother, Scar (a sociopath), duped Simba to believe that he alone was responsible for his father's death. Instead of becoming the new king of the Pride Lands, Simba chose to live in a self-imposed exile, swallowed by the guilt and shame of what he believed had happened in the death of his father. He longed to forget the unforgettable. Yet he was imprisoned by his own incriminations.

Like most clients who attempt to ignore their past, his bondage to it intensified. Simba didn't realize his perspective, beliefs, and understanding of the incident were fallacious. Dr. Rafiki sought out Simba in his place of brokenness and arrived—unexpectedly and unwelcomed—to provide therapy. His treatment plan included shattering Simba's illusion of safety, reminding him of who he was, challenging him to face what he feared, and giving him a vision for his future so he could become who he was meant to be. To address his client's brokenness, Rafiki employed experiential strategies rather than taking one of the more traditional approaches.

Rafiki led Simba on a dark and perilous adventure through a thick jungle. The journey took time and persistence, but they eventually arrived at the edge of a watering hole, where Dr. Rafiki invited and challenged Simba to face his fear. Soon the waves transformed Simba's reflection into that of his father, Mufasa. Clinically Dr. Rafiki reframed the watery image into the truth that Mufasa lives in Simba. Remarkably, Simba heard his father's voice (nonhallucinatory) calling him by name, saying that by denying his own identity, Simba had forgotten his heritage. Mufasa charged Simba to remember who he was and to realize that he was more than he had become.

In the next session, Dr. Rafiki employed what I refer to as the "assault" technique, a provocation technique by using his walking stick to thump Simba on the head:

Simba: Ow! Jeez, what was that for?
Dr. Rafiki: It doesn't matter. It's in the past.
Simba: Yeah, but it still hurts.
Dr. Rafiki: Oh, yes, the past can hurt. But from the way I see it, you can either run from it or learn from it.

Rafiki swung his trusty staff again at Simba's head, but having learned from experience, this time Simba ducked. While Dr. Rafiki might face ethical and legal charges for using this technique today, he provided Simba with a counterexperience to his traumatic paralysis. Living as a victim is a choice. The session ended, but Dr. Rafiki had driven his point home—we can learn from the past without running from it and face the frightening reality.

Dr. Rafiki's experiential techniques forced Simba to face and wrestle with not just his past but his present and future. Simba learned that many of the perceptions that had ruled his thoughts, feelings, and behavior were misguided and mistaken. The bottom line is that Dr. Rafiki's experiential work brought Simba to truth that evicted his deeply held lies by constructing therapeutic experiences that served to reshape Simba's reality.

Far too many counselors fail to consider using experiential SITs because of ignorance or fear. To address these issues, the aim of this chapter is to present a theological and psychological perspective on experiential techniques. My hope is that this exploration into the nature, value, and use of experiential work will awaken your curiosity and enliven your interest in becoming like Rafiki.

THEOLOGY AND PSYCHOLOGY OF EXPERIENTIAL TECHNIQUES

Experience is "anything observed or lived through, an actual living through of an event, individual's reaction to events, feelings" (*Webster's New Dictionary*, 1979). Rogers (1959) viewed experience as all that is going on within a person that is potentially available to awareness. This includes sensory, physiological, and bodily sensations; feelings; cognition; images; motivation; and memories. Greenberg and Van Balen (1998) contend that experiencing is the "synthesized product of a variety of sensorimotor responses and emotion schemes, tinged with conceptual memories, all activated in a situation" (p. 45).

Experience consists of an internal (intrapersonal dynamics/self) and external (relationships and environment) world. If nothing but other people's responses existed, the internal world (self) would be only learned responses of others (Gendlin, 1981). Furthermore, the interpersonal world is more than external events. It is inexorably linked with our feelings and intrapersonal world. In fact, the external world and events of one's life long precede the emergence of a person's sense of self. Consider the experiences of an infant with his or her caregiver as described in attachment theory. Research such as the still face experiment (Tronick, Als, Adamson, Wise, & Brazelton, 1978) demonstrates this connection. Healthy development requires caregivers to be emotionally attuned to a child from infancy. Failure to consistently receive the caregiver's mirroring of displayed emotion, which is generated from the infant's internal state, leads to deficits in brain functioning (cf. Rodrigo et al., 2011) The systemic nature of self and its interpersonal environment implies the dynamically symbiotic relationship between the intrapersonal self and the interpersonal self.

Because of these basic operations, every person is always being himself or herself at any given moment (Greenberg & Van Balen, 1998). Whether our experience is consistent with our normal way of perceiving, thinking, feeling, or acting, at that moment in time we are connected to the environmental context, what is happening inside of us, and how that is being experienced in the moment.

Experiential Therapy

The Bible and experiential techniques. The Bible is replete with experiential exercises. Throughout the Scriptures, many of the experiential methods used by God and the prophets resemble in part those methods found in Haley's ordeal therapy (1984). Haley sought to create a relatively painful and woeful experience for a client that would ultimately decrease the frequency, severity, and presence of the undesirable behavior. The ordeal must be something that the client can do without legitimately being able to object to doing it. One ordeal associated with the theory is directing a client who struggles with insomnia to exercise during the middle of the night when unable to sleep. Accordingly, Haley devised psychologically shocking tasks that, if performed, would be more difficult than having the symptom, thus providing an ordeal that would lead to giving up the symptom. If unsuccessful, the task is augmented in difficulty until its severity exerts influence over the client's problem. Of note is the fact that ordeal therapy is a theory. It is more than a technique to use with clients. The task must be understood and used with comprehension of how it fits with ordeal theory and with your own theory of human functioning.

Experiential work in the Old Testament. Consider the Old Testament patriarchs such as Abraham, Jacob, and Moses who endured ordeal experiences. Perhaps the most well-known was Abraham's ordeal to kill his promised son, Isaac. The cost of this directive from God was enormous. Abraham had a history of disobedience and lack of faith. God chose to test Abraham not for his benefit but for Abraham himself. God's command to sacrifice Isaac was of such a magnitude that Abraham could either choose his old ways or unequivocally obey Jehovah God. He dutifully complied by embarking on the journey that would lead to ultimate heartbreak and sorrow. To Abraham's relief, God stopped the ordeal at the last second. Abraham experientially learned that obeying God is far wiser than following one's own way and that God can be trusted to honor his promises. Moreover, he learned that obeying God leads to blessing and fulfillment of God's promises. So, at least in this context, ordeals can be given as tests with the desired outcome being divine blessing.

Further, many Old Testament prophets, such as Elijah, drove home salient points through experiential interventions. The unclean Naaman was to dunk himself seven times in an unclean river to be cured of leprosy. Angered by the therapeutic request, Naaman left in a fury, regarding the idea with contempt. A servant, however, convinced Naaman to submit to the directive, which ultimately led to healing (see 2 Kings 5).

Experiential work in the New Testament. The Lord Jesus made religious use of experiential strategies, most often in the form of miracles and teaching (cf. Robinson, 2009). You will recall the disciples witnessing the feeding of thousands on two occasions (Matt. 14:13–21; 15:32–39; Mark 6:30–44; 8:1–21; Luke 9:10–17; John 6:1–15), and of seeing Jesus sleep through a treacherous storm, only to be awakened by them clamoring for him to do something. Wiping the sleep from his eyes, he calmed the raging sea (Matt. 8:23–27; Mark 4:35–41; Luke 8:22–25). Additionally, Peter had a miraculous experience of walking on water after Jesus said, "Come" (Matt. 14:22–31).

Worship as an Experiential Process

To me, worship is our paramount experience. In fact, it is our eternal occupation (Rev. 4:8–11; 14:7). Broadly speaking, worship is an activity and state of being that is to be an expression of the whole person. Further, the majestic object of the person's worship shapes a person's experience of worship. A cyclical process ensues as one continues to worship the object of worship, God, so that he is experienced with even greater worth. Worship arises out of an internal yearning for a transcendent experience that cannot be fully described. Only God and the worshiper knows when that created longing touches divine contentment. Worship is a core experience that forms, shapes, and influences our life experiences. Just as the experience of worship reorients and connects each one of us to God as well as other worshipers, therapeutic experiential work reorients a client's perspective of past and current experiences as well as his or her connections to them.

The quality of our worship experience is determined in part by our personal aims. Many people target worship for the experience itself. The intent here is to achieve something that develops or affirms the self. But worship isn't about us; it is completely about God. We worship not to find God or to experience him. We worship because it is the fitting response to the experience of God and his presence. Worship isn't sought but is experienced. It is not a passive experience but is an aesthetic judgment, like what happens when we see a beautiful sunset or a painting. Worship is also a Spirit-enabled and Spirit-infused action that originates outside of us though it is operative within us—something that we cannot conjure up in our own power. When we only desire an experience, then we miss God. When we turn to God, both worship and the substance of growth are experienced. Worship must grow from within, in response to connecting with God. The more we attach to God, the greater the experience of worship, and the more it grows within. Thus, worship is a vehicle toward relational wholeness with God. True worship requires authenticity and intensity. We might never attain the fullness of our personality, but we will still worship God from our extant level of development. Consider the sentiment penned in Psalm 63:1: "O God, you are my God; earnestly I seek you; my soul thirsts for you; my flesh faints for you, as in a dry and weary land where there is no water" (ESV). David is expressing more than a simile. By associating a parched body that craves literal water with a parched soul that craves the living water of God, he is declaring that a life cannot be sustained without God.

Purposes and Benefits of Experiential Techniques

Provides a holistic multisensory approach. The collection of experiential SITs allows you to approach client issues from a multisensory vantage point, tapping into a client's visual, auditory, olfactory, and kinetic processes (Beaulieu, 2003). As Nickerson and O'Laughlin (1982) point out, using a clinical approach that primarily involves just talking limits what can be accomplished. For that reason, Beaulieu (2003) enforces the idea that therapists need to get beyond words and enlist more of their clients' senses (p. 1).

Provides in-moment observation. Experiential techniques are oriented to the present, meaning that they connect clients to their actual issues in the moment. Experiential techniques expose the client's real-life processes in the session. Moreover, you are also observing the client's processes outside of the therapeutic context. It affords both of you the opportunity to reflect on the client's experience in the moment.

We learn through experience. From birth we gain competence by engaging the world around us. Simply put, we learn from experience, and we learn from doing. Experiencing something is a far more effective teacher than teaching concepts. Experiential SITs provide meaningful and active learning as you engage clients in the therapeutic process.

Counseling becomes more concrete. Facts associated with experience are less meaningful than the process of experience itself (Gendlin, 1982). Experiential work makes abstract concepts become concrete and understandable (Jacobs, 1992). For example, Sarah, a sixty-two-year-old woman, presented with a three-year depression following the sudden death of her husband, a pastor. She was the quintessential pastor's wife who had served the Lord faithfully for more than forty years. After six months of therapy, Sarah had made only minor progress. She agreed to an ordeal task whereby she spent thirty minutes a day sitting on her bed with no clothes (she could wrap herself in a sheet or blanket) and suck her thumb. A week later, Sarah sat in her preferred chair and cursed me. Tears streamed down her face as she commented on her assignment: "You are saying I'm a baby." I asked her how she came to that conclusion. "Sucking my thumb," she said. "You are right. I have lived in self-pity for over three years, and I'm sick of it. I've got to move on." Sarah's lightbulb experience transfigured her from being glued to the past to a woman determined to break free and move on. "I want to find a way to help people with grief," Sarah replied. "God can use this . . . but I still wish he was here."

Generates insight and self-awareness. Generating insight and self-awareness can be achieved through a host of SITs. Consider Virginia Satir's (1983; Satir & Baldwin, 1984) use of sculpting. Clients are placed in postures that can activate self-awareness into their functioning within a system. We know from research that moving our bodies into different positions, or even observing the bodies of others in different positions, can evoke different emotions in the brain (Winters, 2008). Thus, insight and change can occur by connect-

ing clients to their bodies. We are embodied souls. In fact, our bodies are temples. Counselors often ignore the body in their work, but to neglect it is to diminish how we were created (out of the earth).

A wonderful question to ask clients is "Where in your body do you feel what you feel?" In this vein, Gendlin (1996) directs clients to attend to the bodily felt sense of a symptom, memory, or issue so that new meanings emerge. Placing a hand on an area of the body where feelings are physically felt raises awareness of an emotion that is somatically experienced. For example, a client disconnected from his feelings retorted, "I guess I just swallow them." While he contemplated what it was like to lose "all" arguments with his wife, I asked him to reflect on his body to find the place(s) that felt that internal experience. He placed one hand on the lower part of his abdomen and the other hand over his esophagus. As we processed his somatic experiences, I asked him to take what he physically sensed into his hands and then to put those sensations into his mouth to allow those sensations to have a voice. He replied, "I hate you [wife] for never hearing me. What I think and feel matters!"

A well-known technique, though not considered experiential, is often used to promote awareness of experience. Mindfulness involves the ability to suspend negative judgments about experience and to maintain flexible, balanced awareness. It allows clients to make fuller contact with a distressful or avoided experience. Rude and Bates (2005) state that it is justifiable to label mindfulness as an experiential technique, "in that such approaches train individuals to enhance awareness of thoughts and sensations toward the goal of gaining perspective and breaking out of scripted perceptions and reactions" (p. 363).

Dramatizes a point. To dramatize a woman's unhealthy dependency on her live-in boyfriend, who was repeatedly abusive, I asked her to stand facing me and place her palms on my palms—as if we were playing patty-cake. I asked her to press her hands against mine, and then I continued to slowly step backward. Soon she was leaning her weight on my hands (it helps to have a personal trainer for this technique). Once she was feeling highly vulnerable, as if she were going to fall, we processed that experience as a metaphor for her relationship with her boyfriend.

Increases clinical intensity and promotes healing. Clients desire to be free of whatever painful feelings and situations are front and center for them in the session. Neimeyer (2009) notes that all "change is initiated in moments of experiential intensity" (p. 67). Creating an emotionally impactful experience that extends beyond cognitions provokes internal dynamics in such a way that they find expression in the session. Although it did not happen during the session, a vulnerability was created for Sarah by removing clothes, sitting on the bed, and sucking her thumb. The ordeal intensified her pervasive feeling of loss so that she connected her profound grief with what was partially keeping her drowning in it.

Bypasses natural blocks to change. Often clients have been practicing and reinforcing unhelpful and unhealthy ways of being and acting for most of their lives. Usually nothing you can say, no matter how wise, will undo the years of this pattern. Whereas traditional therapies emphasize thinking, experiential techniques focus on being and doing. By taking a backdoor rather than a front-door approach, you can bypass defense mechanisms, allowing easier access to the client's inner world. In certain settings, experiential approaches redirect clients from the process of therapy to an activity itself. For example, participants of wilderness programs are so focused on the nature of activities that they are unaware of the personal issues that are emerging and being exhibited.

Experiential work enhances spiritual formation. Experiential work enables clients to undergo a radical, deep-seated transformational change. We can journey our way to become the person that God has envisioned us to be. Just prior to his crucifixion, Jesus illustrated his perspective on the nature of Christianity by washing his disciples' feet. Christ's experiential work was to model that the things that are seemingly trivial are the measure of spirituality. As Chambers (1935, February 25) wrote: "One who becomes broken-bread and poured-out wine in the hands of Jesus Christ for other lives" is one who lives out Christ's example.

CASE STUDIES

Case One

Jan Hampton scheduled a family session for her daughter, Brooklyn (age thirteen), her son, Noah (age eleven), and her husband of sixteen years, Mark. The reported reason for therapy was Mark, who "didn't get it." Jan claimed that Mark was a strong and domineering figure in the family. She contended that he had created a family climate characterized by disengagement, intimidation, anger, and blaming. When expectations were high and enforcement was harsh, Jan and the children learned to feel excessively guilty in unhealthy ways. Underneath their guilt lay a bedrock of shame. The Hamptons reported that Mark was cold and indifferent, being minimally involved with the family. In addition to his job as a high school principal, Mark was also the head coach of the football team. Mark was considered an excellent role model among the African American Christian community.

The children harbored the belief that other families were perfect, but theirs was flawed. The internal stress of the family was shrouded in secrecy yet was exacting an inordinate toll on each member. As the identified patient, Mark offered his evaluation of the entire family's evaluation. Aloofness appeared to mask his hurt. Mark reported that his numerous attempts to engage his family, beginning with his wife and then the children, were all met with a "stiff arm" and "pushback."

Mark constantly feared that others, especially his family, would dislike him. Since he believed that no one could be counted on to fulfill his needs, he disengaged from others and became cynical and domineering. Conversely, sensing that his family—and others—expected something of him that he felt he could not give fueled his aversion even more. While he

had an overwhelming desire to be cared for, ironically his distancing from others served only to confirm his fear. He was creating a similar dynamic in his own family.

Case Two

Thirty-six-year-old Nicki described her problem as "excessive codependency." She described a lifetime of high deference that began in her family of origin and became her constant companion in "all" of her adult relationships. Nicki said that she had never been to counseling before, though she reported struggling with mild to moderate depression. She has had a string of unhealthy and fragile relationships. Her addiction to dysfunctional relationships developed out of a need to find nurturing sources. To Nicki, a bad relationship was better than abandonment. She was shamed about needing to be dependent, yet she wanted to be totally dependent on someone. Currently she has a live-in-boyfriend who is unemployed, emotionally and mentally abusive, and "struggles with overusing" alcohol and other drugs. Nicki is a highly regarded "team player" in the human resource department of a large manufacturing plant, where she works as a benefits coordinator.

EXPERIENTIAL STRATEGIES, INTERVENTIONS, AND TECHNIQUES

Therapy, in and of itself, is an experience. The nature of that experience is different from counselor to counselor and with each individual client. The clinical use of experiential techniques connects to a client's experience within therapy as well as with the experiences that contributed and shaped the issues that need to be addressed. The following section will examine the wide breadth of experiential SITs and equip you to implement them in therapy.

The Scope of Experiential Work

Experiential techniques are used with all populations and therapy formats, including individuals (Degges-White & Davis, 2011), couples and families (Carson, Becker, Vance, & Forth, 2003; Duffey, Somody, & Eckstein, 2009; Hendricks & Bradley, 2005; Murray & Rotter, 2002; Satir, 1983; Satir & Baldwin, 1984; Star & Cox, 2008; Thomas, 2000; Wittenborn, Faber, Harvey, & Thomas, 2006), and group therapies (cf. Chung, 2013; Klontz, Garos, & Klontz, 2005; Klontz, Wolf, & Bivens, 2000). Experiential work is used to address such disorders and issues as depression (Hendricks & Bradley, 2005), domestic violence (Binkley, 2013), trauma (Elliott, Davis, & Slatick, 1998), various addictions (Bornstein, 2004; Klontz et al., 2005), and conduct disorder and antisocial personality disorder (Jones, Lowe, & Risler, 2004).

Clinician Reluctance in Using Experiential SITs

Because of the avant-garde nature of many of these techniques, certain counselors are hesitant to conceptualize, utilize, or embrace them, especially the provocation ones. Beginning counselors tend to shy away from using "more directive and potentially powerful interventions" (Cummings, 1992, p. 23). Attributes of effective counselors include compassion, grace, warmth, and empathic attunement. The nature of people attracted to our profession are inclined to be uncomfortable hearing about unconventional practices, particularly if they seem outside of the bounds of prosocial behavior. To capitalize on the power of these techniques, you will need to shed the shackles of social graces and a need for acceptance and approval. It is essential that you are true to yourself as well as your clients. Any SIT can be customized to fit your personality and range of comfort. Be open to expanding yourself by ethically and appropriately trying on new ideas and techniques.

Using Experiential Techniques

The adoption of certain clinical techniques, of course, depends on the counselor's knowledge, skills, and judgment with the type of techniques being learned. You need to develop your own solid clinical platforms that direct and support a style of counseling that works for you (Jacobs, 1992). Counselors who consider themselves eclectic often do not have well-structured scaffolding on which to build an approach. One part of my platform is the impact of experiences on human functioning. Cognitions, for instance, include beliefs, perceptions, interpretations, and the attribution of meaning. They are most often removed from the experiences that created, shaped, and reinforced them. Addressing experiences puts you in an arena where learning and change occur. The client's internal world can be tapped into, often without the client being able to make complete sense of the therapy in the moment. Experiential techniques are effective because human functioning processes are similar in everyone. Because each client presents with idiosyncratic responses to issues and problems, a wise counselor tailors and customizes SITs to fit a number of variables, including a client's situations, personality, age, and cognitive ability. Sometimes experiential techniques that work well with children will also benefit adults (Landreth, 2012). Although some experiential techniques will work best only with children and others only with adults, many are useful across the lifespan.

Preparation for Experiential Work

This section unpacks important tasks and activities that will prepare you to make the most of experiential techniques.

Develop creativity. Creativity is a transformative process resulting in new ideas that are meaningful and useful (Runko & Jaeger, 2012; Stein, 1953). Duffey, Haberstroh, and Trepal (2009) contend that creativity strengthens connections with self and others and increases authenticity, empathy, expression, and growth. For those who don't believe that they could ever be creative, Carson and colleagues (Carson, Becker, Vance, & Forth, 2003) describe creativity as an openness to being present and intuitive in session, something each one of us can do. Additionally, cultivate an attitude of learning not to fear failing or looking foolish; relatedly, learn to give yourself compassion; learn to dream; learn to ask questions; be curious; and most importantly, partner with the creator God and through prayer ask him to stimulate ideas in your mind and heart.

Be versatile. Too often when a client says, "Ouch," counselors either back off implicitly or say, "Oops, my bad!" (Jacobs, 1992). We know pain is necessary for change. That is why so many of us prefer avoiding change. Experiential techniques often produce uncomfortable levels of anxiety by disrupting problematic patterns.

Supply your office with necessities. Jacobs (1992) recommends outfitting yourself with such things as a whiteboard/large pad; a small chair to reference the little boy or girl inside the client; two extra chairs; and a potpourri of props, including cups, tapes, and shields. In the case of props, Jacobs fleshes out his notion of props by stating that one way to symbolize a client's hole in self-esteem is using paper or Styrofoam cups. You could, for example, illustrate thoughts playing around in a client's head via a digital file, and a shield could be used to show what the client needs to do to protect him- or herself with certain family members. To that list I add video recording sessions and sand tray work, both of which are described later.

In-Session Considerations

Assess for the appropriateness and timing of experiential techniques. Experiential techniques are not fitting for all clients, though they are suitable for far more clients than is typically expected. The timing of therapeutic work captures the art of therapy more than the science. The bottom line is that work is less about timing than the client's readiness and willingness.

Stay with. Far too often therapists do not allow a client to hold a feeling long enough. An experiential psychotherapy phrase that can assist the therapeutic process is "stay with" the feeling associated with the experience. Yontef (1993a) says that counselors need to maintain focus on the client's emerging and present experience as long as that experience is continuing. The client's experience is not to be interrupted by either the client or yourself.

Assess the selection of client material. Since every aspect of therapy is an experience, including therapy itself, there is no limit to clinically relevant content. Some clinical information is ripe for experiential work, such as identifying client processes, themes, obstacles to change, resistance, and much more.

Identify client process. You are likely aware of the difference between content, what is said or done, and process, which focuses on how things are said or done. Presenting problems represent the content in the session. Content is usually subordinate to process. It is impossible to have content without process since how words and behaviors are expressed always accompany content.

Process is expressed in several different ways that allow you to identify them. First, assess the processes that are being expressed from intrapersonal dynamics. Since all of life involves relationships, intrapersonal dynamics are formed and reinforced through interactions with others. In meaningful relationships, they are exhibited through patterned dance steps that carry heightened emotion between two or more individuals. Various examples illustrate processes. A codependent client's process, for example, would be a "door mat," and the person she is usually attached to would be "dirty boots." In the case of sexual acting out, the faithful often sees himself as the "saint" and the unfaithful one as the "sinner."

Processes are also evident in the absence of communication, that is, what is not said. As Watzlawick, Bavelas, and Jackson (1967) quipped, not to communicate is impossible. In other words, communication is more than words. In fact, we communicate far more nonverbally. Thus, silence can be deafening. Others will perceive and interpret any nonverbal communication and attempt to make meaning from it.

Your task is to recognize, label, and interact with client processes. Processes are therapeutically critical since they are leverage in the client's personal individual system or couple/family system. Almost everyone is unaware of his or her processes. Clients report and emphasize the things that were said, done, and felt without any connection to what is happening in them and between them and others.

Processes are experienced viscerally. Feelings and emotions, which connect to the processes, are the underbelly of our thoughts, words, and behaviors. No matter how hard someone attempts to conceal her emotions, she finds a path out. Clues to feelings include body language (e.g., posture, gestures), especially facial expressions, language (e.g., choice of words), and paralinguistics (e.g., tone, rate of speech). A wise therapist is attuned to observing and listening for emotional expression by helping clients identify and express feelings such as "I'm angry," "I'm bad," "I'm sad," or "I'm afraid," to name a few "I-feeling states." Many other psychological processes exist that can be identified, labeled, and used to devise experiences. Your task is to recognize, label, and interact with client processes.

Video-record. The use of video recording sessions allows you to offer feedback to a client, couple, or family. I have sometimes stopped recording during sessions to play back something that occurred (see Geertsma & Reivich, 1983). I have also assigned watching a session at home to reinforce concepts (see Gasman, 1992) or enhance skill development such as active listening (see Benschoter, Eaton, & Smith, 1961).

A Selection of Experiential Techniques

The uses of experiential SITs are limited only by your creative juices. The following uses are found peppered throughout the literature: parables and metaphors (Burns, 2001, 2005; Loue, 2008), writing activities (Pennebaker, 2010), phototherapy (Weiser, 2004), poetry (Gladding, 1979), music (Degges-White & Davis, 2011), art (Degges-White & Davis, 2011; Gladding, 2005; Hogan & Coulter, 2014), sand tray (Dale & Lyddon, 1998), dance (Strassel, Cherkin, Steuten, Sherman, & Vrijhoef, 2011; Winters, 2008), sculpting (Satir, 1983; Satir & Baldwin, 1984), psychodrama (Chung, 2013; Moreno, 1994), equine therapy (Selby & Smith-Osborne, 2013), wilderness and adventure therapies (Jones, Lowe, & Risler, 2004), the use of props (Jacobs, 1992), directives (O'Hanlon & Hexum, 1991), and ordeals (Haley, 1984). Remember that our clinical mission should not be confused with the methods we use. If we are wisely using effective methods of change, we will likely achieve our therapeutic mission. But the SITs are not an end in themselves. The following section will focus on selected examples from this list of approaches and strategies.

Metaphors and stories. God loves a good story! His Son, Jesus, evidenced the power of stories to teach as well as confound his hearers. Unsurprisingly, metaphors have been a long-standing figure of speech used to represent truths, principles, and ideas, and voice poignant emotions. Metaphors use words or phrases to call up relatable, powerful, and lasting images that generate salient emotional experiences in the listener or reader. They create clarity, provide a visual experience, provide an alternative way to think about something, can symbolize new insights, and provide an easy way to grasp an experience that represents a therapeutic thought. Research shows them to be effective in promoting emotional and cognitive change (Gelo & Mergenthaler, 2012; Haynes, Strosahl, & Wilson, 1999). They are effective in part because they bypass the analytical aspects of the mind (Citron & Goldberg, 2014; Wagener, 2017)—they are right-brain focused. As such they can detour client resistance and promote change (Tay, 2012). Metaphors can be shared by client or counselor via oral or written form, whether the client independently tells a story or is prompted by something else, such as photos, music, art, or a book.

I categorize metaphors into two broad types. The first type of metaphor is storytelling. Stories span the continuum from fairy tales, parables, speaker illustrations, and author stories to those used for therapeutic purposes. Everyone can connect to a story; they stir us in ways that sharing information does not. Hamilton and Weiss (2007) aptly say that "stories go straight to the heart" (p. 2). Additionally, stories can work especially well with clients who are younger or who have cognitive difficulties such as traumatic brain injury or recent concussions. Therapists use stories to evoke emotions (Garrett, 2006; Samur, Lai, Hagoort, & Willems, 2015), link actions and events (Binks, Smith, Smith, & Joshi, 2009), provide insight (Wagener, 2017), bypass cognitive processes and defenses (Genuchi, Hopper, & Morrison, 2017; Romig & Gruenke, 1991), establish connections (Abrahamson, 1998), and generate empathy (McQuiggan, Robinson, & Lester, 2010). Stories offer clients new ways to deal with life problems. Your storytelling ability is linked to your imagination and ability to remember stories you have heard or read. Biblically, parables are a euphemism for storytelling. Jesus communicated powerful truths through parables. Not only did they inspire, instruct, and challenge, but they also provoked confusion in the listeners. Confusion is a compelling state of mind that prompts a person to search for meaning.

Second, metaphors can depict a client process. Frank was physically abused by his father, although the soul terrorism he experienced was far worse. As a child, Frank would hide under his bed when he knew his father was coming home or coming up to punish him. Life in his home was both chaotic and treacherous. As a forty-two-year-old, Frank had lived his life in fear, had maintained minimal boundaries, and was disengaged in his attachment. I told him, "Frank, it seems you have been hiding under your bed your entire life. When you were young, the thought of leaving your safe haven was intolerable. As an adult, however, what ideas do you have about what crawling out from under your bed would look like?" The metaphor resonated so much with Frank that his description of his own processes incorporated the phrase.

Props. In my practice, I have found that using various props is beneficial. In fact, nearly all of my clients have reported that they remember the prop more than what I've said (not exactly an affirming remark). The intent of props is to facilitate client learning. They bring to life what might seem too vague or too new of a concept. A clinically used prop illustrates such concepts in a concrete fashion, helping the client pin down the truth. Thus, props are visual analogies of concepts, such as being truly righteous because of the work of Christ (cf. Rom. 3:21–22; 1 Cor. 1:30; 2 Cor. 5:21). As for what to use as a prop, anything. Blocks, plates, pens, a box, Styrofoam cups, vinyl records, rocks, sticks, chairs, and a host of other objects, including card tables. For the Hamptons, I used a card table placed on its side in front of Mark to represent the family dynamic. The analogy was that a wall was built between Mark and the rest of the family. Mark needed the wall in part to protect him from his fear of being inadequate in family relationships. Each of the other family members needed the table to hide from the triggers of their own shame. The prop proved to communicate a powerful message. The experience of each family member was processed in relationship to this dynamic. The experience resulted in stunning insight, except for Noah, who only partially "got it." The words "table" and "wall" were used to label experiences since they anchored a powerful family experience. Another prop I used with an entire family required Chinese handcuffs (see Haynes et al., 1999). Perhaps you remember the colorful woven tube in which one index finger is inserted into each end. The irony of the device is that the more one pulls to release the fingers, the tighter the device grips the fingers.

One final prop that I have made wide use of is "Groucho glasses." When couples, for example, believe any dialogue on a specific topic will evoke negative emotions and disaffection, I may choose to use my Groucho glasses (large glasses with a big nose, bushy eyebrows, and mustache—a caricature of the face of the famed Groucho Marx). The Hamptons could not talk about certain issues without an escalating fight or family members shutting down. I proposed that they could talk about the hot-button issue while laughing. Jan quickly assured me that it would be impossible. To make my point, I handed a pair of Groucho glasses to each family member. They burst into laughter (a welcomed response from their typical interactions). Each family donned the glasses as I then instructed them to talk about the conflictual issue. They could not fight.

Laughing interfered. Even after allowing time for them to habituate to the glasses, they did not fight. Since the topic is a difficult one, keeping yourself composed is important. Encourage participants to get the thoughts and feelings out as they had previously. By becoming a relatively neutral presence, the clients have a free field of expression. Although a bit of a pun, helping clients find a "new lens" to perceive a situation will inevitably change perspectives and interactions.

Phototherapy. Consistent with the adage "A picture is worth a thousand words," you can request clients to bring in photos of selective times in their lives. Nicki created a photo timeline of her life that she believed represented herself at various moments along her lifespan. A supervisor once told me that a picture is a "mirror with memory." The majority of clients select photos that portray darker times. Much later in therapy, having an interest in photography, one client took pictures that characterized God's love and grace toward her, her plans, and who she longed to be. I have found that using photos produces a wealth of clinically valuable information that likely would not have been revealed otherwise.

Sand tray. Sand tray work is a valuable creative experiential strategy that allows clients the opportunity to gain insight, resolve conflicts, remove obstacles, and "say" things that they could not vocalize in talking therapy. It is an expressive and projective technique whereby the client creates a psychological representation of his inner and outer life. Sand tray provides creative space for the client to construct a visual depiction of internal conflicts and distress.

Sand tray is typically considered a play therapy activity. Yet adults have rarely balked at the suggestion of the technique (Landreth, 2012). Adults, however, unwittingly disclose anxiety with such statements as being afraid of not "doing it right" or not being creative enough. It is impossible for a client to do sand tray work wrong. For you, however, the processing and translation of the work can be practiced wrong. Talking too much, assuming an expert position on the client's creation, overinterpreting, taking a negative slant, or not assuring the client is ineffective. If a client seems to get stuck during the activity, simply reassuring her usually does the trick to help her along. For example, "It seems you're stuck. That happens to most people. Many of them have found that just going with their guts and not thinking too much helps."

Sand tray requires the availability and accessibility to such items as various figurines (e.g., people—men/boys, women/girls, disabled people, military personnel, athletes, law enforcement personnel, criminals, medical personnel, monsters, fantasy characters, pirates, action figures and superheroes; animals—jungle, domestic, ocean, historic), buildings (e.g., houses, castles, forts, lighthouses, towers, doors and windows, furnishings), transportation equipment (e.g., cars, trucks, ambulances, fire trucks, trains, boats, planes, construction equipment, roads, bridges), environmental elements (e.g., trees, plants, rocks, mountains), weapons and tools (e.g., miniature guns, knives, hammers), and many other miniatures of various kinds. Clearly, preparing to use a sand tray requires time and effort in finding, purchasing, and storing the items (garage and yard sales are excellent places to start). An ideal office setting allows the client to view and access all items at the same time, which means they should be organized on shelving such as bookcases.

Nicki was excited to use the sand tray. She brushed all the sand aside from the middle of the box and then buried a woman figurine in the space she created. After her sand tray was completed, we processed her work. Nicki and I explored what it represented, focusing on eliciting her feelings and perceptions. I also used a sand tray with the Hampton family. A highly moving moment occurred when Brooklyn and Noah created their own sand tray of what it is like to be in the family. After each created sand tray, I took pictures from different angles. (Although for me these were the days of Polaroid cameras, today cell phone photos can be easily sent for quick copying to a nearby printer.) I would lay out the photos in subsequent sessions to create a metaphor of each family member's experience in the family to prompt movement toward transformation and growth. With couples or families, I use circular questioning to elicit comments from other family members.

Provocation. The root meaning of *provocative* is to "call out." The therapeutic idea is to "call out" various aspects of the client's experience through a number of particularly nontypical techniques. What would it feel like for you to employ any of the following techniques?

- *Playing devil's advocate.* For example, "Perhaps changing is too much work." "Well, if you sought a divorce, at least you would no longer have to try so hard to change your husband."
- *Siding with the client's assertions.* For example, "Well perhaps you've created a strong argument against yourself—that you are indeed unworthy." "That is a good point. If you stopped abusing benzodiazepines, then how in the world would you manage your anxiety?"
- *Exaggeration.* For example, encouraging self-defeating behavior and attitudes. "Perhaps you could continue to avoid agreeing with your wife, because that means you wouldn't be close enough for her to hurt you."
- *Paradox.* For example, to a client who fears failure: "If you don't study for your upcoming math test, we will have a better idea of what would happen if you actually fail." "Well, that doesn't sound pleasant to talk about. Let's talk about something else." "Maybe you should try to think harder about ways to stop worrying in order to come up with a better solution."
- *Jesting.* For example, to a sexually avoidant wife who quit working with the couple's previous counselor after he said, "I don't understand what is so hard about this. Just go down on your husband." As we were working toward deeper levels of non-demanding touch, I said the following to her: "Well, I know the thought of a hand massage with your husband makes you feel overly vulnerable. Gently working toward deeper levels of physical intimacy does

mean having to feel uncomfortable many times over throughout the process. I guess the other approach is to dive into the deep end of the pool where you just go down on him." The statement brought laughter and a willingness to begin with light hand massages.
- *Sarcasm.* For example, "It sounds like you must be awfully special. Everyone else is allowed to be human and make mistakes, but not you. When did you become a god?" "It seems like we are in a power struggle. Is it important to you to win?"
- *Putting the client in a crucible.* For example, "Well, if there really isn't anything left to try and you really are as hopeless as it sounds, maybe we should just give up and accept things the way they are."
- *Suggesting ridiculous ideas or solutions.* For example, "Given how much you want to please your mother, perhaps you should build an altar to her." "I have an idea: what if you told your friends to stop reaching out to you and your family to stop calling to create a completely new way of conquering your addiction, since nothing else has worked?"

In all cases, delivery of the material is very important. In some cases, being straightforward is the right style, whereas in others using a slightly humorous tone is more effective.

An ethical standard across disciplines is to do no harm. Yet to stimulate client change, therapists must stir the waters of the soul. Stirring often feels like a treacherous storm to the client. While counselors are charged with the ethical virtue of doing no harm, effective therapy hurts. Consider the fact that our spiritual healing required Christ's suffering and death. Grace required violence. While you might think that such counseling is harsh, mean-spirited, dishonest, disrespectful, and any number of offensive labels, the exact opposite is true. The basis of these techniques is that clients can change and grow when presented with a challenge. I believe that psychological fragility is both vastly overemphasized and overestimated. When provocation is used, you are actually making contact with the client in an empathic manner.

Like no other technique, provocation can emotionally hurt. It stirs the waters, creating confusion, shock, and the loss of words. Using provocation is not for the fainthearted counselor. Because provocations are avant-garde and bold, the sensibilities of many clinicians may be violated. The purpose of provocation SITs is to lead to change. Despite what some may protest, provocative techniques are not employed to play games.

Using these techniques necessitates six conditions. First, provocative techniques must be consistent with how you understand human behavior. Second, prior to beginning therapy, you must obtain informed consent on the use of these interventions as part of your overall approach. Third, the therapeutic relationship must be strong; attunement is a must. Fourth, you must possess deep respect for the client; hopefully that is a given. Fifth, when planning for provocation, you must explain the technique and gain permission

to use it (by this, I do not mean telling the client you are trying to provoke, but describing the technique that is being used for provocation). Finally, you must obtain supervision to develop competence.

In a family session, Mark's domineering comportment was pronounced. I switched seats with Noah to have access to Mark. I queried him to tell the family the main point in his diatribe that preceded my change of seats. As Mark began to reiterate his point, I pushed on his shoulder, much to his surprise. When he questioned what I was doing, I urged him to continue talking to his family. Soon, not only was the family laughing, but Mark himself was becoming more lighthearted and reasonable. Being prudent in using such a technique is critical because it could be misunderstood.

Sometimes clients unnecessarily acquiesce to their family members and need to find their inner strength to set appropriate boundaries. Either the client or I will identify this acquiescence as being a "doormat." When the timing is right, I get permission from the client to use a provocation to help them experience their problem in a different way. In this technique, I take a pair of old shoes (size 12 or larger filled with concrete work nicely) and ask clients to place the shoes in their laps. My therapeutic intent is for clients to demonstrate ego strength by throwing the shoes to the ground or ending the exercise, thus asserting that they will not be treated like a doormat. Their boundaries become clearly affirmed and appropriately defended. Getting clients to do so, however, takes significant effort and time.

After the client places the shoes on his lap, I do not say anything. If and when I'm asked for the rationale, I thank the client several times for agreeing to the exercise. The typical response will be "It's okay." Throughout the time the shoes lie on the client's lap, I direct conversation toward issues of setting boundaries. At some point in the discussion, the client will likely ask if he can remove the shoes from his lap. I acknowledge how uncomfortable he must be but reiterate that it is comforting to see how cooperative he is with this type of treatment. Interestingly, many clients will continue to acquiesce to the unusual intervention. Most often, however, clients throw or place the shoes on the floor. When a client does so, I stand up and applaud. Moreover, I bestow a gold medallion (a party-favor item) on the client. For many, this is the first time they have "stood up" for themselves. Some clients cry at the revelation that they have been a doormat and let other people's "dirty boots" walk over them. From my perspective, this technique demonstrates the highest level of empathy, since I join the client in his self-perception. This provocative technique accomplishes far more in one session than other traditional and "gentler" approaches.

Ordeals. As aforementioned, ordeals in counseling (Haley, 1984) are used to eradicate a problematic behavior by means of the counselor creating an ordeal (a new directive or task) to create tension with the client's problems. Nicki's "real problem" could be described from different points of view. In one session, it seemed that a real and valid concern was her unmet dependency needs expressed in her overattachment to unhealthy men. After we defined the problem, using Prochaska and DiClemente's (1982) transtheoretical model, I carefully assessed Nicki's readiness to change. Ironically, I did not believe Nicki thought she could change. I told Nicki that I thought her real problem was the fact that she did not think she could change and that she had not yet hit bottom.

To simplify the ordeal, it involved Nicki telling her live-in boyfriend that she wanted to be totally dependent on him and had no desire to change or belief that she could change. As is the case for most clients, she looked stunned but agreed to do what I suggested. Two weeks went by before our next session. She reported that her boyfriend moved out in previous days. She was confused but liked him being out of her apartment. I then asked her that whenever she met a man and began to think that he was someone to pursue, she was to tell him the same thing—that she wanted to be totally dependent on him and had no desire to change. Nicki remained unattached for quite some time, allowing us to work on her preoccupied attachment style and unmet dependency needs. Eventually she met a rather healthy man, and she refused to give him the directive. We processed this relationship over the course of several sessions. After meeting the man, I agreed with Nicki that he was relatively healthy. They did marry, and I had the honor of providing their premarital counseling. Several years later, I received a Christmas card that reported they were doing well. Trading a life of ordeals for one ordeal is an excellent method to find change.

Structured Experiential Techniques

Life and trauma egg. One of my favorite experiential exercises is having a client complete a life and trauma egg that is derived from Murray's (1991) and Carnes's (1997) work. It is an effective and gentle method to establish a person's trauma history as well as noting any negative life experiences. From the egg one can often identify patterns in a person's life and the subsequent coping mechanisms and core beliefs derived from the experiences. Life events develop into a personal covert mission statement that keeps people stuck in an issue.

I typically assign the egg exercise as homework, but occasionally the client and I work on it in session. After explaining the assignment to Nicki, she began by drawing a large oval (the egg) on a piece of paper (see figure 8.1). Outside of the egg in the lower corners of the paper, she listed about eight to ten words that describe her mother on one side and eight to ten words that describe her father in the other corner. In addition, she listed the spoken and unspoken rules from her family of origin up to the age of eighteen in the top left corner. In the top right corner, she listed who represented characteristic family roles (i.e., hero, scapegoat, mascot, enabler, clown, forgotten child, and people pleaser).

Next, using colored pencils and markers, she drew symbols (no words) to represent a traumatic event. Each symbol was contained in a circle or bubble and drawn

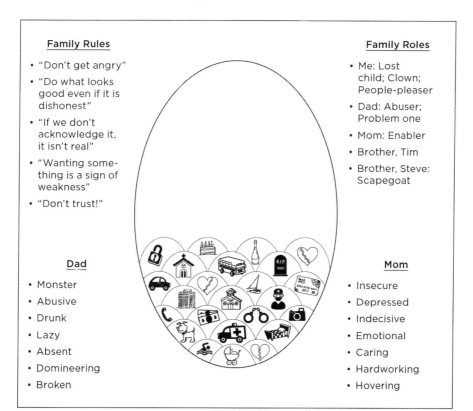

Family Rules

- "Don't get angry"
- "Do what looks good even if it is dishonest"
- "If we don't acknowledge it, it isn't real"
- "Wanting something is a sign of weakness"
- "Don't trust!"

Dad

- Monster
- Abusive
- Drunk
- Lazy
- Absent
- Domineering
- Broken

Family Roles

- Me: Lost child; Clown; People-pleaser
- Dad: Abuser; Problem one
- Mom: Enabler
- Brother, Tim
- Brother, Steve: Scapegoat

Mom

- Insecure
- Depressed
- Indecisive
- Emotional
- Caring
- Hardworking
- Hovering

inside the large egg. We started with her earliest memories and moved chronologically. Nicki also considered any event in which she experienced strong emotions such as anger, sadness, hurt, guilt, shame, abandonment, and betrayal.

In a subsequent session, we began going through her egg. The entire process took two sessions. Some of the processing included noting themes throughout the sessions and attempting to determine her responses to the following: Life is . . . ; People are . . . ; God is . . . ; I am . . . ; and so on. Therefore, I will. . . . Nicki responded with "Life is too hard"; "People cannot be trusted"; "God loves me but doesn't like me"; "I am lost"; and "Therefore, I will continue to get help."

Much later in therapy, Nicki created an "angel egg" that identified the "angels" in her life. Angels can be people, animals, nature, events, achievements, God (e.g., client's faith, Jesus Christ), or any time the client felt joy, comforted, nurtured, and loved. The thrust was to help Nicki embrace those aspects of her life rather than hyperfocusing on the negative. Nicki drew an equal number of angels to the number of trauma circles.

Rituals. Every family therapist and most—if not all—counselors are familiar with the relevance and significance of rituals in family functioning. The Hamptons staged having a family dinner together—a rare occurrence for the family. Though they appeared to be a loving family on the surface, cohesion seemed low. Their lives, especially Mark's, operated in different universes. Jan and Brooklyn's planets aligned closer to each other, though not close to the father's. Noah's planet existed closer to the father's than the others. The idea of creating a dinner ritual would teach them not only how to have a family dinner but provide me with a new avenue of insight into their family dynamics. Because the family looked like a deer in the headlights when I suggested this as a "home experiment," we agreed to role-play a family dinner. Since we didn't have a formal table, the family arranged themselves around a card table. The awkwardness was highly apparent in getting this role play going. With coaching the family began to figure out how to conduct themselves in this novel exercise. In short, the conversation was more fluid between Jan and Brooklyn. Noah was moderately successful at engaging them, but Mark's attempts were ineffective. By working with the family by using the structure of a role play, the family meal produced fruitful insight into their intrapersonal relationships.

Expressive Experiential SITs

Every client brings unique talents and passions into therapy. Depending on your creativity, any client has a facet of her life that is ripe for a creative and experiential technique. Below are several experiential exercises that involve writing, verbalization, and music.

Experiential writing techniques. Writing assignments hold a high therapeutic value that crosses many approaches. You can assign the client to write creatively, structured, or a combination of the two. Below are selective ways to use writing.

Journaling. In each of the case studies, journaling was a requested task. All but

Mark regularly journaled about their experiences with other family members and, most importantly, their internal feelings in relation to those interactions. While Mark said that he didn't "object" to the assignment, journaling was not of value for him and he knew he likely would not comply. I have used many different types of journaling throughout my career. Some involve clients writing with their nondominant hand with the hopes of tapping into childlike states. A structured journal activity requests that clients journal about different aspects of their lives—either several prescribed ones or a singular area. These could include emotional, social, behavioral, or spiritual aspects. A singular area could include one of the previous areas or specific ones, such as life goals, education, occupation, marriage, parenting, addiction, or something else.

Journaling might focus on exploring self, which I call "insight journaling"; documenting particular events, feelings, and so on at specific times; creating a prompt for the client to respond to, such as a question, series of questions, or a sentence stem; writing to a future time or self or to a past self; researching a topic and journaling the information and reflecting on it; blogging—the ideas are virtually unlimited. The value of journaling is that clients are using their personal time to "do the work" of counseling. The data that comes forth from these exercises is beyond valuable.

Letter writing. A client's letter can address a part of the self (e.g., wounded self, scared self, self-contempt, failure, insecurity) or a person currently in the client's life (e.g., parent, spouse, employer, minister). The letter may also be directed to a person previously in the client's life (alive or deceased) or to God. This assignment can also be linked to an empty chair approach, whereby the client reads two letters from polarized perspectives. Letter writing was extremely beneficial to Nicki. She wrote letters to all members of her family of origin, to her current paramour, to past people with whom she'd had romantic relationships, to her future self, and to the part of her that longed to be intimate with God.

Poetry. Admittedly, I'm not passionate about poetry. Yet I recognize and know the therapeutic value of it. Your creativity will produce numerous ways to incorporate poetry into your counseling. You can select a poem to use as a catalyst for the client or, more typically, have the client create one. Recently, a meek and soft-spoken Christian client asked me if he could write a poem after I suggested a form of journaling. In the next session, he read his poem, which was filled with venom and vulgarities. The incongruence between his persona and internal world was obvious. Processing his first poem took several sessions. This exercise was a regular component of our work together. Additional ideas that I have asked clients to consider include writing inspirational prayers and their own psalms of lament or hope.

Experiential vocalizing technique. Firestone (2001) developed an approach to his understanding of personality functioning that he termed *voice therapy*. Many clients with whom I have worked have been robbed of their voices or have repressed or suppressed their voices. Firestone believes that one's internal critic or self-destructive processes need to be expressed. These critical messages have been introjected most typically from parents and other significant figures in the client's life. Wisely, he would ask the client to express these afflicted parts of self by speaking in the second person. The idea is to shift from "I am a loser" to "You are a loser." From my experience, this approach fits well with the conception that we are a composition of parts that form our whole. As with Nicki, I ask clients to enhance their vocal and nonverbal expressions in a dramatic manner. Some clients, like Mark, cannot make the shift from the cognitive voice to the affective voice without spending time working on their feelings.

In his work, *Voice Therapy*, Firestone (2001) notes five steps in the process: (1) identifying negative thought patterns and processes; (2) gleaning insights into the origins of those thoughts; (3) responding to and resisting the voice, in which the client speaks back to the voice defending the self; (4) identifying self-destructive and self-defeating behaviors; and (5) collaborating on ideas to address the patterns that are in keeping with the client's interests, ambitions, and goals.

Culling out the self-destructive processes generally produces an inordinate level of affect, so be prepared. After many months of family therapy, Mark finally tapped into his internal critic. Though the expression of it was extreme and felt overwhelming to Jan and the children, the predominating expressed affect was hurt and sadness. His verbalization of his pain

lasted nearly thirty minutes before he was weeping in his seat. At times during his tormented eruption, Jan, Brooklyn, and Noah were in tears as well. The intervention brought them closure together in a new and healthy way.

Experiential music techniques. Music—and art as well—brings beauty to the human experience. Music is both felt and heard. Music tells a story. A client doesn't need to know anything about music to experience it. Yet the more a client knows, the greater the appreciation and potential of motivation. For example, Steve had once enjoyed writing music and singing. With time and encouragement, Steve agreed to try to write songs that could communicate how he felt. He would write songs that captured thoughts, feelings, motives, and goals and bring them into therapy to play and sing for me. Initially, Steve would assail his work. His shame clouded out his joy, evident in how he initiated playing his music. Though Steve was not a gifted singer, his guitar prowess was quite evident. Early in therapy, his music was dark and depressing. I experienced the music moving me toward sadness. Thus, it is important to stay grounded in the work that we do. In time the tenor of the music changed. Today Steve is playing with a recognizable band with a spirit of joy on his face. Other clients have brought in established music that communicated something to them. Clients who lack knowledge of music, unlike Steve, might not know what they are responding to, but they are still experiencing it. Remember the power of music because God has integrated it into our eternal experience.

Experiential art techniques. Art expresses the creational beauty of God. His artistry is implanted in the human soul as the only bearers of his image in creation. Any art form can be used, even if the client is "art challenged." Collages, for instance, are a very useful technique applicable to children, adolescents, and, yes, even adults. While they can be made in session, they are also useful as homework assignments. If constructed in your office, you will need a significant amount and array of art materials and magazines. Also, have access to natural objects such as leaves and small stones. Collages are projective in nature. They can therefore be linked to any number of issues—for example, representing an ideal self, a specific part inside the client, family of origin, priorities, goals, and the like. Personally, I have primarily used collage making as a projective technique whereby the client creates his or her inner world. Metaphorically, creating a collage can be linked to creating our own reality.

Additional expressive techniques include such art forms as creating three-dimensional models of some aspect of creation, dance, and drama that can be used for clients within the appropriate contexts. The arts communicate. Whether the art form is informing us of truth or falsehood, it creates an experience that reflects aspects of the client's intrapersonal world into the interpersonal world. Younger generations seem to find meaning in art forms more than in words. Words do not hold value in our culture as they once did. Images, regardless of their form, offer salient meaning that we must capture in our clinical work. Be creative.

CONCLUSION

The thrust of these experiential SITs is to expand client self-awareness (e.g., insight, knowledge of self), strengthen self-regulation, and promote change. Experiential techniques consist of a wide range of therapeutic and creative activities, such as expressive writing, phototherapy, psychodrama, music, arts, animals, props, provocation, and processes aimed at promoting healing. Clients can identify obstacles, work through internal conflicts, accept responsibility, gain valuable self-awareness, and improve their sense of self.

Experiential work adds a dimension to the counseling process that is often neglected. Though the counseling field's focus is cognition, neurobiology, and behavior, experiential approaches provide observational data that is the confluence of all other facets of human functioning. Because they arouse "real-time" feelings about former incidents during session time, you are afforded the opportunity to observe a client in action. Our clients' hearts have reasons that their heads do not yet know. Experiential work bridges the heart-head divide.

The genre of experiential techniques requires valuing every person as an image bearer of God. While ethical guidelines specify that clinicians do no harm, the foundational ethic—actually, virtue—of Christian helpers is to love our clients as Christ loves them. While that may be easy to say, in practice it necessitates walking with the Master.

Since infusing creativity in the counseling process is accepted now more than ever (Duffey, 2006/2007) and is found throughout the Bible, I encourage you to become outfitted with a mind-set and skill set for incorporating experiential work into your current counseling approach.

Who knows? If Dr. Rafiki had not possessed an assortment of experiential ideas, Simba might still be hiding in shame and despair in the jungle.

RECOMMENDED READING

Bradley, L. J., Whiting, P., Hendricks, B., Parr, G., & Jones, E. G. (2008). The use of expressive techniques in counseling. *Journal of Creativity in Mental Health, 3*, 44–57. doi:10.1080/15401380802023605

Degges-White, S., & Davis, N. L. (Eds.). (2011). *Integrating the expressive arts into counseling practice: Theory-based interventions* (1st ed.). New York, NY: Springer.

Gladding, S. T. (2005). *Counseling as an art: The creative arts in counseling* (3rd ed.). Alexandria, VA: American Counseling Association.

Greenberg, L. S., Watson, J. C., & Lietaer, G. O. (1998). *Handbook of experiential psychotherapy* (1st ed.). New York, NY: Guilford Press.

Haley, J. (1984). *Ordeal therapy: Unusual ways to change behavior.* San Francisco, CA: Jossey-Bass.

Jacobs, E. (1992). *Creative counseling techniques: An illustrated guide.* Odessa, FL: PAR.

O'Hanlon, W. H., & Hexum, A. L. (1991). *An uncommon casebook: The complete clinical work of Milton H. Erickson, M.D.* New York, NY: W. W. Norton.

CHAPTER 9

Spiritual Strategies

Fernando Garzon, PsyD

He heals the brokenhearted
And binds up their wounds.

PSALM 147:3 NKJV

Christianity changes people's lives. We have two thousand years of evidence for this assertion, so naturally, as Christian counselors, we seek ways to foster the reality of Jesus's transformative power in our work with clients. Many of us were trained, however, in secular programs that either did not espouse spirituality as a valuable resource in therapy or advocated methods from Eastern religious traditions. Thus, we may lack education on specific strategies to build on the strength-based resource of a client's Christian faith.

A wide variety of biblically based strategies, interventions, and techniques (SITs) exist as potential resources for our quest. The biblical counseling literature (e.g., Powlison, 2003), Christian integration/Christian psychology literature (e.g., Appleby & Ohlschlager, 2013; Johnson, 2017; Tan, 2011a; Worthington, Johnson, Hook, & Aten, 2013), and Christian spiritual formation literature (e.g., Foster, 1998, 2002; Willard, 1998) represent valuable sources of information on possible interventions. One important caveat should be noted, however. In this chapter, I recognize the wholly inadequate nature of terms such as *technique, strategy,* and *intervention* to capture the sacred work of the Lord involved in each method described. These are simply the limited terms I have available to explain these profound approaches.

In this chapter I address spiritual strategies. Theological and psychological rationales for using these interventions are considered first. Techniques investigated include sharing Scripture, Christian meditation, Bible reading and memorization, worship, solitude and silence, forgiveness, and Christian inner healing prayer. By no means do these exhaust the wonderful ways God can lead us in our work. This chapter, therefore, serves as an introduction. The case example of Darrell illustrates the application of these methods.

THEOLOGY AND PSYCHOLOGY OF SPIRITUAL STRATEGIES

To address the theology and psychology of spiritual strategies, we must first briefly address the shift that has occurred in psychology. Historically, psychology stood adamantly against religion. Since the early and mid-twentieth century, psychology has become more open to its role in well-being. After thinking through why this shift occurred, we need to consider the broad pluralistic view of spirituality embedded in psychology along with its definition, and finally we should explore the distinctive facets of biblical spirituality.

Many psychological theorists have traditionally pathologized spirituality (see, for example, Freud's 1927 *The Future of an Illusion* and Albert Ellis's 1980 essay *The Case against Religion: A Psychotherapist's View*). These critics, however, valued scientific research, and the studies in the last two decades examining the physical and mental health benefits of spirituality have abandoned the predominant negative or skeptical perspective of religion. More specifically, Koenig, King, and Carson (2012) reviewed thousands of investigations examining the role of faith in physical and mental health and note that the question has shifted from whether spirituality is good or bad to understanding the conditions in which spirituality promotes health and those conditions in which it may harm well-being. Since many different spiritualties exist, clarifying the meaning of this term becomes important.

Spirituality, in the psychological sense, has been defined as the search for that which transcends the self, or the search for the sacred (Hill et al., 2000). This broad pluralistic definition attempts to be applicable to monotheistic Western religions, Eastern religions, and pagan religions alike. Many psychology and counseling texts written on spirituality likewise recognize the diversity of religions and seek to identify potential commonalities among different faiths to apply a universalist perspective. For example, Cashwell and Giordano (2014) propose the following common link between spiritualities: spirit exists. It is "discoverable" within a person who has an open mind and heart. Many don't recognize the spirit within. A path to liberation exists. Following the path leads to rebirth or enlightenment. Enlightenment or rebirth ends suffering. Social acts of compassion and mercy flow from this end of suffering. While mental health professionals attempt to identify commonalities and linkages among spiritualities in an effort to accommodate as many types of clients as possible, the effort becomes problematic when the significant differences between faiths become overlooked or minimized.

Another option is to emphasize the heterogeneous nature of various faiths. We can acknowledge that there are substantial differences between spiritualities that make it important to adapt as specifically as possible to the client's unique characteristics in the secular counseling setting. Conservative Christians have specific cherished beliefs and would likely have concerns with mental health professionals who adopt a universalist style of language and perspective in the exploration of their faith. They might feel misunderstood and be concerned about exposing themselves to demonic deception if a counselor applies Eastern-based spiritual strategies. Christianity has a distinctive spirituality, and the more a mental health professional knows about this spirituality, the more thera peutic strategies can be applied that fit the Christian client's faith characteristics. Admittedly, these characteristics will likely seem foreign to a counselor who is not a Christian. However, this also points to the ethical value of having mental health professionals from a variety of faiths so that specialized multicultural attention to the religious aspects of a client's background can be given when warranted. Referrals to Christian mental health professionals to improve the care of deeply religious clients sometimes makes sense.

Christian spirituality can be defined in numerous ways. Tan (2011) describes Christian spirituality as having several facets. It involves a *deep hunger for God* and a *love for him* based on a personal relationship. God is not a "force" or abstract being who exists in galaxies far, far away. He is a loving Father who enjoys relating to his children. This relationship produces a response of *worship* and *desire to obey* God's good will in a person. It includes *surrendering to the Lord's unfolding work of grace* in our hearts, *being filled with the Holy Spirit, decreasing one's yielding to the sinful nature*, and *the nonlegalistic practice of the spiritual disciplines in both individual and church community life*. Tan adds that Christian spirituality has a biblical, *eternal perspective* rather than a temporal one. It recognizes *spiritual warfare* and uses God's resources such as prayer and Scripture in

the effort to overcome the world, the flesh, and the devil (Eph. 2:2–3). Finally, he notes that there are *mystical aspects and experiences* that increase our Christlikeness, including the "dark night of the soul." Tan's description fits well in highlighting the broader purposes of spiritual strategies from a biblical worldview.

To summarize, clinical psychology and counseling have shifted to being more open to spiritual techniques. Pluralistic universalist approaches to spirituality may not be as effective with Christian clients as adopting a heterogeneous perspective that recognizes the distinctive features of Christian spirituality. Research is increasingly documenting that spiritual strategies can reduce symptoms and cultivate wellness. The growing evidence base provides an important rationale for adding spiritual interventions to secular therapies and justifying billing insurance companies for them. The Bible, however, provides an additional, more meaningful rationale: "Do not be conformed to this world, but be transformed by the renewing of your mind, that you may prove what is that good and acceptable and perfect will of God" (Rom. 12:2 NKJV). Cultivating an intimate relationship with God transforms how we see ourselves and experience others (Nouwen, 1996). In short, these strategies are good for the soul. I hope you will agree with that assertion after reading about my work with Darrell, which follows.

CASE STUDY

Darrell's case has some biographical and treatment elements combined from a few clients in order to protect confidentiality. Darrell is a forty-two-year-old African American, midlevel manager in a software company who recently got a promotion. He struggles with self-doubt about his ability to succeed in his new position, and he is working long hours partly out of his concern about his ability to succeed. He feels guilty for not spending enough time with his wife but sounds like he's convincing himself that his seven- and ten-year-old kids are fine with the amount of time he gives them.

Darrell's father struggled with drugs and alcohol and left the family when Darrell was six years old, never to be seen again. Afterward, Darrell's mother pushed him to excel in school: "You will not go down your father's path. You will make something of yourself and not leave your family penniless!" Darrell vowed he would prove his mother right.

Darrell presents with mixed anxiety and depression symptoms. His treatment consists of traditional cognitive behavioral therapy (CBT), some marital consultations, and interventions arising from a biblical worldview. While CBT elements will be briefly mentioned, this chapter will focus on the spiritual methods involved.

SPIRITUAL STRATEGIES, INTERVENTIONS, AND TECHNIQUES

Sundry approaches arise from a foundation on Scripture. These include sharing Scripture, Christian meditation, Scripture memorization, worship, solitude and silence, forgiveness, and Christian inner healing prayer. Ethical aspects, however, such as informed consent and spiritual assessment must be considered first in their application in professional mental health settings.

Informed Consent

First and foremost, I had to discuss with Darrell the possibility of spiritually based counseling in an ethical manner. Mental health professionals in nonministry settings apply Christian strategies in the context of clear informed-consent procedures that avoid imposing values on the client and yet invite discussion of faith if it is of interest to the client (Tan, 2003). This is done verbally and in a detailed informed-consent document provided to the client prior to therapy. A paragraph on one's Christian background, training in spiritual interventions, and openness to include such strategies can be incorporated into a standard therapy informed-consent form. Below you will find a sample paragraph that can be adjusted to your qualifications:

As my PsyD degree from Fuller Seminary may imply, I have specialized training in working with Christian spiritual issues in therapy. I have continued getting training in this area through workshops and conferences since my graduation. I am comfortable incorporating such practices as prayer, Christian meditation, discussion about the Bible, spiritual disciplines, and Christian inner healing prayer as a part of your treatment if you value these practices and we both feel that they would be helpful in your treatment. Of course, you have the prerogative to include or exclude spirituality from our work altogether.

When I asked Darrell if he had any questions about the informed-consent document, he (like most of my clients) stated that he did not. I still went over key areas, such as confidentiality and emergency contact procedures. Addressing the possibility of spiritually integrated counseling would continue in the spiritual assessment. For further examples and more detail on faith-related aspects of informed consent, see Aten and Leach (2009).

Spiritual Assessment

All Christians are not the same, so when clients indicate an interest in including faith resources in treatment, spiritual assessment should be incorporated as part of the cultural and psychological assessment. One can examine clients' cultural backgrounds in the early sessions and include religious aspects as part of the clinical conversation. Faith history, conversion story, denominational preferences, church attendance, and the presence or absence of practices such as prayer and Bible reading should be included in the assessment. The clinician must discern how healthy or unhealthy clients' views of God are (for example, is God seen in a situation as a source of grace and strength or as an angry judge?). Clients' descriptions of their church experiences along with their nonverbal presentation during such discussion can be useful to help a therapist get a sense of whether their faith communities might be a resource for better cop-

ing. Sometimes clinicians use a variety of measures to supplement session information, such as the Religious Commitment Inventory (Worthington et al., 2003) and the Theistic Spiritual Outcome Survey (Richards et al., 2005). Also important is cultivating relationships with many of the pastors in the area to have a good sense of whether they might be good consultation resources if needed. See Aten and Leach (2009) for further information on spiritual assessment.

In the case of Darrell, he was raised in the Church of God in Christ (COGIC), a predominantly African American Pentecostal church. He accepted Christ when he was twelve and described his private devotional life as sporadic as he grew up. He met his wife at college, who was also from a COGIC background. They both became more committed to their faith after they were married and had children. They used to attend church regularly and occasionally prayed together over life situations, and he would read Bible stories to the kids at bedtime. Over the last three years, however, Darrell worked long hours to get the promotion he now has. He feels distant from God and as though God is demanding and very angry with him. He believes God is angry because he has not been attending church, is not being a good father, and is not "doing well."

Grace, Spiritual Interventions, and Sharing Scripture

Christians can be vulnerable to living in the land of "should." "I should read the Bible more"; "I should pray more"; "I should do this more"; "I should do that more."

Clearly absent is a theological and practical application of grace to themselves. Consequently, when considering Christian spiritual interventions, you must apply these in an environment of grace rather than in a performance-driven context of "should." Without a grace-filled therapeutic context firmly in place, clients can consider interventions and out-of-session activities as more things on the Christian "to-do" list. Darrell was already feeling guilty, with more than a moderate underbelly of shame. He desperately needed to encounter God's grace.

Grace consists of God's unearned, unmerited favor and unconditional love poured out on us through Jesus Christ (Trotter, 1996). Grace spans Christian denominations as a construct and conveys God's acceptance of us where we are at right now even as our lives might feel like a mess. The therapist's compassion, care, conveyance of no condemnation (Rom. 8:1), and support can serve as a vehicle to implicitly convey God's love and grace. Considering grace explicitly through discussion and Scripture study allows clients to change their conceptualization of how God sees them. Darrell was receptive to such activities.

Darrell was very performance driven at his job and spiritually, so I listened empathically to these concerns and then explored with Darrell the concept of God's grace. I was wanting to generate cognitive dissonance for Darrell, as grace would undermine his pressure to perform for God and his sense that God was angry with him. Paradoxically, it might increase his spiritual practices because he would approach them out of a heart of love and thanksgiving instead of to gain God's approval. I invited Darrell to read Romans 8 each day for one week. Since Darrell was not having daily devotional times with God, it was important to make this activity achievable, hence, the small amount of Scripture. This would only take five to ten minutes of his time daily, and together we defined success in the assignment as him completing this three or more days in the week. I encouraged him to pray and ask God to show him his heart for Darrell each time before he read, and then to pause at any portion of this chapter that seemed to speak to him personally and reread it. He could jot down a note about that particular portion if he would like for us to discuss it in our next session.

From examining how I shared the Scriptures in Darrell's situation, we can identify several key learnings about using the Bible in session and creating out-of-session Scripture assignments.

1. To use the Bible to share about grace or any other important and relevant theological concept, we must know the Bible well ourselves, apply a sound hermeneutic, and have our own regular daily time of prayer and reading. This provides a base from which to draw. Sometimes a helpful starting point is a book cataloging Scripture references to various topics (e.g., Hunt, 2014).
2. We implicitly embody grace, forgiveness, and other healing concepts in the Bible through showing love, compassion, and care for the client in the session whether we are talking about God or not.

3. We explicitly explore theological concepts such as grace by tying them specifically to one or more of the client's challenges. This "theoeducation" (Garzon, 2005, p. 116) has similar principles to how we tie psychoeducation to the client's specific symptoms and situation.

4. We must make realistic out-of-session Scripture reading assignments that are small enough and reasonable in frequency to maximize the chances of the client experiencing success in doing the task (i.e., don't expect an hour's worth of reading each day of the week from a client who does not have a regular devotional time).

Christian Meditation

Darrell responded well to reading Romans 8, and part of the next session was devoted to investigating some of his insights on God's grace for his life. We also considered connections between his early upbringing and his sense of God as being angry and very demanding. Through our discussion, he realized that he had transferred some of his mother's performance pressure onto God and his spiritual life. It was premature at this time to make meaningful connections to his father due to the depth of the wound from his abandonment. Clearly, Darrell's past was significant to his anxiety and depression; however, in the early stages of treatment, providing coping skills to manage his symptoms seemed most critical.

Though deep breathing or progressive muscle relaxation might have been useful strategies, I chose to capitalize on Darrell's faith resources. I would use a version of

Christian meditation to lower his anxiety, address some of his maladaptive cognitions about God, and enhance his experience of grace. Despite Christianity's rich history with meditation, some Christians view such activities with suspicion (e.g., Bobgan & Bobgan, 1987; Hunt & McMahon, 1985). Three concerns sometimes occur: meditation is from Eastern religions and is not Christian, meditation involves guided imagery and is therefore New Age, and meditation can open up a person to demonic influence. Information about meditation in the Bible and on the history of meditation in Christianity, as well as on the features of Christian meditation mentioned, can allay these fears.

Meditation is clearly mentioned in Scripture (e.g., Josh. 1:8; Pss. 1:2; 63:6; 77:12; 119:15; 143:5). For example, the Lord admonished Joshua to meditate on his ways so that Joshua would prosper (Josh. 1:8). Psalm 119 repeatedly emphasizes meditating on God's laws, ways, works, creation, and testimonies (vv. 15, 23, 48, 78, 148). Christian meditation has been practiced since the early centuries of the church (Burton-Christie, 1993). Protestant, Catholic, and Orthodox branches of the church all have historical figures who practiced and taught Christian meditation. Some methods are relatively advanced, such as lectio divina and the *Spiritual Exercises of St. Ignatius of Loyola* (see Benner, 2010; and Garzon, 2013, for detailed descriptions of many strategies). Others are more straightforward. I will focus on an easy-to-learn strategy.

In many ways, Christian meditation is distinct from Eastern religious forms.

Unlike Eastern worldviews, the Christian worldview recognizes that God is immanent (always with us), relational, and transcendent. Therefore, we are not alone in our present-moment experience. Instead of just focusing on "emptying" oneself from various thoughts and distractions or looking at them dispassionately, Christian meditation also focuses on filling us with a deeper awareness of God through Scripture or meditation on his character.

The historical grounding and distinctive features of Christian meditation likewise impact New Age worries. (It's not new!) New Age spirituality also uses the imagination in many of its meditations, so some clients fear any forms of Christian meditation that also use the imagination. Only *some* forms of Christian meditation do this. If considering a version that includes the imagination, these concerns can be addressed in several ways. For example, we use our imagination daily without realizing it. If someone says "blue car," most people immediately picture a blue car. If a person says "blue Corvette," that picture changes if you didn't think of a Corvette originally. Someone might ask, "How many windows are in your home/apartment?" Most people would pause and mentally picture each room, counting the windows. Foster (1998) notes that Jesus utilized his listeners' imagination in his usage of parables, and the psalmists frequently applied the imagination in the Psalms (Ps. 23, for example). Nevertheless, "the imagination, like all our faculties, has participated in the Fall. But just as we can believe that God can take our reason (fallen as it is) and sanctify it and use it for his

good purposes, so we believe he can sanctify the imagination and use it for his good purposes" (pp. 25–26).

Thus, we can yield our imagination, as we can our reasoning, for the good purposes of God.

When clients have worries about exposing themselves to demonic influence through meditation, these anxieties can often be allayed by discussing our authority in Christ and suggesting prayer for protection to begin the meditation (see Anderson, 2000, 2013, for more on our authority in Christ). A simple prayer like, "Lord, we ask for your hedge of protection around us," often suffices. Of course, if clients continue to have apprehensions after providing the above information, these should be respected and alternative interventions be done.

As I discussed Christian meditation with Darrell, he initially voiced anxiety about Eastern forms of meditation and the idea that he would be exposed to the demonic. He responded well to my clarifications about meditation's history in Christianity, its differences from Eastern meditation, our authority in Christ, and the ability to open any meditation with prayer for protection. Given his initial fears, I proposed a basic form of Christian meditation that did not involve the imagination, scriptural truth meditation. Scriptural truth meditation has two forms that are clearly supported in the Bible. One form emphasizes meditating on small portions of Scripture and the other on God's character. I give clients a handout that includes the instructions below (adapted from Garzon, 2013).

Scriptural truth meditation. I used scriptural truth meditation with Darrell. To introduce the technique I said, "Scriptural truth mediation helps us pause and quiet ourselves to reflect on a meaningful truth from Scripture. It is useful when we feel stressed, hurried, anxious, or frustrated. To do this effectively, you must not have your smartphone, computer, radio, television, or any other distracting technology around. Get in a comfortable position. Sometimes sitting in a chair with your feet on the floor and your hands in your lap accomplishes this. Pause and ask the Lord to prepare your heart to be open to his truth more deeply."

The following steps are the ones I walked Darrell through next.

1. Ask the client to select a verse or verse phrase that is comforting and meaningful. See the samples below. Simply guide the client through this process. Feel free to contribute other verses that are encouraging as well. Assist the client in finding additional verses if you like.

   Psalm 23:1: "The LORD is my shepherd."

   Psalm 37:7: "Be still before the LORD and wait patiently for him."

   Proverbs 3:5: "Trust in the LORD with all your heart."

   Matthew 11:28: "'Come to me, all you who are weary and burdened, and I will give you rest.'"

   Romans 8:1: "Therefore, there is now no condemnation for those who are in Christ Jesus."

   Philippians 4:13: "I can do all things through Christ who strengthens me" (NKJV).

   1 John 1:9: "If we confess our sins, he is faithful and just and will forgive us our sins."

   1 John 4:8: "God is love."

2. Encourage the client to get comfortable in a sitting position.

3. To prevent the client from becoming distracted, request that he close his eyes or find a spot in the room to focus on.

4. Once the client is positioned to relax, lead the client in a brief breathing exercise. For example, "Breathe in deeply and breathe out, repeating the scriptural phrase."

5. The client is to repeat this step several times.

6. Next, tell the client: "*Quietly ponder the passage, reflecting on its meaning and how it connects to your life now.*"

7. To anticipate the likelihood that the client will become distracted, say, "*Eventually your mind will wander. This is perfectly normal. It's what our brains naturally do, so you do not need to berate yourself.*"

8. Add, "*When this occurs, gently return to the Scripture again and again.*" (Often people receive benefit with only ten to fifteen minutes of meditation.) "Afterward, you may like to write down some of your thoughts. I would be glad to hear about them in our next session if you would find that beneficial."

Stress break. Write down the verse on an index card or load it into your smartphone. When you feel stressed during the day, take out the verse, look at it, take a deep breath, and quietly repeat it in your mind or out loud one to three times. Then return to what you were doing.

Rehearsing any Christian intervention during a session is useful. Darrell and I started with prayer and did scriptural truth meditation for five minutes. He chose a verse of his own that wasn't on the original list, "My grace is sufficient for you" (2 Cor. 12:9). After the experience, he said that he felt relaxed and more aware of God's presence. He was very open to continuing to use Christian meditation, so we set a goal of four times per week with stress breaks as needed daily.

Scripture Study and Memorization

Scripture meditation naturally goes along with Bible study and Scripture memorization; however, clients have busy lives, so use creativity to help cultivate a regular time of Bible study and prayer when it is not already a part of a client's life. Even though Darrell wanted to build his relationship with God, his new position presented challenges for him in carving out a solid portion of his day for a private devotional time. Accordingly, we brainstormed some options. Darrell had a forty-five-minute drive to work each day, so we agreed that this would be a perfect time for listening to Scripture using audio Bible MP3s.

During some sessions, we also used Scripture in the cognitive restructuring of Darrell's faculty core beliefs. Darrell would put the most meaningful Bible verse used in his smartphone so he could view it during the week and memorize it. He also put it on a sticky note that he placed on the

mirror of his bathroom so he could look at it and be reminded of God's love and presence while he was shaving. When he was in situations where a core belief got triggered in public, Darrell would act like he was receiving a text that just came in and bring up the Scripture on his smartphone for support and strength. Through the sticky notes and smartphone strategies, he memorized the verse over time so that he could recite it mentally whenever he needed it.

Darrell also discovered ways to involve his wife. She was reading a weekly devotional that had short daily readings, so he agreed to start reading and discussing those with her in the evening before they went to bed. This activity served a dual purpose of building him up spiritually and increasing his time with his wife. After three weeks of listening to the Bible in his car, memorizing Scripture to counteract maladaptive core beliefs, and having daily devotional time with his wife, Darrell said he was feeling stronger spiritually and closer to his wife. In a marital consultation, she confirmed seeing positive changes in Darrell and noted feeling closer to him as well.

Darrell's experience highlights several principles that are useful in incorporating Bible study and Scripture memorization in therapy with "busy" clients:

1. Be creative. There are lots of ways to incorporate Scripture reading (or hearing) into a client's day even when it appears busy. The next steps help you get started in figuring these out.
2. Assess the client's daily routine. Look for natural downtimes in her day. If a

client drives, takes the subway, rides an exercise bike, or has some other free thinking time, determine whether hearing the Bible or reading it is an option to add to the activity.

3. Use technology and simple props. The smartphone can be a very helpful device for clients to input Bible verses and review. Some software applications are also available that will send a daily verse to the client (e.g., the free You-Version Bible app).

4. Involve spouses and family members when appropriate. Having a married couple do devotionals together can enhance intimacy as well as benefit the client spiritually. The inclusion of another person also increases the likelihood that the activity will take place, much like exercising regularly with a friend increases the likelihood that exercise will be done consistently.

Worship

Whereas Bible study and Scripture memorization are commonly utilized in pastoral care and sometimes in professional Christian counseling, research suggests that mental health professionals seldom recommend worship as a practice for their clients (Ball & Goodyear, 1991; Jones, Watson, & Wolfram, 1992). Indeed, I did not find a chapter on worship or substantial discussion of the topic in any of the professional Christian counseling texts researched for this chapter! The Bible emphasizes that worship requires a sincere heart attitude of love toward God and a desire to walk in his holiness (Pss. 96:9; 103:1; John 4:23–24) combined with a

corresponding action or behavior to reflect those attitudes, such as singing, praise, thanksgiving, or making music (Pss. 96:1; 100:1–4; 150:1–6; 1 Thess. 5:18). Silent adoration can also occur (Ps. 46:10). Worship can take place privately or publicly in community (Eph. 5:19–20; Heb. 10:25). Foster (1998) notes that in public worship we "experience Reality . . . the resurrected Christ in the midst of a gathered community" (p. 158). Denominations have substantial variability in expressions of this practice. Perhaps this variability accounts for some of the reluctance therapists have in exploring worship as an intervention in therapy, although an additional factor may be on therapists' minds too.

This other concern focuses on the potential for role boundary confusion (Richards & Bergin, 2005). Therapists might feel that clients could start looking at them as some sort of "spiritual guru" or pastor instead of a counselor. Such confusion could lead the client to heavily rely on the counselor instead of a pastor and church community for spiritual guidance.

Nevertheless, even with this potential pitfall, encouraging worship represents a powerful addition to treatment when appropriate safeguards are put in place. Safeguards include assessing client practices to ensure recommendations fit the client's comfort zone, following up with the client on any recommended practices to see how they were experienced, monitoring for any role confusion in the client's verbal and nonverbal behavior toward the clinician, and addressing such confusion if it occurs.

I asked Darrell about his worship experiences when he was more active in his faith, and he described the songs, music, and praise in his COGIC services. He acknowledged that he had never practiced worshiping privately in his past individual devotional times, partly because he wasn't sure what that would look like. Consequently, we discussed a variety of practices Darrell could do privately, such as thanking God in prayer for the things he was grateful for, reading selected psalms out loud, and singing worship songs from his church or those he liked on Christian radio. Darrell decided that he could listen to Christian music instead of secular music while he drove to work. He might even sing along with it. This was a good start. Over time Darrell became more open to returning to church services and a small group Bible study. The worship embedded in these Christian community events contributed to Darrell's growing relationship with the Lord.

Solitude and Silence

If clinicians neglect worship as an intervention in counseling, solitude and silence represent additional seldom prescribed practices not only for them, but perhaps for most evangelical Christians in general (Barbour, 2004). The hectic pace and constant noise of modern life choke out God's quiet invitation to meet him in these ways, so we must be intentional if we are to practice them. These spiritual disciplines represent a primary "formative place" for the Holy Spirit's work (Calhoun, 2005, p. 113). Here the Lord prunes away "the forces of society that will otherwise relentlessly mold us" (Ortberg, 2002, p. 84). Indeed, solitude and silence

fit with the Lord's declaration through the psalmist to "be still, and know that I am God" (Ps. 46:10) and Paul's admonition in Romans 12:1–2 not to conform to this world. The practices denote a voluntary separation from all relationships (both face-to-face and social media) and external distractions to cultivate an attitude of "inward attentiveness" to what God is doing in one's life (Foster, 1998, p. 96). Ideally, a person practices solitude and silence away from typical settings like home and work in a place without distractions, such as a retreat center. For Darrell, creativity would again have to be in order.

I considered Darrell's diagnostic features before even discussing this intervention. Darrell had a clear abandonment wound from his father, but his mother was a faithful, consistent, and supportive figure in his life. He showed no features of post-traumatic stress disorder (PTSD) or borderline personality disorder (having high sensitivity and reactivity to feeling alone). Borderlines are not good candidates for solitude and silence! Darrell also had good coping skills for any potential anxiety moments due to the Christian meditation and CBT exercises I had trained him in previously.

As we did with worship, we seized upon Darrell's one guaranteed time alone—his commutes to and from work—to start the process. I suggested that during one week Darrell try an experiment and do one round trip with no distractions—no radio or smartphone on. We would then evaluate what happened at our next session. Darrell was encouraged to pray as he got in the car and welcome the Lord's presence before he drove off. I also clarified that people encounter different things. He may not feel anything. He may have a sense of God's presence. He may get anxious. He may feel something else. God could respond in many different ways, so Darrell would need to trust that God was there with him and just be attentive to his presence while he drove. If he had any distress, he could stop the experiment at any time.

When Darrell returned, he said that driving with no Scripture or radio music felt strange on his trip to work. He got in touch with some mild anxiety, which surprised him. He wanted to speak with God about it, but he remembered he was supposed to be silent, so he just trusted instead as he drove. He commented, "It was weird. I almost felt like I was praying without words. I felt a deep sense of trusting God even though I had this anxiety. I knew God was doing something." He got distracted sometimes in busy traffic, which I assured him was normal. Given his experience, we included solitude and silence as an option of things to do during his commute time.

Forgiveness

Spiritual disciplines such as meditation, Bible study, worship, and solitude inevitably lead one to encounter the Lord's great love and the theme of forgiveness. Sometimes, however, misconceptions about forgiveness must be addressed before a client is ready to consider it (Enright & Fitzgibbons, 2014). For example, forgiveness does not equal reconciliation. A woman who has been physically abused by her spouse does not have to return for further abuse because she has forgiven him. Forgiveness involves only the client. Reconciliation involves the repentance (with clear fruit) of the offender and the slow rebuilding of trust over time. Some clinicians believe forgiveness is a defense against anger. Counseling models of forgiveness clearly contradict this (see below). Enright and Fitzgibbons (2014) note that forgiveness isn't condoning, excusing, or tolerating harmful behavior. It involves fully recognizing that one has been sinned against (or unfairly treated in a secular perspective) and making the choice to willingly relinquish resentment and revengeful responses toward the offender, choosing instead to respond with compassion and love.

Over time Darrell and I explored his relationship with his father. Darrell said that he had forgiven his father for the substance abuse and abandoning the family, but I saw a lot of tension in his posture and limited eye contact whenever we discussed him. When I asked what led Darrell to forgive his father, he said that it was something he knew he needed to do as a Christian. I noted that even though we might decide to forgive someone because it is something we should do as Christians, we can still be left with a heart full of emotions that we feel shouldn't be there, such as anger, hurt, and bitterness. Darrell agreed. I suggested that perhaps there were some things we could do in therapy to help his heart catch up with his decision to forgive.

Two empirically supported counseling models of forgiveness exist: Everett Worthington (2009, 2013—see chapter 26 for greater detail of his model) and

Robert Enright (2001, Enright & Fitzgibbons, 2014). Both are very helpful to learn. Materials written for both secular and Christian audiences are available.

I chose Enright's (2001; Enright & Fitzgibbons, 2014) model to use with Darrell. Enright's model involves four phases to attain emotional forgiveness. These phases are not necessarily linear. A client can work through a phase, go to the next, and then return to the previous phase as new material emerges if necessary. Each phase involves a series of questions, journaling, and structured exercises, and the phases are flexible enough for the clinician to incorporate a wide variety of therapeutic techniques. They include the uncovering phase, the decision phase, the working phase, and the deepening phase.

Phase 1: Uncovering phase. In this phase, help the client to identify the defenses being used to deal with the hurt (like denial, repression, minimization, etc.) and to determine whether those defenses are working to create happiness, a fulfilled life, and a sense of having moved on from the injury. Usually the answer is no. Exploration of the underlying negative emotions then ensues. Anger, shame, and rumination about the offender are key emotions this phase addresses. The eventual goal is to process and release these negative emotions.

Here is a sample journal exercise from Enright (2001, pp. 93–101). The client reads psychoeducational information about common defense mechanisms, such as denial, suppression, repression, displacement, regression, and identification with the aggressor. A series of questions invites the client to consider which defense(s) he currently uses and the consequences of those. For example, "Does your defense mechanism actually hurt you? Are others adversely affected by what you do?" The client makes a list of the ways the defense mechanism hurts him and also hurts others. Our exploration in therapy and the exercises helped Darrell recognize just how much rumination he was doing over the anger and shame he had in connection with his father. Slowly in the therapeutic work these started to lessen.

Phase 2: The decision phase. This is where the client recognizes the problems with previous defenses, realizes that they are not working, and decides to forgive as a way of further releasing these feelings and moving on. A sample exercise involves the client listing the attempted solutions she has used to try to deal with the offense and rating how effective those solutions have been on a 1–10 scale. Here, in the case of Darrell, we have an example of the nonlinear nature of Enright's model. As stated previously, he had already decided to forgive prior to therapy, but he had to start at phase 1 instead of 2 because he needed to recognize the defenses he was using and the levels of anger, shame, and rumination that were in his heart. Even though Darrell had stated that he had already decided to forgive his father, starting at phase 3 would have been a mistake.

Phase 3: The working phase. In this phase, the client reframes the incident, exploring the larger context in terms of the offender and situation. Questions help the client understand the person more in depth (e.g., how stressful were her life circumstances at the time of the offense? Was she abused as a child? Did addictions impact her thinking?). At this point, assist the client in cultivating compassion, sometimes through Gestalt techniques such as the empty chair. However, this must be done carefully, especially in situations of past abuse. A good sign is when the client shifts from condemning the person globally to condemning the person's *actions*. Along with the judgment of behaviors, she begins to see the individual as more complex than just all "bad." When empathy is clear, the client has the ability to "step inside the other person's shoes." A highly useful technique to do this is the well-known empty chair technique (see page 20), or what I prefer to call "chairwork." Though chairwork may have been done in phase 1 to encourage processing anger, shame, and the like, here the purpose is to get a sense of what the offender is like "inside," his weaknesses, frailties, and so forth. Such work should be done cautiously and in small amounts initially. When well timed, it can dramatically increase empathy.

Darrell considered his father's upbringing in an abusive home, early poverty, his unemployment at the time of his departure, and the impact his addictions had on his thought process when he left. Sometimes we would go back to phase 1 to process further anger when it emerged. We also did Christian inner healing prayer in the processing (see below). When Darrell had developed some genuine empathy for his father, I placed an empty chair in front of him and asked him to imagine his father sitting there. I invited him to briefly

sit in the chair to get a sense of what his father might be feeling inside a year after he left the family. I chose this time instead of during the family struggles because I wasn't sure what Darrell might sense. Could he get underneath his dad's frustration in the family so that he wouldn't just feel that his dad was blaming his mother and him? Darrell sat down in the chair, with me watching his nonverbals closely. "He's so alone inside, like he doesn't have anyone in the world . . . so much pain from his own abuse . . . a deep sense of despair at not knowing how to handle his family. He panicked. That's why he left. . . . And now he drowns his guilt for leaving and his own pain [in alcohol and drugs]." When I asked Darrell to return to his seat, he commented on how much more he understood his father now.

Phase 4: The deepening phase. The client examines the larger role of suffering in life (Thomas & Habermas, 2011). He starts to realize that he is not as alone in suffering as he might have thought (i.e., others have experienced traumas and abandonment too, so they can potentially identify with his experience and be a support). He starts to recognize his own need for forgiveness from others, and he considers that God may be using this pain to lead him to a higher calling. This phase often interweaves with phase 3 and takes place both in session through well-timed questions and outside of sessions through journaling homework exercises. Sometimes the client brings up these aspects spontaneously.

The main pitfall to watch for in both phases 3 and 4 is the danger of spiritual bypass (Cashwell, Bentley, & Yarborough, 2007). In spiritual bypass, the client over-spiritualizes the hurtful experience to avoid the "unfinished business" related to the emotional pain of it. As long as the client has meaningfully worked through phase 1, the danger of spiritual bypass is low. When it does occur, you can help the client do further emotional processing using phase 1 strategies. Darrell appeared ready for phase 4.

Darrell could recognize his own need for forgiveness, and he started connecting with online support groups for adults who were abandoned by their fathers. He also sensed a higher calling on his life. He realized that his life was not just about fulfilling a vow he had made to his mother. Darrell also had a call to be the emotionally supportive father to his children that he had never had when growing up. "Oh my God," he cried as he realized this, "I haven't left the family financially, but I have left them emotionally, just like Dad left me!"

Darrell now had great motivation to cut down his hours at work and spend more time with his wife and kids. Indeed, he even started developing a heart for the children in his neighborhood who did not have a father. His work in traditional CBT on his cognitions regarding anxiety at work and financial success versus emotional support of his family dovetailed perfectly into these powerful realizations.

Throughout the phases, prayer and Bible reading helped empower Darrell to do the work. He leaned on grace to look at the painful emotions in his heart in phase 1. He asked God to give him understanding of his father in phase 3 and even prayed for his father ("if he's still alive") in that phase. In phase 4, in addition to seeking help from God at his new position, he was now asking for the strength to be a better husband and father. He also was praying about how to help the fatherless kids in the neighborhood. Another form of prayer, specifically Christian inner healing prayer, was particularly helpful for Darrell when he was dealing with a lot of anger at his father in phase 1.

Christian Inner Healing Prayer

Christian inner healing prayer (CHP) seeks to facilitate a client's ability to emotionally process painful memories by vividly recalling these memories and asking for the Lord Jesus (or God) to minister into this place of pain (Garzon & Burkett, 2002). A wide variety of models exist, and some developers dislike the term *inner healing prayer* for conceptual or theological reasons. The term is used here because of its predominant presence in the literature on these approaches and the general familiarity of the term within some Christian circles. Models of CHP normally have training programs, and more are encouraging meaningful hours of practice under the supervision of someone well trained in the approach. As a researcher of CHP models (e.g., Garzon, Worthington, Tan, & Worthington, 2009), I've noticed a typical pattern for new models. Initially there is a wave of enthusiasm for the approach, followed by theological critique from seminary academia and clinical critique from Christian therapists. These criticisms then normally lead model developers over time to a healthy sharpening of the theological aspects of their approach and increased safeguards in their training requirements to reduce the risk of iatrogenic injury.

The model I used with Darrell was based on the Immanuel approach (Lehman, 2016; see http://www.immanuelapproach.com/ for a variety of resources). This model was developed by psychiatrist Karl Lehman and has influences from attachment theory, eye movement desensitization and reprocessing (EMDR) therapy, and neuroscience. Some of the positives of using this prayer model are that it starts with a positive memory at the beginning, it is nondirective, and it ends either at the peaceful resolution of whatever memories have emerged or the positive memory place created at the beginning; consequently, the client leaves the session in a stable condition. This model also includes a variety of neuroscientifically based coping skills and encourages the cultivation of healthy relationships in the church (Wilder, Khouri, Coursey, & Sutton, 2013); thus, it is more than just a prayer form.

As noted above, Immanuel prayer starts with thanksgiving and the client thinking of a positive memory of something he is grateful for (e.g., the birth of a child, the client's wedding, a deeply meaningful spiritual experience). The client closes his eyes and pictures the scene. The client then prays (at your encouragement) and asks to sense the Lord's presence in the event more fully. The client becomes attentive to any changes in what he sees, feels, and hears in the memory as well as any new thoughts or realizations in it. A wide variety of experiences can occur. When changes lead

to a deeper sense of connection with the Lord, invite the client to ask the Lord for further direction as to anything he would like the client to work on today. The client then follows to that memory. Often this is a painful memory. As with the positive memory, encourage the client to ask the Lord to reveal his presence more fully in this memory. The client again attends to any changes in what he sees, senses, or hears, or any new thoughts or realizations. As these changes take place, a follow-up question is sometimes asked about what the Lord wants the client to know in this situation. For example, sometimes a client will sense the Lord telling him that it wasn't his fault that an abusive situation occurred. When there is a sense of peace and resolution in the memory, the session ends. If more work is needed in the memory processing but time is running out, the clinician invites the client to return to the positive memory where the session started to ensure the client ends at an emotionally positive place and to make sure the client is grounded in the here and now as the session ends. Thus, the approach can take place over a series of sessions when needed.

Complexities can arise in doing the Immanuel approach, so in-depth training is important (see "Additional Thoughts on CHP" on page 195). What follows below in my work with Darrell should not be construed as sufficient information to try the model but rather an introduction to the Immanuel approach CHP type of intervention.

As Darrell shared early in therapy about painful memories of his father's alcohol and drug addiction, along with his father's eventual abandonment of the family, I pondered whether the Immanuel approach might be a useful intervention for him. After Darrell had some clear coping strategies for stress, such as Christian meditation, and had made some progress on his cognitive restructuring, we began processing phase 1 (uncovering) of Enright's forgiveness model. At this point, I introduced the Immanuel approach as a possibility. Darrell checked out Dr. Lehman's website, which included some videos of this approach, and voiced his interest in trying it. I made it clear that this approach did not have any empirical research currently, that processing memories can be emotionally painful, and that alternative secular treatments were available. However, Darrell liked the idea of using his relationship with God to help him deal with his painful history. A separate written informed consent for this intervention tailored after Hunter and Yarhouse's (2009) recommendations was signed.

The first Immanuel session. We met for an hour and a half for the first Immanuel session because it's important to leave time for processing the prayer intervention at the end. Even when the strategy appears very positive, do not assume clients do not have any questions or that they are comfortable feeling the sometimes powerful emotions. It's better to ask them what the prayer was like for them and if there were any aspects that were difficult. Processing any concerns assures that clients have enough information to decide whether more CHP should be considered in future sessions.

As this approach begins at a positive place, we opened in prayer with Darrell expressing thanksgiving to God for the many blessings in his life. He thanked God for his wife, children, new job, a home, food on the table, a good church, friends, and good health. I then asked Darrell to think of a positive memory. It could be current, a few years ago, childhood, whatever he liked, as long as it filled him with joy and happiness.

Darrell chose the birth of his first child. He kept his eyes closed and described the scene of seeing the delivery and his joy at holding his daughter for the first time. *"We know the Lord was with you in this moment of holding your child because he promises to be with us always. Lord, show Darrell more clearly where you were in this experience he is remembering. Darrell, just notice if anything different occurs in the memory."*

Darrell paused, *"I see Jesus smiling. He has his arm around me, and he's looking at my daughter too. He looks back and forth from my daughter to me with such love and joy. It's incredibly reassuring that he's here. I feel so happy."*

I let Darrell enjoy this scene and encouraged him to keep sharing with Jesus how he was feeling in the memory scene. Darrell conversed with the Lord, giving thanks for the birth of his daughter. When I sensed the timing was right, I interjected, "Darrell, ask the Lord if there's anywhere [memory] he'd like you to go to do some work today."

Darrell did this and drifted to the scene of his father storming out of the house for the last time. Darrell described that his mother and father had been arguing, and as his father walked out the door, he yelled, "Goodbye!" glaring at his mother and then "Goodbye!" glaring at Darrell. Both Darrell and his mother started crying when he slammed the door. Tears were streaming down Darrell's face now.

"Darrell, ask the Lord where he was in this scene, to help you know he was present. Look for Jesus in whatever way he chooses to reveal himself here." Darrell again had the sense of the Lord right beside him, putting his arm around him. After he felt this comfort for a time, I encouraged Darrell to ask the Lord what he wanted Darrell to know.

"The Lord says it wasn't my fault. I was just being a little boy, and my father didn't know how to be a father. I didn't cause this. That feels so reassuring."

I encouraged Darrell to keep dialoging with the Lord and asking the Lord any questions he had about the memory. The Lord explained about his mother and father's free will and their level of brokenness (in ways Darrell could never hear from me if I had said the same thing in session in regular dialogue). He reassured Darrell that he was with him and would take care of him and his mother. Somewhere in the midst of this holy conversation, Darrell's tears turned from sadness to peaceful reassurance.

As we approached twenty minutes left in the session, I asked Darrell how he was feeling in this memory with the Lord. "I feel peaceful. Like it's going to be okay. My mother and I will be all right." I invited Darrell to end the time with the Lord with some thanksgiving and then to return to the room, opening his eyes when he was ready. We then explored what the process was like for Darrell, how he conceptualized the experience, and any concerns he had. Darrell had no concerns and expressed interest in keeping Immanuel prayer as a component of his treatment.

Additional thoughts on CHP. Darrell's diagnostic features made this a straightforward example of Immanuel prayer. Some clients are very open to CHP while other clients are more cautious, so assessment, information about the prayer form, and respect for client preferences are paramount. Diagnostic features are critical too. Clients with PTSD, complex PTSD, dissociative features, substance abuse, and other conditions need comprehensive care and careful timing for any interventions like CHP. In regard to the technique itself, the clinician must be careful to be nondirective in the memory processing so as not to risk implanting false memories, and the experiences of the Lord must always align with what Scripture describes as reflective of his character. These are other reasons why this is merely an introduction to CHP in this chapter. The more training clinicians have in trauma treatment and CHP models like the Immanuel approach, the more options they have in providing care for their clients.

CONCLUSION

God is infinite, so the ways he can lead us to use the Bible and his immanent presence with us in therapy are equally infinite. This chapter has merely introduced the broad subject of interventions based on a biblical worldview. The reader is encouraged to use the recommended readings below as resources for additional information.

Clearly, spiritual interventions add dramatically to traditional secular therapies. Through Christ-centered interventions in a CBT therapy context, Darrell did more than just decrease his anxiety and adjust to his new job. He now had spiritual fruit of eternal value as well. He forgave his father, became a better husband, learned to connect emotionally with his family, and developed a deeper sense of calling on his life. Darrell was more in love with his Lord than he had ever been before, and I was more amazed at God's grace and power. This is the impact of the gospel in therapeutic action. This is the value of spiritual strategies in professional counseling.

RECOMMENDED READING

Appleby, D., & Ohlschlager, G. (2013). *Transformative encounters: The intervention of God in Christian counseling and pastoral care*. Downers Grove, IL: InterVarsity.

Aten, J. D., & Leach, M. M. (2009). *Spirituality and the therapeutic process: A comprehensive resource from intake to termination*. Washington, DC: American Psychological Association.

Foster, R. J. (1998). *Celebration of discipline: The path to spiritual growth* (25th anniversary ed.). San Francisco, CA: HarperCollins.

Foster, R. J. (2002). *Prayer: Finding the heart's true home*. San Francisco, CA: HarperCollins.

Garzon, F. L. (2013). Christian devotional meditation for anxiety. In E. L. Worthington, Jr., E. L., Johnson, J. N. Hook, & J. D. Aten (Eds.), *Evidence-based practices for Christian counseling and psychotherapy* (pp. 59–76). Downers Grove, IL: IVP Academic.

Garzon, F., & Burkett, L. (2002). Healing of memories: Models, research, future directions. *Journal of Psychology and Christianity, 21*(2), 42–49.

Johnson, E. (2017). *God in soul care: The therapeutic resources in the Christian faith*. Downers Grove, IL: InterVarsity.

Lehman, K. (2016). *The Immanuel approach for emotional healing and for life*. Chicago, IL: Immanuel.

Tan, S.-Y. (2003). Integrating spiritual direction into psychotherapy: Ethical issues and guidelines. *Journal of Psychology and Theology, 31*, 14–23.

Tan, S. Y. (2011a). *Counseling and psychotherapy: A Christian perspective*. Grand Rapids, MI: Baker Academic.

Thomas, J., & Habermas, G. (2011). *Enduring your season of suffering*. Lynchburg, VA: Liberty University Press.

Willard, D. (1998). *The divine conspiracy*. San Francisco, CA: Harper.

CHAPTER 10

Christian Formation of the Self Strategies

Ian F. Jones, PhD, PhD

> Put off, concerning your former conduct, the old man which grows corrupt according to the deceitful lusts, and be renewed in the spirit of your mind, and . . . put on the new man which was created according to God, in true righteousness and holiness.
>
> **EPHESIANS 4:22–24 NKJV**

Who am I? Why am I here? What is my purpose in life? These are some of the most basic questions we ask ourselves. But these are not new questions. Written on the wall of the ancient Greek temple at Delphi were the words "Know thyself." While the ancient world usually connected awareness of self with the supernatural, the modern view could be summed up in the words of Alexander Pope published in 1733–34: "Know then thyself, presume not God to scan, / The proper study of mankind is Man" (cited in Seabury, 1900, p. 28). But is it possible to truly know yourself without knowing God? Franz Delitzsch (1899, pp. 72–73) said, "Man cannot be estimated psychologically, except as we know something of the position in the world assigned to him by God the Creator." We cannot fully know ourselves outside of an awareness of and relationship with God,

and this understanding is essential to effective Christian counseling.

In this chapter, we will examine some views of the self from biblical, historical, and contemporary perspectives to gain a better understanding of the importance of having a solid biblical view of human nature and development in Christian counseling. We will explore the effect of these views in the counseling context and look at ways that we can provide effective biblical counsel in addressing soul growth and self-awareness.

THEOLOGY AND PSYCHOLOGY OF THE SELF

Views of the Self and Human Nature

A biblical view of the self. Humans were created bearing the image (*selem*) and likeness (*dᵉmût*) of God (Gen. 1:26–27).

197

After forming man, God "breathed into his nostrils the breath of life; and man became a living being (*nepeš*)" (Gen. 2:7 NASB). The breath of God assures life, while its absence means death (e.g., Job 34:14–15; Ps 104:29). Hebrew thought does not envision life apart from the body (Job 19:26–27).

We also possess a "spirit" (*rûaḥ*), which has its source in God (e.g., Job 33:4; 34:14–15; Zech. 12:1). Unlike the *nepeš*, the *rûaḥ* is not bound up with the body or blood and parallels the mind or inner person (e.g., Ps. 77:6 [7]). It expresses the inner psychic emotions of the individual (e.g., Gen. 41:8; Judg. 8:3; 1 Kings 21:5). In Leviticus, the Bible speaks of our "inner self" or soul (נֶפֶשׁ, *nepeš*) (cf. Deut. 4:9; 11:18; 13:3; 28:65; 30:6, 10; Job 7:11). Leviticus 26:15–16 says, "If, instead, you reject My statutes, and if your soul (נַפְשְׁכֶם, *nepeš*) abhors My ordinances so as not to carry out all My commandments, and so break My covenant . . . I will appoint over you a sudden terror" (NASB). And verse 43 says, "'For the land will be abandoned by them, and will make up for its sabbaths while it is made desolate without them. They, meanwhile, will be making amends for their iniquity, because they rejected My ordinances and their soul (*nepeš*) abhorred My statutes'" (NASB). Additionally, Job 14:22 has, "But his flesh will be in pain over it, and his soul (וְנַפְשׁוֹ) will mourn over it" (NKJV).

Nephesh can have a wide range of meanings (Mounce, 2006, p. 670). The Hebrew concept sees the person as a whole, body and soul, including natural and emotional desires. The three passages in question certainly incorporate the inner self or personal aspect of the soul, with Job 14:22 referencing both the physical and inner soul dimensions. For additional support on the Job passage see Alden (1993): "14:22 'Body' and 'soul' (which the NIV renders as 'self') constitute the entirety of a person who suffers—physical pain and mental anguish. It is a sad and sour note for Job to end on, but the book is not over." In the words of J. I. Packer (1993): "Each human . . . consists of a material body animated by an immaterial personal self. Scripture calls this self a 'soul' or 'spirit.' 'Soul' emphasizes the distinctness of a person's conscious selfhood as such; 'spirit' carries the nuances of the self's derivation from God, dependence on him, and distinctness from the body as such" (p. 74).

Unlike other creatures, humans bear qualities and attributes that are unique, including reflecting the image of God, having the ability to communicate with God (Gen. 3:8–19), and being tasked with responsibility for his creation (Gen. 2:15). The psalmist spoke of the uniqueness of our creation: "For you created my inmost being; you knit me together in my mother's womb. I praise you because I am fearfully and wonderfully made" (Ps. 139:13–14). The words "knit together" indicate intentional creation but also imply providing protection. All people have extreme value in the eyes of God.

At our core, we are social beings created with a need for spiritual relationship with God and social relationship with others. God's call on our lives is to know him and his word (Deut. 11:18). The total commitment of the heart and soul or mind

(Heb., *nepeš*) indicates an intentional attitude and action designed to produce obedience to God and primacy on his word.

The self has freedom of choice. God has given us freedom to choose our own way. The presence of the Tree of the Knowledge of Good and Evil in the garden allowed for the free exercise of will, and the consequences of violating the will of God were clearly spelled out. The tree may also represent wisdom and knowledge that could have been attained free of sin and personal experience if Adam and Eve had remained true to God. A full self-understanding comes only through knowing God our Creator in a renewed relationship with him. Life has meaning and purpose, and knowing God affects our self-understanding and relationship to others in all aspects of life. But we have a problem: sin.

The self is fallen and sinful (Gen. 3). When Satan lied and distorted God's word, he cast doubt on God's goodness and led Adam and Eve into a state of rebellion with him. The image of God was now distorted; we are all fallen and suffer the effects of sin, evil, and the curse. Sin permeates, pollutes, and corrupts our lives (physical, spiritual, cognitive, emotional, relational, and behavioral)—all we are and do is damaged by sin (Rom. 3:10–18). Even our world is cursed (Gen. 3:17). Sin leads to suffering, either directly (through active wrongdoing) or indirectly (through victimization or the sins of others).

The fall led to the elevation of the self, a focus on self-interest, and a self-will that resulted in a predisposition to be "inconsiderate of others" and "arrogantly assert-

ing" of our own will (Titus 1:7; 2 Peter 2:10) (Vine, 1989, p. 1024). Self-will sets aside God's will and leads us to "do something arbitrarily without divine permission; to act on one's own decision rather than considering the needs of others and the purpose of God" (Wyrick, 2003, p. 1461). People outside of Christ risk idolatry, elevating themselves at the expense of others: "There will be terrible times in the last days. People will be lovers of themselves, lovers of money, boastful, proud, abusive, disobedient to their parents, ungrateful, unholy, without love, unforgiving, slanderous, without self-control, brutal, not lovers of the good, treacherous, rash, conceited, lovers of pleasure rather than lovers of God—having a form of godliness but denying its power. Have nothing to do with such people" (2 Tim. 3:1–5).

Variations of this view, which actually affirm the value of self-interest, are found in the secular models of human nature, which view man as making choices based on personal desires, as man is considered the originator and god of his own life (Erb & Hooker, 1971). In contrast, Christians have a new nature, which allows them to recognize their worth and self-esteem, but only through the sufficiency of Christ (2 Cor. 3:5). This alternative perspective leads a person toward love and service to others (Phil. 2:3–11).

Menninger (1973) noted that while the use of the word *sin* was prevalent in early church writing and throughout Scripture, it is largely missing in today's society and has become a taboo word. The effect of this cultural change has been to reduce individual moral responsibility. Where previously a person was held accountable for bad or evil behavior, now the blame is likely to be placed on parental child-rearing practices, or sinful behavior is redefined as a sickness and a medical or biological problem requiring the intervention of professional specialists. In contrast, a biblical understanding of sin is essential to effective Christian counseling.

McMinn (2008) argues that Christian counseling, unlike secular counseling, has a third, essential building block for empathy. In addition to active listening skills and a belief in human dignity, biblical counseling adds an understanding of the weight of sin: "Grace cannot be understood without understanding the extent of our sin, and we must have the hope of grace in order to look honestly at the depth of our sin" (p. 18). Understanding one's own sin allows a Christian counselor to communicate with a client in a true spirit of empathetic forgiveness: "The honest language of sin prepares us to see our infinite value in the arms of God, to breathe in the fragrance of life-giving love, and then to offer that love lavishingly to ourselves and others" (p. 48).

The self has capacity to self-regulate. The Bible says redemption in Christ leads to a transformed life and an ability to exercise self-control or self-discipline (Acts 24:25; 1 Cor. 7:9; 9:25; Gal. 5:23; 1 Thess. 5:6; 2 Tim. 1:7; 2:15). Such transformation involves being able to put aside our old self, crucified with Christ, "so that the body ruled by sin might be done away with, that we should no longer be slaves to sin" (Rom. 6:6). "Put off your old self, which is being corrupted by its deceitful desires . . . and . . .

put on the new self, created to be like God in true righteousness and holiness" (Eph. 4:22, 24; cf. Col. 3:9–10). God expects his people to be self-disciplined and to exercise self-control, indicating a sober, temperate, calm, and dispassionate approach to life, having mastered personal desires and passions (Prov. 25:28; Gal. 5:23; 1 Cor. 7:5; 1 Thess. 5:6; 1 Tim. 3:2; 2 Tim. 1:7; 3:3; Titus 1:8; 2 Peter 1:6) (Wyrick, 2003, p. 1460). We are to follow the example of Christ in self-control and self-discipline. In his short letter to Titus, Paul stressed repeatedly the importance of Christians exercising self-control (Titus 1:8; 2:2, 5, 6, 12). Christians must be wise, demonstrate common sense, and control their thoughts, emotions, words, and deeds; and Paul implies that not only are we capable, but all Christians are expected to learn this self-discipline (Lea & Griffin, 1992, p. 284). Self-control is mastered through "purposeful, loving discipline" and training, particularly within the family and within the larger community of faith—God's family (Packer, 1993).

Historical views of the self. In the seventeenth century, Descartes shifted the focus of philosophy to the self. In his view, God may confirm our thoughts, but he is not actively engaged in our lives. Descartes "symbolized the retreat into the individual self-consciousness as the one sure starting point in philosophy. . . . He set up the individual consciousness as the final criterion of truth" (Brown, 1968, pp. 52–53). Later God would be eliminated altogether from post-Cartesian philosophies. In contrast, a number of scholars sought to explain the self and the soul within a biblical framework that allowed for observation and verification.

Prior to the twentieth century, numerous biblical psychologies addressed the nature of the self and the soul (see Vande Kemp, 1984). Delitzsch (1899), for example, examined the nature of the relationship between man's soul and spirit and the Spirit of God, as found in the Scripture. The biblical understanding of the self and the ego (which he distinguished from the spirit and the soul) was unique to the Bible and "intrinsically differs from that many-formed psychology which lies outside the circle of revelation" (p. 17). Delitzsch acknowledged the value of observation and empirical facts, though under the authority of Scripture.

The importance of developing a specifically biblical view of the self and the soul was stressed by Jonathan Langstaff Forster (1873). Forster challenged the prevailing view of human nature, where a psychology of platonic dualism had infiltrated the church, with the separation of the body and the mind, the denigration of the physical realm, and the elevation of the immaterial. Such a view was not scriptural, in particular, because it ran counter to the biblical view of the incarnation of Christ and the future promise of new bodies. "Every religion is based upon a psychology of its own," said Forster. "Before any particular views regarding 'the soul' can be advantageously examined, the meaning intended to be conveyed by the users of that word must be mastered. The Greek mythologists understood one thing by the term 'soul'; the philosophers understood another thing; and the Hebrews, from the entire Biblical context, seem to have understood something to which the former meanings only bore an ideal analogy. The Biblical doctrine of a personal resurrection from the dead is only consistent with the conditions of the *Hebrew* soul and spirit" (pp. 110–111).

Fletcher (1912) observed that while biblical psychology and modern psychology do not have to be in conflict, a complete understanding of human nature begins with a recognition of the role of God in our creation and in our lives. Fletcher believed that biblical psychology is theocentric. When the Spirit of God as the one who creates, sustains, and directly influences man is removed, psychological terms lose their true significance. "To the religious man the psychological language of Scripture is of the highest importance, for it was fashioned by religious experience and expresses, as no naturalistic system of scientific psychology can ever be expected to do, the influence of God upon the mind of man and the reactions of the soul of man in the spiritual environment" (p. 12).

Soul care, counseling, and helping people deal with problems in living were a significant part of the historical church (McNeill, 1951; Oden, 1987; Purves, 2001). Clebsch and Jaekle (1964) identified four historical functions of pastoral care and counseling: healing, sustaining, guiding, and reconciling. *Healing* meant not only actions and instruments, including medications, designed to restore health, but also a recognition of spiritual insights and actions related to the illness. *Sustaining* focused on helping a person, through sympathetic compassion, to endure and to grow spiritually in the midst of the pain and suffering. *Guiding* involved assisting a person to make wise choices in thought and action. The *reconciling* function emphasized healing broken relationships with God and with others, and often involved forgiveness and discipline (pp. 8–9). The self in Scripture and classical pastoral counseling is not viewed as an atomistic, disconnected entity; instead, the healthy soul is intimately and intricately connected with and accountable to God and to a healing community of fellow believers. In fact, research on the effectiveness of counseling has revealed that factors such as the relationship, alliance, and culture of hope cultivated by the counselor are more important than a particular theory or model of counseling (Wampold, 2001). This view stands in contrast to the individualistic modern personality development theories and therapies.

Rieff (1966) claimed that the twentieth century gave rise to the emergence of "Psychological Man" and the "triumph of the therapeutic." Introspection and Freudian analysis became part of a therapeutic culture in the West, and Freudian terms (e.g., *Freudian slip, id, ego, superego, psychoanalysis*, and *defense mechanisms*) became part of our everyday language. The ego psychologies emphasized an autonomous individual, who struggled with internal tensions and drives, while navigating amid the often hostile forces of society. Freud believed that the key to a healthy self resided in strengthening the ego and making the unconscious conscious. Therapeutic engagement in these models focused on the isolated individual, detached from

community and possible social and spiritual support systems.

In the 1960s, the humanistic and self-psychologies took center stage. Maslow proposed a hierarchy of needs, the highest being self-actualization—note the elevation of self and the dismissal of the need for God and community. Maslow (1964) sought to develop his own humanistic religious model of values, in opposition to a biblical worldview: "the highest spiritual values appear to have naturalistic sanctions and . . . supernatural sanctions for these values are, therefore, unnecessary" (p. 36).

At the same time, Rogers (1961) in his person-centered psychotherapy, replaced God with personal experience as the "highest authority": "*Experience is, for me, the highest authority.* The touchstone of validity is my own experience. No other person's ideas, and none of my own ideas, are as authoritative as my experience. It is to experience that I must return again and again, to discover a closer approximation to truth as it is in the process of becoming in me. Neither the Bible nor the prophets—neither Freud nor research—neither the revelations of God nor man—can take precedence over my own direct experience" (pp. 23–24, emphasis in original).

These self-centered models of counseling, arguing for an innate goodness in mankind, along with the rise of relativism, led not to Maslow's *Eupsychia*, or a land of self-actualized people, but to a *Malpsychia*, according to Joyce Milton (2002). Where the fabric of social relationships was being undermined, psychology had become "the new arbiter of values," and friendship and love were disposable items (pp. 281–282). Vitz (1977/1994) sounded the alarm at the effect of these psychologies: "All modern psychological theories of human motivation and personality assume that reward for self (i.e., egoism) is the *only* functional ethical principle. In short, psychology's deep commitment to narcissism, egoism, self-worship, the individual, isolated self—or, as I call it, 'selfism'—has been thoroughly demonstrated" (p. xi).

Selfism is a self-defeating goal for the Christian. It is anti-Christian, and it leads to destruction of families. Vitz argues that psychology has become a religion. In fact, he calls it the "cult of the self" (p. xii). Specifically, he holds that it is based in secular humanism, which rejects God in favor of worshiping self. The focus of his ire is on the humanistic psychologies, in particular, not on the experimental, behavioral, and analytic psychologies.

Social Development of Self

Sociologists have long argued that our personalities do not develop innately and independently; instead, they are shaped by social constraints and forces. For example, children reared in isolation experience considerable problems in adjustment. Our sense of self and identity are inextricably linked to social engagement.

Cooley (1902) referred to our individual identity as the reflected or "looking glass self"—a self that develops through our perception of how others respond to our behavior. The development of the self is a three-stage process: (1) we imagine or observe how our behavior appears to others; (2) we imagine or interpret their

judgment of this behavior or appearance; and (3) we have self-feelings, such as pride or mortification, about these perceived judgments. "As we see our face, figure, and dress in the glass, and are interested in them because they are ours, and pleased or otherwise with them according as they do or do not answer to what we should like them to be; so in our imagination we perceive in another's mind some thought of our appearance, manners, aims, deeds, character, friends, and so on, and are variously affected by it" (p. 152).

To Cooley the self is a social product. He challenged Descartes's focus on individual consciousness through introspection and contemplation ("I think, therefore I am") as the primary foundation for reality and knowledge. The self and self-awareness cannot exist independently, but only through interaction with others. In Cooley's (1909) words, "Self and society are twin-born; we know one as immediately as we know the other, and the notion of a separate and independent ego is an illusion" (p. 5). The self develops most fully in primary groups.

Like Cooley, Mead (1934) believed that social interaction leads to the development of the self. The self is divided into two parts—the "I" and the "me." The "I" is the spontaneous part of the self, and the "me" is the social part of the self. The self develops through continuous conversation between the "I" and the "me." The "me" internalizes the demands of society and gives reflections for the "I" to react to. There are three developmental stages: (1) the imitative stage (first year of life), where the child mimics significant others; (2) the play stage (ages two to four), where the child takes the role of the other—practicing attitudes and actions of significant others; and (3) the game stage (ages four plus), where the child takes the role of the generalized other—internalizing the demands and expectations of society.

Goffman (1959), in his dramaturgical theory, likened our lives to performances in a theater. He described our "fronting" behavior where we engage in "impression management," controlling our image and how we want others in the world to perceive us. But there is also our backstage behavior, seen only by our family and close acquaintances, where we let down the public mask and social roles, and where we reveal who we really are. Goffman called us all "incorrigible con artists," constantly trying to manage and manipulate our images, but ultimately we are unable to avoid this deceptive behavior.

Goffman's view parallels the biblical descriptions of deception in human nature, beginning with Adam and Eve and the first attempt to cover up bad (sinful) decisions and behavior. In Jeremiah 9:8, for example, God observes the deception of his people: "Their tongue is a deadly arrow; it speaks deceitfully. With their mouths they all speak cordially to their neighbors, but in their hearts they set traps for them." Perhaps unwittingly, Goffman also implied that our self-deception makes us incapable of changing ourselves—outside of divine intervention and transformation.

Cooley, Mead, and Goffman provide insight into our human nature, but they fail to address our most basic relationship with our Creator. In contrast, Balswick, King, and Reimer (2005) provide a sociological model of human development from a theological perspective. They contend that God created us for relationship, and the goal of human development is to become a reciprocating self, fully engaged across the life stages in giving and receiving with God and with others. In unity with God and others, we do not lose our individual identity; instead, we more fully come to understand ourselves, others, and God. It is in the process of these relationships that we come to know ourselves more fully, with an ultimate goal of glorifying God and seeking unity with him—"It is essential to remember that the reciprocating self as *imago Dei* is a self under construction, already beloved by God in the present but not yet transformed by eschatological perfection" (p. 246). To spiritually develop, we must utilize our human capacities as image bearers of Christ, and "this will be manifested as we relate to God and fellow believers in a way that provides meaning and guidance for life and a consistently lived Christian ethic" (pp. 286–287).

Worldviews, Human Development, and Counseling

How do you become who you are? What are the processes or stages of your development? To better understand the role of self in counseling, we need to look at the theories of human development. While the theories presented in most modern development textbooks hold a veneer of objectivity, Vandenberg and O'Connor (2005) argue that the "foundational assumptions about human development derive from the historical tension between religion and science, and that appreciation of these origins enables us to recognize shortcomings and problems in the manner in which development is often conceptualized" (p. 190). All secular theories of human nature and personality development rest on a naturalistic worldview that, while attempting to fully describe personality, fails to adequately account for our essential nature. This is true especially given the reductionism basic to naturalism and its underlying philosophical assumptions.

Worldviews as control beliefs. Worldviews shape our beliefs about what we accept as true or false; they act as control beliefs. We would like to believe that we assess new data by objective standards. In reality, we tend to evaluate new information by how well it fits into what we already believe to be true or what fits into our worldview.

Naturalistic or secular counseling separates science from religion and views faith as nonscientific—not needing proof; however, underlying this myth of neutrality in counseling toward religion are philosophical assumptions that reflect biases against religion (Slife & Whoolery, 2006). Christian counselors must recognize these biases as they study theories of human nature and development as well as when they provide biblical counsel. We need alternatives to the self-psychologies and developmental theories that rest on individualism; materialism; rejection of authority; and a focus on techniques to change, correct, or control thoughts and behaviors, while failing to acknowledge the moral and spiritual implications of these approaches.

The naturalistic worldview permeates modern counseling theories. Some of the fundamental assumptions of naturalism are that the world is a closed system; the supernatural does not exist, since all things can be explained within the material world; knowledge is limited to sensory observation, testing, and analysis; humans are assumed to be highly evolved animals, possibly capable of change (behavioral, cognitive, or biochemical) through conditions of cause and effect; history and life have no ultimate direction, purpose, or meaning; there is no afterlife; all religious experiences are explained in terms of irrational beliefs or feelings with natural causes; and morality is based on individual or social preference or standards (Cosgrove, 2006; Sire, 2009).

Webb-Mitchell (2001, pp. 84–88) has identified five characteristics of modern developmental theories that draw from philosophical views found in the Enlightenment.

1. *Individualism*, or the view that the individual is primary, existing for the self, without regard for God or others.
2. *Opposition to authority*, driven by feelings or emotions and personal preferences, with no moral responsibility to others.
3. *The centrality of the mind*, or the elevation of reason and rational abilities.
4. *Natural religion*, in which the spiritual is reduced to rational explanations, and religion becomes another social movement providing group support.
5. *Universalism*, in which the natural predisposition of humans is to create deities and religions for guidance and instruction in life.

In other words, these theories present a particular philosophy that elevates the self and personal preference over relationship to God and others. The implications are that we are not intentionally created for a purpose by a loving, personal creator God. Instead, we are subject to sexual, genetic, cognitive, emotional, social, or moral drives that exclude intentional design or supernatural meaning.

The biblical worldview and personality development. In the biblical worldview, our life story is part of a bigger story with an Author/Creator, a beginning, and an end that gives life meaning and purpose. We come to a fuller self-understanding only through knowing God, recognizing our sinful condition, and seeking reconciliation through Christ (Rom. 10:9–10; Eph. 2:8–9). A Christian understanding of personality development should have features that are distinctly different from secular models.

Alternative models of personality development have been suggested. Webb-Mitchell (2001) provides an outline of a model that views healthy personality development as a Christian pilgrimage. The focus of his model is on becoming more like Christ within the historical church community. The pilgrimage concept is not new. The Scripture speaks of a process of sanctification or spiritual growth (Rom. 8:29–30; 2 Cor. 3:18; Phil. 2:12–13; 3:10–17; 1 Thess. 4:3, 7; Heb. 2:11). In 1678 John Bunyan presented what could be called a model of personality transformation and development in his book *The Pilgrim's Progress from This World, to That Which Is to Come*. In this allegory, we find Christian, who was formerly named Graceless, embarking on a life journey from his hometown, the "City of Destruction," representing this world, to the "Celestial City," or heaven. Christian is an "everyman." The struggles he endured, the problems he faced, and the choices he made are common to all humans on their journey through life.

Webb-Mitchell (2001) outlines five characteristics of the Christian pilgrimage that describe healthy, biblical, human personality development.

1. *Community and its story.* Healthy Christian development is centered in Christian community, growing in Christ's body (1 Cor. 1:10–17; 3:6–11), not in independence and individualism.
2. *Obedience to authority.* The biblical model views healthy development as moving from rebellion toward obedience to God.
3. *We are mind/body/spirit in Christ.* Christian pilgrimage consists of more than the individualistic cognitive, physical, moral stages of development. Instead, it engages the totality of the person, and the self is transformed by the Holy Spirit within a relational community—the local and universal communion of saints.
4. *God in Christ.* Secular models describe the final stage of human development as the ideal in terms of the self, whether it is psychosexual, psychoeducational, cognitive, or even faith development. The end stage is the goal, purpose, or highest expression of the model. In contrast, the Christian pilgrimage moves toward becoming more like Christ and members of his body.

5. *A particular people of a particular God: a kind of universal.* Secular models are presented as universal; however, they lack common agreement, even in their definition of terms. The telos for developmental psychologists is "a refurbishing and recycling of the self, which becomes more civilized and accommodating to all kinds of differences in the world as the years roll on." In contrast, "the telos for members of Christ's body . . . is to grow into the head of the church, which is Christ. Our end is not a completed self, but resurrection" (p. 99).

Fowers (2005) suggests character development as another alternative to the assumptions in secular psychotherapy. He drew from the field of virtue ethics in the areas of personal development, psychological well-being, and the good life. Fowers proposed that character traits make it possible to pursue the good in life. Thus, "psychotherapy can be seen as a process in which individuals reflect on and alter their way of living to be better able to seek what they see as genuinely good" (p. 40). Character development provides a contrast to focusing on changing a behavior or a thought process. "Virtue ethics portrays human activity as (a) pursuing what we see as worthwhile goals, (b) which requires virtues or well-established patterns of character. (c) Virtues manifest themselves behaviorally in actions, (d) that are pursued willingly and spontaneously, (e) based on a clear understanding of how best to act. (f) Enacting virtues involves wise choices about how to pursue the good in specific circumstances. Thus, virtue is multifaceted, with dispositional, goal-directed, behavioral, affective, cognitive, and wisdom-based aspects" (Fowers, 2005, p. 40).

Fowers's approach fits easily within a Christian model of development, focusing on developing new attitudes and habits, identifying what is important in life, and making wise choices.

Roberts (2007) has identified the specifically Christian emotion-virtues of contrition, joy, gratitude, hope, peace, and compassion that can be shaped by the gospel and the Holy Spirit in the development of Christian character. These virtues form a foundation from which a Christian approach to counseling can be developed (Roberts, 2001).

Barna (2011) describes ten stages on a journey to maturity in Christ, in a popular example of a transformational model of development to spiritual wholeness.

1. Ignorant of the concept or existence of sin
2. Aware of and indifferent to sin
3. Concerned about the implications of personal sin
4. Confess sins and ask Jesus Christ to be their Savior
5. Commitment to faith activities
6. Experience a prolonged period of spiritual discontent
7. Experience personal brokenness
8. Choose to surrender and submit fully to God: radical dependence
9. Enjoy a profound intimacy with and love for God
10. Experience a profound compassion and love for humanity

These alternate models provide a basis for Christian counseling that addresses the self and soul growth. The uniqueness of a biblical view of human nature is important. Understanding humans in a naturalistic monist sense or ignoring the biblical model of human nature leaves counselors with therapeutic approaches that define problems and solutions within a humanistic framework dependent on individual and social efforts, void of any awareness of the implication of creation in the image of God and the consequences of the fall.

CASE STUDY

Ben (age thirty-nine) and Alice (age thirty-seven) have been married for fifteen years. They have a son, Billy, age thirteen, and a daughter, Emma, age ten. The given reason for coming to counseling was marital problems, and they made an appointment with Mike, their church counselor, in hopes of salvaging a marriage that appeared to be headed toward the rocks. Personal histories provided at the beginning of the first session revealed the following.

Ben

Ben is the second of three children. His father beat Ben regularly, sometimes without the slightest provocation. His parents divorced when Ben was ten years old. When Ben was a high school senior, he made a profession of faith after he was invited to a church service by a friend. While an active member in the Baptist Student Ministry (BSM) in college, he met Alice at one of the BSM meetings. Immediately after graduation they married, and Ben began working for a marketing firm that specialized in computer technologies. The work has grown more stressful over the years, Ben's expectations for promotion have not been met, and his dream of opening his own business has slowly died. Additionally, Ben has experienced health problems, reminding him that he is getting older.

Amid his work and health frustrations, Ben's relationship with Alice has grown continually distant. They have begun fighting over his sporadic church attendance, his yelling and expressions of anger at the children, and the recent discovery by his wife of his interest in pornography.

Alice

Alice is the only child of loving parents who are still married. She grew up in a protected household where the family was active in church. Alice has experienced few health problems, and she maintains a program of healthy exercise and diet. She was attracted to Ben by his charm and his active involvement in the student ministry. After Alice completed her degree in education and they married and became parents, Alice and Ben decided that she would stay home to raise their children. Their plan also included Alice homeschooling until both children have completed sixth grade.

Alice attends a weekly Bible study, does volunteer work, and is active in her church. Her recent discovery of pornography on Ben's computer and his dismissive reaction to her confrontation have left her feeling empty, betrayed, and confused.

The couple agreed in the first session to set a goal of and make a commitment to rebuilding their marriage and their relationship within a specifically Christian and biblical framework. They also agreed to individual counseling sessions, with Ben meeting with Mike, and Alice meeting with Rhonda, another counselor on the church staff. Mike and Rhonda would meet with the couple together at arranged times throughout the counseling process. The purpose of the individual sessions was to allow a more intensive focus on personal issues that needed addressing with the goal of strengthening the marriage relationship. The remaining portions of this case study will focus on the sessions with Ben.

STRATEGIES, INTERVENTIONS, AND TECHNIQUES TO PROMOTE A CHRISTIAN FORMATION OF SELF

Case Study First Session

In his first individual session, Ben described his frustration with his life.

Ben: I'm not sure what's wrong with me. I'm yelling at my kids, and my wife is upset with me. I wish I could start all over again.

Counselor: And if you could start all over again, what would you do differently?

Ben [*sighs*]: I don't know. I'd probably change jobs. I'd really want to be a better husband and parent, but I never seem to get it right. Alice makes it all look so easy.

Counselor: Since we can't go back into the past, what do you think you need to do now to change things?

Ben: I don't know. I guess I need to quit feeling sorry for myself and start act-

ing like the husband and dad that I am supposed to be. But I've been told so many times that I'm such a screwup.

Location and identification of self. Ben is having difficulty identifying his real problem and accepting responsibility for his behavior. He is willing to commit to being a "good" husband and father but is unsure of what he needs to do. Underlying his difficulty is a basic issue of identity. A model of counseling that addresses the fundamental questions of our identity and our relationship with others is found in Genesis 3 (Jones, 2006). After the fall, God first asked Adam and Eve, "Where are you?" (v. 9). The question implies that there had been a breakdown in their relationship; fellowship with God had been lost. Subsequent events reveal that sin had led to a separation and breakdown in relationship across three dimensions: relationship with God, relationship with others, and relationship with self. We not only try to deceive God and others, we also engage in self-deception. God's follow-up question, "Who told you that you were naked?" (v. 11), revealed that Adam and Eve were receiving information from a new source of authority in their lives that led to actions contrary to God's will.

The Bible speaks of the importance of relationship as basic to our nature; we are to love God and to love our neighbor (Mark 12:30–31). Embracing and applying the greatest commandments will provide a foundational step for Ben in finding his identity in Christ and becoming a godly husband and father. Sociologists have long argued that our personalities do not develop innately and independently; instead, they are shaped by social constraints and forces. For example, children reared in isolation experience considerable problems in adjustment. Our sense of self and identity are inextricably linked to social engagement.

Ben needed a counselor to foster a biblical understanding of his identity so that he can recognize himself not just from the reflection of his peers but from God's view of him. He will need to identify his deceptive behavior and commit to change, but he will also need to acknowledge his inability to make changes at the deepest, spiritual level outside of transformation in Christ and reciprocal relationships with God and the Christian community.

Ben must also come to terms with his developmental and occupational stage in life and the realization that his personal goals may not be achieved. Ben has the classic signs of what is often referred to as a midlife crisis. Levinson (1978, pp. 209–244) identified four polarities affecting a midlife crisis.

1. **The *young-old* polarity**, where the transition from younger to older is met with an awareness of aging and mortality as a man's body weakens, even as, in his mind, he still feels young. Successful transition will require that Ben come to terms with his limitations while embracing the wisdom and maturity that comes with aging, recognizing the power and authority that he holds, and accepting the responsibility of providing godly leadership for his family and the coming generations.

2. **The *destruction-creation* polarity.** This polarity requires Ben's addressing the personal experiences of conflict at his work, the memories of abuse and painful experiences in his development, and the awareness of his own failings and destructive behavior in his family. He must also accept his own mortality while releasing the forces of creativity and productivity imbued by God. Levinson (1978) observes:

> Men at 40 differ widely in their readiness to acknowledge and take responsibility for their own destructiveness. Some have no awareness that they have done harm to others or might wish to do so. Others are so guilty about the real or imagined damage they have inflicted that they are not free to consider the problems of destructiveness more dispassionately and place it in a broader perspective. Still others have some understanding that a person may feel both love and hate toward the same person, and some awareness of the ambivalence in their own valued relationships. In each case, the developmental task is to take a further step toward greater self-knowledge and self-responsibility. (p. 224)

3. **The *masculine-feminine* polarity**, where Ben will need to balance his masculine strength and drive to achieve with the biblical responsibility of demonstrating love, sensitivity, and nurturing toward his family.

4. The *attachment-separateness* polarity, where Ben will need to learn to balance his dependence on others with appropriate self-sufficiency and responsibility for personal growth and spiritual development. "A major developmental task of middle adulthood is *to find a better balance between the needs of the self and the needs of society*" (p. 243, emphasis in original). Levinson (1978) writes:

> In order to care more deeply for others, [a man] must come to care more deeply for himself; caring means that he is mainly concerned not with material comfort and success, but with self-development and integrity. It means that he will exercise authority with greater imagination and compassion. It means that, while he enjoys the power and the tangible rewards of leadership, he gains even greater satisfaction from creating a legacy, enjoying the intrinsic pleasure of work and having more individualized, loving relationships. (pp. 242–243)

The counselor discussed these polarities with Ben. Together they examined the implications in his life, areas of personal control, and possible remedial actions that he could take. Within the biblical worldview, self-development and integrity mean becoming more Christlike in attitudes and actions, and addressing the struggles in life, including broken dreams and expectations, in biblically transformative ways. As part of his spiritual development, Ben will need to understand what it means to live a transformed life in Christ.

Steps to soul growth and transformation. In his epistles to the churches, Paul dealt with problems in a way that provides guidance for the Christian counselor. Roberts (2001) describes three steps in the Pauline approach to counseling that apply to transformation and soul growth.

Assessing the personality of the believer. Lead the client in a self-assessment, identifying and examining the personal traits (behavioral, emotional, cognitive, and relational) that represent the "old self" in connection to the problem (p. 145). This includes distorted views of God that need correcting. The goal is to "put off" these traits and replace them with godly traits and virtues, "accessing and actualizing a personality that has been created for and in believers by virtue of the incarnation, death, and resurrection of Jesus Christ" (p. 137). Help the client identify and explore specific instances where expressions of the "old self" (e.g., anger, selfishness, envy) have led to problems. The focus is on character, not on circumstances.

Clarifying the gospel. Teach your client about the transformed personality in Christ. Communicate "the characteristics of this new personality and convey a practical understanding of how its various emotions, cognitions, and behaviors interact: how forbearance of neighbor flows from and reinforces love of neighbor, how love of neighbor and thankfulness to God both derive from and reinforce love of God, and how love of neighbor and God lead to joy and peace and discernment" (p. 150).

The view should be realistic, not idealistic, as the client is encouraged to imagine becoming more like Christ and to practice godly virtues, even as he acknowledges the presence and temptation of old-self traits.

Teaching therapeutic agency. Help the client follow the biblical path to change through (1) yielding or choosing to obey and serve Christ; (2) walking in Christ by practicing the godly behaviors that are characteristic of the new self; (3) "putting off" and putting to death or intentionally rejecting the vices of the "old self" and "putting on" Christian virtues that are already present in the new self; and (4) walking in the Spirit, setting the mind on Christ, giving thanks, and rejoicing. Activities that can enhance change include prayer, suffering, fellowship, confession, reading and meditation, worship, and works.

Ben had already committed to seeking God's will and finding biblical solutions to his problem, so in subsequent counseling sessions, the counselor assisted him to identify the characteristics of the "old self" that he needed to remove, including his distorted or unbiblical views, and then to examine the transformed godly attitudes and actions that he needed to "put on."

Counselor: Ben, what are some of your thoughts, actions, and emotions that you would consider to be hurting your relationship with God and with Alice? Take your time; give me some examples, and try to be as specific as possible.

Ben: Well, I find myself acting like my father, something I swore I would never do. I get angry with my kids for the little things, or at least what I think

is a fault or bad behavior, and I raise my voice with Alice when we have a disagreement, particularly about disciplining our children. It just seems to spiral out of control. Another thing, of course, is the fact that Alice discovered that I have been looking at porn. I know it's wrong and I plan to stop, but I get stressed out just thinking about all my problems.

With the counselor's assistance, Ben went on to detail exploring his negative thinking before shifting to identifying the virtues and characteristics of the new person in Christ, or what a transformed life would look like. They then worked together to develop a plan for addressing each of these issues.

Doing an honest self-assessment. An honest self-assessment requires recognizing the traits, attitudes, and behaviors that represent the "old self," then identifying the characteristics of the new life in Christ, including your position, function, and calling within the body of Christ. We are examining and self-testing our position and level of faith in Christ (2 Cor. 13:5). This learning process of putting off the old self and putting on the new self requires a new attitude, with a goal of becoming righteous and holy (Eph. 4:22–24).

One outcome of this renewal is honesty toward others, where we humbly recognize our place, responsibility, and role as part of the larger Christian community: "Do not lie to each other, since you have taken off your old self with its practices and have put on the new self, which is being renewed in knowledge in the image of its Creator"

(Col. 3:9–10; cf. Rom. 12:3–5). A number of spiritual activities can enhance this self-assessment and support soul-growth and putting on the new self.

Ben began to list the particular traits, attitudes, and actions that were negatively affecting his relationship to God and to his family. He also began a list of godly qualities and virtues that would replace characteristics of his "old self." From these lists, he worked with his counselor to develop a specific plan of personal and relational growth, and the counselor gave him specific spiritual activities for soul growth.

Spiritual activities for soul growth. To promote a Christian formation of self, basic Christian disciplines are valuable.

Prayer. Clients such as Ben are often unaware of the different forms of prayer and their therapeutic value (Jones, 2007). Prayer can be a form of acknowledging the presence of God and communicating with him at a number of different levels.

Prayers of thanksgiving. "Devote yourselves to prayer, being watchful and thankful" (Col. 4:2). Activity: List all the things that you are thankful to God for and offer up a prayer of thanksgiving for each one of them.

Prayers of confession. Activity: List and confess your sins (Luke 18:13; 1 John 1:9).

Prayers that seek God's blessing, peace, and protection (Num. 6:22–27). Activity: List specific items in your life that you desire God to bless and protect; for example, your family and marriage.

Prayers of petition (Matt. 6:11–13; Luke 1:13) *and intercession on behalf of others* (2 Cor. 9:14). Activity: List people with particular needs, and pray for them.

Prayers requesting that God would grant the right words to say (Eph. 6:19) *and the opportunity to say them* (Col. 4:3). Activity: Identify a specific situation in which you might ask God to give you the right words to say to bring redemptive ends. For example, Ben could ask God to anoint his words as he seeks forgiveness and prompt him for the opportune time to say them to his wife, Alice.

Prayers for protection (Mark 14:38). Activity: Identify specific weaknesses and temptations in your life, and ask God for vigilance to recognize the danger, strength to resist or deal with the issues, and protection from the temptations of the world.

Prayers of contemplation and listening. Activity: Meditate on a passage of Scripture, and allow the Holy Spirit to speak to you.

The counselor emphasized to Ben that these different forms of prayer and the accompanying activities were not simply actions designed for external behavioral change but means of growing in a personal relationship with God. One example of this distinction is reading and meditation.

Reading and meditation. Clients can benefit from two levels of reading the Bible (Johnson & Jones, 2009). Normal reading of the Bible is done at an intellectual level, where the focus is on discovering meaning and changing our thoughts about God, our world, and ourselves. Clients should understand that an intellectual knowledge of the truth is not enough; instead, God's truth must enter our soul (Heb. 4:12–13). Meditative reading is done at a heart level, where our souls are moved and transformed by Gods' Word. The focus at this level is on personally experiencing God; we "search [our] hearts and be silent" (Ps. 4:4) before God. For example, we might focus our meditation on the attributes of God and how these might relate to a personal counseling issue. Part of this meditation might involve memorizing passages of Scripture as a way of preventing relapse into sin (Ps. 119:11).

In addition, numerous books are available that deal with how to handle problems from a biblical perspective. Develop a list of reference books to recommend to clients. In Ben's case, he chose to read a number of books on Christian approaches to dealing with pornography and a book on challenging and changing his thoughts and behavior.

Suffering. While suffering may at first seem contrary to spiritual growth and even harmful, it can provide important lessons (Kellemen, 2007; Thomas & Habermas, 2008, 2011). Ben's counselor led him to examine ways that God can bring meaning to his childhood experiences of being beaten by his father, and perhaps to find ways to help others who have been abused. The purpose in counseling was not to dismiss or diminish the enormous toll that the abuse had exacted on Ben; rather, the counselor helped him to understand the deep connection of his experience with the suffering of Christ.

Community fellowship and worship. Ben has been avoiding church, but connecting with the fellowship and support of believers can provide an important support system. Christians who meet together, particularly in small groups, have the opportunity to share their burdens,

help others, and encourage one another (Gal. 6:1–5; Heb. 10:25). In addition, public worship is a visual demonstration of mutual support and encouragement and a means of equipping "his people for works of service, so that the body of Christ may be built up" (Eph. 4:12).

Confession. Confession involves identifying sinful behavior (thoughts, attitudes, emotions, and actions), accepting responsibility, repenting before God and those people you have harmed, and seeking forgiveness (James 5:16).

Forgiveness and godly actions. One expression of salvation in Christ is found by imitating him in our godly actions and behavior (Eph. 2:10). The action of seeking forgiveness from Alice and demonstrating love and sacrificial leadership toward his wife and children will be an important part of Ben's action plan. The more he dedicates his works or labor to the glory of God, the more he will be transformed into a godly disciple, husband, and father, walking in the way of Christ.

Additional spiritual disciplines. Eck (2002) described thirty-two spiritual disciplines, divided into cognitive, behavioral, interpersonal, worship, and healing categories for potential use in counseling. *Cognitive disciplines* address disordered thought life (meditation, listening, Scripture, study, prayer, discernment). *Behavioral disciplines* (simplicity, frugality, fasting, chastity, body care, saying no/yes) address excessive, out-of-control behaviors (e.g., materialism, gluttony, and promiscuity). Behavioral disciplines such as slowing, Sabbath, solitude, silence, and secrecy address managing stress and finding balance and meaning in life beyond compulsive behavior or pursuit of money or power. Service, servanthood, sacrifice, finding meaning in suffering, and dying to self well are behavioral disciplines that address transcending self-interest through personal growth. *Interpersonal disciplines* such as confession, repentance, forgiveness, submission, and humility help repair and restore broken spiritual and interpersonal relationships. *Worship disciplines* include Eucharist, singing, celebration, fellowship, community, hospitality, and guidance, addressing the horizontal and vertical connections in life. And *healing disciplines* such as witnessing, testimony, and intercession speak to spiritual concerns or brokenness and the desire for spiritual renewal.

The counselor reviewed these disciplines with Ben and helped him to see the tremendous resources available to Christians. Together they identified the ones that Ben was already practicing. The counselor emphasized that he did not expect Ben to use all of the remaining disciplines immediately, but encouraged him to begin to examine them systematically and seek God's direction in selecting and applying them.

Developing a godly attitude and orientation. In Jeremiah 15:19, God confronted his prophet and warned him to repent. The New American Standard Bible provides an interesting turn of phrase in the call to repentance. Jeremiah must learn to "extract the precious from the worthless" before he can become God's spokesman again. Jeremiah must avoid the distractions of the world and instead look for God's presence and speak his words in every situation. We are to recognize and look for the hand of God in all relationships and in all situations (Jones, 2006). God communicates with us continuously in our daily activities, and our responsibility is to look for his actions. For Ben, this means seeing every conversation with his wife and children as an opportunity to communicate in a godly way. Each time he speaks, he needs to remind himself that he is also addressing God; consequently, his words need to be measured and carefully chosen so as to please God. Such an awareness should have a sobering effect on his thoughts and conversation.

After a few weeks of counseling, Ben reported that things were better at home. A review revealed that he had implemented a number of changes, such as reading and meditating on Scripture, praying authentically, paying more attention to his diet and exercise, and reaching out to others for support.

Ben: I've talked with a friend who lives in another state, and we have agreed to become accountability partners. He is further down the path in dealing with porn, and he has been encouraging me. I have also shared with a Christian colleague in my church, and we have agreed to meet together regularly for prayer and support.

Research supports the view that we are not very good at self-assessment, and we tend to deceive ourselves in estimating our abilities. We are naturally inclined to overrate our skills and performance (Dunning, Heath, & Suls, 2004). Accountability partners and a support group can assist Ben in examining his behavior more accurately. In addition, Ben added a software program to his computer to block porn sites, he attended a church-sponsored conference on porn prevention, and he began reading books by Christian authors that provided insight and practical guidance on the subject. He also started a systematic reading of Scripture.

Ben: I thought about our conversation on "putting off" and "putting on," and I have started to do an intentional devotional by reading five psalms a day. I am trying to read them as though God and I are in conversation. I was really affected by David's repentance in Psalm 51, when he asked God to "create in me a pure heart" and "renew a steadfast spirit within me" [v. 10]. I want God to give me that kind of heart. I also found myself really getting into Psalm 86, where David calls out to God and asks for his mercy. Listen to this [reading from his Bible]: "You, Lord, are forgiving and good, abounding in love to all who call to you. Hear my prayer, LORD; listen to my cry for mercy. When I am in distress, I call to you, because you answer me" [vv. 5–7]. He goes on to say, "Teach me your way, LORD, that I may rely on your faithfulness; give me an undivided heart, that I may fear your name. I will praise you, Lord my God, with all my heart; I will glorify your name forever. For great is your love toward me; you have delivered me from the depths, from the realm of the dead" [vv. 11–13]. I read this over and over, and I was hit by the way my heart had been divided and how God has delivered me. Psalm 103 tells me that God's love is "as high as the heavens are above the earth," and that "as far as the east is from the west, so far has he removed our transgressions from us" [vv. 11–12]. As I meditated, I became overwhelmed by the fact that I am forgiven in Christ, and that I don't need to keep dwelling on the mistakes that I have made and keep feeling ashamed and depressed."

Ben's devotional reading was helping him to shift his memory and focus toward a place of protection and peace. The image of building a wall of protection that separated him from temptations and the emotions stirred up by the bad memories of his past worked well in helping him focus on his walk with Christ. Each new activity, such as Bible reading, added another block to strengthen the wall and reduce the possibility of relapse into sinful behaviors. Just doing something does not guarantee a change of heart and an ability to cease being tempted by or engage in self-destructive and unbiblical behavior. But the combination of both external activities, such as blocking software and attending a conference, and internal activities, such as prayer and meditation, helped to consolidate change for Ben in a powerful way.

In a subsequent counseling session, the counselor shifted the focus to dealing with unwanted thoughts and unhealthy thinking.

Counselor: Ben, we have talked about unhealthy and negative thinking that makes you feel miserable or has led to actions that you later regret. You have also read Caroline Leaf's book, *Switch on Your Brain*. So what are some of these "must have" beliefs that get you into trouble?

Ben: I thought about this a bit when I was reading the book. I came up with: *I must have a new job to succeed*; *I need pornography to be sexually satisfied*; *I must get angry when things don't appear to go my way*; and *Life is unfair*.

Challenging thoughts and beliefs. One approach to dealing with Ben's difficulties and temptations is cognitive behavioral therapy. For example, clients can list and examine their beliefs to see if they are rational. McMinn (2007, p. 14) identifies six steps:

1. Identify problem thoughts and feelings.
2. Find dysfunctional automatic thoughts.
3. Help client dispute automatic thoughts.
4. Find underlying core beliefs.
5. Help client dispute core beliefs.
6. Help client maintain gains.

Problems arise when we attempt to define the standards that constitute rational thought. Roberts (1987, 2001) has pointed out that the central virtues, such as mutuality in relationships, calmness, responsibility, and self-acceptance, have different meanings and implications when compared to a biblical worldview. The secular view is that thinking that leads to pleasure and a stress-free life is of the highest order and is there-fore the most rational. However, this goal runs counter to a biblical worldview, where honoring God and pursuing his kingdom are the highest values, regardless of cost, including pain and suffering. A Christian approach to cognitive therapy will require evaluating, translating, and transposing the steps into an explicitly biblical worldview (see Johnson, 2007, pp. 231–239).

The apostle Paul, for example, experienced severe beatings, floggings, stoning, imprisonment, dangers from shipwrecks, and abuse from religious leaders and government officials (2 Cor. 11:23–29). His behavior that led to these experiences would be considered irrational and his thinking delusional or unhealthy by a secular psychotherapist. In fact, he would probably be encouraged to challenge his thinking and develop new beliefs that reduced the likelihood of physical injury. But Paul's highest goal was not the achievement of a tranquil life by avoiding suffering and conflict with others at all costs. In his biblical worldview, he believed that God's grace is sufficient, and he pressed on toward a heavenly calling and goal (2 Cor. 12:9–10; Phil. 3:14). Paul had an eschatological view in which he saw his present suffering as transitory and not worth comparing to the glory to come (Rom. 8:18).

Leaf (2013) describes five steps to changing thoughts and behavior. First, gather your thoughts and actions that you want to change, and look for the underlying motivations. Examine one at a time over a period of seven days. Second, shift to a focused reflection for the next one to three weeks, setting aside a few minutes every day to study what is stimulating you to think and act in a certain way. Third, write your thoughts in a notebook or journal and write a plan for change. Fourth, start applying your plan during the day, revisiting the thoughts and behaviors, and updating your strategies. Fifth, set a goal each day based on your plan. As you achieve success in one area, move on to the next goal. Leaf notes that her twenty-one-day "brain detox plan" is not guaranteed to be successful on the first attempt and often requires ongoing repetition.

Garner (2014) has used a similar series of practice steps for musicians who want to overcome stage fright. She points out that repetitive practice is required to re-wire memories in the brain: "As a musician practices, updated information concerning the work is re-formulated and integrated through the amygdala. Repeated practice (called 'elaborative rehearsal' in scientific terms) interweaves new layers of knowledge with each playing of the piece, creating a tapestry within the memory that can endure the pressure of a live performance" (p. 54). After acquiring the memory of the behavior or thought that you want to change, you practice what you want to say or do. Each thought or preferred behavior is broken down into small parts to examine and practice. Finally, the parts are consolidated and reinforced in the memory through further examination, analysis, and practice, leading to a desensitization of the experience of performing. In addition, a person can imagine his or her performance—practicing in the mind, and introduce potential stressors (imagined situations of what could go wrong). Breathing techniques and other stress-reducing exercises provide additional assistance in changing the unwanted thoughts and behavior.

Seven practical treatment tools can assist clients in challenging distorted thinking and developing healthy biblical thinking (Pearce, 2016, pp. 187–188).

1. Renewing your mind: Transforming your will and thoughts, as you plant the truth of God in your soul
2. Changing your mind: Repentance (Gk., *metanoia*) before God and taking every thought captive to "make it obedient to Christ" (2 Cor. 10:5)
3. Finding God and the blessing in suffering: A "redemptive reframing" of problems to discover that God is at work, even in the darkest of times
4. Reaching out and connecting: Learning to embrace the covenant community, sharing with and caring for one another
5. Letting go and letting God: Learning to hand over all of your problems to God, confessing your sins to him and receiving acceptance and forgiveness
6. Saying thanks: Expressing gratitude and recognizing the many blessings God has given you
7. Giving back: Learning to love and care for your neighbor through acts of service

A key to success with these procedures is the importance of repetition (practice, practice, practice) in challenging unwanted beliefs and rehearsing and practicing new beliefs, which must be followed by exercises and activities that engage and affirm the new life in Christ.

Ben continued to identify thinking that led to negative consequences. In the beginning, he practiced these thought and behavior exercises in the counseling session, where he could role-play situations with his counselor. He continued his contact with his accountability partners, and he intentionally worked to restore and improve his relationship with his wife and children. In addition, he became more active in his church and volunteered to work with one of the social ministry groups.

CONCLUSION

While the case study presented a number of successful changes in Ben's life, the reality, as he would freely admit, is that there have been setbacks. He still gets discouraged at times, and the temptations and personal challenges have not disappeared. What is different, however, is that he now has the tools and spiritual resources to deal with his problems, and he no longer feels adrift and alone. He can trace his development from putting off the old self to putting on the new and becoming more like Christ. Secrecy, guilt, isolation, stress, and anxiety have been replaced with a sense of confidence, community, and joy.

This chapter has examined some biblical approaches to soul growth and the development of a sense of self. A biblical view of human nature recognizes our creation in the image of God and the consequences of sin and the fall. Secular approaches to human development present a fragmented view in which the individual is autonomous or strives for independence, with no acknowledgment of a personal Creator and a sense of spiritual purpose. In contrast, healthy human development, within the biblical worldview, requires redemption in Christ and transformation from the old self to the new self; a shift from autonomy, egoism, and self-centeredness to a self that is more fully realized in dependence on God, a goal of holiness, and a relationship with the community of believers. This understanding allows for the use of a number of robust strategies and techniques in counseling.

The first task of counseling is to clarify a person's relationship to God, self, and other (neighbor). This self-assessment involves helping the Christian client understand the nature of transformation in Christ, particularly as it applies to current problems and issues that have initiated the counseling process. Counseling strategies are designed to help the client follow the biblical path to change. These procedures include spiritual activities such as prayer, Bible reading, meditation, confession, community engagement and fellowship, worship, and ministry to others. Additional techniques include reframing issues, problems, and situations so as to discover ways that God may be speaking to and teaching the client, and learning to evaluate and change unbiblical and untrue thoughts and beliefs.

The overall challenge is to embrace a biblical worldview that acknowledges the presence and work of God in all areas of life, including counseling. Such counseling helps people engage and apply Scripture in all areas of their personal lives and continually grow in personal spiritual maturity and faith within the body of Christ.

RECOMMENDED READING

Balswick, J. O., King, P. E., & Reimer, K. S. (2005). *The reciprocating self: Human development in theological perspective*. Downers Grove, IL: IVP Academic.

Barna, G. (2011). *Maximum faith: Live like Jesus*. Ventura, CA: Metaformation.

Kellemen, R. W. (2007). *Spiritual friends: A methodology of soul care and spiritual direction* (Rev. ed.). Winona Lake, IN: BMH Books.

McMinn, M. R. (2007). *Cognitive therapy techniques in Christian counseling*. Eugene, OR: Wipf and Stock.

Pearce, M. (2016). *Cognitive therapy for Christians with depression: A practical tool-based primer*. West Conshohocken, PA: Templeton.

Powlison, D. (2003). *Seeing with new eyes: Counseling and the human condition through the lens of Scripture*. Phillipsburg, NJ: P&R.

Welch, E. T. (1997). *When people are big and God is small: Overcoming peer pressure, codependency, and the fear of man*. Phillipsburg, NJ: P&R.

CHAPTER 11

Coping Skills Strategies

Amanda M. Blackburn, PsyD
E. Nicole Saylor, PsyD

Peace I leave with you; my peace I give you. I do
not give to you as the world gives. Do not let your
hearts be troubled and do not be afraid.

JOHN 14:27

As mental health clinicians, we often seem to major not in our chosen subdisciplines but in the development of coping skills. Much of what occurs in the therapy room focuses on facilitating a client's ability to healthily respond to life's stressors, losses, and even celebrations. The Christian counselor is uniquely positioned to support clients in developing coping skills while also making meaning of suffering. Doing so can build resilience and expand an individual's capacity for dealing with life's challenges. These may include daily, intermittent stressors or persistent, critical, or prolonged challenges. Such a working model—to honor the complexity of people, problems, and processes—must encompass a holistic approach that also seeks to incorporate the existential task of making meaning of suffering within the context of a biblical belief "that in all things God works for the good of those who love him, who have been called according to his purpose" (Rom. 8:28).

When we use a holistic approach to coping, we acknowledge and address the meaning-making purpose of suffering and coping for our clients. Doing so requires that we incorporate techniques that respond to all dimensions of coping: intrapsychic, physiological, psychological, and social (Pargament, 1997). Coping may simply be viewed as "a response aimed at diminishing the physical, emotional, and psychological burden that is linked to stressful life events and daily hassles" (Snyder & Dinoff, 1999, p. 5). However, a holistic approach acknowledges that while some types of suffering may be eradicated, others are only lessened and as a subcategory are merely managed or tolerated. This elevates the importance of making meaning of the *why*, *how*, and *what now* questions related to stress and suffering in the counseling room.

THEOLOGY AND PSYCHOLOGY OF COPING

Culturally, we tend to embrace the idea that suffering is abnormal, an anomalous occurrence that offends our otherwise positive life expectations. We generally expect to avoid suffering, and have some misinformed notion that if God truly loves us, he will protect us from what is difficult or painful (Thomas & Habermas, 2008, 2011). Alternatively, we view suffering as evidence of a lack of God's love or as punishment for our poor behavior. This is diametrically opposed to the presentation of suffering in the Bible, which indicates that we are called to suffer. That suffering is neither the eradication of joy nor an indication of living outside of God's will (Thomas & Habermas, 2008, 2011). Rather, suffering is a multifaceted experience that is inevitable in this broken and sinful world. Schmutzer (2016) highlights that "because popular faith views suffering as failure, people need permission to grieve" (148).

Scripture points toward an understanding that suffering can be a path to sanctification; feeling the deep emotions of suffering can be a spiritual experience. The entirety of the Bible is rife with examples of suffering, of interruptions, of painful situations filled with profound psychological and spiritual pain intermingled with joy and a striving for shalom—the way things ought to be. We read of Job's catastrophic loss of his family, belongings, and even the support of his friends amid his loss. We witness Bathsheba's rape at the hands of King David. We observe the desperation, isolation, and pain of the many afflicted that Jesus heals. Suffering is established as something that even the sinless Son of Man, Jesus Christ, experiences at the hands of a broken world (Thomas & Habermas, 2008, 2011). Therefore, while we may experience pain, stress, or suffering as natural consequences to some individual choices, our collective sinful state would result in inevitable pain and loss even if we were capable of truly holy perfection.

The disconnect between our poorly developed theology of suffering and the "empirical reality of evil triumphant" (Mandolfo, 2014, p. 114) provides a critical gap in coping which the Christian counselor must fill. Clients may lack a vocabulary for grief, loss, and pain. They may also have dismissed even simple coping mechanisms in the name of naively optimistic and deeply misguided beliefs that "bad things will not happen to me." Thus, we find that clients may benefit from both the teaching of cognitive and behavioral coping skills, along with meaning-making interventions that address providing a vocabulary for suffering, naming loss, and helping a client to modify their expectations and theology in regard to suffering.

Therefore, coping skills may help alleviate the physiological and sometimes the psychological pain of suffering. However, some situations and some people will need coping interventions that extend more deeply into the existential questions of suffering. For example, behavioral interventions, breathing exercises, and modifying cognitive appraisals may help a young man cope with the felt experience of losing his wife to cancer by decreasing panic attacks, improving his daily functioning, and elevating his moods. Yet he may require other interventions such as lament and religious rituals. He may need to change expectations and deeply held cognitive beliefs about suffering and God's role in loss in order to develop resilience. These prepare him to go on facing life yet offer no guarantees that he won't encounter further loss.

As counselors, we face the task of balancing symptom relief (a necessary and highly valuable goal) with meaning making. This allows clients to expand their capacities for tolerating and even thriving under incredibly difficult circumstances. Over our past ten years of experience, it seems that some individuals crumble under the collective weight of stress and grief. Others develop an increased capacity for tolerating and functioning in situations of profound pain, without losing the ability to continue to be vulnerable to both the joys and pains that life has to offer. As mental health professionals, we must find the critical place where each client is in need. Sometimes we must alleviate pain to properly assess and engage the situation. At other times, the pain is so large, chronic, or recurrent that full relief of the suffering is an absurd goal. Hence, we must engage questions of theodicy and resilience, of making meaningful lives with the hurt.

Cognitive Appraisal Process and Coping

The cognitive appraisal of events is a key component in how we experience and respond to stressful events. When an event happens in life, we experience it, and then we take action (Lazarus & Folkman, 1984). The cognitive appraisal process occurs in two steps. The first step is *primary appraisal*, in which an event is labeled as (1) something good or beneficial, (2) a challenge, or (3) a threat of possible harm. Once an event is appropriately categorized, then we can react. This is when *secondary appraisal* occurs; we choose what to do about the event, or how to cope with it. Often, secondary appraisal results in choosing to respond with behaviors that are either problem focused or emotion focused. In any case, once an event is appraised as a challenge or stress, a disruption to functioning occurs, and stress results.

Appraisal can be influenced by an individual's history and current life situation, situational and cultural contexts, and spirituality and religion. For example, what to one individual is the supportive silence of a friend holding space is to another a punitive silence and lack of caring from a trusted other. As mentioned above, the commonly held assumption that stress or the unexpected is "bad" and that "bad things won't happen to me" can further contribute to cognitive appraisals being more negative and resulting in greater disruptions in functioning and subsequent higher levels of stress.

Stress: Psychological and Spiritual Functioning

The dual process of stress—our appraisal of an event and resulting categorization of that event as a "threat" or "challenge"— results in the disruption of our homeostasis. When we appraise events as unexpected, overwhelming, or threatening, this causes changes in the physiological processes of our bodies. Our psychological well-being can be negatively impacted, and our relationships and social structures may be disrupted. Stress may be internal in origin, perhaps in response to cognitive dissonance, a biological dysfunction (depression, for example), or other internal stressor. Stressors may also be from the external environment, in the form of unmet expectations, threats to survival, loss, or other sources. Regardless of the source of stress, action is required to restore balance in order to return to previous levels of functioning or to create a "new normal" in light of new circumstances (Lazarus & Cohen, 1977).

Impacts of stress. The physiological changes that occur as part of the body's stress response indicate that stress, in fact, has intrapsychic, physiological, psychological, and social implications. Under stressful circumstances, the sympathetic nervous system (SNS) creates comprehensive change, from the brain throughout all of the body's systems. Muscles tense; respirations increase; the heart pumps harder and faster; and blood vessels to the large-muscle groups increase blood flow, resulting in higher blood pressure. Meanwhile, the endocrine system works in concert with the brain to make adrenaline, noradrenaline, and cortisol course throughout the body to incite these changes. The body is flooded with glucose from the digestive system, a needed energy source for fighting or running from the perceived threat. Noncritical processes, such as digestion, slow down, focusing the body's energies and resources solely on the task at hand: survival (American Psychological Association, n.d.).

Throughout the lifespan, children and adults can usually identify this subjective experience of fear or anxiety, named the "fight-flight-freeze" response. While the awareness of and response to fear and anxiety differs at various stages of development, research indicates that the impacts of stress are far more pervasive than mere arousal. Stress is known to cause a release of glutamate, a neurotransmitter that inhibits synaptic receptors key to memory (Lei & Tejani-Butt, 2009). Much of this activity happens in the limbic system, a portion of the brain that is responsible for "functions necessary for self-preservation and species preservation" that "regulate(s) autonomic and endocrine function, particularly in response to emotional stimuli" (Swenson, 2006, n.p.).

The brain is constantly creating new neurons. However, new neurons in the hippocampus may die when exposed to the body's physiological response to stressful social events (Thomas, Hotsenpiller, & Peterson, 2007). Moreover, the hippocampus appears to create more myelin, the insulating sheath on neurons, than new neurons when under duress. This indicates that the brain focuses on making faster signal loops between existing connections, rather than making new connections, during periods of stress. Therefore, those under chronic stress may experience memory and learning difficulties (Chetty et al., 2014). These findings indicate psychological dimensions to stress that impact cognitive processes, selective attention, and even the very architecture of the brain.

Further, cortisol, also known as the stress hormone, increases activity in the amygdala, the portion of the limbic system responsible for processing emotional stimuli (Vaisvaser et al., 2013). Stress may also shrink the gray matter of the brain in specific regions of the medial prefrontal cortex, a brain region implicated in emotional regulation, self-control, and information processing (Yuen et al., 2012). With memory and cognition dampened, and the amygdala processing more information, there is a biological explanation for the heightened emotional responses observed during stressful events. In addition, Van der Kooij and colleagues (Van der Kooij et al., 2014) found that stress activates specific enzymes that literally result in individuals being less social, avoiding their peers, and having increased difficulty in comprehension and memory. Here lies the evidence of the further impact of stress on the intrapsychic, psychological, and social aspects of the individual.

From stress to coping. In the June 2000 edition of *American Psychologist*, preeminent researchers summarized the field of stress and coping, and specifically called for focus of investigative inquiry to shift toward clinical applications (Somerfield & McCrae, 2000). Since that time there has been an explosion of inquiry, with nearly 340,000 peer-reviewed articles on stress or coping in the interim. Most of these are focused on a specific type of coping (e.g., religious coping), or the development of coping within in a particular population (e.g., cancer patients).

Teaching coping skills is the appropriate clinical response for clients experiencing stress. Knowing that stress has impacts that are intrapsychic, physiological, psychologi-

cal, social, and spiritual, the wise clinician anticipates this need and develops a wide range of skills for helping clients relieve symptoms across these four domains. However, clinicians must also acknowledge that some stress and pain are to be endured, and no amount of skills-based intervention will lessen the intensity or duration. In such cases, coping may focus on resilience, increasing a client's capacity for tolerating pain and stress, and making meaning. It is these circumstances that a person can sacredly reinterpret to facilitate adaptive functioning and spiritual growth (Sisemore, 2015).

Under stress, the brain clearly engages primitive coping methods that focus on the key goal of survival. Yet most clients present in the therapy office either with stressors that are not truly life threatening or at a time after a life-threatening stressor or encounter is in the past. With the threat of survival not being preeminent, the first line of coping interventions often involves engaging the parasympathetic nervous system (e.g., breathing exercises, progressive muscle relaxation) to calm the arousal initiated by both acute and chronic stressful events. These physiological interventions are key for turning off the lower-order mammalian brain so that higher-order reasoning can be engaged. Through these exercises individuals can regain use of cognitive skills essential for memory, using higher-level reasoning and processing of emotions, and break out of the social dampening and isolation patterns that stress induces in the brain and in the body to follow.

Beyond physiological interventions, coping must activate the psychological and intrapsychic domains. Some interventions combine these with the physiological techniques (i.e., meditation, mindfulness). Such interventions include assessing and addressing cognitive attributions and thinking errors that occur intrapsychically. They also include understanding the origins of such coping, so that they can be dismantled and healthier attributions and coping styles be reconstructed in their place.

Subsequently, the engagement of social coping emerges. As referenced previously, the social realm can often be a source of stress or contribute to the maintenance of stress. Further, the impacts of stress can lead to isolation and disengagement, cutting the client off from accessing the positive impact of social support on mind, body, and soul. Therefore, coping interventions must move beyond the individual and look to the collective, with interventions that consider interpersonal, relational, and social aspects of coping (e.g., social mapping, developing or accessing social support networks).

Finally, religious coping emerges as the frame that fully encompasses the meaning of stressors. Religious coping can be healthy or adaptive in times of stress (Pargament, Falb, Ano, & Wachholtz, 2013). Beyond symptom relief, religious coping can support an existential understanding of stress and suffering that contributes to healthier relationships, greater capacity for coping with future stressors, and weathering well situations beyond one's control. Sisemore (2015) describes what Pargament's (1997, 2007) model of spiritual integrative psychotherapy includes: "Pathways to conservation of the sacred

include knowing (spiritual study), spiritual acting (rituals, ethics, etc.), relating to others in community, and experiencing the sacred through prayer, meditation, and other disciplines" (p. 260). These aspects are especially effective for situations that extend beyond symptom relief and into life-altering, typically painful events that exceed any individual's capacity for control. Pargament's approach seems to truly embody Christian thinker Frederick Buechner's (2004) sentiment: "Here is the world. Beautiful and terrible things will happen. Don't be afraid."

Understanding Strategies and Techniques for Coping

Coping skills derive from two main schools of therapeutic intervention: psychodynamic and cognitive behavioral approaches. Psychodynamic approaches tend to focus on developing ego strength for the utilization of mature and adaptive defense mechanisms over immature and ineffective ones. Psychodynamic approaches also emphasize healthy patterns of interaction in relationships as a source of coping strength. Cognitive behavioral approaches include dialectical-behavioral therapy (DBT; Linehan, 1993), which is most often used to manage more entrenched emotional dysregulation. However, its principles and interventions target the skills and capacities that form the foundation of healthy coping. Similarly, cognitive behavioral strategies are of great utility for developing coping in response to specific clinical symptoms. They also apply to developing and increasing an individual's capacity for further healthy coping.

Coping strategies help us minimize and adapt to the negative stress reactions we have when the demands of life exceed our internal and/or external resources. Successful coping strategies work by diminishing the amount of stress or anxiety a person is experiencing. However, successful strategies that reduce stress might not always be healthy and wise. As a result, coping is often conceptualized with clients as *adaptive* (i.e., healthy) versus *maladaptive* (i.e., unhealthy).

Adaptive coping provides helpful feedback, as this coping helps the person monitor stress or actually reduce her anxiety in the midst of the stressor. Adaptive coping strategies include behaviors like utilization of social support, good exercise and sleep habits, deep breathing or other relaxation techniques, and humor. Maladaptive coping strategies are just a temporary panacea that may momentarily reduce anxiety but do not help in separating the stressor from the anxiety. In fact, these types of negative coping actually maintain the anxiety the person is trying to avoid. Maladaptive strategies might include using illicit drugs, promiscuous sexual behavior, or numbing behaviors like television or video games. Professionals also often divide coping strategies into the following categories: appraisal-focused, problem-focused, and emotion-focused strategies. Most persons utilize a mixture of all of these types of coping when experiencing a significant stressor.

Appraisal-focused coping involves changing how one thinks about a problem or stressor in order to reduce anxiety. This often involves "reframing," or choosing to think about the stressor differently in order to reduce perceived stress. Problem-focused coping attempts to eliminate the cause of the stressor or learn problem-solving skills. We use problem-focused coping when we perceive we have some control over the problem. Such coping is often referred to as external, indicative of its focus on factors external to the client. Emotion-focused coping is used when we perceive we have little to no control over the problem. This approach aims to modify and modulate the distressing emotions someone feels as a result of their stressor, often referred to as secondary coping.

Strategies and interventions are easiest to understand and utilize when considering the primary goal of the intervention—from calming our bodily response to stress (e.g., breathing) to changing how we think about a problem (e.g., cognitive management), and improving and utilizing good social support (e.g., interpersonal skills). Because counselors often teach coping strategies to clients as therapeutic interventions, the use of categories can be helpful to better understand some components of coping. To better assist in the clinical application of coping categories, we have divided the interventions into the four categories set forth by Pargament's (1997, 2013) framework of coping: physiological, psychological, interpersonal, and religious.

CASE STUDIES

Case One

Dan is a forty-five-year-old married man with three nearly grown children. The youngest is in her senior year of high school. Dan has been a pastor for twenty years. Recently he has been experiencing exercise-induced panic attacks. After several visits to the local emergency room and a full cardiac evaluation, there is no indication of any medical cause for his symptoms. His panic has recently generalized to his work, and he has persistent fears that he is going to die of a heart attack like his father. He has had panic attacks while preaching to his congregation and has become avoidant of the public speaking duties of his job.

Case Two

Aryn is a twenty-one-year-old college senior with a series of unhealthy dating relationships and one-night stands. Although he performs well academically, social situations with friends and potential girlfriends cause him significant anxiety. After a stressful interaction with his roommate or a "bad" first date, Aryn goes online to dating websites to "hook-up" with a local female for promiscuous sex. Afterward he feels incredibly guilty since he is a Christian and believes sex is best reserved for marital relationships.

Case Three

Susan is a middle-aged, Caucasian woman with a history of poor coping skills. She has a history of high-functioning alcohol abuse and self-harm (i.e., cutting) behaviors. She has a conflictual marriage and two school-aged children. When she feels anxious or overwhelmed, she often ends her day with drinking a bottle of wine alone in her kitchen.

Case Four

Leslie, who is approaching sixty years of age, is a twice-divorced mother of three children who are in their thirties. Her oldest son, Camden, her only child from her first marriage, was killed in a serious car accident caused by an impaired driver. Camden's two children, Leslie's grandchildren, were in the car. Her seven-year-old grandson, Mason, suffered a traumatic brain injury. Although Mason survived, his functioning was greatly diminished. Camden's wife, Keelah, is temporarily living several hours away with Mason while he completes residential rehabilitation at a facility. Camden's daughter, Allie, was unharmed by the accident. She is living several hours away with her other grandparents while her mother and brother pursue rehabilitation. In addition to her grief and loss, Leslie is acutely depressed and unable to attend work regularly. Leslie is battling loneliness, as she was closest to Camden among her children and the two shared a special bond from their several years as a family unit prior to Leslie's remarriage and the birth of her next two children.

STRATEGIES, INTERVENTIONS, AND TECHNIQUES FOR IMPROVING COPING SKILLS

The following section describes various categories of coping strategies according to their focus. Some strategies, interventions, and techniques (SITs) teach modulation of the physiological, and some, of the internal world, while others focus on social relationships. Finally, religious coping and the practice of lament are discussed. Each category will provide examples of ways to incorporate the SITs with our chapter's case studies.

Physiological Management Skills

Physiological management skills can be used to manage the fight, flight, or freeze responses of the nervous system. Some of these behaviors help to slow down our breathing and heartbeat or reduce tension in our muscles. Most can be done alone or in a group and in various contexts. The most common are breathing and muscle relaxation. From the case examples, Dan can clearly benefit from first learning some skills to allow him to manage his fight or flight responses so that he may then engage higher level skills to address the underlying stressors that are taxing his previously sufficient levels of coping.

Breathing. Breathing exercises help activate the parasympathetic nervous system (PNS) by "turning down" the sympathetic nervous system (SNS). When we encounter a stressor or threat, the SNS is activated—breathing and heart rate speed up and cortisol pumps through the bloodstream to prepare us to fight or flee the situation. The SNS keeps us alive by activating the physiological systems (e.g., muscles) that react to keep us safe. For instance, the SNS is helpful when one steps out in front of a speeding car and needs to quickly jump over the curb to the sidewalk for safety. However, this is not a helpful reaction when initiating a difficult conversation with a friend or sitting for a final examination, or when Dan is walking to the pulpit to deliver a sermon. Breathing exercises can help to calm someone who is not in a threatening situation but whose body is reacting as if he is in danger.

Breathing exercises can first be as simple as sitting or lying in a comfortable position and paying attention to the act of breathing. The next step involves intentionally inhaling through the nose and exhaling slowly through the mouth. This is followed by taking deep "belly breaths" that utilize the diaphragm, inhaling for a "two-count" and exhaling for a "four-count." The important part with counting is that the act of exhaling is taking longer than inhaling. Once comfortable with the breathing, the client should set a timer and breathe this way for five to ten minutes or until he feels noticeably calmer. Several mobile phone apps, podcasts, and breathing visualizations are available on the internet to help facilitate these skills.

Dan managed quite well with breathing exercises in his course of treatment. After initial mastery of breathing techniques, we integrated a somewhat unique exercise to help make his breathing both prayerful and physiologically calming. He utilized the Jesus Prayer, a common prayer from Eastern Orthodox traditions. The full prayer is, "Lord Jesus Christ, Son of God, have mercy on me, a sinner." For Dan, we shortened the prayer to "Lord Jesus Christ, have mercy on me." This prayer, paired with deep inhalations and exhalations between the phrases, served the dual purpose of connecting this simple biological intervention with a deep meaning for Dan.

Muscle relaxation. Muscle relaxation skills help to relax by first tensing various muscle groups and then relaxing each muscle group. A common type of muscle relaxation exercise is called progressive muscle relaxation (PMR). It has been shown to be a helpful coping tool, as it significantly decreases symptoms of anxiety, burnout, depression, and perceived stress (Sadeghi, Sirati-Nir, Ebadi, Aliasgari, & Hajiamini, 2015; Scholz et al., 2016; Zaeri & Zaeri, 2015).

Dan also utilized this physiological style of coping. He found this intervention especially helpful for releasing muscle tension prior to sleep at night. He also utilized PMR at the gym when he would find that his appraisal of his increased arousal from physical activity would start to drift into panic about a heart attack. He especially liked that he could utilize this technique in a public setting or while driving, without any evident outward signs to those around him.

For more resistant clients, educating the client on the functioning of the nervous system and arousal can provide the needed justification for a trial of PMR. Counselors will likely find the most success from doing such exercises first in session and then asking the client to practice at home. The physiologically calming experience is usually quite rewarding and reinforces practice for most clients. It can feel awkward and unusual to practice breathing or relaxation in session. Acknowledging the awkward and uncomfortable responses can help alleviate reluctance to be awkward.

Guided imagery. Guided imagery is the use of verbal prompts to assist a client in creating a visual image of a peaceful or relaxing location in her mind. While such interventions may include some mindfulness-based prompts to attend to imagined sensory experiences (tastes, smells, sounds), the true intent is to engage the client's body in a parasympathet-ic state, allowing for slowed breathing, muscle relaxation, and emotional calm. Such techniques are shown to aid in the management of stress, to decrease anxiety and depression symptoms, and to reduce blood pressure. The content of guided imagery provides the opportunity to personalize the intervention for individual client needs. You can use scripts that focus on relaxation, rewriting scripts for anxiety-provoking events, or even for invoking a client's "worst case scenario" to be experienced and engaged in vivo to be addressed in session.

Dan's case provides the opportunity to create visualizations for a wide range of purposes. He may be aided by creating relaxing scenarios to use in managing his sympathetic arousal, as well as scenarios that imagine him succeeding at his triggering events (giving a sermon without panic symptoms) or navigating the worst case scenarios (having a panic attack midsermon).

Intrapsychic and Psychological Skills

Intrapsychic skills help manage stress by attending to our internal processes while psychological skills help attend to our thoughts, emotions, and perceptions. These are both coping strategies that are done individually and can be done in multiple contexts and situations. The following are commonly practiced intrapsychic and psychological coping strategies.

Self-compassion. Sometimes an especially difficult component of a challenge is one's internal dialogue of self-criticism or shame. People commonly have the perception that others are better able to cope, manage, and respond to stresses. Self-compassion is an important intrapsychic coping skill, as it attends to one's self-perceptions and evaluations of current struggles. Self-compassion is: (1) *self-kindness* or "the ability to treat oneself with care and understanding rather than harsh self-judgment"; (2) *common humanity*, which refers to "recognizing that imperfection is a shared aspect of the human experience rather than feeling isolated by one's failures"; and (3) *mindfulness*, or "holding one's present-moment experience in balanced perspective rather than exaggerating the dramatic story-line of one's suffering" (Neff & McGehee, 2010, p. 226).

In a Christian context, such approaches can be framed in the context of both receiving and giving grace. For a client who claims a Christian faith, examining the underlying assumptions of how she believes God views her can be an effective way of identifying attributions she holds. Self-criticism or shame may originate from distorted views of God's love and difficulty accepting the grace afforded via Christ. The practice of self-kindness and ability to accept common humanity are potential indicators of one's ability to radically accept grace and forgiveness. The practice of mindfulness can help to calm.

Aryn constantly struggled with self-compassion. While he was easily able to offer grace to others, he found himself his own harshest critic. Aryn's first step in treatment was to offer himself the same grace and understanding that he so quickly offered to others. Counseling sessions often focused on normalizing Aryn's anxiety and encouraged him to remember that everyone struggles with something. Together we practiced having a broader perspective when Aryn experienced significant social anxiety, rather than succumbing to the downward emotional spiral that often resulted when he believed his "social life was over."

Mindfulness. Similar to but independent from the mindfulness portion of self-compassion, mindfulness refers to the state of being aware of one's thoughts, feelings, bodily sensations, and environment. Some trauma-informed therapies may call this practice grounding. Mindfulness is present-focused on self and surroundings rather than focusing on the future (i.e., what lies ahead) or obsessing about the past (i.e., what just happened). Mindfulness skills include the activities and behaviors that help one obtain a state of mindfulness. For example, it may include paying attention to sensory input in the present moment: *What am I seeing? What am I hearing? What am I tasting? What am I feeling? What am I smelling?* A common activity to introduce mindfulness is to eat a small treat (e.g., a raisin or peppermint candy), first paying attention to what it looks like, then slowly chewing and paying attention to all the taste sensations, what the treat sounds like as it is chewed, and so on.

Mindfulness is a helpful coping strategy that can be practiced in various settings, making it an accessible reality for many experiencing stress or negative symptoms like anxiety. Mindfulness also has both mental health and physiological benefits

(Davidson et al., 2003; Weinstein, Brown, & Ryan, 2008). Some research has even shown that mindfulness is as effective as taking medication to prevent relapse of major depression symptoms (Segal et al., 2010).

Aryn worked for many sessions on grounding, or mindfulness, practices. Aryn first practiced in session by paying attention to all of his sensory experiences in the counseling room (e.g., *What did he see when he looked around? What did it feel like to sit in his chair?*). Aryn's initial experience with these types of present-moment observations was difficult as he realized he lived most of his life quite disconnected from his present experiences. He was usually so busy obsessing about past experiences or worrying about future social interactions that he missed what he was experiencing in the present moment. Aryn was eventually able to begin using mindfulness during stressful social interactions (e.g., conflict, first dates) and realized he had a much better idea of his physiological, emotional, and psychological state—which enabled him to better care for his anxiety in the present moment. As Aryn was able to notice, attend to, and cope with his anxiety, his promiscuous sexual encounters subsided.

Cognitive restructuring. Any thought process can be laden with errors in thinking. Two common cognitive distortions, overpersonalizing and all-or-nothing thinking, can create additional stress when trying to cope with stress. Overpersonalizing occurs when a person blames himself for any problem or challenge that arises, even in situations that are beyond his fault

or control. This is problematic because it creates a state of overly negative self-blame, which often results in feeling stuck instead of activated to take action and solve the problem. Another distortion, all-or-nothing thinking, occurs when things are perceived as either all good or all bad. This is problematic because things are rarely great or horrible (*My roommate is perfect, or my roommate situation is the worst thing ever to happen to me*). Often situations and variables are somewhere in between (*I really like some things about my roommate, but some aspects of her cause me much stress*).

One cognitive management skill to assist with these types of thinking errors is cognitive restructuring. Cognitive restructuring assists in minimizing the common "thinking errors" that occur when we cope by identifying and confronting these distortions. Cognitive restructuring takes a client through an easy process with a few simple steps. First, identify the challenging or triggering situation (e.g., a professor critiques her paper and gives her a bad grade). Second, identify the emotional response (feeling embarrassed and angry). Third, identify any automatic thoughts that accompany the emotional response (*How could I have messed up like this? I am such a loser*). Next, identify evidence that supports ("I wrote the paper late at night the day before it was due and did not have it proofread before submitting it") and contradicts ("This is just one assignment, and I have done well in other aspects of the course; I am a worthy person, and I have value as a person even though I did not do my best work") the automatic thoughts. Finally, cognitive restructuring requires identification of a more objective, balanced assessment of the situation ("This paper was not my best work, but I can pass the course. My worth is not defined by my performance in this class"). Following this process, it is helpful to identify the current emotional state and ability to think more clearly about the stressful situation. While cognitive restructuring is a coping strategy by itself, this strategy can also influence the development and identification of additional problem-solving coping strategies.

One limitation to cognitive restructuring is that acute emotional discomfort can interfere with activating the higher order thinking that it requires. Interventions that address autonomic arousal (as discussed above) and presence (i.e., mindfulness) may be necessary prior to engaging in cognitive restructuring. Similarly, after successful use of cognitive restructuring, clients may find that there still exist ever-present stressors or persistent relational problems that warrant intervention. At this juncture in therapy, relational interventions, such as psychodynamic approaches or existential approaches like lament, may be warranted. Yet cognitive restructuring and similar cognitive behavioral interventions are an important step in self-awareness and coping skill development.

Aryn's most commonly used cognitive distortion was all-or-nothing thinking. After a bad date, he often told himself, *I am such a loser that I'll never get a date, and I'll never get married.* After admitting this to me, Aryn explored other, less extreme, possibilities after an undesirable outcome. For example, *This date didn't*

turn out anything like I expected, but I learned some things I'd like to do better next time. Eventually Aryn was able to realize that while some dates might not end as he had hoped, he was likable and worthy, and he was able to learn the necessary skills for a fun first date. While this intervention did not eradicate Aryn's all-or-nothing thinking, the practice helped provide him with the capability of identifying unhelpful thinking patterns.

Pro-con lists. I also taught Aryn how to create a pro-con list, which helped him to create some emotional distance from stressful situations and to come up with solutions that might reduce stress. The task is simple and familiar to almost everyone. Clinicians may ask a client to divide a piece of paper in half, titling one side "Pros" and the other side "Cons." The client is then instructed to list all possible solutions, categorizing them into a positive (i.e., Pro) or negative (i.e., Con). While this coping strategy can be helpful, it is often victim to common cognitive distortions or errors of thinking, such as *mental filter* (i.e., obsessing about negatives while ignoring positives), *emotional reasoning* (e.g., *I feel stupid, so I must be stupid*), or *should* (i.e., setting goals for things that you "should" be) statements. Should any of these common distortions be identified during the creation of a pro-con list, you can further reinforce the previously mentioned cognitive management skills.

Aryn was first able to utilize this strategy when he realized he was emotionally overwhelmed at the thought of telling his current roommate that he did not wish to room together. Initially the thought of having this difficult conversation caused so much anxiety that he almost agreed to live another year with a roommate whom he strongly disliked. During a counseling session, Aryn and I created a list of the benefits of having this potentially conflictual conversation (i.e., the pros) and also the difficulties or drawbacks of the conversation (i.e., cons). While Aryn dreaded the conversation and the possibility of angering his current roommate, he realized the possibility of living together one more year felt significantly worse. After looking at his pro-con list and coming to this realization, Aryn felt empowered to go ahead with the conversation.

Goal setting and goal action. Another cognitive management strategy, goal-setting is a beneficial coping tool, for it assists in solving a problem and working toward a reduced-stress state. Goal-setting is the process of identifying, outlining, and pursuing steps to solve a problem. Goals need to be collaboratively established between client and counselor so the client has ownership and feels empowered to take action. First, the goal needs to be identified: "I would like to be more physically active." Next, a starting point and subsequent steps are identified: (1) Purchase inexpensive workout clothing and shoes. (2) Purchase a gym membership near my house. (3) Begin going to the gym two evenings per week after leaving work. Steps toward a goal should be small, specific, measurable, realistic, and achievable. All goals should have a timeline or deadline. Finally, any potential obstacles that may create stress or make obtaining the end goal difficult should be identified ("I occasionally have

social commitments in the evening after work"; "I am embarrassed to take an exercise class"). The final step is to take action on the first step.

Aryn worked on several goals throughout counseling. One of Aryn's first goals was to ask a girl in his Communications 101 course out for coffee. To help Ayrn feel confident to meet this goal, we broke this goal up into several smaller steps that felt doable for him. First, Aryn decided to get a haircut, purchase a new shirt, and look up the location of a local artisan coffee shop. Aryn also identified potential obstacles to completing his goal, including the overwhelming anxiety he would feel when talking with his female classmate after class. To overcome this obstacle, we role played the conversation until Aryn felt comfortable about his introduction, small talk, and eventual request for a date. Once each of his smaller steps was accomplished and obstacles were overcome, Aryn was able to ask his classmate out on a date.

Social Coping Skills

We are not alone in the world (e.g., Deut. 31:6; Ps. 68:5–6; Prov. 18:24; Isa. 41:10). God created us as relational beings, and we live in community with others (e.g., Gen. 1:26–31; 2:15–24). People are more easily able to regulate their emotions, calm down, and self-soothe (i.e., emotional co-regulation) when they have a trusted, safe person to help them do so (Butner, Diamond, & Hicks, 2007; Mancini, Luebbe, & Bell, 2016; Saxbe & Repetti, 2010). Moreover, research notes the importance of positive emotional co-regulation in children's development of executive functioning and coping skills (Herbers, Cutuli, Supkoff, Narayan, & Masten, 2014; Lougheed, Hollenstein, Lichtwarck-Aschoff, & Granic, 2015). Thus, being in relationship with others and having the necessary skills to do so are critical social coping skills.

Accessing social support. One of the most difficult tasks for many is to ask for help. However, when one experiences significant challenges, setbacks, or grief in life, one of the most helpful tasks is to reach out to a friend or loved one. Social support is often researched in relationship to one's coping strategies and quality of life, as it is so integral to success in both categories. We assess new clients' current and past social support during the intake process, as we know its importance in success of the counseling process. Moreover, we are aware that clients with limited social support will rely more heavily on the counseling relationship during recovery (Leibert, Smith, & Agaskar, 2011). Accessing social support may present as calling a friend, going to church, attending a therapy group, or emailing a parent to receive support, validation, and hope with a current life challenge.

Susan had difficulty letting others know she was struggling with anxiety. She felt ashamed at her behavior and alone in her pain. I encouraged Susan first to reach out to a trusted friend to ask for prayer for "a struggle." Later in the process, Susan felt more comfortable to tell her friend she was struggling with alcohol use. Once Susan received unconditional support and encouragement from her friend, she found herself willing to try a church-based twelve-step program I recommend-

ed for those struggling with addictions or unwanted behaviors. As her group normalized her anxiety and helped her to identify newer, healthier coping strategies (instead of abusing alcohol), Susan then felt empowered to let her church small group know and to ask them for prayer and support. While Susan was initially understandably hesitant to report her struggles to the group, the more she asked for help, the more she realized that her burdens were easier to bear when she was in community with trusted others.

Interpersonal effectiveness skills. Interpersonal effectiveness skills are used to create and attend to healthy relationships, which include any skill or behavior that improves our social interactions. Individuals with strong interpersonal skills are able to attend to both verbal and nonverbal communication in other people while assuring their own responses are appropriate and relevant for their current social situation. Other important interpersonal skills include asking for things and the ability to say no to a request. Interpersonal effectiveness skills help someone approach relationships and social situations in a calm, intentional manner instead of reacting impulsively to distress or anxiety. Interpersonal effectiveness skills are often taught in clinical and educational settings to populations with known interpersonal deficits, including those struggling with emotional dysregulation (Linehan, 1993), older adulthood (Martin, 1999), and many types of cultural adaptation.

Marsha Linehan (1993) describes three types of effectiveness within an interpersonal exchange. *Objective effectiveness* refers to the goal of the interaction. *Relational effectiveness* refers to the goal of a conflict-free relationship. *Self-respect effectiveness* refers to the goal of respecting oneself in the social interaction, which often looks like valuing one's needs and priorities as much as one values her peers' needs and priorities. Usually each type of interpersonal effectiveness is given certain priority for the specific goals of any social interaction.

Susan struggled to ask for help in relationships because she lacked the confidence necessary to maintain healthy relationships. She worked with me on interpersonal effectiveness skills to gain more confidence in her social interactions, especially during interactions with her husband. Susan became aware that she found it stressful to ask her husband for things she needed. As a working mother with two children, Susan needed occasional time away to relax or connect with a friend over coffee. Even though her husband encouraged her to meet a friend for dinner, Susan felt selfish in accepting his offer to stay home with the children for the evening. Interpersonal effectiveness skills helped Susan to respect herself and value her needs while sorting through the details in a respectful dialogue with her husband.

Cultural rituals. Remembering that all client coping strategies (from cognitive management skills to interpersonal effectiveness) and choices occur within a cultural context is essential. Successful coping cannot be removed from both cultural and religious influence, which provide a filter for clients' coping strategies and cognitive appraisals (Pargament, 1997). Protestant Christians may seek out community (i.e., accessing social support) through a church small group or Bible study during times of stress. Catholics, on the other hand, may participate in the sacrament of confession. Jewish communities practice "sitting shivah" after the loss of a loved one, where the community gathers around and nurtures the grieved family or individual. Native American communities have rites of passage that assist in coping with developmental transitions. Many cultural or religious groups have cultural-specific coping practices; however, knowledge of these group norms does not predict the behavior of one individual (Sisemore, 2015).

Religious Coping

Religious coping involves the act of turning to religious beliefs when confronted with a challenge, stress, or loss (Nelson, 2009). Religious coping attempts to better understand and create meaning during stress and suffering. This meaning making often enhances relationships, creates a greater capacity for coping with future stressors, and helps one to endure and manage the challenges that are outside of control. Research demonstrates that many people seek out faith during challenging or stressful times (Hogg, Adelman, & Blagg, 2010; Schuster et al., 2001; Walsh, 2002). While some have labeled this act as a psychological defense (Freud, 1937; Vail et al., 2010), most current research agrees that religious coping is not psychologically defensive but rather adaptive (Pargament et al., 2013). Several studies have indicated that engaging in religious practices in times of crises may result in better outcomes than for those who are less religious (Park, 2005), and that greater meaning seems to result from religious coping (Emmons, Colby, & Kaiser, 1998).

Positive religious coping includes beliefs that "God or one's high power will use the experience to strengthen one's faith, seeking help from clergy or spiritual support from others, and engaging in religious helping" (Ahles, Mezulis, & Hudson, 2016, p. 228). Positive religious coping can also be either internal (e.g., prayer, meditation, forgiveness) or external (e.g., attending community religious services, volunteerism or charity, and practicing forgiveness; Plante, 2009). Plante also suggests several tools that are neither internal nor external but are common practices: acceptance of self and others and becoming part of something larger than oneself. These types of religious coping interventions are a helpful part of the counseling process for clients who adhere to a religious worldview.

Leslie's situation was complex, and when she came for counseling, her coping was extremely poor. While initially physiological and cognitive interventions were helpful in managing her acute symptoms, her suffering clearly reached more deeply into themes of loss, anger at God, anger at the perpetrator of the incident, and trying to make sense of the catastrophic trauma that happened to her family. Although Leslie had long been involved with a specific church community, her son's death propelled her to attend to long-held feelings of mistrust and loneliness, and she felt judged and unwelcome at church. She

quickly found a new church where she felt unconditionally accepted. Through this process, she was able to increase her attendance at congregational events, develop new relationships of support, and more fully focus on her spiritual experience of God through faith rituals. Her church rallied to support Leslie, helping her with repairs to her home, serving as companions at events, and even joining her for meals to ease the loneliness of her son's absence and her grandchildren's distance. The congregation also hosted several fund-raisers to support Mason's medical expenses, which gave Leslie a sense of meaning and purpose. She even vulnerably approached some fellow church members about joining her in her struggle to forgive the perpetrator of the accident.

Lament. Some situations cannot be made right. Some pains are physically or emotionally chronic; some losses are perpetually recurrent. Lament provides a process for clients to engage with God in relationship, to increase their comfort with discomfort. As an especially significant form of religious coping, lament is central to coping for the Christian context for clients of all faiths. While other coping approaches from the physiological, psychological, intrapsychic, and social context of life may expand our capacities for coping or alleviating pain, lament will guide you or your client in making meaning of suffering.

Lament can reclaim the language of suffering so that there is a "shift from Christianity as a 'faith of answers' to one more willing to find mystery in painful stories and uncomfortable questions" and as "a powerful tutor to help the suffering lean into the tensions of faith and doubt" (Schmutzer, 2016, pp. 148–149). Suffering is disorienting, and lament facilitates the making of meaning in the wake of such disorientation. Scripture provides a model for engaging our cries of pain and for relief brought by the Creator.

For example, the Psalms contain laments for the individual as well as for communal loss. The heartfelt cries for relief and redemption, as well as anger and doubt are evident in Psalm 130:1–2, "Out of the depths I cry to you, LORD! Lord, hear my voice. Let your ears be attentive to my cry for mercy." Similarly, collective psalms of lament often reflect a feeling of being abandoned or rejected, as in Psalm 74, which begins, "O God, why have you rejected us forever?"

Hall (2016) provides a five-step process for engaging in the sacrament of lament: *address to God*, *complaints*, *request*, *motivation*, and *confidence in God*. The address to God is a call to him to invoke intimacy, inviting him into the painful place so that the individual does not have to face suffering alone, nor hide in shame or guilt. The complaint follows, where the source of suffering and the emotional experience of the lamenter are to be brought to God. Following the address and the complaint comes the request; this is the transition from lament to hope. The request is one for not only the deliverance from suffering, but the delivery from lack of meaning and purpose. The motivation then focuses on the character of God and who he is, as well as the reasons why the petitioner believes God should intervene and respond. Finally, the lament concludes with an expression of confidence in God, praise. Rochester (2016) has well thought out case examples in the same special issue of the *Journal of Spiritual Formation and Soul Care* that examine the application of lament in counseling.

For Leslie, the grief and pain of her loss was monumental. Her coping potential was quickly exceeded. She often railed angrily in sessions about wanting answers from God, answers from the perpetrator, and even answers from her deceased son. She had no vocabulary for discussing her loss, and she even felt intense guilt and shame at times that she should express such sentiments toward God or others. The concept of lament was completely unfamiliar to her, although she had become a Christian early in her life. I (Amanda) invited Leslie to explore her thoughts behind why she viewed intense or negative emotions as sinful. As her comfort with her emotions and vulnerability in session increased, she became increasingly open to the belief that God wanted to also be present in these emotions with her. This is what empowered her to seek out a faith community that was congruent with her new understanding of God as loving Comforter.

While Leslie did not participate in the formalized structure of lament, she did invoke the various stages in her process of recovery. Leslie's prayer life transformed dramatically. Over the course of counseling, she had periods where she cried to, railed against, begged and pleaded with, requested of, and praised God in her prayer journals and personal prayers. She also had a faith community of Christians who were accepting and supportive of this wide range of emotions and process of transformation. As a result, Leslie's coping expanded. She came to see that her intense grief and its various felt components were not barriers to her functioning. While the pain remained intense, she came to view it as a reminder that she was to practice self-care, turn to God with openness, and engage her faith community. She no longer experienced shame or guilt for having the very normative experience of grief and loss. She engaged in lament, processed her emotions, and developed a new vocabulary. The result was greater intimacy with God and a more internalized faith. She became more comfortable with the discomfort that she was not immune from further loss, but that future losses did not have to be weathered alone from others or apart from God.

CONCLUSION

Coping is one's current and long-term capacity to respond to, survive, and thrive within the chaos and complexity of life's stressors and losses. Coping strategies and interventions should promote resilience and meaning making in helping clients deal with situational and chronic stressors,

as well as complex and traumatic losses. Offering a holistic coping model to your clients, honor the complexity of people, problems, and processes. They provide your clients the space to wrestle with their own theology of suffering.

Coping can be physiological, psychological, relational, and religious. The coping strategies and interventions presented in this chapter address one's behaviors, cognitions (i.e., thoughts), emotions, metacognitions (i.e., what we think about what we think), meta-emotions (i.e., attitudes about how we feel), and culture (Lazarus, 2000). Moreover, religious coping strategies allow a client to draw on their faith practices and communities during difficult times. While many forms of coping may assist in the removal of pain, lament moves people deeper into relationship with God to increase their comfort even as their pain endures. The interventions in this chapter provide an overview but are not exhaustive of the multifaceted ways that we cope, grieve, and move forward. The experienced professional develops competencies with a wide range of coping interventions that focus both on symptom relief and meaning making in addition to maintaining self-care practices to expand her own capacity for coping.

RECOMMENDED READING

AnxietyBC. (2016). AnxietyBC: Home. Retrieved May 25, 2017, from https://www.anxietybc.com/

Barton, R. H. (2006). *Sacred rhythms: Arranging our lives for spiritual transformation.* Downers Grove, IL: InterVarsity.

Bourne, E. (2016). *Coping with anxiety: Ten simple ways to relieve anxiety, fear, and worry.* Oakland, CA: New Harbinger.

Brantley, J., McKay, M., & Wood, J. C. (2007). *The Dialectical Behavior Therapy skills workbook: Practical DBT exercises for learning mindfulness, interpersonal effectiveness, emotional regulation and distress tolerance*. Oakland, CA: New Harbinger.

Burdick, D. (2013). *Mindfulness skills workbook for clinicians and clients: 111 tools, techniques, activities and worksheets*. Eau Claire, WI: PESI Publishing and Media.

Coe, J. (2016). Special issue: Suffering and the Christian life. *Journal of Spiritual Formation and Soul Care*, *9*(2). Retrieved from http://journals.biola.edu/sfj/volumes/9

Halloran, J. (2016). *Coping skills for kid's workbook: Over 75 coping strategies to help kids deal with stress, anxiety and anger*. CreateSpace Independent Publishing Platform. https://www.create space.com/

Jones, A. W. (1989). *Soul making: The desert way of spirituality*. New York, NY. HarperCollins.

Linehan, M. M. (2015). *DBT skills training handouts and worksheets*. New York, NY: Guilford Press.

Scazzero, P. (2014). *Emotionally healthy spirituality*. Grand Rapids, MI: Zondervan.

Sittser, J. L. (2003). *When God doesn't answer your prayer*. Grand Rapids, MI: Zondervan.

Sittser, J. L. (2004). *A grace disguised: How the soul grows through loss*. Grand Rapids, MI: Zondervan.

Stavlund, M. (2013). *A force of will: The reshaping of faith in a year of grief*. Grand Rapids, MI: Baker.

Warren, T. H. (2016). *Liturgy of the ordinary: Sacred practices in everyday life*. Downers Grove, IL: InterVarsity.

CHAPTER 12

Attachment-Oriented Strategies

Gary Sibcy, PhD[*]

> Come to me, all who labor and are heavy laden, and I will
> give you rest. Take my yoke upon you, and learn from me,
> for I am gentle . . . and you will find rest for your souls.
>
> **MATTHEW 11:28-29 ESV**

Attachment theory is based on God's design that human beings come into the world completely helpless to take care of their own needs, and that to develop as a person, they must rely on others who are stronger, wiser, and loving. This relationship begins at birth with the parent(s)/caregivers and then extends to others (teachers, friends, spouse, and ultimately God). Attachment is a powerful relationship that not only affects how a child learns to think and feel about himself and others but literally shapes the brain's capacities to regulate emotions, read and understand other people's feelings and intentions, and engage in enduring intimate relationships. This attachment relationship also sets the foundation for us to experience a sense of confidence needed to explore the world and feel that life has meaning and purpose, and to have the capacity to experience both empathy and intimacy with others without losing our sense of self-identity.

Attachment theory is not itself a theory of counseling and psychotherapy. Instead, as we will see, attachment theory is a meta-theory: it is a theory that helps us make sense of other theories. It does not directly compete with other theories as much as helps us understand when and why one theoretical orientation and its associated therapeutic strategies, interventions, and techniques (SITs) is more appropriate than another. For example, when two people come to therapy for clinical depression, attachment theory may help us better understand which SITs will most likely work for one client while another counseling approach would be more appropriate for

---

[*] Special thanks to Nils J. Palma, PhD candidate, for his assistance with this chapter.

the other. For example, one client with more of an avoidant style of attachment was triggered by a job demotion and now suffers from highly self-critical thoughts and retreats from his wife, family, and friends. Attachment theory would help us see that cognitive behavioral therapy (CBT) may be most useful in this case, with its focus on breaking patterns of perfectionistic, self-critical rumination patterns of thinking, followed by attention reallocation strategies for helping him reengage his work with an improvement mind-set. Once his mood is stabilized, attachment theory would suggest helping him form stronger attachment bonds by drawing from interpersonal therapy techniques and strategies. These would help him to see how his retreat from others actually increases his emotional distress, and that engaging and talking with others about his concerns in a balanced way can actually improve his mood and protect him from relapsing back into depression whenever he experiences some kind of professional setback. So attachment theory provides a powerful framework for conceptualizing cases and selecting appropriate treatments.

THEOLOGY AND PSYCHOLOGY OF ATTACHMENT

At the heart of a Christian worldview is the belief that God is a relational being. In fact, the concept of the Trinity is inherently relational. God also created human beings in his image and declared that a person is not complete in a state of alone-ness. We were designed by God, without a doubt, to be in relationships.

Another key Christian doctrine involves the balance between God's transcendence and his immanence. God is an all-powerful and all-knowing being who transcends both space and time. At the same time, God is immanent: present in this very moment. John the Baptist exclaimed, "The kingdom of God has come near" (Mark 1:15). Immanuel is translated, "God with us." He is accessible to us in this very moment, and as we see below, this omnipresent availability forms the basis of our ability to regulate anxiety and experience a sense of peace that is beyond our comprehension.

So, at the core of Christian anthropology is the notion that God created us as relational beings. It is not surprising, then, that within the scientific study of human development, top researchers and theorists like Stanley Greenspan, Allan Schore, Dan Siegel, and many others tell us that language and cognitive skills (even math-related concepts) as well as emotional and social skills are all learned and developed through dynamic, interactive, affectively charged relational exchanges. Relationships literally shape the brain's capacity to function. In fact, the brain is a relational organ (Cozolino, 2014)

Attachment and the Secure-Base System

The basics of attachment may be best understood by understanding what I call the secure-base system (see figure 12.1).[†]

---

† This concept is adapted from a number of key sources, including but not limited to Ainsworth (1978); Bowlby (2012b); Powell, Cooper, Hoffman, & Marvin (2016).

On the left-hand side of the cycle, you notice the secure base. In early childhood, children use their parent as a source of security. When a child feels secure, her exploration system is activated, and she experiences a sense of confidence and curiosity to explore the world around her. In the background, she needs her parent to watch over her, delight in and encourage her exploration, set limits on her behavior if needed, and be available to her if she feels threatened or in trouble. On the far-right side of the circle, if she feels threatened from some internal or external source, the exploration system is immediately deactivated, and the attachment system proper is turned on. Notice that these two systems are incompatible: when one is on, the other is off. When the attachment system is turned on, it generates anxiety, and the child signals to the parent that there is a problem and she needs help. Proximity-seeking behavior is what she uses to get closer to her mother (crying, walking/running, lifting her arms), and she and her mom engage in a goal-corrected partnership to help her experience a safe haven (for young children, literally melting into a parent's embrace). Once felt security is achieved (which may take only a few seconds), the child launches back to the top of the cycle and is out exploring the world.

In the early years of life, children progress around this circle thousands of times. Young children experience safe haven and secure base through physical proximity to their caregivers. But over time they may be able to experience secure base in a more symbolic way over greater distances (e.g., talking, a telephone call, a text message). It is through this secure-base system that the person develops the capacities described above. On the top of the cycle, the child's sense of self-confidence and identity form. This is where a child learns autonomy and self-direction while, at the same time,

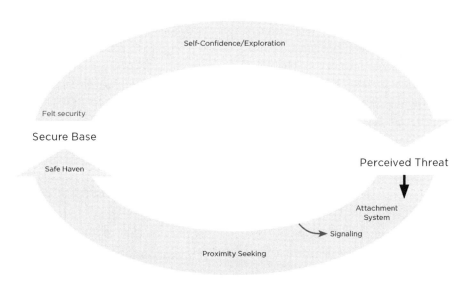

Figure 12.1. SECURE model

learning self-control and the ability to live within limits. On the bottom side of the cycle, the child's sense of other is molded. Here he learns how to appropriately manage his emotions and to work collaboratively with others to solve problems and manage stress, anxiety, sadness, and anger. The bottom is where he learns that others are trustworthy, reliable, and accessible in times of need.

This secure-base system is internalized by the child into what is referred to as an internal working model (IWM; Bowlby,1988) and forms a set of beliefs about himself (*Am I worthy of love and capable of experiencing intimacy?*) and others (*Can I trust others to be there for me in times of trouble, and can they help me?*) (Clinton & Sibcy, 2002). It also wires the brain for experiencing intimacy, coping with stress, and regulating emotions (Clinton & Sibcy, 2012).

Styles of Attachment

Based on the child's experiences in the secure-base system, these internal working models are organized into different patterns or styles attachment (Ainsworth et al., 1978; Bartholomew & Horowitz, 1991; Main & Hesse, 1990). Four primary patterns have been identified: secure, avoidant, preoccupied, fearful-avoidant.

Secure attachment. Children with secure attachment are able to effectively use their parents as a secure base for exploring the world, and when they are emotionally distressed, they can effectively use their parents to help get calmed down. From these experiences, they develop a positive sense of self (*I am worthy of love, and I can explore the world and make a contribution to society in a meaningful way*) and a positive sense of others (*I can count on my attachment figures to be reliable, accessible, and trustworthy, capable of meeting my needs and helping me in times of duress*). One's sense of self and sense of other synergistically interact with each other in a way that promotes a balance between experiencing a sense of self-definition and identity and experiencing a sense of enduring closeness and intimacy. Securely attached individuals can move fluidly and flexibly between the exploration system and the attachment system, based on what is happening in their lives. Those with secure attachment are able to experience their emotions, both positive and negative, without becoming overwhelmed and resorting to defensive and sometimes destructive behaviors to compensate for their inability to cope effectively with their feelings.

Avoidant attachment. Avoidant attachment develops when children's parents overemphasize the top of the cycle, pushing their children to become independent and autonomous even when the children do not feel a sense of security. These parents are often overly concerned that if they don't push their children to behave independently early, the children will become too clingy and dependent. Moreover, when the children are on the bottom side of the cycle and signaling attachment anxiety, the parents often ignore these signals and can be quite rejecting, cold, and harsh. The result is individuals who avoid experiencing their attachment-related emotion. In other words, their attachment systems are underactivated, and their exploration systems are overactive. Avoidantly attached persons tend to depend on their environment (things, money, fame, achievement, addictions), rather than relationships, to regulate their emotions. Consequently, they have difficulty experiencing empathy and durable intimacy with others. It's important to note that these individuals can be very friendly and outgoing; the difficulty comes in feeling close to others, especially in times of need.

Preoccupied attachment. Preoccupied attachment occurs when the caregiver discourages the child to explore the world. The parent is often threatened by the child's autonomy and so unwittingly and unknowingly sabotages his efforts to launch from a secure base. Also, parents may feel quite anxious and overwhelmed, and so the child finds himself in a role-reversed position of attempting to take care of a parent's emotional needs. When on the bottom of the cycle, the child experiences the parent as unreliable and unpredictable. At times, the parent, if she is feeling good, can be supportive and caring. But on other occasions, the parent can get overwhelmed and angry with the child for being needy.

Consequently, the child learns that to get his parent to respond to his needs, his emotions must be intense and even dramatic. The result is a child with a negative sense of self (*I'm not worthy of love, and I'm uncomfortable with autonomy and exploration*) and an often idealized sense of other (*I desperately need others to take care of me, but I must be in great need in order for her to respond to my emotions*). Unlike the avoidant, the preoccupied person's exploration system is underactivated, and his attachment system is hyperactivated. Even when his caregivers are responding to his needs, the preoccupied person may have difficulty feeling relief or feeling loved. And because he does not feel others respond with enough affection and concern, he may use defensive measures (oversubmissiveness, anger, clinging, demanding) and destructive behaviors, such as threats, self-injury, or promiscuity to soothe his emotions.

Fearful-avoidant attachment. Fearful-avoidant attachment, sometimes referred to as disorganized, occurs when a person has experienced difficulties on both sides of the circle. This often occurs in abusive environments, where caregivers place the child in a biological paradox, where the parent, the child's secure base, becomes the child's source of threat. The result is that biologically the child is motivated to (1) "run away" from the threat and to (2) seek comfort from her secure base. The child literally does not know if she is coming or going, and so the solution is to disconnect from her experience. This is believed to be the genesis of dissociation. Another result is that the child has a negative view of herself (*I'm unworthy of love, and I'm uncomfortable with autonomy*) and others (*I cannot count on you to help me in times of stress*). She may rapidly vacillate between both strategies of avoidance and preoccupation: "I don't need you; go away! Please don't leave me; I can't live without you." Finally, a child with fearful avoidance struggles with both autonomy and intimacy, and she may find herself strangely attracted to people who are likely to reenact abusive behavior.

Attachment in Scripture

Many principles behind attachment theory are illustrated through stories found in the Scriptures that reflect how parents shape a child's behavior (see Deut. 6:20–25; 1 Kings 14:12–13). In other cases, such as in the lives of King Saul and King David, the Scriptures illustrate various themes of attachment.

In the Old Testament, we see that when confronted by the prophet Samuel (1 Sam. 15), King Saul excused his behavior using a reasoning that closely follows the logic of a person with an ambivalent attachment style—Saul was afraid of being rejected because he already thought himself flawed. By contrast, King David took responsibility for his sin when the prophet Nathan called him out for his adulterous behavior (2 Sam. 12). David's secure attachment style gave him confidence to admit the truth, which we may assume was because his relationship with God was based on trust, and he was confident in God's willingness to forgive his sins and restore David's relationship with him.

The New Testament is filled with references to attachment themes that illustrate both sides of the secure-base system. For example, as noted in the epithet, Jesus portrayed himself as a haven of safety for those on the bottom side of the cycle, encouraging those who are weary and in need of comfort to come to him to find rest. Note that this requires that believers acknowledge their pain and needs, a task that is difficult for those who are more avoidant. Similarly, Jesus said that those who are at the bottom of the cycle and who are vulnerable enough to acknowledge their thirst (emotionally, spiritually) should "come to me to drink," and for those who do, "Out of his heart will flow rivers of living water" (John 7:38 ESV). Note that after people drink from Jesus's water, a river of living water flows, implying the person launches to the top of the cycle and takes this peace, joy, and security with them and offers it to others. The act of launching to the top of the cycle with the heartfelt knowledge of Jesus as their secure base and source of confidence is poignantly illustrated in Matthew 28:18–20, when Jesus told his disciples to "go" into the world and carry out God's purposes with the knowledge of his eternal presence, "And behold, I'm with you always, to the end of the age" (ESV).

Finally, in Philippians 4:4–7, Paul described key aspects of the secure-base system: He began by stating that we should rejoice because we know that "the Lord is near." Thus, he is our ever-present secure base from which we launch onto the top of the cycle, experiencing positive emotions and reasonableness. But notice that when we get on the bottom of the cycle and our attachment system is activated, instead of getting preoccupied with anxiety, fear, dread, and fretful worrying about all that could go wrong, we are to acknowledge (i.e., signal) our concerns to God and through "prayer and petition" (i.e., proximity-seeking behavior) bring those concerns to him. The result is the experience of great peace, which is beyond our understanding (i.e., safe haven).

Attachment Styles and Pathology

Attachment styles are relatively stable across the lifespan. Typically attachment security promotes psychological and emotional health and can act as a source of resilience in times of stress. In some ways, attachment security is equated to emotional and psychological health like the body's immune system is to our physical health. The immune system does not protect us from exposure to pathogens, but when exposed it protects against diseases. Though it sometimes prevents illness altogether, when an illness does occur, a healthy immune system attempts to keep the illness process at bay unlike those with a compromised immune system. Likewise, attachment security does not protect people from stressful life events, but they help us cope more effectively with stress so that it doesn't result in the onset of psychological and emotional disturbances.

Research does not demonstrate that attachment insecurity directly causes psychopathology and maladjustment. In fact, these insecure styles of attachment appear to be effective ways of managing the anxiety stress that result from insensitive, rejecting, chaotic, and sometimes abusive parenting. The difficulty is that if these patterns of attachment carry forward and are not somehow offset by alternative sources of secure attachment (e.g., family, friends, teachers, coaches, youth pastors), they can increase one's vulnerability to various forms of maladjustment. Alan Schore (1994), arguably the John Bowlby of our day, teaches that attachment security is tantamount to emotion regulation and healthy self-development. In contrast, attachment insecurity results in emotion dysregulation. Current research suggests that it is emotion dysregulation that is at

the heart of most forms of psychopathology, especially anxiety, depression, and emotional disorders (Barlow et al., 2011).

The current research on all forms of anxiety disorders and depression show that there is a great deal of overlap of symptoms between them (e.g., Brown & Barlow, 2009; Barlow et al., 2011; Kring & Solan, 2010). Additionally, there is a great deal of comorbidity among different disorders. For example, those who have anxiety disorders are increasingly at risk for developing depression over the course of their lifetimes. Also, it is very common for people who suffer from a depressive disorder to also experience significant co-occurring anxiety. Interestingly, researchers also found that treatments designed to target specific disorders (e.g., panic disorder) help reduce symptoms of other co-occurring disorders (like generalized anxiety disorder symptoms), plus they help improve mood symptoms. Moreover, affective neuroscience suggests a common underlying brain structure for all anxiety and emotional disorders, characterized by two features—overreactive limbic system circuits and underactive cortical structures such as the prefrontal cortex—resulting in limited inhibitory control of the limbic system.

Triple vulnerability. Research (e.g., Barlow et al., 2011; Suárez, Bennett, Goldstein, & Barlow, 2009) has shown three interactive factors involved in the progression toward the onset of disorders like anxiety and depression. The first is known as a generalized biological vulnerability in one's temperament, involving traits such as neuroticism, negative affectivity, behavioral inhibition, and avoidance. In some instances, this vulnerability may lie dormant until the individual experiences substantial stressful life events. The second factor arises from environmental risks, which can result in attachment insecurity, poverty, neglect, and the like. This creates what is known as a generalized psychological vulnerability, resulting in an individual who feels the world is uncontrollable and unpredictable. Finally, the third factor involves the specific psychological vulnerabilities that may arise in the context of stressful life events resulting in the disorder-specific symptoms.

So attachment itself is not equal to psychopathology. However, when it is combined with underlying biological vulnerabilities and challenging, stressful life events, it can result in the emergence of psychopathology. Let's take a closer look at how patterns of attachment can contribute to the development and maintenance of anxiety, depression, and emotional disorders.

Attachment avoidance. People with higher degrees of attachment avoidance tend to be concerned about problems centering on self-definition. If they develop problems with anxiety and depression, those problems are usually triggered by concerns about perceived failure, such as financial difficulties, work performance complaints, a lack of recognition, or a loss of status. They tend toward perfectionism, often holding themselves to unrealistic standards of performance. Likewise, they also tend to be emotional perfectionists, having very little tolerance for normal negative emotions such as anxiety, sadness, and grief.

Consequently, these individuals engage in both experiential and relational avoidance. Experiential avoidance is a known marker for maintaining both anxiety and depression. Experiential avoidance involves the person actively attempting to push out of their awareness negative thoughts, feelings, and images related to the stressful life event. Relational avoidance is failing to let others know about their distress. They keep it to themselves and turn away from others. Both of these processes interfere with the necessary emotional processing of the event and stunt the activation of effective problem solving, leading to heightened degrees of psychological and emotional distress and/or emotional numbness. This can activate another layer of defensive strategies, where the avoidant resorts to various forms of emotionally driven behaviors such as addictive habits (alcohol, drugs, sexual acting out, etc.) to assuage their pain. This comes full cycle as the consequences of these behaviors creates another wave of stressful life events.

Take Bob for example. He had received a poor evaluation at work from his supervisor. He was completely floored by the event and soon started experiencing depressive symptoms. He tried to ignore these feelings and not think about how upset he was about what had happened. His wife knew he was suffering, but he would just tell her he didn't want to talk about it. He eventually turned to watching some pornography on his phone, waiting for his wife to go to bed and then telling her he'd come in later. Once she discovered the pornography use, she became very angry and threatened to leave him. It was only then that he sought help.

Attachment preoccupation. Those with attachment preoccupation tend to be concerned about relatedness issues on the bottom of the cycle. They are typically stressed by life events such as relationship breakups, rejection, abandonment, anger related to jealousy, and other relationship concerns. Unlike the avoidant individual who pushes experience away, those with preoccupation tend to get flooded by and entangled in their internal experiences. Because of their fear of such emotional dysregulation, they may engage in a great deal of avoidance and safety behaviors.

Avoidance is the tendency to move away from experiences that are uncomfortable. Preoccupied individuals have very little tolerance for normal levels of anxiety and experience these feelings as dangerous and overwhelming. The difficulty with avoidance is that while in the short term it helps a person escape negative feelings (this is referred to in behavioral terms as negative reinforcement), in the long term it only intensifies those negative feelings. And it increases the likelihood that the next time you're faced with the feared situation, you will use the same methods of escape used previously. So, for example, if you are afraid of elevators because you fear they may get stuck and you will not be able to breathe or that you will have a panic attack, whenever you encounter an elevator you immediately take the stairs and tell yourself you needed the exercise anyway. Your anxiety about the elevator will immediately abate, and you may even feel good about the fact that you are getting some additional car-diovascular exercise. But in the long run, it reinforces your fear of elevators and your belief that something bad would have happened had you got on. Also, it will increase the likelihood that the next time you are faced with the choice of riding the elevator or taking the stairs, you will automatically take the stairs.

Another strategy to address preoccupation is the use of emotionally driven behaviors (Barlow et al., 2011). Unlike avoidance, which is designed to prevent emotional activation, emotionally driven behaviors are things people do once negative emotions have been triggered. Emotionally driven behaviors are designed to alleviate emotional distress by giving the person a sense of false security. These operate through the same mechanism as avoidance. A classic form of emotionally driven behavior comes in the form of compulsions. A client of mine who suffered from obsessive-compulsive disorder would get the intrusive thought (obsession) that his hands were contaminated with the deadly Ebola virus. This created tremendous anxiety, and so he used a combination of both avoidance and safety behaviors. Avoidance behavior was that he refused to touch any doorknob. Safety behaviors (or compulsions) involved excessive handwashing and eventually turned into wearing latex gloves like those used in medical settings.

Those with preoccupation may also attempt to use experiential avoidance as a way of not feeling certain kinds of emotions because they feel such emotions are threatening to their relational concerns. Jill recently took a job with an employer who was very impressed by her willingness to make sacrifices for the company. He would often ask her to carry out various tasks after hours and even on the weekends when she was supposed to be spending time with her family. She soon developed significant anxiety in the form of panic attacks, which would come out of the blue. She was unable to see any connection between her panic attacks and the frustration she was feeling toward her boss. When she came for therapy, her main concern was her panic anxiety. However, as I helped her gain increasing control of it, we turned our attention to her concerns about her job. We soon discovered that like many others suffering from anxiety disorders, Jill was afraid of the emotion of anger. In her experience of an emotionally chaotic and enmeshed family background, expressions of anger created serious problems. This opened the door for working on how to be appropriately assertive and set clear boundaries.

Fearful avoidance. Those with fearful avoidance patterns may vacillate between using both avoidance and preoccupation strategies. Like those with preoccupation, they desperately long to merge themselves with another person while at the same time employing avoidance strategies to keep others at a distance. Like preoccupied individuals, fearful avoidants are terrified of abandonment, often obsessing about the possibility of being rejected, betrayed, and left alone. They are also prone to use experiential avoidance strategies. These become extremely problematic to those who have experienced traumatic events because they prevent those people from emotionally and cognitively processing those events in a way in which they are able to "make sense" of them in their overall life narrative (Briere & Scott, 2015).

Finally, those with fearful avoidance are more prone to utilize what are called tension-reduction behaviors, which are extreme forms of the emotionally driven behaviors described above. These include behaviors like cutting, burning, binging, purging, extreme forms of sexual acting out, and excessive drug and alcohol use. These behaviors can actually be forms of both negative and positive reinforcement—negative reinforcement in that they help the person escape painful negative affect of states, and positive reinforcement because many of these behaviors involve the addition of pleasurable experiences. For example, when a person cuts, the body releases endogenous opioids, which not only take away the experience of pain but also cause the person to "feel good." Consequently, once these behaviors are started, they are difficult to stop. Further, they tend to escalate in frequency. Moreover, many of these behaviors lead to secondary consequences that in the long run lead to more stress.[†]

CASE STUDY

Recall the case of Cindy described in chapter 3, "Cognitive-Based Strategies." As Cindy made progress using CBT to allevi-

---

† Note that these different maladaptive emotional regulation strategies described above can be used by each of the different patterns of attachment. For example, those with primarily avoidance strategies can use tension-reduction behaviors.

ate her panic symptoms, she began to discuss long-standing concerns she had about her relationship with her husband. In her mind, she felt that her husband was more concerned about playing his internet-based video games with his buddies from around the country than he was about her. She decided to speak up and tell him how she felt. She told him that she felt he was addicted to these video games and that she believed he had an addictive personality in which he absorbed himself in everything but close relationships. She went on to tell him that she was jealous of these games and felt that they were like a mistress with whom he was having an affair: "You look forward to spending your time and your emotional energy with them more than me." This strategy backfired, her husband saying that she "blows everything out of proportion," and that she needs to "get a life." This only reinforced Cindy's belief that expressing her negative feelings was a bad idea and that she should keep her feelings locked away.

STRATEGIES, INTERVENTIONS, AND TECHNIQUES FOR ATTACHMENT-BASED ISSUES

Note that attachment theory is not necessarily wedded to any specific set of counseling strategies and techniques. A number of assessment strategies and instruments have been devised to help study attachment across the lifespan, and these have been modified and integrated into various treatment models. Attachment theory instead provides an integrative guide or road map for helping therapists better formulate cases and select treatment strategies

that will help accomplish specific therapeutic tasks. Accordingly, rather than calling these strategies, interventions, and techniques (SITs) for attachment, I'll refer to them as attachment-oriented or attached-informed SITs.

Therapeutic Attunement

Your first task is to create an environment in which the client will accept your presence as that of a helper who has his best interest in mind (Thomas & Sosin, 2011). Since clients carry their internal working models of attachment into all their emotional and social interactions, they will interact with you out of their style of attachment. As Schore (1994) notes, our affective interactions of attachment shape our brains for life.

The goal, according to Solomon and Siegel (2003), is to provide the "client a relationship foundation and specific experiences that help to promote complexity during the session and eventually to have the ability to self-organize and move toward complexity outside the sessions" (p. 5). For this reason, as with all cases, you need to exhibit compassionate empathic attunement to each client and his or her narrative as it unfolds before you. Attunement occurs through mutual gaze, voice rhythms and inflections, and other bodily responses between you and the client.

Therapeutic relationships are best established by targeting a client's right brain. Schore (2012) contends that emotional communication moves between a caregiver's and infant's right brains. Our IWMs of attachment reside in the right hemisphere of the brain, which is strongly connected to our nervous system and body. It processes not only current emotion, but emotion coded as bodily and relational memory. The right brain has been called the "the well-spring of passion, creativity, imagery, primary process thinking, and unconscious process" (DeYoung, 2015, p. 37). Early relational wounds damage the right side of the brain. Thus, as counselors, we must target client right-brain experiences by speaking right-brain language, which is not logical, rational language. When we use left-brain interventions, we often run into resistance or an inability to move past the troublesome feelings because such logic is misattuned to the site of emotions.

DeYoung (2015) argues that it isn't what we explain or interpret to the client but how we are with the client right brain to right brain, especially in affectively stressful moments. Clients must experience our empathy, regulation of our own affect, the ability to receive and express nonverbal communication, the sensitivity to register very slight changes in another's expression and emotion, and immediate awareness of one's own subjective and intersubjective experiences (Schore 2012). DeYoung (2015) writes, "A person who can't solve personal and social problems in right-brain ways will come to rely on left-brain, explicit analytical reasoning. But left-brain analysis will only contain and manage, not solve emotional and interpersonal problems" (p. 38). She goes on to say, "Change comes from the right-brain challenged client as he is able to contact, describe, and regulate his own emotional experience" (p. 38).

SECURE Model

In Bowlby's classic text, a *Secure Base: Clinical Applications of Attachment Theory* (1988, 2012), he outlines five core tasks of attachment-informed counseling. I incorporated these tasks into the SECURE model of change as depicted in figure 12.1 (Sibcy, 2007; Clinton & Sibcy, 2012). Within this model, therapy is not simply a transfer of factual knowledge to the client. Rather, it is fundamentally an integrative model of counseling that takes seriously the role of the therapist as an image bearer of God. The therapist helps establish a therapeutic context in which the client acquires skills needed to improve his or her ability to experience and regulate strong emotions and to participate in empathic, warm, enduring intimate relationships.

The SECURE acronym identifies six clusters of empirically based, biblically informed attachment-related tasks that are derived from a wide range of theoretical orientations and can be applied to nearly all forms of psychopathology, including complex disorders such as chronic depression and various trauma related syndromes. These six tasks are **s**afety, **e**ducation, **c**ontainment, **u**nderstanding, **r**estructuring, and **e**ngagement.

Safety. This is the key to any model of therapy. It refers to the secure-base function described earlier in the secure-base system. Here the therapist fosters a therapeutic alliance, which involves a nurturing collaboration in which the client begins to explore the story of why she decided to come and receive help. This is a very important therapeutic task because it helps identify where the pain is that the patient wants help with more immediately. So, for example, in Cindy's case it was clear to me in the first session that Cindy had difficulty with assertiveness and boundary setting. However, her main motivation for coming to therapy was her panic attacks. It was important that the therapist help her with those panic attacks first before addressing her interpersonal difficulties.

Safety also involves gathering information, doing a diagnostic assessment, and setting clear treatment goals to which the client is open and willing to commit. Additionally, the clinician provides a certain amount of structure to the session, which may involve setting agendas early in a session, identifying specific problems to work on, and securing the client's commitment to work on those problems. Finally, the clinician must help clients understand their problems in a way that makes sense and instills a sense of hope. This is an ongoing process throughout the course of therapy, by which the therapist provides a secure base from which clients can explore their problems and make linkages between their current problems and past relationship experiences.

Education. This can involve small psychoeducational tasks by which the counselor helps the client make sense of current problems. For Cindy, helping her make sense of how panic attacks work within the cognitive behavioral model gave her a sense of hope, and it also provided a springboard to teach her various types of coping skills. Once her panic attacks began to subside, I then explained how the fear of feeling certain negative emotions like anger could fuel panic anxiety. This created a clear rationale for her to begin working on effective communication skills. Cindy was taught numerous cognitive, emotional, and behavioral skills over the course of treatment. In our lives and for our Christian clients, we frame these as "spiritual formation skills" in that they facilitate conscious contact with God. They allow us to move from problem-focus to God-focus. Among the skills are behavior training, distress-tolerance skills, emotion-regulation skills, and attention-regulation skills/mindfulness training.

Containment. Containment extends the aspect of the safety construct further. Therapy involves the balance between two factors: support and challenge. Support provides emotional regulation to explore new challenges. Effective therapy involves creating a balance between emotional activation and emotion regulation. This is referred to as the therapeutic window (see figure 12.2). This is a crucial aspect for attachment-based therapies because once emotion is activated, it activates the attachment system. This involves the IWM where the person's implicit relational beliefs are also activated. They are prone to expect you as a therapist to handle their negative feelings much like their previous attachment figures. Helping a person regulate their emotions within the context of a therapy session can be an important strategy for revising their IWM about themselves and others. But this requires sensitivity and skill on your part.

In figure 12.2, the left-hand side is emotional activation between 0 and 10. On the bottom is the length of a therapy session in minutes. The therapeutic window is the optimal amount of emotional activation in which the client can learn new skills for handling his emotions and, implicitly, revise his IWM about an attachment figure's trustworthiness and willingness to help him regulate.

The solid line represents the therapist underchallenging the client. The session is mostly factually oriented. Although it keeps the client from feeling badly, it doesn't really challenge him to learn new strategies for healing. If this were to repeat itself over many sessions, the client might begin to question the usefulness of therapy.

The line with consistent dashes depicts the data from the therapist overactivating the client's emotional system. This is too much challenge and not enough support. In some instances, a novice therapist may think that he really had a good session because the client could "get in touch with her feelings," but she was left feeling completely dysregulated at the end of the session. This unfortunately can retraumatize clients, making them feel ashamed, unworthy, and unsafe.

The inconsistent dashed line represents the therapist finding the therapeutic window. There is a moderate degree of emotional activation, and the therapist can help the client lower the emotional intensity before the end of the session. Operating within the therapeutic window is key to all effective therapies. In many ways, it reflects the secure-base system described above. The therapist helps the client feel secure enough to explore new territories. Once emotion is activated, the therapist helps the client learn how to calm herself down and effectively cope with the task without using maladaptive strategies such as avoidance, emotionally driven behaviors, or dissociation. Through repeated journeys into the therapeutic window, the client can learn new skills for managing negative emotions and revise her IWM.

In Cindy's case, for example, by helping her with her panic attacks, I established myself as a secure base for her to then explore how to experience anger and turn it into effective assertive behavior. We began to practice new communication skills within the safety of the therapeutic session.

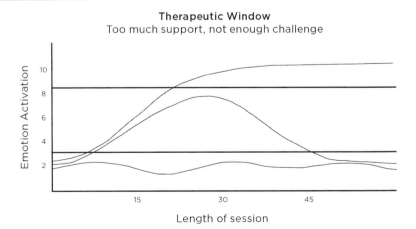

Figure 12.2. Therapeutic window

Once she became increasingly comfortable with the strategies within the session, she began to practice them out of session in real-life settings. In Bob's case, discussed early in the chapter, my first task was to teach him strategies to manage his presenting problems, namely, his impulses to use pornography and poor communication with his wife. Then we turned our attention to his difficulties with handling negative feedback from others and reducing his overuse of perfectionism. This became somewhat scary to him because whenever he thought of modifying these perfectionistic attitudes, he became flooded with feelings of shame and inadequacy.

Understanding. As Cindy's sense of safety improved, she was better prepared to engage in the process of narrative repair. This involved her telling her stories and linking current patterns of thinking, feeling, relating, and communicating with previous relationship experiences. This can involve the use of the significant-other history (McCullough, 2000) or adult attachment interview and other narrative based procedures (Steele, Steele, Sroufe, & Jacobvitz, 2008). It can also involve helping clients see how old patterns of relating were potentially healthy at the time but now create more difficulties. Further, it can involve helping clients see how relationships are two-way transactions and how to appreciate the consequences of their interpersonal behavior. Essentially, we begin to help clients see that they unintentionally and unknowingly create much of the interpersonal pain experience. Finally, through the process of understanding, we begin to help clients learn how to differ-

entiate between toxic attachment figures from the past and current relationships, especially the therapeutic relationship.

Restructuring. Ultimately, from an attachment model of therapy, the goal is to help clients develop coherent narratives that help them make sense of their existence in light of God's redemptive story in their lives. This restructuring process is sometimes referred to as schema reconstruction. Restructuring can involve the use of multiple strategies that involve modifying maladaptive, self-defeating patterns of thinking, feeling, behaving, and relating to others. It involves helping clients engage in personal experiments that can generate new "data" that may restructure and transform negative, rigid, globally negative beliefs about themselves and others. This type of interpersonal exposure occurs both in and out of session. Here we practice new patterns of relating to others while giving up old patterns of avoidance, blame, and defensiveness. It also involves fostering forgiveness of oneself and others.

Below are procedures developed by James McCullough (2000) in an empirically supported treatment package for treating chronic depression. The treatment combines cognitive, behavioral, and psychodynamic principles together in a unified practice model. It is only one of many examples of models that can be used to accomplish attachment tasks in therapy. These strategies (e.g., significant other history, transference hypotheses, interpersonal situation analysis; discipline personal involvement, and interpersonal discrimination exercises) were applied to Cindy's case and helped her overcome her chronic sense of interpersonal helplessness in her relationships and especially in her marriage.

First, explore the significant-other history. This involves asking the client to identify four to six people in her life who played a significant role (for good or ill) in who she is today. This must include both parents if they were physically involved with her early childhood, and the person's spouse if she is or ever was married. In most cases, begin by discussing the client's relationship with her mother. Ask the client to describe her relationship with this parent during early childhood, and ask her to describe what it was like being around this parent. Listen for words or descriptions that may be useful to explore the emotional nature of the relationship. Also, encourage the client patient to give autobiographical memories of specific events that occurred between her and the parent. After about ten or fifteen minutes, you ask: "How do you think this relationship affects who you are today? What stamp has this relationship left on you?" Here you both explore how the relationship influences the way she thinks about herself, others, and her emotions. Repeat this with each of the subsequent significant others.

Second, at the end of this interview, which can span the course of two to three sessions, form in your mind—not with the client—a transference hypothesis. This is based on the idea that certain emotionally charged relational events that occurred in childhood are likely to recapitulate themselves in therapy at some point. Four different transference themes commonly occur in therapy relationships:

(1) intimacy—connecting while struggling with abandonment; (2) expression of negative emotions—sharing negative feelings toward others backfired; (3) mistakes—mistakes or breaking a rule received severe criticism or punishment; and (4) disclosure of private material—private material that was revealed to other people was used against them. In Cindy's significant-other history, she remembered her parents arguing frequently. In the way she remembers it, her mother was a very critical and demeaning person. Whenever she would verbally attack her father, he would explode into fits of cursing and start breaking things. She concluded that expressing negative feelings, especially anger and frustration, led to scary explosive behavior from others, especially men. The transference hypothesis for her was: *If I express negative feelings to Dr. Sibcy, he will get angry and upset with me.* Based on this transference hypothesis, I began keeping my eyes peeled for a therapy "hot spot," which was some occasion in which Cindy might express negative emotion toward me in therapy.

Interpersonal discrimination exercises (McCullough, 2000). Once a hot-spot situation is activated in therapy, use this as an opportunity to help the client differentiate past toxic relationships from the present therapeutic relationship. This involves asking the client a series of questions: (1) Ask how the client's significant others that were identified in the significant-other history would have responded to the current situation. (2) Ask the client how you (as the therapist) responded to her in the current situation to differentiate how you handled it compared with those from the past. (3) Ask the client, "What does this say about our relationship?" (4) Ask, "What do you think this says about future relationships?"

In Cindy's case, a situation arose out of her arriving fifteen minutes early for therapy. I was in a therapy session with a new client who needed to be hospitalized due to suicidal intent. Though I informed my receptionist that I was running late, she failed to tell Cindy, who sat in the waiting room for some time. She eventually left. In the next session, she acted as if nothing had occurred. She said that I was too busy to see her. After some prompting, she told me that she was really upset and hurt about what had occurred. I encouraged her to be more specific about what she meant by "upset and hurt." I told her, "If I had been in your shoes, I would have been really angry. They could have at least given me the courtesy of informing me that my counselor was running late because of an emergency." Her eyes moistened as she heard me validate her concerns. She then admitted to being angry about not being valued and respected. I again empathized with her, saying, "Yes, that makes total sense to me. Again, I would have felt the exact same way. And now that you bring this up, I also feel badly because I didn't follow up with my receptionist and update her on the fact that I was going to have to reschedule with you because of an emergency situation. I just assumed that she communicated that to you without checking it out."

We then transitioned into talking about other events that had occurred since the last session. Toward the last twenty minutes of the session, I initiated the interpersonal discrimination exercise (McCullough, 2000). I asked Cindy to remind me again of how things would go in her relationship with her father if she expressed negative feelings. She responded that she in fact never really did express these feelings to her father because she was so afraid that he would react to her like he did her mother. Then she described how angry and scary he would become when he did this. When I asked her how her husband would handle it, she quickly described how he would minimize her concerns and tell her she was blowing everything out of proportion. I then asked her to describe how she felt during those events. This activated her emotional system, and she was clearly in the therapeutic window. Then I asked her, "Cindy, how did I handle it when you expressed your frustration about your last appointment?" She noted that I was very understanding and had validated her feelings, taking her concerns seriously. I asked her to describe very specifically what it was that I did that gave her that impression, to draw her attention to specific behaviors that occurred in the session and how these were different from her father's and those of other significant others. This was a very important strategy. Unless I drew attention to the disparity between Cindy's past and the present, in the context of emotional activation, she would likely leave the session and remember it in a more negative light. She would very likely just incorporate the event into her IWM, thinking that I was upset and angry with her for her having expressed these feelings. But by drawing her attention to what actually happened in the session and perceptually anchoring her into what actually happened, I provided her with a very powerful opportunity to revise her implicit expectations for how people will react to her when she expresses her feelings.

I then asked Cindy what this implied about our therapeutic relationship. She could at least verbalize that she felt it was safe to express her feelings and that she and I could talk about the strategies for handling possible challenges in the therapy relationship. Finally, I asked her to reflect on how this might affect other relationships down the road. This was difficult for her to elaborate on, because in her mind, at least at that time, she believed that others would not necessarily be so validating. I told her that I understood, but hopefully, down the road, she might discover some new possibilities.

Interpersonal situation analysis (see McCullough, 2000). To transform our clients' IWMs, we also need to focus on how they currently handle relationship conflict. People with any of the three insecure attachment patterns struggle with understanding how their interpersonal relationship patterns can lead to the negative outcomes they expect from others. For example, it's very common with people suffering from both anxiety and depressive disorders to move into a passive hostile stance in which they stuff their negative feelings, especially anger and frustration, and disengage from others. The unfortunate consequence of this is that others are unable to understand their behavior and are likely to become more dominant and hostile or disengaged and rejecting.

For those with more fearful avoidant patterns of attachment, they are also prone to dissociate or perceptually check out from interpersonal relationship events. The effect is that they no longer pay attention to what is actually happening between them and the other person. The interpersonal situation analysis is designed to help people focus during interpersonal events and also better understand the relationship between their interpersonal behavior and their consequences.

The situation analysis involves seven steps (i.e., situational description; interpretations of the situation; description of personal behavior; identification of the actual outcome; identification of the desired outcome; asking, "Did you get the desired outcome?"; asking, "Why?") There are also two phases to this task. The first is the elicitation phase, in which you help the client effectively describe what happened. The second is the remediation phase, in which you teach the client new skills.

Step 1: Situational description. Identify a "slice of time" and describe a relevant interpersonal event that has a beginning, middle, and end. In Cindy's case, this took some time because she was used to describing interpersonal situations in global, negative, rigid patterns. Recall that Cindy stated that no matter what she says to her husband about his video games, he "goes off at me, saying that I blow everything out of proportion and that I need to get a life." I eventually helped her identify and describe a recent event. This was challenging because the task involves describing the event without infusing commentary and interpretation into the description.

Those interpretations are elaborated in step 2. The following is Cindy's situational description:

> The other evening, after dinner, my husband got up from the table and put his dishes in the sink. He then walked to the downstairs door and looked at me and said, "I'm going downstairs to play my game." I just looked at him and said, "Okay." He went downstairs to play his game, and I went to bed.

As we looked at this event, it was important for us to identify the last thing Cindy did in relationship to her husband. She initially thought that it was when she went to bed. But we focused on when she looked at him and said, "Okay," just before he went downstairs to play his video game.

Step 2: Interpretations of the situation. In step 2, I helped Cindy identify three interpretations she made in that situation by asking her: "What thoughts were going through your head in the situation? What did you think was happening? What did you think you should do?"

Cindy came up with three interpretations: (1) "Here we go again. He's going to go play his video game and leave me here all alone." (2) "He doesn't really care about my feelings and what I want." (3) "What's the point in saying anything?" It is important to note that in this step, you don't challenge these thoughts.

Step 3: Description of personal behavior. Whereas in step 2, Cindy described what was going on inside her head at the time of the event, step 3 encouraged her to shift her perspective to describe what her behav-

ior would look like from the position of an objective observer. You may want to ask a client, "If I had a GoPro camera mounted on the wall that recorded this event, or if your husband had a GoPro mounted on his forehead and we were watching that on the screen in front of us, what would I see you do?" This is a challenging task, especially for people with long-standing depression and a history of interpersonal trauma. It's difficult for them to imagine what their behavior looks like to others. Initially Cindy said that she was very angry and upset. "Would I be able to see that looking at the film of you in that situation?" I asked. She said, "Oh, I guess you wouldn't have been able to see it because I didn't show any expression of anger or frustration." "Okay, Cindy, but what would I see on the film?" I asked. "You would have seen me nod my head up and down as I said, 'Okay,' in a passive, quiet voice."

Step 4: Identification of the actual outcome. In this model, an "outcome" refers to the last behavior the client did in the interpersonal situation. For Cindy, it was when she said, "Okay," to her husband when he declared that he was going downstairs to play his game. It's important to note that in this model, "outcome" is a behavior that the person has 100 percent control over. So Cindy had 100 percent control of whether she said, "Okay," or not.

Step 5: Identification of the desired outcome. I asked Cindy, "If you went back to step 4 and could replace the actual outcome with something different, would you?" It is here that you begin the remediation process. Cindy's desired outcome was that her husband stop playing video games.

First, it was important to clarify whether she simply wanted him to give up his video games or wanted him to spend time with her. This implicitly challenged her black-and-white, all-or-nothing thinking. She said that she wanted her husband to spend time with her.

This was a good first step. Second, it was important to help her see that getting her husband to spend time with her was not something she had direct control over, so it couldn't be her desired outcome. Instead, I asked Cindy what was the best way for her husband to know what she wanted in this situation? As is commonly the case, she contended that she shouldn't have to tell him what she wanted. "He should just know." I empathized with this: "I agree with you 100 percent. You shouldn't have to tell your husband that you want to spend time with him." I then explained that we can live in one of two worlds: Shouldville or Realville. In Shouldville the world is the way it ought to be. You don't have to tell people what you want or need; they simply get it and respond to it effectively. I also pointed out that there are many other wonderful benefits of Shouldville, such as grass never growing over three and a half inches, eliminating having to spend hours of our weekend mowing, and traffic lights always being in perfect synchrony whenever we're rushing from one side of town to the other. But, I continued, we have to live in Realville. And here we must mow our grass and daily tolerate those diabolical traffic lights that delay us. We also must tell the people we know best, like our spouses, what it is that we want, need, like, and don't like.

Cindy objected, declaring that it doesn't matter what she says to her husband, nothing works. "No matter what I say to him about what I want registers in his mind. All he cares about is his video games." Again, this is a very common belief by those with chronic interpersonal helplessness. It is here that we have conversation about getting one's desired outcome. I often use a baseball analogy.

Counselor: Cindy, I don't know if you care much about baseball, but let's just use it as an example. If a baseball player wants to get a base hit, what would be his desired outcome?

Cindy: To hit the baseball.

Counselor: Okay, but does a batter have 100 percent control over whether he hits the baseball?

Cindy: No, I guess not.

Counselor: That's right. In fact, the best baseball players in history only get a hit 30 percent of the time. The other 70 percent of the time they get out. So the best players only get a hit on average three out of every ten times at bat. But in order to get a hit, what is it that the baseball play must do? If he's going to hit the baseball, what does he have to do that is 100 percent under his control?

Cindy: I guess swing the bat.

Counselor: That's right. He has to take good swings at good pitches. That is 100 percent under his control. If he doesn't do that, there is no possible way to get a hit. Now, the same thing applies to social situations like yours. If you ask your husband to spend time with you, you might strike out. But if you don't ask, you are almost 100 percent certain not to get what you want.

Most people realize that the player must swing the bat to get a hit. I clarify that response by telling the client that the player needs to take good swings at good pitches in order to get a hit. But that doesn't mean he will get a hit. It only creates the best possibility. But I also point out that a baseball player doesn't get depressed if he strikes out while taking good swings at good pitches. He may be disappointed, and this may inspire him to spend more time in the batting cage practicing his swings. But the player who stops swinging the bat gets depressed, telling himself as he walks away from the plate, "See, no matter what I do, nothing works for me." Before long he stops going to the plate and eventually stops even showing up to the stadium for the game.

Our goal at step 5 is to identify what a good swing looks like in the situation. We worked on it, and Cindy finally came up with this: "I would like it if we could find some time to spend together this evening."

Step 6: Ask, "Did you get the desired outcome?" I first asked Cindy if she received her desired outcome. Of course, the actual outcome must be clearly named: "In your actual outcome, you shook your head up and down and told your husband, 'Okay.'" Second, I stated what Cindy's revised desired outcome was: "You revised your desired outcome to wanting to say to your husband, 'I would like it if we could find some time to spend together this evening.' Did you get your desired outcome?"

Although the answer is obvious, it is important that Cindy explicitly state, "No." This sets the stage for step 7, where we want the client to see how her interpersonal behavior in this situation made it nearly impossible for her to achieve her desired outcome.

Step 7: Ask, "Why? Considering what went wrong and why, what could you do instead?" This step comes immediately on the heels of the client's response to step 6. Once Cindy said, "No," I followed up with, "Why?" The reason we ask the "Why?" question is to help clients attend to the fact that they don't get their desired outcomes when, in fact, they don't ask for it or they don't speak up. It's very common for clients to object: "It doesn't matter what I do; I won't get it anyway." It's important to realize that people who don't suffer from chronic interpersonal helplessness easily see the reason why they didn't get their desired outcome. But those with more impairment often do not get it. For example, a client might say, "I didn't get my desired outcome because my husband went downstairs and played his video game, and I went to bed." In such situations, ask, "What is it in this situation that you didn't do that you had to do in order to get your desired outcome?" Like Cindy, in most cases this question allows clients to see that the reason they didn't get their desired outcome was failing to speak up.

We then returned to step 2 to remediate Cindy's thinking. Avoid debates with clients about whether their thoughts are true or not. Instead, Cindy and I focused on whether the thought helped her to obtain her desired outcome. To do this, we train clients on how to produce an *action-read*. This involves the client looking at a situation in such a way that it tells her what is actually happening, and asking, "What do I want?" and "What do I need to do to get it?"

Cindy could see that each of her three interpretations was ineffective. I read to her each thought and then asked, "Did this thought help you obtain your desired outcome?" Cindy replied, "No, I guess I didn't." After demonstrating that each of the interpretations was ineffective, I asked, "If you wanted to get your desired outcome, to tell your husband that you wanted to spend time with him this evening, what would you have to tell yourself to do in this situation?" Cindy realized that she needed to speak up to her husband in a friendly and inviting way about what she wanted him to do.

Given the amount and complexity of the information from conducting situational analyses, I either write them on paper or type them on a computer screen so the clients can see the flow of the conversation in front of them. I also use colored fonts/markers for clarity. I marked Cindy's desired outcomes in green, and then I asked her: "Let's imagine that you are back in that situation. Your husband has his hand on the door and looks at you and says, 'I'm going downstairs to play my video games.' What would you say to him?" I encouraged her to read the highlighted statement to me (word for word). Clients often feel the same kind of interpersonal fear they feel in the actual situations. This is a form of interpersonal exposure in that the client is almost always in the window of tolerance.

At this point, we role played this situation in a very safe way. When Cindy stated her desired outcome in the role play, I gave her a fist bump and a positive reinforcing statement: "Way to go! You did it!" Almost immediately her countenance brightened, and she felt like she had accomplished something in the session.

Remind clients to practice these skills only within the safety of the four walls of therapy. Once your clients feel confident enough, they can try the skills in their day-to-day life. This is consistent with the attachment secure-base system. We are not trying to force clients to the top of the secure-base cycle before they feel ready to do so. Many therapists are tempted to pressure the client to practice these skills outside of therapy: "Okay Cindy, so how about the next time your husband starts to go play his video game, you speak up and tell him what you want?" Chronically depressed clients will very likely tell you they will try but won't follow through. This will only place undo strain on the therapy relationship, because when they fail to do so (as they most likely will), you will represent just another person they have disappointed. It may even result in them missing the next few sessions.

Engage. The final component in the SECURE model is engagement. As clients are able to learn skills for regulating their emotions and/or managing their relationships more effectively, we encourage them to risk reconnecting with their lives. For some clients with more acute onset types of problems, this can happen fairly quickly once their symptoms begin to abate. Once they start feeling better, they return to the relationships, the hobbies, the goal-directed activities they used to engage in prior to the onset of their symptoms. For those with more chronic, long-standing problems, this can be a challenging task as their identity, in terms of what they like, what they don't like, what feels meaningful and purposeful to them, is underdeveloped. Thus, some need additional skills for learning how to make friends, identifying hobbies and points of interest, and connecting with a larger support network.

For example, once Bob's symptoms were stabilized, I needed to help him plug into a broader support network of male friends. He took up exercise and started playing tennis. He signed up for tennis lessons and joined tennis leagues where he met new male friends he could spend time with. This became a healthy alternative to assuaging his loneliness with pornography and other addictive behaviors. He and his wife were also able to plug back into a local church and began attending some church-based small group meetings that helped them learn more about their faith and provided a place to share their concerns and prayer requests with friends. This went a long way in increasing Bob's comfort with self-disclosure. Interestingly, as he began to keep track of prayer requests made in the group, he noticed over time that God responded to these prayers in powerful ways he did not expect to see. He learned that prayer was not so much about trying to get God on board with his agenda but ultimately about him becoming more sensitive to God's purposes. Eventually Bob began asking God to help him learn how to be the most effective he could be at work not to get praise from his boss but to be a testimony to God's work in his life. Interestingly, his work performance improved, and paradoxically his self-confidence improved as well.

Attachment-oriented counseling therapies focus on the impact of childhood relational trauma on the adult (Solomon & Siegel, 2003). Among the various therapies that work in the treatment of attachment-based disorders are interpersonal psychotherapy and mindfulness-informed CBT (Luyten, Fonagy, Lemma, & Target, 2012). According to Briere and Scott (2015), the client has to develop a new way of looking at himself before he can begin to change.

Interpersonal Neurobiology (IPNB)

Another attachment topic that clients need to learn about is how a person's brain functioning impacts their feelings, thoughts, and behavior. This is known as interpersonal neurobiology (IPNB). One of the attachment-based therapies that I have found effective is derived from the work of Siegel (2012; see also Solomon & Siegel, 2003). Interpersonal neurobiology is a field that studies the interaction between relational experiences and the developing mind. Throughout the person's development, the brain generates complex neural networks through interactions with others and the environment that result in a system that responds to external stimuli and allows for internal regulation (Solomon & Siegel, 2003). Understanding how the organization of one's brain was impacted by early experiences can help clients become more objective about their own feelings, thoughts, and behavior.

Narrative Strategies in Attachment Therapy: Remembering the Story

Train to self-soothe. As the client gains the skill to self-regulate, it is advisable to ask the client to remember her story (Foa, Hembree, & Rothbaum, 2007). This is often a difficult period as the narrative recall will activate painful memories and attachment behaviors that would increase her arousal, but is nevertheless necessary. One of the key steps during office sessions is to introduce the use of self-soothing techniques every time the client's narrative is becoming too painful to recall or narrate. This period takes several weeks as the person learns to integrate her episodic memory (memories associated with emotions; a person's autobiographical memory) with her implicit memory (primarily unconscious and includes memory about carrying out procedures, such as riding a bike or playing an instrument). Do not set a time frame in which to accomplish this step as the client will do this for you. What is important is that you provide emotional support and assurances to the client that she will get better. Remember, the person cannot heal what she does not feel.

Reframe the story. As the client gains the ability to narrate the story with minimal discomfort, it is important to help her understand that those memories will never go away. However, it does not mean that the client would continue to experience the pain. At this stage, begin to teach her how to reframe the meaning of the story so that she is able to identify the growth that came from her experiences. Usually during this phase the client will address topics related to forgiveness, grace, and acceptance. Avoid the temptation to tell her what she should do, but instead rely on Socratic questioning to help her formulate her own answers.

Though discussion of the mentalizing technique is beyond the scope of this chapter, it is useful in attachment work. Simply put, mentalization is a process whereby people learn to understand both their intentions and those of others (see Allen & Fonagy, 2006; Allen, Fonagy, & Bateman, 2008). By increasing a client's mentalization capacity, improvement should occur in her affective regulation. Cindy mentalized the unsatisfactory experiences she had with her husband. My goal was for her to learn how to feel clearly, as opposed to thinking clearly, which has its own place in therapeutic work. Attuning with her distant family relational history, her history with her husband, and her current patterns of experience, she was able to develop new capacities to feel the connection between those histories and patterns. (For more information on mentalizing see Sibcy, 2017).

CONCLUSION

Attachment-oriented strategies recognize that interpersonal concerns are behind many of the mental health problems that counselors treat. Therapies such as interpersonal psychotherapy and mindfulness-informed CBT have proven valuable in the treatment of multiple disorders such as anxiety and depression. In the Bible Jesus spoke about old wineskins that could not contain new wine because they would burst (Matt. 9:17), and we could say that a person's original IWM is like the old wineskin that bursts when we are faced with a new context. Our brain is a complicated and precious organ that God gave us so that we could relate to him and to one another. According to IPNB, it is designed to maximize relations. When given erroneous or deficient information in the context of its original development, it encodes behavioral rules that continue to conform with that context until remediation occurs. Through attachment-based counseling, the counselor helps people develop new IWMs that are flexible, adaptable, coherent, energized, and stable.

RECOMMENDED READING

Bowlby, J. (1988). *A secure base: Clinical applications of attachment theory*. London: Routledge.

Briere, J., & Scott, C. (2015). *Principles of trauma therapy: A guide to symptoms, evaluation, and treatment* (2nd ed.). Thousand Oaks, CA: Sage.

Brisch, K. H. (2002). *Treating attachment disorders: From theory to therapy*. New York, NY: Guilford Press.

Clinton, T., & Sibcy, G. (2002). *Attachments: Why you love, feel and act the way you do*. Nashville, TN: Thomas Nelson.

Clinton, T., & Sibcy, G. (2006). *Why you do the things you do: The secret to healthy relationships*. Nashville, TN: Thomas Nelson.

Clinton, T., & Straub, J. (2010). *God attachment: Why you believe, act, and feel the way you do about God*. New York, NY: Howard.

Farnfield, S., & Holmes, P. (2014). *The Routledge handbook of attachment: Assessment*. New York, NY: Routledge.

Grossman, K. E., Grossman, K., & Waters, E. (2005). *Attachment from infancy to adulthood: The major longitudinal studies*. New York, NY: Guilford Press.

Karen, R. (1998). *Becoming attached: First relationships and how they shape our capacity to love*. New York, NY: Oxford University Press.

Siegel, D. J. (2012). *The developing mind: How relationships and the brain interact to shape who we are*. New York, NY: Guilford Press.

PART 2

Population-Based Strategies

CHAPTER 13

Child-Focused Strategies

Kevin B. Hull, PhD

See that you do not despise one of these little
ones. For I tell you that their angels in heaven
always see the face of my Father in heaven.

MATTHEW 18:10

Children are continuously developing. The physiological, emotional,
and cognitive states of children are constantly growing and changing, pushing
them developmentally forward so that
new levels of awareness, relationships, and
abilities can be achieved. Moreover, children are helpless and must have help to
get their needs met. Children are at the
mercy of their caregivers; they have little
say over what happens in their daily lives.
Children are also affected by the environment to which they are exposed but have
little ability to change it or flee. Children
cannot control who enters their lives or
who leaves; they have little to no control
over when relationships begin and end.

The combination of developmental
changes and needing to rely on others to
meet their basic needs make children at
risk for emotional and mental distress. The
American Counseling Association (2011)
reported that 5 percent of all children in
the United States between the ages of four

and seventeen were found to have "serious
difficulties with emotions, concentration,
behavior, or being able to get along with
other people" (p. 2). Additionally, the
American Counseling Association (2011)
reported that in the United States, 5 to 9
percent of children, which represents millions of children, "have a serious mental
disturbance" (p. 3), and 75 percent of children who suffer from behavioral and emotional conditions are not provided with
adequate mental health care.

Children require a counseling approach that is strategic and fitted to their
unique needs. A therapist who works
with children must possess a multifaceted
approach due to the vast developmental
milestones of childhood development and
all the potential challenges that accompany these milestones. Cognitive, emotional, and social development, as well as the
attachment process and self-development
are all part of the developmental journey
of childhood. This chapter provides the

reader with an overview of effective counseling techniques that address the mental, emotional, behavioral, and spiritual challenges of children. Specific strategies and techniques are tied to one or more of the six cases.

THEOLOGY AND PSYCHOLOGY OF CHILDHOOD

The developmental milestones of childhood are numerous and complex. The stages of development are designed to propel the child forward so that new challenges can be faced and mastered. A child's developmental foundation rests on physical needs being met and on emotional security (Maslow, 1970). These create an optimum environment for the stages of cognitive development (Piaget & Inhelder, 1969), attachment (Bowlby, 1969, 1982), emotional development (Berk, 2006), moral reasoning (Kohlberg, 1976), and psychosocial development (Erickson, 1963). The most basic psychological needs of children that are necessary for emotional and cognitive growth are a sense of safety and security. These needs are filled through nurturing relationships with caregivers. Receiving comfort when hurt or scared provides children with a sense of safety that enables them to achieve developmental milestones. Children who do not have a sense of safety cannot develop or learn properly and often develop psychological, emotional, and social problems (Bowlby, 1969, 1982).

Self-development, one of the most significant developmental tasks of childhood, is made up of many factors and stages. Harter (2012b) identifies six key features of self-development during childhood that fall under three main categories: self-awareness, self-agency, and self-continuity. Self-agency, the sense of having control over one's thoughts and actions, is critical as the child develops the idea that his behaviors impact others and situations around him. Self-continuity describes the revelation that the child's self has "physical permanence over time" (Harter, 2012, p. 683). Abuse, trauma, neglect, and negative attachment patterns can significantly disrupt or halt self-development, as well as create negative and false self-attributions that become embedded in the child's thinking and behavior (Cicchetti & Toth, 2006). As the child approaches adolescence and eventually advances to adulthood, these problems can multiply and create significant attachment and self-esteem problems as well as cognitive and emotional difficulties (Bretherton & Munholland, 2008).

The Bible affirms the developmental process, acknowledging that children require nurture (Prov. 22:6) and training (Eph. 6:4). Left to themselves, there may be trouble (Prov. 29:15). Admonitions to parents are plentiful (Prov. 1:8–9; 19:18), reflecting how children absorb the modeling around them and revealing that the environment can affect a child's development and functioning. The New Testament in particular teaches that Jesus was "indignant" at how the disciples were chasing away the children (Mark 10:13–16); he told the crowd that the "kingdom of God belongs to such as these" (v. 14), and that one could not attain heaven if one were not "like a little child" (v. 15). Jesus then "took the children in his arms, placed his hands on them and blessed them" (v. 16). God also reveals through Scripture his compassion for the fatherless (Ps. 68:5–6) and special judgment reserved for those who do harm to children or lead them astray (Matt. 18:6). Fathers are specifically warned not to "exasperate" their children but to "bring them up in the training and instruction of the Lord" (Eph. 6:4).

The Bible provides examples of wayward children, such as Eli's sons (1 Sam. 2), as well as the grief of King David over his wayward son Absalom (2 Sam. 18:33). King Ahaz is another example of a son who chose not to follow his father's godly example (2 Kings 16:2) and ignored God's commands. Conversely, the parable of the prodigal son (Luke 15:11–32) gives hope to parents of wayward children and demonstrates a hopeful faithfulness and reliance on God to deliver the young person. Scripture also demonstrates extraordinary young people who walked with God and were blessed by God. Miriam helped steer the course of Moses's life by approaching Pharaoh's daughter to find a Jewish mother to nurse him (Ex. 2:7), while Joseph (Gen. 37), Samuel (1 Sam. 3), David (1 Sam. 16), and Josiah (2 Kings 22) are examples of young people who were important to God and obedient to him, and played a key role in the course of history.

CASE STUDIES

Case One

Jenny is a six-year-old black female who has been diagnosed with reactive attachment disorder. Her adoptive parents report that she has been removed from three schools in the past year and that she has intense anger outbursts in which she is inconsolable. She was adopted at age three after being removed from her family due to physical neglect and emotional abuse. They are worried because she has never bonded with them.

Case Two

Timothy is a nine-year-old white male who has been brought to counseling because of his aggressive behavior toward his mother and peers at school—this after being told by his father three weeks ago that the father never wants to see Timothy again. Timothy told his mother that he feels "worthless" and that he hates himself.

Case Three

Caitlyn is a twelve-year-old Hispanic female who reports being afraid to spend time at her father's house. Her father has recently remarried, and Caitlyn told her mother that the new wife does not speak to her and that it makes Caitlyn feel uncomfortable. When she tried to talk to her father, he screamed at her and told her it was her fault and that she is "spoiled and selfish." Caitlyn has been having nightmares every night for the past month.

Case Four

Bobby is an eight-year-old black male who is refusing to attend school. He fights his mother every morning, and if she tries to take him to school, he refuses to get out of the car. School staff have attempted to pull him from the car, but he hits and bites them and then runs away. When they make him stay at school, he attacks the teacher, destroys the classroom, and lashes out at peers. He told his mother, "I am stupid and I hate school."

Case Five

Andrew is a ten-year-old Asian male who is being bullied at school. His mother and father report that Andrew's classmates push him down and make fun of his Asian heritage by imitating his accent and making fun of his "slanted" eyes. The family recently moved from Japan and are shocked at the way Andrew is being treated. The school has been absolutely no help at all. The parents are very frustrated and are considering homeschooling Andrew.

Case Six

Tristan is an eleven-year-old white male who has been sexually abused by a paternal uncle for the past year. He finally reported the abuse to his parents two weeks ago, who took the necessary steps with law enforcement and are following up with recommended counseling. Tristan's father's side of the family has completely rejected him, saying that he "is a liar and a troublemaker." Tristan has nightmares, wets the bed, and refuses to eat, play with friends, or go to school.

Case Seven

Abbey has experienced conflict with a classmate who has wronged her, but the classmate now has apologized to Abbey. Abbey is lashing out angrily toward her mother and siblings. When Abbey is questioned by her mother, Abbey tells her that as a Christian she knows she must forgive the classmate but does not want to.

STRATEGIES, INTERVENTIONS, AND TECHNIQUES FOR COUNSELING CHILDREN

The techniques presented in this chapter are a simple overview of the main counseling approaches with children. Due to the vast nature of child counseling, it is beyond the scope of this chapter to cover every technique in detail. Thus, the goal is simply to expose the reader to the primary techniques used with children. The strategies and techniques in this chapter are categorized in terms of those that deal with building the therapeutic alliance between the child and the therapist, those that relate to the inner development of the child, those that deal with specific problems, and finally, group counseling.

Techniques to Establish the Therapeutic Relationship

The therapeutic relationship is considered to be a key element in the foundation of successful counseling in general (Thomas & Sosin, 2011); however, in counseling children, it is considered by many to be the foundation on which all change, growth, and healing rest (Bowlby, 1988; Crenshaw & Mordock, 2005; Hull, 2011). Scripture recognizes this by emphasizing the role of relationship in human friendship (Prov. 18:24; Col. 3:12–14) as well as a believer's relationship with God (John 1:10–13; 1 Peter 3:18–22; 1 John 1:3–4). The following elements of creating a solid counseling relationship with a child client will be discussed: establishing a sense of safety, active listening and attending, identifying the problem, and confidentiality.

Establishing a sense of safety. Children are taught by parents that most strangers are dangerous and to avoid them. How confusing it is for a child who is brought to a stranger by her parents for counseling and being told that she must talk to the counselor! The therapist working with children must be skilled in quickly shifting the child's perception of potential "stranger danger" to that of a trusted advocate. I tell parents who bring their children to me for counseling, "Without a sense of safety, there can be no learning or healing, and thus there can be no change." Children must feel safe to benefit from the counseling process because trust cannot be built until the child feels safe. While the therapeutic alliance is emphasized in nearly every form of counseling, with children it is of utmost importance (Ackerman & Hilsenroth, 2003; Hull, 2011; Saunders, 2001).

The two key elements of safety for the child in the counseling process are (1) the therapist as a safe presence and (2) the counseling room as a safe place. The therapist must present qualities of safety in a calm tone of voice, make eye contact with the child, and provide clear explanations of the boundaries and expectations. The therapist must also be aware of the physical differences in being a "big person" and make himself grounded to the child's level by sitting on the floor or kneeling in front of the child while making introductions and conducting the initial interview. The counseling room must be one that "should contribute to a client's feelings of comfort and ease" (Henderson & Thompson, 2011, p. 86), regardless of what theoretical approach drives the counseling process. For example, items that are inviting to children, such as smaller chairs and tables, open spaces for sitting and play, as well as toys that are age appropriate and easily within reach, help establish a sense of safety and confidence that the adult will be understanding. The Scriptures are full of reminders of the central role that safety and emotional comfort play in the life of human beings. Examples abound in the Old Testament (e.g., Ps. 91) and in God's care for the Israelites, as well as in the New Testament and in Jesus's words to his disciples, "Surely I am with you always, to the very end of the age" (Matt. 28:20).

Active listening and attending. Active listening is a process of communicating with another person that promotes understanding (Hutchby, 2005). This means that the therapist concentrates on the child in an undivided way. By fully attending, the therapist provides open-ended questions ("Tell me about your day") with paraphrasing and summarizing ("So, you're glad that the bully and his family moved away"), and with encouraging responses ("That helps me understand what happened. Could you tell me more about that?"), all of which support the child's telling of the event. Encouragement can be nonverbal, such as a nod of the head or facial expressions that let the child know the counselor is following his story. Jesus modeled compassion for children and invited children into his personal space when he told the disciples, "Let the little children come to me" (Matt. 19:14; Luke 18:16).

Identifying the problem. Caregivers bring children to counseling because there is a problem that is not going away. The therapist must determine what the problem is based on the caregiver's perspective and gain the child's view of the problem. The therapist must also assess what has been done to alleviate the problem thus far, and what, if any, strategies have been useful. Sometimes all will agree as to what the problem is. Sometimes the view from the therapist's perspective will differ from that of the caregiver. In the case of eight-year-old Bobby who refuses to attend school, it appears that the mother is doing all she can at this point. Bobby needs to go to school, and something is blocking him from going. In the case of twelve-year-old Caitlyn who ultimately refuses to go to her father's house and is exhibiting withdrawn behavior, Caitlyn's father sees the problem as his daughter being "selfish and spoiled." The therapist, however, might view her behavior as truly fearful and avoidant. Even when a problem seems straightforward, sitting with the child to understand the problem from her vantage point is of utmost importance, as this becomes a building block of the therapeutic alliance and leads into the problem-solving stage.

Confidentiality and therapist loyalty. Standards of care demand that therapists who work with children maintain confidentiality always, with certain exceptions, such as the voicing of self-harm or abuse (American Counseling Association, 2005; American Psychological Association, 2010). However, confidentiality in child therapy is not always so clear. Caregivers understandably want to know what is being done and said. At times, other parties may be involved, such as divorced parents or grandparents acting as caregivers. Custody situations can cause difficulty for counselors when it comes to confidentiality. However, most adhere to the rule that regardless of custody, getting permission from both parents prior to working with the child helps to avoid custody-related problems. Counselors need to know their state's guidelines regarding confidentiality and custody issues. The therapeutic alliance, which is built on the ability of the child to trust the therapist, can be damaged by such intrusions. Many believe that the therapist should protect the minor (Stone & Isaacs, 2003), while laws and other ethical standards give parents full accessibility to records and information because children lack the maturity to make decisions without parental involvement (Ware & Dillman-Taylor, 2014).

One way to deal with this issue is to explain to parents the importance of confidentiality and have them waive their confidentiality rights (Bennett et al., 2006) through the Health Insurance Portability and Accountability Act (HIPAA) Privacy Rule. This rule allows the therapist to assure the parent that the regular restrictions to confidentiality will be observed (e.g., self-harm, abuse allegations) should they arise during therapy. This allows the child to fully bond with the therapist and embrace the therapeutic experience as theirs alone (Bennett et al., 2006).

Techniques to Develop the Child's Representation

A child's self-representation is characterized by how the child thinks and feels about herself and how she sees others and relates to them, and it contains the elements of self-worth, self-confidence, and an overall sense of competency (Harter, 2012b). The development of self-representation begins in infancy and is fostered by loving and nurturing environments that give the child a sense of safety. These environments provide opportunities for the child to grow through a trial-and-error process, all the while encompassed in supportive relationships (Ferrer-Chancey & Fugate, 2003). A major conflict that arises during development is the emergence of shame and guilt as the child develops the desire for control and autonomy (Erikson, 1950). Shame and guilt have different cognitive, emotional, and behavioral characteristics (Tangney & Dearing, 2002). Shame tends to be directed at the self, while guilt arises over something one has done (Parker & Thomas, 2009), and both are useful in guiding the child to make good choices and increase the child's self-acceptance and understanding, as well as helping the child accept limitations and increase striving through the developmental process. From a biblical perspective, shame and guilt lead one to accept one's limitations and ultimately find one's purpose and identity through Christ (Eph. 1:5; Col. 2: 9–10).

Disruptions to the development of self-representation, such as loss, trauma, or sudden change in stable relationships (divorce), can have temporary or long-term effects on the child's emotional, psychological, social, spiritual, and academic functioning. The admonitions of Scripture related to raising children with the concepts of "training" behavior (Prov.

22:6) and teaching biblical concepts (Deut. 11:19) directly relate to building up a child's identity and creating a solid foundation of knowledge that leads to healthy thinking and behavior. The following approaches contain techniques that assist the therapist in helping to develop a child's healthy self-representation.

Play therapy. Play therapy has its beginnings in psychoanalytic theory and is well documented as an effective approach for children suffering from emotional, cognitive, and social difficulties (Koocher & D'Angelo, 1992; Leblanc & Ritchie, 2001). Play therapy is useful in helping children in therapy develop a healthy self-concept, particularly in the areas of emotional problems and low self-worth (Hull, 2011). While there are many theoretical variations of play therapy (Child-centered, Jungian, Adlerian, etc.), the basic idea is that since children lack the ability to communicate as adults can, play is the instrument of healing and communication and allows the child to see the problem from a safe distance. The therapist affirms the child's behavior in the play, joining in the play if invited, and tracks the child's actions ("Now you are putting the robber in the prison that you built out of Lincoln Logs") (cf. Hull, 2016) to let the child know that the therapist is attentive and engaged (C. E. Schaefer, 2001). Play therapy is not recommended for medical or biological problems, and the effectiveness of play therapy can be affected by many factors, such as the quality of parenting or the structure of the home environment.

Principles of Christianity can be integrated into the play process. The concepts of sin, forgiveness, and salvation can all be played out with children. I use play to help children put thoughts and feelings regarding Christianity into words. For example, many children are afraid of death and dying but know that heaven is waiting through the sacrifice of Christ should anything happen to them or their parents. The child is given the opportunity to choose toys that represent family or loved ones, and the child plays out the "death" of the toy and the process of the "dead" toy going to heaven and receiving new life. Through playing out this process, the child experiences the loss and the reassurance of heaven through play, and thus the faith of the child is reinforced and strengthened.

Sand tray. One of the classic tools of play therapy is the sand tray. The sand tray is a valuable tool used in play therapy with both children and adults to help develop a healthy self-concept (Richardson, 2012). The sand tray allows the child to create a make-believe world by filling the sand tray with whatever objects made available by the therapist. The child is free to add to or take away from his world without interference from the therapist, and the world belongs to the child, along with the interpretation of what is created. The child is free to experiment and works through emotional problems like guilt, shame, fear, or sadness, and self-worth is built through the process of ownership of the creation and the freedom to manipulate the sand tray "world" (Richardson, 2012).

Homeyer (2016) says that the sand tray therapy room must contain three key elements: "A tray with sand, a miniature collection, and water" (p. 247). The tray can be any size or shape, but many recommend a rectangular tray, and it is ideal that two trays be offered to the child: one with dry sand and one that the child can fill with water. Miniatures are used to create a landscape. Miniatures may be toy animals, figures of people, or any other theme a child may find useful (Homeyer, 2016). The intricate details of sand tray techniques are too many to discuss here; however, further reading may be found in the recommended reading section at the end of the chapter.

In the case of Andrew, sand play was an effective tool to help him build up a sense of self-worth, which led to him feeling empowered to deal with the bullies. He chose several army figures, dug a trench complete with bunkers, and placed "good" soldiers facing "bad" soldiers. Initially, the sessions involved chaos and destruction as the "bad" soldiers demolished the "good" soldiers, their bunkers, and supplies. Over the course of seven sessions, the "good" soldiers built better bunkers, developed better weapons, and soon began crushing the "bad" soldiers and their supply bunkers. At school, Andrew stood up to the bullies and called on teachers for help when the bullying occurred. His mother noticed that he was more confident and no longer afraid to go to school.

Computer, video, and tablet games. Modern technology offers play therapists several tools, from tablets to video and computer games. Children of today enjoy computer, video, and tablet games, and the games have become a part of children's everyday life. Video and computer games are an effective way to help children suffering from emotional disturbances (Hull, 2009), and app-based games provide the play therapist with effective ways to build a therapeutic alliance and increase coping skills/resilience (Hull, 2014).

For example, Tristan was fearful of meeting his therapist due to his mistrust of adults. However, when the therapist offered a tablet to Tristan, he was delighted because of his familiarity with tablets; he had one of his own at home. The therapist instructed Tristan to look at the apps and to pick a game that he would like to play. Tristan was excited to see Minecraft (Mojang), a game that he played often at home and with his friends. The therapist invited Tristan to create his own world and name it. When the therapist used another tablet and joined Tristan in Minecraft, Tristan's nervousness about coming to counseling disappeared, and a bond between Tristan and the therapist instantly formed. Over several sessions, Minecraft was used, and the two of them added to Tristan's world and worked together to create stores of resources and explore the landscape. While playing Minecraft, Tristan became comfortable talking about what happened to him and told his story. Tristan's Minecraft play reflected his feelings about himself as he was very hesitant and fearful at the beginning stages of play. He lacked the confidence to do much exploring, and instead his character stayed tucked safely in the house that he and the therapist had built. The therapist used his character to invite Tristan's character to explore the landscape, and as Tristan became more confident in his play, his confidence in himself outside of the playroom increased.

Tristan's mother reported that his bedwetting and nightmares had stopped after a few weeks of coming to therapy, and after a month she told the therapist that he had formed new friendships in the neighborhood and that teachers said Tristan was more social at school.

Video, computer, and app-based games all have themes of overcoming challenges, relying on resources for help, and "leveling up" of attributes (Hull, 2014). Minecraft is rich in these qualities. The element of joining the child in play adds another dimension that was helpful in the therapist bonding with Tristan and using themes from the game to build up Tristan's self-worth and confidence. For example, the therapist used the "monsters" in the game, such as creepers, skeletons, and zombies, to represent the negative thinking and feelings that come from experiencing terrifying events. As Tristan battled these monsters and overcame them, the therapist would ask him to identify a negative thought about himself that Tristan had overcome and replaced. Similarly, when Tristan surveyed a building that he built or a cave that he explored, the therapist would prompt Tristan to identify the positive thoughts and feelings that came from seeing his work and accomplishments. The therapist used the metaphor of his relationship with Tristan and the themes in the game of working together to show Tristan how relying on others for help can instill feelings of hope and receiving love. Tristan talked about the many friends and family members who cared for him and supported him during this difficult time.

Strategies, interventions, or techniques (SITs) derived from Gestalt. The Gestalt approach, made famous by Fritz Perls, focuses on the underlying causes of behavior and emphasizes awareness to deal with the present rather than focusing on the past (Henderson & Thompson, 2011). The Gestalt therapist guides children to accept responsibility for their actions and be self-aware through techniques that promote insight and problem solving (Yontef & Jacobs, 2008). Many techniques can be used with children, such as using "I" language, substituting "won't" for "can't," taking responsibility (Henderson & Thompson, 2011), and perhaps the most famous, the empty chair technique. The purpose of this technique is for a client to work out unfinished business. The client sits in one chair and speaks to the other chair that represents the personal work that is left undone.

A variant of the empty chair is the two-chair technique, which is a back-and-forth process in which the child acts one part and then moves to another chair to act out what another part or person may say or do. For example, Caitlyn is extremely fearful of her father. The empty chair was used by the therapist to have Caitlyn voice her fears and frustration in the safety of the therapy office with the encouragement of the empathic therapist ("Daddy, I'm scared of you and confused, and it hurt me that you called me selfish"). She then moved to the other chair to play the role of her father ("I have a new wife now, and you are going to have to learn to get along with her"). While this exchange did not automatically create a solution to the problem, Caitlyn felt empowered by voicing her true feelings, and she began the path of acceptance of a situation that she could not change but must endure. Over the next few sessions, she reported that she had gone to visit her father, that she could talk with his new wife, and that things were going better.

From a Christian perspective, there is much that contradicts the Gestalt approach (Jones & Butman, 2011), from the emphasis on humanistic thinking and reliance on the self to the elevation of self-awareness. However, some elements of Gestalt do align with Scripture, such as the idea of taking responsibility for actions. For example, for a child who wants to blame others for how he feels, you could request that the child complete sentences with blanks, such as "I'm feeling _____, and I take_____ percent responsibility for how I feel." This technique creates a sense of ownership and increases awareness of others, and the Golden Rule of Luke 6:31 ("Do to others as you would have them do to you") can be applied. Gestalt techniques of changing negative and critical self-thinking can be connected to Scriptures that speak of renewing the mind and following Christ (Rom. 12:2). The empty chair technique can be adapted to work with any conflict related to spirituality and Christianity.

I have used the empty chair technique but modified it and included the use of hand puppets or stuffed animals when working with children. This is useful when the child is struggling with conflicts (the case of Timothy and his father rejecting him), opposing feelings (the case of Bobby refusing to attend school but knowing he has to go), or sudden changes like parents getting divorced or the loss of a family member or friend, as in the case of Caitlyn or Tristan. The child chooses a puppet that represents himself in one emotional state (such as angry or sad) or as another person (such as a brother or friend). The child places that puppet or stuffed animal in a chair. The child then sits in an opposite chair with a puppet or stuffed animal and talks to the chair that holds the puppet the child has chosen that represents another emotional state or person. The goal is that the child will develop greater insight into why he feels the way he does or will better understand another's behavior. For example, Abbey wanted to follow Christ's example of forgiveness and was troubled by her feelings of not wanting to forgive a classmate. Abbey was experiencing anxiety and became aggressive toward her family members. Upon entering the playroom, Abbey chose a puppet (a crab) that represented her feelings of selfishness and anger and a girl puppet that represented her classmate. The crab puppet talked about having been hurt and how it kept its claws ready to snap when the person came near because it did not want to be hurt again. Abbey then switched chairs and used the puppet of the girl to explain how she had been jealous of Abbey because Abbey had both parents and got to go on trips with her family. Abbey explained to me that the girl had voiced this, but until Abbey played out the scene with the puppets, she did not grasp the meaning of the girl's words. The technique helped Abbey see the situation from a different perspective, which made forgiveness a real possibility. Abbey's anx-

iety and aggression immediately extinguished, and she reported to me that she grew in her faith. She added that it helped her see that it was possible to live out her faith; she no longer felt discouraged.

SITs derived from individual psychology. Individual psychology, founded by Alfred Adler, has beneficial techniques in helping a child develop a healthy self-concept. Individual psychology sees children's problems as attempts to gain superiority to balance feelings of inferiority. Negative behaviors serve as a necessary part of the child's daily life because the child gets something from the behavior that perpetuates the occurrence of the behavior (Henderson & Thompson, 2011). Individual psychology identifies four goals of misbehavior: attention, power, revenge, and inadequacy. The therapist identifies the goal of the child's choices and confronts the child regarding what she is gaining from the behavior. At this point, the therapist may use a variety of individual psychology techniques, such as encouragement (Mosak & Maniacci, 2008), which involves accepting the child as she is and noticing her effort as opposed to the outcome. The therapist may also use logical consequences that allow the child to experience natural outcomes of her behavior ("I chose not to mow the yard as Dad asked, so now I have to do it during volleyball practice, which means I will not get to play in the next game").

Adlerian play therapy is another technique used to encourage the child to see himself as capable and valuable. This serves to raise the child's self-worth so the child builds social connections and creates a sense of bravery to face new situations and challenges (Kottman, 2009). For instance, Timothy believes he is "worthless" because of his father's rejection of him. The therapist sees him as discouraged and, through playing tablet games, finds that Timothy is insightful and smart, and is good at navigating new situations. The therapist and Timothy create a "circle of friends" using LEGO minifigures that represent all the people who care about Timothy. While building a statue of himself using wooden blocks, Timothy can verbalize his value and worth through remembering aloud all the times when he made good choices and helped others. Through playing with toy fire trucks and pretending to respond to a fire using a building made of Lincoln Logs, Timothy can identify the people he has in his life to whom he can reach out when he feels sad and discouraged. Over ten sessions, Timothy is doing better in school and no longer lashes out angrily at others. He can verbalize his feelings about his father, and he admits to feeling sad. He can also connect with others and is trying out for a soccer team, a sport he has never played before.

Alfred Adler's "individual" approach is much opposed to Christianity, and the original theory had no place for God or Christ. However, much like Gestalt techniques, individual psychology and the principles described by Adler integrate well with Christianity in several ways. These include the concern for the welfare of others, the idea that one's lifestyle affects one's relationships, and the view that humans in general are purposeful and goal directed (Jones & Butman, 2011). Adler's

emphasis on courage fits nicely with the Christian admonition of courage through relationship with God (Josh. 1:8–9) and the power to live without guilt or fear of death through Christ's ultimate sacrifice on the cross. The principles of Adler that are embedded in the individual approach concerning the importance of helping others also align with the admonition of Christ to be aware of others' needs and to help them (Matt. 5:16, 42; Luke 6:31). Because children naturally battle fear during key developmental periods, therapists can integrate principles of Scripture into Adlerian play therapy to emphasize courage and thus negate fear. For example, in the case of Bobby who is afraid to attend school, the sand tray could be used to play out a scene from the Bible involving Joshua and the Israelites who had to trust God in defeating the great city of Jericho. To Bobby, school represents a large, unconquerable city that is always in his way. Playing out how the Israelites' trust of God enabled them to find courage to take the city could provide Bobby with the courage to face school each day.

Techniques for Specific Problems

The following techniques are useful for specific problems, such as behavior problems, distorted patterns of thinking, and trauma, grief, and loss.

In chapter 6 of this text, Dr. Thomas masterfully outlined the main ideas and techniques of the behavioral approach. This section will examine the behavioral approach with children for addressing specific problems and particularly focus on how therapists can help parents provide behavioral interventions for their children. Interventions such as rewards and punishments and systematic desensitization will be discussed here.

Consider the case of Bobby who is refusing to go to school. While the therapist may uncover fears over time that contribute to the defiant behavior, which may be dealt with by using play, individual, or Gestalt approaches, the main issue is that Bobby needs to attend school, and his mother needs behavioral interventions to assist her in getting him there. The therapist first taught the mother the basic components of the behavioral approach, beginning with explanations of reward and punishments for undesired behaviors (see Thomas, chapter 6). Using the techniques of shaping, and by helping the mother establish a token economy (Thomas, chapter 6), Bobby could earn tangible rewards by not fighting his mother in the morning and getting to school in a relatively compliant manner.

The therapist also used systematic desensitization (Thomas, chapter 6) with Bobby through establishing a "stimulus hierarchy" (Henderson & Thompson, 2011, p. 271) in which the therapist used LEGOs to build Bobby's house and school, and assessed Bobby's level of anxiety as he got ready in the morning, left home, and got closer to school. Using a LEGO minifigure to represent himself, Bobby imagined walking through the steps of getting ready, leaving the house, and standing in front of the school. During therapy sessions, Bobby was taught to relax by the therapist using relaxation techniques at each stage of the

hierarchy as Bobby approached the situation using the minifigure. Bobby's anxiety was significantly reduced when he approached the real-life scenario of getting ready, leaving home, and going to school, and he found he could relax himself and resist the urge to flee upon reaching the school building.

From an integrative perspective with Scripture, the behavioral approach and Christianity both value stewardship, responsibility taking, and the key roles of habit and reinforcement in daily living (Jones & Butman, 2011). The behavioral approach from a Christian viewpoint has several applications for counseling children. Scripture discusses the importance of training children and the role of parents in giving rewards and consequences, and it also gives somber warnings to those who fail or refuse to learn to control behaviors that may get them into trouble later in life. Scripture also demonstrates the role of relationship in teaching and changing behaviors, as well as stressing the importance of parents modeling the behavior they are attempting to get their child to demonstrate. Using a behavioral approach that aligns with Scripture provides Christian parents with alternatives and a variety of methods for changing behavior, instead of focusing on negative consequences like spanking.

For example, in the case of Jenny, diagnosed with reactive attachment disorder, the adoptive parents realized that spanking was not only ineffective in shaping Jenny's defiant behavior, but it seemed to make her behavior worse. Similarly, putting Jenny in time-out made the parents feel as though they were in time-out due to having to hold her down and sit with her in the time-out chair. It was just one more situation that Jenny controlled.

Jenny's therapist helped Jenny's parents understand the motives behind Jenny's behavior and why she acted out. Comprehending motives is not part of a behavioral approach but rather is part of psychodynamic and some cognitive behavioral approaches, but it proved helpful to create relationship and understanding between Jenny and her parents. The therapist helped them realize that Jenny was defiant because she felt safe if she perceived that she was in control. Once this was communicated by the therapist and understood by the parents, the parents and the therapist put together a positively oriented reward and consequence system that was communicated to Jenny when she was calm. For making good choices, such as doing her chores without being asked or doing her homework, she received a token. Her tokens could be collected and "cashed in" at the end of the week to earn a special reward, such as playing a game with her parents or going to the park to ride bikes with them. If Jenny was defiant or acted out, a series of consequences was implemented by the parents, such as loss of privileges, which resulted in a loss of tokens. Jenny could "earn" back privileges with appropriate responses, such as writing an apology or volunteering to do an extra chore. The concept of justice was modeled through Jenny's parents as they praised her effort to control her emotions and modeled relationship while delivering a consequence that helped Jenny see that she was in charge of her reactions and choices.

Over time, Jenny could control her outbursts, which had lessened in length and severity, and she improved her relationship with her parents. Through setting boundaries, rewarding positive behaviors, and consistently following through with consequences, Jenny's parents were established as the authority figures but were also seen by Jenny as loving figures whom she could trust to protect her. After a while, Jenny no longer required a reward system, as her desire to please her parents and remain in open relationship with them reflected her relationship with God.

SITs derived from cognitive therapy, cognitive behavioral therapy, and rational emotive behavioral therapy. The approaches of cognitive therapy (CT), cognitive behavioral therapy (CBT), and rational emotive behavioral therapy (REBT) have similar qualities of making a person aware of destructive, irrational, and negative patterns of thinking, and teaching the person to change those into rational and positive messages (Henderson & Thompson, 2011). These approaches are effective with children (Banks & Zionts, 2009). In fact, one study found that REBT was more effective with children than with adolescents (Gonzalez et al., 2004). REBT and CBT contain a behavior component that allows therapists to specifically address behavioral problems in addition to managing negative thought patterns that directly impact the child's emotional state. CBT is particularly effective with children suffering from depression (Henderson & Thompson, 2011). Depressed children tend to exhibit an external locus of control ("outside events and circumstances control me"). Gilman and Chard (2007) demonstrate how thoughts, emotions, and behaviors can be changed through "teaching, role play, and storytelling" (Henderson & Thompson, 2011, p. 429).

For example, Timothy is in a depressed state after feeling abandoned by his father. Timothy's thought process has elements of self-blame (*If I had worked harder and been a better kid, Dad wouldn't have left; this is my fault*), which results in feelings of sadness, despair, and guilt. His behavior of aggression toward his mother and peers at school is related to his negative feelings, which are related to his destructive patterns of irrational thinking. Timothy's therapist used a whiteboard to draw out the thoughts and connected feelings and then encouraged Timothy to challenge the accuracy of the main thought (*My dad leaving is my fault*). The therapist talked with Timothy about the choices and control that adults have compared to children to show Timothy that in reality his father's choice had nothing to do with Timothy. The therapist used role play and the scenario of Timothy choosing to keep or get rid of his dog, Stickers, to enforce the choice aspect of Timothy's father choosing not to see Timothy. ("Stickers can't make you keep him or get rid of him—that is your choice"). Timothy wrote his new thought about his father on the whiteboard ("My dad has chosen to move away and not see me because that is his choice"), and together he and the therapist identified the new emotions connected to this positive, rational, truth-based thought: relief, self-satisfaction, and hope. While Timothy still felt anger and some sadness, the self-

blame and guilt over feeling responsible for the situation were gone. Thus, he no longer exhibited aggression toward his mother or peers at school.

The approaches of REBT and CBT are compatible with Christianity in that the Bible encourages a person to recognize that thoughts and feelings influence a person's behavior. Regarding children and the approaches of REBT and CBT, several applicable strategies align with a Christian approach. Fear is a common emotion that children face during the developmental journey. Worrying is a common behavior that results in all sorts of problems. Scripture is clear in the admonition not to allow fear to dominate a Christian's mind and lifestyle (Phil. 4:6–7; 2 Tim. 1:7) and in saying that worrying is also wrong (Matt. 6:25–27; Luke 12:25). Taking steps to eliminate fear and worry are paramount to being in relationship with God and doing his will. Children are at a key point in development to learn this and benefit from the results of being able to eliminate fear and worry from their daily living.

For Christian children, I have used Scripture verses as a foundation and the techniques of REBT or CBT to make the application of the verse possible in the child's life. For example, one of the issues that arose with Tristan that added to his emotional struggles was his worrying about whether his salvation was secure. The main trigger for him was fear that his sins were not forgiven. This is a common issue that arises for Christian children. Tristan and his counselor examined verses that addressed this fear, which helped to form a solid foundation of truth based on what the Bible tells believers. For example, 1 John 1:9 ("If we confess our sins, [God] is faithful and just and will forgive us our sins and purify us from all unrighteousness") was a powerful verse that left no room for doubt or fear for Tristan.

The counselor and Tristan also examined theological statements by great theologians based on the truths of Scripture, such as this quote by Oswald Chambers (1935): "By the supernatural grace of God I stand justified, not because I am sorry for my sin, not because I have repented, but because of what Jesus has done" (p. 223). The verses and quotes formed an absolute truth for Tristan. Then the counselor and Tristan identified Tristan's irrational thoughts. Through the foundation of Scripture and theological statements, a context was created for why irrational thoughts could be labeled irrational. Because of a child's place in brain development, targeting irrational thinking and replacing those thoughts must be done in a way that the child can see and understand, such as drawing/writing them out on a whiteboard or a piece of paper. Together the counselor and Tristan developed an arsenal of positive, truth-based thoughts that blasted the framework of irrational thoughts that held the feelings of fear and behavior of worry in place. Tristan grew in his faith, and his parents noted that his nightmares ceased and his self-confidence grew, resulting in better school performance and improved relationships with peers and family members.

Solution-focused brief therapy. Many counseling approaches that are effective have one common element: time.

Working with children requires sufficient time to build trust, orient the child to the process, and allow the therapeutic process to create growth and healing. However, in some settings, such as schools, hospitals, or areas where war or a natural disaster has occurred, or if there are constraints due to managed care, time may be limited. Solution-focused brief therapy (SFBT) is a good fit for children who are developmentally on target and have sufficient cognitive and language skills (Nims, 2011). SFBT helps the child identify solutions to problems in a way that creates a different perspective and thus increase coping skills and self-efficacy. The basic idea of SFBT is that the main problem usually stems from poorly defined goals (Sklare, 2005). By using the "miracle question" (Nims, 2011, p. 2), scaling (rating success attempts from 0 to 10), making goals better defined and reachable, identifying exceptions (when something happened previously that contained a small part of a solution or positive outcome), and reinforcing the child's efforts, the therapist equips the child with new patterns of thinking. The stage is then set for new behaviors to overcome the challenges the child is facing.

SFBT is compatible with expressive forms of play therapy, such as art and the sand tray. Nims (2011) discusses his technique of "wow and how" (p. 4), in which the therapist affirms to the child what she is experiencing to provide encouragement ("wow"), and then follows it up with a "how" question designed to get the child to instill coping skills. For example, Jenny's therapist noticed that Jenny got ready for school that morning with no problems

("Wow, you don't like going to school, but you got ready today without getting upset") and followed it up with a statement to increase coping and insight ("I wonder how you did that this morning"). Jenny responded, "Well, I knew that I had to go, and that I won't get my reward if I can't control myself."

Jenny's response shows that she is developing the ability to contain her emotions and make good choices. At this point, the therapist praised her efforts and instructed Jenny to draw her room that morning and what it felt like to feel the emotion but not act out. She drew herself with a "tornado in my tummy" and then drew a thought bubble above her head in which she drew a "tornado vacuum cleaner." She explained that the vacuum was her thinking of not getting her reward, and that when she had that thought, she discovered that the "tornado in my tummy was gone, and I just got ready for school." Jenny's therapist asked her how it felt before the "tornado" disappeared, and she picked the number 8 (on a scale of 0–10, where 0 is no disturbance and 10 is extremely disturbing). Then she picked the number 2 to signify her feelings after she had imagined the vacuum cleaner. Next, the therapist instructed her to draw her classroom and various places on the school campus. He instructed Jenny to draw herself at school and what she could do to make the same thing happen at school that happened at home. "What would have to happen for you to feel a '2' at school?" She drew herself smiling, with only a big orange circle where the tornado had been, and with a thought bubble over her head in which she drew a vacuum cleaner. When

asked to explain, Jenny responded, "My teachers let me go to the reward box when I make good choices, and when I thought of that, the tornado stayed away because that thought is like the vacuum cleaner."

From a Christian perspective, SFBT contains many strategies that help Christians live as Christ and thus live in a future-oriented way (Frederick, 2008, p. 413). SFBT has many elements that are useful when counseling children from a Christian perspective. First, the Bible gives us many examples of God solving problems. He gave the Israelites food, water, and healing, as well as protection from enemies. In the New Testament, Jesus provided food to the crowds, turned water into wine, and healed the sick. The sacrifice of Christ is the ultimate solution to the problem of sin separating humans from relationship with God.

Second, while God provides divine wisdom and supernatural intervention at times, Christians are instructed to get wise counsel (Prov. 12:15; Heb. 4:12) and to use common sense (Prov. 10:13; James 1:22–25) in solving day-to-day problems. Children face all sorts of problems, from school difficulties to complex social situations. While they can seek help from adults, they often must learn to solve problems on their own. Helping a child understand that God is a constant help, but that there also are adults to call on, and that God has given each person the ability to think and solve problems is crucial in helping the child experience an increase in self-confidence, self-worth, and faith.

I have worked with many young people who are bullied and tell me that God feels very distant because they do not feel an immediate solution to their problem. "Is he there?" "Does he care?" they ask. Through art and sand play, the attributes of God can be examined. Attributes such as his caring for the animals, knowing the hairs on our head, and sending his own Son to die for us are just a few of the attributes that can be shared through directive play. For example, Andrew's difficulty with bullies can leave him feeling very alone, as though God has forgotten him. Andrew needs to know that God is not simply watching and doing nothing; he is using the experience to prepare Andrew for something. He has provided Andrew with people to help him and a mind with which Andrew can plan and make decisions. Bible passages that involve bullies can be found in the stories of Esther, Ruth, and David and Goliath. Techniques like storytelling and narrative therapy (see Recommended Reading) can also be powerful SFBT tools to strengthen children's faith and increase their coping skills. I have shared with children like Andrew that even though God promised victory over enemies like Goliath, David still had to face him. But David did so armed with the confidence that God was with him in the endeavor, and by defeating Goliath, David displayed the power of God before a heathen people.

Trauma, grief, and loss issues. A large percentage of children require psychotherapy services due to experiencing grief because of a traumatic event or loss. Divorce of parents, loss of a loved one or pet to illness, and having to move away from a school, home, or friends are common ex-periences for children in today's culture. Children are often victims of emotional, physical, and sexual abuse. Therapists must be prepared to help children understand the emotion of grief as well as other emotions that come with trauma and loss. As noted earlier in the chapter, trauma and loss can halt or severely disrupt the reaching of developmental milestones that are vital for future stages of growth and self-development (Harter, 2012). By addressing these issues and by providing children with the ability to understand and cope with trauma, grief, and loss, their development can continue, and they can gain self-understanding.

Children struggle to process negative emotions that seem confusing. They often attribute negative emotions to flaws in their character, resulting in low self-worth and self-loathing. Children need coping skills to help them overcome the negative effects of trauma and loss. Children at various stages of development struggle with expressing themselves verbally, which puts them at risk of increased emotional suffering when experiencing a trauma. Also, children may not have supportive environments that provide them with emotional comfort following a traumatic event or loss, which may result in acting out through negative behaviors, causing problems academically and socially.

The cases of Tristan and Timothy represent acute loss of significant family members. Timothy and Tristan benefited from counseling in that negative emotions were processed and both experienced a shift in perspective (Timothy: "Dad left, and that was his choice—it had nothing to do with me"; Tristan: "A bad thing was done to me, but it wasn't my fault") that increased coping and increased self-worth in both of the cases. Tristan and Timothy also demonstrate the need for intervention, because both are at key points of development, as referenced earlier. Both are able to process the emotions and continue on their developmental journeys better equipped for the future as a result of the counseling interventions they received.

Play therapy and grief/loss. Play therapy is an effective approach to help children deal with grief and loss (Hull, 2011). Child-centered play therapy allows children to construct their own worlds through the sand tray, art, or building materials like LEGOs or Lincoln Logs and then to explore grief at their own pace and in a personal way. For example, Tristan experienced grief over the loss of family members who now want nothing to do with him. The playroom represents a place where he can use play to work through the terrifying feelings and thoughts of rejection. His therapist, in the child-centered approach, sits as Tristan explores the room. The therapist also reflects on Tristan's discoveries ("You've found the drawing and art supplies. Those are for you to use if you wish") to affirm his curiosity and exploration. As Tristan engages in playing with a toy or toys, the therapist affirms his play through statements that give Tristan empowerment and confirmation of his behavior ("Now you are building a house with the LEGOs. You put the figures in there to keep them safe"). Through this process, Tristan finds that he is free to express himself, release negative thoughts and emo-

tions, and find empowerment that leads to better coping and behavior.

Prescriptive play therapy (Schaefer, 2001) enables the therapist to construct a play environment to deal with a specific type of loss. The therapist strategically offers toys that she knows will be suited for the child based on what the child has experienced. The play therapist working with Timothy knows that the themes are rejection and acute loss due to Timothy's father rejecting him. On entering the playroom, Timothy sees a table with LEGO blocks and minifigures with some drawing paper and markers next to them. The play therapist directs Timothy toward the table and tells him that today Timothy can choose from the drawing and art supplies or build with LEGOs. As Timothy begins to draw, he tells the therapist what his father said to him. The play therapist then asks Timothy to pick a LEGO minifigure to represent himself and one that represents his father and to play out how the conversation went. At this point, the play therapist is like a movie director but still gives Timothy the freedom to be in control of the action and what Timothy chooses to share.

Through play, Timothy experiences the emotions of sadness, anger, and frustration from a safe distance and also with a sense of control. If the emotions become too intense, he can make the minifigure that represents himself fly away or possess superstrength that enables him to smash the building he just built. Play also enables Timothy to play the role of his father through being in control of the minifigure that represents his father. This results in greater awareness and perspective taking, which can be healing for Timothy in resolving the conflict between feeling rejected and accepting the reality of how his father has treated him. The therapist can also direct Timothy to challenge negative statements made by the father (*"You are a worthless son"*) and create truth-based statements that preserve and build up Timothy's sense of value and worth.

While becoming a certified play therapist is recommended to ensure proper training and expertise, certification is not required for a certified/licensed counselor to use play in his counseling work. However, for a therapist who plans to use play therapy for a large portion of his work, the certification process provides specific training and expertise along with supervision that ensures that necessary skills are gained. Details regarding becoming a registered play therapist can be found in the Recommended Reading.

Faith integration for children experiencing grief/loss. Comfort for believers is found all throughout Scripture (e.g., Isa. 53:4; Matt. 5:4), and the hope of an eternal home with our Father is foundational to the Christian faith. These truths serve to shatter the effects of grief and loss. "Brothers and sisters, we do not want you to be uninformed about those who sleep in death, so that you do not grieve like the rest of mankind, who have no hope. For we believe that Jesus died and rose again, and so we believe that God will bring with Jesus those who have fallen asleep in him" (1 Thess. 4:13–14). Integrating aspects of faith into work with children who are experiencing grief and loss is a powerful way to increase the child's coping skills and to provide hope that goes beyond the temporal earthly realm in which we are bound.

Scripture verses that speak of hope and comfort can be added into play therapy by using art to draw and color a picture that represents the verses. Solution-focused techniques and cognitive techniques can also be used to incorporate the verses to undergird new patterns of thinking, which bring about confidence, hope, and reassurance. Stories from the Bible using characters who have suffered loss and experienced grief can also be used in play: Job losing his children, David's grief over Saul turning against him, and Jesus's reaction to hearing that Lazarus was dead. Reality therapy is also effective in helping a child understand that grief is normal and is a part of loving someone or something. Explaining the physiological components that create the grief response can be useful to help the child understand that experiencing grief and all the sensations that come with it are normal. This can be done through art and drawing out parts of the brain to increase the child's understanding of what the grief process is and why it happens. Younger children may not be able to appreciate how their grief is affected by physiological processes, but the use of art and building materials can be useful for younger children to help them process their grief.

CONCLUSION

Counseling children is no small task. Children are quickly and constantly developing new behaviors and patterns of thinking as their neurological and biological systems propel them toward adulthood. While challenging, counseling children is one of the most worthwhile and rewarding parts of the field. Effective counseling with children requires counselors to be equipped to address their behavioral, psychological, and neurological needs. Effective techniques come in many forms, and a skilled counselor uses a variety of these techniques to help children heal and grow in order to reach key developmental milestones. Counselors who work with children have a unique privilege in helping prepare those of the next generation to be psychologically healthy and confident to face the challenges of adulthood.

RECOMMENDED READING

Axline, V. (1964). *Dibs: In search of self.* Boston, MA: Houghton Mifflin.

Green, E. (2014). *The handbook of Jungian play therapy.* Baltimore, MD: Johns Hopkins University Press.

Hull, K. (2009). Computer/video games as a play therapy tool in reducing emotional disturbances in children. *Dissertation Abstracts International, 70.*

Hull, K. (2011). *Play therapy and Asperger's syndrome: Helping children and adolescents grow, connect, and heal through the art of play.* Lanham, MD: Jason Aronson.

Hull, K. (2016). *Where there is despair, hope.* Lynchburg, VA: Liberty Mountain.

Kottman, T. (1995). *Partners in play: An Adlerian approach to play therapy.* Alexandria, VA: American Counseling Association.

Lawson, D. (1987). Using therapeutic stories in the counseling process. *Elementary School Guidance and counseling, 22,* 134–142.

Oaklander, V. (1988). *Windows to our children: A Gestalt therapy approach to children and adolescents.* Highland, NY: Center for Gestalt Development.

O'Conner, K. J., Schaefer, C. E., & Braverman, L. D. (2016). *Handbook of play therapy* (2nd ed.). Hoboken, NJ: Wiley.

Turner, B. (2005). *Handbook of sandplay therapy.* Cloverdale, CA: Temenos.

WEBSITE

Association for Play Therapy. http://www.a4pt.org/

CHAPTER 14

Adolescent-Focused Strategies

Andi J. Thacker, PhD

[God] has made everything beautiful in its time.

ECCLESIASTES 3:11

Nothing seems quite as daunting to parents, youth pastors, helping professionals, or teachers as the adolescent years. Recently I was speaking to a group of parents at my church, and a parent made the comment that it feels as though rearing an adolescent is like parenting an alien life form. Although this statement was quite amusing to those gathered, it was evident that many could identify with the experience of this parent. In my private practice, I often have parents who seek help, saying, "She is a totally different person this week than she was last week. I just don't know who my kid is anymore." Even though as adults we have personally been through adolescence, for some reason this unique period of development remains a daunting enigma. Popular media outlets often report on the negative side effects of adolescence, highlighting less-than-desirable behaviors.

Counselors and helping professionals are not immune from this experience. Yet Scripture and science alike point to a Creator who intentionally set apart the period of adolescence to be a unique developmental stage that can be a prelude to a productive and healthy adulthood. Knowing how to meet the therapeutic needs of adolescent clients and help families navigate this unique season of life can be a challenge for helping professionals. The purpose of this chapter is to provide you with therapeutic strategies, interventions, and techniques that can be utilized when working with adolescents. In this chapter, you will find an overview of adolescent development and a theological integration of the use of activity therapy, as well as recommendations for utilizing activity therapy with adolescent clients. Brief case vignettes will be used to illustrate different aspects of activity therapy with adolescents.

THEOLOGY AND PSYCHOLOGY OF ADOLESCENCE

God, in his creativity, set apart certain periods of time in the lifespan that are characterized by specific developmental processes. At birth an individual is completely dependent on caregivers to sustain his life. But eighteen months later that same individual will be walking, talking, and able to feed himself. During late childhood and adolescence, an individual will undergo significant physical, cognitive, and socioemotional changes that qualitatively change the way he views life, makes decisions, and engages in relationships.

From a theological perspective, some of the characteristic features of the adolescent stage are a reflection of how humans are image bearers of God. The writer of Genesis 1:26–27 references human creation, stating that "God created mankind in his own image, in the image of God he created them." Scholars have debated this concept, some saying that only the material aspects of man reflect God's image and others contending that only the immaterial aspects reflect God's image. For the purposes of this work, this concept will be viewed as being twofold, that is, that the total being of an individual is created in God's image (Ryrie, 1999). Man's physical body, as well as man's nonphysical attributes, such as his intelligence and ability to make decisions, reflect God's image (Ryrie, 1999). Balswick, King, and Reimer (2005) propose that across the developmental lifespan, being image bearers of God is lived out in what they term "the reciprocating self," meaning that "the self that in all its uniqueness and fullness of being engages fully in relationship with another in all its particularity. . . . It is the self that enters into mutual relationships with another, where distinction and unity are experienced simultaneously" (pp. 48–49). As each member of the Trinity is in constant

and perfect communion with one another, there is also distinctiveness between each member of the Godhead (Ryrie, 1999).

During adolescence, central tasks of development include identity development and differentiation from parents. Even though differentiation is a developmental task of adolescence, differentiation does not mean isolation or complete independence but rather navigating the changing relational landscape with parents and growing closer in peer relationships (Balswick et al., 2005). Adolescents are learning how to be in community with their parents and peers yet be distinct and differentiated, growing in a greater sense of self-concept.

Further, during adolescence, individuals experience a growing ability and responsibility to make decisions for themselves and be self-directing. The idea that humans reflect God's image by having agency or the ability to make decisions is reflected greatly in adolescence when teenagers are presented with opportunities to make choices. From childhood to adolescence and onward into emerging adulthood, an individual's opportunity to make decisions grows and expands to include more facets of one's life. For example, a toddler has few opportunities to make decisions for herself, but as she grows into childhood, those opportunities to exercise agency grow and continue to grow through adolescence, culminating in emerging adulthood when she quite possibly could be making most decisions for herself. Adolescence is a time when her agency can flourish as she explores her identity. This specific aspect of development exhibits how individuals as image bearers reflect the characteristic of God also having agency (Evans, 1990).

Understanding the Lord's unique design during each developmental stage informs a counselor about developmentally appropriate practices. In this section, I will explore the unique qualities that characterize the stage of adolescent development.

Adolescent Development

Adolescence has traditionally been viewed as a period of human development characterized by "storm and stress" (Santrock, 2015). However, more recently researchers have highlighted the creative ingenuity of adolescents as an opportunity for great growth and exploration (Siegel, 2013).

Determining the age at which adolescence begins and ends has become increasingly ambiguous in light of new concepts of emerging adulthood and increased scientific knowledge of brain development (Broderick & Blewitt, 2010; Siegel, 2013). Gil (1996) reports that adolescence has generally been defined as a time between ages ten and twenty-one; however, he limits the period to age eighteen because a person is considered a legal adult at that time. For the purposes of our discussion, adolescence will be defined as ages thirteen to eighteen. Some of the strategies, interventions, and techniques discussed in this chapter are applicable for use with preadolescent clients, ages ten to twelve, as well as emerging adult clients, ages nineteen to twenty-five.

Erik Erikson (1950, 1963) described the major developmental task of adoles-cence as identity versus identity confusion. During this time, adolescents are exploring different roles, values, attitudes, and preferences in an attempt to define their identities and seek greater independence from their families in anticipation of autonomy in adulthood. However, to focus on independence from family would be too narrow a view of adolescent growth and development. Balswick, King, and Reimer (2005) describe the proclivity of adolescents to prefer time with friends over time with family as a normative aspect of adolescent development. Although independence from family is a natural outgrowth of adolescence, because of the inextricable human need for connection, the need for close interpersonal bonds with peers is absolutely crucial to healthy adolescent development. Because of these aspects of adolescent development, treatment of adolescents should include an awareness of identity formation, increasing autonomy and independence, and a growing sense of peer group connectedness.

Siegel (2013) utilizes the acronym ESSENCE to describe the key features of adolescence. ESSENCE stands for "emotional spark, social engagement, novelty seeking, and creative expression" (Siegel, 2013, p. 12). During this period of development, the brain is undergoing a renovation in which many changes are occurring. These changes will essentially lead to more cognitive control, greater emotional regulation, increased self-understanding, and greater social functioning (Siegel, 2013). These specific changes are related to the dramatic transformations that occur in the prefrontal cortex of the adolescent brain.

In addition to this, neurons (brain cells) will make more connections in the brain, but the brain will also begin the pruning process in which the number of basic neurons is reduced to create more efficient functioning. Additionally, the process of myelination will occur to increase the coordination and efficiency of neuronal connections (Miguel-Hidalgo, 2013; Siegel, 2013). Adolescents are also more likely to engage in risk-taking behavior because of their bent toward novelty seeking identified by Siegel (2013). Increased novelty seeking is due in part to changes within the brain that lead to neural activity utilizing dopamine, which creates a drive for reward coupled with a lower baseline secretion of dopamine in the brain (Siegel, 2013). Further, adolescents exhibit hyper-rationality in which they are aware of the risks of behaviors yet place more emphasis on the possible positive outcomes of such risky behavior (Siegel, 2013), lacking the greater self-awareness and self-regulation abilities that future brain development will provide. Because of this, adolescents are more prone to impulsive behavior, novelty seeking, and possibly addictive behaviors.

Characteristic of this life stage is the tendency for adolescents to push away from their parents in preparation for launching, coupled with an increasingly closer connection to peers. Therefore, peer relationships and seeking ways in which to demonstrate autonomy occur frequently in adolescence (Clark & Rabey, 2009). The push and pull of autonomy-seeking behavior can sometimes create distress between the adolescent and parent, as well as angst within the parent-child relationship. Helping parents and adolescent clients navigate this normal yet stressful experience is crucial in therapy.

Also inherent to this life stage are the physical changes ushered in by puberty. During this time, an adolescent's brain will begin to be stimulated by the hypothalamus to produce sex hormones (Broderick & Blewitt, 2010; Santrock, 2015). The production and release of these will trigger a series of changes in the body that will, in the end, result in multiple bodily changes and the ability for an adolescent to be sexually reproductive. Inherent to the process of puberty is also the emergence of sexual attraction and sexual identity. A discussion on this specific area is beyond the scope of this work, but Yarhouse and Hill (2013) provide a developmentally thorough and theologically sound explanation of this aspect of adolescent development.

This discussion of adolescent development, while not exhaustive, demonstrates the "remodeling" that occurs in the life of an adolescent (Siegel, 2013). For a more robust explanation of adolescent development, please refer to Recommended Reading. Understanding these basic changes is crucial to the therapeutic process in that therapists play the role of educator for both adolescent clients and their parents. Providing useful information on normal development eases parental fears and helps manage parental expectations of their adolescent child. Further, reminding parents that the characteristics inherent to this developmental stage are a God-created reality confirms the belief that we were created by an infinite being who created with intentionality and purpose. This information is also helpful to the adolescent in that it helps the client navigate the sometimes rocky waters of "remodeling" that will occur (Siegel, 2013).

All of these changes indicate that adolescence is a time of immense transition. For some, adolescence is a time of excitement and eager anticipation of the future. But for others, it is characterized by confusion, relational discord, and possible negative consequences that accompany risk-taking behaviors. Therapeutic services offer a great opportunity for adolescents and their parents to navigate these issues well.

Theology and Creativity

Every aspect of life testifies to a theology of creativity. From nature to humanity, God's creativity and design are on display for all to witness (see, e.g., Gen. 1; Rom. 1). As humans, we are set apart and unique from all other creation because of the *imago Dei*, meaning we bear God's image (Ryrie, 1999). Humans share in the likeness of the Father by exhibiting a desire and ability to create (Bauer, 2013). Furthermore, we have the opportunity to participate in God's creativity, as well as demonstrate personal agency as we share in the process of artistic expression (Hart, 2000). God made us as creative agents, meaning that we are innovative, imaginative, inventive, artistic, and resourceful. This same creativity and sense of agency, knit into the very being of humanity, is present within the therapeutic relationship and can act as a catalyst in the therapeutic process.

As mentioned previously, Siegel (2013) has highlighted the creative nature of adolescence. Some of the most culturally defining and imaginative ideas were brought forth in the minds of adolescents. Teenage inventors have developed methods to transport refrigerated vaccines without electricity or ice, provide clean water sources for underprivileged regions, and screen for communicable diseases (Wheeler, 2016). These examples of adolescent ingenuity and creativity are only a small example of the powerful ideas that have sprung forth from developing minds. Therefore, the use of creativity within adolescent counseling creates an environment in which adolescent clients can comfortably express themselves.

Furthermore, some research has indicated that expressive therapies allow a client to access different aspects of their personal experience that might not be readily accessible with exclusively talk therapy (Badenoch, 2008; Kestly, 2014). For these reasons, activity therapy offers a therapeutic context in which adolescent clients can thrive therapeutically and developmentally.

CASE STUDIES

Case One

Casey is a fifteen-year-old female who presented for therapeutic services due to depressed mood and withdrawn behavior. Casey reportedly has not exhibited previous behavioral or emotional concerns and lives in a stable home environment. Casey has recently begun therapeutic services with me. I had already conducted an initial intake session with Casey's parents.

After explaining the therapeutic process and limits of confidentiality, I obtained Casey's informed assent to proceed with therapeutic services.

Case Two

Jake is a thirteen-year-old boy who presented for therapy due to aggressive behaviors at school. Jake's mother reported that he is very bright yet has been struggling socially with peers, as evidenced by disagreements in the classroom and withdrawn behavior from friends. Jake's mother reported that she is recently divorced from Jake's father and has full custody of Jake. Jake's father is reportedly inconsistent in his involvement in Jake's life. Jake is an only child.

Case Three

Lauren is a sixteen-year-old female client who presented for counseling due to issues related to being adopted. She came to counseling approximately six months ago and completed fifteen sessions with me prior to beginning group activity therapy. Heather is a seventeen-year-old female client who started counseling approximately five months ago, shortly after her parents divorced. Heather completed twelve individual sessions with me prior to starting group activity therapy. I suggested group activity therapy for these clients because of their similar developmental stage and the presenting issues related to family concerns. Further, I continued to work with both clients individually in addition to group activity therapy. Additional information on selecting group participants can be found in Bratton and Ferebee (1998).

STRATEGIES, INTERVENTIONS, AND TECHNIQUES FOR COUNSELING ADOLESCENTS

Counseling methods and techniques guide you in your therapeutic practice. Various strategies, interventions, and techniques include cultivating a relationship with the adolescent, parental involvement, and creating a sense of autonomy or ownership for the emerging adult. The following section outlines specific guidelines and principles for working with adolescent clients and their parents. Following these guidelines, I revisit the case vignettes and outline examples of how to implement these practical strategies and interventions with the clients described in the previous section.

Beginning the Relationship

The beginning of any therapeutic relationship should be characterized by relationship building with the client. Scripture highlights how God created people for relationship and that through relationship one finds healing (Pyne, 2003; Thompson, 2010). The story of the Bible highlights how God created humanity within the context of both vertical and horizontal relationships in that we were created to be in relationship with God and our fellow humans (Gen. 1:26–27). However, the entrance of sin into the world marred these vital relationships, resulting in relational rupture (Thompson, 2010). The ultimate form of repair of this rupture came in the form of substitutionary atonement when Christ willingly died on the cross in our place (Ryrie, 1999). From this, we see a foundational example of the cycle of hurt and healing in our world. Sin causes relational rupture, yet relationship brings repair and healing. The therapeutic relationship is a context in which this pattern plays out regularly. To achieve this type of relational repair, building a strong therapeutic alliance with both the adolescent client and the client's parent(s) is crucial.

Building a strong therapeutic alliance involves several techniques. You demonstrate empathy, genuineness, and unconditional positive regard, creating an environment in which the client can feel safe and understood (Fall, Holden, & Marquis, 2010). The concept of unconditional positive regard is akin to the theological concept of grace. Lightner (1991) references grace as God's kindness or favor to those who are undeserving. Whereas a counseling relationship is not between an almighty perfect being and an imperfect creature, showing grace or unconditional positive regard to a client demonstrates Christlike love and builds a sense of safety and trust in the therapeutic relationship. An atmosphere of safety allows the client to freely explore life issues and circumstances while knowing you are fully accepting of his personhood.

Other techniques involved in relationship building include reflecting feelings and reflecting content. The importance of the therapeutic relationship cannot be overstated in adolescent counseling because adolescent clients do not typically present for counseling on their own volition. Generally, parents of adolescent clients have initiated therapeutic services without gaining the support or consent

of the adolescent. Thus, building strong therapeutic relationships can help adolescent clients gain a willingness to participate in therapy. Furthermore, approaching the therapeutic relationship with a spirit of patience is necessary. Because adolescents, generally speaking, do not initiate therapy like adult clients, the progress and pacing of the relationship may be much slower. This can feel discouraging; however, it is developmentally normal because of the therapeutic circumstances.

Relationship building does not cease once a therapeutic alliance is established. Rather, these same skills and techniques continue throughout the entirety of therapeutic relationships and serve to provide clients with an experience of "feeling felt" (Thompson, 2010). "Feeling felt" is the experience in which clients perceive that you truly understand their experience and "get them." This experience not only builds trust in you and the therapeutic process, but it also creates healing neurologically for clients (Badenoch, 2008; Thompson, 2010).

Parental Involvement

An integral aspect of any counseling with minors is involvement of parents or main caregivers. For the purpose of this discussion, I will use the term *parent* to identify those individuals who are legally responsible for the care of a minor client.

From a legal and ethical perspective, in many states clinicians must obtain written consent to provide treatment to a minor client (Sanders, 2013). Based on this requirement, clinicians must have contact with the parent(s). Additionally, it is important that the parent(s) feel connected to the clinician as well as to the therapeutic process. Without the support and participation of the parent(s), it is unlikely that therapeutic services will be successful (Kottman, 2003; Ray, 2011). You can foster a sense of connectedness with parents by maintaining appropriate and timely parent consultations.

Meet first with the parents. The initial therapeutic appointment should be reserved for meeting with the parent(s) solely without the adolescent client present. The purpose behind excluding the minor client in the initial parent consultation is to allow the parent(s) the opportunity to speak candidly about the presenting problem (Ray, 2011). Further, it allows the therapist to gain an understanding of the parents' expectations for therapy. Often parents enter therapy with expectations that might be beyond the ability of the therapist or the scope of the therapeutic experience. Having the opportunity to level set for the parents builds appropriate expectations and helps avoid frustration regarding unmet expectations further into therapy. Obtaining a detailed developmental history of the adolescent client during the initial parent consultation is imperative. This will guide your conceptualization and treatment planning of the client. Additionally, it will allow you to have a better sense of the presenting problem, any developmental delays, and the nature of the parent-child relationship.

Adolescent sessions and parental consultations. I recommend conducting individual therapeutic sessions with the adolescent client approximately three to four times following the initial parent consultation. After the third or fourth individual session with the adolescent, you can conduct a parent consult to inform the parent(s) of treatment updates, client progress or regression, or possible parenting skills to implement. Follow-up parent consultations can be conducted with or without the adolescent present. I recommend that you seek to include the adolescent client in parent consultations so as to contribute to a sense of trust within the therapeutic relationship. This sense of trust could be violated if an adolescent client perceives that you are sharing with the parent(s) what she has said in confidence. Although the parent has the legal right to the information shared in the counseling session, it is not realistic to expect the adolescent client to share candidly if the counselor shares every detail of sessions with the parents. Parents often will be in favor of a degree of privacy between the counselor and adolescent client to foster trust (Sanders, 2013). At times, this guideline might be unavoidable due to the circumstances of the situation.

The importance and impact of contact with parent(s) of minor clients goes far beyond that of legal requirements and extends to include the benefit of the adolescent, parent(s), and other family members within the home. For this reason, parent(s) should be regarded as active agents in their adolescent's treatment. Additionally, due to the relational nature of the parent-child dyad, adolescents often present for therapeutic services with relational challenges within the parent-child relationship. For this reason, utilize this relationship to bring healing and restoration within the parent-child dyad.

Additional Considerations with Parents

Handle parent feelings with care. A unique aspect of working with adolescents is that a clinician must also be prepared to work with the client's caregivers. In my clinical experience, and in my personal life as a mom, I have found that the role of parent is one of the most sanctifying and challenging God-ordained experiences that an individual will encounter. Parenting provides a consistent reminder of one's human finiteness and frailty. Quite often the parents who have entered my practice present with a myriad of emotions about the situation. While feeling love and concern for their children, parents might also feel anger, despair, inadequacy, excited anticipation, fear, and so on. It is of utmost importance that you handle parents' feelings with care and concern, being mindful of the challenging nature of parenthood.

The strategies outlined below can be helpful tools to impart to parents. However, listening to any objections or concerns a parent might voice regarding the effectiveness or applicability of the presented strategies is imperative. Whenever making recommendations to parents, I always post these suggestions as optional tools that might be beneficial in their parenting toolbox. I want to support and facilitate the parents' autonomy to choose what strategies and tools fit best for their family relationships.

Choice giving. One of the crucial tasks during adolescence is a pushing away from parents to establish a sense of increasing autonomy for launching (Broderick & Blewitt, 2010; Siegel, 2013). However, adolescents still have a need to remain connected to their parents (Clark & Rabey, 2009). This natural movement away from caregivers while still needing to remain connected can create a certain degree of anxiety for parents. To help with this transition, encourage parents to provide the adolescent with age-appropriate responsibility to increase good decision making and encourage an increasing level of independence. One option for facilitating autonomy and independence is teaching parents to utilize choice giving. Choice giving is a strategy that can be utilized with young children as well as older adolescents. Choice giving has a twofold function in that it provides the opportunity to learn how to make decisions and can be used for disciplinary purposes (Landreth & Bratton, 2006). Parents should provide their adolescent children with age-appropriate opportunities to make decisions in order to encourage independence. An example of this might be the adolescent client deciding what elective classes to take in school or what extracurricular activities to participate in. The end goal is that the adolescent will move toward increasing autonomy so as to be able to make wise decisions when he launches from the home.

Just as they would do with younger children, parents of preadolescents and adolescents should utilize choice giving when disciplining them. Choice giving for disciplinary purposes allows adolescents the opportunity to build an internal locus of control in which they practice making decisions and bringing themselves under control (Landreth, 2012; Ray, 2011). Using choice-giving language for disciplinary purposes, such as "If you choose to be late for your curfew, you choose not to use the car tomorrow night" is encouraged. The parent allows the adolescent the opportunity to make this decision knowing that her decision has consequences either way. This practice has the inherent goal that the adolescent will begin to role play consequences of behavioral choices and further understand the relationship between cause and effect and personal responsibility.

Contract setting. Another area of concern for parents of adolescents is boundary setting. At times, an adolescent and his parent will present for counseling with specific areas of concern regarding inappropriate behavior. Many times parents present feeling helpless and uncertain of how to set and maintain appropriate boundaries for their adolescents. Using contract setting helps the parent and adolescent client have a clear understanding of the expectations and boundaries within the family atmosphere (Sells, 2004). When using contract setting, parents identify the top two to three concerning behaviors of the adolescent to address. In conjunction with the adolescent and parents, you help facilitate a discussion in which the parents and adolescent decide on appropriate consequences for these behavioral concerns. The behavioral concerns or boundary violations, along with the consequences, are recorded and posted in a public area in the home. Having a predetermined plan allows the parent to feel empowered, and it allows the adolescent ownership in the discipline process. Participating in contracting with parents allows adolescents the opportunity to role play consequences prior to engaging in behaviors that would violate family rules.

Balancing faith discrepancies. My experience has been that many parents seek counseling services with a Christian counselor due to religious beliefs. Whereas parents might be Christian, the adolescent client might not always ascribe to the parents' religious beliefs. When integrating psychology and theology, I seek to honor both the wishes of the parents and the wishes of the adolescent. To do this, I am respectful of the parents' preferences that I will maintain a certain Christian ethic in my practice, while also being mindful of the adolescent client's desire not to explore the subject of spirituality. I follow the client's lead and will explore spirituality and religion to the extent that the adolescent client is willing. However, my biblical worldview guides my actions as a clinician and informs my viewpoint of human creation and the world.

Activity Therapy with Adolescents

Activity therapy is to adolescents as play therapy is to children. Where play therapy serves to reach the child client's unique developmental level, activity therapy does the same for adolescents. In this way, activity therapy serves to bring forth the inner world of an adolescent that may otherwise be kept guarded from others. Activity therapy builds a bridge between a client's inner world and his concrete experience, allowing for greater mastery over life circumstances that might be experienced as unmanageable (Rubin, 2005). Furthermore, because activity therapy utilizes multiple senses, some feelings and thoughts that are out of the client's awareness or that are difficult to express can surface (Bratton & Ferebee, 1999).

Due to the nature of activity therapy, metaphors and symbols in creative expression provide a nonthreatening manner for the client to express self (Bratton & Ferebee, 1999; Rubin, 2005). The experience of counseling can be anxiety provoking for any client, especially an adolescent who has not willingly chosen to attend counseling. Sitting across from another can sometimes feel threatening and overwhelming for the client. Having the opportunity to move one's body or be creative in session can lessen the pressure felt by the adolescent. Further, Malchiodi (2007) has indicated that the use of expressive therapies allows the client to progress toward action, express feelings and thoughts, and implement new ways of acting.

Activity therapy can be utilized in a directive or a nondirective manner. A directive activity therapy approach is where you select and initiate activities with the client. A nondirective therapeutic approach occurs when you allow the client to lead and select specific activities. Frequently, a blend of both directive and nondirective therapeutic approaches is used. Bratton, Taylor, and Akay (2014) recommend that the counselor take a flexible approach in terms of directive versus nondirective activities. Specifically, you monitor the client's unique needs and developmental level, and you are guided by a personal theoretical orientation (Bratton et al., 2014).

In the case of nondirective activity therapy, having multiple activities on display and available for the client to select from is helpful. Examples of this might include expressive arts and crafting supplies, such as paints, modeling clay, colored pencils, markers, pens, developmentally appropriate color pages, knitting materials, and so forth. With more directive activity therapy, you will present a specific activity for the client.

One example of activity therapy is utilizing expressive therapies or expressive arts. Expressive therapies allow for the experience of the client to be expressed as a symbolic representation of his inner world (Rubin, 2005). When expressive activities are used in this manner, the activity serves a similar function to the role of play in counseling with children. As play is the natural form of communication for children (Landreth, 2012), the activity becomes, for the adolescent, the form of communication, and the created product becomes the client's words. Utilizing activities in adolescent counseling can serve as a means to an end or an end in itself. Activity therapy can serve as a way to lessen the client's anxiety, for all the energy is not focused on talking, and can also allow the client and the counselor to gain new insights into the inner workings of the client. Themes regarding how the adolescent client feels, experiences life, and behaves can emerge through expressive activities. Oaklander (1988) explains how activity and creativity serve as a means for projection and how projection originates within the person and illuminates what the client cares about and the client's sense of self. Many times the progression of the healing process is evidenced in the created activities of the client when these types of expressive activities are utilized repeatedly in the therapeutic relationship. For this reason, maintaining photographic records of the client's created work is valuable.

Structuring and implementation. As you maintain the role of supportive companion on the client's journey of self-exploration, you should follow several guidelines when utilizing creative expression in therapy. To begin, structuring of the session is vital to allow time for instructions, creative expression, and processing. Allowing time during the session for processing to occur is essential, although a client may not always be able to assign words to the metaphor and meaning of her creation. Allowing time to process one's creation provides the opportunity for the client to debrief the activity and reflect on the experience (Crane & Baggerly, 2014). A general guideline for session structuring is to allot five minutes for instructions about the activity, twenty to twenty-five minutes for the activity, and ten to fifteen minutes for processing. Giving a client a five-minute warning prior to the end of the allotted activity time is helpful so she can wrap up her creative process. If expressive activities are being utilized in a group therapy setting, the time allotted for sharing and processing should be increased to account for each group member. I recommend allotting more time for a therapeutic group than for an individual therapy session.

Processing. When beginning to process the client's activity, allowing the client to assign meaning to his creation and avoiding placing personal projections on the created work is vital (Lombardi, 2014).

Suspend your judgment and avoid making interpretations while translating what you hear and see from the client (Oaklander, 1988). The client is the expert on his creation, and you only need to seek to gain a deeper understanding from the client's unique perspective. Additionally, honor the vulnerable expression of the client evidenced through the activity and, therefore, do not touch the client's creation or give evaluative feedback about the product. When processing the client's created process, ask open-ended questions about the client's experience of creating, as well as how the client feels about the overall product. Examples of these questions might include "How did it feel to participate in this activity?" or "How do you feel when you look at what you created?" Because of the deep and reflective nature of expressive activities, using therapeutic pacing that is slow enough to allow for sufficient time for the client to reflect and process is crucial. You can also ask processing questions regarding aspects of the client's created activity. These types of questions might include "What do you notice about this part of your creation?" or "What's going on in this part of your work?" Additionally, noticing the client's process while creating is helpful—specifically, any emotional responses exhibited while creating or the amount of time allocated to a specific aspect of the activity. If a certain aspect of the process appears particularly meaningful, note this to the client and ask if he can share about what was being experienced during the creation process.

Through the process of creating, a client's inner world will be projected through the activity (Oaklander, 1988). Many times this inner state comes forth in the form of a metaphor. When beginning to process a client's experience and creation, initially remaining in the metaphor is key (Oaklander, 1988). If the client is developmentally at a place in which abstract processing has begun and he demonstrates emotional readiness, you can move out of the metaphor into the practical application of this experience to the client. Remember that moving out of the metaphor brings the vulnerable subject matter into the present realm, and that can increase anxiety for the client (Oaklander, 1988). Be sure to evaluate the readiness of the client prior to moving out of the metaphor (Bratton et al., 2014).

Prior to the end of the session, allow a few minutes to check in with the client. This time allows him to continue feeling that you understand, as well as allowing him time to move out of the affective realm into a more cognitive realm. Moving into the cognitive realm allows him the opportunity to move out of the therapeutic space and proceed into the next activity for the day without feeling completely exposed emotionally.

Creative materials. When utilizing activity therapy, specifically creative activities, following guidelines regarding what type of artistic medium should be used at certain junctures in the therapeu-

tic process is essential. Landgarten (1987) suggested that counselors start clients with the most controllable medium and then progress to the least manageable medium. Because less controllable means of artistic expression can elicit strong and surprising emotions, beginning with a medium that creates less threatening feelings is helpful (Bratton et al., 2014; Landgarten, 1987). Bratton and associates (2014) further suggest that counselors account for the amount of structure presented in an activity and how much the activity relates to the client's issues, the directness of their questions when processing, and the combining of different media into one activity. A visual representation of Landgarten's (1987) guideline is provided in table 14.1.

Consider several factors when deciding how to progress therapeutically with different expressive mediums. Also, consider the artistic medium that is most effective for the client, considering that clients show preferences for certain types of creative supplies. Some clients might prefer materials such as modeling clay more than drawing supplies. Allowing the client to lead in this area is important, and utilizing a different artistic medium each week is not necessary (Bratton et al., 2014). However, following the guidelines of progressing through the use of materials from more manageable to less manageable, as noted below, is important.

Table 14.1. Landgarten's Guidelines

WWet clay	Water colors	Soft plasticine	Oil pastels	Felt marker (thick)	Collage	Hard plasticine	Felt marker (thin)	Colored pencils	Lead pencil
1	2	3	4	5	6	7	8	9	10

Therapeutic space. When utilizing activity therapy, the therapeutic space has to be arranged in a manner conducive to this approach. Conduciveness includes but is not limited to therapeutic materials and furniture arrangements. Displaying expressive materials and activities in the office allows for spontaneous creative expression. Be sure to utilize expressive materials that will not interfere with the integrity of the space. Specifically, I advise that you not include materials that might cause damage to the therapeutic space. Including such materials would create an environment in which you are not able to be fully accepting of the client and permissive with the creative process. If space and finances allow, additional resources, such as a stage with costume materials, a woodworking area, sewing supplies, or other physically expressive activities can be useful with adolescents. Additional information regarding the therapeutic space can be found in Bratton and Ferebee (1999).

Because of the nature of activity therapy, you should utilize a great deal of personal creativity in developing and implementing expressive activities. Many scholarly resources discuss the use of expressive activities, such as poetry, drama, photography, music, and movement, in counseling. A list of resources regarding specific expressive activities, as well as methods for processing these activities, is available in Recommended Reading at the end of this chapter.

The counselor. The person of the counselor is a crucial aspect of the therapeutic process. As a carpenter would seek to maintain the integrity and usefulness of the tools he uses, so you must seek to do the same. The counselor is one of the greatest "tools" utilized in the therapeutic process (Thomas & Sosin, 2011). Diligently working to know oneself and understand how the therapeutic process influences you is essential.

Utilizing expressive therapies adds a new element to the therapeutic experience for both client and counselor. I urge my supervisees to gain personal experience utilizing each artistic medium prior to incorporating the medium into therapeutic practice. The rationale for this practice is to further increase self-understanding but also to help them empathize greater with the client's experience. Rubin (2011) explains that in-depth knowledge cannot be attained from simply reading about the subject of expressive therapies; rather, the counselor must gain knowledge through experience by interacting with as wide an array of artistic media as possible.

My own training in the area of expressive therapies began in my doctoral program, where I had the opportunity to participate weekly in expressive activities. This process deepened my appreciation for expressive therapies, increased my self-understanding as a person and a counselor, and provided me with a rich understanding of the therapeutic process as it relates to expressive therapies. Whereas experiencing expressive therapies in a university setting is not an option for some counselors, the act of incorporating the personal practice of expressive therapies is possible.

You can accomplish this goal in several ways. One way is to seek therapeutic services from a counselor who is experienced in the area of expressive therapies. Another way to accomplish this goal is to find a supervisor who is trained in expressive therapies and will utilize this modality throughout the supervision experience. You can also participate in a small consultation group in which each week the group utilizes and processes a specific expressive medium. Finally, seek more formal training by attending seminars or university classes that specifically teach expressive modalities. Whereas activity therapy is an effective avenue for facilitating therapeutic healing, other therapeutic techniques and modalities are also very helpful when working with adolescents. Many therapeutic modalities allow for integration of different therapeutic techniques. Therapeutic activities can be integrated into a wide range of theoretical orientations to bolster the positive impact of the therapy for the client. Additional resources for evidence-based treatment of adolescents is listed at the end of the chapter.

Case One

My office is equipped with a table for expressive activities, as well as an area for sand tray therapy. I introduced the concept of activity therapy to Casey by explaining that sometimes certain activities like expressive arts can be helpful to the therapeutic process. I asked if Casey would be willing to try an expressive activity. Casey somewhat reluctantly agreed, and I provided Casey with instructions. I shared with Casey that she would have about twenty-five minutes to work on her drawing, and then she would have time to process her drawing. I asked her to draw a picture of

her life. After twenty minutes, I gave her a reminder that she had five minutes to complete her drawing.

After twenty-five minutes, I began the processing phase of the session. To begin, I asked Casey to observe what she created and notice any feelings she had as she looked at her drawing. I was careful to pace her questions and reflections in a slow manner so as not to overwhelm her and to provide ample time for client reflection. Casey reported feeling sad when she looked at her drawing. I asked her to share about what she drew. She shared that she drew her life, which she described as "lonely." Casey explained that she drew herself alone in a world where everyone passes by and does not notice her. I was intentional to reflect the feelings and emotions stated by Casey. Throughout the processing time, I was intentional to allow Casey to assign meaning to her drawing by asking her to describe aspects of the drawing. I did not label parts of the drawing as "the lonely part" or the "sky" or "sun" until Casey had done so. Casey and I spent the remainder of the session processing parts of her drawing. Because the therapeutic relationship had just begun, I chose not to explore in depth the loneliness she reported feeling. Specifically, I spent the majority of her time reflecting her feelings and not asking what was causing her to feel lonely. I made this decision so as to continue working on establishing the therapeutic alliance prior to asking more directive reflection questions. To wrap up the session, I asked Casey how she was feeling after completing the activity. I thanked Casey for her honesty and vulnerability.

Because the therapeutic relationship was not yet established and I did not yet know how Casey would handle the expressive activity, I was intentional not to move too quickly with her. During the early stages of counseling, focusing on building a strong therapeutic relationship is vital. Additionally, many activities utilized can help improve conceptualization of the client. Because Casey voiced feeling lonely, it was crucial that I sought to "see" and "be with" Casey in a manner in which she felt valued and understood.

Parental involvement is a critical aspect of therapy with minor clients. Because the relationship with Casey was new, I progressed by conducting two more individual sessions with her then conducting a parent consultation. Because of her age, I allowed Casey to choose whether she would like to be present for the parent consult. I wanted to facilitate an atmosphere of trust and safety, communicating to Casey that I would not keep secrets from her by disclosing aspects of her counseling to her parents without her knowledge. During the parent consultation, I would provide a time for Casey's parents to voice concerns, comment on progress observed, or ask questions. I would also facilitate an opportunity for Casey to share with her parents anything she would like to share. The purpose of this time with the parents and the adolescent client is to model healthy communication skills and facilitate parent involvement in the therapy process. The subject of loneliness came to light from Casey's first session. If this topic persisted in subsequent sessions, it might be appropriate to address this theme with Casey and her parents to discuss possible social support networks that might be beneficial for Casey.

Case Two

At this point, I had completed four sessions with Jake. During the first four sessions with him, I noticed his unique interest in building and creating. Jake was immediately drawn to the building materials like LEGOs and large cardboard blocks. During the first few sessions, Jake proceeded to create an object and then destroy the object. I was consistent to reflect Jake's feelings while constructing and deconstructing. During the fifth session, I asked Jake to create an object that represented anger. During the creation process, I noticed that Jake became angry when he could not manipulate the materials in the manner in which he desired. When it was time to process, I asked Jake to share about what he created. Jake described the object he created while I continued to attend to him and remain within the metaphor. I suspected that part of Jake's anger was due to his parents' divorce and his father not being as involved in his life. However, because Jake was in the developmental stage and because he had not voiced this being the cause of his anger, I chose to remain within the metaphor during the entire processing time. I allowed Jake to assign meaning to what he created and sought to reflect back the information that he was providing. At the end of the session, Jake spontaneously destroyed the object he had created.

There are differing opinions regarding the therapeutic use of certain building materials like LEGOs. I have found that LEGOs allow for creativity and construction within the therapeutic setting. Be sure to utilize building blocks and LEGOs that allow for creativity and that are not part of a set to build a specific object.

With this client, I sought to follow his natural inclination toward building materials. I did not seek to introduce other creative mediums because he continued to be drawn to the building materials. It is not necessary to introduce new creative mediums every session.

Through the first few sessions, I was able to observe the client's anger and utilize creative expression to explore this feeling. Furthermore, I did not explore beyond the scope of the metaphor because of Jake's developmental stage. Remaining within the metaphor allowed the experience and process to be manageable emotionally for him. Exploring beyond the metaphor would bring the reality of the situation to the forefront and would be too anxiety provoking at this point in therapy for Jake. I chose to continue to remain in the metaphor while processing activities with him and sought to reflect the experience of anger represented in his creative expression.

Because Jake's father chose not to participate in the therapeutic process, all parent consults were conducted with Jake's mother. Jake was given the option of attending parent consults; however, he chose to wait in the waiting room. To protect Jake's privacy, I did not disclose specific behaviors or statements Jake made during session. I did share with Jake's mother the theme of anger that Jake was working on in session. This provided an opportunity for his mother to share about areas where she had observed his anger manifest at home and in school. I suggested that Jake's mother practice naming Jake's emotions in the moment to help him feel understood. Because Jake had acted out aggressively in anger by breaking or throwing toys, I taught Jake's mother limit setting and choice giving to facilitate self-responsibility and create appropriate boundaries for Jake's behavior. I chose to follow up with Jake's mother every three to four sessions to monitor therapeutic growth and provide parenting support.

Counseling with minor clients often means working with divorced parents and blended families. The counselor must be aware of legal caveats associated with each individual case. Specifically, consulting the legal custody agreement provides guidelines for how a professional can proceed therapeutically and which parent can and must provide written consent for treatment. Counselors should consult with legal experts where there is confusion regarding the legal caveats of a counseling situation.

Case Three

I had conducted five group activity sessions with Heather and Lauren. Because of the nature of the relationship between both of the clients and me, and because of the deep relationship between the clients themselves, the group experience was rich with deep processing and interpersonal connectedness.

One of the goals of a group activity is that group members will gain an increasing amount of self-direction and be free to utilize internal resources (Bratton et al.,

2014), so I was flexible in allowing these clients to be self-directive in the creation process. Expressive activity media were displayed in the counseling room in an inviting manner in which both clients felt free to utilize different materials. During the sixth session, Lauren and Heather decided together to create collages around the theme of helplessness and loss of control since much of the therapeutic time to this point had been spent processing those things. To allow for ample time to create and process, I structured their group activity sessions in increments of one hour and fifteen minutes. After creating for approximately thirty-five minutes, the clients began to process their activities. Initially Heather shared about her collage, followed by Lauren; however, because of the depth of the therapeutic relationship, the dialogue that followed was a back-and-forth flow between the two clients. I continued to listen actively but allowed opportunity for both clients to lead the process. I made note of similarities between the clients' experiences as well as how the theme of helplessness and loss of control impacted their current functioning. Because of the emotional and developmental readiness of both clients, I was able to move beyond the metaphor represented in the collage activity to explore more direct applications that emerged from their collages. To conclude the session, I asked both clients to reflect on their experience in the session and allowed time for both to share their experience with the group.

Conducting group activity therapy sessions is more of an advanced therapeutic skill due in part to the need to attend to more than one client. However, group activity therapy can be extremely beneficial to adolescent clients. Because of the social engagement aspect of adolescence, group activity therapy is uniquely suited to meet their developmental needs (Siegel, 2013).

One unique aspect of activity therapy is that the client may become more self-directive in the therapeutic process (Bratton et al., 2014). This will hopefully occur in a group therapeutic process as well. As illustrated above, once a group or client has established a stable therapeutic alliance, the client can become more of an active agent in the activity selection process. I allowed both clients to lead in the session and decide what activity to pursue. Throughout the time, I was consistent to attend to the emotional needs of each client and reflect the stated themes evident from the process. As the therapeutic relationship continues, the counselor must be mindful to maintain good attending skills and also be verbally reflective of the process that is occurring in the group dynamic. As with the case vignette, when clients show readiness developmentally and emotionally, the counselor can pursue processing on a deeper level that at times might go beyond the metaphor represented in the creative activity. As with every activity, the session should be brought to a close by checking in with clients about their experience and summarizing key points of the session.

Group activity therapy provides a unique opportunity for adolescent clients to connect with one another and gain peer support in a safe environment. Parental involvement in therapy is also very important when working with groups. Although the adolescent clients are participating in group therapy, the parent consults should be conducted individually to maintain appropriate confidentiality for clients. I chose to conduct parent consults with each set of parents every three to four group sessions. During the parent consults, I updated Heather's parents and Lauren's parents on their child's individual progress.

In the case of my client Heather, because her parents had recently divorced, I provided the option to meet with her parents together or separately to respect their relational boundaries with one another. Her parents chose to meet at the same time with me to promote effective co-parenting. This allowed me the opportunity to brainstorm with Heather's parents how they could promote consistency for her as she lived part-time with each parent.

While meeting with both sets of parents individually, I provided recommendations that group activity therapy continue because the intervention was beneficial to the therapeutic growth of both clients. I discussed with each client's parents evidence that demonstrated how their child was benefiting from group activity therapy. Heather presented with more emotional regulation, and Lauren demonstrated an increased ability to connect relationally with Heather and other peers at school. Further, I was careful to monitor whether either client was ready to terminate individual therapy and continue solely with group activity therapy.

Additionally, I provided time for the parents to provide feedback on their child's progress, voice concerns, and ask questions. It is not uncommon for parents to be curious about the other client in the group and ask questions about that client's progress, goals, behavior, presenting problem, and so forth. This curiosity at times grows out of a natural concern of parents that their child might be getting close to another adolescent who might negatively influence their own adolescent. In these moments, reflecting on the parent's concerns for her own child and reassuring her that groups are carefully selected with the well-being of all clients in mind is important. Further, one of the roles of the counselor is to model and discuss healthy relationship boundaries and monitor the group dynamic to prevent or address unhealthy relationships or behaviors. However, it is imperative that the counselor maintain confidentiality and not discuss the other client's progress with the parents, even though some parents will persist in seeking information about other group members. Gently and respectfully enforcing boundaries on confidentiality and HIPPA at all times is essential.

CONCLUSION

God created humans in his likeness as image bearers to be creative agents. Because of this innate creativity, utilizing creative expression within the therapeutic context allows for a deep and rewarding therapeutic experience that can bring forth healing on many levels. Adolescent clients are uniquely primed to benefit from therapeutic services that incorporate creative expression and can benefit greatly from this type of therapeutic technique.

RECOMMENDED READING

Green, E. J., & Drewes, A. A. (2014). (Eds.). *Integrating expressive arts and play therapy with children and adolescents.* Hoboken, NJ: Wiley.

Kendall, P. C. (Ed.). (2011). *Child and adolescent therapy: Cognitive-behavioral procedures* (4th ed.). New York, NY: Guilford Press.

Landgarten, H. B. (2014). *Family art psychotherapy: A clinical guide and casebook.* New York, NY: Routledge.

Malchiodi, C. A. (2006). *Expressive therapies.* New York, NY: Guilford Press.

Oaklander, V. (1988). *Windows to our children: A Gestalt therapy approach to children and adolescents.* Highland, NY: Gestalt Journal Press.

Rubin, J. A. (2005). *Child art therapy* (Deluxe ed.). Hoboken, NJ: Wiley.

Rubin, J. A. (Ed.). (2016). *Approaches to art therapy: Theory and technique.* New York, NY: Routledge.

Sweeney, D. S., Baggerly, J. N., & Ray, D. C. (2014). *Group play therapy: A dynamic approach.* New York, NY: Taylor & Francis.

CHAPTER 15

Couple-Focused Strategies

FREDERICK A. DIBLASIO, PHD

Do not be conformed to this world, but be transformed
by the renewing of your mind, that you may prove what
is that good and acceptable and perfect will of God.

ROMANS 12:2 NKJV

When a person says "I do" to vows at the altar to become one with another human being, seldom do they comprehend the depth to which God will knit them together. The connection produces in-depth and ongoing spiritual, emotional, and neurobiological changes through life that pave the way to spiritual, cognitive, and physical oneness. Because the marital relationship requires such strong intimacy, problems often develop as two different human beings attempt to connect as one. This chapter will challenge the reader to consider the place where this oneness exists, along with all the emotions, cognitions, and volitions involved—in the brain of each partner. A new and exciting horizon is at hand where understanding the neurobiology of strategies will lead to counselors finding treatments that work most effectively. As brain-imaging technology has advanced in recent years, a pioneering movement in treatment strategies is occurring that

paves the way to deepen healthy cognitive, emotional, and behavioral interactions, as well as increasing empathy and acceptance between partners. At first the chapter's neurobiological orientation is not what the reader may have expected; however, the chapter will tie the neurobiological information into very practical and useable strategies.

Couples treatment, by and large, has shown in the research literature to be effective in helping couples resolve relationship problems (Sexton, Datachi-Phillips, Evans, LaFollette, & Wright, 2013; Stratton et al., 2015). In particular, cognitive behavioral therapy (CBT), integrative behavioral couple therapy (IBCT), and emotion-focused therapy (EFT) are showing increasing research evidence of effectiveness (Fischer, Baucom, & Cohen, 2016; Gurman, Lebow, & Synder, 2015; Lebow, Chambers, Christensen, & Johnson, 2012). Although rates of effectiveness are difficult to accurately predict, at least

70 percent of couples positively benefit from couple therapy (Lebow et al., 2012).

A common aspect of CBT, IBCT, and EFT is that they advocate a time of calming of the natural defensive posturing that comes when partners are in conflict. The calming leads to better access to cognitive, emotional, and behavioral responses that work for, rather than against, the relationship. The added feature is that these techniques promote acceptance and empathy for the other, which are critical ingredients to a healthy relationship. Emotional regulation of couples during difficult times promotes satisfying and healthy partner relationships (Kirby & Baucom, 2007). Couple therapy approaches that advocate for acceptance-based techniques are more effective than traditional therapies that promote excessive ventilation of unfiltered emotional exchange (Christensen, Atkins, Baucom, & Yi, 2010).

God designed the human brain to achieve intimacy and oneness with him and our spouses and connection with the body of Christ. One article posits that humans are neurologically "wired to connect" (Fishbane, 2007, p. 395). Brain research has made great advances in understanding emotions and cognition related to relationships (Kandel, Schwartz, Jessell, Siegelbaum, & Hudspeth, 2012). However, the crossover to the clinical practice literature is lagging behind (DiBlasio, Hester, & Belcher, 2014). Although some have attempted to connect neurobiology and the understanding of the brain to couple therapy (e.g., Roberts & Koval, 2003), the therapeutic/clinical empirical research is virtually nonexistent. The natural progression of research of CBT, IBCT, and EFT therapeutic approaches is likely to eventually include an in-depth exploration of the common-sense principle that all three approaches share certain brain-related processes. The known science of the brain, especially as it involves the limbic system and human response, is well developed (Kandel et al., 2012). Therefore practitioners are encouraged to use this science in developing techniques to help couples. Counselors are constantly faced with difficult and challenging situations where neurobiological science may be of use to help couples understand how the human brain works to form both positive and negative interpersonal neuropathways. Discovery of how the brain works allows for new strategies and tools for counselors not only to help couples in conflict but to help couples form new behaviors that assist them through their future marital dynamics.

Based on the belief that the brain is God's wonderful creation gift to humans, this chapter first provides a biblical overview of marriage and biblical support for the integration of neurobiology for helping couples. This is followed by a brief case study that will be utilized to demonstrate the techniques discussed throughout the chapter. Next, I present biblical/neurobiological techniques for couples that have produced repetitive positive results in my clinical practice. Although the body of neurobiological research about brain structures and functions is well developed, the reader is cautioned that little research is currently available that empirically tests the effectiveness of the techniques described herein.

More and more counselors are trained in systemic approaches that consider the biopsychosocial-spiritual aspects of humans and their interpersonal relationships. It is time for theory development to establish a look into neurobiological clinical approaches that then can be empirically tested. And in the final section before the conclusion, I present several systemic techniques for helping couples to forgive, improve their fit together, negotiate, set realistic expectations, and restore love during conflict.

THEOLOGY AND PSYCHOLOGY OF COUPLE COUNSELING

God has an exalted view of marriage according to Genesis 1:27–28; 2:18–25; Malachi 2:14; Matthew 19:3–6; Mark 10:6–9; 1 Corinthians 7:2–5, 10–16, 27–40; Ephesians 5:21–33; Colossians 3:18–19; Titus 2:4–5; Hebrews 13:4; and 1 Peter 3:1–9 (Broger, 1991, p. 246). The verses above describe that from the beginning God designed marriage as a lifelong, committed, and monogamous relationship between a man and a woman. Each was made to become one with the other and grow in devotion to become one with God through Christ. Marriage requires a dedicated sacrifice of self to the well-being of the other.

One of the problems with professional couple counseling is that many secular approaches encourage humans to find happiness and follow their hearts. Although on the surface this may sound healthy, seldom does the pursuit of self-focused happiness produce what it takes to sustain strong, healthy, and Christlike bonding in a monogamous relationship. In fact, Jeremiah 17:9 says that the "heart is deceitful above all things and beyond cure. Who can understand it?" While there can be found much rejoicing and happiness in marriage, the pursuit of self-happiness is not the goal but a by-product. One of the main goals of the Christian life is to love God "'with all your heart, with all your soul, with all your strength, and with all your mind,' and 'your neighbor as yourself'" (Luke 10:27 NKJV). The first and foremost primary neighbor is the spouse.

It is hypothesized here that God created humans physically, neurologically, emotionally, cognitively, and spiritually with the capacity to love. This is part of what Scripture means when it describes humans as "fearfully and wonderfully made" (Ps. 139:14). Further, it is hypothesized that throughout life, humans were designed to increase in the depth of their love for him and others. This is in part via a brain that has the developing ability to become increasingly efficient to love throughout life. The following sections are only hypothesized ways that the human brain may be designed to develop an ever-increasing love transformation, especially in marriage.

Biblical Renewing of the Mind and Neuroplasticity

Christians are better prepared to achieve this love of God and others if they become transformed: "Do not be conformed to this world, but be transformed by the renewing of your mind, that you may prove what is that good and acceptable and perfect will of God" (Rom. 12:2 NKJV).

Although this renewing is obviously spiritual, perhaps it is also manifested as neurological changes in the brain as the Christian repeatedly conforms to the ways of God through thought and behavior.

Interestingly, science has proven that the brain through the life span is constantly developing and forming efficient neuropathways through neuroplasticity. Neuroplasticity is the ability of the human brain to grow stronger through use and stimulation, much like muscles and bodies do when adapting to physical demands like exercise. With brain plasticity, like physical exercise, there needs to be enough repetitive stimulation, simply known as *firing*, of the targeted brain structures to create an increased protein synthesis of neurons. This causes neurons to grow and link together in the brain to eventually form a rigid new neuropathway. The human brain is highly adaptable and will make physiological and neurological changes to accommodate our thought life and behaviors. In neurology, the changes are simply called *plastic changes* because like plastic it can be shaped to almost any form that it is purposed to become. However, also like plastic, once it becomes rigid, the brain has a relatively permanent accommodation that can have the potential to last throughout life (although it may weaken somewhat if not often used). Once plastic changes develop, the brain becomes trained to accommodate neurological flow and firing that is most efficient to accommodate the repetitive thought sequences and behavioral patterns.

In essence, as Christians bring "every thought into captivity to the obedience of Christ" (2 Cor. 10:5 NKJV) and meditate on what is true, just, pure, lovely, of good report, virtuous, and praiseworthy (Phil. 4:8), they may be transforming their brain via neuroplasticity to become stronger and more efficient in these areas. The "renewing of the mind" is a free-will choice to do God's will (Josh. 24:15; John 7:17). Christians are directed in the Scriptures to use this liberty to "serve one another" in love (Gal. 5:13). It is hypothesized that in God's mercy, he created our brains with all that we need to make this choice and to sustain it through a lifetime. With increased use, these pathways become stronger and more efficient for loving God, spouses, and others. Serving one another becomes more "natural," so to speak, so that our natures become more like God's as we are "being transformed into the same image [as God] from glory to glory" (2 Cor. 3:18 NKJV).

A Biblical View of the Amygdala in the Limbic System

Let's start with a user-friendly review of how our brains experience the world around and within us. The limbic system is our neurological system for emotional responses, memory formation, and interpretation of our environment as it relates to pleasure and survival.

At the center of the limbic system are two small brain structures called the amygdala, each about the size of an almond, which are located lower in the brain with one to the left and one to the right. Feelings that are stimulated by the amygdala are often referred to in modern society as a person's "heart." The amygdala is often stimulated throughout the day by external circumstances, both positive and negative. The external cues are taken in by one or more of our five senses, which then cause the amygdala to fire, and from there several amazing things happen simultaneously. The amygdala is stimulated via the senses but can also be stimulated by internal thoughts. For example, one starts thinking about an upsetting and unresolved incident with the partner, thus activating the amygdala, resulting in deep, upsetting feelings. Alternatively, as thoughts of tenderness and love are focused on, the amygdala is pleasantly stimulated.

One of the purposes for the amygdala is to provide an automatic, autonomic, conscious, and unconscious mechanism for instinctual self-protection, including emotional and psychological survival. It is hypothesized that God instilled love for self (e.g., Luke 10:27) in the very essence of our neurobiological creation, resulting in the natural instincts of humans to protect themselves, seek food and shelter, and even to seek protection from emotional harm. As an example of physical danger, suppose a tree branch begins to crack overhead. We instinctively look in the direction of the dangerous sound while simultaneously moving out of the way. The sense of hearing communicated directly with the amygdala, which caused the amygdala to communicate directly to the brain stem for appropriate automatic self-protective and evasive physical movement of the body. In other words, we did not have to think with logic about the action our limbs and muscles took to avoid the falling branch. Our effort to stay physically safe was a reflexive action. Not only did God

create us with the automatic movement, but he also designed in us a chemical/hormonal (adrenaline and cortisol) release of energy that provides alertness and strength to accomplish the task sufficiently.

When humans are emotionally hurt or under emotional threat, the amygdala is activated much like it is when under physical threat. In emotional conflict with a spouse, the amygdala calls for the release of adrenaline, which causes survival alertness and increasing strength while the amygdala simultaneously sends messages to the adrenal gland to release cortisol— the stress hormone. Ironically, the power of these two chemicals combined begins to dull rational and empathetic thinking in the brain in favor of decisive one-track thinking for self-preservation. Further, this release of chemicals disrupts the usual flow of automatic regulatory signals from the prefrontal cortex that promote loving and thoughtful treatment of our spouses. After all, the brain is in survival mode, responding as if under attack. All this can lead to marital partners saying and doing things that are more harmful to the relationship, which in turn causes a pattern of neural firing in the other that is also detrimental to the relationship, creating an interactive circle of elevating frustration and anger. Couples often can identify negative amygdala activity when it is described as that negative "surge" that wells up inside during conflict. Fortunately, God gives humans cognitive control over the emotional center so that we do not have to sin. First Corinthians 10:13 says, "No temptation has overtaken you except what is common to mankind. And God is faithful; he will not let you be tempted beyond what you can bear. But when you are tempted, he will also provide a way out so that you can endure it." The amygdala will calm down in a few minutes if we take a time-out and/or a time for prayer leading to the settling of defensiveness and combative urges.

CASE STUDY

Ray and Mary Hall

Ray and Mary are an African American couple in their midthirties with two young children. This couple came to counseling after Ray's discovery of Mary's affair. Ray said that the hurt and shock caused him to seek after God, and as a result he made a commitment to the Christian faith, while Mary was a devout Christian believer for most of her life. Uncharacteristically of Mary, after ten years of faithfulness to Ray, she got involved in an emotional and physical relationship with a Christian friend of the family after he offered her compassion and empathy for her struggles with Ray. Ray demonstrated a host of oppressive, controlling, and narcissistic qualities throughout their marriage. Mary capitulated to the control and suffered silently throughout the years, finding refuge in raising her two children.

In the fourth session of therapy, the couple completed a lengthy forgiveness session described below (also see DiBlasio, 2000a, for conducting forgiveness sessions in cases of marital infidelity). Ray formally forgave Mary for the affair, and Mary forgave Ray for his controlling and oppressive behaviors and lack of empathy over the years. The follow-up therapy focused on Mary building trust once again with her husband and learning new and loving ways to speak up in the marriage. Ray focused on controlling his oppressive nature and anger. During the therapy, the Halls appreciated the brain information and agreed to allow the therapy to be focused on strong Christian integration and neurobiological intervention.

STRATEGIES, INTERVENTIONS, AND TECHNIQUES FOR COUPLE COUNSELING

Neurobiological Education and Contracting

As we age, we learn more about our bodies that helps us in times of problem treatment as well as prevention. Take as an analogy the man with acid reflux who discovers that if he eats within an hour of bedtime he will experience reflux throughout the night. His remedy is to avoid eating before bedtime; if he makes an exception, he stays up an extra hour. Once people understand their physical health, they can make healthy plans for prevention and adjustments if problems develop. He makes a "contract" with his doctor and himself to follow this simple treatment plan and avoids complicated medical treatment and drugs. For example, during a time of negative hyperarousal, a client is taught that the initial surge is the response of the amygdala going into self-survival mode. This then becomes a cue to calm the amygdala down with focus on pleasant memories or some distraction. One client who was a baseball fan told me that he distracted the surge by focusing on the imagery of a slow-motion swing hitting a perfect pitch.

Interestingly, as significant as the brain is to human emotional relationships and thus treatment of couples, seldom do counselors educate clients or develop treatment plans with the brain as a central focus. If couples understood better the functions of the brain, they would gain new insight and tools to control and regulate how they respond to their partners. It would also help them gain awareness of how to interpret their partners' times of emotional reactions. As a parallel related to physical pain management, one study found that when patients received and used pain neuroscience education, the result was a decrease in pain and improved physical performance (Puentedura & Flynn, 2016, p. 408).

Neurobiological education alone is not enough to produce effective change. Part of this strategy requires clients to form a contract in which they agree with the counselor to follow a treatment plan that addresses their problems. Effective client contracts are those in which clients freely agree to pursue a treatment or suggestion without pressure from the counselor.

Throughout the treatment, Ray and Mary commented on how helpful it was to hear about the brain in a way that they could understand. It gave them hope that they could become better with each other and that the brain would form new neuropathways to maintain the improvements. They understood that with the power of the Holy Spirit and the fruit of the Spirit of love, joy, peace, forbearance, kindness, goodness, faithfulness, gentleness, and self-control (Gal. 5:22–23), their brains could form neural pathways to strengthen unity and love throughout the marriage. It gave them a profound hope that major and permanent changes were possible. The Halls readily agreed that they would each work on retraining their brains and give up focus on attempting to retrain the other. They also agreed (contracted) that follow-up discussion about the brain would become a regular part of almost every weekly session.

Cortisol-Control Intervention and De-escalating Conflict

Cortisol is meant to dull the signaling from the amygdala to the higher order cognitive structures so that the person stays in an instinctual survival mode, thus inhibiting logical cognitive thought that can get in the way of fighting or fleeing danger. One client, after completing treatment, went on to train for an elite military fighting group that performed special worldwide combat operation missions. Previously in his marital therapy he worked on his need to control the release of cortisol during times of anger at his wife. A year later he reported appreciation for the couple therapy that focused on cortisol control and learning to calm oneself during marital crisis situations. He reported that he was more advanced than others in the training because of what he learned in the therapy. His military trainers made recruits aware that cortisol had to be controlled because the flooding of cortisol as aroused by the amygdala would dull their cognitive abilities to discern wisely in combat situations. They taught that when entering into a zone to stop a terrorist, if cortisol was too high, a soldier may mistake an innocent bystander reaching for his passport as a terrorist reaching for a gun. As a result, recruits are trained to calm their amygdala in combat training situations, and actual cortisol levels are monitored by medical personnel to see if they are successful at lowering their cortisol.

Typical responses after cortisol release in marriages are to walk away in anger and frustration; to become sullen and withdrawn emotionally, which is another way of fleeing; or to provide agitated verbal defense, which is usually done in tones and communications that show anger, upset, and irritation. It is hypothesized that the cortisol elevation, in and of itself, produces the external stimuli that further influence the rise in cortisol of the other partner. Chronic release of cortisol is associated with depression, hypertension, sleep deprivation, migraines, decreased resistance in the immune system, chronic fatigue, and a host of other physiological and psychological disorders.

The well-known verse: "'Be angry, and do not sin': do not let the sun go down on your wrath" (Eph. 4:26 NKJV) has produced many exhausted marital partners as they struggle through the night with high-pitched emotional and sometimes volatile arguments in an effort to resolve the issue between them. Interestingly, research shows in such encounters that depriving couples of sleep has detrimental effects on the couples' ability to manage conflict (Wilson et al., 2017). Couples are relieved to hear that the amygdala of the brain can be calmed and anger released in a matter of minutes. Thus, the anger is settled before

sundown, and the work of resolving the problem can wait until the morning.

Ray and Mary practiced during sessions when negative emotional spiraling would occur. They were asked to pause for a moment and to read the behavioral cues that one or both were having an *amygdala moment*. As an example, Mary, in a response she was giving, inadvertently criticized her husband, and the negative change in Ray's facial expression was noticeable. I said to Ray, "By looking at the negative look on your face as your wife was talking, I wondered if your amygdala just fired." Ray was surprised that it was that obvious, and he explained that he recognized that his amygdala fired because he felt an intense desire to set the record straight about how his wife's comments about him were not true. Ray was encouraged to let his amygdala settle a bit before he spoke as practice for controlling his anger. After a few minutes of conversation between Mary and me, Ray very appropriately was able to point out to his wife the critical comment she made that sparked his amygdala response. I called attention to how much calmer and softer Ray's voice became when compared to just minutes earlier. After affirming Ray for his success in calming his amygdala, I stated: "You are now ready to have a meaningful conversation with Mary about your feelings about the criticism." Ray said that her comments "hurt" his feelings, which was a significant improvement for Ray who seldom was able to express anything but anger at his wife during times of conflict. Mary was moved to empathy for her husband, apologized for the unintended criticism, and went on to reinforce the high level of success Ray had made in recent weeks.

In the therapy, Ray was slowly understanding that his negative feelings could be discussed, but he needed to avoid the immediate rapid rise in negative amygdala-driven intensity to avoid becoming controlling and oppressive. On the other hand, through such interventions as the above, Mary was beginning to be more alert to her husband's hurt feelings and to recognize that she needed to avoid premature emotional or physical withdrawal. Helping couples to regulate the right therapeutic level of negative emotional sharing in the session is the responsibility of the counselor (Weeks & Fife, 2014).

As a word of caution, some counselors have sought to encourage much raw and unfiltered expression of negative emotions in therapy offices to achieve "catharsis" or ventilation. Interestingly, the release of cortisol and adrenaline in emotional situations can sometimes reach a level that hinders the peace and love of God and love of spouse. The counselor should take charge of helping couples regulate negative emotions and help the couple regulate a therapeutic balance.

Managing the Hippocampus

When the amygdala activates in response to negative reactions from a spouse, it automatically communicates with the hippocampus, where unpleasant memories and the negativity they evoke are stored. In response, the hippocampus signals back to the amygdala memory of emotional data that is used by the amygdala to interpret the current perceived threat by comparing it to previous similar situations in the past. The more negative experiences stored in the hippocampus, the greater the intensity of the perceived danger of the current threat. The amygdala automatically signals the hippocampus for emotional memory input from history. The communication between the two structures is immediate, direct, and ongoing to keep the amygdala on high alert to respond to the threat at hand using automatic, historical, and emotional data.

For example, if during a fight a mate called the partner cruel, hurtful, and verbally abusive names, even though forgiveness was achieved, the experience is unconsciously relived when this same person comes anywhere close to the vocal tone and facial looks of that time. It is the brain's way of quickly interpreting current threat with past information in order for the person to move to self-protective behaviors. The scarring of hurtful memories accumulates through the years by various interpersonal situations and is filtered to the amygdala at lightning speed.

Couples are made aware that they should not "feed the hippo" an unhealthy diet that leads to permanent relationship scarring. Negative treatment of the other through loud voice, vindictive statements, and exaggerated critical accusations is not emotionally healthy for either the one expressing them or the one receiving. In fact, given the amount of cortisol that fires and the negative searing of the hippocampus, an argument can be made that only loving communication hits the mark for healing. Sometimes the partner was not involved in the original creation of the wound.

Such was the case with Mary, as she was wounded by her parents and siblings during childhood. The scars from these previous wounds were stored in the hippocampus and became fodder for interpreting hurtful events in her marriage.

The good news is that the hippocampus is not just for negative and hurtful memories, but it is also the place for the positive and pleasurable ones. When I was a child, I loved my summers at a camp that was off of the South River in Annapolis, Maryland. To this day, the smell of a river brings a wave of pleasurable feelings of my youth. In this case, automatically and within split seconds the amygdala picks up the smell and signals the hippocampus. The hippocampus feeds the amygdala data of past association with the smell and pleasant feelings, and simultaneously the amygdala signals for the release of oxytocin, which adds to the pleasurable feeling. In addition, many other things are being signaled by the amygdala. Among them is a signaling to the prefrontal lobe, which provides return signaling for enhancement or inhibition of the amygdala activity, and to the higher-ordered brain structures, which contain memories and thoughts that also provide enhancement or inhibition. Now the pleasurable memories are in full swing, enhanced by the interactive activity of several brain structures but completely under the control of free will to continue or to stop.

Because of Ray's verbal outbursts and occasional destruction of property in anger and Mary's unfaithfulness, I cautioned the couple that these memories become permanently etched into the hippocampus

and resurface subliminally during conflict and times of perceived threat. Just making the Halls aware of these *automatic implicit reactions* of the brain produced a cognitive awareness that their marriage did not need any more negative scarring interactions. Further, it made them aware that the immediate surge of fear or anger has a negative tie to history. As Ray improved during the therapy, there were times when Mary would become fearful, go into what I labeled a "fog," and become overly emotional, confused, and capitulating when Ray was slightly irritated. Mary was able to recognize that in these times she could not trust her feeling level because her amygdala was being overly stimulated by her hippocampus, which had many stored fearful reactions from the oppression she experienced as a child and from Ray's oppression of her. In these crisis times, Mary was able to put things into perspective by not depending on her "gut" fearful feelings but instead focusing on the new, safer reality that had been created in the marriage.

Helping Couples to Create Oxytocin Moments

God in his infinite wisdom created humans to be attached to one another in love, and no greater interpersonal human lifelong bond exists than the bond of marriage. The connection is much greater than solely an emotional bond. One key function of the amygdala is to activate the secretion of oxytocin, an attachment/love hormone, between husband and wife that bonds them together in a deep neurobiological way.

As mentioned above, the amygdala is stimulated by both threat and pleasure.

A pleasurable experience causes the amygdala to signal the pituitary gland for the release of oxytocin. Several interactional behaviors increase the likelihood that oxytocin will be secreted: eye contact, physical touch, kissing, hugging, cuddling, sex, massage, petting a dog/cat/etc., receiving acts of altruism, performing acts of altruism, giving empathy, and receiving empathy to name a few (see Kuchinskas, 2009). Notice how many of these examples fit the category of loving behaviors. Oxytocin is the key hormone involved in a baby attaching to the parent. In marital partners, one of the highest times of mutual strong flooding of oxytocin is during sex, especially just before and during orgasm. Through sexual intimacy, God provides a neurological signaling for the release of an attachment hormone, which in turn not only brings pleasure, love, and attachment to the relationship but increases the likelihood for lifelong monogamy. Oxytocin is known to increase contentment, mellowness/calm, security, bonding and attachment, positive social interaction, empathy, loving behaviors, growth, and healing. At the same time, it reduces anxiety and stress, depressive mood, blood pressure, and insecurity.

Interestingly, this major hormone known to emanate from interpersonal human contact that can potentially change the nature of a marital relationship is seldom known or discussed in the context of a couple's counseling. Keeping the concept front and center is helpful, and at times asking clients to take a moment to consider how they might boost oxytocin in the other should be a regular part of the therapeutic encounter. Looking for ways to promote it for the couple at home and finding opportunities during sessions to directly refer to it and encourage it is important. Obviously, focusing on it is not only beneficial for the routine maintenance of the relationship but can be healing and restorative during times of stress, anger, and hurt. Part of why "a soft answer turns away wrath" (Prov. 15:1 NKJV) may very well be that the soft answer is oxytocin producing.

The focus on understanding and utilizing the release of oxytocin is an essential part of a *neurobiological-integrated couple therapy*. Among other things, Ray and Mary found the information about God's design of giving men and women a neurobiological chemical to assist in lifelong attachment fascinating. They felt empowered by knowing that each had the power to produce togetherness by such simple things as extending touch and kind words. In addition, it gave them a way to counteract the flow of cortisol in the other. Many Christian couples benefit from the recommendation of useful easy-to-read resources to help promote practical tips for building up the marital relationship (for example, see Wheat & Perkins, 1980).

During therapy sessions, Ray and Mary readily complied each time a therapeutic request was made for them to provide oxytocin moments for the other. In time, it was noticeable that the couple increased in their self-motivated and spontaneous actions to create oxytocin moments. The following are a few brief examples of directives during their sessions.

1. "Mary, I noticed Ray's pit bull look [a fun way that Ray and I described his cor-

tisol shooting moments]. Do you think he needs a little oxytocin?" Response: Both smiled, and Mary reached over and gently held his hand. (By the way, a love seat is a must for couple therapy.)

2. "Mary, as you talk about the hurt from your childhood, would you mind if Ray puts his arm around you?" Response: Ray compassionately looked at his wife, put his arm around her, and the two moved closer to one another.

3. "Ray, I noticed a real sincerity in what you just said. Would you look at Mary and consider turning that into a spiritual commitment to her?" Response: Ray turned to his wife, held her hand, looked into her eyes, and with a gentle voice made a commitment to her. This was followed up with praise and prayer. A nice by-product of praise and joyful prayer is likely another source of oxytocin release.

Treating Personality Disorders with a Neurobiological Intervention

There are two surprising statistics regarding personality disorders: first, about 9 percent of the general population have a personality disorder (PD) (Lenzenweger, Lane, Loranger, & Kessler, 2008), and second, about 46 percent of clinical cases have one or more persons who have PD (Zimmerman, Rothschild, & Chelminski, 2005). This means that a majority of couple therapy cases will involve presenting problems that are more related to the PD pathology than to problems in communication or other routine issues.

A neurobiological breakthrough in research has occurred regarding personality

disorders, but so far the advances of this research have not yet sufficiently crossed over to the mental health professions. Evidence is mounting as differences are being found in PD subjects' brain structures, brain function, and neurological connectivity between structures, especially the limbic system and the structures that provide higher-ordered limbic control functions (DiBlasio et al., 2014). It was discovered that when PD subjects were compared to normal controls that "(1) PD subjects have connectivity dysfunction of signaling between and within brain structures (e.g., Rüsch, Bracht, Kreher, Schnell, Glauche, Il'yason, & Tebartz van Elst, 2010); (2) communication dysfunction occurs between the frontal cortex and the limbic system—especially with emotional executive functioning (orbitofrontal cortex) and cognitive executive functioning (dorsolateral prefrontal cortex) (e.g., Salavert, Gasol, Vieta, Cervantes, Trampal, & Gispert, 2011); and (3) brain structures are smaller, with grey and white brain matter being less in volume (O'Neill, D'Souza, Carballedo, Joseph, Kerskens, & Frodl, 2013)" (DiBlasio, in press).

I have frequently noticed in clinical practice that the PD partner continued to repeat the same mistakes without learning from the consequences of his or her behavior. Although the above research was not available at the time, I suspected that, like an academic learning disability where brain abnormalities interfere with learning, PD was a problem of learning related to emotions and interpersonal situations that were also related to brain abnormalities. This lead to the formulation of *emotional and interpersonal dyslexia* (EID), an approach that has proven effective in my clinical practice. Because a full review of the theory and techniques of EID is beyond the scope of this chapter, the reader is referred to DiBlasio and colleagues (2014) for a more complete presentation of this approach for treating PD clients from a Christian perspective. Among the techniques to address EID, the following four stood out in the Hall case.

Diagnosis and explanation. Prior to the couple's therapy, Ray was called narcissistic by his wife and his wife's siblings, which he said only infuriated him. However, after a strength-based delivery that complimented his strengths of intelligence and articulation, and affirmed him as someone having that "x-factor" (that something special that is not found in ordinary people), he received the diagnosis of narcissistic personality disorder (NPD). He was encouraged and hopeful because he learned that the diagnosis had an explanation and that there was a practical treatment plan of retraining his brain that made a lot of sense to him.

Support and teamwork from the spouse. Mary was also hopeful because the diagnosis made some sense out of the past ten years of Ray's self-centered behavior, and for the first time Ray was owning his controlling behaviors and committing to a treatment plan for recovery. Mary was able to follow through in setting loving boundaries at home as practiced during the therapy. Ray felt respected when I asked if he wanted to give permission for his wife to do her part in helping him. In a healthy way, Mary was able to detach her sense of security from Ray's negative moods and show him empathy instead of the antagonism and withdrawal she had displayed for so many years. The couple was also able to renew a better sexual life together as the sense of teamwork caused both to become closer.

Building new neuropathways and no longer trusting the "heart." Ray had many interpersonal strengths that he used in his running of a small consultation firm that he could count on and use in his marriage. One of those strengths was that Ray was known to be able to achieve whatever he determined he wanted to achieve (this is also part of the "x-factor" described above). This determination was used for motivating Ray to build new pathways and not to trust his negative feelings about Mary. Ray understood that his EID was at its worst with Mary because she was his best friend. Each time he took a time-out and avoided acting from impulse on his negative feelings, he understood he was developing neuropathways that would over time become healthy and strong.

Using an accountability person. During the forgiveness session, accountability persons were chosen by mutual agreement for both Ray and Mary. Ray, with Mary's full support, chose an elder from their church who reached out to Ray during the marital crisis. The elder and Ray meet weekly for an early morning coffee, where they pray together and Ray checks out some of his thinking about Mary to make sure he is thinking realistically. In addition, Ray did well at becoming more patient to save discussing tough issues with Mary for his weekly counseling sessions. After a few weeks, he reported that he could tell his brain was being re-wired because it was becoming easier to be more patient and empathetic with Mary.

Clinical Use of Forgiveness

Although focusing on the present and future of the relationship is tempting, couples are often stuck in the hurts and offenses of the past. Counselors are encouraged to offer a structured forgiveness session (e.g., DiBlasio, 2000a; 2013) for the purpose of helping couples resolve past issues. It is critical that couples self-determine whether to be involved in such a session as well as determine the timing of it. Correspondingly, bringing up the issue at the start of treatment is important so that couples who choose to attempt it can also decide whether they would prefer it in the beginning, middle, or end of the therapy. Many Christian couples choose to have the long five-hour session at the beginning of therapy. Almost without exception, the session leads to forgiveness and paves the way for a therapy that is able to resolve additional problems quickly. One of the basic reasons for this is because forgiveness is central to the Christian faith. God the Father forgives humans who believe in and are committed to Jesus (John 3:16).

The following summarizes several main points about interpersonal forgiveness:

Approximately 24 verses are found in the Scriptures that directly use the word "forgive" (or some variation of the word) and a handful of interpersonal examples of forgiveness, such as the prodigal son (Luke 15:11–32), that do not directly use a variation of the word forgive. The overwhelming and connecting theme of Scriptural forgiveness is that we are to forgive as the Father has forgiven us (Col 3:13). Jesus taught that humans must forgive one another, and that God's forgiveness is associated with our forgiveness of others (Matt 6:12; 6:14–15; 18:21–22; 18:35; Mark 11:25; Luke 6:37; 11:4).

Since unbelievers and believers can make a decision to forgive in a moment in time (for example, at the bedside of a dying person), we therefore know that God has created humans with the free-will ability to forgive immediately, despite possible countervailing negative emotions. This decision process is enhanced for Christians because they have the power of the indwelling Holy Spirit. Jesus said, "For if you forgive men their trespasses, your heavenly Father will also forgive you. But if you do not forgive men their trespasses, neither will your Father forgive your trespasses" (Matt 6:14–15). Interestingly, these verses immediately follow the Lord's Prayer (Matt 6:9–13) and in context can be considered Jesus wanting to bring a special emphasis to the importance of interpersonal forgiveness. Additional Scripture teaches: (a) unforgiveness is sin (Rom 1:31; 2 Tim 3:3); (b) Christians have been forgiven a great debt (symbolic of forgiveness through Christ) and therefore we may not be unforgiving of others (the story of the unforgiving servant found in Matt 18:23–35); (c) Christians are to interrupt their prayer and take care of forgiveness issues (Mark 11:25) (given that we are to pray "unceasingly" [1 Thes 5:17] immediate forgiveness is implied); (d) resolve offenses before bringing gifts to the altar (Matt 5:23–26); (e) love suffers long (keeps no record of wrongs) (1 Cor 13:4); (f) must forgive frequently (Matt 18:21–22) and even if offended multiple times (Luke 17:3–4). No Scriptures were found to show that God promotes a process of making a decision to forgive over a period of time. (DiBlasio, 2010, pp. 291–292)

The first three steps of the forgiveness session are these:

1. Definitions of forgiveness are discussed.
2. The focus on each person having the opportunity to seek forgiveness for his or her wrongful actions is established.
3. The treatment process is introduced, and the couple decides whether to participate. These steps help to prepare the couple for the session and provide an opportunity to define and discuss forgiveness, learn about decision-based forgiveness, and decide if they want to participate in a session where decision-based forgiveness is utilized. Decision-based forgiveness is the letting go of the need for revenge and the releasing of negative thoughts of resentment and bitterness. Because each person is able to make a free-will decision on the offense for which they want to seek forgiveness, accountability is increased, and defensiveness is reduced. Usually this is new to couples who heretofore spent a fair amount of negative energy and emotion trying to convince the other of his or her offenses. When left to make an independent and free-will choice, a person almost always choses the very offense that the spouse would have chosen for them. Just by owning the offense, the offender has a positive start toward achieving forgiveness.

After these initial steps, one spouse is chosen to begin steps 4 through 12 in sequence. The spouse with the more serious offense is asked to start. At the completion of this segment, the other spouse begins steps 4 through 12. The steps are as follows:

1. Offender states the offense.
2. Offender provides explanation.
3. Questions about the offense are addressed.
4. Offended person gives emotional reactions.
5. Offender provides empathy to the offended person.
6. Offender develops a plan to stop/prevent behavior.
7. Offended person identifies with the offender's hurt.
8. Emphasis is placed on choice and commitment involved in letting go.
9. Offender makes a formal request for forgiveness. After both have completed their turns through the steps, focus is placed on step 13.
10. The couple completes a ceremonial act to celebrate the forgiveness decisions made.

The following describes three of the above steps from the Hall case study.

Step 5: Offender provides explanation. I began step 5 by getting Ray's permission to dig deep and to try to get a full explanation of Mary's unfaithfulness. The free-will permission given by Ray made him a key participant with me in an exploration of the problem. This helped to minimize his defensive and hurtful reactions as he assumed the position of understanding the factors that went into the affair. Mary was genuinely repentant, and with many tears and sobbing she described the affair and the deception she used to cover up her wrongdoing. When asked to provide an explanation, she was able to connect to a lifelong unfulfilled desire to be loved and valued. Her father and a couple of older siblings were described as narcissistic, which led to a childhood of neglect and emotional abuse. In addition, Mary developed an acquiescing personality and found it hard to say no to family and friends.

Despite this history and Mary's knowing that Ray was self-centered as they were dating, our discussion helped her to see that perhaps she was blindly drawn to Ray, in part, because of the subliminal self-sabotaging propensity to be in an oppressive relationship. After ten years of marriage and being controlled and criticized by Ray, one day something "clicked off" in her after one of Ray's anger outbursts when he threw the electronic video game machine down the steps because the children were fighting over it. While Mary was telling her story, Ray began to cry with a true sense of empathy for her suffering under years of his mistreatment. This show of deep empathy was something that

Ray reported he had never had before in his life with anyone. Although we would like to think it was the technique, there is nothing like the convicting power and the softening of the heart brought about by the Holy Spirit.

When it was Ray's turn to choose an offense (remembering that Mary completed steps 4 through 12 before Ray took his turn), he was quick to admit his cruel and controlling nature throughout their marriage. He was quick to recognize that ever since his childhood he was self-centered, and once he locked on to what he wanted, he was "a force to be reckoned with." Interestingly, Ray's mother and brother had the same controlling and critical propensity. After a discussion of how his brain may be working and how he could build new neuropathways for anger control, both partners saw the information as revelatory and found hope that Ray could actively retrain his brain.

Step 9: Offender develops a plan to stop/prevent behavior. Mary developed the following plan with the assistance of Ray and myself: (a) Mary was to completely cut off the relationship and *all* contact with the other man, and if he were to somehow reach out to Mary, or if there was incidental contact, Mary committed to report the information immediately to Ray. (b) Mary (and Ray) were to have a complete "sunshine" policy with each other. This meant that their lives were open books for one another, including phone, computers and social networks, letters, and passwords. (c) Mary gave Ray permission to periodically check up on her to make sure she was honoring their marriage and not being deceptive about such things as her where-abouts and activities. Checking behavior is typical for the nonparticipating spouse; however, when it is built into the plan, it creates less negativity, and each time the check is enacted and nothing is revealed, it helps to build trust. Given that Ray had a problem with control, Ray gave permission to me to monitor him closely so that he would not abuse this permission. (d) Mary was to find a mature woman to meet with regularly by phone and in person for prayer, advice, and accountability. (e) Ray and Mary decided that certain articles of clothing worn during the affair should be given to a charity or thrown away.

Improving the Fit between Marital Partners

Achieving agreed-upon complementarity in relationship. When couples connect, they each bring certain personalities, skills, and talents to the relationship. Part of the attraction that led to the initial draw of one to another has something to do with this fit. For example, it is not unusual for a slightly introverted person to ultimately fit best with someone more on the extroverted side. The metaphor I use with couples is the geometrical concept of supplementary angles, that is, two adjacent angles that together equal 180°. Couples have a number of fits across a wide array of subjects. Examples of subject areas include family decisions, financial wisdom or financial management, social-life initiation, child-rearing involvement, emotional intimacy, physical intimacy, advocacy for needs, general power in the relationship, assertiveness, and resolving conflict.

On some matters one may be an obtuse angle (greater than 90°), while on others be an acute angle (less than 90°).

Mary and Ray were asked to choose several subject areas important to them. Of the areas they chose, control and decision making was one of the more significant ones. I explained the concept of supplementary angles, and obtuse versus acute angles. Then I asked them to privately write down their own estimates of angle size for themselves, as well as their perception of each other. Interestingly, couples often predict similar answers. It is not required that the total equal 180°, since, for example, it is possible to have both partners as obtuse angles in a subject area (these areas are usually wrought with conflict) or a combination of acute angles that do not equal 180°.

Even though couples write down their answers independently beforehand, there is usually a high level of agreement in the ratings when they are shared during the intervention. In fact, Ray and Mary perceived exactly the same on all angles. Before treatment, Ray was narcissistic in the relationship and wielded a lot of power. He dominated much of the decision making without empathy. Both Ray and Mary rated Ray as 150° and Mary as 30°. When asked what degrees they aspired to achieve, they again independently chose the same ideal of Ray at 100° and Mary at 80°. This is a very typical devout Christian perspective because many Christian couples desire for the husband to have greater control as the spiritual leader, but it also promotes a significant amount of control for the wife. Note how in Proverbs 31:16 (NKJV) that the wife "considers a field and buys it; from her profits she plants a vineyard" indicates that in biblical times woman had significant involvement in finances, land negotiations and acquisition, and agricultural labor. Although counselors sometimes are tempted to influence couples toward 90°/90° goals, couples must have self-determination in relation to their faith, desires, and culture.

Next, we discussed the systemic principle of work Ray and Mary needed to do together. This included Mary "finding her voice" and becoming more decisive while Ray purposely pulled back control. If Ray did not pull back enough, Mary would have more difficulty growing in the size of her angle because Ray was blocking the growth space. The strength of this technique increased throughout therapy as it became a mutually agreed point of reference to navigate through issues of decision making and other therapeutic issues.

Accepting and tweaking personality. Counselors use various personality measures to ascertain the personalities of clients. I prefer to use the model first developed by Hippocrates (the father of medicine) in 360 BC of melancholic, sanguine, phlegmatic, and choleric. Often part of the subliminal expectation that spouses develop about their mates is that their mates be more like them. However, if this were to come about, the spouses would likely not get along at all. God built humans differently and gave them different giftedness to fulfill a function and become part of the body of Christ (1 Cor. 12:12–27).

Although Ray was diagnosed as having narcissistic personality disorder, this should not be relied on to determine his identity. As Ray improved, more of his natural positive choleric personality emerged in the family. Ray was a successful businessman in a field where his choleric decisiveness, leadership, and boldness to take calculated risks has historically led to profitable results. The negatives that can come with this personality type of being judgmental, critical, negative, and moody was evident in Ray toward his family. His wife was sanguine, loved to entertain people, and loved to see others happy. The negative side of her personality was that she was a bit scattered, would take on too much, and would become upset when her husband would not help in the fun family things she created often on the spur of the moment. As the couple improved, they were asked to "celebrate" the personality of the other and at the same time focus on tweaking their own negative personality aspects out of love for the other. They were also encouraged to think about how their personalities fit together to bless each other and their children.

Coaching Couples in the Art of Negotiation

Negotiation and compromise coaching. I attended a wedding where the Honorable Donald Lemons, now Virginia Supreme Court Chief Justice, gave the homily to my niece and the man she was about to marry. He mentioned how most couples come into marriage thinking of it is a 50/50 proposition and asked the groom and bride to press the palms of their right hands together representing a 50/50 marriage. He then metaphorically represented adversity by slicing his open hand upward between the palms of the couple and easily sliced through their "marriage." He said marriage needed to be 100 percent by both parties and asked them to represent that by interlocking fingers of their pressed palms. At that point, he could not slice through the grasped hands. I have found over the years that couples have benefited from this little exercise and have accepted the challenge to bring 100 percent effort to the relationship. Any time a technique combines a word picture or metaphor for clients, it deepens the spiritual, cognitive, and emotional experience.

From childhood, we are often taught to find the middle ground of compromise during times of conflict with others. We naturally seek that 50/50 position in the negotiation. While sounding right and desirable, marriage seldom benefits from this approach. If a couple are at an impasse, it is usually because they are relatively far apart on their feeling and/or thinking of the issue at hand. When I see this in therapy, I ask the couple to rate their position on a scale from 1 to 10. On some issues, the couples are closer than they think, making the work at hand easier. But sometimes they rank their positions at the extreme opposite ends. Since compromise does not have to be 50/50, it may be that one partner is more capable (or more willing) to take seven to eight steps up the scale while the other manages only two to three steps on a given issue, and on another issue it may be vice versa.

Couples who get out of the 50/50 expectation on marital issues open new vistas of opportunity to minister and assist the other. They find the beauty in the teamwork of two working together in the spirit of Ecclesiastes 4:9–10: "Two are better than one, because they have a good reward for their labor. For if they fall, one will lift up his companion" (NKJV). Once couples develop a repertoire of negotiation possibilities, they begin to lose interest in the stressful pursuit of always trying for the 50/50 mark. Although be alert for a partner who consistently does not want to take more than a couple steps on a majority of issues. Sometimes the consistent unwillingness of a spouse to compromise more than one or two steps on issues may be an indicator of a personality disorder.

Another use of a rating system comes into play when couples spend a lot of goodwill capital fighting over the perception of quantity or rating of a situation that does not mean much in the long run. For example, a couple may get quite upset because one believes a situation happened three times while the other believes it to be seven times. In this case, for the sake of argument, you can suggest that the couple just accept that it was something in between three and seven and focus instead on the underlying issue. Usually couples are not being deceptive when they recall their perceptions (see "Creating Tolerance for Perceptions" in chapter 20). People perceive the same reality in different ways, often a reflection of their personalities, life experiences, and automatic implicit reactions from the hippocampus. Couples find it interesting when the counselor refers to the different perceptions of reality by saying, "Your mate's reality may not be your reality, but it becomes part of your reality because you have to deal with his/her perception" (this wisdom originally came to me from a client from years ago).

Helping Couples to Reduce Expectations

Couples often come to therapy with a mind-set of how far short their marriage is from the way a marriage should be. I have always found this an interesting concept because we derive the way a marriage "should be" by some set parameters deep in our convictions. Often these convictions are too ideal for the majority and do not accommodate for the special uniqueness of the blending of the two personalities. Couples are particularly struck when the counselor compares having an ideal of how the other should be to having an emotional affair with a person who does not exist.

One of the early psychologists, William James (James, 1890), thought of happiness as a ratio of perceived reality divided by expectations. This is represented by the formula Happiness = Perceived Reality ÷ Expectations. Therefore, if Mary perceives Ray's score of husband success as 7 on a ten-point scale, and her expectation of the relationship is a 10, then the ratio is 7 ÷ 10 (represented by the fraction 7/10), in other words, 70 percent happy. However, it is human nature to overly focus on how far short the other falls from expectations—in this case 30 percent unhappy. One way to improve the ratio is for the rater to immediately readjust his or her expectation to a lower level, ideally to a 7 (now 7/7 or 100 percent happy). This move generally leads to more internal happiness for the individual and at the same time provides

nurturance and acceptance to the partner. Ironically, improvement occurs when a person receives more acceptance and less criticism from the spouse, and thereby the reality becomes better than before.

Stroke-Kick and Relationship Restoration

In another case, Sarah was seeking forgiveness about numerous times of planning events with family and friends without notifying or even warning her husband. The husband was growing angry and resentful that despite his requests to be included in the planning, the wife continued to secretly plan the events because she feared her husband would not let the event occur. The word *manipulative* came to my mind as a way to help the wife identify with the gravity of the behavior. However, to blurt out this word would do more harm than good. It was time to build Sarah up (stroke) so that the helpful insight (the kick) could be received. In many cases, the cadence is more like: stroke, stroke, stroke, and kick followed by more stroking. I said to Sarah, *"I have been impressed with your serving nature toward your family and your outreach to your friends [stroke 1]. You seem to have the spiritual gift of hospitality [stroke 2], and it seems that people enjoy being with you [stroke 3]. However, the word manipulative came to my mind as you were describing your offense toward your husband [the kick]. Can you explain why I thought of the word manipulative?"*

I encourage couples to practice this concept of stroke-kick with each other, as well as with their children. Sometimes wanting to deliver a kick to a spouse is negatively amygdala-driven, and the mate finds it difficult to be patient to attempt to get the kick out in a way that it will be received. In these instances, couples are asked to allow some amygdala calming time so that they can better deliver a stroke-kick approach.

Similar to the stroke-kick is the need for couples to develop and constantly focus on relationship restoration skills during times of tension and conflict escalation. Relationship restoration skills involve the direct intent to do or say something during tense moments to show the other that he or she is valued and loved. Not only is this a direct topic for education and monitoring during the therapy, but it also needs to be modeled by you. For example, I created tension by pointing out Sarah's manipulation. Sarah, with tears welling up in her eyes, said that she agreed that she was manipulative and that her sister had just talked about that with her prior to the session (often the Holy Spirit will be at work even before clients come in for their sessions). In an effort to attend to relationship restoration, I said, "However, your intent is not to be manipulative, because I can tell you are a person who deeply desires to serve and make other people happy."

CONCLUSION

One theme Scripture for this chapter is from Romans 12:2: "Do not be conformed to this world, but be transformed by the renewing of your mind, that you may prove what is that good and acceptable and perfect will of God" (NKJV). The word *transformed* in the original Greek means to have a *metamorphosis*, much like a caterpillar turning into a butterfly. From a neurobiological perspective, this is what occurs through neuroplasticity. In other words, if humans do not conform to the world but instead think and behave in godly ways, the brain will form new neuropathways that will cause the brain to be renewed and become more efficient at serving and loving God, their spouses, and others.

It is time for counselors to use the advancing science in neurobiology to create clinical/spiritual techniques that consider a fuller understanding of the brain by couples. This chapter presented several techniques that integrate the basic understanding and use of the limbic system, such as calming the amygdala, managing the hippocampus, controlling cortisol release, and promoting the secretion of oxytocin. In addition, several systemic techniques were presented, such as the clinical use of forgiveness, promoting the art of negotiation and compromise, and helping couples to fit better together to improve the oneness of marriage. Techniques that focus on the integration of cognition and emotional, behavioral, spiritual, and neurobiological aspects, as well as on the mutual reciprocity involved in systemic dynamics, hold much promise for meaningful and godly therapeutic encounters with couples.

RECOMMENDED READING

DiBlasio, F. A. (2013). Marital couples and forgiveness intervention. In E. L. Worthington, Jr., E. L. Johnson, J. N. Hook, & J. D. Aten (Eds.), *Evidence-based practices for Christian counseling and psychotherapy* (pp. 232–254). Downers Grove, IL: InterVarsity.

DiBlasio, F. A., Hester, C. P., & Belcher, J. L. R. (2014). Emotional and interpersonal dyslexia: Thoughts toward a neurological theory of personality disorders. *Journal of Psychology and Christianity, 33,* 374–384.

Gurman, A. S., Lebow, J. L., & Snyder, D. K. (Eds.). (2015). *Clinical handbook of couple therapy* (5th ed.). New York, NY: Guilford Press.

Ripley, J. S., & Worthington, E. L., Jr. (2014). *Couple therapy: A new hope-focused approach.* Downers Grove, IL: InterVarsity.

Weeks, G. R., & Fife, S. T. (2014). *Couples in treatment: Techniques and approaches for effective practice* (3rd ed.). New York, NY: Taylor and Francis.

Wheat, E., & Perkins, G. O. (1980). *Love life for every married couple: How to fall in love and stay in love.* Grand Rapids, MI: Zondervan.

Worthington, E. L., Jr. (2005). *Hope-focused marriage counseling: A guide to brief therapy* (Rev. ed.). Downers Grove, IL: InterVarsity.

CHAPTER 16

Family-Focused Strategies

Frederick A. DiBlasio, PhD
Amanda G. Turnquist, MSW

Speaking the truth in love, we are to grow up in every way into him who is the head, into Christ, from whom the whole body, joined and held together by every joint with which it is equipped, when each part is working properly, makes the body grow so that it builds itself up in love.

EPHESIANS 4:15–16 ESV

After God created Adam, he saw that it was not good for man to be alone. He then created Eve (Gen. 2:4–24). The two joined together in a perfect spiritual, emotional, and physical lifelong monogamous union. The arrangement was just right for the procreation of children. The concept of family was not new at creation, for there always was and always will be God the Father, Jesus the Son, and the Holy Spirit. Further, before creating humans, God created angels. What God created in heaven and on earth reflects his divine nature of being relational and family-oriented. Although we do not deserve it, his desire is to live with believers and followers of his Son for eternity. We are the family of God.

We get a foretaste of this eternal sense of belonging and interconnectedness by growing up in a family. As adults, we have the privilege of becoming one with our spouses and having our own biological and/or adoptive children. However, when sin came into the world, it corrupted the full and perfect harmony that God had planned for family life. One of the modern ways we address sin and conflict, resolve family problems, and assist families through crises is through family therapy.

Family therapy has proven to be an effective intervention for families with young children, adolescents, and adult children facing a variety of obstacles (Carr, 2014; Sprenkle, 2012; Robbins, Alexander, Turner, & Holliman, 2016). Research points to significant positive effects through functional family therapy (FFT) and systemic family therapy (SFT; Carr, 2014). Brief strategic family therapy, multidimensional family therapy (MDFT), and multisystemic therapy (MST) produced statistically significant positive results as well when compared to groups that received no intervention (Sprenkle, 2012). Therefore, while family therapy takes a variety of forms, it is an effective approach for families experiencing a variety of difficulties.

Though empirical studies have found that family therapy is efficacious for all members of a family, one study found that older youth, compared to younger children, are responding best to this form of therapy for a variety of issues (Baglivio, Jackowski, Greenwald, & Wolff, 2014). When functional family therapy was used in community settings, it proved effective in reducing recidivism rates among adolescents and sustaining positive effects up to fourteen years after the family participated in the therapy (Carr, 2014; Robbins et al., 2016). As family members begin to understand the role they each play in the struggles of any other family member, they begin to work better together and form healthier patterns. Research is catching up with what counselors have already discovered: family therapy is a compelling approach to address a variety of relational issues and problems. It also potentially saves a significant amount of money in long-term health costs for family members (Sprenkle, 2012).

In this chapter, we first present a theology and psychology of families and family therapy by taking a scriptural look at the systemic dynamics of hierarchy and reciprocity. This is followed by a brief history of the development of systems-oriented family therapy. A number of traditional strategies and techniques as well as retooled approaches are presented along with some new applications to modern-day understanding of family relationships, human neurobiology, and the Christian faith. Case studies are used to illustrate many of the strategies and techniques presented.

THEOLOGY AND PSYCHOLOGY OF FAMILIES AND FAMILY THERAPY

Systemic Dynamics: Hierarchy

One of the classic principles of family therapy is realigning family hierarchy so that parents are in charge of their children. This order of family life is supported in numerous Scriptures that promote parents to be caring, nurturing, and loving to their children by providing for their needs, teaching them right from wrong, leading them spiritually to honor and worship God, and using godly discipline to help them learn (Deut. 6:6–7; Prov. 13:24; 22:6; Matt. 7:11). Children are viewed by God as a "heritage from the LORD" (Ps. 127:3–5), and he established procreation as a key aspect of marriage (Gen. 1:28).

Ephesians 5:22–6:4 gives an order to family life. Although considered controversial because of the word *submit* and the declaration that the husband is "head of the wife" (5:23), these verses are often taken out of context by those who overly focus on those two concepts. It is no coincidence that the verses about family order are preceded with Ephesians 5:18–21: "Be filled with the Spirit, speaking to one another in psalms and hymns and spiritual songs, singing and making melody in your heart to the Lord, giving thanks always for all things to God the Father in the name of our Lord Jesus Christ, *submitting* to one another in the fear of God" (NKJV, emphasis added).

Family members are to attend to "making melody" in their hearts and to submit their own self-oriented pleasures and desires in deference to the well-being and cohesion of each member. If followed, the man would likely be a self-sacrificing husband and father in the example of Christ, the wife a faithful and self-sacrificing partner and mother, and the children self-sacrificing and obedient to the parents. Not all families are configured in this ideal way, given that some families have only one parent, some have no children, and some children live with relatives or friends. Nonetheless, the concepts of love and unity, and "speaking to one another in psalms and hymns and spiritual songs, singing and making melody in your heart to the Lord" (Eph. 5:19 NKJV) still applies.

Systemic Dynamics: Reciprocity

Interactions between people in a group involve simple and complex mutual reciprocity in exchanges of behavior with one another. Reciprocity is simply the concept that human behavior does not occur in a vacuum but instead is highly influenced as a response and interconnectedness to others. Families can greatly benefit from one another's strengths as well as suffer greatly from each other's negative qualities because of the way that close family dynamics can magnify negative traits and the sin nature. Families are small communities that are united in identity and deeply interconnected. In considering these traits of families, some striking similarities can be noted between family units and the "body of Christ" (1 Cor. 12:12–27). The family unit can be thought of as a microcosm of the body of Christ. Jonathan Edwards, a leader in the Great Awakening of the 1700s, once said, "Every Christian family ought to be as it were a little church, consecrated to Christ, and wholly influenced and governed by [His] rules" (Vaughan, 2007, p. 186).

Like the body of Christ, families are broken by sin and therefore made up of sinners in need of a Savior. Also, like the body of Christ, family members have unique strengths and weaknesses that impact their relationships and functioning as they strive for unity. The metaphor of the body of Christ as a human body is helpful for understanding church dynamics and will now be used as a tool for understanding family dynamics as well.

Systemic family therapy focuses on how the system created by the family through healthy and unhealthy dynamics impacts the emotional and relational health of the family members. The apostle Paul wrote, "If one member suffers, all the members suffer with it; or if one member is honored, all the members rejoice with it" (1 Cor. 12:26 NKJV). Therefore, a struggling child may be the reason for seeking family therapy in the first place, but as Paul pointed out about the body of Christ, all members are suffering as that child suffers. In addition, seldom does a symptom stand in isolation, but instead contributory dysfunctional behaviors can be found in other members of the family. The counselor's role is to identify the unhealthy contributions and point them out to the family, while also identifying strengths to lean into. As family members become aware of the unhealthy patterns and begin to work on them, the entire body benefits and begins to work together more wholly.

The importance of unity and uniqueness within a family is also highlighted through these verses: "If the whole body were an eye, where would be the hearing? If the whole were hearing, where would be the smelling? But now God has set the members, each one of them, in the body just as He pleased. And if they were all one member, where would the body be?" (1 Cor. 12:17–19 NKJV).

When family members work together, they are the most effective. Division within families can take root quickly. However, families are called to work toward unity. It may not mean that members always like each other, but that they see their interconnectedness within the family system and use that for the benefit, not the harm, of the family. Note that unity does not mean sameness. Uniqueness within families is beautiful and part of God's design for the family (1 Cor. 12:18). Through a strengths-based approach to family therapy, these unique strengths are pointed out so that the family may be able to see and appreciate one another better.

Brief Historical Overview of the Pioneers of Family Therapy

Although professional therapy was popularized by Freud in the early 1900s, the concept of professional work with families did not evolve until the mid-1950s. At that time, the United States government was awarding grants to fund studies/experiments to find cures for schizophrenia. Some recipients of this grant money believed that schizophrenia resulted from dysfunctional dynamics within the family. Murray Bowen was one recipient who used the research money to hospitalize entire families of a schizophrenic member, believing a systems-theory-derived thought that dysfunctional family dynamics produced a schizophrenic member. Although these experiments failed to bring answers to schizophrenia, it became a path for Bowen to expand his systems thinking, which led to his pioneering effort in developing a systems approach to family therapy. John Weakland, Gregory Bateson, Jay Haley, and others from Palo Alto, California, received grant support for their study on family communication patterns, which also failed to cure schizophrenia. However, they discovered that intervening in the communication and interaction patterns were essential elements in correcting family dysfunction. Jay Haley became a pioneer and leader in the family therapy field as he became the director of the Mental Research Institute (MRI) and the first editor in the 1950s of the prestigious *Family Process* journal. He was significantly influenced by Milton Erickson, who believed that an effective intervention to solve a client problem was to approach it subliminally and thereby decrease the type of client awareness that would produce defense mechanisms to resist the effort at positive change.

In the 1960s, several other principal people rose to the level of pioneers in family therapy. Virginia Satir, who studied under Bowen, left the East Coast to set up a family practice in Palo Alto and used aspects of the communication model advocated by Weakland, Bateson, and Haley. In addition, Salvador Minuchin came to the United States and brought with him the systemic ideas of family dysfunctional structure and patterns, and developed with others *structural family therapy*. Jay Haley left Palo Alto in the late 1960s to join Minuchin and others at the Philadelphia Child Guidance Clinic, where they went against the grain of individual psychodynamic talk therapy, which had dominated professional counseling for more than sixty years. Harry Aponte and Cloé Madanes also joined the Minuchin group and later splintered off to make significant and pioneering contributions to family therapy. Haley and Madanes married and moved to the Maryland area in the mid-1970s to open their own family therapy training program, where they developed a brief problem-solving approach of *strategic family therapy*. Both Minuchin and Haley emphasized that effective clinical training needed to be accomplished by having a team of people in one room calling in instructions during a live family session in the adjacent room. This was accomplished by using the one-way mirror room equipped with phones for a supervisor to call the therapist in real time to offer suggestions and insights. For a more thorough look at the pioneers mentioned here, see Nichols and Davis (2017).

Some of the thoughts and techniques described in this chapter are rooted in my (Fred's) interaction and exposure to some of these pioneers over the past three to four decades. Whereas it is easy to cite the person, it is more difficult to be precise as to dates and location, and as to whether the information was from private discussions or presentations. Therefore, sometimes you will see a particular family therapist pioneer cited without much other citation information. Henceforth the first person pronouns used in this chapter refer to me.

Systemic Thinking

A systemic perspective usually accounts for the relatedness and interaction of a complex array of variables. Using it as a framework, clinicians attempt to make sense of the human experience and decide how to attempt to bring about change in dysfunctional behaviors. It is a view of the world that studies the interconnectedness of people with each other and the environmental and biological forces that influence the total life process. People are always affecting the world around them and, at the same time, are being affected by it. The human condition is in part defined by personality and other internal factors and in part defined by a complex web of external factors. (DiBlasio, 2000b, p. 285)

In the theory explosion that occurred in the 1950s and 1960s, as indicated in the previous section, the pioneers of family therapy were mostly systemic thinkers, and to this day the field of family therapy is largely systemically oriented. I remember that Minuchin used a metaphor of an ice explorer with a sled and team of dogs headed northward to reach a destination.

Interested to find out how far he traveled in the first few minutes of his trip, he checked his directional equipment and discovered that he was slightly farther south than when he first began. The reason for the southward movement was that he was on a gigantic iceberg that was headed south slightly faster than his dogs could head north. Minuchin emphasized that the movement of the metaphorical iceberg, or the family context, is a chief factor in designing intervention. He advocated a therapy that not only considered the emotions and behaviors of the individuals involved (the sled headed northward), but also considered the profound effects of reciprocal interactional patterns as influenced by community, culture, and other important contextual concerns (the movement of the iceberg).

Family dysfunction can often reach a homeostasis where family members and their reciprocal interactions and the other contextual concerns implicitly act interdependently to influence a sequence of behaviors between members. Helping families to unlock from dysfunctional patterns is most effective when therapy focuses on strategies to change the dynamics of the people involved. For example, a third grader who "fears" going to school may have a parent who is overprotective. The child's fear accommodates the overprotectiveness and vice versa. The overprotectiveness may in part be influenced by a less than satisfying emotional intimacy with the less involved parent. The less involved parent may be subliminally influenced to be less involved because of the amount of overprotectiveness of the other parent and vice

versa. One value that can bring the parents together is the common interest and concern about the child's problem. This mutual concern may preoccupy the private time the couple share together and become enough to keep the marriage emotionally stable. Implicitly, this subliminal connection is a point of camaraderie for the parents that unwittingly acts to increase the need for the child to have a problem. In addition to the above, the therapist must determine how the school, community, and other contextual issues factor into the equation. Thus, an individual therapy for the child's fears may be like driving the sled northward on an iceberg if the systemic considerations of the family dynamics and the context are not considered and dealt with simultaneously. "Systemic thinking focuses on the concept that the whole takes on a life that is more than the sum of its parts. At the same time, the part cannot be fully understood without understanding the context in which the part exists" (DiBlasio, 2000b, p. 285). Moreover, a comprehensive, systemic approach carefully considers culturally relevant factors that are significant to the family (Richeport-Haley, 1998).

CASE STUDIES

Case One

Jason and Kelly Shaw, both in their midthirties, are parents to two children, Mark, age ten, and Kelly, age four. Jason and Kelly fight frequently, many times in front of the children, as they struggle to communicate with each other. This is especially difficult because Mark has taken on a parental-child role and constantly interrupts Jason and Kelly when they do try to work something out. Mark pushes the limits at home, often demands reasons from his parents about simple requests, and lately has been arguing with school teachers.

Case Two

Janice Kent is a divorced forty-one-year-old raising her three teenage children: Christine, age seventeen, Sam, age fifteen, and Joey, age thirteen. Janice is very religious, and to the frustration of her children, she spends much of her time at church meetings, service projects, and Bible studies. The case was referred for family therapy to help the children adjust to the recent divorce and to address Sam's recent experimentation with marijuana. Now, as a single parent, Janice finds it difficult to manage the behavior of her children as they have become less respectful and often argue and debate with her.

Case Three

Jacob Stone, age forty-eight, and Molly Stone, age thirty-eight, have two children: John, age twelve, and Steven, age nine. The parents called for therapy because Steven demonstrated unusual fear of thunderstorms. Jacob and Molly's relationship has been strained since the loss of a child at birth two years ago. Since the loss, Molly has overly cuddled Steven, a subject of many arguments between Jacob and Molly. On the other hand, Jacob emotionally drifted away and became more distant to Molly and his sons after the death of their third born.

Case Four

Randy Mills, age fifty, and Sandy Mills, age forty-eight, were involved in couple therapy with me for conflict in their marriage. As their marriage improved, they requested help with some acting out behaviors of some of their five children, especially Jill, a fourteen-year-old freshman, who displayed unsavory characteristics of her father, including stubbornness, impatience, and at times lack of anger control.

STRATEGIES, INTERVENTIONS, AND TECHNIQUES FOR FAMILY THERAPY

Several treatment strategies have withstood the test of time over the years of my clinical practice. These strategies were influenced by several schools of thought and theoretical considerations, especially systemic thinking, structural family therapy, strategic family therapy, cognitive behavioral therapy, social learning theory, the person-of-the-therapist model, experiential family therapy, and neurobiological theories, to name a few. Like many Christian counselors, I start with Scripture as I consider the integration of various schools of thought and techniques. Before I integrate a technique, it must be again filtered through Scripture to ensure spiritual soundness. Below are several techniques that have been effective mainstays. First, the techniques will be defined and explained, and then they will be put into context through examples. These techniques are intertwined and interrelated and operate together to accomplish a therapeutic goal as made obvious by the case material.

Enactments and Inducing Enactments

In many therapeutic encounters, counselors discuss behaviors and problems that occurred in the past or have the family consider how they may respond to future situations. Although helpful, the more powerful intervention occurs when the behaviors and conflicts are addressed in real time during the therapy session through *enactment*. Enactments refer to manifestations of patterns and behavioral sequences that are occurring live so that they can be observed by the counselor, and thereby predisposed for direct intervention to address them. Thus, the counselor can work with actual family interactions as they are happening. Consequently, the family is afforded the opportunity to practice more functional methods of relationship in the moments when learning is at its peak efficiency. People tend to learn the most at the time they are doing the "real thing" rather than merely talking about it (Edgar, 1969). Of all the methods of therapeutic learning, such as discussing the issue, hearing how to respond in the future, and role-playing a better way to interact, none is as effective as working with the problem as it is happening in real time.

You should relish the moments when spontaneous enactments occur and, in most cases, give the enactment priority for therapeutic intervention. You may choose to *induce an enactment* by asking the family to do or discuss something that is likely to evoke the family dynamics in the session. For example, a counselor may induce an enactment of the family's typical dysfunctional communication simply by asking the family to discuss their plans for the summer, knowing that it might reveal dysfunctional patterns of communication, power, hierarchies, and boundary issues.

Using Directives

Directives are tasks that the counselor asks a family to do in session or to accomplish at home. For example, the counselor might ask a father to sit next to a son and empathetically listen to the son's thoughts about the family rules, or ask a mother and father to meet privately for fifteen minutes twice a week to coordinate and evaluate a new child discipline procedure. Typically, directives are aimed at building a healthier pattern of behavior between family members that will replace a dysfunctional pattern. Directives work best when done routinely in every session. Repetitive practice of healthier behavioral sequences brings about new structure and patterns. Throughout the history of modern-day family therapy, strong repetition of positive corrective patterns of behavior between family members during therapy has been considered vital in accomplishing therapeutic change. Obviously, repetition creates new habits of interactions. In the past few years, I have become more aware that this repetition has a neurobiological effect on the family members involved. The repetition causes certain firing in brain structures that can lead to neuroplasticity, creating new brain pathways (see chapter 15 for more information on neurobiology).

Interrupting Dysfunctional Patterns

When counselors notice a dysfunctional pattern manifested in the session, they should give a specific directive to the family or do something to disrupt their current dysfunctional pattern. This technique may need to be used a few times before the family begins to operate this way at home. Dysfunctional patterns are often ingrained in family structures and must be disrupted many times and replaced with more functional behaviors. Pointing out the dysfunctional pattern before interrupting it is necessary for the family's understanding of the dysfunction with the hopes of righting it.

Interrupting dysfunctional patterns is usually best done in subtle ways. I remember being supervised by Harry Aponte via a one-way mirror. After the session he said to me, "Sometimes you use a sledgehammer when a needle will do." He was referencing my tendency at the time to be too abrupt and direct. As an example, in one case, while the parents were obviously trying to win me over to accept their complaints of each other, I abruptly interrupted them and directed them to face each other to discuss the issue. The sudden transition for them to deal with each other stifled them and produced awkward silence. A subtler way to bring the desired result would have been for me not to comment to the speaker, but instead to look to the other person in silence. This nonverbal cue usually causes the speaker to turn to the other parent and promotes interaction between the two. Aponte helped me understand that in that case it was better for me to use subtler ways to accomplish the same interruption and to establish a new way for the couple to interact. This is especially true when addressing par-

ents in front of their children, because an authoritarian-like interruption from the counselor may put parents in a degrading, lower hierarchical position. In addition, the more direct approach can put the parents in a childlike position by the unintentional "parenting" of the parents by the counselor.

Setting Healthy Boundaries

To help my students understand the implicit nature of boundaries, I ask for a volunteer to come up front and discuss with me the things they did to make it to class. A volunteer comes forward and begins to tell me the particulars of her journey to arrive to class on time. As the volunteer starts talking, I interrupt and ask if the student trusts me enough to close his/her eyes and to stay perfectly still (I sometimes imagine that volunteers feel like the proverbial audience volunteers at a carnival who are blindfolded and an apple placed on their heads for an archery demonstration). I face the class and, without looking, stretch forth my arm and wave it frantically in front of the student's face. My fingertips narrowly miss the nose of my poor volunteer, who only feels the breeze caused by the rapid flutter of my hand. I then tell the class that I was not worried about hitting the student in the face because in the United States we have an automatic physical boundary set off in our brains (likely under major direction from the prefrontal cortex) of about three feet for conversation with most people. This distance is a bit closer when it involves a loved one or an adult to a child. The distance is culturally influenced—that is, some cultures stand closer and others farther away. We have a built-in boundary about our physical proximity when interacting with others.

Just as strong as physical boundaries, people have psychological, emotional, and interpersonal boundaries. Sometimes the boundaries are too close, often referred to as enmeshed boundaries, and sometimes the boundaries are disengaged or not close enough. An example of an enmeshed boundary is a mother who constantly talks for her fourteen-year-old son, while the son is overly dependent on the mother to speak for him. An example of a disengaged boundary is a teenager and parents who avoid each other and seldom share information and emotional connection. "For proper family functioning, the boundaries of subsystems must be clear. They must be defined well enough to allow subsystem members to carry out their functions without undue interference, but they must allow contact between the members of the subsystem and others" (Minuchin, 1974, p. 54).

In general, parents should operate as executors of the family and have a close cohesion to one another. The most common boundary intrusion occurs when a child becomes a parental child and/or a parent becomes more childlike. When children interfere in the parental subsystem, they not only cause divisiveness with the marital dyad but also put themselves in a pseudomature position. Although subliminal and likely not at conscious awareness, the child is burdened by this role, which inhibits normal development. When parents become more childlike, they do not have enough hierarchical influence necessary for leading and caring for their own children. Children under such conditions become more insecure, lose respect for the authority of parents, and are prone to treat parents as siblings.

Case study one. Several of the above techniques were used with the Shaw family. Mark, the oldest of Jason and Kelly's children, was a parental child who was often in the middle of the parents' relationship. Likewise, in part due to the deteriorating intimacy between Jason and Kelly, the parents would inappropriately involve their son in parental matters. The hierarchy of the family was displaced through this pattern as the three were on the same hierarchical plane.

In one intervention directive, I asked the parents to discuss their thoughts about new approaches to rules for the home while their two children and I observed the conversation. I expected that such a directive would induce an enactment where parents would find it difficult to avoid involving Mark and vice versa. Mark and mother were enmeshed. In addition, the directive set up an opportunity to establish a healthy boundary between the parental subsystem and Mark, as well as provide an opportunity for interrupting the dysfunctional pattern and promoting a functional pattern of the parents as the executors of the family. This type of directive was repeated in different ways throughout the therapy.

At first it was difficult for Mark to avoid giving input to the parents' discussion (this was the enactment of the family pattern), so I interrupted this pattern by saying, "Mark, you, your sister, and I are going to just observe and not interrupt the discussion between your parents. I'll come over and sit next to you and your sister, and that will help you to remember just to listen." Interestingly, a few minutes later Kelly was at a point of slight disagreement with her husband, and she looked over at Mark as an unintended nonverbal cue for Mark to interject. Mark quickly started to verify his mother's perspective. I reminded Mark of the rule to just listen but this time gave him and his sister a pad of paper and pencil and asked them to write down their observations and quietly show them to me as their parents continued to talk. Both children started to write and show me notes, to which I quickly wrote replies. As the three of us were engaged in note sharing, the parents continued their discussion without the mother's implicit invitation for Mark to intervene or Mark's interruption. The goal of the intervention was to keep Mark from interrupting Jason and Kelly and to engage in kid business instead of parent business. It was less important for me to follow the parents' conversation because I was helping the family alter dysfunctional structure and replace it with structure that emphasized healthy boundaries.

Use of Nurturance to Elevate Hierarchy

As noted earlier, nurturance is critical in the parenting process. Interestingly, a by-product of the parent giving nurturance is an elevation of hierarchy. A common problem in families struggling with dysfunctional patterns is a disturbance in the parent-child hierarchy. Various approaches to family therapy, especially structural

family therapy and strategic family therapy, attempt to realign the family hierarchy so that parents are on a plane above their children. When parents and children are on the same level, confusion results, and a child's negative symptoms get more powerful (see Madanes, 1981, for a helpful understanding of power in families). When undue power is given to children and leadership is weak, insecurity is fostered. As much as children, including teenagers, might complain and argue otherwise, loving and appropriate power undertaken by parents increases the security, safety, and well-being of youth.

This technique centers around the idea that nurturance should be brought into family therapy sessions as a way of establishing parental hierarchy, interrupting negativity, and creating positive therapeutic moments for a family. Nurturance would be used by directing parents to perform some nurturing act toward their children, such as in the case below where the mother was asked to hug her children and reassure her support of them. The nurturing act has the side benefit of promoting the release of oxytocin, the love/attachment hormone, in the brain for both the nurturer and the one being nurtured.

Case study two. Hierarchy in single-parent families is often a problem because the parent tends to respond to one or more of the children in adult ways, prompting some children to take on a parental-child role. It is not unusual for children to systemically step into the role of the absent parent while also filling the single parent's need for companionship. Sometimes children were already fulfilling this function prior to a divorce, and the couple splitting up induced an expansion of the problem. This was the case in the Kent family, as the mother often responded to her teenage children in adult ways yet at other times argued and debated with them much like an older sibling.

The Kent family was a case being supervised at the Haley/Madanes clinic by Clinical Director James P. Keim. About twenty-five of my graduate students and I were behind the one-way mirror and were allowed to give input to Keim as he called in supervisory comments to the counselor. The teenagers accused their mother of thinking that they were "worldly," a negative term she often used to describe people who are involved in sinful and immoral behavior. Although the mother never referred to her children as worldly, we surmised in the observation room that at some implicit level the children were anxious that their mother would reject them because they smoked cigarettes and because Sam was also experimenting with marijuana.

By their tone of voice and assertive posture, it was obvious that the two older children wanted to argue with their mom and escalate the discussion into a negative interaction. After our discussion about the probable fear of the children that their mother would reject them, Keim called the counselor and instructed her to ask the mother to hug each child while individually assuring them that she would never reject them. Nurturance was thus conveyed through congruence of speech and action and a physical demonstration of affection. This created a powerful and

intimate moment for each child with their mother while also reinforcing Janice's place of power in the family's hierarchy. Janice got up from her seat and approached each child individually to show each child motherly love and nurturance. The use of nurturance disrupted the pattern of the children comforting the parent because it reestablished the parent as the nurturer.

Christine and Joey welcomed their mother's embrace as she vowed never to reject them. Sam (the fifteen-year-old experimenting with marijuana) was initially ambivalent about his mother's task of hugging, offering her a fist bump instead. Keim quickly called in to instruct the counselor to have the mother sit next to Sam and embrace him in a hug until he was convinced that she would not reject him. Interestingly, as Keim was talking privately to the counselor over the phone, Sam good-naturally whispered to his sisters, "Call from the hotline—mother has to hug the son—mother has to hug the son." This brilliant insight and playful comment showed both Sam's understanding of the therapeutic process and his desire to be hugged by his mother instead of the more superficial fist bump that he had initiated. When the mother sat next to her son, Sam fully embraced his mother's hug, and the two were motionless as they quietly enjoyed the serenity of the embrace for several minutes. I will never forget the look of peace on both of their faces; I count this as one of those therapeutic moments that I still can visualize in my mind. Not only did the use of nurturance help to elevate the mother's hierarchy, but it also helped to break down physical and emotional walls that were established between the mother and her children. Moments like this cause the amygdala of both parents and children to signal for the release of oxytocin, the love/attachment hormone, and creates a pleasant memory stored with positive affect in the hippocampus.

Empowering Parents to Win the Process and Outcome

I picked up this technique of empowering parents to win the process and outcome from Cloé Madanes decades ago and have used it successfully with families since then (including using it with my own children as they were growing up). She viewed it as a technique to promote an "old-fashioned" value that would become one of the hallmarks of strategic family therapy, which was to help put parents in charge of their children (see Keim, 1997, for this and other techniques to address oppositional children). A harmful cycle is created when children act against the authority of their parents, and the parents respond with feeling powerless over their own children. This feeling of powerlessness then causes further resistance and disobedience by the children and further perpetuates the powerless and helpless parenting attitude.

The *process* of an interaction is all of the behavioral sequences that occur within the parent-child interaction. The *outcome* is the final disposition of the result of the interactions. Many parents with difficult children find that they can usually win an outcome through the escalation of power, which often involves louder voices, numerous threats of punishment, or in the case

of younger children, physical control. Not only does the child witness a model for negative and aggressive behavior, but also the dramatic human contact acts as a positive reinforcement. According to social learning theory, social reinforcement via human contact, even when negative and angry, is so powerful that it can reinforce the child's negative behavior. In addition, when a child is engaged in a battle with a parent and the process becomes negative, the parent and child are on the same hierarchical plane, and the relationship becomes much like sibling to sibling rather than parent to child. If this pattern persists, the parent and child may not maintain the healthy hierarchical difference necessary for healthy child development.

Winning the process would involve the parent controlling negative emotions and behaviors, and maintaining loving authority, which causes the parent to win the process of the interaction. When a parent argues with a child, implicit to the context of the argument is the notion that the child is of equal status as the parent and has the right to resist. In such cases, the parent loses the process, and the only way to win the outcome is for the parent to overwhelm by emotional or physical force.

The example I give to my graduate students is of a fourteen-year-old daughter who begins to dress a bit more provocatively. This draws the attention of the mother (or father) as she walks down the steps to leave the house. The exchange between daughter and mother becomes intense as both exchange harsh words. If the daughter then walks out of the house to meet with friends anyway, the mother loses the process and the outcome. If the escalation continues until the daughter stomps up the stairs and changes her clothes, the mother loses the process but wins the outcome. If the parent lovingly and respectfully discusses a more appropriate outfit choice for her daughter, which causes her to go and change, the mother wins both the process and the outcome. However, if the daughter continues to resist, the mother is to say calmly, "We can talk about this later, but for now we are finished discussing it, and you may not leave the house until you change your clothes," regardless of whether the daughter changes or decides not to go out, and the mother still wins the process and outcome.

Staying Focused on the Presenting Problem

With the popularization of systemic work, counselors became eager to show family members their many systemic dysfunctions and how to fix them. It is still difficult for counselors to shake loose from the erroneous supposition that if they provide sufficient education and insight about dysfunctional patterns, family members will gain convincing insight and change. Whereas this might be true in some cases, giving direct insight too early in the treatment is not usually effective. Although family members may politely receive the counselor's insights about their problems, seldom does hearing about the interactive systemic dynamics cause well-entrenched patterns to change. If this were so, therapy could be transformed into presentations with PowerPoint slides and completed within a few hours of seminar with the

family. In addition, in cases where parents are at their wits' end with an acting-out child not obeying, the last thing they need is a counselor overly focusing on all of what they did wrong to contribute to the child's behaviors. In fact, parents coming in for family treatment often fear that counselors will blame them for the child's problem. Often family-focused counselors cast the net too wide and attempt to capture solutions for a vast array of family dysfunction. As a result, the therapy loses focus and power to resolve the problem at hand.

Haley and Madanes emphasized that therapy should start by keeping the focus on the presenting problem and choosing a treatment strategy to resolve it in as brief a time as possible (see Haley, 1991). For example, in the case of the Stone family above, the presenting problem is the child's fear of thunderstorms. Therefore, the intervention should stay focused on resolving the fear and the dysfunctional behaviors it produces. In this case, there are many other issues, such as grief related to losing a child at birth, the depression of parents, the parents in conflict with one another, and so forth. If the parents choose, these issues can be addressed later in the therapy, but first the treatment should be designed to resolve the child's fear of thunderstorms. Interestingly, sometimes as a child's problem is resolved, the parents' relationship worsens. In some cases, the parents unwittingly sabotage the success of the child because of a subliminal and systemic pull on the child to have a problem to maintain marital connection. If this were to happen, the counselor might say to parents: "You both have done a great job in helping your child over the problem. The improvements are very noticeable. During the last few sessions, I noticed that your teamwork with each other was tougher for you than before. Would you like to meet for a few couple counseling sessions to discuss this and to work on your relationship?"

Increasing Involvement of the Peripheral Parent

When there is an acting-out child or child with a presenting problem, often one parent is more involved than the other. At times, this involvement can be dysfunctional and intense, causing an enmeshed relationship between the parent and the child. Given this intensity, the other parent implicitly slides to a more peripheral position. However, systemically it could be said that the drift of one parent to the periphery influences the other parent to be overly involved. The relationship of the two parents tends to become stressed and less intimate as they drift a bit apart. I found myself not agreeing with Haley's relative abandonment of this technique by using it only in some cases of a stepparent needing a boost in hierarchy.

Often I have found that mothers tend to be overly involved in child problems, and fathers take on more peripheral roles. Christian families in this condition are spiritually out of sync, and a therapy that focuses on fathers becoming more involved is welcomed by Christian families because the goal is biblically sound. As long as the therapy assigns the mother a significant role to assist in the process, Christian parents are not as likely to have marital conflict over the father becoming more involved. Not only does the case study in the next section demonstrate parent coaching, but it also provides an example of rearranging involvement levels of parents.

Parent Coaching

In my earlier family therapy cases, when I received a referral because of a child's presenting problem, I would automatically schedule a family therapy session that included the parents and all of their children. Now I invite the parents to come without the children for the first session to explain the problem to me and for an assessment of a treatment plan. Often I offer to help the parents become the counselors under my coaching and guidance. This helps to maintain the parental hierarchy, makes the parents more competent, and spares the child from need for direct professional treatment. If this coaching effort fails to eliminate the presenting problem, I renegotiate with the parents to meet with the family. However, this approach usually works for mild to moderate problems, and meeting with the family is not necessary (note that severer cases often require direct work with the child and sometimes the other siblings).

Case study three. Molly Stone called for therapy for Steven, their nine-year-old son who was unusually afraid of thunderstorms. He would get very nervous whenever it rained for fear that a thunderstorm was approaching, and he wanted to be as close as possible to his mother. After hearing more about the problem, I offered to coach the parents in becoming parent counselors for their son as the first strategy to use, which could be followed by an appointment with the son if the parent counseling was not effective. Jacob and Molly readily agreed, and the coaching began in the first session and the second part in another session.

The directives included a desensitization program, and other treatment strategies were discussed. One of those other strategies was for the father to spend more positive time with his youngest son, the one who had a fear of thunderstorms, to help build the son's security and identity. Mother, on the other hand, was to "balance the scales" a bit by spending more time with their older son. Given that the mother understood that this maneuver would allow the father more involvement, she was happy to cut back on her overinvolvement with the younger son in favor of this new role. I helped to seal the deal by empathetically and kindly pointing out to Molly that since she had been so worried and invested in Steven's fears and anxieties over the past year, she had somewhat neglected her relationship with her older son. Molly readily embraced the directive to focus more on her older son, which she understood would be supportive of her husband's involvement with Steven. The parents reported that they faithfully enacted the plan, causing the child's fears to abate within one month.

I invited Jacob and Molly in for a third session to discuss future plans and suggestions to maintain gains made. With the parents no longer connecting over the child's problem, they were more conflictual and at odds with one another and demonstrated a need for some couples work. Ironically, the child's improvement brought the marital conflict more to light. We renegotiated a contract to start a short-term marital treatment.

Coaching How to Administer Time-Out for Children

Sometimes parents who come in for the initial consultation appointment as described above bring concerns about children who are disobedient and difficult to manage. Many times, coaching on how to apply a loving time-out procedure works to resolve the disciplinary issues. The first step is to discuss that the word *discipline* is a form of the word *disciple*. I ask the parents if they are willing to make a commitment to each other that instead of managing their children they will commit to disciple them for the kingdom of God. This means that instead of giving priority to the hustle and bustle of life, they will take the time to work and disciple their children in "the way they should go" (Prov. 22:6). Interestingly, time-out procedures do not take a great amount of time once children are trained for them.

Family meeting to explain time-out. Any family meeting first requires that parents are on the same page. Parents presenting a united front that reflects a well-thought-out strategy and a commitment to stay consistent is critical. The presentation not only reviews the specifics of how time-out works but includes a calm and loving explanation of the biblical call for family life and godly order. The parents clearly review the procedure below so that children are prepared for it. Children do better when changes are known in advance, and they have consistent structure to rely on.

If a parent has made mistakes in the past with angry outbursts during discipline procedures, this is the time for that parent to offer a heartfelt apology and seek forgiveness. This forgiveness request has the added benefit of establishing security with the children, as they become hopeful for a closer relationship with the parent (see DiBlasio, Worthington, & Jennings, 2012, for information on forgiveness intervention with children, adolescents, and families). The parents should demonstrate that the change in the discipline format is an effort to guide and love the children more deeply.

Any new direction for family structure and discipline should have an incentive built into the program. Working with acting-out youth in a residential program for the early years of my clinical experience helped me to realize that building a relationship with each child on my caseload was critical. I found that just five minutes of friendly contact during positive times caused both them and me to feel good about our relationship (also see chapter 15 for the neurobiological oxytocin such contact produces). A by-product of these purposive times of contact was that the residents acted out much less. I encourage parents to dedicate the time needed for this one-to-one time and when possible to focus on the child's strengths and spiritual giftedness.

Procedure. Three fundamental steps are needed to enact the time-out procedure.

1. Set a private pretend practice time for each child. Parents should make this a fun time in which parents and child role-play a violation and parents work through the steps below with the child. This not only educates the child on the procedure but allows him to experience participation and cooperation, which gives him some ownership of the procedure.

2. When a child commits a violation, calmly request that the child go to the time-out chair or mat. The location must be in a safe, open area such as a family living room. Set a timer for the age-appropriate time, in many cases one-minute for each year of the child's age (i.e., six minutes for a six-year-old). While keeping the child in sight is important, there should be no discussion or direct contact between the parent and child. If the child does not complete the time-out sufficiently, add more time. The parent should have backup consequences ready if the time-out is not properly handled by the child. These consequences are determined and administered later. Certain violations need to have time-out *and* a follow-up with further consequences because of the seriousness of the violation.

3. After the time-out, discuss the violation and why the child thinks the violation was wrong. Ask the child for alternative positive behavior that may have avoided the violation. This should be followed by an apology and a request for forgiveness. Extend forgiveness, and seal the restoration with a hug.

Case study four. Sometimes the initial referral is not about the children but is instead a need for marital therapy. Such was the case for the Mills family. Randy and Sandy were involved in marital therapy for eleven months. After finding therapy helpful to resolve their marital crisis, especially Randy's impatience and anger toward his wife, they requested help with disciplining their children. Randy relied on spankings as the main form of discipline. Sandy, on the other hand, did not discipline her children enough, resulting in them being rude and disrespectful to her. Systemically this added to the pressure on Randy to hold the children accountable for their disrespect of their mother, which further fueled Randy's anger and impatience. After the significant improvement of Randy's relationship with Sandy, the disrespect of the children toward their mother became particularly frustrating for him, resulting in increased spankings. Instead of inviting the children for a family session, I encouraged the use of parental coaching focusing on the time-out procedure above.

In the second session of the coaching, Randy and Sandy reported a high level of success with the approach. Four of their five children received a time-out, and the couple reported no repeats of the previous disrespectful behavior. Randy, using the maturity, empathy, and control he developed during the therapy toward Sandy, was able to generalize it to the children. He took leadership in presenting to the children the plan the couple agreed on in the previous session. They reported that in tears Randy offered a sincere apology and requested forgiveness of his children for his previous anger and impatience with them. This in turn brought his whole family to tears as they witnessed his godly sorrow and humility. In a follow-up session one month later, the parents reported much-improved behavior and respect from their children.

CONCLUSION

An association is made between family life and Scriptures that focus on the body of Christ. This association is made because the family is a fundamental unit within the overall church structure that calls members to "grow up" in Christ, to be "joined and held together," and to be "built up in love" (Eph. 4:15, paraphrased). The structure of ideal family life reflects oneness and love between marital partners and the bringing up of children who respond to them with honor and obedience (Eph. 5:22–6:4). Although not all Christian families have two parents or children, all families are called to unity, love, and growth in Christ.

When families run into difficulties, life conflicts, or developmental transitions, they sometimes need professional counseling and guidance. For Christian families, this intervention is best done using biblical principles, a systemic approach, and a careful integration of theories and therapy. The systemic perspective considers the interactive effects that occur between family members and the contextual issues of the situation. Patterns between family members develop and are maintained from the mutual reciprocity of behavioral exchanges between them. Pointing out dysfunctional patterns and asking members to change is not enough. Effective intervention requires interrupting dysfunction as it occurs and replacing it with something functional on the spot. Repetition and practice are necessary for the new patterns of behavior to take hold through neuroplastic changes occurring in the brains of family members.

Techniques that help parents develop loving, competent, and nurturing patterns of behavior help restore a rightful and secure order to family life of parents being in charge of their children. As parents increase in these qualities, children become stabler and securer, which causes an increase in their positive behaviors. In turn, as children demonstrate positive behaviors, even more nurturance and love from parents toward their children are evoked. Instead of vicious cycles of dysfunctional behaviors promoting more dysfunctional responses, families achieve a positive spiraling and mutually supportive cycle of God-focused relationships.

RECOMMENDED READING

DiBlasio, F. A. (2000). Systemic thinking and therapeutic intervention. *Journal of Marriage and the Family: A Christian Journal, 3*, 281–300.

Haley, J. (1991). *Problem solving therapy*. San Francisco, CA: Jossey-Bass.

Keim, J. P. (1997). Strategic family therapy of oppositional behavior. In F. M. Dattilio (Ed.), *Integrative cases in marriage and family therapy: A cognitive-behavioral approach*. New York, NY: Guilford Press.

Madanes, C. (1981). *Strategic family therapy*. San Francisco, CA: Jossey-Bass.

Minuchin, S., & Fishman H. C. (2004). *Family therapy techniques*. Cambridge, MA: Harvard University Press.

Nichols, M. P., & Davis, S. D. (2017). *Family therapy: Concepts and methods* (11th ed.). New York, NY: Pearson.

PART 3

Clinical Issue–Based Strategies

CHAPTER 17

Family of Origin–Focused Strategies

Frederick A. DiBlasio, PhD

And we know that all things work together for
good to those who love God, to those who are
the called according to His purpose.

ROMANS 8:28 NKJV

As parents age and reflect on their years of bringing up children, they realize that they have been on a journey of many twists and turns of family life. The memories vary between heartwarming, happy, and unforgettable moments to the crises and immense heartaches they wish they could forget. The ups and downs of family life and the relationships children forge with their families of origin become ingrained in the fabric of their identities. As children become adults, they carry the legacy of their family of origin into their own families through the patterns of the past. Some of these patterns are positive and promote God's will for our lives, while others are dysfunctional and need to be resolved. One popular belief of counselors who do family of origin work is that to achieve resolution of ongoing dysfunctional patterns acquired in the past, family members need to tackle the issues head-on

and resolve them with the original family members with whom the issues developed in the first place.

Family of origin therapy is an effective method for a variety of scenarios, including but not limited to couples' conflicts, attachment issues, and roadblocks experienced by counselors with particular populations. When people begin experiencing problems with their partners and/or children, they often focus on their current relationships to resolve the issues and do not consider the patterns of the past. This is not always effective when the issues stemmed from something deeper, such as a learned behavior from their families of origin. For example, when a partner struggles to communicate, this may be in part because his childhood models for family communication were dysfunctional. Knapp, Sandberg, Novak, and Larson (2015) state, "Hostility during conflict in family-of-origin negatively impacts couple relationships cyclically: children from openly hostile family-of-origin environments are more likely to have difficulty communicating effectively with future romantic partners" (p. 19). Therefore, these negative communication patterns are perpetuated until someone recognizes them. Family of origin therapy may help adults in their spouse-to-spouse or parent-to-child dysfunctional communication patterns in the current family once they recognize and break the cycle with members of their family of origin. This knowledge opens a space for adults to work on repairing relationships, seeking and granting forgiveness, and forming new patterns.

In addition to helping improve current family interactions and interactions with others, examining one's family of origin is effective for addressing many different internal difficulties. When individuals take a family of origin perspective, they begin to see how dysfunctional family relationships of the past affect their current sense of well-being and internal problems of self-esteem, contentment, security, career stability, and so forth. For example, negative sibling interactions in the family of origin can lead to lower self-esteem and higher anxiety (Knapp et al., 2015).

After an overview of theology and psychology of family of origin work, this chapter will focus on techniques and strategies for family of origin therapy. This includes sessions where adult children and their parents meet in a long therapeutic session to address and resolve old family issues, and individual/couple sessions where counselors work to assist clients to recognize and restructure old family of origin patterns that adversely affect their current relationships. Before the conclusion of the chapter, I present two cases that demonstrate the direct use of the strategies and techniques.

THEOLOGY AND PSYCHOLOGY OF FAMILY OF ORIGIN

The Bible provides examples of the importance of families of origin. In the family of Jesus, we can assume that Jesus, as the oldest son, had a responsibility for his mother, Mary. We don't have any information about Joseph, Mary's husband, beyond the time that Jesus was in the temple teaching at age twelve (Luke 2:41–52). Joseph most likely was not alive at the time of Jesus's crucifixion, because on the cross Jesus assigned "the disciple whom he loved" to take his place as Mary's oldest son (John 19:26–27). This disciple immediately took Mary to his own home. In addition, in Jesus's parable of the prodigal son, the family structure shows two adult sons living with their father with the anticipation that when the father died they would inherit his wealth and property. However, the younger son asked for and was granted his portion in advance. Multigenerational families living together are described throughout the Scriptures and to some degree still exist today.

Times have changed, and adult children, their spouses, and the parents are much less interconnected than they used to be. Historically, there were large agricultural communities that included one's immediate family, such as spouses and their children, and living with them or nearby would be grandparents, parents of the spouses, and siblings and their families. However, some countries and cultures still practice the historical tradition of extended families being strongly connected and interdependent. For example, in the Lancaster, Pennsylvania, area, it is not unusual for entire extended Amish families to live on the same or adjacent farms. As each child marries, a house is built for the new couple on neighboring land. Great respect and honor are paid to the elderly family members, and physical, emotional, and spiritual support abound.

One of the most devastating family of origin issues is when parents have adult children who reject God. Even King David had quite an ordeal with his rebellious adult son Absalom, who committed adultery with David's wives and attempted to overthrow his kingdom and kill him (2 Sam. 15–19). Absalom became greedy, adulterous, and murderous despite his father's lifelong love for him. Unfortunately, parents cannot make decisions for their wayward adult children regarding their faith or living a life pleasing to God. Each person must make his or her own decision to accept and follow Jesus in order to be saved (John 3:16). Ruth Graham (1999) provided a reminder to parents struggling with a prodigal adult child: "Remind [the parents] gently, Lord, how you have trouble with Your children, too" (p. 144).

Another interesting family of origin example is the story of Joseph, his brothers, and his father (Gen. 37:1–50:26). Out of jealousy, the older brothers sold seventeen-year-old Joseph into slavery and reported to their father that Joseph had died. Many years later, after many trials and tribulations, and through the divine providence of God, Joseph saved Israel from starvation and famine. When his brothers came to him for food, he eventually forgave them and brought them and their father into Egypt to care for them. Interestingly, Joseph spiritually concluded about the abuse he received: "You [my brothers] meant evil against me; but God meant it for good, in order to bring it about as it is this day, to save many people alive" (Gen. 50:20 NKJV). Here are some of the implications of family of origin issues from the story of Joseph and his brothers: (1) Close ties and mutual support of the brothers and father were evident through their adult lives. (2) The father had a place of honor and leadership throughout the adult lives of the brothers. (3) Evil behavior of siblings can lead to devastating consequences for an individual. (4) Adults can forgive the abuses of childhood. (5) God can shape past childhood abuse into something that brings honor to him in one's adult life.

Regarding the psychology of family of origin, we have learned that the experiences of childhood with relationships and circumstances, in part, can lead to certain patterns children develop that they take into their adult lives. Sometimes Christians enter the therapeutic encounter greatly wounded from the pain and abuse inflicted by family members during growing-up years. Counselors can barely help but feel significant compassion and empathy as stories unfold that cause them to ask, "Why, God, did a child of yours suffer so?" To make matters worse, many adult children still face emotional abuse as adults in three distinct ways. The first is the ongoing disparaging and denigrating treatment throughout adulthood from dysfunctional parents and/or siblings. The second is a propensity for some abused and neglected children to grow up and subliminally find a mate and/or others who continue the abusive pattern. And third, the adult internalizes the abusive treatment and stays stuck in an implicit self-abusing and self-sabotaging position throughout life. Another factor complicating the mix is that some adult children have personality disorders or other mental health problems that further complicate how they respond to interventions related to the above three areas. Whereas various opinions exist about the answer to the suffering question posed here, Christians can be assured that suffering at the hands of family of origin members from the past will somehow "work together for good to those who love God, to those who are the called according to His purpose" (Rom. 8:28 NKJV). Keep in mind that Romans 8:28 is a message for a foundation of hope and needs a context of Holy Spirit leading filled with love and empathy, and thereby it should not become a sound bite to immediately give grieving counselees out of context.

Research has shown that when people work on their attachments to their partners, some of the negative aspects of their relationship can be connected to dysfunctional communication patterns evident in each partner's family of origin experiences (Busby, Gardner, & Taniguchi, 2005; Knapp et al., 2015). This provides hope for clients as they begin to understand the extent of the negative impacts their families of origin may have had. Further, conflicts in marriages are better understood as

spouses explore the patterns of communication in their families of origin (Topham, Larson, & Holman, 2005). Sometimes dysfunctional patterns can be traced back through the generations (McGoldrick, 2011). Knowledge of dysfunctional patterns within their families of origin often validates clients in their own feelings, brings them insight, and empowers them to make changes. Bowen was instrumental in providing a theoretical framework for helping practitioners to think about intergenerational patterns (Bowen, 1978; Kerr & Bowen, 1988). Likewise, Framo was a pioneer in advocating that intense short-term therapy with family of origin members can produce lasting positive results (Framo, Weber, & Levine, 2003).

Family of origin work has also proved helpful to counselors' self-development as they begin their own practices and come up against impasses with certain client populations (Aponte & Kissil, 2016; Deveaux & Lubell, 1994; Winter & Aponte, 1987). Counselor supervisors are often the first to notice dysfunctional patterns when their supervisees get stuck with certain cases because of supervisees' unresolved family of origin issues (Haber & Hawley, 2004; Winter & Aponte, 1987). For example, if a counselor grew up in a family where infidelity of a parent was an issue, the counselor may struggle to work with clients who are unfaithful to their partners. Once these feelings and reactions are recognized, the counselor could likely work with a supervisor to resolve their personal issues as they provide counseling to clients (Aponte & Kissil, 2016; Haber, & Hawley, 2004; Winter & Aponte, 1987).

CASE STUDIES

Case One

Frank Thompson and his wife, Jane (Woods) Thompson, a couple in their early forties, came for marital therapy to address conflicts within their marriage and to discuss struggles with their twelve-year-old daughter who was disobedient and argumentative. Jane was irritable, critical, and impatient toward her husband and her daughter. Jane was diagnosed as having dysthymia (note that the current DSM-5 [American Psychiatric Association, 2013] has relabeled dysthymia to persistent depressive disorder), and Frank was diagnosed as having adjustment disorder with depressed mood. Jane's primary symptoms were irritability and chronic dissatisfaction and negativity toward life in general. She was particularly moody and critical in her interactions with her husband. Jane reported that she avoids her family of origin, which consists of Jake Woods, her sixty-two-year-old father; Mike Woods, her thirty-eight-year-old brother; and Kathy (Woods) Sattler, her thirty-six-year-old sister. This avoidance intensified after Jane's mother died three years previously. During the therapy, Jane agreed to have a family of origin session, and therefore the case information below will focus mostly on Jane, her family of origin sessions, and results of a six-year follow-up.

Case Two

Karen Tussey, a single, twenty-eight-year-old female, started therapy because of depression and adjusting to a breakup with her boyfriend. She was discouraged because she tended to attract men who were impulsive and narcissistic. During individual therapy, it became apparent that she unwittingly chose men who, like her father, were self-centered and critical. On the other hand, she was stable, responsible, and mature and withstood the abuse and neglect without complaint, much like her mother did from Karen's father throughout Karen's growing-up years. She reported that John Tussey, her fifty-nine-year-old father, was critical and rejecting of her for all of her life. For as long as she could remember, her father had referred to her as "fat" and "not too smart." In recent years, he belittled her occupation as a kindergarten teacher and would suggest that she should be more like Ted, her thirty-year-old brother, who was a successful computer software engineer. On the other hand, Mary Tussey, Karen's fifty-seven-year-old mother, was supportive of Karen and often made excuses for John's negative behaviors and criticisms.

STRATEGIES, INTERVENTIONS, AND TECHNIQUES FOR COUNSELING FAMILY OF ORIGIN ISSUES

To start this section, I review how Framo and Aponte approach family of origin work and then move from there to strategies and techniques that I have developed and used in family of origin practice. Sometimes I build off of the models of Framo and Aponte with my own adaptations, and in other places I present a different thought or approach. Framo's work is an important resource in developing my thinking about conducting family of origin sessions. If you want to begin conducting such sessions, I suggest that you absorb Framo's (1992) book on the topic. However, over the years, I have developed my own style of conducting the session and thereby include below some selected strategies that have proven to be effective in my practice, some of which contradict the following section on Framo and Aponte.

Therapeutic Approaches of Framo and Aponte

James Framo dedicated much of his professional career to family therapy, focusing specifically on family of origin. Harry Aponte is a pioneer of family therapy and trained counselor using the person-of-the-therapist model, which involves a focus on family of origin influence on counselors' practices.

Logistics and length of Framo's family of origin sessions. Framo's model advocated for a onetime long (approximately eight hours) therapy session divided between two consecutive days, involving the original family members. The purpose of the session is to work through past issues to improve familial relationships. He viewed the session as helpful for families who have positive relationships as well as for families with deep hurts who may have little contact with one another. All of the information provided in this section comes from *Family-of-Origin Therapy: An Intergenerational Approach* (Framo, 1992) or my memory from films and a presentation Framo made at a conference.

The session is ideally conducted by male and female cocounselors for any gender differences to be accounted for and to allow the counselors to work off each other. When I heard Framo present on having two counselors of different genders, he focused on two aspects to explain this recommendation. First, he said that the family of origin patterns are so strong that when alone a counselor can be easily and unknowingly drawn into family dysfunction. This is less likely to occur if two counselors are working together on avoiding such a pitfall. Second, he explained, "There are some things that women go through that only women can understand, and then there are some things that men go through that only men can understand." At this point, I thought he was finished, but he was not, as he continued on: "Then there are some things that women go through that only men can understand, and some things men go through that only women can understand."

The overarching goal of the therapy is to improve family relationships. This will look different depending on the individual relationships within each family. As counselors guide the session, family members begin to see that their problems are more intertwined than they may have thought. Family members often believe that they were isolated in their problems until they realize that other members felt similar hurts and that they contribute to each other's hurts in ways they did not realize. These realizations are not for the purpose of blaming members but for addressing past hurts and anger so that family members can come to a more compassionate understanding of one another.

The family of origin session has three parts, which are divided over the two consecutive days. The goal of the first part is to build rapport with the family members and reduce their anxiety. The session is sometimes months in the making, due to having to overcome resistances, coordinate schedules, and arrange travel for those coming long distances. The cocounselors spend the first minutes getting to know each member on a surface level and establishing some connections on which to build trust. Counselors might ask each one in turn about their occupation and whether they have a favorite hobby, being sure to make efforts in the discussion to engage and appreciate each family member.

The second portion is when the bulk of the work is done. In many cases, this is the work of adult children resolving anger and finding more compassionate understanding of their parents. This often includes discussing the parents' marriage, relationships with children, and any other agenda items brought by the family. Another goal of this portion is to shed a different light on some of the events of the past and hopefully reframe situations such that the adult children can see parents realistically and as fallible human beings.

The third and final portion of the Framo session ties the themes of the session together with the goal of encouraging the family as they leave. Framo had each family dyad discuss their relationships with the goal of strengthening them. After particularly difficult sessions, parents especially may feel discouraged and as though they failed in their parenting, so Framo suggests ending the session on a high note by concentrating on the strengths of the family members in order to encourage them.

Family of origin sessions require effort on the part of the cocounselors and each family member just to be there and go through with it. However, once the eight hours are complete, families have at the very least experienced something together and hopefully shared in some healing and helpful interactions. Framo offered to the members of the families to come back for individual sessions or sessions with one other member to work through issues brought up during the family of origin session, which he said about 10 percent of families did (Framo, 1992, p. 73).

Aponte's person-of-the-therapist model. The person-of-the-therapist model developed by Aponte uses the family of origin as well as other formative relationships as tools for clinicians to better understand themselves in order to better use themselves as clinicians. The following information in this section comes from *The Person of the Therapist Training Model: Mastering the Use of Self* (Aponte & Kissil, 2016), *The Person and Practice of the Therapist* (Winter & Aponte, 1987), and my training and conversations with Harry Aponte and Joan Winter.

When counselors run into consistently difficult client themes or populations, it may be because of some sort of unresolved issue in the counselors' past. Aponte points out that this issue affecting one's life and clinical work may stem from the counselor's family of origin. If so, clinicians consider what past themes stand out for them as they were growing up that may be impacting their practice. Examples of impactful themes may be alcoholism, a difficult relationship with a parent, or a traumatic death in the family. If unresolved at some level, these themes may begin to influence a counselor's practice with clients who struggle with similar issues or remind the clinician of a particular person.

The first step to overcoming these therapeutic difficulties is becoming aware of them. Once counselors are well aware of their own adverse personal history and the ways it impacts their practice, counselors can work on these personal issues. While the past cannot be changed, counselors become better helpers when they attempt to improve their personal relationships with their own family of origin members, reframe their past situations, and work through unresolved difficulties. This allows them to develop a more effective use of self. After such personal work, counselors may decide that certain client populations are still too difficult or triggering. However, Aponte taught me that in most situations counselors have places of brokenness that with good professional supervision can be resolved concurrently as they are evoked with certain client situations. Either result is viewed as a professional success because counselors will better understand themselves and how best to serve clients. The person-of-the-therapist model helps connect one's personal life to practice in order to be a better clinician while also producing personal growth.

Benefits of Long Sessions

Over the years, I have found significant benefits in using long sessions. However, I have modified them to occur in one day and not over two consecutive days as advocated by Framo. Family members and myself find it much more convenient to set aside a day rather than two for the session. Usually a session will run for two to three hours with a ten-minute break in the morning, followed by a quick lunch, and then meet again for two to three hours with a ten-minute break in the afternoon. Although today's norm is to have therapy fit into a fifty-minute hour, I have found significant value in using longer sessions, especially for family of origin work. Below I make the case for using longer sessions by using metaphors drawn from plot designs used by playwrights for theatrical productions, as well as the concept of the inertia effect to cause momentum in therapy encounters.

Have you ever noticed that counseling sessions are similar to dramatic productions? For centuries, playwrights (as well as other writers and novelists) developed stories with predictable patterns of presentation. Freytag (1900) captured this pattern by putting it into a five-stage sequencing of dramatic structure that has since become known as Freytag's Pyramid. First is the *introduction*, in which the setting, characters, and the characters' stories are initially introduced. This constitutes the prologue (Freytag, 1900, p. 115). Second, there is *rising action* where the plot starts to develop as characters in their context become active in the buildup of the story: "As to the scenes of this rising movement, it may be said, they have to produce a progressive intensity of interest; they must, therefore, not only show evince [clear] progress in their import, but they must show an enlargement in form and treatment" (Freytag, 1900, p. 128). This is followed by the *climax*, which "is the place where the results of the rising movement come out strong and decisively; it is almost always the crowning point" (Freytag, 1900, p. 128). The fourth stage is the *falling action* (the return), in which there is a de-escalation in the story preparing for the wrap-up. During this time, there is often "clear insight into the life of the hero" (Freytag, 1900, p. 135). And finally, we have the *dénouement*, a time where final results, conclusions, and resolutions are made known and analyzed.

Modern-day therapeutic sessions, influenced by insurance coverage, other restraints of economic reality, and a culture that leans toward getting the most possible in the shortest amount of time, have unwittingly followed Freytag's Pyramid. For example, ten minutes are spent on social warmup, agenda setting, and catching up since the previous week (the introduction); fifteen minutes are spent focusing in on a concern/topic more intensely (the rising action); ten minutes are spent at the crowning moment where change and insight is at its most productive stage (the climax). At this point the counselor looks at the clock and realizes that with only fifteen minutes left, the session needs to de-escalate quickly and be summarized (the falling action). The final minutes of the session consist of bringing the session to a conclusion that provides security and accomplishment to the family (the dénouement). Hearing the lobby door open at the fifty-minute mark, which is inevitably the counselor's next clients, reminds the counselor to stand up

and say goodbye, hopefully with enough time to finalize notes and make it to the bathroom (this last item has become increasingly important as I age).

Having started professional counseling in the 1970s (the 1960s if counting camp counselor days), I experienced a time when counseling sessions were not always on the fifty-minute timer. During the 1970s, we spent more time with families. Social workers were particularly interested in conducting family sessions during home visits that would often last two or three hours. In addition, we conducted group therapy sessions that often lasted just as long. What I noticed about these former times and the current times of five- to six-hour family of origin and forgiveness sessions is the benefit of an *inertia effect*.

In physical science, an inertia effect is when an object is set in motion and tends to keep moving at a constant velocity with less effort. Momentum is achieved. For example, have you ever helped push a car to the side of a road? Getting the car to start rolling takes quite a bit of effort and strength (the rising action), but once the car gets rolling, someone had better jump in to steer (the climax) because the car is now moving, requiring much less effort to keep it rolling when compared to the first push. In short, the most productive work of a therapeutic session is accomplished in the climax portion. In other words, once the session is intensifying and moving in a positive direction, momentum has been achieved that creates propulsion toward accomplishing therapeutic objectives. The longer the family is moving in this state of momentum the more therapeutic objectives are being met. In the fifty-minute-hour session, not long after reaching the most productive part of the session, counselors begin to apply pressure to the metaphorical brakes to slow the momentum in order to prepare for stopping the session. Imagine how much more work could be done in a longer session where full advantage and attention is paid to the most productive part. I make the argument that one long session is often more productive than numerous fifty-minute sessions spread across a few weeks. As a side note, when clients can make the economic sacrifice (since insurance companies will usually cover only a portion), I prefer to meet with regular counseling sessions every other week for two-hour sessions. Sometimes the balance of reduced travel, car and road expense, and time off of work can somewhat offset the economic disadvantage of less insurance reimbursement to the client. Reducing fees is also helpful to make the longer sessions feasible.

Circumstances That Lead to Scheduling Family of Origin Sessions

Family of origin sessions usually come about in one of three ways: (1) While doing couple's therapy, issues would come up that reflect long-standing patterns that predated the marriage and were evident in the spouse's family of origin. (2) During an individual therapy session, unresolved issues and patterns of the past come to light. (3) Once I started doing family of origin sessions, some families began to call directly for the purpose of resolving issues with their original family.

Counselor Conviction and Enthusiasm Is Contagious

When I heard Framo present on family members resisting participation, he said something that really stuck with me. At first only about 10 percent of his clients agreed to arrange a family of origin meeting. As he witnessed significant healing in the lives of clients who completed the sessions, especially couples in marital therapy, he began promoting the family of origin sessions with greater enthusiasm. As a result, nearly all of his individual and couple cases would request that the session be arranged. This highlights the point that if counselors are enthusiastically convinced of the treatment they provide, clients are more willing to attempt and to benefit from the treatment.

Spouses and Other Relatives Are Not Invited

The family of origin session is exclusively for adult children and their parents. Sometimes a grandparent or other relative who was living in the home throughout the growing-up years of the children is invited because he or she was an integral part of the day-to-day life of the family. When attempting to arrange a session, clients often inquire about whether spouses can participate. Spouses are not invited to attend a family of origin session. Spouses were not part of the original family, and their presence and participation can interfere with the work needed to be done between family members. Sessions can be videotaped or audio-recorded, and if written permissions of participants allow it, spouses can watch or listen to the session after the fact.

Creating the Invitation to Participate

Clients are often a bit doubtful that certain family members will participate. I help my clients practice how they will extend the invitation. Many clients prefer email, so I encourage them to draft a request for me to review with them before sending. The email message needs to address "hooks" that are often unintentionally embedded that can influence a family member not to participate. Consider this hypothetical email message, which would cause this invited family member to want to stay home:

My counselor suggested that I approach you and the rest of the family to see if you would be willing to participate in a family of origin session. It is a session where we can share our thoughts about our growing-up years and especially provide me an opportunity to share all the heartache and pain that your behavior has caused me.

It is not unusual for clients to have a negative viewpoint regarding whether a family member would agree to come. In fact, sometimes if they were to frankly ask certain family members to come, they indeed might get a refusal regardless of how they ask. One way to improve participation response is to get permission to contact family members directly. I have found that when I get a list of some strengths from the client about family members beforehand, I can use those strengths to engage them during telephone calls. When I make direct calls to family members, explain the importance of their participation, and

describe what they can expect to happen during the session, nearly all family members agree to attend.

Some important tips for these phone calls include the following:

1. Prepare a written script/notes to help you feel less nervous (at first these calls can be scary for the counselor to make).
2. Find the best phone number and time to call.
3. Be strength-based, positive, supportive, and encouraging.
4. Let family members know how important their participation is to help the counselor gain adequate insight into the family.
5. Be sensitive to the desires and feelings of all family members.
6. Guarantee that this will be a onetime session and that there will be no pressure for the family member to attend other sessions.

As random examples of the above, the counselor might say things like these during the conversation: "Your involvement will help me get a balanced perspective. A mother's (father's) mature insight sheds much light on the situation." "Your son told me that you are very articulate and have a talent for describing situations and events. I could really use someone with that skill in the session." "If I were in your shoes and came to the session, I would be afraid that the counselor would pressure me to come to weekly sessions. I guarantee this is just a onetime event." "Although we will attempt to deal with any problems from the past, we will spend time focusing on the positive and some of the pleasant memories." "My goal will be to help everyone feel safe." "Your daughter said that as a single parent, you raised three rebellious teenagers at once. I have got to hear how you managed to do that!"

Creating Tolerance for Perceptions

Writer and critic Edmund Wilson once said, "No two persons ever read the same book." Regardless of how many people read the story, each walks away with a variety of perceptions and interpretations about the contents of the book. When it comes to family members recalling the narratives of family life and events from the past, perceptions are usually uniquely different. Many factors are at play to produce idiosyncratic memories of events. A sample of a few considerations include (1) personality differences (e.g., someone who is melancholic may view an event with more exacting negativity than others); (2) gender differences (e.g., a father's brain may have compartmentalized the events and thereby did not experience the same amount of stress as the mother); (3) difference in developmental stages (e.g., a nine-year-old child at concrete operational thought may have a much less abstract and limited view than a teenage child who experienced the same event); (4) implicit reactions formed in the brain's hippocampus (e.g., someone may store memories with varying degrees of pleasure or stress, causing memories to be colored by differing emotional experiences at the time); and (5) the effect of the event weighing differently on the in-

dividuals involved (e.g., the child who was abused the most by the older brother will directly recall the events with more pain and suffering).

After reviewing how perception difference is common in families, I request that the family consider an agreement that family members respect the integrity of others' perceptions of past events and circumstances, especially when they differ. For example, the counselor might say:

Whenever families get together, they bring very individualized memories of past events and circumstances. Therefore, members recalling the same event and time period will have different perceptions based on their personalities, how they process ideas and emotions, and how the event affected them. Can we all agree to allow each of us to have our own perceptions without questioning integrity or motives? In many cases, it is not important to get all the facts. For example, it usually does not matter if something happened three times versus eight times. But instead, let's search for themes and unresolved feelings and issues and not worry as much about getting others to agree with the entirety of our perceptions.

Discussing Pleasant Memories

Beginning the session on a positive note is vital, so I ask participants if they would take turns sharing a pleasant memory from the past. This icebreaker creates a positive start to the session and orients family members to dialoguing with each other. As memories are reminisced, I ask questions to get members of the family involved with each other in a close and meaningful way. For example, you might ask, "What went through your heart as tears came to your dad's eyes when he reported the pleasant memory about you?" Interestingly, sharing of positive memories evokes the amygdala in the brain to signal for the release of oxytocin, which is a hormone in humans that assists in bonding and attachments between people.

Self-Accountability Segment

All too often people come to counseling ready to address the problems they perceive in others without enough exploration in self-accountability for what they contribute to the issues. For the most part, when clients are invited to focus on their own wrongdoing and/or mistakes in a nondefensive setting created by counselors, they choose the very things that family members would have picked for them to emphasize. Instead of a room full of blamers, the family gets a group of people willing to admit their responsibility and therefore are better prepared to act as participants in resolving problems. Also, "confessing to one another and taking responsibility for one's actions in resolving conflict has strong biblical support" (DiBlasio, 2013, p. 237). Furthermore, "it is difficult to genuinely grasp one's own participation in the problem while simultaneously defending oneself from the accusations of another" (DiBlasio, 2013, pp. 237–238). Be cautioned that some people who have personality disorder(s) may not do well in self-accountability. To begin this section of the session, you might say something like the following:

Family life is not perfect. Whereas families have many strengths and highlight moments, there are also problems and numerous heartaches. Sometimes there are major issues that go unresolved for years. Family members coming to a session like this often want to address the mistakes and hurts mostly caused by others. This ends up causing much defensiveness and is counterproductive because it is hard to take ownership of a problem someone else has put into your lap to address. When each family member gets to choose which offense or wrongdoing he or she wants to address, there is often more self-accountability to make corrections and to seek forgiveness. In this part of our session, I would like to challenge everyone to put on the table a past issue or problem for which you can claim significant self-accountability.

Stay Resolution Focused

When I present on conducting family of origin sessions, I tell my students and others that these sessions practically run themselves, especially as the family moves toward the resolution stage. Keeping the family on task is imperative. To start the family moving toward resolutions, consider saying (if true), *"I have been impressed with the outpouring of your hearts and your feelings today and the ability of members to focus on self-accountability. Many things came up today that seemed to have been issues previously left unsettled for years. Now I suggest that we consider what might be the solutions to some of these issues. Who would like to start?"*

Often families intuitively move toward forgiveness and steps for a forgiveness session can be enacted (see clinical use of forgiveness below and also DiBlasio, 2013). Particularly important before forgiveness is sought is that the family member is assisted in developing a plan to stop or prevent the offense in the future.

Although I cannot say exactly why it works, something very special occurs in family of origin sessions toward the end that seems to break through years of misery and controversies. Several things, probably working in tandem, come to mind when trying to unravel the mystery: (1) Much prayer is used by family members, supporters, and counselors for God to work a healing in family relationships. (2) God is pleased to have his children "speak the truth in love" (Eph. 4:15) to one another and to live out Matthew 18:15–16 (in love approach a fellow Christian about his or her sin). (3) Most sessions involve seeking and granting forgiveness, which is one of the core heartbeats of the Christian life. (4) Perhaps the long time under the inertia effect described above provides enough momentum to catapult hurdles that have bogged down the family for so many years. (5) When a session is predicated on achieving self-accountability and a nondefensive environment, participants may be more motivated. (6) The effort that goes into arranging and getting to the session, and the potential it holds for lasting healing has family members working harder out of the high expectations to resolve the issue. (7) Realizing that a family meeting of such magnitude may not easily come around again leaves members with a feeling of urgency to get the job done right.

Spiritually Embracing the Past

Knowing that "[God's] eyes saw my substance, being yet unformed. And in [His] book they all were written, the days fashioned for me, when as yet there were none of them" (Ps. 139:16 NKJV), is comforting. Further, God will never leave us or forsake us (Heb. 13:5). God knows everything about us—even every hair on our head is numbered (Matt. 10:30). Sometimes we do not fully understand the reason for suffering this side of heaven, but we can rest assured that God will fit all things into a pattern of good for those who love him (Rom. 8:28).

Joseph's story mentioned above is an excellent example of how years of unfair treatment (starting with treachery against him by his siblings from his family of origin!) and tremendous suffering and persecution were God's methods for redemption of the Israelites from overwhelming starvation. Great empathetic care must be taken when discussing the hurt and pain from clients' past and current suffering. Therefore, the following suggestion always prioritizes this empathetic care when assisting clients. I encourage Christian clients to embrace their past, because every moment of it we were in the Savior's everlasting arms (Deut. 33:27), and God uses our past to accomplish his present and future plans for us—"Yea, though I walk through the valley of the shadow of death, I will fear no evil; for You are with me; Your rod and Your staff, they comfort me" (Ps. 23:4 NKJV).

I remember working with one grandmother who at the age of seventy was raising her seven-year-old grandson. The boy's mother (the grandmother's daughter-in-law) died from a heroin overdose, and the father (the grandmother's son) was a drug addict who caused significant problems for them. She was greatly distraught thinking about the "dismal" future of her grandson I talked with her about embracing the past using some of the Scriptures above. And I was able to share my personal story of how God saw me through living with very disturbed parents, physical abuse, and poverty while I was growing up in Baltimore City, and how that became a platform for my understanding and loving people with personality disorders and other mental disorders. She said it touched her and greatly helped her when I said, "If I could, I would not change one minute of my past, because now I see where God used it to prepare me for my counseling ministry." The grandmother better understood that her grandson was in the good hands of God.

When Family Members Have a Personality Disorder

In some family of origin sessions, family members struggle with one or more members who have personality disorders. As mentioned in chapter 15, about 9 percent of the general population have a personality disorder (PD), and about 46 percent of all clinical cases have one or more persons who have PD. Just one PD member in a family, not to mention two or more, can be the catalyst for years of much pain and suffering for the rest of the family. According to the American Psychiatric Association, "A personality disorder is an enduring pattern of inner experience and behavior that deviates markedly from the expectations of the individual's culture, is pervasive and inflexible, has an onset in adolescence or early adulthood, is stable over time, and leads to distress or impairment" (2013, p. 645). It is imperative that you not only build into your approaches and strategies PD assessment and diagnosis but that you also develop treatment plans to help other family members cope and understand how to avoid repetitive dysfunctional cycles.

A breakthrough in research shows that PD is a result of neurobiological abnormalities, and treating PD as emotional and interpersonal dyslexia (EID) has been effective (see chapter 15 and DiBlasio et al., 2014, for further explanation and research citations). First, the credit for changes goes to God, the healer of the human heart and mind. God is very pleased when Christian clients with PD attempt to retrain and renew their brains to form neuroplastic changes that lead them to be godlier and more loving (Rom. 12:2; 2 Cor. 10:5). I suggest that the reader review the following techniques and strategies from chapter 15 that can be applied to PD situations: "Treating Personality Disorders with a Neurobiological Intervention," "Diagnosis and Explanation," "Support and Teamwork from the Spouse," "Building New Neuropathways and No Longer Trusting the 'Heart,'" and "Using an Accountability Person."* In addition, the second case

---

* Other helpful strategies from previous chapters. The reader may also want to review the following techniques that can be applied to family of origin work: chapter 15: "Biblical Renewing of the Mind and Neuroplasticity," "A Biblical View of the Amygdala in the Limbic System," "Neurobiological Education

below, the Tussey family, gives an example of a family with a father who had a personality disorder.

CONNECTION TO CASE STUDIES

Many of the strategies and techniques discussed above become evident in the case studies. In both the recommendation for the clients to participate in the family of origin session grew out of revelations made in their individual/family therapy. Also, both cases involved follow-up individual sessions.

Case One

In the Woods's case, therapeutic work also included a follow-up session between Jane and her father. Jane's normal personality was that she was choleric and melancholic, which among the many strengths of such a personality has several negatives, including a propensity to be more judgmental, to have a low-level of satisfaction with self and others, and to be prone to depression. For as long as Jane can remember, she has always struggled with low-level depression and occasional major depression. Frank had an easygoing phlegmatic and sanguine personality that was more optimistic and understanding, but also acted to enable his wife's depression (see systemic effects in chapters 15 and 16). As the therapy started, to become more effective in assisting the couple to become less con-

flictual, Jane became more depressed and negatively refocused on her daughter even though her marriage was getting better and her daughter made positive behavioral progress. Two major factors played a part in Jane's depression: (1) she was still grieving her mother's death, which occurred from a heart attack three years earlier when her mother was age sixty, and (2) she was diagnosed with a rare fatal blood disease and was told by her doctors that she would likely not live to see her grandchildren (given the age of her daughter, that would be only ten to fifteen years left to live at the time of the family of origin session).

Even with an increase in depression, Jane understood that the marriage and her daughter's behavior were significantly better. Although Jane was receiving psychiatric medication for depression, she continued to decompensate. In the process, she brought up the cutoff she had in her relationship with her father since her mother's death. We renegotiated the contract for therapy to focus on this and Jane's other individual issues, and in the process, I suggested a family of origin meeting between Jane, her father, and her two siblings.

The meeting was scheduled for a five-hour period in one day. During the pleasant-memory phase, the father mentioned how independent, precocious, and graceful Jane had been as a little girl. He added, "Even when she fell, she fell gracefully." These comments brought pleasant

and Contracting," "Cortisol-Control Intervention and De-escalating Conflict," "Managing the Hippocampus," "Helping Couples to Create Oxytocin Moments," "Clinical Use of Forgiveness," "Accepting and Tweaking Personality," "Negotiation and Compromise Coaching," "Helping Couples to Reduce Expectations," "Stroke-Kick and Relationship Restoration"; chapter 16: "Systemic Thinking," "Enactments and Inducing Enactments," "Using Directives," "Interrupting Dysfunctional Patterns," and "Setting Healthy Boundaries."

tears to Jane, who later said that she was not used to hearing supportive things from her father.

During the self-accountability portion, the father brought up that he was an "emotionally absent father" because he focused too much on his career and left too much of the parenting to his wife. He called it his "sin of omission." Jake Woods's thirty-eight-year-old son, Mike, expressed anger toward his dad for not being supportive of him during his childhood. While Jane and her sister observed, I asked the father and son to turn their chairs toward each other to see if they could get somewhere with this problem. The father was particularly strong and mature at receiving his son's anger while being repentant and empathetic, and we worked through to the point where the father asked for and received forgiveness from his son. This process took most of the remaining time of the session. I remember thinking that Jane was likely going through a positive vicarious experience watching the productive way her brother and father moved to resolution. At the end of the session, I recommended that the father and Jane make an appointment with me to meet alone to work through their issues with one another. The youngest sister expressed satisfaction growing up and indicated that she had no residual issues that needed resolution.

During the individual follow-up a week later, Jane and I processed the family of origin meeting. She said that she wanted to get her "claws" into her father, and that she hated him (so much for my thoughts that the gains made by brother and father would be a positive vicarious experience). Given

her intense feelings, I suggested that we should hold up on any further meetings between her and her father until we had done enough individual work to prepare for such a meeting. Although not intentional on my part, my reluctance to schedule a follow-up may have had a paradoxical effect on Jane. That is, being told that she was not ready might have acted subliminally to promote Jane's desire to be ready. In addition, and probably more relevant, I asked her, "What is your faith position about your hatred toward your father?" I could tell by the look on her face that she was having a revelatory moment, likely a moment that was Holy Spirit inspired. She gave me a metaphor that explained those seconds after my question. She said, "When you asked the question, it was like I was up in a plane where the ground was blocked by massive clouds, and then the clouds parted and I could see clearly all the way down." She continued to explain that she was convicted that hatred of her father was not at all acceptable to God. She continued to express that this was the moment that she gave up her hatred toward her father. I responded, "I think you are now ready to meet with your dad."

Jane immediately wrote a nice letter to her dad asking if he would like to schedule the follow-up meeting. Her dad, not having yet received the handwritten letter in the mail, called a day later and asked her the same question. God was already at work, and I was filled with anticipation over what was to come. Much like what occurred between Mike and the father (perhaps the vicarious experience did help after all), Jane and her father worked through the issues in a loving forgiveness format.

During the discussion, Jane explained that her father was capable of being emotionally available to her younger sister, which caused Jane confusion as to why he did not offer that to her. The father told Jane something he had never discussed with her about the younger sister. He said that the younger sister had developmental problems from birth and was physically weak, frail, and often sick. This resulted in both parents having tremendous worry as they overinvested in the younger sister's care just to help her survive childhood. Jane and her brother were unintentionally neglected. The father said that Jane and Mike were physically and emotionally strong and independent, and it did not occur to him that they needed his attention as well. The explanation helped to set the stage for Jane's granting of forgiveness to her dad. With my help, the father developed a plan to prevent him from repeating his past mistakes. I could tell the father was committed to following the plan because he was careful to write each part down on a small pad of paper he carried in his pocket.

When it was Jane's turn to seek forgiveness, she used the analogy she had heard from her father more than once. He said that she was "prickly like a porcupine" when around him. She was able to explain that her childlike jealousy over the favoritism the father and mother demonstrated toward the younger sister made her feel unwanted and unloved. Jane told her father that the pattern was deeply ingrained in her, and that she was not always aware when she was being "prickly." Jane asked her father to give her a nonverbal cue if she slipped and became prickly in the future. The father suggested the tug-of-the-ear gesture used in the game of charades (the sign for "sounds like"). The father granted forgiveness to his daughter's request for it, and intuitively they hugged. While hugging, the father said that this was the first time they had ever hugged. He explained that he grew up in a family of "emotional telephone poles" where physical affection was not expressed, and that he carried that into his own raising of children. He mentioned how different things were since he became a Christian because when it came to anyone else (but not his own children), he freely demonstrated physical affection. Although the hug between father and daughter was beautiful to witness, a bit of sadness washed over me when I thought about so many wasted years.

In an effort to understand the long-term effects of a family of origin intervention, I invited the family to meet once again six years later. During this session, the improvements made during the intervention were still evident. Before the intervention, the family could not spend more than a few minutes together even during holidays, and the father would not see much of his grandchildren. Not only was the family getting together for extended periods, including regular visits with his grandchildren, but the father also invested in a beach town vacation home where the entire family would vacation together. The father reported that he was faithful in sticking to his plan over the six-year period and pulled out a tattered piece of paper on which he originally recorded his prevention plan. He said, "I keep this on my car visor, and occasionally while waiting for a light to change I pull it down to read it."

Perhaps the most astounding development was that Jane was healed of her rare blood disease, and as of this writing, she is not only alive but is enjoying being a grandmother of a two-year-old. Whereas we cannot say with any conclusiveness that the improved condition was a result of giving up hatred and seeking and granting forgiveness, we do know that health improvements after forgiveness are validated in the research literature (Lutjen, Stilton, & Flannelly, 2012; Lawler et al., 2005).

Case Two

During the therapy, Karen was slowly making progress, as indicated by an increase in hopefulness, lessening of depression, and coming to insight that the recent failed relationship with her boyfriend was part of a maturation process to become emotionally healthy. She was convicted to end her propensity to develop relationships with self-centered and unstable men who eventually brought her much disappointment and heartache. In one session, she talked about her relationship with her father and the constant ridicule she received from him. In almost every interaction she had with him, he would call her "fat" and comment on his perception that she was not very intelligent. This and other mean comments from him throughout her entire life left her with much self-doubt, poor self-esteem, and anger over his cruelty. She reported that as a child, she remembered seeking after his approval only to find that she could never measure up.

As Karen was receiving this type of treatment growing up, she noticed a stark difference in how her father treated Ted, her older brother. Because he was athletic and handsome and did well academically, Ted was treated by her father with much favoritism. As she started to describe her father, it was obvious that he might have a moderate case of narcissistic personality disorder (NPD). When Karen mentioned he was mean, critical, and judgmental, I asked her if she would like me to give a few other possible descriptors, many of which I thought she might agree applied to her father. As I went down the symptoms of NPD and about a dozen other associated features that often go with NPD, she was wide-eyed with amazement and asked, "Do you know my dad?" I do this to help clients understand from the beginning that personality disorders are very predictable because they result from brain abnormalities and emotional and interpersonal dyslexia (EID) (see chapter 15 for more details).

By understanding this, Karen could begin her journey in developing a healthy understanding of the possible brain abnormality involved, setting healthy boundaries, and not basing her self-esteem on the faulty misperceptions of her father. The metaphor I used with her to explain the misperceptions involved was to imagine if someone were to tell me that I was three feet tall. Right away I would know that this was not true, and if the person insisted that it was true, you could bet that his ruler was crooked and bent. Further, it would be a bit irrational on my part to believe that a measurement coming from such a distorted measuring device represented my true height. I cautioned Karen, as I do all my clients, that I cannot make a diagnosis based only on reports from family members. However, it is ethically sound to circumspectly discuss the symptoms of a disorder and let the patient make her own judgments. In such cases, clear communication must occur with the client that professional diagnoses can be rendered only when you professionally meet with the person.

As Karen was working on undoing years of her internal distorted reality and also working toward setting healthy boundaries with her father, I suggested a family of origin session. She immediately thought that her father would never attend. I asked if she wanted to sign a release that would allow me to call her father. He agreed to come, which shocked the rest of the family. As mentioned above, resistant family members often respond differently to a strength-based and positive approach coming from someone outside the family.

After the greeting and social warmup stage, each member took turns recalling a pleasant family memory. Then I asked for members to participate in the next part of the session, which involved self-accountability for something negative that they now regretted. I purposely asked Karen's mother if she would go first and then proceeded clockwise around the room so that Karen's father would be last and therefore would have a lot of time to think. When it was Karen's father's turn, he could think of nothing that he did that needed to be processed with the group. Jaws seemed to drop as the other three family members were stunned that the father who caused the most problems in the family could think of nothing to report.

Although this at first seemed countertherapeutic, it actually served as a highlight of the session. Karen reported in our processing session after the family of origin meeting, "Seeing Dad be absolutely clueless about the harm he has caused opened my eyes to how true it is that he might have a brain problem." From that moment on, Karen was able to follow therapeutic directives more earnestly and was able to stop internally entertaining her father's criticisms. In time, she actually developed compassion and empathy for him. Karen's individual therapy progressed nicely as she broke out of her depression and gained a better self-identity. Note that depression and negative self-esteem often coexist, and when there is improvement in one, the other tends to improve. On the sixth individual session after the family of origin session, Karen and I agreed that she no longer needed therapy. She reported that even family and friends had commented on her improvements.

Because of Karen's long pattern of getting involved with the wrong type of men, we agreed that if she were to become serious about a relationship, she would consider setting an appointment to discuss the situation. Fortunately, she did follow through with short-term treatment when a romance was developing and ended up marrying a mature and kind man who did not show symptoms of any mental health disorder. The next time I heard from Karen was about four years later. After saying "Hello," she started to cry. She was sobbing and barely able to catch her breath to tell me that her father had just died. As I began to console her, she clarified that her tears were tears of joy. She said, "After our family session, I was struck with how disabled my dad was. I approached him with more love and understanding. We were able to work things out. I found that I was the one needing to change, to become more Christlike and loving toward him. I'm calling to say thank you because I had four years of a much better relationship with my dad because of the counseling."

CONCLUSION

As children grow up and move away from parents and siblings to forge new families, they take with them years of interactions and patterns of behavior. Adult children carry both implicit healthy and unhealthy ways of relating in their new romantic relationships. Although not always aware of it at first, some old dysfunctional patterns begin to play out between partners and over time filter down to biological or adopted children. These patterns are strongly entrenched in systemic dynamics with the family of origin and are best dealt with by intervening with the people with whom the problem developed in the first place.

Family of origin therapy paves the way for transformation of adult family relationships through forgiveness and reconciliation. God is about the work of forgiving and reconciling his children to himself through Jesus his Son. Therefore, the ways in which we can mimic these patterns in our earthly family relationships bring him glory. Breaking dysfunctional patterns through family of origin therapy not only influences those directly involved but can have a ripple effect for generations to come as dysfunctional cycles are broken and healthier patterns are formed. The therapy brings families together in ways in which they may not have been able to do in a traditional week-to-week therapy. Counselors who help counselees to resolve longstanding conflict and to bring years of unforgiveness and anger to an end preform one of the nobler undertakings and eternally rewarding efforts of the counseling profession. God clearly wants peace and love in the body of Christ, especially between family members (e.g., John 13:34–35; Rom. 12:18; 1 John 4:7), and as a result, an unhindered relationship is possible with him (Isa. 59:2; Matt. 6:14–15).

RECOMMENDED READING

Aponte, H. J., & Kissil, K. (2016). *The person of the therapist training model: Mastering the use of self.* New York, NY: Routledge.

Framo, J. (1992). *Family-of-origin therapy: An intergenerational approach.* New York, NY: Brunner/Mazel.

Framo, J., Weber, T., & Levine, F. (2003). *Coming home again: A family-of-origin consultation.* New York, NY: Brunner/Routledge.

Kerr, M. E., & Bowen, M. (1988). *Multigenerational emotional process.* In M. E. Kerr & M. Bowen (Eds.), *Family evaluation: An approach based on Bowen theory* (pp. 221–255). New York, NY: W. W. Norton.

Searight, H. R. (1997). *Family-of-origin therapy and diversity.* Washington, DC: Taylor & Francis.

CHAPTER 18

Family Conflict–Focused Strategies

Linda Mintle, PhD, LCSW, LMFT

> What causes fights and quarrels among you? Don't they
> come from your desires that battle within you? You desire
> but do not have, so you kill. You covet but you cannot
> get what you want, so you quarrel and fight.
>
> JAMES 4:1–2

Family relationships are complex, powerful, intense, and often challenging. Since Eden, conflict has been a basic element of human nature. It is inevitable. In fact, one could say that the family is a system in conflict. Opportunities for differences and disagreements are commonplace given the frequent contact family members have with one another. In addition, stress associated with family changes—for example, a new baby, separation, a child beginning school, moving or changing jobs—also gives rise to conflict situations.

Unresolved conflict can breed mistrust and add to the stress of family gatherings. Those disagreements influence the quality of family relationships but also the social development and future adjustment of children. For example, the presence of serious family conflict is a predictor of depression and substance use in adolescents (Reinherz, Giaconia, Hauf, Wasserman, & Paradis, 2000). The more conflict can be resolved and handled in constructive ways, the better the opportunity for healthy family relationships.

Thus, it is not the presence of conflict that is of concern, but how conflict is handled. This chapter focuses on goals and intervention strategies for family conflict aimed at improving relationships. Counseling families through the conflict process will not only help with conflict management but will also grow intimacy within a family system.

THEOLOGY AND PSYCHOLOGY OF FAMILY CONFLICT

Kramer, Boelk, and Auer (2006, p. 794) define family conflict as "interpersonal tension or struggle among two or more persons whose opinions, values, needs or expectations are opposing or incompatible." This interpersonal tension presents in various ways depending on who is involved in the family conflict. For example, a conflict between siblings might be handled differently than a conflict between child and parents.

Family conflict is influenced by resources and power. According to social conflict theories, conflict is characterized by the quest for resources. Individual family members act according to their own interests, needs, and values in order to secure resources they deem important or desirable. Different family members often want different things (e.g., children want to stay up late, and parents want them in bed early) or want the same things but operate with limited resources (e.g., children compete for parents' time, the father's job interferes with helping his wife with her elderly parents). Because power and resources are distributed and negotiated, fairly or unfairly, control theory asserts that family conflicts result from an individual's need to secure and maintain power and control within a relationship(s). Unequal power and limited resources create conflict over issues of boundaries, roles, and organization. Members often disagree on actions that should be taken and on which resources should be used. Power struggles result. A common example is disagreement over how to manage finances or when the balance of power and resources is tipped because a family member struggles with an addiction or mental illness.

A family development approach addresses the importance of conflict as it relates to stage transition in the normal course of family life. As families move from one developmental stage to another, roles must be constantly renegotiated, making conflict points likely. In their book, *The Changing Family Life Cycle*, Carter and McGoldrick (1989) outline common family stages, the emotional processes involved in each transition, and second-order changes in family status that are required to proceed developmentally. Common stages of family development include leaving home, marriage, families with young children, families with adolescents, launching children, and families in later life.

The key is to be aware of emotional processes and manage changes during transition points. Communication is needed to prevent family members from alienating each other. A breakdown in communication around conflict can disrupt the system. Thus, developmental transition points are ripe for conflict to occur and should be considered when conducting a family evaluation.

System theory holds that family relationships are best studied holistically and interactionally, accounting for hierarchies and subsets and the larger context in which people operate. Family conflict has the potential to disrupt the entire system and lead to stability or dysfunction. All members of the family are affected, and the system self-regulates through feedback (Gurman & Kniskern, 1981). Therefore, assessment should include the system as a whole, as well as subsystems.

System theory also purports that interpersonal interactions have a content and process component. What is said (content), and how it is said (process), are both evaluated when observing family interactions. Attending to the process includes observing interactional patterns. For example, Gottman, Coan, Carrere, and Swanson (1998) discovered that the processes of helping couples to de-escalate during conflict and to make effective repairs are both important to marriage satisfaction. Other process factors, such as self-soothing and starting a conflict with a soft approach were determined to impact the person's ability to listen to the content during conflict. Thus, the family therapist listens for content but is also observing the process unfolding in the room.

Biblical guidelines regarding conduct and attitude inform treatment and address how and what is said as well. The mandate to go to the one with whom you have conflict (Matt. 18:15–17) supports the notion not to avoid or appease family members. Conflict is to be addressed.

In terms of peacemaking, the process begins with prayer, asking God for wisdom and the courage to have difficult conversations. James 1:19 speaks to the need to be "quick to hear, slow to speak and slow to become angry." Proverbs 12:15 reinforces the importance of listening, "The way of fools seems right to them, but the wise listen to advice."

Each family member is to take responsibility and not be driven by pride, self-centeredness, or defensiveness. Dialogue is guided by the directive to speak the truth in love (Eph. 4:15), understand the power of the tongue (James 3:1–12), and be kind, compassionate, and forgiving (Eph. 4:32).

Forgiveness is not optional in the Christian faith; rather, we are commanded to forgive often and liberally (Col. 3:13). Forbearance is substituted for retaliation, and the restoration of all family relationships is desired. Reconciliation is God's heart.

Moreover, change is always possible. When God transforms a heart, it is much easier to work on solutions and forfeit the need to be right or to be offended. God's grace is sufficient, and family members can be reassured that God will give the strength needed to make change no matter how difficult the situation. Prayer is also a powerful tool. Families should be encouraged to pray together for unity and healing.

When family members have difficulty dealing directly with each other over conflict, a third party may intervene, forming a triangle to stabilize the tension (Minuchin, 1974). The goal is to help the two family members deal directly with each other and detriangulate the third party. Bringing in a third party when two people are unable to resolve a conflict is also prescriptive of the way to deal with conflict outlined in Matthew 18.

Koerner and Fitzpatrick (2009) note that because the family is a socialization unit, children adopt certain conflict styles that they carry to the rest of their interpersonal relationships. Wilmot and Hocker (2014) add that the patterns of behavior used during conflict are activated without much thought. Social learning theory supports the idea that family conflict styles are learned and passed on through generations unless there is intentional change. These styles are not right or wrong but are a reflection of the learning that takes place in a family system (Wilmot & Hocker, 2014). However, some styles are more effective at preserving relationships, promoting empathy, and listening, as will be noted.

Zimet and Jacob's (2001) modeling theory further supports that children learn behavior patterns in their families, and parents are the models for parental conflict behavior. Consequently, children who witness constructive parental conflict styles learn how to regulate their emotions, problem solve, read the emotions of others, and develop positive social behavior. Those children who learn negative conflict styles experience negative effects. Assessment of conflict styles as they relate to family interactional patterns is needed.

Since family conflict is normal and a part of all relationships, how family members deal with conflict is critical to healthy family functioning. The counselor's task is to help family members relate positively to one another when conflicts arise and build a climate conducive to working through difficulties and stress. When conflict is handled well, people grow and change is possible. Issues can be solved, reconciliation is possible, and intimacy deepens. Still, conflict can create discomfort or tension among family members. Regulating those feelings of tension is also an important part of helping families confront differences and work through disagreements.

When family conflict is handled poorly, it can tear families apart. To assist in conflict management, the therapist interrupts toxic behavioral patterns and redirects interactions in ways that de-escalate conflict and build positive patterns. Strat-

egies to de-escalate conflict, such as using humor, taking responsibility, controlling tone and body language, and employing calming techniques, can be practiced. In cases where family members lack specific skills needed to address conflict in a healthy fashion, teaching skills related to assertiveness and problem solving is helpful.

Coping strategies used to deal with conflict impact physical health and may lead to longer life. Fabricius and Luecken (2007) found that family conflict can have long-term health consequences, such as high blood pressure, immune suppression, and premature aging. Of particular importance is the way anger and avoidance are handled. Data support that the overexpression of anger and avoidance can lead to cardiovascular, endocrine, and immune system problems (Kiecolt-Glaser & Newton, 2001). Stress can be reduced using interventions that focus on calming down physical arousal. Teaching family members to use relaxation methods, such as deep breathing, time-outs, distraction techniques, prayer, and meditation, is helpful for self-soothing. For angry thoughts, biblical guidelines, such as not giving vent to anger, allowing God to be the judge of a person, resisting the urge toward revenge, and taming the tongue, can be discussed and practiced.

Despite the negative physical and psychological effects of poorly handled conflict, not all family members are willing to work through interpersonal conflict. Some refuse to reconcile their differences and hang on to unforgiveness despite biblical mandates to address differences, forgive, and pursue reconciliation with each other. Both the Bible and psychological research have much to say regarding unhealthy consequences of poorly handled conflict.

Finally, building trust is essential in order to address conflict issues and encourage family members to commit to work through problems. During conflict, trust is a mitigating factor against possible negative effects. Family secrets, betrayals, emotional neglect or harm, inconsistency, and unreliability all erode trust. Distrust breeds insecurity. Therefore, if breaches of trust exist, those issues must be addressed to build a climate for conflict to be discussed.

Attachment and Conflict: Early Family Influences

Since family conflict can negatively impact attachment style and potentially affect future relationships, attachment styles are assessed. Emotional security theory (EST) posits that it is the meaning of interparental and family conflict that relates to a child's assessment of emotional security. Since negative family conflict has the potential of undermining child adjustment, the goal is to foster a child's emotional security to positively impact adjustment.

Cognitive contextual theory developed by Grych and Fincham (1990) can be used to explain children's responses to interparental conflict. This theory contributes to our understanding of family conflict by addressing the meaning associated with conflict interactions. The way people make sense of conflict is influenced by experiences, recollections, and interpre-

tations. These experiences form appraisals that influence the causes and consequences of a disagreement. So when family members perceive a conflict to be threatening or negative, appraisals and meaning are associated with emotional response and coping (Lazarus & Folkman, 1984). Cognitive behavioral therapies address these appraisals, expectations, and meanings given to a specific conflict event.

Cultural attitudes and norms also affect meaning. For example, preserving harmony at all costs is an expectation in Asian cultures that may lead to lack of confrontation and inner feelings kept to oneself (Zhang, 2007). A grandparent and teenager can develop misunderstandings due to not understanding each other's generational context. Culture is like an iceberg. Most of it is not in our awareness on the surface but is present below the surface. Therefore, it is important to assess both the meaning of conflict and the way it is viewed in the larger cultural context in which the family operates.

Overall, the successful management of conflict requires affect regulation, problem solving, and other neurocognitive skills. These skills are influenced by attachment, an innate need to be connected to an attachment figure. The nature and quality of the parent-child bond gives rise to the type of attachment that forms in a child's life. Attachment, whether secure, ambivalent, or avoidant, affects how conflict is handled in a family system.

Attachment is formed by the interaction of one's unique genetic makeup and specific experiences in the environment. It begins in utero with the release of maternal hormones on the developing fetus that can create certain neurobiological vulnerability in some cases (Glynn, Wadhwa, & Sandman, 2000). As an individual continues to develop, the external influence of the family system becomes a major social influence in the forming of attachment. According to Bowlby (1988, 2012b), coping is impacted by the quality of the early attachment, which in turn sets the stage for social relationships later in life. To form a secure attachment, children must experience a sense of security as well as physical and emotional regulation with caregivers who are accessible and available. A secure base allows children to explore their world, remain curious, and eventually develop a sense of self-confidence and autonomy.

Neurocognitive skills, such as emotional regulation, social skills, empathy, compassion, problem solving, and flexibility, are positively influenced by feelings of security and safety. Secure attachment influences emotional and social development, including how a child thinks about self, others, and the world. When parents are at ease with the child's growing sense of autonomy and curiosity, the child develops positive beliefs about others and the self. Core beliefs are stored in the emotional memories of the limbic system and later retrieved as implicit memories. When various experiences (e.g., conflict) threaten a sense of security, negative emotions such as anxiety and anger arise. When intense emotions are triggered, the caregiver's job is to help calm and regulate the child's emotional intensity by validating the distress and providing safety and comfort. Consequently, the child learns

self-regulation and emotional regulation, skills needed for conflict management. Through a secure attachment, the child develops a positive sense of self and others.

Caregivers who are not attuned to the emotional experiences and core beliefs forming in their child's development may interact in ways that are avoidant or dismissive. The child then develops a negative view of attachment needs and experiences unpleasant emotions without support. The lack of response and subsequent negative beliefs prompt children to become overly autonomous or independent and develop a negative view of others. When the caregiver is unable to provide security, the child is at risk for later mental health problems. In fact, exposing children to chronic feelings of insecurity puts them at risk for developing maladaptive psychological patterns as adults (Diamond & Muller, 2004; Zimet & Jacob, 2001).

When caregivers are emotionally immature and not meeting their own needs, an ambivalent attachment with the child results. In this type of attachment style, the child is more preoccupied with the parent's needs, feels unsafe to explore the world, and develops beliefs that care for his needs is unpredictable. The child feels anxious and eventually preoccupied himself. A good example can be seen in family work with a teen diagnosed with an eating disorder, a depressed mom, and a distant father. If the mother's depression isn't addressed and the father distances, the teen feels anxious and becomes preoccupied with the needs of the mom and lack of attention from the father. Eating disorder symptoms serve the purpose of bringing the parents together to work on the teen's problem but do not address interpersonal difficulties related to attachment. The result is ambivalent attachment.

In families with severe neglect, abuse, and/or chaos, children develop a fearful/disorganized attachment style. Caregivers become the source of fear and anxiety rather than calmness and reassurance. This creates ongoing internal conflict and releases stress hormones throughout the body. To survive, these children often disconnect or dissociate, impacting brain connections involved with self-awareness, narrative memory, and rational problem solving (Schore, 2000). The result is poor coping, mood regulation problems, and behavioral control issues, all conflict contributors (Schore, 2001).

Feelings of safety, protection, and security are formed over time based on parents' relationships and the family as a unit. Affect is important and at the heart of the emotional security hypothesis. Emotional security theory contributes to our understanding regarding the effects of conflict on children in terms of security and adjustment (Cummings & Davies, 2011). This theory purports that emotions, conditions, and behavior mediate the impact of conflict and are related to emotional security. Security is strengthened during conflict when there is calm discussion, support, humor, problem solving, and physical and verbal affection. Reactivity, perception of family relationships, and behavioral responses to conflict are components of security.

Applying attachment theory to conflict, Davies and Cummings (1994) note that parental conflict, especially destructive forms, undermines emotional security and healthy family relationships. These effects are evidenced by emotional, social, cognitive, and physiological dysregulation. A way to gauge these components is to observe a child's emotional reactions during conflict. Emotional security theory defines those behaviors that elicit positive versus negative emotional reactions during conflict as "constructive."

Exposing children to constructive conflict in families can be beneficial and lead to feelings of security. For instance, McCoy, Cummings, and Davies (2013) found that constructive marital conflict was correlated with positive school adjustment. Thus, constructive conflict management between parents can provide a needed modeling of healthy ways to manage conflict.

Since conflict activates attachment style, those with secure attachments tend to see conflict as less threatening and to recover better from conflict compared to those with avoidant or anxious attachments (Pistole & Arricale, 2003; Salvatore, Steele, Kuo, Simpson, & Collins, 2011). Since attachment styles are learned patterns of behavior, they can be unlearned. Generational patterns can be changed.

Generally speaking, the following are true when it comes to attachment style:

- Secure family members have low avoidance of conflict and low anxiety.
- Preoccupied family members who worry about what others think need constant approval, doubt their own worth, and have anxiety around conflict.

- Family members who deny a need for closeness and minimize the importance of relationships avoid conflict and have little anxiety over doing so.
- Family members who are fearful and don't trust are highly insecure, tend to avoid conflict, and are anxious about it.

Finally, God reminds us that we are secure in our relationship with him (John 10:28–30). We are constantly on God's mind (Ps. 139:2), and he delights in us (Ps. 37:4; Zeph. 3:17). He promises never to leave or abandon us (Heb. 13:5). Therefore, we can live in the peace of knowing that as we work on our family relationships, we have a secure base in Christ. The personal, living, and active God exchanges insecurities for his security. He provides the ultimate corrective experience for insecurity and ambivalence for all family members.

Conflict Styles

Family members also have conflict styles that have been learned over time. The handling of conflict is based on unspoken and spoken rules. These rules govern the way family members communicate concerning conflict (Gottman,1993; Gottman & Levenson, 2002).

Gottman conflict styles. Gottman identifies three functional styles of couple conflict—avoidant, volatile, and validating—and one dysfunctional style—hostile. According to Gottman (1993), it is the mismatch of these styles that makes conflict more problematic. For example, the avoider wants to avoid, but the volatile

wants to pursue, often in an intense way that is overwhelming to the avoider. When family members identify their styles, they can look for mismatches. Once mismatches are discovered, members must find ways to accommodate each other to work through differences.

Avoidant style. Avoiders prefer not to deal directly with conflict nor talk about their differences. If they present their side, they do not push for more to happen. They make no attempt to persuade or convince the other. They are not angry regarding avoidance but believe that the positives of their relationships outweigh the negatives. Thus, they focus on the positives, prefer to avoid conflict, and tend to believe time will resolve most issues.

Volatile style. This style is often evidenced by passionate, competitive, and intense words. Volatiles are clear about their opinions and have no problem arguing and persuading. Sometimes during conflict they laugh, but then they go back to disagreeing. Volatiles show both positive and negative emotions but manage to keep warmth and positive feelings from overtaking negative ones. Two people who are volatile types deal with differences head-on and see themselves as equals. At times they can be aggressive with each other. Their style is to be honest and to use conflict to better understand each other and strengthen their relationship. Even though their eruptions can be dramatic, they don't inflict emotional pain on each other and lovingly reconcile.

Validating style. Validators prefer to discuss difficult issues in a way that uses self-control and brings solutions. They want to understand the other and make empathic statements that validate the other's opinions and emotions. They listen and show support. In the end, validators compromise. Busby and Holman (2009) determined that a validating style is superior to other styles in terms of couple satisfaction and stability.

Hostile style. People with a hostile style are defensive, critical, and contemptuous. They typically blame others and personally attack both character and behavior. This leads to a lack of connection and over time creates major problems in relationships—separation, divorce, loneliness, and unhappiness. This is a problematic style that leads to significant difficulties like detachment and disengagement.

Thomas-Kilmann conflict styles. Thomas (1992) developed a conflict taxonomy that is similar to the above but includes five conflict-handling styles (avoider, competitive, collaborative, compromiser, and accommodator) classified according to two underlying dimensions of intent—competition and collaboration styles. According to Thomas (1992), family members can use all five styles to handle conflict but rely on one more than the others given their temperament and experiences.

Out of this taxonomy, Thomas and Kilmann (1974) developed an instrument that assesses behavior in conflict situations and can be given to family members to help identify their styles. The instrument looks at two factors, assertiveness and cooperativeness. These two dimensions of behavior are used to define five conflict styles. Each of these styles has advantages and disadvantages in interpersonal situations.

Assessing styles can help family members be aware of their patterns and explore alternatives when their style isn't working. Since the avoider style is discussed as part of Gottman's conflict styles, we'll begin with the competitive style.

Competitive style. The competitive style is one in which members go after what they want, regardless of the needs of others. It is an "I win, you lose," type of style that challenges family cohesion. This style isn't effective in terms of deepening intimacy. A competitive style can easily become problematic when a person pulls out all the stops in order to win. Competitive tactics include lying, sarcasm, denial, attacking, criticizing, denigrating, and threatening. Basically, it is doing whatever it takes to come out on top even at the expense of the other person. A little competition may stimulate two people to work on a problem, but this style itself isn't conducive to building safety and trust.

Collaborative style. A collaborating style utilizes assertiveness but also cooperation. This conflict style looks for the resolving of difference in a way that satisfies all parties. It is based on trust and self-disclosure. Collaborators learn from each other by digging in and exploring issues around conflict.

Compromising style. Related but not the same is the compromise style in which there is win and lose for family members. This style is usually characterized by partially meeting the needs of each person involved in the conflict. A compromiser looks for middle-ground solutions, splits the difference between two positions, and makes concessions.

Accommodating style. The accommodating style fits those who are naturally more agreeable than others. They usually concede during conflict if the other person makes a good argument. People who accommodate are able and willing to give up their own goals and ideas for the sake of working together. They make adjustments or give in but run the risk of building resentment because their needs are not considered. So while accommodation is a positive relationship trait, it has to be balanced with the expression of needs. Accommodation and compromise do help keep the peace but should be used when a person feels he or she can live with the solution. Otherwise resentment may grow. When a family member is not assertive but cooperative, she is accommodating and yielding to another family member's point of view. The demands of others are met, but the individual's needs are not.

In both the Gottman and Thomas-Kilmann models, the importance of identifying a primary style and assessing the use of that style is useful for conflict management. Family members can recognize the mismatch and work toward accommodating each other's styles.

A conversational orientation is one that allows family members to be open and conversational regarding feelings, attitudes, and the like. A conformity orientation is one that does not allow open conversation but is built on having the same beliefs. When a family has both a high conversational and conformity orientation, they are considered consensual. They go for consensus but do so by discussing issues in an open way. In these families, emotional expression is welcomed and support is provided. However, they do not want disagreement.

Families characterized by high conversational orientation and low conformity allow open talk but don't push conformity. These families are considered pluralistic. They welcome disagreement and discussion, but because conformity is not required, negative emotion is not vetted. When the conversational orientation is low and conformity is high, these protective families want obedience and not much talk. Since there isn't much communication, family members avoid and use negative emotions in direct and indirect fighting.

Finally, a family with low conversation orientation and low conformity is characterized by low interactions and considered to be laissez-faire. Family members are not emotionally connected, so conflict rarely comes into play.

Parenting Styles

In addition to understanding the conflict and attachment styles of each family member, the way parents deal with conflict often relates to the style of parenting they employ. Parenting styles can be defined as those behaviors and attitudes that determine the emotional climate of the way parents and children interact (Seigler, Deloache, & Eisenberg, 2006). Baumrind (1973) categorized parenting styles into three basic types: authoritarian, authoritative, and permissive. These styles relate to the warmth, support, and acceptance offered to a child, as well as the degree of parental control (Maccoby & Martin, 1983).

Authoritative parents express warmth, support, and nurturing but also exercise a balance of control and demands. Authoritarian parents are low on warmth and use a great deal of control. This type of family environment often leads to competition (Takeuchi &Takeuchi, 2008). Permissive parents are high on warmth and acceptance but have low control. Of the three, authoritative parenting is the parenting style believed to be best for children's outcomes related to school achievement, adjustment, and self-efficacy. Parent training can help parents make changes in their parenting approaches and adopt a more authoritative style.

Conflict can develop when parents have different parenting styles and disagree as to how to parent. For example, if a permissive parent wants to allow a child more freedom and independence, and an authoritarian parent believes this is not a good idea, conflict erupts over the amount of freedom given to the child. Such parenting differences have an impact on children, and they may feel distressed, confused, and not supported by their families (Kerr & Bowen, 1988). Therefore, one of the goals of family work is to assess parenting styles and work toward developing a more authoritative parenting style.

For this to happen, assessing each partner's values, experiences, and beliefs related to their own upbringing is necessary. Begin by asking questions related to family of origin, and how each partner was parented. Ask questions like "Who was the disciplinarian? Who made the rules? What happened when one parent disagreed?" Talk about the primary values

each parent holds. Then help each partner see where differences exist and how these differences may result in their own conflict and conflict with their children. Next, talk about the different parenting styles and the impact of each on parent-child relationships. Finally, merge the two styles into a cooperative or compromising effort that has the best interest of the children in mind. When children see their parents operating with a unified style, conflict decreases.

Stages of Conflict

According to Galvin, Braitwaite, and Bylund (2016), family conflict follows six different stages: (1) The first stage, prior conditions stage, considers the history of the relationship because historical issues can trigger conflict for any number of reasons. (2) The frustration awareness stage is characterized by frustration over a blocked need or concern. (3) The active conflict stage is when the conflict is apparent based on verbal and nonverbal messages given. (4) The solution or non-solution stage is when parties either find a solution or the issue remains unresolved. (5) The follow-up stage is defined as the actions that follow the conflict and affect future interactions. (6) The resolution stage is the final stage in which the conflict no longer exists or doesn't impact the family. During these progressive stages, family members can disengage, give in, shift the focus, or be interrupted by outside people as well. The therapist helps keep family conflict from derailing and promotes engagement from the beginning stage to the end.

CASE STUDIES

Case Study One: Family Conflict

Jim and Susan are parents to twenty-one-year-old Sarah. Sarah is an only child who graduated high school with honors. She now attends a university several hours away and has visited home only a few times during her first two years at college. Jim is retired military and has a job in cyber security. Susan is a stay-at-home mom who has taken on odd jobs to help pay for family expenses. The family is Caucasian with mixed European ethnic roots. Sarah has a history of bulimia beginning in high school, but she was able to keep her symptoms under control and a secret from her parents. Sarah describes her father as controlling and demanding, requiring obedience to rigid rules. Her mom is passive and rarely asserts herself in the marriage or in family decisions. Sarah began losing significant weight at college, vomiting several times a day. Her weight loss was so apparent that the student health nurse referred her for inpatient care at the university hospital. There she was diagnosed with bulimia nervosa and major depression disorder and was hospitalized.

With Sarah's permission, her parents were notified and asked to attend regular family therapy sessions. When questioned about family conflict, Sarah replied, "We don't have it. It's my dad's way or no way. He is controlling, but mostly fair, although I don't think my mom likes his rules. He is easily upset when either of us does things apart from his way. My mom just lives with it, but she doesn't look happy. In fact, she seems sad most days. She has been in and out of psychiatric hospitals for most of my life."

During the first session, a family genogram was drawn with information provided by all members. The father was positive for substance use and the mom for depression. When questioned about the father's drinking behavior, the mom said little, and Sarah talked about how much her dad's drinking bothered her mom. The dad denied that drinking was a problem. Furthermore, all three family members had not discussed Sarah's bulimia or the mom's multiple past hospitalizations for depression. Conflict avoidance was the style used to deal with numerous conflicts between different family members. In terms of attachment styles, Sarah had formed an anxious, preoccupied attachment with her parents, feeling emotionally hungry for nurturance and support. Her family life-cycle transition to independence was difficult. She constantly worried about her mom's unhappiness and felt responsible to fix her. How would her mom function without her? And she was afraid to oppose her dad.

Sarah's mom described a fearful and avoidant attachment, having grown up with a verbally abusive father with whom she had distance because he frightened her. Sarah's father's attachment style was dismissive and avoidant. Whenever the mom tried to question his rigid rules, he would emotionally pull away and drink more frequently. As a result, she withdrew. Emotional distance characterized the couple's relationship.

During the second session, the father tried to reason with his daughter regarding her weight loss and vomiting. The mother remained silent regarding the daughter's symptoms but chose to comment on her husband's drinking. When she did, tension filled the room. She told her husband that he had no right to address the daughter's eating disorder when he was using alcohol in the same manner. Sarah inserted herself into the discussion (triangulation) and made a bargain with her father. If he would stop drinking for a week, she would stop vomiting. He agreed, stating it would be easy since he didn't have a problem. The next week, the parents returned for the family session. The father reported no drinking for the entire week. Sarah reported a significant decrease in vomiting. The mom said nothing and appeared withdrawn. The day following the session, the father called the family therapist to tell her that the mom was hospitalized for a suicide attempt. What happened?

Case Study Two: Marital Conflict

Daniel and Rachel found themselves constantly bickering in front of their children. Voices were raised. Unkind words were spoken. Blame was prevalent. Tension filled the air. Both were unhappy and considering divorce. The children often found themselves in the cross fire of disagreements. Unless the family made changes, the likelihood of divorce was a reality.

In terms of conflict styles, David and Rachel were both volatile, bordering on hostile at times. While their styles matched, the level of contention was high and filled with contempt. Their critical, defensive, and contemptuous behaviors left the pair disillusioned with the marriage. The two found themselves moving apart from each other.

In reviewing their histories, both came from chaotic homes in which fighting and bickering were the norm. Fighting was viewed as a way to stay connected to each other in the relationship. As long as they were fighting, they were talking. Yet the consequences of regular fights left both feeling those insecure attachments from childhood. Both adult spouses remembered times when they thought their parents would divorce. Rachel vowed she would not fight like her parents and hated the way she was behaving. She talked about how her sisters cowered under the harsh words of her father and often hid after dinner. She was the sibling who tried to take a stand against the fighting. Yet her father's constant criticism left her feeling insecure.

In Rachel's current marriage, she blamed David for instigating fights and not helping to calm her down. David knew he was acting like his father and also reminding Rachel of her father, but he didn't know how else to handle disagreements. He, too, recalled a childhood of feeling unsure as to whether his parents would go the distance in their marriage. When he was in high school, his parents divorced. He was afraid Rachel and he were headed down the same road. Both of his brothers were divorced.

When the couple came for martial therapy, both acknowledged childhood pain around their parents' fighting. They were aware that their behavior followed a similar pattern but didn't know how they arrived at such a negative place and wanted better ways to deal with conflict.

While their conflict styles matched, little was resolved, and both were growing more negative in the relationship.

STRATEGIES, INTERVENTIONS, AND TECHNIQUES FOR FAMILY CONFLICT

Conflict is one of the strongest indicators when it comes to assessing psychological adjustment in children and family (Amato & Keith, 1991). In fact, the risk for a number of emotional and behavioral problems is found in exposure to family conflict (Grych & Fincham, 1990). As noted, a family's ability to navigate conflict impacts the adjustment of all members.

In fact, destructive family conflict can result in higher rates of depression, anxiety, and alcohol use among the adults (Cummings & Davies, 2002). These outcomes have potential negative effects on both children and adults in terms of physical and psychological health, well-being, and family relationships. For example, Keller, Cummings, Davies, and Mitchell (2008) found that destructive marital conflict tied to parental drinking negatively impacts children, family functioning, and adjustment. While individuals are responsible for their use of substances or eating disorder symptoms, disorders develop in the context of relationships.

Assessing Disorders in Relationship Contexts

In case study one, the family originally organized around the father's drinking and controlling behavior. The mother withdrew and became depressed, feeling powerless to make her husband change. His rigid approach to relationships also triggered fear and avoidance from her childhood. This passivity led to depression, as she felt powerless to make changes in the way Sarah and she were treated. Sarah internalized self-doubt and felt responsible for her mom's unhappiness. This exacerbated her eating disorder and depression. The observed helplessness of her mother made her anxious and depressed. She felt equally powerless.

Growing up in a family in which problems were avoided contributed to Sarah hiding her struggles and maintaining the eating disorder. She knew that her mom was sad about her dad's drinking and emotional disconnection, and she didn't want to add to her misery. In addition, Sarah was insecure about leaving home and developing independence (the family stage of launching). While she wanted to be more self-sufficient, the stress and pressure of decision making, problem solving, and dealing with other relationships resulted in more bingeing and purging. She had little success negotiating decisions with her father. The eating disorder was an outlet for the stress and the powerlessness she felt.

In the hospital, Sarah became more in touch with her emotions and need to separate from her parents. She realized that she felt guilty for leaving her mom to go to college. She did not trust her father to be attuned to her mom's emotional needs. She also realized that she avoided conflict with her father, fearing he was too powerful to confront. Her developmental task was to become separate but attached. To do so required Sarah to address multiple issues.

Sarah's dad did not know how to deal with his wife's growing depression and drank even more in response to the increasingly emotionally distant relationship. In an effort to be more assertive about her own needs, Sarah decided to confront her father's drinking. As Sarah began to address the conflict with her father, I commented on how Sarah and her father behaved more like a marital couple than the mom and father dyad. The mom sat silent and allowed Sarah to confront her husband. Structurally, Sarah was functioning as the marital partner, not the daughter trying to emotionally leave home. She was triangulated into the marital intimacy problems. Sarah's decision to insert herself into the marital conflict by making a bargain with her father to stop drinking failed to account for the repercussions on the family system. Unconsciously, Sarah would do what her mother could not do—be the empowered wife who could get her father to stop drinking. While her step to assert herself with her father was a move toward more independence, it had systemic consequences.

Sarah's mom, rather than Sarah, needed to be empowered to address the marital conflicts of drinking and distance. When Sarah assumed her mom's role and had success getting her dad to stop drinking for a week (a task her mom had never accomplished), the mom felt even more failed in her attempts to provoke a change of behavior in her husband. This feeling of failure and hopelessness prompted the suicide attempt. The mother became "the patient" around which the family would need to rally. However, this incident pro-

vided an opportunity to restructure the marital subsystem and detriangulate Sarah to work on her goals of separation/individuation. The spouses had an avoidance-avoidance pattern, so I needed to engage the mom and dad in the marital conflict. To do this, I supported the mom's concern regarding the seriousness of the drinking behavior and encouraged her to talk about the impact the drinking had on their relationship. She was lonely and wanted more connection with her husband but was unsure how to accomplish this.

I also validated the importance of the husband accepting his wife's influence and asked if he thought her concerns were valid. He did but expressed uncertainty as to how to deal with his depressed wife. Work on the insecure and dismissive attachments of the couple ensued. When the mom talked about the impact of drinking and distancing, and her husband listened, her depression began to lift. The husband agreed to address the drinking without being dismissive of his wife. With my help, the husband was able to talk about the loneliness and fear he felt regarding his wife's depression—a feeling that often cued his drinking. I also helped connect these feelings to familiar ones from both childhoods, helping the couple see the attachment histories and their influence on family relationships. Sarah was now free to focus on her eating disorder and related issues. Once the drinking was addressed, the parents were able to assist Sarah in the task of providing appropriate support and nurturing related to the eating disorder. Because of her dad's sobriety and attachment work, Sarah was able to emotionally release her mom to his care and was free to pursue her own development. The mom's depression continued to lift as she felt more competent and empowered to address her husband and nurture her daughter. In this process, the family was able to work on their conflict skills, changing from avoidance or distance to a model of engagement that allowed all members to take responsibility and work at more effective interpersonal strategies.

Because family members are often locked in dysfunctional patterns around conflict that perpetuate problems, your role as counselor is to bring about change by affirming strengths, monitoring distance and closeness, keeping emotional reactivity down, addressing attachment needs, identifying conflict styles and stage, addressing family life- cycle issues, and reframing experiences.

Psychological Models Promoting Family Change

In case one, the family work utilized elements of emotionally focused family therapy (EFFT) to deal with affect and attachment issues, the Maudsley approach to provide emotional support and guidance regarding the eating disorder, structural and Bowenian family therapy to strengthen subsystems and support separation/ individuation, and dialectical behavior therapy (DBT) to boost interpersonal effectiveness skills.

Building skills with dialectical behavior therapy. Dialectical behavior therapy (DBT) offers skill training modules that can be used in a number of individual and interpersonal areas that relate

to conflict work (Keller, Cummings, & Davies, 2008). In cases like the above, the skill training components of DBT were very helpful given a lack of interpersonal skills needed to work through problems. The skills of mindfulness and tolerating distress, interpersonal effectiveness skills, and emotional regulation were helpful in strengthening engagement and regulating affect. Each skill in the DBT model is composed of specific strategies taught in a group or individual session. For example, the skill of tolerating distress has four strategies: (1) how to distract oneself, (2) how to self-soothe, (3) how to develop a pros and cons list that helps one understand the benefit of tolerating pain, and (4) how to improve the moment via positive mental imagery. The "how tos" are broken down into specific behavioral steps, taught, practiced, and recorded. They are then reviewed with the therapist for discussion and further application.

Family Therapy

The Maudsley approach is a family-based treatment developed for adolescents with eating disorders and young adults living at home (Lock, LeGrange, Agras, & Dare, 2001). Parents play an active but positive role in dealing with a child who has an eating disorder. This approach allows the family to participate in the patient's recovery by helping the child with weight stabilization, returning the control of eating back to the patient, and establishing a healthy identity. Instead of coming together to bicker over their daughter's dysfunction, the parents united on their parenting role and worked as a healthy subsystem. They shifted the attention to a positive parenting model that was collaborative.

The family met for twenty treatment sessions over a twelve-month period. The therapist encouraged Sara's parents to help restore Sara's weight. During the beginning of treatment, a family meal was conducted to observe family interaction patterns and assist the parents in helping their daughter eat more. Parents were coached to be empathetic but firm about the need to eat. The therapist modeled this position, showing parents how to avoid being critical but affirming their child's struggle with eating. When the child was eating more, maintaining weight gain, and not restricting food, phase two of the approach was initiated.

During phase two, therapy shifted to the impact of the eating disorder on identity and autonomy. Appropriate parental boundaries were established, and a reorganization around the child's growing autonomy was addressed. Overall, the parents played an active role in the child's healing with the coaching of the therapist.

Shifting the family pattern from one of conflict avoidance to one of engagement was critical. This family used conflict avoidance to resolve tension and anxiety. Family conflict included marital and parenting issues, as well as family challenges related to untreated mental health issues (substance use, eating disorders, and depression).

Other types of family therapy can be used to improve communication and change dysfunctional patterns related to a number of problems, including conflict.

Most models of family therapy address interactional patterns, communication styles, and individual issues that impact the system. Recurrent family patterns are identified, and individual behavior is understood in the context of the family system. Family members are repositioned to function in more flexible ways and establish a new homeostasis.

Detriangulating. Structural and Bowenian work included detriangulating Sarah from the marital triangle and strengthening the marital relationship. Sarah repeatedly involved herself in conflict issues between her parents as a way of dissipating tension in the family. According to Kerr and Bowen (1988), families are composed of a system of interlocking triangles. This process of triangulation into parental conflict has been shown to internalize and externalize problems concurrently over time, thus contributing to Sarah's sense of responsibility (appraisal) and emotional dysregulation characterized by eating disorder patients (Grych, 1998). Sarah's appraisal (thoughts), emotional process, and triangulation played roles in mediating her parents' conflict. The strategy was to take Sarah out of the middle of marital conflict and redirect spouses to address each other.

Finding a Voice, Sense of Self, and Mastery

Furthermore, a mediating factor in conflict management is a person's ability to execute action that meets his or her goals. This idea relates to Bandura's concept of self-efficacy and is important in the development of self and self-image (Bandura,

1977). According to Canary and Canary (2013), interparental conflict affects a child's self-efficacy in terms of believing that she can manage conflict situations. The higher the self-efficacy, the more adept the child is with positive strategies to manage conflict. Thus, counseling also focused on Sarah's development of a stronger sense of self and use of her voice as she continued to separate through a healthier attachment with her parents. She was challenged to identify her needs, voice them, and practice autonomous behavior even if she failed.

Affect Regulation to De-escalate the Negative

To improve emotional security in this family's relationships, emotion-focused family therapy (EFFT) was chosen because it combines affect regulation and attachment theories with systemic and experiential approaches. It is based on the assumption that negative interactional patterns are reflective of emotional states and attachment issues (Johnson, Maddeaux, & Blouin, 1998). The goal is to reestablish connection between family members by creating new emotional and interactive experiences. Focusing on the creation of secure attachment, family members are helped to regulate emotions, problem solve, and communicate (Johnson & Lee, 2000).

To accomplish the goals of EFFT, I worked with the family to de-escalate negative interactional patterns and affect. In the case above, this was done by validating the mother's sadness over her husband's drinking and by talking about her desire to connect with her husband. This led to new ways for her to engage with her husband in the therapy room. When the husband was able to talk about his anxiety over his wife's sadness and ambivalence regarding intimacy, he softened and became less controlling and distancing. For the first time, underlying needs of intimacy and attachment were addressed.

Changing the interactional patterns. While this case evidenced an avoider-avoider pattern of conflict, the pursuer-withdrawer pattern is a common pattern in many families. Once the withdrawer is able to express needs and wants, engagement increases and the pursuer becomes more vulnerable with needs and wants as well. In this new experience, communication and problem solving improve (Johnson, 2004). New interactions are experienced, consolidated, and integrated. In terms of parent-child interactions, parents then become coaches of resolving conflicts (Johnson & Denton, 2002).

Recall case two, in which Daniel and Rachel were experiencing marital conflict over parenting. Since parents are models for intergenerational transmission of conflict styles and patterns, working on couple conflict benefits all family members. Two approaches are useful in working with attachment histories, conflict styles, negative emotions, and dysfunctional patterns that block a couple's ability to navigate conflict.

The Gottman Method

The first is the Gottman method (Gottman & Silver, 2012), in which couples are coached to manage their arousal and interactional patterns. The emphasis is placed on disarming conflicting verbal messages, removing barriers that result in conflict gridlock, increasing empathy and intimacy, and expressing respect and affection. Daniel and Rachel had volatile conflict styles that resulted in an escalation of conflict. Without intervention, the escalation of conflict could move the couple toward divorce. Thus, the couple needed to decrease arousal patterns. One strategy toward that end is to teach the couple to self-soothe using the techniques below.

De-escalate conflict. During conflict, a therapeutic goal is to down-regulate negative affect to keep conflict from escalating. In that process, Gottman identifies negative cycles that maintain attachment insecurity, with the aim of breaking the cycles and uncovering unacknowledged longings and dreams. He also speaks to the importance of making repairs by using remorse, forgiveness, and other repairs such as humor.

Physically soothe self and partner. In keeping with the Gottman method, the counselor explained to the couple that physiological changes in the body take place when emotions run high (e.g., increased heart rate, secretion of adrenaline, and an increase in blood pressure). During these physiological changes, it is difficult to maintain a conflict discussion. Thus, Daniel and Rachel were to employ calming strategies when conflict interactions began to escalate. Calming strategies included a short (five- to ten-minute) time-out, deep breathing (three to five minutes), humor, and distraction or refocus to reengage the thinking part of the brain. Both would take a brief time-out and count backward from ten—a distraction technique that worked to diffuse their emotion and decrease their heart rates. Once calmer, they would reengage the conflict topic.

Reduce the four horsemen. When couples fight, videotaping the interaction is helpful. The Gottman method includes observation and assessment of a conflict interaction looking for the presence of the "four horsemen" (criticism, defensiveness, contempt, and stonewalling). Couples are coached to reduce criticism with a gentle startup; replace defensiveness with taking responsibility; replace contempt with humility, appreciation, and respect; and stop stonewalling by using self-soothing techniques. During the course of therapy with Daniel and Rachel, the therapist stopped interactions by using a bell to signal that one of the four horsemen was in operation. The couple had to continue the conflict dialogue without the negativity and reengage in a new way.

Up-regulate positive affect during conflict. Up-regulate positive affect during conflict as a way to balance positives and negatives in the relationship. For this couple, turning toward each other when conflict presented and limiting the use of the four horsemen and replacing them with the antidotes listed above was important.

Build positivity during nonconflict times. This was done by attending to the couple's friendship and intimacy and building positivity to strengthen connection. They needed a positive base from which to address problems. Having positive interactions with a partner in order to build a "bank account" of positivity from which to draw on during more challenging moments is vital. Through Gottman's research, he observed that healthy couples have a five-to-one ratio of positives to negatives in their relationships. Couples do best with conflict when they have a positive feeling about their relationship. To build this positivity, the couple was directed to build a love map for each other. Love maps relate to how much a couple knows the intimate world of the other and can recall positive moments of the relationship. In addition, the expression of fondness and admiration was encouraged.

In his research, Gottman discovered that 69 percent of couples' conflict does not get resolved. Therefore, his method teaches couples to use conflict management skills and acceptance when dealing with ongoing conflicts. For example, Daniel and Rachel identified a conflict related to disciplining their children. They had little agreement on parenting styles, which led to loud fighting in front of the children. Prior to beginning intervention regarding the specific conflict, I asked each of them to state three to five things they appreciated about the other. The strategy of stating appreciation and gratitude was used to build positivity prior to addressing the conflict.

The couple was then coached not to persuade, problem solve, or compromise when the conflict was raised. The goal was to delay responding to a discipline issue until both could calm down, talk about consequences, and deliver the consequences as a united parenting front. First, Daniel was to listen to Rachel's thoughts, feelings, and needs or requests related to the issue. Once Rachel felt that Daniel ful-

ly understood her position, it was Daniel's turn to speak and Rachel's turn to listen. In this form of active listening, each partner repeats what he or she heard from the other. Both the speaker and listener are responsible for staying calm. Daniel wanted to deliver punishment to the children immediately, fearing that any delay would make the punishment ineffective. He did not feel there was time to consult with Rachel when a child was acting out, but his punishment was often severe and delivered harshly. Rachel similarly stated that swift punishment was key to effective results and did not want to delay action until she could talk to Daniel. Rachel remembers how ineffective her mother was with punishment because she was too dependent on her father to make decisions. Consequently, she felt her children would not respect her and learn to listen to her.

To prevent escalation and flooding of emotion (Gottman & Silver, 2012), a pulse oximeter was used to measure heart rates and oxygen concentration during a conflict discussion. A person is flooded with emotion, inhibiting listening, when the heart rate exceeds 100 beats per minute (bpm) or the oxygen concentration falls below 75 percent (in which case one should go to the hospital, as organ failure begins to occur below 80 percent). When Daniel and Rachel began to talk about discipline issues, they had to stop talking and utilize their calming techniques for twenty minutes. After they calmed down, they reengaged in the conflict discussion with more awareness of the issue, tolerance of the other's position, and better understanding of what was driving their actions.

Rather than criticize the other, each partner stated his or her wishes in neutral terms as a need. Being able to stay calm and listen was key and helped build empathy.

Daniel and Rachel were able to acknowledge that they heard each other and had a good understanding of each other's positions. Their next step was to problem solve and negotiate their differences. During this time, it was important for each spouse to stay open and consider compromise. Rachel acknowledged that she often responded too quickly and later regretted her actions. She was open to slowing down and discussing consequences with Daniel when possible. Both agreed they needed to deliver consequences in a calmer fashion. Daniel was willing to pause and consult with his wife as he worried that he was too reactive and harsh. A compromise was to wait five minutes, have a brief discussion regarding the consequence in order to come to consensus, and deliver the consequence in a calm manner.

The above goals are accomplished through a detailed method based on Gottman's (1999) sound relationship house theory. This theory stresses the importance of knowing your partner through friendship, expressing fondness and admiration, turning toward the partner, and building a positive relationship when conflict is not present. Six conflict skills are taught to the couple: beginning with a soft startup, accepting the wife's influence, making effective repairs during conflict, de-escalating, compromising, and learning to soothe the self and the partner. The Gottman method has several levels of training for clinicians to learn and apply in detail.

Daniel and Rachel realized that they rarely showed fondness or admiration toward each other and were no longer attuned to each other's needs. They were so wrapped up in fighting that they lost sight of positive expressions of love and affection. Thus, I assigned the two to recapture their friendship by doing things they used to enjoy doing together, talking about positive moments of their day, and checking in with each other as to how they were feeling. Rachel worked on beginning a conflict discussion by gently asking to talk about an issue. This was easier for her once she reengaged with her husband on a friendship level. Daniel realized that his wife's input was important when dealing with the children now that they were able to address problems in a better way. When hurtful words were said, each apologized, agreeing to tame their tongues (cf. James 3:1–12) and exercise forgiveness. Often the couple resorted to a brief time-out to practice calming down in order to listen. Both had reactive styles of responding to issues and wanted to make changes.

The Gottman method also teaches couples how to process a fight using a six-step approach that includes sharing feelings, describing each partner's subjective reality, sharing attachment issues, checking emotional arousal (flooding), acknowledging responsibility, and problem solving a way to make the fight better. These steps lead to a new experience in which spouses are attuned, engaged, and responsive, operating from a secure base from which to have future conflict discussions. These steps were helpful for Daniel and Rachel.

Creating a Safe Haven

This couple was also helped using Sue Johnson's (1996) emotion-focused therapy (EFT), in which a sense of safety and support was built as the couple better understood the role of emotions in their relationship and created safe havens for corrective experiences to occur. Johnson's EFT targets the building of secure attachments and repairing emotional hurts and wounds. I engaged in emotional coaching by translating feelings and needs of the person during the therapy interactions. I explained and taught constructive alternatives to ineffective patterns of interactions.

I discussed with Daniel and Rachel their fighting pattern of attack and attack. Both used the attack mode to avoid painful and difficult emotions. I then explored feelings around the attacks and learned that Daniel felt like a failure in that he was yelling just like his father. He recalled how painful it was to hear his dad yell at his mom. She would cry and not talk for days. Rachel talked about watching her sisters cower under the harshness of her dad. She was determined to fight back and not become depressed like her sisters. The pain that each partner felt in their own child experiences helped build empathy toward the other. As a result, they were open to changing their attack-attack mode of dealing with conflict. Fighting was reframed in terms of attachment; it kept them engaged, connected, and feeling strong. Moreover, fighting did not resolve issues and had the potential to activate the negative feelings they had as children in their own children. This awareness led to a better understanding of each other's needs,

a deeper intimacy, and more positive conversations as to how they could help each other feel securer and more connected without fighting.

Part of the work is to clarify emotional responses associated with underlying attachment issues and interactional positions, validate attachment needs and fears, heighten key experiences, build empathy, and clarify feelings and needs. Similar to the Gottman method, this approach leads to emotional engagement and a safe haven in which to address conflict.

Make Repairs

Both Johnson (2003) and Gottman (2011) speak to the importance of making effective repairs when conflict is in play. Daniel and Rachel felt forgiveness was an important part of the repair process. Neither liked the actions and words they used when they became reactive during a fight. Both recognized the power of those words to linger long after a fight ended. Thus, they often had to apologize and work on controlling their words. Eventually the couple used prayer to begin a conflict discussion and found this helpful in staying calm and respectful to each other. In addition, couples and family members who can be empathetic when negative emotions arise, tolerating those emotions and developing a better understanding of why those feelings occur, build an environment conducive to dialoguing about conflict.

Build Friendships

In family assessment, an often overlooked area is the role friendships can play when it comes to reducing stress. Here is an example of how a conflicted couple can behave as friends, adding a needed layer of support to family members.

Rachel: It seems like my dad was so critical of what I did. He was constantly on me about my grades and studying. This just made me want to yell back at him.
Daniel: Maybe he really cared about your future. Next time you talk to your dad, maybe you could ask him why he pressed you so hard. Maybe you can both understand each other a little better. I would rather have a dad who cares than one who doesn't. And trust me, dads can help when you really need them!
Rachel: I guess you're right. I know he cares. I should try to talk to him instead of avoiding him. He is important to me. I will try. Thanks for listening. I know you understand because your dad yelled a lot at you.

Friendships can be a source of emotional support and provide a secure base for individual family members when conflict occurs. Thus, the ability to develop friendships and use them for support can have a positive impact on those experiencing family conflict as well (Johnson, 2003; Rogers, 2004). For Rachel, having a husband who was able to talk through problems outside of the marriage offered stress relief and support.

Finally, it should be noted that when conflict is harmful and threatens the security of a family member, the unsafe behavior must stop. Unsafe behavior includes destructive behaviors such as physical and verbal aggression, withdrawal/avoidance, verbal and nonverbal anger, and insults. The safety of family members must be considered before conflict interventions are made.

Assigning the Family Practice

Structured practice often helps families with conflict skills and interactions. When a family has the goal of improving conflict skills, this model can be explained with a couple or all family members. Here is a ten-step process that can be given to a family as a homework assignment. When a minor conflict arises, ask the family to follow these steps:

1. Arrange a time and place to discuss the conflict.
2. Have each person state the conflict issue in objective, behavioral terms.
3. Stay focused on the issue, not on past offenses or problems.
4. Establish guidelines to respect each other in the dialogue, for example, no name-calling or yelling.
5. Allow family members to take a time-out or a moment to calm down if emotions run high.
6. Brainstorm solutions and rank which of the solutions makes sense to try.
7. Anticipate problems with each solution, and identify the obstacles.
8. Implement a solution, and get feedback.
9. Evaluate the solution. Did the conflict resolve? Why or why not? Were there underlying issues that were not addressed? Try again with a different solution or approach if needed.
10. Evaluate the process. Did family members feel comfortable bringing up difficult issues? Why or why not? Was the

conflict handled in a positive way? Did the conflict keep from escalating? Will family members be willing to try this again?

Becoming a Peacemaker

God calls us to be peacemakers in our families (Matt. 5:9). Making peace includes regularly addressing conflict issues. Families may confuse making peace with avoidance. This was the case with Daniel and Rachel. *At one point, Daniel and Rachel were loudly debating over which of their Christmas parties to attend. Both spouses had office parties scheduled on the same evening. As they continued to discuss the conflict, Daniel's mother, who was standing nearby, inserted herself physically between the couple. She stretched out her arms and said, "Blessed are the peacemakers. Now stop fighting." Daniel and Rachel looked confused. "We are not fighting. We are having a conflict over Christmas parties and working our way through it. Please, let us talk, because we want to come to a decision." When the dialogue ended, Daniel went over to his mom and asked what her reaction was about. Why did she feel a need to stop them from talking? His mom told him that conflict was scary when she was a child. Her father was abusive, and she could not tolerate any disagreements. The Bible has helped her see that she needs to be a peacemaker and stop disagreements. Daniel said, "Mom, I think you have a wrong understanding of what is means to be a peacemaker. Peacemakers don't avoid disagreements. They handle them in ways that honor God."*

Daniel was right. To make peace requires time, respect, patience, humility, listening, and a willingness to change. Here are seven steps to help families address the peace process when family conflict occurs.

1. *Peacemakers make the move toward peace.* The biblical directive in Matthew 18 instructs believers to go to the person with whom they have conflict. This directive prevents triangulation, escalation of the problem, and growing resentment. If the reluctance to confront is based on lack of trust or concerns over escalation, practice in the therapy room will help families build confidence to eventually bring up issues at home. Regardless of which setting, the family should set up a time to discuss the problem and not avoid.

2. *Begin the conflict with prayer.* One way to immediately de-escalate a conflict is to begin with prayer. Prayer calms the physical body as well as prepares the heart to listen. When family members invite God into the problem through prayer, God's wisdom and direction are sought. This is a way to soften hearts and be empowered through the Holy Spirit. This also sets the atmosphere and teaches the family to depend on God in all things.

3. *Listen to understand the perspective of the other person.* Often people who hurt, hurt others and don't listen. Rather than focusing on being right or defending a position, listening to the concerns of those in the conflict informs the issue at hand. When a family member takes the time to understand the perspective of the other person, it builds empathy and reduces reactivity.

The greatest example of this is Jesus. In the middle of his pain on the cross, he focused on us, not his own pain.

4. *Take responsibility.* With conflict, each member needs to look at his or her behavior before pointing a finger at the other. Family members are encouraged to focus on their specific part of the problem. Did they respond well or become defensive, accusatory, or blaming? Did they take a self-centered position? Are they hanging on to anger and unforgiveness? Did they say things that require an apology? Reinforce the idea that members cannot control other people but can control their own reactions. Was the reaction godly? This is the part each of us will be accountable for one day. James 4:1–2 provides insight into the question of what causes fights and quarrels. The answer has to do with the desires that battle within us. Those battles are often our selfish, prideful desires. When family members are self-centered, irritation and conflict increase (cf. Ps. 139:23–24). At the root of much unresolved conflict is pride. Proverbs 13:10 tells us that pride only leads to arguments. When a family member is determined to be right and does not take responsibility for his or her actions, pride is usually at the root. C. S. Lewis (1977) described pride as a spiritual cancer that eats up the very possibility of love, contentment, or even common sense.

5. *Speak the truth in love (Eph. 4:15).* This is reinforced in the Gottman research regarding a soft startup. Proverbs 15:1 says that a soft answer turns away wrath, but a harsh word stirs up anger. When the truth is not spoken in love, it brings hurt, not reconciliation. Scripture tells us that the power of life and death is in words. By a family member's words, he or she can build up or tear down. Peacemakers respect those who disagree and do not tear them down. Colossians 3:8 gives guidance to our words: "But now you must also rid yourselves of all such things as these: anger, rage, malice, slander, and filthy language from your lips."

6. *Forgive often and every time.* At the root of many ongoing conflicts is an unwillingness to forgive each other. Forgiveness is an individual act and does not require reconciliation. It is a step toward reconciliation and a command given by God. It is also a choice and, for many, an emotional process that requires healing. Encourage family members to forgive and ask for forgiveness, for this is a biblical directive and will cause division if not applied.

7. *Work on solutions.* The focus is often to change the other person rather than to work on a conflict solution. When members cannot solve a conflict, they must learn to disagree in respectful ways. Again, Scripture has much to say about how words are used and how to disagree in a godly manner. Peacemakers build a bridge rather than a wall. This happens when a person is kind, loving, empathetic, and filled with God's grace. Peacemakers also look for solutions and are willing to compromise. Peacemakers practice making peace. They allow their children,

friends, and other family members to engage in conflict and move toward conflict resolution. When solutions aren't found, peacemakers work to preserve relationships and at times agree to disagree.

CONCLUSION

Conflict avoidance is not a desired style. Your role is to assist families in developing positive ways to dialogue and interact when conflict arises. Doing so requires attending to issues of power and resources, cultural factors, and individual psychological issues that may be impacting the family system, while assessing attachment styles, conflict styles, the stage of the conflict, and the family development stage. Interventions include elements of EFFT, EFT, DBT, the Gottman method, and structural and Bowenian family therapy. Biblical guidelines that govern individual and interpersonal behavior are helpful in de-escalating negative conflict patterns and making repairs that help families heal, develop secure connections, and become peacemakers.

RECOMMENDED READING

Gottman, J. M., & Silver, N. (2012). *What makes love last? How to build trust and avoid betrayal.* New York, NY: Simon & Schuster.

Johnson, S. M. (1996). *Creating connection: The practice of emotionally focused marital therapy.* Florence, KY: Brunner/Mazel.

Johnson, S. M. (2008). *Hold me tight: Seven conversations for a lifetime of love.* New York, NY: Little, Brown & Co.

Lock, J., Le Grange, D., Agras, W. S., & Dare, C. (2001). *Treatment manual for anorexia nervosa: A family-based approach.* New York, NY: Guilford Press.

McKay, M., Wood, J., & Brantley, J. C. (2010). *Dialectical Behavior Therapy workbook: Practical DBT exercises for learning mindfulness, interpersonal effectiveness, emotion regulation, and distress tolerance.* Oakland, CA: New Harbinger.

Mintle, L. S. (2015). *We need to talk.* Grand Rapids, MI: Baker.

CHAPTER 19

Domestic Violence–Focused Strategies

Lynne M. Baker, PhD

The Lord examines both the righteous and the wicked.
He hates those who love violence.

PSALM 11:5 NLT

Domestic violence, or intimate partner violence, is a widespread occurrence of global proportion. The World Health Organization (WHO) estimates that worldwide, of those women who have been in a relationship, approximately one-third have experienced some form of physical or sexual violence perpetrated by an intimate partner. This information is even more disturbing when one considers the fact that a great many cases of domestic violence remain unreported. As a result of shame, fear, or personal, family, or cultural considerations, women endeavor to handle the situation alone (Baker, 2010a; Sue & Sue, 2013). The impact of domestic violence on children compounds the problem. While domestic violence is not always perpetrated by men against women, women generally form the greater proportion of victims (McAllister & Roberts-Lewis, 2010).

In view of this fact, this chapter addresses domestic violence from the perspective of female victims, although a number of the principles can be used to highlight difficulties within various relationships and assist victims to review their situation and decide on the most appropriate course of action. My desire is that through consideration of the information provided and the strategies outlined, counselors will be able to more effectively assist those who have suffered as a result of domestic violence in their journey toward recovery.

THEOLOGY AND PSYCHOLOGY OF DOMESTIC VIOLENCE

Jesus, described as the Good Shepherd (John 10:11), comes with the promise of abundant life. In stark contrast, domestic violence is a destructive force that results in violation and deprivation. It may therefore be paralleled with the role of the thief whose motivation is not one of love, but is instead self-centered and self-serving, with the intention only to steal, kill, and destroy (John 10:10). As such, domestic violence may be categorized among the works of darkness. To understand domestic violence within this context more effectively equips both the counselor and the client to identify the nature of the behavior and respond in a manner befitting such an affront to divine intention.

An Overview of Domestic Violence

Domestic violence is a heinous violation of someone's humanity. It permeates the very being of an individual to the deepest levels, including but not restricted to physical, emotional, psychological, and spiritual functioning. Domestic violence affects many individuals and families irrespective of race, social standing, or religious faith (McAllister & Roberts-Lewis, 2010; Nason-Clark, 2009; Popescu & Drumm, 2009; Roberts-Lewis & Armstrong, 2010; Todhunter & Deaton, 2010). Domestic violence is a crime, but it is often hidden behind closed doors, cloaked in shame and silence. The client must have great courage to come forward and reveal her personal circumstances.

Domestic violence is an umbrella term that refers to behavior by a perpetrator that is usually designed to exert power and control over the victim. Domestic violence must be understood not as a single event but as a pattern or lifestyle choice for the perpetrator, which can manifest in many different forms, including physical, verbal, sexual, financial, social, and spiritual abuse. While at times a single behavior may appear quite innocuous, such as a look, gesture, or comment, it frequently forms part of a cluster or pattern. Intimidation, domination, and coercion are central themes when considering domestic violence (Baker, 2010a; Cares & Cusick, 2012; Miles, 2000, 2002). Baker (2010a) relates the stories of various women who reported physical abuse occurring only once in their relationship, yet both verbal and emotional abuse were significant, and the threat of further physical violence loomed constantly.

The cycle of violence further confuses the issue. While there are a number of models for the cycle, which vary considerably in the number of stages identified, the three stages originally identified by Walker (1979) are sufficient to grasp the concept. They include the building up of tension, the explosion, and finally a stage of loving contrition. The stage of loving contrition, sometimes referred to as the honeymoon period, is probably the most confusing for the victim. The perpetrator may show remorse, bring gifts of flowers or something else that is meaningful to the victim, beg for forgiveness, and promise not to behave in such a way again. Life may seem very pleasant for a time, and the victim will often want to believe that everything will eventually be fine, but ultimately the cycle continues, resulting in increased power for the perpetrator and disempowerment for the victim. Endeavoring to survive in such conditions has a significant impact on the self-esteem and overall psychological health of the victim and inevitably exerts influence on the decision-making process (Lin-Roark, Church, & McCubbin, 2015).

Children, too, become trapped in the ongoing nature of domestic violence. While the depth of damage to children in both the short and the long term is yet to be fully understood (O'Brien, Cohen, Pooley, & Taylor, 2012), studies indicate that even very young children are at risk of later facing difficulties related to adjustment (Graham-Bermann & Perkins, 2010), together with subsequent health (Kuhlman, Howell, & Graham-Bermann, 2012) and behavioral (Cole & Caron, 2009) issues. Howell, Miller, and Graham-Bermann (2012) also identified a negative impact on the beliefs and attitudes of young children who had witnessed domestic violence. Many thought that violence was "common, justifiable, and often the only way to contend with problems" (p. 951). The impact of domestic violence on children can be more fully grasped if you take the time to imagine the trauma experienced by the young girl whose mother regularly hides under her bed to escape the physical beatings of her father. You might also consider the concerns of a young mother whose three-year-old daughter seemed to be deliberately hurting herself. According to the mother, the child rarely witnessed the explosive outbursts of her father, yet the mother did suspect that her little daughter's behavior was in some way connected with the physical violence and continuing abuse that permeated the household.

Biblical Perspective

The Bible is replete with examples and comments regarding the outcome of violence and the consequences for those who perpetrate it. Violence is clearly depicted as unwise, as sin, and as the pursuit of the wicked (Prov. 4:14–17). The wise are instructed to avoid the behavior and lifestyle of the wicked for whom evil has become a sustaining force. Drawing on Proverbs 4:17, Ross (1991) describes evil as "the diet of the wicked" (p. 925), and those who engage in it will eventually face the judgment of God (Ps. 11:5) (Purkiser, 1967; Schaefer, 2001). VanGemeren (1991) depicts those who practice violence as "disregarding the rights of others" and living "at the expense of others" (p. 486). Referring to Proverbs 10:6, Ross (1991) points out that even the language or speech of violent people cannot be trusted. In short, they are liars.

The prophet Malachi denounces the use of violence (Mal. 2:16) and reprimands those whose lifestyle is one of hypocrisy and questionable moral standing (2:17) (Alden, 1985). The book of Jonah (3:8) links the concepts of evil and violence, and in an effort to escape the judgment of God, the king cries out for the inhabitants of Nineveh to turn away from both evil and violence (Ellison, 1985; Peisker, 1966). Even though this cry pertains to a setting other than domestic violence, it remains clear that even a heathen people had the capacity to realize that violence is something that God neither admires nor desires.

Beyond actual physical violence, the Bible further cautions against allowing anger to rule one's behavior, declaring that the person who yields to anger is a fool (Eccl. 7:9) and creates conflict (Prov. 15:18). Harper (1967) describes anger as "the enemy of clear thinking and sound judgment," with the capacity to "destroy [persons'] interpersonal relations and their reputations as responsible persons" (p. 573). This notion is well supported when considering the account of Nabal and Abigail (1 Sam. 25). Here we see the juxtaposition of the selfishness and anger of the character Nabal against the wisdom and subsequent generosity of his wife, Abigail. The reputation of each was well known within the community. Nabal is described as "surly and mean in his dealings," whereas Abigail is declared to be "an intelligent and beautiful woman" (1 Sam. 25:3). As the story unfolds, we see both characters in action—Nabal fully living up to his reputation as a fool, while Abigail acted quickly and very wisely to prevent disaster from coming on her household. Ultimately Nabal the fool was destroyed even to the point of his own death as a result of his own selfishness, greed, and anger.

From a New Testament perspective, the apostle Paul emphasizes the need for appropriate communication and the avoidance of any speech that may be considered "corrupt" (Eph. 4:29 KJV). Taylor (1965) explains the term "corrupt" here as meaning "putrid, vile, morally unwholesome" (p. 224). Wood (1978) uses the word *rotten* and extends the overall meaning to include "malicious gossip and slander" (p. 65), a concept that is further accentuated in Ephesians 4:31. Similar thoughts are echoed in Colossians 3:8, referring to anger, malice, and even "filthy language," together with the imperative to strip away these things until there is no trace remaining (Nielson, 1965), and discard them as one would a "filthy garment" (Vaughan, 1978, p. 213).

Interestingly, the Bible is equally descriptive regarding the manner in which one should consider another person. Wisdom is to be prized above gold or silver (Prov. 16:16) or expensive jewels (Prov. 8:11). It is strongly linked to understanding (Prov. 3:13; 4:5; 23.23, 24:3). Proverbs 16:32 indicates that the person who "is slow to anger is better than the mighty; and he that ruleth his spirit than he that taketh a city" (KJV). This is the person who is able to exercise restraint over his/her emotions. This is the person who embraces wisdom. The concept of the individual who is able to accomplish this being greater than one who is strong and able to conquer a city presents a very powerful image in an era when "military prowess was held in high regard" (Ross, 1991, p. 1012). The very convincing juxtaposition of light and darkness is offered by the author of Ecclesiastes to describe the yawning gulf that separates wisdom and foolishness (Eccl. 2:13).

With this in mind, it is interesting to consider Proverbs 11:12 in the light of domestic violence. This Scripture, as found in the King James Version, declares plainly that the person who "despiseth his neighbour" is without wisdom. Depending on the translation used, one could substitute any of the following terms: *belittles*, *finds fault*, *reviles*, *puts down*, *derides*, *denounces*, or *speaks scornfully*, for the word "despiseth." Further, using the same premise, the word "neighbor" here may refer simply to another person. In short, any behavior that undermines another person—including one's spouse—is unacceptable and quite foolish. In fact, how much more should one consider, nurture, and protect one's spouse—physically, emotionally, spiritually—in every way possible?

Throughout Ephesians 5, the apostle Paul highlighted the need for unity within the Christian church. He considered themes of love, light, and wisdom as a foundation for positive Christian behavior and later addresses the need for appropriate domestic relationships (Taylor, 1965) structured within the framework of mutual submission (Eph. 5:21) (Arnold, 2002). In verse 25, Paul moved away from the cultural norms of the time with the instruction "Husbands, love your wives, just as Christ also loved the church and gave himself up for her." This instruction refers to an ongoing love that is paralleled to the form of love that Christ has for his church and has exhibited through his sacrifice. Such love "involves passion, undying devotion, sensitivity to need, and self-denial" (Taylor, 1965, p. 242). It highlights not only the commitment of Christ to his church and the requirement for husbands to love their wives but also reflects the attitude displayed by Jesus toward the women of his day.

Examples of Jesus's treatment of women can be clearly seen throughout the Gospels. Jesus broke with tradition as he encouraged Mary's desire to sit with his disciples and listen to his teaching rather than fulfill her correct societal duty of assisting her sister, Martha, with the preparation and serving of food (Luke 10:38–42) (Strauss, 2002). Mary's choice, although praised and sanctioned by Jesus himself, was well outside the norm and also considered to be culturally inappro-priate. Jesus further broke with tradition when he chose to converse with the Samaritan woman at the well (John 4:7–9). Even though she was a Samaritan and was considered a woman of low standing in her own community, Jesus not only engaged her in conversation but communicated meaningful spiritual insight.

Yet another example of Jesus's attitude toward women is seen in his deeply compassionate response to the desperation of a woman considered to be ceremonially unclean due to her medical condition (Matt. 9:20–22; Mark 5:25–34; Luke 8:43–48) (Lake, 1975; Wilkins, 2002). Interestingly enough, the Bible does not even name this woman. She is known only as "a woman . . . who had been subject to bleeding" (Luke 8:43), yet Jesus publicly acknowledged her presence and gently encouraged her. According to the existing laws, not only should this unnamed women have been in "ritual isolation" (Garland, 2002; Liefeld, 1984, p. 917), but her action would have rendered Jesus unclean (Sanner, 1964). Thus, his caring response as opposed to an angry reprimand would, without doubt, have both shocked and challenged the thinking of the crowd, particularly that of the religious leaders.

Once again considering Paul's instruction for husbands to love their wives in the same manner as Christ loves his church, a further understanding of this form of love can be seen in the imagery of the shepherd described in Psalm 23. Remembering that Jesus referred to himself as the "good shepherd" who "lays down his life for the sheep" (John 10:11), most would agree that the shepherd in this psalm is a representation of Christ, and when one considers the role of the shepherd in relation to the sheep in his care, the prevailing image is one of loving devotion. It is the duty of the shepherd to nurture the sheep and provide for them. The shepherd is ever watchful and alert and is expected to protect the sheep. Ultimately the sheep are able to rest peacefully in the care and guardianship of the shepherd, who does not flee at the first sign of difficulty but rather honors his commitment (Baker, 2010a). While this may appear to be a rather tall order, it is nevertheless a clear depiction of the commitment of Christ to his church and therefore offers a vivid illustration of the expectation Paul extends to husbands.

Examination of the Scriptures reveals that Jesus, as the absolute epitome of Christian living who exemplified the perfect will of God, his Father (John 5:30), demonstrated a love, care, and respect for women that was completely incongruent with the traditional societal position of his era. His example continues to stand as a model for modern society.

CASE STUDY

Margo is sixty-five years old and has been married for thirty-eight years. She is actively involved in her church, and her husband is a deacon. She describes a significant level of ongoing verbal and psychological abuse within her marriage. It commenced quite early in her marriage and has escalated considerably over the years. Margo is very committed to her Christian faith and has a strong desire to live by the standards set down in the Bible. Her beliefs include the need to continually forgive her husband for his treatment of her and also to remain married, for her marriage is viewed as a sacred covenant before God.

STRATEGIES, INTERVENTIONS, AND TECHNIQUES FOR DOMESTIC VIOLENCE

When developing suitable interventions, a range of strategies and techniques may be employed. The following approach is designed as a guide for the therapist and may be adjusted according to the specific needs of the client. It is not designed as a one-size-fits-all method, nor is it rigid in application, but rather affords both the client and counselor a comfortable level of flexibility. Further, it allows for as little or as much time as is required to fully explore each individual aspect of the situation and encourages the counselor to attach value to the faith and foundational beliefs of the client and to operate within that framework.

Assisting the Client

One of the most significant steps toward healing comes from the realization that domestic violence is not the fault of the victim. It is nothing that the victim does or is that causes the perpetrator to behave in the manner chosen. Many victims of domestic violence believe it is their fault that the perpetrator treats them in an abusive and disrespectful manner. While this is certainly understandable in the light of the blame that is constantly directed toward the victim by the perpetrator, the realization that this is not the case can bring immense relief and even result in a turning point—a lightbulb moment—empowering the victim to move forward and take a step toward freedom.

How you can assist. In cases of domestic violence, the safety of the victim and her children is paramount, so assessing safety is essential. Questions such as "Do you feel safe?" "What would help you to feel safe?" "How safe do you feel in going home?" and "What do you think he would do if you left?" are all helpful when it comes to assessing the immediate safety issues relevant to the client. The question "What do you think might happen if . . . ?" is particularly useful if you wish to offer a thought for the client to ponder. It also allows the client the opportunity to take a breath and freely consider the idea you have gently presented and offer her own response.

As much as cases may be seen as similar in many ways, each individual client is unique, so you need to develop a clear understanding of the worldview of the specific client and elect to operate within that framework. To accomplish this, it is necessary to explore that worldview in addition to exploring the importance of faith to the person within that worldview (Nason-Clark, 2009). This can prove challenging, but it is not impossible. For the Christian woman, faith may be described as "extremely personal" and "uniquely individual" (Baker, 2011, p. 25). Therefore, avoid any apparent criticism (either intentional or unintentional) of her faith or any suggestion that she should give up her faith or ignore its basic tenets. Even though you may not entirely understand the operation

of a particular faith, for some women such faith is the only support available, and it can offer a level of stability in times of turmoil and crisis. Thus, it should be nurtured and respected. Pargament (2002) suggests that the benefits of religious faith and the associated coping strategies are linked to the level of commitment of the individual (see also Brown, 1994).

The ABC's of Providing Support

The following "ABC" guide is designed as a basic structure to help you, as the counselor, move through some of the issues that may be relevant to Christian clients.

A: Acquire knowledge (and with it understanding). The first requirement is for you to acquire relevant client knowledge. Some counselors use the word cue *at* to the effect that they acquire the appropriate knowledge to determine where the client is *at*. This means developing an understanding regarding the worldview of the client and how the client relates to her faith and to God. Doing so assists in acquiring a more complete sense of how the client is currently managing or coping with her situation.

The responses at this point will be varied. Some clients will see God as a loving father while others may see him as a strong authority figure. The Bible may be considered a guide for life or as the ultimate and final word of God, which cannot be challenged regardless of the circumstances (Baker, 2010a). Additionally, it is important to determine the general coping style of the client. This can range from a coping style that defers to God in all things and trusts that he will work things out for the good of the individual (Bickel et al., 1998; Maynard, Gorsuch, & Bjorck, 2001; Pargament & Brant, 1998) to a more active coping style in which the person does everything within her power and accepts that God is there and has given her the mind and will to operate effectively (Bickel et al., 1998; Maynard et al., 2001; Pargament & Brant, 1998). Between these two styles is the collaborative coping style in which both the individual and God are considered to play an active role in the problem-solving process (Pargament, 1997). For example, the person may pray for guidance, wisdom, or direction and expect God to respond appropriately. A very practical outworking of this style might be as straightforward as the individual, through prayer, requesting insight or guidance from God as to what action she could take, followed by meeting someone who provides her with the name and contact details of a knowledgeable counselor—you. The collaborative approach may be viewed as the individual having made the request to God, God having provided the necessary information (via whatever means), and the individual subsequently fulfilling her part by following up and making an appointment and then gaining relevant information and insight as a result.

The most significant coping strategies reported by the women in a study I conducted (Baker, 2010a) were maintaining a strong relationship with God and praying, which usually work hand in hand for the Christian. Furthermore, many of the women interviewed explained that they needed to focus on something specific to continue functioning. I reported that

despite ill health and an extremely difficult marital relationship, one respondent (Mary) maintained a fairly basic routine, focusing predominantly on the needs of her children to help her "keep it together" on a daily basis. Mary methodically worked through her daily routine of taking the children to school, keeping the house tidy and in order, and later collecting the children from school in the afternoon. Her mind was firmly focused on the essential aspects of her schedule for each day, knowing that she had specific responsibilities. By maintaining order, Mary was able to deal with each task or issue as it occurred (Baker, 2010a).

In conjunction with this coping strategy, Mary continued to link her faith with action by creating her own prayer book in which she collected copies of prayers she liked or felt were significant for her. She was able to draw strength and encouragement by reading or praying the words of inspiration. She also read a variety of stories about others who had faced and overcome extremely difficult challenges in their lives (Baker, 2010a). While Mary developed this strategy for herself, a separate organization identified as Set Free Ministries recognized and utilized the benefits of prayer and prayer partnership with a regular support person as part of its domestic violence intervention program (Danielson, Lucas, Malinowski, & Pittman, 2009).

B: Identify blocks or barriers. The counselor can pinpoint any potential religious barriers that may be blocking positive action on the part of the client. Potential blocks or barriers may exist in the form of beliefs or religious teachings, such as the marriage covenant is forever binding; God does not approve of divorce and even disapproves of any individual who makes that choice; constant forgiveness is mandatory regardless of the offense or the number of times it occurs; and women must remain subject to their husbands in all things (Popescu et al., 2009). Discovering such barriers does not mean that you should dismiss the beliefs of the client but rather should move toward building an understanding of the beliefs and how they impact the thinking and subsequent actions of the client (Nason-Clark, 2009). "While this step may take some time, it is nevertheless important to consider the area closely, as any or all of these beliefs can operate within the worldview of one individual" (Baker, 2011, p. 27).

C: Clarify theological understandings. The counselor should address and clarify any possible misconceptions previously identified as a barrier to positive action, remembering also that the client may not be well versed in issues of theology but may simply be believing things she has heard or been told directly by either the perpetrator or members of the clergy. If the client adheres strongly to Scripture, it is best to challenge any misconceptions in the light of biblical teaching. For example, the concept that God hates divorce is drawn directly from the Bible (Mal. 2:16). However, this is only one section of the verse in question. The 1984 edition of the New International Version of the Bible presents the complete verse as follows, "'I hate divorce,' says the Lord God of Israel, 'and I hate a man's covering himself with violence as well as with his garment,' says the Lord Almighty." If a client is able to develop an understanding of the biblical concept in its correct context, this discovery in itself can act as a catalyst for further discovery and foster gradual release from some of the difficulties she has been facing. The story of Rachel (Baker, 2010a) highlights the importance and power of such a revelation. I reported that this woman who had attended church regularly for many years and had heard many sermons had only ever heard or been taught the first portion of the Scripture in Malachi and had endeavored to live her life accordingly, thus remaining captive in an abusive relationship. The realization of the context brought not only a fresh understanding but also a new sense of freedom and liberty in how Rachel was able to approach her situation.

Applying the ABC Model to Margo

A: Acquire knowledge. In conversation with Margo, concentrate on building rapport with Margo and validating her experience. Support can be easily conveyed and rapport developed by utilizing some of the key concepts of the person-centered approach to therapeutic practice: congruence, unconditional positive regard, and empathic understanding (Corey, 2017), and making every effort to accurately understand the thoughts and feelings of the individual (Ivey, Ivey, & Zalaquett, 2018). This includes developing a clear understanding of the particular coping strategies employed by the individual. It is highly probable that Margo may embrace a collaborative approach to problem solving and overall coping by seeking professional assistance from either a counselor or psychologist and/or a medical practitioner, while also petitioning her heavenly Father for the most appropriate strength, guidance, and outcomes. The essential nature of the person-centered approach is strongly supported by women who have been victims of domestic violence and maintain that among the central issues relevant to receiving useful and effective assistance is the need to be heard and the need to be believed (Baker, 2010a; King, 1998; Miles, 2000; Walker, 1994).

This acquiring knowledge step can sometimes take a considerable amount of time. Often women in this situation have never spoken to anyone of their experiences, and once the taboo of speaking is removed and acceptance and a sense of validation are present, a great deal of information coupled with the associated emotions can cascade forth in a veritable Niagara. Mixed with an overwhelming sense of betrayal is the question of "Why?" "Why has this person who has promised to love and cherish me behaved in such an appalling and abhorrent manner?"

In the case of Margo, the confusion as to how her husband can possibly serve as a deacon in their church, offer the sacrament, and present a loving front to all within the community and then change so completely when out of the public eye is very apparent. The incongruence of the behavior (that of a perpetrator of domestic violence) with the label of "Christian" (which her husband embraced without hesitation) is something that she does not understand. It makes no sense to her at all. She has searched her heart, questioned her own behavior, and done everything possible to lovingly support him, meet his requirements, and care for his needs, yet nothing changes. For Margo, the Bible is not only a guide for living but also an authoritative source of instruction to which one should adhere—this is viewed as part of living a Christian life. The confusion, however, does not necessarily end here. It may also extend to the question of why God, a loving Father, would permit behavior that impacts so heavily on her and her children, and is clearly against his overall desire for humanity.

B: Identify blocks or barriers. After listening to Margo share her story—a story of anger, aggression, manipulation, and ongoing abuse perpetrated by her husband—and exploring Margo's worldview with particular attention to her faith, you may discover some more prominent areas that are worthy of deeper consideration. For example, women who hold a strong Christian faith will often punctuate their stories with information from the Bible—either explaining the principles or clearly quoting verses of Scripture that relate to their predicament. Such information may be drawn from many years of faithful church attendance and Bible study, from well-meaning members of the clergy, or alternatively from the perpetrator who wishes to maintain control over the actions of the victim and takes delight in using both the content and weight of Scripture to exert his authority. These are sometimes the concepts that keep victims of domestic violence, and ultimately their children, trapped in difficult, dangerous, and intolerable situations (Miles, 2002). These are also the areas that require further exploration.

You may be told that the Bible states that one must constantly forgive, all of the time, repeatedly, regardless of the offense. Scriptures that may be quoted relate to the need to forgive "seventy times seven" (Matt. 18:22 KJV) or "seven times in a day" (Luke 17:4 KJV). While such instructions were never intended as a mathematical exercise, these are the words that frequently resound in the minds of the women. The concept of marriage as a sacred and indissoluble union combined with Scripture references such as "'I hate divorce,' says the LORD" (Mal. 2:16 NIV 1984) and "Let not the wife depart from her husband" (1 Cor. 7:10 KJV) can prove extremely difficult for women of faith who are or have been victims of domestic violence. These, together with teachings from the Gospels of both Matthew (19:9) and Mark (10:10–12), which indicate that anyone who divorces and remarries is guilty of committing adultery, create another very significant barrier for those who are confronted with domestic violence (McAllister & Roberts-Lewis, 2010; Miles, 2002). You may indeed discover that Margo's husband is guilty of using these and similar Scriptures to control and manipulate Margo's thoughts and ultimately her choices regarding her marriage. Perpetrators of domestic violence frequently use whatever means are available—including the Scriptures and any possible sermon material—to undermine and control the victim. It is not unusual for women in this situation to second guess both their thoughts and actions, even going so far as to question their ability to live an acceptable Christian life.

C: Clarify theological understandings. Clarification does not mean dismissing the Scriptures, ideas, and explanations offered by Margo but rather exploring those ideas as a process of discovery and contextual understanding. Once again, the counselor should work within a Rogerian framework and trust that Margo has the ability to discover and resolve her own issues (Geldard & Geldard, 2012). For victims of domestic violence, encouraging ownership of the new thoughts and ideas is important, as this allows them to act from a position of conviction, strength, and empowerment, which has previously been denied them by the perpetrator. While in one sense the client may prefer or expect to be told what action to take, it is far better for her to work through the information and options herself and come to a suitable conclusion or solution on her own (McAllister & Roberts-Lewis, 2010). This does not negate your role as a counselor but provides the necessary support and nurturing environment for clear decisions to be made and relevant action to be taken. It allows the client to develop faith in her newly understood view and to embrace the view as her own as opposed to something she has simply been told or taught. In short, if you talk the client into something, even if the information is completely accurate, it is highly probable that someone else (possibly the perpetrator or even a well-meaning friend) will be able to talk her out of it. The old expression "when push comes to shove" is quite apt. When the road becomes difficult—and it will—the woman needs to be able to be confident that she has made the best decision possible in her individual situation.

The concept of forgiveness. In Margo's case, clarifying understanding would involve considering the Scriptures as they relate to forgiveness and assisting her to gain a fresh understanding relevant to the context of domestic violence. Issues to be considered would include the concept of forgiveness in relation to genuine repentance, common misconceptions pertaining to forgiveness, and the act of forgiveness in connection to future decision making (Baker, 2010a).

When one considers the idea of repentance and the subsequent plea for forgiveness, one might be excused for assuming the individual who committed the offense is genuine in his desire to be forgiven and is also committed to following an appropriate course of action in the future and making every effort not to reoffend. Barabas (1981) maintains, "The normal conditions of forgiveness are repentance and the willingness to make reparation" (p. 289). This is frequently not the case with perpetrators of domestic violence (Miles, 2000; Rinck, 1998). The question that might be asked centers around the difference between repentance and remorse. Is the perpetrator genuinely repentant or instead using the ploy of apologies and the stated desire for forgiveness as a means by which to continue his reign of terror?

A simple example serves to illustrate this point quite succinctly. If a person walked toward you, stood calmly in front of you and kicked you in the shins, and then apologized, you might let it go. If a short time later that same person repeated the action and gave another apology, you might let it go a second time. However, if the same person continued to behave in the same manner daily, you would hopefully arrive at the realization that the offender was in no way sorry or repentant for actions that were evidently a choice.

Likewise, it is necessary to consider whether Margo believes that the charitable and Christian act of forgiveness also includes forgetting or excusing the offense (i.e., the continuing abuse), engaging in mediation, or seeking reconciliation regarding the relationship. Margo may have been instructed that forgiveness means she is obligated to attend couple counseling, attend mediation, and engage in whatever activity is necessary to maintain the relationship. This is a very daunting prospect, as any of these options continues to place her in the presence and under the control of the perpetrator without any real hope of a positive result. Casey (1998) indicates that when forgiveness is connected to forgetting the offense and simply moving on with life, it "does not free a person from abuse, but only perpetuates it" (p. 228). It does so by "relieving the abuser of any true responsibility to examine his behavior and to change" (Cooper-White, 1995, p. 256).

Forgiveness, although ultimately a critical step toward healing, is best presented as a process (Miles, 2002). It takes time—time to feel physically, psychologically, and emotionally safe, and time to work through the hurt, the disappointment, and the seemingly ever-present sense of betrayal that has permeated the very being of the individual. This understanding of forgiveness should be clearly conveyed to the client. Forgiveness should never be viewed as a magical event that takes place on command. It is vital that you never push the client to forgive the offender. Doing so can be highly detrimental to the client's journey to wholeness, lead to the client abandoning treatment, and leave the victim feeling inadequate and a failure in her Christian life.

As Margo begins to realize that forgiveness requires genuine repentance and does not necessarily mean that she must remain in the relationship or continue to endure the abuse, feelings of guilt and failure at her own inability to forgive in an instant every occurrence of abuse can begin to dissipate. The benefit of time, and the opportunity to work through the pain of the abuse and betrayal she has suffered, is more likely to lead Margo to the place where she is gradually able to forgive. This applies both to the perpetrator as well as those to whom she has turned for assistance but who may have instead provided both inappropriate and damaging counsel.

The concept of marriage as indissoluble. Margo has also expressed concerns regarding her lifelong commitment to her husband and the promises she made before God in her marriage vows. These concerns need to be addressed so that Margo is able to scrutinize her own thoughts, feelings, and beliefs around the concept that marriage is forever—regardless. Separation with a view to divorce is extremely difficult at the best of times. There are many things to consider, including incredibly strong emotional issues, which are frequently compounded by religious (Bent-Goodley, St.

Vil, & Hubbert, 2012; Popescu et al., 2009; Roberts-Lewis & Armstrong, 2010) and even societal expectations of the woman (Tshifhumulo & Mudhovozi, 2013; Wendt & Hornosty, 2010). The opinion of scholars is diverse, and such diversity continues across denominations and even to individual members of the clergy. Thus, it is difficult to arrive immediately at a decision or a conclusion when considering opinions that range from no option at all for divorce to divorce as a necessity (with or without the option to remarry), to even the possibility of annulment, depending on one's denominational perspective (Baker, 2010a).

In the initial instance, it would be advisable to explore the specifics of Margo's foundational beliefs around marriage. According to Margo's understanding and religious perspective, is there an option for separation or divorce? Under what conditions might Margo believe this to be possible? The institution of marriage was designed as a blessing, but in the case of domestic violence, it is obviously not a blessing. Marriage, if viewed as a reflection of the love Christ has for his church, is meant to be a union in which husbands are encouraged to love their wives "just as Christ loved the church" (Eph. 5:25). Once again, in the case of domestic violence, this level of love and commitment is entirely absent. Zodhiates (1984) maintains that "it is not possible to love and mistreat a person at the same time" (p. 109). One significant conversation that appears to assist women who are fully committed to their marriage and the vows they made and do not wish to be guilty of breaking those vows, centers around the consideration of when and how those promises, and ultimately the marriage agreement (or covenant), might be broken.

The issues surrounding the possibility of separation and/or divorce, even in the case of domestic violence, are multifaceted and particularly sensitive. Many believe that the marriage covenant is broken at the time of the divorce, a teaching that often results in a sense of condemnation and failure for the woman who wishes or chooses to seek a divorce from her husband. Eilts (1995), however, offers an opinion to the contrary, highlighting the fact that the marriage covenant has clearly been broken by the violent and abusive actions of the perpetrator who has completely dishonored the marriage vows. This position is supported by a number of authors (Alsdurf & Alsdurf, 1998; Miles, 2000, 2002; Sprinkle, 1997). If one is to embrace this perspective, then in the case of domestic violence, divorce does not break the marriage covenant but becomes the legal acknowledgment of the already broken covenant (Baker, 2010a, 2010b).

Reconciliation as an Option

Even if the client has chosen to leave the perpetrator, she may still be under pressure to reconcile the relationship. This may be the result of foundational beliefs regarding either forgiveness, marriage, or both. It may also come from the influence of others, including well-meaning friends, members of the clergy, and of course the perpetrator. In cases of domestic violence, reconciliation is extremely difficult, often impossible. It can also be quite detrimental to the victim, for it once again places her in a very vulnerable—and possibly even dangerous—position (Baker, 2010a). This option must be considered with great caution and only with the best interests of the victim as the central issue—remembering always that the individual client is considered to be the expert in her own situation.

As an example of undue and inappropriate pressure to reconcile, Baker (2010a) reports the case of Joanna, a wife and mother of four, who elected to separate from her perpetrator husband with a view to seeking a divorce. Joanna was subsequently asked to step down from all active involvement in her church when she refused to contemplate a future reconciliation with her husband. Her involvement in the music ministry had contributed significantly to Joanna's ability to cope with her situation. Joanna was unacceptably vilified, and ultimately she was revictimized in a misguided effort to force her into an unwanted reconciliation.

If a client wishes to consider the option of reconciliation, the option should be fully and very carefully explored. It should take into account the past and present behavior of the perpetrator, successful involvement in support programs, and the existing evidence of long-term and well-sustained change together with an ongoing demonstration of serious commitment to that change. Beyond this, and of paramount importance, is the physical, mental, and emotional safety of both the client and her children. This level of change takes a great deal of time. It does not nor should it be expected to occur quickly. In one such case, eventual reunification took place after a period of seven years (Hegstrom, 2004).

Your Personal Work

Self-awareness is a term frequently associated with the role of the counselor. Your worldview and belief system are an important component when considering the best interest of the client (Ballantine Dykes, Kopp, & Postings, 2014; Corey, 2017; Geldard & Geldard, 2012; Sheperis, Henning, & Kocet, 2016).

In the case of Margo, for example, if you have a clear view that divorce is sin and that the marriage vows are permanently binding regardless of the conditions of that marriage, it could be extremely challenging for you and possibly even detrimental to Margo. A personal bias of this nature on your part may influence your approach with Margo, including the alternatives discussed. Margo may also be sensitive to the covert approval or disapproval of the counselor when considering the action she should take. Ideally, Margo should feel completely free to choose her own course of action based on her own thoughts, experiences, and convictions. Therefore, careful consideration of your own beliefs regarding religious concepts, including issues around forgiveness and marriage, is recommended (Baker, 2010a; Popescu et al., 2009).

You may wish to take time to explore your own view of marriage and the origin of that belief. Is it a societal or religious construct learned through family or perhaps later in life? Has your view changed over time? What were some of the contributing factors to that change? Is your belief system likely to influence the manner in which you would approach or guide a client? Similar questions could be applied to your understanding of forgiveness with particular respect to forgiveness as a process, the connection between forgiveness and repentance, and how the act of forgiveness may impact any decisions made by or expected of Margo.

Work for the Client

The process of clarification can be assisted through the use of guided reflection. Margo may be encouraged to consciously reflect on her own beliefs. Baker (2010a) provides a range of pertinent questions relevant to both forgiveness (p. 109) and marriage (p. 134) that may be used to foster reflection and discussion. You may use these and similar questions as discussion prompts during a session or alternatively afford the client time to work privately to develop thoughtful responses that will form the foundation for further discussion. Forgiveness topic questions include exploration of the client's experiences of forgiveness and any expectations that may have been placed on her by others; any concerns she may have regarding forgiveness; any possible roadblocks that may hinder her ability to be able to extend forgiveness to key people—for example, the perpetrator or those who have judged her harshly; and any assistance she feels she may want in relation to her progress.

After taking the opportunity to reflect on the various aspects of the topic in question, Margo may now be asked how she might explain the concept of forgiveness to a friend in light of her current understanding. Offering an explanation in her own words will help Margo to articulate and further clarify her understanding. And doing so may also lead to additional thoughts for reflection or discussion. In relation to marriage and/or the option of divorce, questions focus on the reality of the client's relationship and how that compares to the biblical expectation for marriage and the previous experiences or understanding of the client regarding the concept of divorce. Unlike Margo, the client may have already chosen to obtain a divorce but still carry a great deal of guilt and condemnation as a result of that decision. To obtain a deeper understanding of these issues, both you and the client may benefit from reading the appropriate chapter(s) of *Counselling Christian Women on How to Deal with Domestic Violence* (Baker, 2010a). This option offers the benefit of providing relevant information on the required subject and blending it with the practice of reflection. It thereby allows Margo the time and freedom to clarify her thoughts, reconceptualize her beliefs in the light of new information, sort through her options, and determine a course of action most suitable for her individual situation.

Further Assistance

Having developed an understanding of the faith perspective of the client and the manner in which faith operates in her life, it is possible for you as the counselor to utilize this insight to create additional intervention strategies that are effective for the specific client. Typical religious coping strategies, such as maintaining a strong relationship with God, prayer, and reliance on Scripture (Baker, 2010a), may manifest differently between individuals. Prayer, for example, may offer a time of quiet seclusion that temporarily removes the person from the immediate pressure of the environment, affording her the inner strength to con-

tinue. It may also offer a sense of security working hand in hand with the belief that eventually the situation will be resolved. As previously mentioned, Mary (Baker, 2010a) liked to read and created her own collection of inspirational prayers. Others may choose to write poetry that emulates the Psalms and expresses a deep cry for assistance or perhaps conveys the depth of their anger, frustration, or despair. Each of these types may constitute a form of prayer.

A variety of intervention strategies may be employed to assist clients, but ultimately it depends on the individual client and the specific needs of that client as to which options or techniques are employed. For example, a client who is comfortable with writing may engage well with the journaling or letter-writing process and possibly find benefit in reading sections of the entries during counseling sessions. In this way, thoughts and feelings may act as a foundation for further discussion and exploration. Alternatively, a client who is more interested in drawing or art may find the process more effective utilizing her own means of expression. Irrespective of the method chosen, the aim is to support the client in the discovery and expression of her feelings and in doing so assist her to gradually move forward.

Note that while some women rely heavily on their faith to be able to cope with the often debilitating rigors of domestic violence, others are unable to do so (Nason-Clark, 2009) and may struggle with a sense of being let down either by their faith, their faith community, or even God. Understanding the specific value that faith represents to an individual client can also help you to realize the degree of loss that can be experienced when a woman is feeling not only betrayed and violated as a result of domestic violence but also completely disillusioned in relation to her faith.

In the majority of cases, women who are or have been victims of domestic violence want to be able to tell their stories. They want to be heard and to have their feelings and experiences understood and validated. They want people to know that they have done everything within their power to make the relationship work as it should.

CONCLUSION

Domestic violence cannot be ignored either by society in general or by Christian communities. While it may occur behind closed doors, its pervading presence poses a challenge to the entire community. Domestic violence is not restricted to any particular person or group of persons but impacts individuals in a way that undermines their mental, emotional, and physical well-being. The effect of domestic violence is far-reaching. It not only touches the individual involved or the home in which that person lives but influences family dynamics and impacts significantly the children involved and their relationships with others both inside and outside the home. Such behavior is clearly condemned from a biblical perspective, and those who have suffered as a result of domestic violence require support and encouragement to be able to find restoration and reestablish their lives in an environment free from fear. To this end, counselors have the opportunity to assist clients to explore their experiences, thoughts, and feelings, and eventually regain their confidence and move forward to find healing and become survivors.

RECOMMENDED READING

Abrahams, H. (2010). *Rebuilding lives after domestic violence: Understanding long-term outcomes.* London: Jessica Kingsley.

Baker, L. M. (2010). *Counselling Christian women on how to deal with domestic violence.* Bowen Hills, Queensland: Australian Academic Press.

Crippen, J. (2015). *Unholy charade: Unmasking the domestic abuser in the church.* Tillamook, OR: Justice Keepers.

Kroeger, C. C., & Nason-Clark, N. (2010). *No place for abuse: Biblical and practical resources to counteract domestic violence* (2nd ed.). Downers Grove, IL: InterVarsity.

McMullin, S., Nason-Clark, N., Fisher-Townsend, B., & Holtman, C. (2015). When violence hits the religious home: Raising awareness about domestic violence in seminaries and amongst religious leaders. *Journal of Pastoral Care and Counseling, 69*(2), 113–124. doi:10.1177/1542305015586776

Rinck, M. J. (1990). *Christian men who hate women: Healing hurting relationships.* Grand Rapids, MI: Zondervan.

WEBSITE

The RAVE Project: http://www.theraveproject.com/index.php

CHAPTER 20

Forgiveness-Focused Strategies: The REACH Forgiveness Model

EVERETT L. WORTHINGTON JR., PHD
STEVEN J. SANDAGE, PHD
JENNIFER S. RIPLEY, PHD

He has shown you, O mortal, what is good.
And what does the LORD require of you?
To act justly and to love mercy
and to walk humbly with your God.

MICAH 6:8

Forgiveness is crucial for living—God forgiving humans, who receive the gift of forgiveness (called *divine forgiveness*), humans forgiving other humans (called *interpersonal forgiveness*), and humans forgiving ourselves when we have responsibly dealt with our wrongdoings (called *responsible self-forgiveness*). Transgressions occur within relationships, but forgiveness is granted by one party within the relationship. For example, we sin against God, and God forgives. We are hurt by another person, and we forgive; or perhaps we hurt another person, and that person forgives us. We wrong another person, and we then might forgive ourselves. But because the context of the transgression is interpersonal or relational rather than individual, people sometimes equate forgiving with saying, "I forgive you," or think that if they forgive an offender it necessarily means that they must reconcile with the person. Neither of these is accurate.

Theologically, in divine forgiveness (Worthington, 2003), God the Father forgives on the basis of the finished work of Jesus the Son's restorative justice on the cross. The Holy Spirit convicts people of their sin (and also prompts people to forgive others). Jesus is willing to take on the burden of sin to which all humans contribute, and he forgave (and forgives) those who hurt him (during his life on earth and throughout human history). The Holy

417

Spirit is active in all people's experiences of divine forgiveness, their willingness to forgive others, their desire to seek forgiveness from others, and their responsible forgiveness of themselves. Divine forgiveness is thoroughly Trinitarian.

In person-to-person forgiveness, the transgression might be one-sided, in which a person offends or hurts an innocent person. More often transgressions are reciprocal harms inflicted by two people on each other. Regardless of how complicated or long-lasting the trail of mutual harms, each incident is forgiven by an individual (or one individual forgives the offender, which forgives the sum of wrongdoing). Person-to-person forgiveness is an *intrapersonal* experience that occurs within the skin of the forgiver (though it occurs in interpersonal context).

In self-forgiveness, wrongs done to others must be responsibly dealt with (Worthington, 2013). Thus, the psychological experience of self-forgiveness is more about being an offender than a victim. Responsible self-forgiveness requires confessing to God, making amends to the person wronged by taking responsibility for wrongdoing, apologizing, providing empathic understanding of the harm done, valuing the person enough to want to forgive, and offering to make restitution to the offended person. It also requires following through to restore some sense of justice (by making amends), and (perhaps) asking for forgiveness. Sometimes the person one offended or hurt communicates his or her forgiveness (or unwillingness to forgive). Sometimes wronging someone creates a moral injury within the wrong-doer, who cannot forgive the self until that psychological and moral injury is dealt with. When all of these preconditions are met (or at least set in motion)—taking care of one's wrongdoing before God, making amends, and seeking to repair psychological and moral damage to the self—then people can seek to forgive themselves.

Human forgiveness, whether of another person's wrongdoing or self-forgiving for one's own wrongdoing, is difficult. Scripture tells us that Jesus requires forgiveness of others, and common sense tells us that if we wrong others, we should seek divine forgiveness first, seek to repair the social damage second, and deal with our psychological damage third; but even with assurance of God's forgiveness taking care of our moral guilt, there are lasting consequences (2 Sam. 12:13–18) that can lead to self-condemnation (Ps. 51) and thus a need for self-forgiveness.

While Scripture tells us to forgive, we find much in God's general revelation (of which psychology is a part) regarding specifically how we might decide to forgive and experience emotional forgiving. Worthington (2003) has developed a five-step intervention to promote forgiveness that has been used effectively for more than twenty years by people all over the world to help them experience forgiveness. People can forgive without using the model. We have done so since the beginning of time. But the model can help people forgive more quickly and thoroughly.

People inevitably experience barriers to blessing others by offering forgiveness and barriers to their own physical and mental health, relationship satisfaction, and spiritual freedom by failing to forgive. Worthington has sought to provide a way to obliterate those barriers and thus help people reach what God wants them to be. REACH Forgiveness is a five-step intervention aimed at promoting forgiveness. When people forgive consistently, they experience better physical health, mental health, relationship quality, and spiritual freedom, and all of those benefits have been supported by a total of more than a thousand scientific studies. REACH Forgiveness—one way of promoting forgiveness—has been repeatedly tested using the highest standard of empirical evidence—the randomized controlled trial. A recent meta-analysis (Wade, Hoyt, Kidwell, & Worthington, 2014) highlighted seven findings. First, REACH Forgiveness (Worthington, 2006; Worthington & Sandage, 2015) is an evidence-based practice in psychology (Worthington, Johnson, Hook, & Aten, 2013). Overall, REACH Forgiveness is used equally as much as the process model of Enright and Fitzgibbons (2014) and used equally to all other interventions combined. Second, REACH Forgiveness is equally effective, per hour of intervention, to any treatment. Third, besides helping people forgive, it decreases depression and anxiety and increases hope. Fourth, the duration of the intervention is directly related to its efficacy. Fifth, it is available in Christian-accommodated (Greer et al., 2014; Lampton, Oliver, Worthington, & Berry, 2005; Worthington et al., 2010) and secular versions (for both, see www. EvWorthington-forgiveness.com), which are equally effective. Sixth, it can be used in individual psychotherapy, couple therapy, family therapy, psychoeducational groups, and do-it-yourself workbooks, but most of the studies supporting its efficacy have been in psychoeducational groups and in do-it-yourself manuals. Seventh, it can be applied to forgiving others and forgiving oneself, though in the present chapter, we will focus on forgiving others.

THEOLOGY AND PSYCHOLOGY OF FORGIVENESS— A RELATIONSHIP

Centerpieces of Christian Living

The centerpieces of living the Christian life are love, forgiveness, and humility. Divine love began in the Trinity before creation (Volf, 2005). The triune God was not surprised that humans, created in God's image and never losing that blessing, would fall from grace. So God's plan from before the beginning of time was love and forgiveness, both manifest in the humble sacrifice of Jesus. Divine love of God reaching out to humans, divine forgiveness, and divine humility of Jesus in laying down his life for others were mirrored in humans' natural responses to God—love of God, sacred humility, and receiving of God's forgiveness. Those dispositions undergird the patterns for Christian interaction with other Christians and those who do not name Jesus as Lord.

Forgiveness Defined

Forgiveness of others is two separate, often-related experiences. These are best thought of not as two halves of forgiveness but as two different types of forgiveness.

Decisional forgiveness is a behavioral intention to refrain from seeking revenge and to treat an offender as a valued and valuable person (Davis et al., 2015; Exline, Worthington, Hill, & McCullough, 2003; Worthington, 2003). A person can make a sincere decision to forgive and maintain it throughout life, yet they may feel emotionally bitter, resentful, hostile, hate-filled, angry, and anxious when they think of the transgression. That suggests a second type of forgiveness, *emotional forgiveness* (Exline et al., 2003; Worthington, 2003), which is emotionally replacing unforgiving emotions with positive, other-oriented emotions like empathy, sympathy, compassion, or love for the offender. Decisional and emotional forgiveness happen inside people's skins. While a few people define forgiveness as involving the interpersonal interactions, most psychologists consider this to be a conflation with reconciliation (Freedman, 1998).

Scientifically, forgiveness is usually understood using a stress-and-coping model (Strelan & Covic, 2006; Worthington, 2006). In that model, a stressor is appraised and leads to stress reactions and subsequent coping responses. Decisional and emotional forgiveness are two of many coping responses to the stress of being transgressed against. The offense is considered the stressor. An offense creates an *injustice gap*—the perceived difference between the way a person would like a situation resolved and the way it is now (Davis et al., 2016). Big injustice gaps are hard to forgive—small injustice gaps, on the other hand, are easy. Offender acts, such as apologizing, offering restitution, and responsibly admitting to wrongdoing, reduce the injustice gap. However, repeatedly offending, refusing to take responsibility, or showing disrespect for the victim increases the injustice gap. The injustice gap is part of the appraisal of the stressor along with whether it is likely to be threatening or can be managed. The stress reactions involve physical responses (such as the release of cortisol), emotional responses (e.g., anxiety, depression, or anger), cognitive responses (e.g., blame or negative attributions about the offender's personality), and behavioral responses (e.g., lashing out or withdrawing).

Forgiveness—an internal coping response—is often confused with other experiences (see Enright & Fitzgibbons, 2014; Worthington, 2006). For example, forgiveness is not *saying*, "I forgive you," which could be said only to set the offender up for unsuspecting acts of revenge. Saying "I forgive you" is interpersonal; forgiveness is intrapersonal. Likewise, forgiveness is not *reconciliation*, which is restoring trust in a relationship (another interpersonal process). Thus, a woman who is abused physically might forgive her abuser, but she should not return to the relationship (i.e., reconciliation) if the abuser is not trustworthy. Additionally, forgiveness is not to be confused with other internal and external coping responses to perceived injustice, such as (1) getting justice or seeing justice done, (2) turning the matter over to God for divine justice or (3) relinquishing it to God simply because one knows that the matter should be handled by God, (4) forbearing (refusing to react negatively to offense to maintain group harmony),

(5) accepting and moving on with life, (6) excusing (giving legitimate mitigating reasons for one's offense), and (7) justifying (arguing that one's wrongdoing was okay because the victim had offended previously) (Worthington, 2006).

A Christian Theology of Forgiveness

The Bible clearly tells us to forgive—unilaterally (Matt. 6:12, 14–15). Worthington (2003) has outlined a Christian theology of forgiveness, and Worthington and Sandage (2015) have outlined a theology of forgiveness within relational spirituality. Volf (2005) argues that we have a God who is altruistic—a giving God. And we are to forgive as God forgave, altruistically.

But—here's the rub. The Bible does not specify *how* to forgive (Worthington, 2010). That is not its concern. Its concern is to tell what must be done to maintain great relationships with God, with others in and out of the Christian community, and within our own psyches. The Bible promotes faith, but it also commends God-oriented action. We are encouraged to put off bad behaviors and put on good behaviors (Eph. 4: 22–24; James 1:21–25), and in many instances we are given specific instructions, especially in the Old Testament.

The forgiveness that Jesus requires of Christians in the Matthew 6:12, 14–15 passage is probably decisional forgiveness (Worthington, 2003). This is supported by the passage giving the parable of the unforgiving servant (Matt. 18:21–35). That parable ends, "This is how my heavenly Father will treat each of you unless you forgive your brother or sister from your heart" (v. 35). From our twenty-first-century perspective, we often equate "from your heart" to mean emotions, but Worthington (2003) has suggested that in antiquity it meant a decision of the will. This is supported by the parable; no mention of—or implication of—emotion is evident. Worthington has further argued that God does not *require* emotional forgiveness, which is much less susceptible to human will or responsiveness to God's prompting than are decisions. God *requires* decisional forgiveness, and God *desires* emotional forgiveness. More fully developed theologies of forgiveness can be found in several other sources (e.g., Jones, 1995; Shults & Sandage, 2003; Volf, 2005; Wright, 2006).

Forgiveness Interventions

Interventions to promote forgiveness differ from forgiveness as it naturally occurs. Interventions are intended to help people move through a scripted progression of experiences that have been shown over time and over different populations to reliably promote forgiveness in many people. In the remainder of this chapter, we discuss one way that forgiveness might be instigated—the REACH Forgiveness method. This model has been developed by being jointly informed by Scripture and psychology. We believe it is consistent with Christian experience. Helping people forgive is analogous to building a concrete structure. Like building a structure of concrete, we do not pour the concrete (representing forgiveness) onto the floor and will it into a perfectly shaped pillar. Rather, we use wooden forms (representing in this case the REACH Forgiveness model of forgiveness intervention) to shape forgiveness, and we count on God to pour the lasting concrete of forgiveness into our lives.

We look at three contexts of the many in which this model could be used: in psychoeducational groups (in which individuals, who happen to be in groups, are led through exercises and experience forgiveness as individuals), in couple counseling, and in family counseling. We did not tackle all modalities to help people forgive. For example, we did not provide cases for (1) individual psychotherapy (two extended cases are found in Worthington & Sandage, 2015—one in-depth psychotherapy and one short-term psychotherapy; another extended case can be found in Worthington, 2006), (2) do-it-yourself workbooks (Greer et al., 2014; Harper et al., 2014), or (3) online do-it-yourself interventions (Nation, Wertheim, & Worthington, 2017). Nor did we provide cases for (4) process groups, which are unstructured groups that depend more on group discussion and on individual members of the groups interacting to confront and promote self-confrontation of other group members (see Wade et al., 2017), or (5) couple enrichment in groups of couples (Ripley & Worthington, 2002). We did not cover (6) one couple meeting with a couple consultant (for a case study, see Worthington, Mazzeo, & Canter, 2005; for a research study, see Worthington et al., 2015). Finally, we did not deal with (7) self-forgiveness (Griffin et al., 2015; Worthington, 2013). Self-forgiveness can be vital in issues like affairs, accidental self-injuries in which one was at least part-

ly to blame for one's own injury, mortal injury incurred in combat, or engaging in self-injurious behavior like alcohol or drug abuse. However, in the current chapter, we thought it would be repetitive. In addition, all of our interventions are applicable to nontargeted hurts—that is, they are not targeted to people with specific forgiveness issues (like incest) but apply to people who have different hurts. We have, for example, conducted research in which REACH Forgiveness was targeted specifically at patients with a diagnosis of borderline personality disorder (Sandage et al., 2015). That treatment occurs within the protocol of dialectical behavior therapy (Linehan, 1993), but generally our interventions are not targeted narrowly.

CASE STUDIES

While all three of the authors of this chapter have done individual, couple, and family therapy, we each took responsibility for writing about just one area. Worthington dealt with psychoeducation (drawing primarily from Worthington, 2006), Ripley with REACH Forgiveness within the hope-focused couple approach (see Ripley & Worthington, 2014), and Sandage with family therapy (drawing primarily on his experience and Worthington and Sandage, *Forgiveness and Spirituality in Psychotherapy: A Relational Approach*, 2015).

Forgiveness in Psychoeducational Groups

We will not present a specific case here. See the section on strategies and techniques for common interventions across cases, including explanation of each step of REACH Forgiveness.

Forgiveness in Hope-Focused Couple Therapy

The Jacksons truly wanted to forgive each other and move forward in their marriage, but a big offense reared its ugly head whenever they experienced stress—in marriage, work, or parenting. Michael was the obvious offender. He had lost his job in January, and unable to face Louisa, he took out loans, opened new credit cards, and raided an investment account to keep the family afloat for five months. Louisa had been preoccupied with twins who had arrived two months early and with being sole caregiver for her elderly grandmother. Louisa discovered the financial offenses when a tithe check to their church bounced. Michael continued to try and cover up. They had a huge fight. Louisa told the church accountant and pastor about the offense without Michael's permission. After a month of fighting, offenses, and church drama, the pastor wisely referred the couple for counseling.

Couple counseling was difficult for all involved. Once the initial shock and defensiveness wore off, Michael and Louisa felt stuck. Louisa felt she had been betrayed when she was vulnerable. Michael felt betrayed (because of Louisa's disclosure) and offended that Louisa couldn't understand and forgive him. After all, he had forgiven her for an infidelity in their engagement ten years earlier. They were sensitive to all offenses now.

Their therapist, Nicole, started by identifying their current and past pattern of offenses. They resisted forgiving based on past offenses. The couple's valuing of love was weak before Michael's initiating offense because both were focused on other things than marriage. They had lived parallel lives for four years. Michael struggled with empathizing in session, which offended Louisa. Twice he seemed to withdraw emotionally from any attempts to apologize and forgive. Slowly they began to empathize with each other, own responsibility for their own parts of the offenses, and offer forgiveness. They developed understanding of their patterns of offense and committed to preventing future problems. After termination, Nicole said it was one of her most difficult couple cases. Michael and Louisa almost dropped out twice. In the end, Nicole felt good about the outcome for them.

Forgiveness and Relational Spirituality in Family Therapy

Robert (age sixty-two, Swedish American) and his son Eric (age thirty-eight, Swedish American/Anglo-American) pursued family therapy together to see whether they could heal hurts, resentments, and a relational cutoff that had lingered for a decade. Robert was an evangelical pastor who had been largely estranged from both Eric and Eric's sister Rachel (age forty). Three years prior, Eric had moved back near Robert. Robert had lost his wife, Mary, to cancer six years earlier. Eric and Rachel had each attended their mother's funeral but had only sporadically talked with Robert since then. They shared similar complaints about Robert, particularly from their childhoods. Eric lamented,

"He was always more committed to success in ministry than to our family. In later years, Mom started referring to his church as 'the other woman.' . . . And he was hard on us. He expected perfection to make him look good to the church but wasn't interested in us. The worst part was rage that would explode often, always following some setback with his ministry. I think he wanted reassurance from us that he wasn't a failure, but he was impossible to be around at those times. I remember pitching in our state tournament in high school. Dad stayed home because he was having a fit and was working on an angry letter to a denominational official."

Robert owned that he had been self-absorbed, too focused on ministry, and neglectful of his family prior to Mary's death. Mary had stabilized him, though also had probably enabled his narcissistic behavior. As her cancer progressed, Robert's church suffered an ugly split. He lost his position as senior pastor in a takeover by three associates. Historically, he had a series of previous pastorates where he helped increase attendance through his charisma and dynamic preaching, but he had managed to move on to a new church as relational conflicts were brewing. Losing both Mary and his pastorate at the pinnacle of his career sent him into a serious depressive episode. Several years of individual therapy helped him confront himself about his narcissism, insecurity, and dysfunctional patterns of attachment avoidance. Now, remarried and pastoring a small congregation of mostly seniors, Robert felt humbled. He hoped to repair his relationship with Eric and have more

regular involvement with his grandkids (Eric's children). He wanted the same with Rachel, but she lived across country and wasn't open to family therapy.

STRATEGIES, INTERVENTIONS, AND TECHNIQUES SPECIFIC TO PSYCHOEDUCATIONAL GROUPS

Techniques Specific to Psychoeducational Groups

REACH Forgiveness in the present chapter is treated within a Christian context. However, it is also effective with people who do not name Jesus as Lord. There has been much research on REACH Forgiveness within Christian context (for one example, see Lampton et al., 2005) but even more within a purely secular context (for an overall meta-analysis including both populations, see Wade et al., 2014).

The major differences are the contexts. In the Christian version, we attribute the work of the Holy Spirit in building that forgiveness into the Christian's character. In Christian groups, we emphasize humility (Phil. 2:1–9). Definitions of decisional forgiveness are justified by Scripture (Matt. 6:12, 14–15). We suggest Scripture-based motivations for forgiving, like Scripture-based compassion and love, even love for one's enemies (Matt. 5:44) and unilateral forgiveness offered freely. Altruistic forgiveness is framed as motivated by agape love. We might suggest commemorating successful forgiveness by nailing a paper with the written offense to the cross or burning it as an offering to God. In the generalization phase of helping people, we use twelve steps to become a more forgiving Christian and identify heroes of forgiveness (who often include biblical characters) and pray for the offender. In practice, the Christian and secular groups look and feel similar, but in the Christian setting, forgiveness is sacred, giving it more emotional heft. Even if secular REACH Forgiveness is used with explicit Christians, research has shown that Christians in secular groups still did the same things that were being recommended in the explicitly Christian groups—prayed for their enemies, forgave because God said to, and consulted Scriptures. They did what we hope all Christians do—resist abandoning their faith at the door of a secular intervention and use it whether the psychotherapist mentions faith topics explicitly or not.

Most work is done with a relationship partner. People spend most of their effort in such groups working with a single person who happens to be seated next to them. If people know each other, we encourage them to pair with someone that they do not know very well. This pairing is crucial because it means that virtually anyone can effectively lead a REACH Forgiveness group. Because most of the therapeutic work occurs as group members discuss experiences with each other, the leader does not have much "counseling" to do. Research (Lin et al., 2014) has found that post-master's counselors differ little from pre-bachelor's students in forgiveness outcomes.

Literally anyone can benefit from REACH Forgiveness groups. But people with very severe problems or traumas sometimes are so emotionally engaged that they monopolize group time. We encourage people to work with individual psychotherapists to resolve traumatic issues. Nevertheless, Sandage and colleagues (2015) have shown that people with borderline personality disorders benefited from REACH Forgiveness experiences. People with severe disturbances can also work on forgiveness using web-based interventions (Nation et al., 2017) or do-it-yourself workbooks (Greer et al., 2014; Harper et al., 2014; for cost-free access to the workbooks, see www.EvWorthington-forgiveness.com). Such materials can be effective adjuncts to psychotherapy or psychoeducational groups, or they can substitute for psychotherapy if a person does not wish to attend a group or counseling. They can also be resources for church members eager to become more forgiving people.

Preliminary work. At the beginning, ground rules of confidentiality and civil, supportive communication are covered. People select a *not completely forgiven hurt* to work with throughout the group. They write a brief description of the hurt, complete ratings of current forgiveness using questionnaires that have substantial psychometric support, and commit to work on that event throughout treatment. The questionnaires—the Trait Forgivingness Scale (TFS; Berry et al., 2005), and two that assess forgiveness of the event they selected, called the Decision to Forgive Scale (DTFS; Davis et al., 2015) and the Transgression-Related Inventory of Motivations (TRIM; McCullough et al., 1998)—can be self-scored and will be revisited at the end of the group.

Icebreaker (and a covert therapeutic intervention). The work in the group begins with an activity to ease the tension, facilitate group cohesion, and start people thinking about forgiveness without feeling threatened. Each participant describes a favorite dessert and tells the most serious transgression he or she has completely forgiven. The dessert exercise gets people talking and laughing. The description of a forgiven serious transgression sets a norm of disclosure, which establishes the group as one that takes forgiveness seriously. The leader "whips" around the group, starting at some random place and progressing in order. Importantly, the leader begins the whip at random places every time he or she whips for discussion.

Lectio divina. To ground a Christian REACH Forgiveness group in Scripture, we use a modified version of *lectio divina* (versus inspirational quotes in secular groups). The leader reads one of six scriptural passages about forgiveness, then whips around the group, and each member reacts with a word. The leader reads again, and the whip (beginning in a different place) has people respond in a two- or three-word phrase. Depending on time and size of the group, the leader might repeat asking for responses of one-sentence ideas.

Create a working definition. Using a common working definition of forgiveness is important. So we do not ask participants to share their definitions, which they tend to overcommit to. We want them to accept two working definitions—decisional and emotional forgiveness. To elicit agreement, we provide fourteen possible definitions.

Twelve are incorrect, such as defining forgiveness as seeing justice done or as reconciling the relationship. On the back of the list, we describe why the twelve incorrect definitions are not right and why the two correct ones are. People discuss all fourteen with their relational partner.

Invite decisional forgiveness. We invite people to make a decision to forgive. Importantly, do not attempt to coerce a decision to forgive. This is not the time to quote Matthew 6. Most Christians already feel guilty at not being able to experience forgiveness, which they often define as emotional peace when thinking of the harm done to them. Instead, return to a decision to forgive after working through emotional forgiveness.

The leader invites participants to stand and imagine that they are holding the "grudge" they are seeking to address within clasped hands. The hands, tightly squeezed, are held outstretched from the body, which creates muscle tension and tiredness. The leader drones on about the burden of carrying transgressions around, the weight of the feelings, the discomfort of holding unforgiveness, and the desire to just let go of the unforgiveness. When the group leader feels tired, he or she invites the participants to release the grudge and let it fly away and then drop the hands. The leader tells the group that this represents physically the way they might feel emotionally when deciding to forgive and experiencing emotional forgiveness—free and light—and promises to revisit a decision to forgive near the group's end.

Use REACH Forgiveness steps to move toward emotional forgiveness.

Although psychoeducational groups provide experiences that all participants do at the same time, each person moves toward emotional forgiveness at an individual pace. Most people make substantial gains in both decisional and emotional forgiveness, and in becoming a more forgiving person by the end of the group, but a few just open the door to change. A few blast through the door at a run, while most move with deliberation so that within a six-hour session most people have reached what they consider a 75 to 95 percent reduction of the unforgiveness they held at the start of the session. As we talk you through the steps of REACH Forgiveness (below), we focus on the strategies and techniques of the group leader and on the decisions the leader must make, not the experiences of the group participants.

R = Recall the hurt. We seek to help people tell their story with the understanding that they try to be as objective as they can. Often they are not able to be objective because the pain, anger, or offense they experience is extreme. The leader keeps time as pairs take turns sharing their "objective" accounts of the harm.

E = Emotionally replace negative with positive emotions (empathy and other replacement emotions). Helping the person gain a different emotional perspective is the key step. Using an empty chair dialogue can often achieve this (Greenberg et al., 2008). The leader explains the empty chair dialogue and demonstrates it on a fictitious harm that he solicits from the group. At least five changes of the chair are used in the demonstration. Then the pairs take turns with one person "working" and the other observing. The working partner has a fifteen-minute dialogue with the imagined transgressor, moving back and forth between two chairs. They talk about what was learned, and then the other partner works for fifteen minutes with an empty chair.

Other methods of seeing things from the transgressor's point of view can be used. These might include (1) narrating a "letter" ostensibly that could have been written from the transgressor to the victim (group member), (2) asking what the transgressor might say if defending herself, or (3) asking what hurts the transgressor might have experienced to lead her to inflict the hurt on the group member. After several exercises to promote empathy, the group leader whips around to get group members to summarize their learning. When promoting empathy does not help, sometimes people can be invited to experience sympathy, compassion, or love, which can change the emotional valence.

A = Altruistic gift of forgiveness. The leader invites people to reflect on a time when they offended someone who forgave them. They reflect on how being forgiven made them feel—which usually brings descriptions of freedom, lightness, and release. The leader asks whether they would like to give an altruistic gift of forgiveness not deserved by the offender.

Here is an important intervention. The leader asks group members to express—in percent—the degree that the emotional unforgiveness they felt at the beginning of treatment has been changed. They might say, "Eighty percent of my unforgiveness is now gone." Who the group leader begins the whip with is important because as people place a number on the amount of their forgiveness, it becomes more real to them. Over the course of the group, the leader should try to determine who might be most positively experiencing forgiveness, and the leader should start the whip with that person. Starting with a person who has experienced a high level of forgiveness will set the tone for others.

C = Commitment to the forgiveness experienced. People make some kind of statement about their commitment to forgiveness—to the therapist, to the group, to their partner or child or parent, or simply in completing a forgiveness contract that only they themselves see. It is possible to use rituals to solidify the forgiveness experienced. For example, we often ask people to write on their hand in ink a "shorthand" label of the transgression they are trying to forgive. Then, during a break, they try to wash it off. Some wash it clean; others, not quite. This then becomes an object lesson that the leader makes explicit: "If you didn't forgive 100 percent in going through the REACH Forgiveness, go through it again (like you will wash your hands again to get off residual ink)."

H = Hold on to forgiveness when doubt occurs. People are prone to doubt that they have indeed forgiven a perpetrator. Their natural, emotionally conditioned bodily response to pain is anxiety and anger, which they associate with seeing or thinking about the perpetrator. But feeling anger and fear at seeing an offender is not the same as unforgiveness. It shows that one's God-designed body is working

to protect oneself from future dangerous situations. People commit to the forgiveness experienced in step C so that they can H (hold on to forgiveness). To do so, they are taught methods, like distraction, to control rumination.

Reinvite decisional forgiveness. After people have worked through emotional changes, it is easier for them to make a conscious decision to forgive. That decision can also be commemorated in a ritual, such as writing the offense on a paper that is offered to God.

Twelve steps to a more forgiving person. After working through the five steps to REACH (emotional) Forgiveness and reconsidering making a decision to forgive, people are given the opportunity to customize their learning to fit their personalities. People complete these twelve steps in writing. The first step is to identify ten events in their lives in which some unforgiveness remains. In other steps, they work through those events. Becoming a more forgiving person is achieved by God working on promoting forgiveness in many (or all) of the person's relationships. The exercises are different for each event. For example, in one, the person might pray for the person who hurt him. In another, the person might write how he would work through each of the steps of REACH Forgiveness to forgive that person. He might also do something like imagine Jesus entering a room with himself and the person who hurt him, or identify heroes of forgiveness.

Complete the final self-assessment. People complete the questionnaires—the TFS, the DTFS, and the TRIM—that they completed at the outset of the group, and they can self-score to see the amount of progress they made. Many find much forgiveness has occurred, and seeing changes on questionnaires makes the changes seem even more real.

STRATEGIES, INTERVENTIONS, AND TECHNIQUES SPECIFIC TO COUPLE THERAPY

We use the REACH Forgiveness model within the hope-focused approach (HFA) to couple therapy or enrichment (see Ripley & Worthington, 2014; Worthington, 2005). The HFA is based on promoting hope in couples and couple therapists. It seeks to do so by teaching a strategy of faith, work, and love (Gal. 5:6). In practice, the HFA has two halves—a communication and conflict-resolution part called Handling Our Problems Effectively (HOPE) and a second part called Forgiveness and Reconciliation through Experiencing Empathy (FREE). We situate REACH Forgiveness within a four-step reconciliation process (i.e., FREE). We see forgiveness and reconciliation as integral to the hope-focused approach. Both help couples restore a stronger emotional bond by improving communication, practicing conflict management, and building commitment. By the time couples seek counseling, many have already decided to divorce. They might see couple counseling not as a road to healing but as a dutiful step to justify divorce.

Couple enrichment. We completed several randomized clinical trials that establish the efficacy of the REACH

Forgiveness model within couple enrichment. For example, in 2002 Ripley and Worthington used REACH Forgiveness with groups of couples in a five-hour couple-enrichment model. Forgiveness did not produce as many positive effects as did conflict management and communication training. Discussing forgiveness brought up past hurts and reactivated conflicts even in the couples ostensibly seeking enrichment. One leader could not effectively manage the conflict in a group. We subsequently changed to one therapist working with one couple on enrichment (see Burchard et al., 2001; Worthington et al., 2015).

Couple therapy. Ripley et al. (2014) used either the Christian-accommodated or the secular hope-focused approach with Christian couples. While no differences were found in outcomes related directly to the marriage, Christian couples did make more gains in Christian value-related areas using the Christian-accommodated treatment. The research was summarized in Ripley and Worthington (2014), which also provided a rich account of 88 new interventions. In 2005 Worthington had composed descriptions of more than 125 interventions. In the following sections, we examine using REACH Forgiveness with couple therapy (an extended case in couple enrichment is given in Worthington et al., 2005).

Assessment

The first step of couple counseling for REACH Forgiveness may seem counterintuitive. Couples often want to jump directly into "How can we change?" But we have found that more power comes from beginning with a thorough assessment and developing a plan of action before change is attempted. Recall the Jacksons. Michael had hidden financial debt from Louisa, and unkind words and actions from both partners followed the discovery. It seems Nicole should immediately address the offense. But she shouldn't. Few couples are ready at first to consider forgiving.

Thus, the first step in the hope-focused approach is to assess the couple's strengths and weaknesses, their presenting problems, the nature of their relationship, and their motivation to forgive and reconcile. The counselor interviews the couple together (sometimes separately, too, if there are red flags like abuse or recent infidelity), gives them questionnaires, and writes a report of the results. This not only supplies much information the therapist did not have at the outset, but it also engages many people who are not enthusiastic about counseling. Assessment and feedback provide a self-help fact-based plan that couples quickly see can usually better be accomplished with the help of a therapist than on their own. The feedback report also repeats and solidifies an understanding that the couple needs help with love, work, and faith. This sets up intervention. A thorough description of assessment and feedback, including model reports, is found in Worthington (2005) and Ripley and Worthington (2014).

Therapeutic Tasks throughout the Hope-Focused Approach

Stabilization. For couples still in the turmoil of an offense, the first goal, usual-ly begun during the assessment phase but continuing throughout couple therapy, is stabilization. Helping the couple "stop the tornado" is important. Partners may even need to separate for a week or more. The Jacksons were taught time-out strategies. They brainstormed ways they already self-soothe when strong negative feelings arise. Nicole helped them identify watching sports, exercising, and taking time-outs as strategies to distract them from escalating negative feelings. After a few weeks of emotion regulation, they addressed forgiveness.

Learning about forgiveness as a life issue in the context of one's relationship with God. Even when things are stabilized, couples with moderate to severe offenses typically engage in an offense-defense pattern. The first step toward forgiving is to talk about offenses broadly without the emotion of a hot conflict. Many Christians feel (and also believe) it is their duty to forgive others but do not pair this event with compassionate love, or with gratitude for receiving forgiveness from God. Both partners should talk about offenses and forgiveness in their lives prior to their relationship: What did they learn about forgiving while growing up or in previous relationships? The counselor listens for positive skills like making apologies, forgiving, and reconciling. The counselor might ask, "What might God want to help you learn by thinking back on your forgiveness experiences?" By accessing personal strengths and purpose in life, the couple might seek to employ their potential instead of remaining stuck in defensiveness.

Another way to keep emotion lower is to talk about God's forgiveness of each. The counselor can usually contrast previous experiences with apologies, forgiveness, and reconciliation with God's relationship with the partners. Partners reflect on their confessions to God and God's forgiveness of their sins. Some partners benefit from discussing the difference between how they *feel* about their sins against God and divine forgiveness compared to what they *know* about God's forgiveness. They might react emotionally to God as a disapproving parent, a task master, or an uncaring distant figure. By illuminating these feelings, counselors can parallel this with the couple's experience in their relationship: Do they feel that their partner judges and disapproves? Do they wonder whether they can ever please the partner, no matter how hard they work? Do they long for a warm, close relationship but feel distant?

When partners engage in such reflections, they often see their own relationship in a different light—one that ought to be but usually (given that the couple is in couple therapy) is not a forgiving relationship. The parallel between their emotional experience of God and their partner relationship often unsticks partners, getting them to change their condemnation toward each other. This can be true even for those with nontraditional religious beliefs. Some exercises might help. Partners might do the following:

- Write their sins on paper and burn them
- Confess to clergy and receive words of forgiveness

- Engage in atoning actions, not for forgiveness but to honor God
- Show gratitude to God for forgiveness of past sins
- Confess to God their own offenses in the presenting problem

Some couples are uninterested or unwilling to use their relationship with God as a means to explore offenses and forgiveness. An alternative is to work through offenses and forgiveness with a *successful* relationship in the past.

A counselor may spend weeks or months focusing on forgiveness with God or others from the past. It might seem that little has been done on the presenting problem. However, after focusing on forgiveness indirectly, through relationship with God and others, the counselor usually sees the couple softened in relationship with each other and ready to engage in forgiveness and reconciliation. In my (Jen's) experience, partners often forgive and reconcile on their own during the process of focusing on other relationships. Why? Couple therapy that focuses on offenses, defenses, and hurt is difficult to traverse for all involved. The partners need to be open to change, to want to attach lovingly to their spouse, and to be willing to look at their own contribution to cycles of offense. Indirect interventions allow partners to empathize with each other. For example, Michael can feel empathy when Louisa confesses that she feels deep hurt and anger at her parents for not caring for her grandmother and leaving her "holding the bag" in caregiving—even when her twins were born early. Louisa might be able to see the complexity of her external situation—

how she is both offended by her parents yet guilty over her angry words to her parents. As she confesses to God, and perhaps to the spouse and counselor too, Michael can support and encourage her as a fellow sinner. And he can encourage her both to seek and give forgiveness. Michael's role is to be supportive, empathic, and humble (which is necessary for forgiveness)—and when it does not stay that way, Nicole encourages him to return to a stance of love.

Reconciliation. Reconciliation is restoring trust in a relationship, which requires mutually trustworthy behavior. If one person is not trustworthy, the reconciliation cannot be achieved. Worthington (2003) identified four planks in a bridge to reconciliation. These involve *decisions* about whether, when, or how to reconcile. They also include *discussions* about transgressions, which require people to use their communication and conflict resolution skills as well as confessing, apologizing, working to make restitution, and seeking forgiveness. The last two are *detoxifying* the relationship and building *devotion*.

REACH Forgiveness. If the couple is interested and feels ready, they can work through the REACH model for their presenting problem. First, we teach the REACH model not on a "hot" conflict but on a wrong each experienced before he or she met the partner. Each identifies an early wrong, and the counselor works through the REACH Forgiveness steps much as in a psychoeducational group (or as it is used in individual psychotherapy). The partner acts as an empathic support during the learning. After the method is learned, it can be applied to hot topics.

1. The Jacksons briefly (R) *recall the hurt* of the financial offense and subsequent fighting and gossip. They attempt to be more neutral than they might feel.

2. Next they (E) *emotionally replace* negative emotions with positive emotions through empathy with their partner's experience, pressures, and personal struggles that led to the offenses. Worthington (2006) adduced substantial evidence that successful emotional forgiveness first reduced the negativity and later became more positive.

3. They can also reflect on their own previous experiences in counseling—how it felt to have offended others and God, and their longing to have things made right. The counselor asks whether they would like to give this gift of freedom, motivated from their agape love, by (A) *altruistically* giving the gift of forgiveness to each other. They might both decisionally forgive and experience emotional forgiveness.

4. The couple can apologize and (C) *commit* to forgiving each other. Some education on the distinctions between decisional and emotional forgiveness is often helpful if they feel ready to apologize and forgive but not ready to fully emotionally forgive. In couple counseling the process is more interactive and reactive to the couple than in a psychoeducational group.

5. A final step in forgiveness counseling, (H) *hold on to forgiveness*, should inoculate partners from unnecessary reinjuries for the offense. The counselor will normalize negative feelings about past hurts in relationships when

they come up. When couples are physically tired, they can learn about how resource depletion can cause negative emotions about the offense to flare up again. That doesn't mean they didn't genuinely apologize and forgive. They can explore ways to manage negative emotional flare-ups.

STRATEGIES, INTERVENTIONS, AND TECHNIQUES SPECIFIC TO FAMILY THERAPY

Structuring Goals and Relational Interactions in Family Therapy

Clients in family therapy sometimes hope, however unconsciously, that the therapist will quickly orchestrate a magical healing moment that achieves mutual forgiveness and reconciliation. This was Robert's hope at the outset of therapy, though Eric was much more cautious and tentative. It is particularly important in cases like this one to (a) clearly state initial, achievable goals and (b) negotiate ways of structuring relational interactions both inside and outside sessions so further hurts are less likely to recur. This can promote healthier boundaries, better differentiation, and the possibility of safer and more constructive attachment dynamics as the family tries to move forward. Our relational spirituality model (Worthington & Sandage, 2015) suggests that forgiveness typically results from increases in attachment security and differentiation. Forgiveness can then promote relational growth.

You can ask each family member, in turn, to articulate his or her goals. The psychotherapist should record them spe-cifically on a notepad. In this case, Robert initially said, "I hope Eric can forgive me for these many years of being a difficult and distracted father and realize I am different now. . . . I want to be connected to him and to be part of his family life so my grandkids can know their grandfather—know I love them. . . . God is the ultimate healer, and I want God to be pleased with our family's efforts to forgive and heal."

Eric: [*stating more modest goals*] I want to see if it's possible for my dad to spend time with me, Anna [Eric's wife], and my kids without preaching his theological and political views. . . . I want him to consistently show up when we make plans. . . . I would like to get over my anger with him . . . but I need to be convinced he "gets it" and can own his stuff.

Counselor: [*validating*] I'm glad you are each so clear on your goals. It's helpful for me to hear these from each of you. When I consider where each of you is coming from, I am struck that your different goals each make tremendous sense to me. Yet I find in cases like yours that it's important that I help each of you initially focus on what you can personally control so that you don't get overly focused on what the other person is doing since you can't control that. Does that make sense?

[*Eric and Robert both nodded.* (If they did not agree, it would be important for the therapist to explain the differentiation-based rationale for focusing on personal responsibility for their own behavior.)]

Counselor: So here is what I suggest. It sounds like you each would like to work toward forgiveness. You are currently having some interaction with one another, and you both want those interactions to be more positive. Correct? [*Both nod.*] I suggest we try to define some specifics of the interactions that will work best for both of you in the short term, and then I can help each of you figure out how to best manage yourself and your emotions during these interactions, not so that they will go perfectly but so that you can make progress over time.

The counselor then helped Robert and Eric collaborate in naming specific behaviors that could be helpful when they spent time together. Eric asked his dad to keep the topics of theology and politics off limits when they got together. Like Robert, Eric was a Christian but had become a progressive Catholic and Democrat. That involved tensions in relation to Robert's conservative evangelicalism and Republican politics. Eric also asked that they schedule structured times together roughly every week or two around one of the kids' sports activities and that Robert not just drop by the house unannounced or fail to show up when they did make plans. The counselor did not initially comment but made a note of the historical, attachment-related parallel of Eric's reactivity to Robert being inconsistent with his grandkids' sports activities and the memory Eric recounted of Robert skipping his key playoff game.

Normalizing Differences and Anxiety

Another important intervention early in family therapy is to normalize differences and anxiety about differences. Clients often carry a fantasy that there may be some way for all to "get on the same page" so they will not have to manage the differences that create relational anxiety. Normalizing the reality that differences will always exist and that anxiety is a common emotional response to differences frames the need for each person to develop practices for the emotion regulation of anxiety and other challenging emotions like shame, anger, or disgust. This type of emotion regulation is a key part of differentiation.

Eric: So he (Robert) comes to Marco's soccer game and is sitting next to Anna. She mentioned that he missed a couple practices that week with a cold, and Dad launches into telling her, "You can't let him stay home with a cold!" Dad, I don't need you telling us how to parent our kid!

Robert: Don't I have the right to offer some advice?

Counselor: Are you asking that as a genuine question, Robert?

Robert: I guess so. . . . I should be able to offer some wisdom based on my life experience.

Counselor: I still can't tell if you are asking a question or making an assertion.

Robert: [*somewhat flustered*] I'm doing both.

Counselor: [*matching Robert's direct style*] Pick one.

Robert: Okay, Eric, do you not want my advice about things like that? Why even get together?

Eric: No, Dad, I'm not looking for advice or feedback about parenting. When we get together, I want to spend time enjoying the activity without you trying to correct me or Anna.

Counselor: Robert, is that something you can do, or do you believe you need to give feedback even if not solicited? [By framing this as an honest question, the counselor maintains a differentiated position between the two and also invites Robert to wrestle with himself and his values rather than simply acquiesce.]

Robert: Yeah, I can abide by that. My therapist has been helping me see that I often feel I have to do things or direct people and that I have trouble believing people might just want to hang out. I know you are good parents, Eric. I get caught up in my own ideas sometimes.

Counselor: This seems like a good opportunity to notice some of the inevitable differences that pop up in family relationships. Eric, you and Anna were comfortable handling Marco's illness and other obligations. And Robert, you had other ideas about what you might do in their place. Robert, do you remember what was going on inside you when you were there with Anna and she shared that about Marco?

Robert: I felt worried because I knew Marco had struggled to make the team and wasn't confident about his play. I want to see him succeed. It concerned me that he might fall behind.

The counselor teased out awareness of both Robert's and Eric's anxiety. Each was then asked about coping strategies he could employ to regulate or soothe his own anxiety in future enactments of similar patterns. This was a *leveling intervention* that established some similarity between Robert and Eric while furthering normalizing the idea that they may cope differently. The idea that these kinds of conflicts are rooted in difficulties managing anxiety can indirectly make it easier to forgive as each realizes hurtful behaviors are not always driven by conscious intentions.

Detriangulating

Differentiation-based family systems approaches emphasize the potential problems of triangulation and the need for detriangulating. This clinical strategy is particularly helpful in forgiveness (see Worthington & Sandage, 2015). Conflictual or unstable dyads often seek a third party for stabilization. A family therapist is always a triangulated figure. Triangulation is not always problematic. It depends on whether the triangulated party can be adequately fair and differentiated in helping the two parties further develop their relationship constructively. Dysfunctional triangulation keeps unforgiveness locked in place.

Robert and Eric each engaged in some unhelpful triangulation. After some initial progress in their interactions outside sessions, Robert relapsed into some impatience and directive behavior when Eric remained emotionally distant. He sent Eric a link to a sermon from one of his own pastor friends that basically mandated forgiving others and suggested that one's own salvation depended on quickly releasing resentments "before the sun goes down." When Eric raised this in session, Robert blurted out, "God wants us to forgive each other!" The counselor responded, "Robert, I'm not going to argue with you about what God wants. But I am concerned you are playing a power card there and crossing a boundary when you try to tell your adult son what God wants him to do. *Wouldn't it take greater faith to let God work and just stay in your own lane?*" Robert was eventually able to identify his own impatience and underlying anxiety that Eric might not ever really forgive him. Vulnerability about his own desire to be forgiven proved more effective with Eric than Robert's triangulation of God.

Eric also used triangulation subtly. In one session, he said, "*Dad, none of my friends' fathers try to tell them how to live or what to do! Why can't you be like Emil's dad? He is just supportive without trying to control his life.*" Such negative comparisons are shaming. In this case, the counselor said, "*Eric, comparing to other fathers is not helping you convey your own longing to your dad. It may feel like you need some other people in your corner to make your case, but what if you tried just speaking from your heart about what you want?*"

Facilitating Grief and Empathy

Grieving and empathy can be valuable interrelated pathways toward forgiveness (Worthington & Sandage, 2015). Family therapy clients are sometimes surprised that as they succeed in improving their relationships, they may start to feel sadness that represents the need to grieve. This proved the case for Eric and Robert. About eight months into therapy, they had made progress in developing positive patterns of interaction with some growing closeness. While they both enjoyed this progress, it also set the stage for both to feel sad about the years of conflict and cutoff. Eric initially voiced this in a moment of vulnerability in a session as he teared up and said, "Sometimes I feel pissed . . . or sad that we couldn't connect when I was growing up. We wasted a lot of years."

Robert initially responded to this defensively, feeling judged. But the counselor diverted the conversation more productively.

Counselor: Eric, I heard you say you feel sad. What do you feel sad about?

Eric: I'm sad that we went so many years without connecting. I'm glad we're making progress now, but at certain moments I feel a wave of sadness and regret. Maybe I shouldn't feel that, but I do.

Counselor: Robert, what do you feel inside when you hear this? I imagine it's hard to take in Eric's longing to have experienced more of this kind of connection with you.

Robert: [*tearing up*] I feel guilty. It's painful to think about the ways I failed.

Counselor: [*sensing a productive softening*] Robert, what do you want to say to Eric about these past disappointments in your relationship?

Robert: [*turning to Eric*] I'm sorry for how I failed you as a father. I didn't understand how to relate, and I can see that did a lot of damage.

Helping family members grieve past disappointments and hurts with each other can simultaneously provide an opportunity to facilitate empathy and forgiveness.

CONCLUSION

In the present chapter, we have described the flexible REACH Forgiveness model of leading people—Christians or non-Christians—through therapeutic or psychoeducational experiences that promote forgiveness for those willing to forgive. Although forgiveness can be addressed in longer courses of treatment (see Worthington & Sandage, 2015), it is often addressed in psychotherapy in shorter bursts of one or two hours or perhaps in groups or workbook assignments of seven hours that are adjuncts to treatment. Few people present for treatment for forgiveness-only psychotherapy. In most instances, forgiveness arises in the midst of treatment for other issues, like depression, anxiety, and personality disorders.

The relationship between time spent trying to forgive and the amount of forgiveness experienced argues strongly for practices to suggest group and workbook options that their patients can take advantage of either free online (www.EvWorthington-forgiveness.com) or for prices of group treatment that typically are less per hour than for individual or couple therapy. We also hope that practitioners see that these interventions can be practiced within the church itself, with groups even being conducted by laypeople who have been shown to have about equal efficacy as trained professionals (Lin et al., 2014). Forgiveness as a Christian virtue is something we all need and is a gift that we as mental health professionals can give to the church as well as practice in a more intensive way in our business.

RECOMMENDED READING

Ripley, J. S., & Worthington, E. L., Jr. (2014). *Couple therapy: A new hope-focused approach*. Downers Grove, IL: InterVarsity.

Worthington, E. L., Jr. (2003). *Forgiving and reconciling: Bridges to wholeness and hope*. Downers Grove, IL: InterVarsity.

Worthington, E. L., Jr. (2005). *Hope-focused marriage counseling: Guide to brief therapy*. Downers Grove, IL: InterVarsity.

Worthington, E. L., Jr. (2006). *Forgiveness and reconciliation: Theory and application*. New York, NY: Brunner/Routledge.

Worthington, E. L., Jr., & Sandage, S. J. (2015). *Forgiveness and spirituality in psychotherapy: A relational approach*. Washington, DC: American Psychological Association.

CHAPTER 21

Shame-Focused Strategies

JOHN C. THOMAS, PHD, PHD

> Do not be afraid; you will not suffer shame.
> Do not fear disgrace; you will not be humiliated.
> You will forget the shame of your youth
> and remember no more the reproach of your widowhood.
>
> ISAIAH 54:4

Shame is "apt to be found in all corners of the therapy room" (Tangney & Dearing, 2011, p. 377). Encountering, processing, and engaging shame is necessary for healing in most clients. Within the shame trove of psychological research, there is a paucity of research on "how to best recognize, manage, treat, or capitalize on shame in the therapy hour" (Tangney & Dearing, 2011, pp. 375–376). Nevertheless, it is a present and abiding condition. Because shame is so incredibly widespread both within and outside of the clinical office, counselors are wise to become increasingly more competent in the area of shame.

To develop an accurate and proper understanding of the origins and outcomes of shame, this chapter presents psychological and theological perspectives. Additionally, counselors must be sensitized to shame-prone client stories and choose effective strategies and techniques to promote healing.

THEOLOGY AND PSYCHOLOGY OF SHAME

Shame is a negative self-conscious emotion that shapes and maintains a person's identity. The vocabulary of shame is extensive, including feeling "ridiculous, foolish, silly, idiotic, stupid, dumb, humiliated, disrespected, helpless, weak, inept, dependent, small, inferior, unworthy, worthless, trivial, shy, vulnerable, uncomfortable, or embarrassed" (Tangney & Dearing, 2002, p. 378). Shame differs from embarrassment and shyness, carrying severer personal and social consequences.

From a personal and clinical perspective, people with shame look different. Perhaps the most common are those who seem insecure, lack confidence, are self-punitive, and have an air of fragility. Other shame-ridden individuals seem perfectly normal until you get to know them, and the underlying shame seeps to the surface.

Still others present as if they could never have bad breath; every aspect of their lives is maintained to appear as if they are totally together. They might be godly, overly kind, and generous. Finally, deep shame can make some oblivious to others; they are entitled, blaming, and lacking in empathy. The common thread in all of these is a self-centered shame.

Clarifying Shame

Shame and guilt. A common misconception is that guilt is the same as shame. The two emotions may be activated by the same event, clouding clarity. Guilt is behavioral focused, that is, it says, "I did a dirty thing," while shame is person-focused, that is, it screams, "I am a dirty person." The feeling of guilt is produced when a person fails to meet a standard, though it might not reflect an accurate appraisal of the situation. Guilt is associated with remorse, sorrow, and sadness (Powlison & Lowe, 2012). It produces reparative strategies with corrective behaviors. In contrast, shame cowers in the shadows (Dickerson, Gruenwald, & Kemeny, 2004; Schmader & Lickel, 2006) with a petrifying terror of exposure. The felt experience is that nothing can be done to correct shame.

Thompson (2015) says that "guilt stands on the platform of shame" (p. 143). Perhaps this is because shame is considered developmentally preverbal, with guilt emerging later (Parker & Thomas, 2009) through moral development. Because shame exists before language, it is impervious to argument and logic. It is rooted in emotional reasoning, not cognitive

reasoning. Thus, shame is more pervasive because it is rooted in the total self and present before words are available to articulate it. Ironically, shame is unconcerned with facts or evidence, rooted in a distortion of truth. Originally, Satan triggered shame by distorting and twisting truth. The result of shame's birth was that humanity would perpetually feel "exposed, vulnerable, devalued self-being, scrutinized, and found wanting in the eyes of a devaluating other" (Zaslav, 1998, p. 155). Self-loathing accompanies shame, and no behavior or repentance can atone for it, though many try.

Shame-Based Identity

When assessing shame, we must distinguish between the experiencing of a shameful event and having a shame-based identity. Shame associated with a specific event or issue, such as the circumscribed shame of someone walking in on you while you are changing clothes, is temporary, and feelings usually diminish soon after. The most destructive type of shame, however, is a shame-based identity in which shame experiences contribute to our forming and knowing who we are. Internally, shame is experienced in terms of "I am" statements. Some common ones are these:

- "I am bad" (unforgivably sinful, disgraceful, damned, disgusting, dirty, perverted).
- "I am defective" (flawed, damaged, broken, a mistake, ugly, pathetic).
- "I am incompetent" (not good enough, loser, ineffective, inadequate, weak, useless, powerless).

- "I am unworthy" (insignificant, inferior).
- "I am unlovable" (unappreciated, unacceptable, unwanted, pitiful).

Shame is corrosive because the "I ams" are further intensified by additional components. For example, "I am bad" is strengthened by adding, "Regardless of what I do, even if what I do appears good." Shame-riddled people "know" that they will be found out. The person lives in a constant state of "knowing" he will be rejected whether from a real or imaginary disapproving public (Behrendt & Ben-Ari, 2012). Shame always wants to shelter itself in some form.

Moreover, one reason that shame is so pervasive is that it was the direct by-product of original sin. Adam and Eve's shame was not only emotions-based, but it was also an objective reality. In that sense, we are all shame prone and have an identity that is linked to a sinful nature. Our first ancestors were both guilty for violating God's mandate, but they were also shameful before God. Though Adam and Eve were no longer innocent before God, they were still image bearers. In the space between innocence and being exposed as naked and disturbingly different, shame found root. The bottom line is that toxic shame is the work of the Evil One, not God (cf. John 10:10).

Shame and pathology. Understanding the role shame plays within psychopathology is necessary in order to apply effective treatment methods (Pineles, Street, & Koenen, 2006). Research strongly indicates that shame is more positively correlated with psychological disorders and offers a better explanation of those disorders than guilt (Dickerson et al., 2004; Pineles et al., 2006). In and of itself, shame is not pathology. Chronic shame, on the other hand, produces a myriad of psychological and personality disorders (e.g., Ashby, Rice, & Martin, 2006; Fergus, Valentiner, McGrath, & Jencius, 2010; Harder, Cutler, & Rockart, 1992; Schoenleber & Berenbaum, 2012; Tangney, Wagner, & Gramzow, 1992; Wetterneck, Singh, & Hart, 2014). Guilt is unassociated with psychological symptoms (Dearing & Tangney, 2011) that can include suicide, the ultimate demonstration of a craving to escape (Blum, 2008; Fullagar, 2003). When adequate attunement and responsiveness to a child's distressful emotional reactions are absent, it can lead to traumatic states and psychopathology. DeYoung (2015) writes, "The isolating experience that turns painful events into long-term pathology is also the experience that creates acute dysregulation and intense shame" (p. 67).

Healthy and unhealthy shame. An expedient means of conceptualizing shame is a continuum of healthy to unhealthy shame. Healthy or functional shame is primarily event and character based, whereas unhealthy or dysfunctional shame is identity based. Healthy shame can motivate us toward godliness and emotional growth. It is a response to the recognition that one is wanton before God. Healthy shame reminds us that we are not infinite, that we have limitations and weaknesses and are sinful, which can prompt and motivate godly living (cf. Joel 2:27; Luke 14:9; Eph. 5:12). In contrast, unhealthy shame is a perniciously deep, internal experience in which a person's sense of self is corrupted by believing and feeling inherently flawed, unacceptable, unlovable, and/or worthless. In excess, shame is intrinsically maladaptive with a core motivational desire to avoid, hide, or escape (Blum, 2008). It produces a self-destructive cycle that increases personal and social chaos. Its hallmark is a conviction in and preoccupation with perceived defects that produces and reinforces itself with compound interest. Since shame was the first experience of Adam and Eve after choosing sin (Gen. 3), it is encapsulated in our DNA (ontological shame). We live in a tragically broken world. Sin vandalized shalom.

Though not the subject of this chapter, the Bible also depicts people and nations whose unhealthy shame and sinful actions metastasize into shamelessness (see Jer. 13:27; Zeph. 2:1; 3:5; Mark 7:20–22; Rom. 1:27; 1 Peter 4:3). In Hosea 4:18, the prophet describes how behavior can degenerate to enjoyment: "They love shame more than honor" (NLT). People may be shameless over a particular act (e.g., sexual acting out) or over patterns of behavior (e.g., manipulating others), or they may be shameless in the sense of lacking a social conscience. In other words, healthy shame is a gift and motivator of change and growth.

Internalized and externalized shame. Another distinction regarding shame is the difference between internalized and externalized shame. Internalized shame (trait shame) is associated with one's personality disposition and character rather than a specific situation (Harmon & Lee, 2010)—being both healthy and unhealthy. It often develops through dysfunctional interaction with attachment figures during the prenatal, infancy, and formative years (Claesson & Sohlberg, 2002). Internalized shame can be deeply integrated into one's worldview, shaping self-perception. It develops one self-insult at a time and is absorbed by a person with no conscious awareness. The messages seep into the soul, polluting one's sense of personhood, resulting in the shamed discounting of self-capabilities, abilities, achievements, and potential. Jung (1957) described shame as "a soul-eating emotion" (p. 23). As it roots itself in the fertile ground of the soul, it fuses with an accumulation of memories, conditioning events, fantasies, thoughts, beliefs, expectations, and other phenomena (Zaslav, 1998); it colors the images of everything (Thompson, 2015). The repetition and barrage of such messages weave shame into the fabric of the soul (Shadbolt, 2009). The shamed person is trapped in a recursive emotional feedback loop of self-perpetuating shame. Since shame is interpreted and experienced through the lens of prior internalized shameful schemas, there is an automatic response to accept the distortions as truth—further reinforcing the person's disposition to the shame experience (Claesson & Sohlberg, 2002; Harmon & Lee, 2010). When a person perceives his "real self" as defective (i.e., shame identity), the feeling is intolerable. Internalized shame not only puts its stamp on a person's identity but forms it.

The torrent of feelings produced by shame becomes a powerful regulator of behavior; this is known as externalized shame. For example, the shamed person develops behavioral patterns that are consistent with the defective beliefs about self. Carol depicted this pattern. She was raised in a highly abusive family that included sexual violations from her father, stepfather, brothers, and her mother's boyfriends. As an older teenager, Carol moved to a city where she became a prostitute.

Shame is interpersonal. Psychologically, shame is a broad term that may refer to an internalized emotion ("to feel shame"), cognition ("I am bad"), body sense ("a sense of shame"), and an interpersonal encounter ("to shame" and "be shamed").

A shame-contaminated core self is associated with relational abreactions and maladaptive social behavioral patterns. Shame often produces reactions that are out of proportion to the situation, directed at self, at others, and most typically at both. When an abreaction is triggered by another, the shamed person may become verbally or behaviorally aggressive, emotionally dysfunctional, and even suicidal. Once the externalized shame is accepted as truth, the manifestations are like those of internalized shame, a motivational drive to hide, escape, and disappear (Harmon & Lee, 2010).

The earthly inception of these patterns is found in the family of origin in which each child is socialized. Children then fall into roles that typically continue into adulthood. Potter-Efron (2007) says that the most common or false selves' roles associated with shame are: "good girl/boy," "naughty one," "difficult one," "crazy one,"

"rebel," "superachiever," "scapegoat," "rescuer," "victim," "responsible one," "clever one," "dumb one," and "clown."

The Emotional Outcomes and Defenses of Shame

Shame may be accompanied by high-intensity emotion or no emotion at all. It often binds with other emotions, creating a cocktail of afflicted emotions that produces a disorganizing effect. Everyone will experience and express shame-based emotions in different ways and through different emotions. Emotional and attitudinal markers of core shame include distress (profound sadness, anxiety, anger, rage), pride (arrogance, grandiosity, entitlement, self-righteousness), low empathy, contempt (self-loathing), negativity (cynicism, blame shifting, including hyperfocus on negative aspects of something/someone), unfavorable attributions of other people (critical, judgmental), envy (prompted by hostility associated with feelings of inferiority), rigidity (legalistic, rule-governed), and perfectionism to distract others from the shame.

To defend against the overwhelming feelings produced by a shame identity, the shamed disavows and distances self from the painful reality of being damaged to the core. Being known is a risk that is too great to bear. For safety, shame-based individuals construct a false self. They might act as though they deserve success, love, affirmation, and so on, but it is pretense. The incongruences between how they feel and how they act leads them to see themselves as impostors—"If they only knew who I am or what I really did, they would never. . . ."

It is this self that Christ said that we must die to (cf. Luke 9:23–24). The old or false self is to die so that the new self can find true life.

A trancelike state emerges as shame takes hold and is triggered into operation. Unaware that shame has been awakened, the person unwittingly covers up undesirable parts of herself, attempts at defending self-operating under the shame radar. Consider Adam and Eve who clothed themselves with fig leaves to hide their bodies from each other, their protection of dry, crumbling leaves epitomizing the futility of concealing shame with defense mechanisms. They only provide an illusion of safety and are self-defeating. Ironically, attempts to hide and protect from the overwhelming and excruciating feelings of shame intensify it and are self-defeating.

Shame Is a Right-Brain Experience

Relational experiences such as attachment are encoded in unconscious internal working models that reside in the brain's right hemisphere (Schore, 2000). The right brain is deeply connected with the body and nervous system, processing emotions coded as bodily and relational memory as well as current emotions. Right brain brings context, emotions, emotional expression, and intuition to a client's story, whereas left brain involves the plot, structure, and order. DeYoung (2015) writes that right-brain language is "the well-spring of passion, creativity, imagery, primary process thinking, and unconscious process. It can also be the site of massive dissociation from emotional and attachment stress—from

whatever is too painful to know viscerally and emotionally" (p. 37). When people say that there is a discrepancy between the "head" and the "heart," they are actually saying that there is a discrepancy between the logic of the left brain and the emotions of the right brain. Left-brain dominance is seen when logic, thoughts, ideas, and speculation are primarily present in the client's discourse. Shame is implicit because it is right-brain dominant.

Thus, the right brain is the home of early attachment damage, leading to at least affect dysregulation and potentially to mental disorders. "A person who can't solve personal and social problems in right-brain ways will come to rely on the left-brain, explicit analytical reasoning. But left-brain analysis will only contain and manage, not solve emotional and interpersonal problems" (DeYoung, 2015, p. 38).

CASE STUDY

Isabella sat in my office with two "failed marriages" and a profound sadness. Though forty-one years old, she appeared older. Isabella presented with a persistent and pervasive sadness and reported feeling unhappy and "vacant" for "no identifiable reasons." She "talked with" her pastor during the dissolution of her marriages but thought that the pastor was getting too "friendly." Isabella called him a "godly man" despite his sexualized behavior. She attributed his behavior to her "seductive" clothing and sending out the "wrong signals." This only reinforced Isabella's sense that God was unsafe, distant, unavailable, and judgmental.

Isabella's relationships were turbulent, but more saliently, romantically intense. Historically, her neediness prompted men to run away because she was too much too soon. Relationship problems stemmed from the anticipation of rejection, and she invited abandonment with her neediness. She blamed herself for every relationship failure. Currently, Isabella "*is not in a relationship*," but "*longs*" to be.

Traumas riddled her past, any one of them sufficient to create dysfunction. Isabella was the last of twelve siblings born to a Hispanic family who "*didn't want*" another child. Throughout her formative years, she was unwelcomed and repeatedly described as a "pain in the ass." She was unfavorably compared with her brothers and sisters, blamed for "everything," and given more responsibility and fewer privileges than her siblings. Isabella cannot remember her mother saying a kind word or showing physical affection. Her mother ignored her, and her father, whom she said was a perpetual philanderer, beat her. The introjected messages led Isabella to conclude she wasn't enough, never measured up, was an inconvenience, and was powerless to change anything.

When Isabella became pregnant at fifteen, her boyfriend blamed her and physically assaulted her. Her parents were furious, calling her a "slut" and a "worthless piece of s***." Both tried to force Isabella to get an abortion, but Isabella believed that the baby would make everything right. Isabella left home and moved across the country to live with an aunt. After the birth of her son, she eventually lost custody to her aunt as an "unfit" mother. Isabella's natural inclination to self-criticism metastasized into self-hatred and then to self-destructive behavior. Soon she was addicted to alcohol and "pills." Impersonal sexual encounters were peppered throughout each month.

At intake, Isabella was sober, had obtained a satisfying job, and was attempting to repair her relationship with her son. Since childhood Isabella feared that every rejection was proof of her unworthiness, which intensified the fear of rejection and abandonment. She lived in fear of being judged, criticized, ignored, or dismissed. As her counselor, I was pulled into her darkness. I found myself walking upstream in a raging river. Passive-aggressiveness masked her terror. At times, she decompensated into gut-wrenching wailing, scooting her chair into the corner of the office, screaming in anguish, "I'm so sorry. I'm a bad girl." Each tear was an indictment. She lived life marinating in shame.

STRATEGIES, INTERVENTIONS, AND TECHNIQUES FOR SHAME

Therapeutically, shame is one of the most challenging issues to treat. The underlying dynamics of shame and its concomitant behaviors are not well understood by many counselors, in part because clients are adept at masking shame despite the excruciating internal experience it creates. In fact, the denial and disguise might be so ingrained that defenses must be identified and lowered before the shame can surface. This is especially true for those who have survived neglect, abuse, and trauma. Thus, the nature of shame doesn't augur well for identification and exploration of shame-prone clients, especially early in therapy. Subsequently, often feelings of shame are nearly invisible to many clinicians.

Shame cannot be eliminated without intentional intervention. Therapy, in and of itself, over time can reduce shame through talking about shamed aspects of self within a safe and supportive environment. Though shame-based individuals have a common core of presentation, each has a unique signature, scripted behavioral complexes of emotions, cognitions, behaviors, and defenses.

The strategies, interventions, and techniques (SITs) can be categorized into five broad therapeutic tasks: (1) establishing a therapeutic bond; (2) entering the story; (3) recognizing, exploring, and identifying themes of shame; (4) processing and addressing the shame; and (5) facilitating spiritual formation. Prior to unpacking the tasks, however, we will begin with an essential counselor personal task.

Prerequisite Work: Explore, Understand, Process, and Own Your Own Shame

To move toward wholeness and effectively work with shame-prone clients, become aware of your own shame. Accept it as part of you. Unproductive countertransference may find expression in anxiety, anger, resentment, contempt, and the like. For example, you may collude with the client to avoid working on shame (Lewis, 1971) in order to circumvent triggering your own.

Often when you experience shame, so does your client. You might have telltale thoughts like these: *I'm not helping this person, I don't know what I'm doing,* or *I'm never good enough.* Rather than getting sucked into your shame vortex, be mindful of it and use it to consider what the client might be experiencing. Reflecting on your own reactions and responses to shame, the defenses you use, and potential countertransference gives insight into and empathy for clients. Also, being self-compassionate and, most importantly, breathing in and embracing God's extraordinary acceptance of you through Christ will naturally transfer to the client. At times, self-disclosure of our own shame is a powerful technique to normalize client shame. Allowing clients to see your own fallenness and humanness through authenticity neutralizes any bestowed omnipotence by the client.

In my human sexuality class, I ask clients to write their sexual autobiography. Exploring your sexual story brings things from darkness to light. It is the best means of making peace with it. A process to use is to start with your earliest memory and develop specific, key experiences and situations that shaped who you are as a sexual person. Relate which events you have struggled with and wish could have been different. Consider those people, relationships, and influences that helped shape your attitudes/values about your body, masculinity/femininity, and sex at various points of your development. Recall specific messages or incidents that created some of your attitudes, values, and priorities. Consider how sexuality was handled in your family of origin. Reflect on how early sexual experiences impacted you. Consider particular incidents that brought insight and growth and those that provided wounded-ness. Consider any unfinished business that may need healing or further growth. Finally, connect your story to being a counselor and how it has impacted, or might impact, your work. By knowing their sexual history and journey, counselors are better equipped to monitor their own physical, behavioral, emotional, and cognitive experiences—especially within the context of therapy.

I believe, along with DeYoung (2015), that a requirement to show that we have faith in the counseling exploration process is to tell our life story sufficiently enough to have a free and open relationship with our own internal narrative about our self and about our self-in-relationships. Therapists who have not worked through their own issues of shame, whether sexual or general, and disconnection from themselves cannot be effective in taking clients to that territory. You need to be in emotional possession of your own story before you can help clients tell integrative narratives (DeYoung, 2015).

In sum, when therapeutic safety is vetted by the client, the focus shifts to accessing shame and overcoming avoidance and hiding. Become an emotional container for the client's pain, feelings so overwhelming that they need a reservoir to hold them. It is so much easier to explain to clients what their problems are than it is to tirelessly stay empathically present and therapeutically attuned to them.

Therapeutic Task 1: Establishing a Therapeutic Bond

A therapeutic value is establishing a secure bond with a client. Shamed clients approach counseling from the history of their relational experiences. Though shame is internal, it is also interpersonal. It is created and maintained through the perception of experiencing the shaming gaze of others. From the standpoint of the theory of the mind (see Premack & Woodruff, 1978a, 1978b), shamed people believe that others think about them in the same way as they think about themselves. Thus, shame involves both the shamed and the shamer (Elise, 2008). Whereas fear activates attachment behaviors, shame typically deactivates attachment behaviors (Hughes, 2007) to create safety through distance. When shaming occurs in one's family of origin, walls of protection are built to fortify against threat. Skepticism and cynicism either prompt an "I don't dare care" or "You only want to get close to hurt me or get something from me" attitude. Even attempts by significant others to affirm or validate the client are brushed aside; nothing is accepted at face value. A lifetime of being devalued is naturally resistant to change.

Practice attunement: presence, empathy, and reflection. Presence is palpable. Empathic responding is an effective means to create safety and provides your clients a taste of feeling God's constant presence. You must do more than feel for your clients; they must experience compassionate, empathic attunement. Hold up a mirror of what the client feels and experiences so that she may see it and eventually come to understand it. Clients need a therapist to be emotionally present to their soul dysregulation and fragmentation in a way that makes them feel deeply, wholly understood and that can lead to reconnection and reintegration of the self (DeYoung, 2015). Simply stated, the task is to *be with* them. This is especially true when facing a client's intense self-loathing. Over the course of time, however, attunement to a client's helplessness, hopelessness, and self-disgust is the best chance for the client to learn what it means to be accepted, validated, and nurtured. As we are fully present providing soothing to shame-prone clients, we model the foundational processes of how to soothe themselves and be attuned to their own needs. Simple statements such as "That makes sense," "Yes, I hear you," and "That sounds horrible" are powerful tools to develop attunement.

Expect shame-prone clients to manifest resistance and create power struggles. Isabella longed for what I was offering her via basic skills, but her self-perception of being inadequate, loathsome, and unwanted interfered.

Hyperfocus on being nonshaming. Timeless fears of abandonment and worthlessness are carried into therapy with deep misgivings about being exposed and found wanting. The voices of historical harmful messages drown out caring and loving messages by the therapist or anyone else (Catherall, 2012). Moreover, anticipatory shame is often more powerful than the shame itself. Understandably, Isabella assumed she would be rejected. She fortified her vulnerability with a defensive stance against everything I said or did, including my greeting at the beginning of the session. I was being measured by unidentifiable expectations. Up against her

terror, I was trapped in a crucible of having each comment interpreted by Isabella as validation of her unworthiness, unlovability, and innate badness.

Ironically, the truth is that everyone is vulnerable—it is part of the human experience. Attempting to show yourself as the exception to all those who have historically shamed the client can be a losing enterprise. Assume that shame-prone clients have no reason to trust you (Harper & Hoopes, 1990). In the case of Isabella, the world of formative encounters that laid the relational template for her shame-based identity necessitated that I look for every opportunity to build an interpersonal bridge. What I consider a helpful opening was received by Isabella with little trust:

Coming to counseling requires a lot of courage. It is hard to admit needing help. Some people won't tell another about personal issues; it says a lot about you, Isabella, that you are willing to face your issues. When I went to counseling, I was anxious and had sweaty hands and a rapid heart rate. All that distress, and I do this for a living! Also, while I want clients to trust me because I believe I'm trustworthy, I struggled to trust my counselors because they had not proven themselves to me. So I realize that I must earn your trust, Isabella; I hope I can. The bottom line is that I know what it is like to sit in your chair. I know just how hard it can be. I am blessed by your courage to make an appointment.

Be Christ incarnate for each client. Identify any leaning toward being judgmental, intrusive, pushy, or frustrated with slow progress. Clients regard Christian counselors as an incarnate sense of what they deeply need through Christ (Thomas & Sosin, 2011). Be hospitable to shame-prone clients such as Isabella, viewing them as guests. Perhaps they will come to perceive that God might see them in the same way (Thomas & Sosin, 2011).

Monitor the communication. Guard your verbal and nonverbal responses. Since language is imbued with meaning, shamed clients often interpret messages as shaming. While your wording may not even closely approximate shame, these clients are sensitized to hyperfocus on being judged. Fear of exposure might negatively reframe handshakes, casual comments, questions, humor, and affirmations, arousing suspicion, diffidence, or stiffness (Harper & Hoopes, 1990).

Check in. Ensure that clients are not misreading or misinterpreting. I typically lead with something like, "Isabella, I want to check in with you to ensure that we are on the same page. It is easy for me to misunderstand someone else, and I don't want to cause you needless pain by saying something that didn't set right with you." If Isabella doesn't believe I'm safe, she will never reveal her most wounded parts. If she cannot speak her shame, it will remain internalized and autonomous (Kaufman, 1992). Careful attention to basic counseling skills facilitates safety.

Avoid attempting to "talk clients out of it." Most shame-prone clients will react negatively if you attempt to show them that they have worth. Attempting to "talk clients out of feeling bad" leads to loss of credibility (Harper & Hoopes, 1990). Left-brain strategies will often fail, especially early in therapy.

Be human. Allowing clients to see your faults, inadequacies, and anxieties might assuage shame. Present yourself as a fallible human being (FHB) who needs God's mercy and grace as much as anyone.

Keep no secrets. Part of building a safe haven is to let shame-prone clients know that you will not keep secrets from them (Harper & Hoopes, 1990). Encourage them to ask you anything about what is happening in counseling. On one hand, they might think of this as a setup, but consistent honesty slowly builds trust. The bottom line is that shame-prone clients need you to be a major thread in building a dependable web of safety over the course of treatment.

Create a no-man's land. The concept of "no-man's land" (see Haley & Hoffman, 1967) is that the rules of society do not apply to the therapeutic space. The counseling office is a neutral zone where typical social etiquette does not exist. You need to ask what would be considered socially inappropriate questions. Also, shame can find a voice when the office space is a place to feel seen, heard, valued, and affirmed unlike the outside world.

Prepare for tests. Most clients test our trustworthiness, but the shame-prone carry it to the doctoral level. It took nearly six months of counseling for Isabella to trust me. Over the course of that period, she tested the waters of my trustworthiness. Allowing Isabella room to work out her anxiety of being judged, abandoned, or betrayed progressively led to disclosure. By consistently allaying her anxieties, Isabella increasingly exposed shaming messages while monitoring my reactions. Some clients are conscious of these tests while others, such as Isabella, are not.

Prepare for post-session effects. I prepared Isabella for the likelihood that she would experience both shame and anxiety from opening up in each session. Of course, post-session shaming serves to reinforce shame.

Therapeutic Task 2: Entering the Client's Story

Humans are storytellers. It is through story that we express our personalities, emotions, afflictions, strengths, weaknesses, passions, values, and life themes. We all have a story that we tell ourselves that creates meaning from the past and the present as well as portending the future.

Transformation through story. When clients share their stories, they are moving toward change. Isabella came to realize that telling her story is the first step. Culling out themes and eventually finding alternative or preferred stories not only helps the counselor make sense of the client but offers insight and opportunities to connect the client to God's story. When Isabella continued to share her story, she gained mastery over it. Over time, she was able to feel her story, own her story, and integrate her story into her whole life.

Right-brain language and connection. Since shame is primarily implicit, it is right-brain dominant. The left brain involves the plot, structure, and order of the story. It is the right brain, however, that brings context, emotions, emotional expression, and intuition. Client stories

are fashioned in both sides of the brain. At this stage of counseling, the feeling-oriented right side of the brain is of most importance. Attempting to speak logic to a right-brain-controlled story will be as successful as speaking pig latin to an English aristocrat. Simply enter the world of the client's story. Accept the unacceptable, and possess a curious interest in the story's unfolding. Moreover, engaging in a client's story reminds us that we are "fellow travelers" (Yalom, 2002).

Right-brain language requires being sensitive to your clients' vulnerability, reflecting their needs and fears when it is possible to do so without shaming them (DeYoung, 2015). Right-brain language involves the stories, metaphors, images, and feeling words that evoke visceral emotions. Rational wisdom will not be effective with clients. Instead, clients need healthy and consistent mirroring they never received from their parents.

Therapeutic Task 3: Exploring, Recognizing, and Labeling Shame

Shame presents in a variety of ways, necessitating the exploration and assessment of its unique nature in each client. You must know the status of their shame and distress. We attempt to decipher how clients avoid expressing their vulnerabilities and how they protect themselves from the terror of being known. Clients like Isabella bristle at the mention of shame. They hear that something else is wrong with them rather than a "diagnostic label" for much of their suffering. Due to fear of exposure or disconnection with feelings, Isabella was not forthcoming in admitting shame. This was complicated by the reality that Isabella's shameful feelings were split off, being regarded as unacceptable and appalling parts of herself. Disconnected from the afflicted part of herself, Isabella avoided distressing feelings, particularly childhood experiences that contributed to them.

Isabella's case highlights the importance of a quality assessment. Pay attention to what is said as well as to what is not said. Can the client tolerate afflicted emotions? Is she able to provide stories that express the language of both hemispheres of the brain? Does the client talk so much that you cannot find space to talk? Sometimes making the statement "I wonder at times if it's a bit scary for you when I ask you how you're feeling" (DeYoung, 2015) will pause the client enough to consider risking exploration of feelings. Clues to shame are found in nonverbal communication. You might choose to use shame-oriented inventories. Though not designed to measure shame, the Distress Tolerance Scale (Simons & Gaher, 2005) measures a client's beliefs or feelings about being in distress—specifically tolerability, appraisal, absorption, and regulation. The information is highly useful in treating shame.

Assess family of origin. Shame-proneness develops within the context of family as well as other meaningful relationships. It is intergenerationally transmitted unconsciously, necessitating exploration of early life experiences and family dynamics. Pinto-Gouveia and Matos (2011) note that research suggests shame-proneness is linked to "early negative rearing experiences . . . such as aban-

donment, rejection, emotional negligence or emotional control and several forms of abusive, critical and/or harsh parental styles" (p. 281). Subsequently, shame becomes woven into a person's autobiographical memory as "conditioned emotional responses, with an impact in the formation of self-relevant beliefs, in attentional and emotional processing and with neurophysiologic correlates" (p. 282).

Since shame arises out of early interactions with significant others, children may introject a negative self-representation if those interactions are shame based (Pinto-Gouveia & Matos, 2011). The internalization process embeds and consolidates beliefs, schemas, attitudes, values, and mind-sets that shape the strengths and struggles of self. For shame, internalization engenders a shame-proneness, which likely stems from some form of trauma.

Based on DeYoung's (2015) narratives, Isabella's family of origin was assessed to determine the dynamics of shame. Culling out historical shame is critical to get at the roots. Many roads can lead to shame, such as making unwise and sinful choices (e.g., Adam and Eve, David), the shameful acts of family members (e.g., Eli over son's sins), victimizing others, betraying and abandoning others (e.g., Judas, Peter), and culture (e.g., woman with bleeding issue).

Not all shame is caused by harsh, shaming parenting. I've had many clients who couldn't find evidence of such parenting. In these cases, they know that their parents loved them. Yet something was off. Parents might be too anxious, troubled themselves, preoccupied, or unaware of how to create intersubjective space necessary to "nurture cohesion, self-awareness, and confidence in their children" (DeYoung, 2015, p. 66).

Assess conversations. Explore how conversations occurred in the family as well as the nature of them. Many family members miss the experience of reliable conversation among themselves in which they feel recognized and understood (DeYoung, 2015). Consider these useful questions: "What happened when people in your family had conversations?" "What was it like around the dinner table when you were eight to ten?" "Were family members open about what they wanted?" "Were they good at listening?"

Assess stories about emotions in the family of origin to explore how emotional vulnerability was handled: given our neurobiological wiring, anything that is perceived as a threat activates the attachment system. When that system involves insecure attachment styles, emotional vulnerability is felt. Consider asking such questions as these: *"What happened when people in your family had emotions?" "Remember a time when a parent was there in a calming way, even though you couldn't fix a problem." "Tell me about times when your parents were upset themselves and talked about what they were feeling." "What happened when somebody in your family made mistakes?" "What happened in your family when family members had differences?" "How was conflict worked out in your family?"*

Assess needs. Narratives about needs can be assessed by asking: "What happened in your family when you needed something or expressed a need?" "Was it fine to want and need something and hope to get it? Or was it important not to need too much?" "How were family members who asked for what they needed viewed by others?"

Determine level of knowing. Knowing refers to understanding how another feels, being in contact with another's subjective world, and having a right-brain connection. Consider whether your client seems to know his parents as people, whether the client feels the parents know him, and how well the siblings know each other.

What is missing? Determine what is missing in your client's story. Children feel shame when what they need to feel human is withheld. Parental attunement is what is often missing with shame-prone clients such as Isabella. When your client was a child, no one was there to regulate his emotions within a tolerable range or help him integrate emotions into words. Thus, events are not connected with emotions. Memories are not woven into felt autobiographical experiences (DeYoung, 2015). When parents are not "in tune" with their children, such children develop with compromised abilities to regulate their own emotions and with a compromised sense of being whole.

Assessment with Isabella helped her sort out what she needed from her parents, what she actually got, and what implicit relational knowing her experiences laid down. Isabella's parents failed to attune to her distressed feelings of sadness, anxiety, and anger, and in fact they invalidated her, leaving Isabella to believe her feelings were wrong and untrustworthy. She was not heard or soothed. Her needs didn't matter. Isabella was conditioned to associate fear and abandonment with intimacy and caregiving. Relationships were not linked with safety or security, leading to her seeing herself—not her parents—as bad. Family shame overshadowed everything in her life. Part of my work was to help Isabella identify who spoke the messages and how those have played out through her life (cf. Sanderson, 2015). Isabella identified and documented spoken and unspoken rules as well as the consequences for violating them.

Another critical dimension that is often missing or seriously lacking is a biblical understanding of God's character, including grace and holiness. As I examined Isabella's early life experiences, she recalled examples of what others said and did that made her feel "less than" or "not good enough." Through faith-oriented living, she masked her mistrust of God. We know that how people attach to others reflects how they attach to God. Modeling God's true character of love, patience, and the like was one means toward repairing her attachment with God.

Genograms are useful, particularly to systemic therapists, for gathering relevant family information and, most importantly, relationship dynamics. They are also valuable for focusing on specific issues such as historical shame. Information gleaned from the aforementioned questions and techniques shed light via the visual depiction of the family on shame patterns and their generational passing.

Elicit unexpressed and avoided shame. Facing the avoidance. Just as Adam and Eve's reaction to shame was to hide hastily behind bushes and fig leaves, shame goes off the grid. Imagine shame cowering under social anxiety, depression, envy, diminished empathy for others, aggression, violence, and even premature termination from counseling (Stadter, 2015) to name a few locations. Thus, mine the shame out from underneath the client's awareness and ability to reach on her own.

Be aware of escape plans. Counseling shamed-prone clients requires them facing what they fear most. Self-protection and self-preservation, which are the natural responses to shame, are toxic. Facing the monster, on the other hand, leads to healing; it is "when shame reaches the light of day that the healing process can begin" (Tangney & Dearing, 2011, p. 378). I use the concept of an escape plan that we unwittingly create to avoid or withdraw from the pain. Isabella's escape plan included introjecting self-blame and disguise. By attributing blame to herself, she found an illusion of control. Worse is that Isabella feels shame for feeling shame. Everyone is a potential perpetrator to her shameful sense of self because she believes that eventually her "real defective self" will be seen.

Draw them out. Stadter (2015) offers several ways of sensitively inquiring about unexpressed content. "I've been reflecting on the very significant topics we've been discussing this past month, and I was wondering if any areas come to mind that we haven't talked about." "You've really been pushing yourself to explore topics that are intensely painful. Can you imagine anything that you wouldn't feel you can bring in here?" Relatedly, Stadter says that it is often wise to explore issues when the client is more controlled and emotionally stable. He says, "Strike while the iron is cold" rather than hot (p. 64). For example, "Two weeks ago you got drunk again and lied about it to your AA group. Maybe we could explore that a bit more today" (p. 64).

Drawing the client's untapped and unexpressed content and feelings out is fraught with barriers and obstacles. Isabella lacked words to voice her shame (Sanderson, 2015). Between her fear of exposure and compensatory "fig leaving," there was little opportunity to explore or release shame. By covering her shame, Isabella not only insulated her deepest woundedness from help but ironically augmented it by inadvertently perpetuating a never-ending cycle of pain.

Not all clients need drawing out, however. For clients with preoccupied/ambivalent attachment, stories continually pour out as if a water pipe exploded with the incredible force of pressure from painful emotions. Their narratives represent protests of being dismissed, misunderstood, and victimized. In such cases, clients need containment more than exploration.

Explore feelings. Difficult issues are most often emotionally clouded. The stench of shame leads people to blind themselves to it. It is masked and camouflaged in many different ways. Thus, finding shame requires careful excavation. As archaeologists investigate places to unearth the fragile clues of a culture's past, we, too, search for the links of our clients' present lives with their pasts. Feelings, like behavior, are artifacts of the forged patterns of living. Exploring and understanding clients' uncomfortable, distress-ful, and overwhelmingly painful feelings will lead us to the roots and foundation of shame. If the client can recognize and understand her feelings, she is in position to change them.

Relatedly, helping clients put feelings to words and words to feelings moves them toward becoming more fully integrated people. Research has shown that putting emotions into words, or labeling affect, correlates with decreased neural activity in the fear center of the brain (i.e., amygdala).

Isabella's disconnection occurs between conscious awareness and the emotional abyss, though much closer to the latter. Isabella was unaware of anger over the way she had been treated from childhood to the present. Moreover, she was unaware of her fears. Isabella learned that the loneliness she felt in relationships was due to her constant fear of abandonment. Humiliation was a prevailing theme in her life; everything about her was a target of ridicule. Not only has shame been a dominant theme for Isabella's life, but the cascade of feelings such as depression, anxiety, anger, and the like that emanated from that shame have made a compound of complexity to treat. These emotions require processing, a vital task in the healing process. Since emotions have adaptive qualities that guide and direct people toward accessing and meeting basic needs and goals, Isabella had to face the feelings she feared most.

Given the vulnerability associated with revealing the ugly self, many methods are required. A number of particular questions proved useful for Isabella. "I wonder if it is scary when I ask you how you are feeling" (validates the feeling of exposure). "As you were talking about how critical your mother was to you, I'm aware of how degrading that must have felt" (a means of directing the client to her internal experience).

My goal was to facilitate a process by which Isabella could label the past. Linking present feelings and beliefs to antiquated and obsolete messages is a step toward diminishing their control of the internal self. Isabella, like all shame-prone clients, needed to evict her childhood messages out of her head and heart. After months of exploring and processing her past, we settled on the label "soul terrorism" to embody the crippling effects of her family's maliciousness.

Ask, "What happened?" Counselors too often accept vague statements by clients without linking them to events and details. When a client tells you about his feelings, follow that up with "What happened?" For instance, "Isabella, when you started feeling so lonely on Friday, what happened earlier in the day?" "What was going on when you noticed feeling lonely?"

Focus. Gendlin (1982) believed that clients have a "felt sense" that, if noticed, could open the door to deeper understanding of feelings. This technique uses relaxation processes to prepare the client to focus on feelings, thoughts, or situations. Next, the client scans her body to notice a "bodily sense" connected to the associated feelings. I asked Isabella to place her hand on the side of her stomach, where one of her bodily senses occurred, to determine whether that spot could tell her what she was feeling. I then asked Isabella to amplify her feelings. When she sensed anger,

I encouraged her to exaggerate it. The goal is to learn that even extremes of feelings can be stewarded. Isabella learned that feelings do not have to paralyze her or prevent her from better living. Amplification was also useful when Isabella would gloss over feelings. Bringing her back to the ignored feelings with amplification gave shame the voice it demands.

Encourage journaling. Therapeutic journaling is a well-worn technique that has tremendous impact on the shame-harboring client. Many methods exist that are beyond the scope of this chapter on how to employ journaling, but the connecting thread is the purposeful reflection of feelings and enhancement of self-awareness.

Use the time-machine elevator. A useful metaphor is imagining a unique elevator that takes a person back in time. The number of floors descended correlates with how far back the client is going. Isabella, a forty-one-year-old woman, decided to go back to eight years of age, thus thirty-three floors. After Isabella pushed the elevator's button, I gently and slowly directed her to descend. She experienced the sensation of slowly moving back through time with each floor. Arriving at the eighth floor, the elevator doors opened, allowing Isabella to step into her past. At this point, you can take the client in a number of different directions, such as looking around to discover a memory, to reenter a previous experience, or simply to observe the past. Facilitate as many details as possible, including thoughts, feelings, images, sensations, the five senses, and behaviors experienced at that time and in the present reexperiencing of it. Strive to bring the entire memory into high-definition focus. Then you can ask what the client is noticing, seeing for the first time, and so on. Often asking where God is in the experience is useful, as well as the client's awareness of faith and spirituality in the process.

Listen for longings. Along with feelings of shame is a longing. Isabella's longings were not just for what was lost but for what never was. An unmet need keeps life frozen in time. In many respects, Isabella's shamed feelings related to unmet needs that called to be thawed.

Longings can be embedded in many issues, including self-sufficiency, dependency, and sinful actions. Separate longing for what is legitimate versus illegitimate. Often longings are so intertwined that untangling them seems impossible.

Affiliated with longing is anguish of what might never be or never was. Disappointed desire is a life-shaping force (cf. Prov. 13:12). Emotional longings are often layered. When one longing is operative, others may be activated as well. A sad reality is that many shame-based individuals cannot recognize all their losses until they have addressed other pathological patterns that block access to the shame. Personal longings and plans are blocked by the unresolved grief, which remains mostly unconscious (Scharff & Scharff, 1987). The experiences of loss are typically buried under an array of unwieldy issues and life patterns, such as parents who were not physically or psychologically present, lost relationships, dashed dreams, and repetitive failures.

I explored Isabella's longings by querying who she would like to be, not who she believes she must be or who she currently is. Isabella listed unwanted identities and her ideal identities with two columns: unwanted (how she doesn't want to be perceived) and ideal (how she wants to be perceived). Next, I assessed their origin, the beliefs and messages that underlie them, and how they direct her behavior (Sanderson, 2015).

Voice the pain. When appropriate, gently challenge a client's reluctance to voice the pain. Shame must be given a voice; it must be drawn out to speak the messages that it carries. Simply, shame must be externalized (Hulstrand, 2015). "Isabella, I don't know the deep layers of pain inside of you. But I do know that getting it out is the only way to stop its coercive and cancerous presence. God wants to set you free from the lies and bondage of the Evil One. It begins by bringing it out of darkness and voicing it into the light." Putting shame into words with a safe person can eventually free a client from shame's prison.

Use the empty chair. One means of voicing shame is to get under the compensatory strategies and secondary emotions to the primary shame by speaking it. For example:

You are angry and bitter at your mother for the abhorrent way she treated you. It is hard to feel and live with anxiety, but it is easier than feeling the enormous shame of feeling belittled, dismissed, devalued, and treated as a nonperson. More importantly, God wants to loosen the grip of things that prevent us from moving forward, worshiping him freely, and maturing in Christ. There is an exercise that many others have found helpful when trying to make sense of their feelings. It certainly doesn't fit everyone, nor does it always work to perfection. It involves two chairs; the one you sit in and another that you will speak to about. . . . Strangely, speaking to an empty chair can remove the fog over actual feeling, give insight, and bring a level of healing. What thoughts do you have about this technique?

Find a hole in the armor. Often clients have a crack in their defense system that offers a way in. This might be in the form of a self-affirming statement that can be a launching point to diminish shame (Hulstrand, 2015). For Christians, faith in Christ and holding on to the gospel is the best launching pad.

Understanding the implications of the gospel of Jesus Christ. The good news of the gospel is more far reaching than being saved from our sin (cf. Rom. 5:8–11; 6:23; 1 Cor. 15:1–8; 2 Cor. 5:14–19). Isabella and I explored how the gospel's power can transform her shame beyond her conversion experience. We explored that peace with God procures the fuel for experiencing the peace of God. We are called to live a life that is worthy of the gospel (Phil. 1:27–30), but that is often hindered by shame, which focuses on our unworthiness—not in the sense that everyone is unworthy of God, but that Isabella was particularly unworthy. Learning the depth of how the gospel is the grace of God (Acts 20:24) is a process that continues throughout life. Resting in the perfect grace, mercy, and love of Christ as opposed to basing our view of God and ourselves

on our own feelings, performance, or sinning can only produce freedom from self. I helped Isabella learn that she could preach the gospel to herself and could more fully understand that the cross is the proof that she is loved and embraced by a God who will never abandon her. She was then able to effectively and consistently challenge the messages of her toxic shame. She was also asked to journal about the tasks of the Messiah and what implications they had for her: to bind the brokenhearted, to set the captives free, and to restore what has been taken away (see Isa. 61:1–3).

Therapeutic Task 4: Processing and Treating Shame

One processing strategy is to feel the shame. Bradshaw (1988) believes that feeling any feeling is shame reducing. Feeling feelings, however, is only a means to an end. Clients need to learn shame regulation. Isabella fed her emotional dysregulation by repetitively telling herself negative, contemptuous, and defective self-statements. She needed to face her internal critics to find redemption and healing. Yet the process also temporarily intensifies the emotional distress. Ultimately Isabella had to accept her painful emotions without self-condemnation and come to know those terrifying feelings.

Next, clients must translate into words their preverbal, global reaction to shame, thereby expediting the development of a more logical, differentiated thought process. Clients need to reevaluate their global negative self-attributions. Most flaws, setbacks, and transgressions do not warrant global feelings of worthlessness or shame.

For example, Isabella found that replacing her beliefs about suffering, which generated negative self-attributions, with a biblically based theology of suffering (Thomas & Habermas, 2008, 2011) reframed and shed new light on her shame.

Below are several techniques to address shame-based thinking, feeling, and behavior. Many of them are derived in part from dialectal behavioral therapy (Linehan, 1993), attachment theory, and Bowenian therapy (Bowen, 1976, 1978).

Cognitive and affective strategies. Isabella's treatment included cognitive, experiential, and systemic work. Cognitively, shame-based thinking is patterned for each person. Regardless of the specifics, shame is filled with dire self-predictions, selective focus on negative aspects of events, negative explanations of others' behavior, and rigid rules about how people should behave. Shame-riddled clients need to know that they are not their thinking or feelings. Every thought or feeling cannot be trusted because they are not based in absolute reality. Clients must be taught principles that aid in understanding what they think and skills to accept what they feel rather than relying on their thoughts and feelings to determine reality. Additionally, learning emotional regulation skills helps develop emotional vocabulary and emotional communication skills (DeYoung, 2015).

Psychoeducation: neuroplasticity of the brain. Shamed-prone clients need education on a host of issues, but I will highlight just one. To convey how the brain can change, I use the analogy of green grass that is trampled into a dirt path from repeated foot traffic. Likewise, the brain creates paths based on repeated self-messages. Once established, the pathways become entrenched and intractable to change. Grass seed can be sown on the trodden paths, but it takes time, effort, care, and boundaries to protect the newly sown seed and fledgling new grass. This technique sets the stage for cognitive strategies later in treatment.

Shame boxes technique (Sanderson, 2015). Shame-based messages must be contained and hindered from replaying in the mind. Isabella was asked to find and decorate a small box. She wrote down each shame message on slips of paper, folded them, and placed them in the box. When ready, Isabella scheduled twenty to thirty minutes to look at one strip and allow shame feelings to arise, journaled them, and rated the percentage of perceived truth. One by one we processed each message. Each week Isabella rerated the perceived truth of each message until it lessened to an acceptable percentage. Ultimately she learned that tolerating a level of shame is possible.

Impact exercise. Additionally, Isabella wrote down the impact of each message on her life. Creating two columns, she documented in the first column ways that she had surrendered control of her life to each message. The second column held truths from the truth box.

Truth box. This box contains messages of truth including scriptural support. While Satan distorted truth to make us shameful, it is the truth of who we are in Christ that can set us free. Following the processing of each shame message, Isabella created a new message that linked with biblical and objective reality. Here is an example:

Whereas I once thought I was worthless, I KNOW that I am invaluable to God! Luke 12:6–7 teaches me: "Are not five sparrows sold for two pennies? And not one of them is forgotten before God. Why, even the hairs of Isabella's head are all numbered. Fear not, Isabella, because you, Isabella, are of more value than many sparrows."

Isabella then recorded these truth messages in the second column of the impact exercise, noting how the truth impacted her when she acted on it.

Parts are parts technique. Another useful technique is derived in part from the work of Schwartz (1995, 2001), who developed a model that attempts to understand each person as a cast of parts. Clients are to become masters over their parts. Although his model suggests specific labels for each part, I customize it. For Isabella, the introjected shame is only one cast member, not all of them. Isabella's shame part (actually many shame parts exist) became dominant. Eventually Isabella was able to discount and distance herself from those shamed parts. This concept is also linked to voicing the pain by helping each shamed part find words. Moreover, it helped Isabella realize that the self-condemnation and poor choices were only parts of her, not her whole self.

Practice of vulnerability technique. Brown (2004) studied both men and women to bring greater clarity to what dispels shame-based thinking and behaviors. Her discovery, while not unique to psychotherapy, revealed that the practice of vulnerability is one of the most effective ways to uncover feelings of shame and dispel the cognitive distortions of isolation and hiding. Homework is assigned that challenges clients to do an agreed-upon activity (or activities) that pushes them into the "horror zone." This might include going to restaurants by oneself, which was assigned to Isabella; asking someone out; speaking in public; exercising assertiveness; sharing a shameful issue with someone; or any legitimate activity that tends to provoke shame in the client.

God and self-compassion. The human brain responds to encouragement, kindness, and compassion. It turns off the brain's alarm system, allowing for self-regulation. Neff (2011) encourages us not to see ourselves as a problem to be fixed but rather through the eyes of self-kindness. Doing so allows us to see ourselves as human beings who are valuable and worthy of care. King Solomon wrote, "Anxiety in the heart of man causes depression, but a good word makes it glad" (Prov. 12:25 NKJV). We can offer such words to ourselves as well. Isabella thought of the most compassionate person she has known and how that person conveyed compassion. She was instructed to note any feelings and sensations in association with the memory. Then she was to imagine treating herself in similar fashion to how the identified compassionate person would or did treat her. She was asked what words and expressions of compassion she would use.

Receiving God's compassion toward us and directing compassion to ourselves promotes emotional resilience (Gilbert & Proctor, 2006), decreases distressful emotions, including shame (Germer &

Neff, 2013), and reduces psychopathology (Barnard & Curry, 2011; MacBeth & Gumley, 2012). As noted earlier, the gospel reminds us that we are loved even when we lived in ways that displeased God (cf. Rom. 5:8). Isabella also journaled such passages as Psalms 86:15; 103:8; 145:8–9; Isaiah 49:13; 2 Corinthians 1:3; and many others that continued to deepen her understanding of what she possesses through the gospel of Jesus Christ.

Meeting with Jesus technique. Salient information, insight, and healing are accessible by imaging a conversation with Christ (non-Christians can image a mature and wise person, though it isn't the same). Isabella was not comfortable in creating our own imagery. So, after a brief period of relaxation, I guided her to imagine seeing Christ and his disciples walking a dusty and dirty path on their way to a village. From her vantage point of sitting on a small hill, she noticed that Jesus directed his disciples to sit down under several large shade trees. To her surprise, rather than joining them, Jesus walked across the path to sit down next to her. Isabella was offered the opportunity to play that scenario out in her mind's eye. She could ask a question and/or listen to what he had to say, though I suggested that Jesus might be the one asking questions. Isabella was to take in the experience, the wisdom, and bring it with her back into the office, where it was explored.

Two-chair critic: criticized dialogue technique. Framing Isabella's internal conflict as consisting of different parts—an internal accuser, internal victim, shamed self, and a godly self—allowed her to explore each part by itself and against other parts. Neither one represents their whole self, just parts. Greenberg, Rice, and Elliott (1993) suggest a two-chair technique that invites client parts to a controlled dialogue. The intent for Isabella was to heighten awareness of the internalized messages she had integrated into herself, to provide an avenue for expressing affect, and to engender an experiential impact. This was accomplished by having the internal accuser and judge sit in one chair while the internal accused and defendant were assigned the other chair, facing each other. The inner critic voice is rarely questioned and might have found life from parental messages. When in the inner critic chair, Isabella was a harsh prosecutor, levying evidence to prove her defectiveness. Isabella's typical reaction to these allegations was either to concede that the criticism was true or, at least initially, retort the critic's shaming voice. From the accused chair, Isabella's internal critic levied her own barrage about what it was like to be criticized.

Three-chair soothing: self-dialogue technique. A variant of the two-chair technique was having Isabella talk to the critic and shamed self (derived from Sutherland, Perakyla, & Elliott, 2014). Isabella spoke truth and showed compassion to the inner critic and inner accused parts. I stationed Isabella between the other two parts, as a counselor would in the two-chair technique. I took the other side so that I was looking directly at her. Likely, you will need to help your client find language that soothes the critic and accused—in other words, doubling. A goal was to assist Isabella in understanding that both of the parts are wounded, each expressing their pain differently. Also, the "evil one" (see Job 1–2; John 10:10; Rev. 20:7–10) has hijacked the accuser's voice to infuse it with biting and destructive powers to brainwash the other part. Isabella chose to speak first to her shamed part.

You feel awful. You feel like you are worthless, that there is nothing good about you. You don't just feel bad about things that you have done that were sinful and wrong; you feel like you are wrong—that there is nothing good about you. Those are lies from the Devil. What is true is that God loves you. His Son has covered you and every part of me with his righteousness. . . . God can only see us through his Son, Jesus's, righteousness, not your unrighteousness. Without Christ no one is good; we are all bad. You cannot possibly be worse than anyone else. I love you, and I will take compassionate care of you with God's help.

To the accuser, Isabella said:

You are angry and hateful. You voice and act out your anger. The way you express your hurt and what you say is harsh, sinful, and harmful. . . . It is destructive. It reflects the hate of the Evil One. You are a liar just like the Devil. You are not just destroying the accused part but yourself as well. Your behavior masks the real pain and shame you feel. It is okay to say that you are hurt and that you are mad. It is not acceptable for you to take out your own hate on other parts of me. I'm grateful for

what you are trying to tell me—for the important information I need to know about having good boundaries. But the shamed part is not the enemy; the Devil is. You must stop believing his lies.

To both:

Both of you need to find healing through reconciliation. To honor the feelings and thoughts of the other part . . . there is wisdom in both. Most of all, you both need to accept the wisdom of God as well as the truth that he loves, likes, and delights in all of us. He, too, hurts with our hurt. He doesn't want either of you, nor me, to stay stuck. He is the hope for all of us. Together we can reflect God's truth. Glorify him. He will be our God; we will no longer make our pain our god.

Eventually Isabella brought these parts into the service of the Lord. Whether joyful, happy, sad, angry, or shamed, the focus would be God. Using a fitness analogy, I also told her that as the truth-based muscle becomes strong and stable, the accuser muscle weakens. Continued working out of the truth muscle is required. In reality, however, eliminating all distressful feelings is not the goal (Thomas & Habermas, 2008, 2011). In the case of Isabella, the initial work was helping soothe feelings, to create softer feelings, and most importantly to let the life of Christ permeate her soul. In doing so, she moved into union with Christ, especially in his death and resurrection.

A final note on soothing: soothing calms the inner self as well as effectively reduces physiological hyperarousal in conjunction with relaxation techniques. As the autonomic nervous system calmed, Isabella also ameliorated her interpersonal functioning through diffusing conflictual situations.

Letter techniques. Venting is an important part of getting in touch with feelings and identifying themes. Isabella was paralyzed by strangled feelings of shame. She needed to give those feelings a voice, something that was conditioned out of her. Isabella was instructed to write a letter to each person who mistreated her (these letters are never mailed) about an event that triggered pain and shame, describing what the person did that was hurtful, how she felt about it, what issues in her life came out of it, and how she was going to allow God to use those issues to grow her for his service. Once she had expressed herself, Isabella's next step was to release and surrender the shame to Christ. Many counselors stop at simply expressing the feelings, which might only activate them. Isabella took the culled-out pain and handed it over to the God whose Son died for everyone's shame. Isabella also took time to replace the negative affect with positive affect associated with embracing grace and mercy, acceptance, forgiveness, and God's goodness. Isabella was also encouraged to write a letter to her wounded self, using her dominant hand to access the right side of her brain. At times, she created dialogue, switching from the dominant hand to tap into her older self and her left side to give the wounded child self a say in the conversation. Other times, she only wrote with her nondominant hand to focus on the child's voice. Finally, Isabella wrote a letter to her past self and then to a future self—a preferred story, if you will. I asked her to incorporate how God would guide her in her journey to a new or maturing future self, then write a gratitude letter to God for his grace and guidance.

Radical acceptance technique (Linehan, 1993). To find freedom clients must learn to let things come as they are, that is, to accept reality without judgment. Wang and Tan (2016) found that practicing non-judgment yielded a temporary suspension of guilt and shame-based judgment, and also created an experience of God's compassion. Suspending judgment helped clients to see the whole picture by providing space to notice God's compassion for struggles and suffering. Isabella learned to perceive her circumstances without putting demands on them, feel present emotions without trying to escape them, and observe thoughts without trying to control them. Moreover, bringing the gospel of Jesus Christ into mindfulness (i.e., focusing on the cross) grounds the technique in our biblical worldview.

Mindfulness. One way to accomplish the above is through mindfulness, which facilitates feeling shame with no escape plan. The clear focus on the present moment with the future hope in physical communion with Christ allows for a rich application of mindfulness to be given to Christian clients (Wang & Tan, 2016). Isabella learned how to view her feelings without seeing feelings as facts. Using Ecclesiastes 7, where Solomon pens the stunning words that sorrow is better than laughter, also reframes distressful feelings. Rather than avoiding afflicting emotions, the client takes a welcoming approach to them.

Mentalization. Mentalization captures the process by which people make sense of the world by imaging how other peoples' state of mind can influence behavior (Allen, Fonagy, & Bateman, 2008; read about "theory of mind" to better understand this process). Schore (2003a, 2003b) maintains that how parents regulate their child's emotions has a profound impact on a child's internal experience of shame. Through mentalization, the child and client are able to feel clearly, which isn't the same as thinking clearly, though to feel one must also think. Shame-prone clients experience affect dysregulation. Like Isabella, they can learn to think about affect, not just feel it. For example, Isabella realized she thought, *Since I cannot make happen what I need, I feel bad. Therefore, something is bad about what I need and what I feel, which means something is wrong with me. I know this isn't true even though it feels true. I will simply accept that I feel it as true.* The goal is to facilitate the process of feeling shamed without the affect dysregulation. Such feelings are embraced rather than avoided. Everyone can learn to hold their fears, anxieties, and defenses.

Opposite-action technique (Linehan, 1993). When we feel distressful emotions, we naturally act consistent with that emotion. The goal was to encourage Isabella to act opposite from her proclivity to seek out men and become dependent. She learned that this impulsivity blocked the process of finding peace of self.

Acting "as if" technique. Similar to opposite action is Adler's technique to encourage clients to act the way they desire to be. People live their lives as if the constructs they hold are absolute truths or facts rather than situationally based constructs. Similarly, Kohlenberg and Tsai's (1994) functional analytic psychotherapy focuses on shamed clients engaging in behaviors such as public speaking that challenge the shame by developing new skills and abilities. The rationale for this technique is that when clients develop skill and flexibility in situations that typically evoked toxic shame, the new behaviors desensitize the intensity of shame. Devising ideas about how Isabella could act if she was shame-free switched the focus from maladaptive constructs to adaptive ones. She monitored herself physically (e.g., head up, shoulders back, controlled facial features), psychologically (e.g., confident, secure), socially (e.g., healthy boundaries), and spiritually (e.g., relating to God through gratitude). This homework was processed and tweaked throughout her sessions.

Negative affect tolerance technique (Linehan, 1993). Emotional regulation is a central skill for the treatment of many disorders. Rather than engaging in her shame-inducing processes, Isabella learned how to step back and observe her thoughts and feelings with mindful nonjudgment. Refocusing on the facts rather than on her evaluation of them helped Isabella develop an ability to identify and describe her internal world. An aspect of this work required Isabella to develop tolerance for negative affect (Tangney & Dearing, 2002).

Finding the exceptions technique. Isabella also sought to find exceptions to her pattern of shame-inducing inner dialogue.

Probe client statements to determine generalizations, deletions, and distortions. These are cognitive filters that impoverish our understanding of the world (see Bandler & Grinder, 2005; Grinder & Bandler, 1976; Thomas & Sosin, 2011 for more detail).

Pros and cons list technique (Burns, 2008). Isabella identified the advantages and disadvantages of endeavoring to be a "perfect person." While this isn't possible for anyone, there is a point of diminishing returns. For Isabella, becoming a "perfect person" is more far-reaching than being a "really good" person or a "godly person." I taught Isabella to accept herself as a fallible human being, which is the basis for needing a Savior and Sustainer.

Setting boundaries intervention. Shame had crippled Isabella's ability to set boundaries, assert, and respect herself. External boundary setting is impossible unless a person has developed the ability to have internal boundaries. Boundary techniques can be geared toward helping clients develop internal and external boundaries. External boundaries involve systemic work whether working with the client individually or with the family system.

Rebuilding a new identity strategy. For Isabella, having a bad identity was better than having no identity at all. I asked her if she wanted to choose to remain the person that she was or become a new person who lives in the mercy, grace, and identity of the Creator. The payoff would be a significant shift in the manifest nature of her life. A new vantage point would reorient her current view of self, others, the world, and God. Exploring the ways

in which God describes our new identity also helped Isabella. These included being a daughter in Christ, a soldier of the cross, a priest, a servant of the King, and a citizen of heaven. Additionally, just as Saul became the apostle Paul and just as we receive a new name in heaven representing a new identity (Rev. 2:17), Isabella could become a new person. She must wash away the soot of an adulterated childhood and subsequent choices. Mahrer (2004) contends change comes from no longer being the person with the problems and bad feelings. The problems or bad feelings are not the targets. Rather, Isabella could become a person who lives from a core of Christ. She could become a whole being who has godly desires and ungodly desires, euphoric and dysphoric feelings, functional and dysfunctional behavior, and a past littered with relational trash and treasured friendships.

Universal limitations intervention. Part of healing for Isabella was understanding and accepting limitations and weaknesses as part of the human experience. They remind us that we are not God. We accept that in our broken state God accepted, loved, liked, and delighted in us. These areas are ones to put under the grace of God and grow through spiritual formation.

Enriching and using the support system strategy. In addition to the normal benefits of a quality support system, Isabella asked her support members for feedback on her strengths. Then she described what she would think about another person with those assets. As a side note to the support system, I also asked Isabella to create a list of who she is in Christ along with a verse or two that accompanies that truth.

Both of these lists were to be reviewed three times daily.

Task 5: Spiritual Formation

Spiritual formation might not seem like a treatment strategy, but it is a fundamental set of experiences to promote life transformation. From a clinical perspective, spiritual formation can be reframed as resilience and coping strategies.

Biblically based theology of self-intervention. While many Christian clients have a biblically based, cognitively stable theology of humanity and God, their emotion-based theology overrides it. Isabella believed that she was not worthy of serving God. I worked with her to eventually accept that God doesn't want us to be acceptable to him, just surrendered and abandoned to him. Like all shame-prone clients, Isabella needed to transform an emotionally charged theology such as her struggle with God's love and delight over her into congruence with her espoused beliefs. The goal is for her biblically based theology to eventually dominate her heart.

God's soothing intervention. Identified and fortified strengths can be soothed by God rather than another. In the case of Isabella, she would learn a healthy God concept, develop self-compassion, and comprehend a balanced view of her weaknesses and limitations.

Spiritual discipline strategies. Spiritual disciplines such as prayer, solitude, fasting, and worship are powerful strategies that promote emotional and spiritual health and well-being. Isabella was taught that worship is about our individual response to God; it isn't about us but about God. It reflects our commitment to God and our focus on him. Worship music is only one natural response of adoring God. Isabella used worship music as a means of moving outside of herself. She also meditated and journaled on passages such as Colossians 3:1–2 and Philippians 2:5–8.

CONCLUSION

No single chapter can identify and unpack all SITs or detail their workings. My intent was to introduce counselors to a spectrum of ideas and tools from which you can address client shame. Remember that while healthy shame is effective for regulating behavior, unhealthy shame hijacks mental, emotional, and spiritual vitality. Shame-prone people overinterpret incidences as confirmation of their unworthiness. Messages, too, filter through a self-concept that establishes and sustains them as bad, unlovable, defective, selfish, inept, and/or any other unfavorable attribution. Accordingly, these mind-sets root the chronic, excessive, intense, and unatonable, debilitating toxin of shame in the soul, squeezing out life-giving truth. It is this insidious, cunning, and baffling nature of shame that makes it an intractable clinical issue.

Since shame was birthed in original sin, it is part of the human condition and likely present in a collection of disorders and issues. Because it is in the DNA of fallen humanity, shame—like original sin—is susceptible to the gospel's life-changing influence. Tap into the willingness, courage, and valor of truth—ideally through pressing into the presence of Christ—to find soul-soothing and restorative healing.

RECOMMENDED READING

Bradshaw, J. (1988). *Healing the shame that binds you*. Deerfield Beach, FL: Health Communications.

Dearing, R. L., & Tangney, J. P. (Eds.). (2011). *Shame in the therapy hour*. Washington, DC: American Psychological Association.

DeYoung, P. (2015). *Understanding and treating chronic shame: A relational/neurobiological approach*. New York, NY: Routledge.

Fossum, M. A., & Mason, M. J. (1986). *Facing shame: Families in recovery*. New York, NY: W. W. Norton.

Harper, J. M., & Hoopes, M. H. (1990). *Uncovering shame: An approach integrating individuals and their family systems*. New York, NY: W. W. Norton.

Tangney, J. P., & Dearing, R. L. (2002). *Shame and guilt*. New York, NY: Guilford Press.

Thompson, C. (2015). *Anatomy of the shame: Retelling the stories we believe about ourselves*. Downers Grove, IL: InterVarsity.

CHAPTER 22

Trauma-Focused Strategies

Heather Davediuk Gingrich, PhD

For he has not despised or scorned
the suffering of the afflicted one;
he has not hidden his face from him
but has listened to his cry for help.

PSALM 22:24

Trauma is everywhere. The news is full of stories of natural disasters, war, terrorism, domestic violence, and child abuse. The National Center for PTSD (2016, Oct. 3) reports that approximately six out of every ten men (60 percent) and five out of every ten women (50 percent) will experience at least one trauma in their lifetime, often within the context of relationships. Within the United States alone, one in six boys and one in four girls is sexually abused before the age of eighteen (US Department of Justice, n.d.), and 31.5 percent of women have experienced at least one incidence of intimate partner violence (Breiding, Basile, Smith, Black, & Mahendra, 2015). Unfortunately, the statistics for child abuse (Tracy, 2011) and domestic violence (Drumm, Popescu, & Riggs, 2009) within conservative Christian circles parallel those of the general population. Christian counselors, therefore, need to know how to treat trauma survivors.

There are two broad categories of trauma. The first includes victims of natural disasters, combat trauma, and single-incident trauma, which often result in a diagnosis of post-traumatic stress disorder (PTSD). The second encompasses chronic, relational trauma, such as child physical, sexual, psychological, or spiritual abuse or neglect and is referred to as complex trauma (CT). Complex trauma has a more complicated presentation. The added complexity is in large part due to CT occurring during a particularly vulnerable stage of psychological development when relational attachments are formed. For example, children are learning how to regulate their affect and to integrate their experiences into a sense of self and identity (Putnam, 1997). Furthermore, CT often occurs at the hands of someone (e.g., parent, pastor, teacher, coach, camp counselor) who is supposed to be a source of safety and protection rather than a source of harm (Courtois & Ford, 2009).

Recommended treatments for PTSD are primarily behavioral and cognitive behavioral techniques. Treatments for CT, on the other hand, are multifaceted because the focus needs to be broader than dealing solely with post-traumatic symptoms. The focus of chapter 6 in this volume is behavioral techniques, many of which are relevant to the treatment of PTSD. *Treating Trauma in Christian Counseling* (Gingrich & Gingrich, 2017) also looks at specific treatment approaches for various types of trauma. Therefore, in this chapter on strategies for trauma treatment, I primarily will focus on CT, making comments where applicable to strategies for working with PTSD.

THEOLOGY AND PSYCHOLOGY OF TRAUMA

Trauma can have devastating effects on its victims. The diagnostic criteria for PTSD in the *Diagnostic and Statistical Manual of Mental Disorders, 5th edition* (DSM-5; American Psychiatric Association, 2013) give a good indication of what victims suffer. The intrusive recurring symptoms, such as flashbacks and nightmares, are some of the most disturbing to individuals. Avoidant symptoms, such as staying away from places or people that can potentially trigger intrusive symptoms can impact day-to-day life and negatively impact functioning in significant ways. Alterations in arousal can also be problematic, particularly hyperarousal, in which a traumatized individual's nervous system is on high alert, resulting in sleep disturbance and overreactions to perceived

danger where there actually is none (e.g., a car backfiring and the person pulling out a weapon in an attempt to protect himself). Alterations in cognitions and mood can be severe in that traumatized individuals often blame themselves for the trauma, resulting in self-hatred, or they experience severe depressive or anxiety symptoms.

As mentioned above, CT survivors often experience the above PTSD symptoms along with many other symptoms. These include intense feelings of guilt and shame, impairment in identity formation, inability to develop secure attachments with significant others, difficulty trusting people, problems with affect regulation, feelings of hopelessness about recovery, and physical problems related to the abuse (Courtois & Ford, 2009; Herman, 1997).

God's original intention for us was to enjoy intimacy with him and his creation. It was only after Adam and Eve's sinful disobedience, resulting in expulsion from the garden of Eden (Gen. 3), that humans began to undergo hardship, including traumatic experiences. The Bible talks about natural disasters, such as the great flood in the time of Noah (Gen. 6–8), and the windstorm that caused the collapse of the house that killed all ten of Job's children (Job 1:18–19).

Scripture includes relational trauma in addition to natural disasters. The rape of Tamar by her half-brother Amnon in 2 Samuel 13:1–19 is a heart-wrenching account of the devastation caused by sexual assault. When she realized that Amnon intended to rape her, Tamar's shame was apparent as she begged him, "Don't do this wicked thing. What about me? Where could I get rid of my disgrace?" (vv. 12–13). Her depression and despair are apparent in verse 19 where Tamar put ashes on her head, tore her robe, and "went away, weeping aloud as she went," and in verse 20 where we are told that she "lived in her brother Absalom's house, a desolate woman."

Tamar's story is just one of the biblical narratives that Davidson (2011) refers to as he goes through the Old Testament and discusses the passages that speak about sexual abuse. He looks at what the Old Testament laws state regarding rape (e.g., Deut. 22:25–27), goes through the Pentateuchal narrative involving sexual abuse (e.g., Gen. 19, 34), and looks at sexual abuse in the Prophets and the Writings (e.g., Judg. 19; 2 Sam. 11). His conclusion is that the Old Testament consistently portrays *"God as the defender, comforter, healer, and vindicator of the abuse victims.* There is an implicit call in the Old Testament for God's people to actively join him in standing on the side of those who have been sexually abused" (p. 153).

Schmutzer (2011) shows how the New Testament writers draw on the foundational principles laid down in the Old Testament with respect to sexuality. For example, he looks at Paul's emphasis on holiness (1 Thess. 1:2–10; 4:3–8) and doing God's will (Rom. 12:1–2; 1 Cor. 6:20; Eph. 6:6) as the basis for sexual ethics. I would add that these same principles are applicable to relational trauma of any kind.

While Scripture is clear that God knows us (Ps. 139:1; Matt. 10:29–31) and cares about us in our pain and distress (e.g., Pss. 23 and 89, among many others), trauma survivors often have difficulty

believing it, just as the psalmist often did (e.g., Ps. 88). It is not unusual to hear from clients' questions such as, "Why did God allow my husband to die in the tornado while my neighbors' husbands lived?" "As a young child I prayed to God to protect me, but he didn't. I was raped hundreds of times over the years. Where was God?"

There are no easy answers to these questions, but Scripture is not silent on the matter. Peterman and Schmutzer (2016) in their book, *Between Pain and Grace: A Biblical Theology of Suffering,* focus on a biblical and textual, as opposed to a philosophical, discussion of pain and suffering. Following are some of the key topic areas they examine, along with the Scripture references they suggest support their assertions. They discuss the suffering of God (Gen. 6:5–6; Ex. 3:7–10; Num. 14:2–5, 9–13, 19–20; Jer. 9:1, 10; 13:7; 14:17–18; Hos. 11:8–9) as well as the emotions and suffering of Jesus, including his compassion (Matt. 9:36; Luke 7:13; Rev. 5:6), grieving anger (Mark 3:5), fear and anguish (Luke 22:39–46), and discontent (Matt. 17:14–17; Mark 7:34). The authors discuss the importance of lament, citing passages from both the Old and New Testaments. Another focus is that of redemptive anger in Scripture, using the examples of Joseph (Gen. 42–50), Jesus (Mark 3:5; John 2:13–22), and Paul (2 Cor. 11:29).

While trauma survivors' anguished questions about God may sound like theological questions, in my clinical experience they are actually heartfelt cries for understanding and expressions of felt rejection, abandonment, and betrayal. While at some point, addressing the theology may be beneficial, until most of the memories have been processed, an empathic response that reflects the intensity of the client's pain is more likely to be appropriate.

In her book on trauma and suffering, Langberg (2015) recognizes that Christians, in our desire to come up with answers to these difficult questions, have a tendency to state biblical truth to people in pain despite the fact that "speaking the truth is not sufficient alone" (p. 111). She outlines six principles (pp. 111–119) modeled by Jesus that offer some guidance as we accompany trauma survivors in their journeys toward healing.

- *He left glory.* Just as Christ left the familiarity and comfort of heaven for our sake, so we should be willing to enter a traumatized individual's world, even if it is out of our comfort zone.
- *He became little.* In leaving glory, Jesus also "reduced himself in size, power, impact, words, and potential to help (Philippians 2:6–7)" (p. 112). Langberg suggests that we need to set aside some of what we think we know, and become "little" enough to enter into another's experience and not "swoop in, tell people what to do, and take over" (p. 112).
- *He entered darkness.* Just as Christ entered the darkness of this world, so we must enter into our clients' darkness of depression and despair and sit with them in it until we can gradually help move them to a different place—the light.
- *He did not get lost in darkness.* Jesus brought God's character into the darkness with him. Similarly, we need to bring love, compassion, and grace with us.

- *He did not abandon us.* Even when in anguish while nearing the cross, Jesus did not run; he stayed and accomplished what he began. Langberg points out that sometimes we begin well at journeying with trauma survivors, but frequently we do not hang in there for the long haul. Clinton and Langberg (2011) capture this concept with the words "staying power" (p. 312).
- *He did not catch our disease.* Jesus did not allow our darkness to destroy him; he stayed emotionally and spiritually healthy. We, too, must watch that we do not fall into despair in the process of working with people who have experienced such horrific things. Langberg suggests that keeping the perspective that we are working for and with God as we come alongside suffering individuals, rather than viewing ourselves as doing the work, will go a long way toward keeping ourselves safe.

CASE STUDY

Helen's flashbacks had become unbearable. In desperation one night, she sat down in the middle of a busy highway, expecting a fast-moving vehicle to hit and kill her, thereby ending her living nightmare. But miraculously, within seconds of a truck smashing into her, Helen was pushed out of harm's way by what she concluded could only be an angel.

Mere days after her discharge from the psychiatric ward of the hospital where she had been admitted on a three-day hold because of her suicide attempt, Helen ended up in my office. She was thirty-five years old and presented as hardened and tough. Having had negative experiences with previous therapists, Helen only showed up because the flashbacks continued to torment her, and a caring Christian nurse who had connected with her in the hospital recommended that she see me.

While the flashbacks created the most distress, hosts of other symptoms eventually were revealed. Flashbacks by day became nightmares by night, contributing to the insomnia that resulted in only three hours of sleep a night for many years. Helen was hypervigilant to danger, her nerves continually on alert. She warned coworkers never to approach her from behind or touch her unannounced; when one woman forgot and touched her shoulder to get her attention, Helen punched her coworker so hard that she required medical attention and almost pressed assault charges.

Helen's emotions fluctuated between rage, terror, despair, anxiety, and depression. She had been addicted to drugs and alcohol for many years and described having had many sexual partners of both genders. Yet she had great compassion for wounded children and animals whom she treated with the utmost gentleness.

It took years for Helen's story to come out in its entirety, in part because of the sheer quantity and severity of trauma in her history. Additionally, she had amnesia for much of her trauma, which came back to conscious awareness in fragments. What emerged was an account of physical, psychological, sexual, and spiritual torture at the hands of both family members and strangers from the time she was a very young child. Helen lived to tell it only because she ran away as a young teen and lost herself in the streets of a big city.

STRATEGIES, INTERVENTIONS, AND TECHNIQUES FOR COMPLEX TRAUMA

The standard of care for the treatment of individuals who have experienced CT is a three-phase model (Courtois & Ford, 2009). While authors use different labels for the phases, they agree about what each phase involves. In the first phase, which I call *safety and symptom stabilization*, the first task is developing safety—safety within the therapeutic relationship, safety from others, and safety from self in terms of self-destructive/suicidal behaviors and the tyranny of symptoms. Once safety and symptom stabilization have been attained, the second phase, *processing of traumatic memories*, can be entered. Trauma processing involves integrating dissociated components of each memory, as well as integrating each traumatic experience into the survivor's sense of self and identity. In the final phase, *consolidation and resolution*, the focus is consolidating the growth attained in previous phases as well as helping survivors navigate the many changes in their relationships and interactions with broader societal systems that will be inevitable due to the changes that have taken place in them. Techniques for this phase are not trauma specific.

For more information about the process of counseling CT survivors (CTSs), including a discussion of the impact of early childhood trauma on development and the implications for treatment, see my book *Restoring the Shattered Self: A Christian Counselor's Guide to Complex Trauma* (Gingrich, 2013). While there is overlap in therapy techniques over the phases of treatment, I will discuss specific techniques under the phase in which they are most useful.

Phase One: Safety and Symptom Stabilization

Not all CT clients will be willing or able to work through all three phases of the healing process because the process takes not months but years. However, even if you do not conduct long-term therapy, you can do phase one work. Often the overwhelming intrusive post-traumatic symptoms, such as flashbacks and nightmares, are what prompt a CT victim to seek help. These same symptoms are often the most challenging for clinicians to help their CT clients manage. Therefore, phase one will be given greater time and attention than phases two and three. While the core issues will not be addressed if you only do phase one work with a counselee, increased symptom containment can help an individual function better, even if full healing does not take place.

Ensuring safety within the therapeutic relationship. CT, by its very definition, is relational trauma, usually at the hand of someone who is in a position of trust (e.g., parent, uncle, pastor, teacher, coach). Therefore, it involves a sense of betrayal (DePrince et al., 2012; Freyd, DePrince, & Gleaves, 2007). In Helen's case, almost all of the adults in her life abused her as a child, making her suspicious of everyone. Only her desperation enabled her even to enter my counseling office.

You may need to put forth significant amounts of time and effort for a CTS like Helen to feel safe with you. The task is all the more difficult if any of the perpetrators were lay or professional counselors (which, unfortunately, is all too common). Not only is developing a sense of safety essential before trauma processing can begin, but the therapeutic relationship in and of itself can be the source of the greatest healing for CT survivors who have been harmed in the context of a relationship. Therefore, paying attention to the strategies discussed below is paramount.

Developing rapport. The facilitative conditions of empathy, respect, and authenticity that you learned in your foundational counseling skills classes will be particularly important in establishing the therapeutic relationship. Biblical narratives of how Jesus related to the Samaritan woman at the well (John 4:4–26) and to the young man who was not willing to give up his riches to serve Jesus (Mark 10:17–22) are good examples of how to do this. Specific techniques such as *empathic reflection (i.e., reflecting content and feeling), using appropriate genuineness and self-disclosure, having a nonjudgmental attitude, and being emotionally present* are essential. Books that focus on teaching basic microskills (e.g., Sbanotto, Gingrich, & Gingrich, 2016) will be helpful in familiarizing you with such techniques.

These basic skills were essential early on in my work with Helen. Although she portrayed a tough exterior, consistent empathic reflection lowered her defenses sufficiently that I could recognize the gentleness and pain that were just below the surface. At the time, my counseling office was located in a faith-based educational setting, so it was clear that I was a Christian without me verbalizing it. Sensing that religion and spirituality were sensitive areas for Helen, I was careful to let her initiate any discussions in these areas. Although I was genuinely myself in the relationship, my decision to limit self-disclosure in the areas of spirituality enabled Helen to begin to feel safe within our therapeutic relationship.

Being and remaining a safe person. Building rapport helps a client to feel safe, but you must actually **be** a safe person and **remain** safe in order not to further damage a CTS. Specific strategies involve the following:

Remember that every client is unique. Just because something worked well for one client does not mean that it will necessarily work for another, even if they are both CT survivors. I learned this the hard way. Having made unusually fast progress with one of my first CT clients, I promised a new client a timeline for healing that was totally unrealistic—an error that contributed to the client prematurely terminating therapy.

Know your limitations. While there will be a steep learning curve when you begin to work with CT survivors, you can benefit your client if you *seek out appropriate training opportunities, read in the field, and get trauma-sensitive supervision.* However, if you are in over your head despite seeking guidance, *refer out to an expert.* While at times I felt overwhelmed while working with Helen, I took courses, read what was available, consulted with experts, and found a peer supervision group

that enabled me to do good work with her, despite facing new therapeutic challenges.

Warn of impending change. Any change from the familiar will be potentially unsettling for a CTS because her abuse was often so unpredictable. Therefore, giving warning in advance of anything different is important. This could include anything from you attending a conference and missing a session to putting up a new picture on your office wall or changing appointment times.

Every time I went on vacation or had to cancel a session, Helen felt as though I was abandoning her. Progress was made only after dozens of situations over several years of warning her in advance that I would be away, reminding her that I would be back, and then reinforcing the fact that I *did* come back once I had returned. A particular challenge was informing Helen (after seven years of therapy with me) that I was making a geographical move to the Philippines. I told her four months ahead of time, after which I spent the entire four months doing grief work and helping her deal with abandonment issues. This not only ensured that we terminated the therapeutic relationship well but also modeled a healthy ending to a relationship, the first time any relationship in Helen's life had ended with proper closure.

Keep appropriate boundaries. Getting caught up emotionally (i.e., experience positive transference) with CT clients is easy to do. The therapeutic work is often intense and punctuated by one crisis after other. Over the course of years together, an increased intimacy will invariably develop that can be helpful but can also result in you letting down your guard and crossing boundaries. In the worst-case scenarios, these infractions could be sexual in nature. But more commonly, they take the form of informal contact outside of sessions, extended phone or email contact between sessions, extended session times (without preplanning), using touch too liberally, or becoming more like friends than therapist and client (which limits your helpfulness as a therapist).

While my role as Helen's counselor was always clear to us both, I was aware that Helen had become special to me. In a sense, we had developed some crisis intimacy because of the intense nature of the trauma processing, the fact that she had not shared the details of her trauma with anyone else, and the severity of her symptoms, which I was helping her manage. While this intimacy is unavoidable and can be helpful in terms of the level of trust it engenders, I have no trouble understanding how counselors who are emotionally vulnerable because of situations in their personal lives could end up unintentionally misusing the relationship with a CTS to meet their own emotional needs. Therefore, *regularly check your own mental health* through *getting your own counseling, working on self-of-the counselor issues with a supervisor, or asking for feedback* from mentors, friends, or family members who know you well.

Keep confidentiality. If the CTS feels as though you have broken confidentiality, the therapeutic relationship will be impaired or destroyed. Make sure that you *clearly outline the limits of confidentiality* in your informed consent statements so that if you have to break confidentiality

(e.g., in the case of a high suicide risk) the relationship can be mended. When those who care about a survivor of CT (e.g., a family member or pastor) contact you out of concern, you will need to *obtain written consent* to discuss the client with them. If no such permission exists, you can listen to the concerns but then make sure you *inform your client* of the contact.

Safety from others. Do not assume that your CT client is currently safe. Victims of child abuse run an increased risk of being victimized later in life. Therefore, assess for intimate partner violence (see Watson, 2017). CTSs may be so accustomed to severe abuse that they do not identify the emotional, sexual, or psychological abuse by a spouse or romantic partner as problematic.

Some CTSs have experienced ritual abuse and mind control by perpetrator groups that may still be victimizing them. This may occur without the CTS being consciously aware of the ongoing contact. See Miller (2012) for tips on how to recognize the signs of this kind of ongoing abuse. No individual, not even a counselor, can keep another person safe. But if you are aware of the danger, you can work with the CT client to develop safety plans that can help to reduce the risk of harm (e.g., monitoring phone calls, not traveling to geographical areas where prior abuse has occurred, cutting off contact with suspected perpetrators).

Although Helen had cut off all contact with her abusive family many years prior, there came a time when her father discovered where she lived and began sending cards and gifts that appeared innocent.

However, these contained covert messages intended to draw her back to the abusive community from which she came. Helen came to the conclusion that discarding such mail unopened was the safest way for her not to be adversely impacted by the contents.

Safety from self and symptoms. CTSs sometimes feel that they are at the mercy of their own self-destructive or suicidal impulses as well as their post-traumatic symptoms. Just as in Helen's case, it is often the intrusive reexperiencing symptoms such as flashbacks or nightmares, or the hyperarousal symptoms such as hypervigilance to danger, or intense spikes of anxiety that motivate a CTS to seek help. While behavioral interventions, such as exposure therapy/prolonged exposure therapy and mindfulness techniques can be somewhat beneficial, I have found some lesser-known techniques to be particularly valuable. Both types of strategies will be discussed in this section.

Behavioral techniques. Many of the strategies discussed in chapter 6 of this book ("Behavioral Strategies") are applicable to work with survivors of any type of trauma, including CTSs. Of particular benefit are those that fall under the heading "Exposure and response prevention (ERP) techniques." The hallmark of the intrusive and hyperarousal post-traumatic symptoms is anxiety. In fact, anxiety is so pervasive that PTSD was previously categorized as an anxiety disorder (American Psychological Association, 2000).

Exposure therapy, or prolonged exposure therapy, is frequently used to desensitize trauma clients from their anxiety (Briere & Scott, 2013). These ERP techniques are utilized extensively for treatment of PTSD and are often the main or only strategies used. The idea behind exposure therapy is to expose clients to situations that serve as trauma triggers, that is, expose them to environmental cues that can elicit a fear response that is associated with the trauma (Briere & Scott, 2013). Sometimes exposure is paired with *relaxation* techniques to help lower a client's anxiety and defuse the trauma triggers. However, for CT, these techniques can be helpful as an adjunct to other strategies but are not sufficient in themselves because post-traumatic symptoms are only one aspect of the total symptomatology for CTSs (Courtois & Ford, 2009).

Mindfulness. While Christian counselors need to be cognizant of the Buddhist worldview from which the concept of mindfulness originated, its use as a therapy technique is not dependent on adherence to Buddhist thought. In fact, Tan (2011b) points out that "contemplative spirituality has, for centuries, emphasized the sacrament of the present moment or self-abandonment to divine providence in every moment and every area of life," and he makes reference to many Christian authors who describe types of prayer that are consistent with mindfulness techniques (p. 243). The application of mindfulness to CTSs is related to the overwhelmingly intense emotions of guilt, shame, anger, hatred, depression, and the like that are so commonly experienced. Christian clients, in particular, frequently are prone to judging all negative emotions as sinful. However, disavowing particular feelings does not make them go away; it just creates further difficulties. Being mindful of emotions means to be aware of them and examine them, but from an emotional distance, without judging whether they are right or wrong (Segal, Williams, & Teasdale, 2013) or, in biblical terms, sinful or not. The idea is to acknowledge what *is*, and accept that the emotion is there, as a way of gaining some control over it.

While Christian clients may not be comfortable acknowledging that they hate their perpetrator, for example, using mindfulness allows them to acknowledge it; like it or not, the hatred is there. Once acknowledged, choices can be made as to what to do with the hatred. This may involve *trauma processing* so that the reasons behind the hatred are identified, or *cognitive behavioral techniques* if the hatred is based in misconceptions or irrational beliefs.

To illustrate, if Helen hated men, she would first need to *become aware* that the hatred was there without automatically pushing it away. Once she *acknowledged the intensity* of the hatred, we might process particular trauma memories of which Helen had not previously been conscious, in which men were the perpetrators. Now that Helen recognized the source of her hatred, we could also use some cognitive behavioral techniques to dispute the lie that *all* men are perpetrators and, therefore, *all* men should be hated.

Strategies that make therapeutic use of dissociation. The DSM-5 (American Psychiatric Association, 2013) definition of dissociation is "Disruption of and/or discontinuity in the normal integration of consciousness, memory, identity, emotion,

perception, body representation, motor control, and behavior" (p. 292). Simply put, dissociation is compartmentalization, or disconnection among aspects of self and experience.

Early childhood trauma impacts development in numerous ways (Arnold & Fisch, 2011). One of these is related to disruption in the normal developmental process of learning to integrate aspects of self and experience (Putnam, 1997). Findings from neurobiological research have shown such lack of integration in the brains of CTSs (e.g., between the amygdala in the right hemisphere of the brain and the hippocampus in the left hemisphere of the brain; see Struthers, Ansell, & Wilson, 2017). For this reason, CTSs tend to dissociate more than individuals who do not have a history of CT. See Gingrich (2013) for more information on dissociation, including the continuum of dissociation (i.e., from normal to multifragmented dissociated identity disorder), how various components of specific traumatic memories can be dissociated, how attachment theory is helpful in explaining dissociative symptoms, and how early childhood trauma is associated with increased dissociation.

While dissociative symptoms can create a lot of distress for CTSs, their increased ability to dissociate can be put to good use in therapy. The following strategies potentially will be extremely helpful for CT clients.

Use of "parts of self" language. Most CTSs experience some degree of identity confusion and fragmentation. An extreme example of such lack of integration in the self is seen in CTSs who dissociate to the extent that they fit diagnostic criteria for dissociative identity disorder (DID; formerly multiple personality disorder). Those with DID experience severe dissociation, feeling as though there are totally different people who take control of their bodies (American Psychiatric Association, 2013).

Even CTSs who do not have DID, however, often experience some degree of personality fragmentation (Steele, Boon, & Van der Hart, 2017). It is as though traumatized child parts remain frozen in time, not recognizing that the individual is now an adult. In a CTS with DID, such child parts may present as a separate alter personality, with a different name, different life history, and so on. In CTSs who use dissociation without having developed a full-fledged dissociative disorder, such dissociated parts of self are more like ego states or self-states. This type of technique is called "parts work" by some authors (e.g., Pressley & Spinazzola, 2015) and "ego state therapy" by others (e.g., Shapiro, 2016), while still others tend toward the language of "self-states" (e.g., Howell, 2005; Noricks, 2011).

As an example, I introduced the idea to Helen by saying something like this:

We all have different parts of ourselves. Some of these are more like roles. For example, I'm operating out of my counselor part right now, but I also have a wife part, musician part, and so on. These are parts of me that I'm consciously aware of, just as you're most likely aware of some parts of you. But there are other parts of us that we may not be as familiar with. For

example, although you have no idea why you have been startled awake at 4:00 the past few mornings, some part of you likely knows what's going on.

Although non-CTSs may find this kind of talk somewhat strange, my experience has been that CTSs relate well to it—it fits their experience of themselves in that they often feel fragmented, as though there are different "parts" that make up their sense of self and identity. In fact, many CTSs have thanked me for giving them language to use that helps them to describe what they have been experiencing all their lives.

View symptoms as attempts at coping. Understandably, CTSs very often interpret their symptoms as all bad; they just want them to go away. If, however, symptoms are viewed as attempts at coping with the horror of their trauma, or as warning signals that something needs attention, the destructive power of the symptoms is greatly reduced. I think a good analogy is that of a railway crossing. When a train is coming down the tracks, the red lights flash, and a loud dinging noise resounds to alert people to the impending danger of a coming train. The problem is, that with intrusive reexperiencing of posttraumatic symptoms, the warning system gets activated even when there is no longer any danger (i.e., when there is no train coming).

The EPR techniques discussed in the previous section are very helpful with trauma survivors who have not experienced CT. These techniques are not as effective with CTSs because of the existence of the traumatized self-states of which the client may not be aware. It may be that the adult client is going through the EPR protocols, but the child part of self that actually experiences the anxiety is not necessarily a part of the process. However, recognize that these symptoms have had an important function in the past (i.e., letting child CTSs know that a train *is* coming), as well as currently (i.e., letting adult CTSs know that they have been struck by a train and could be again, or that although they survived, they have injuries that still need tending).

This is what happened with Helen's early morning terror incidents. During phase two work, a traumatized child part reported that on a regular basis her father had entered Helen's bedroom about 4:00 a.m. and had sexually assaulted her. The child part's terror had been leaking through to adult Helen, partly as a cry for help. In phase one, however, the goal is not to reveal the details of the trauma, because that could result in premature trauma processing. Rather, the goal is to help the client temporarily contain the symptom through a process of contracting with either the client's system as a whole or an individual part of self. The elements that are involved in making such contracts are outlined below.

Make contact with dissociated parts of self. Accessing the part of self that is associated with a particular symptom both increases awareness of the meaning behind the symptom (in phase two) as well as provides an opportunity to better contain the symptom (in phase one). I had already been using the language of "parts of self"

with Helen, so making contact with the terrified child part was not difficult. The conversation went something like this:

Heather: *Helen, I know that waking up terrified in the early morning hours like you've been doing is very disturbing to you. We've talked before about the fact that we all have parts of ourselves that we aren't aware of. What would you think of trying to connect with the part of you that knows what is going on?*

Helen: *Sure, I'll try anything! But how can I do that?*

Heather: *Well, I'd invite all parts of you to listen in as I talk. After pausing for a while, I'd introduce myself, and then I would ask if I could talk with the part of you that knows what is happening.*

Helen: *How will I know if that part of me is listening?*

This might sound very strange indeed to a nondissociative client. However, as mentioned previously, CTSs tend to be more dissociative than most. So while the idea of connecting with a different part of self might be new, the sense that other parts exist generally fits well with their lived experience. Counselors can facilitate such connections by helping CTSs to listen inside and pay attention to thoughts, internal voices, or impressions that could signal that a part of them is attempting to communicate. Once such a connection has been made, it is often easier for CTSs to recognize the presence of a dissociated part of self. Ultimately the goal is to teach clients this skill so that they can negotiate with parts of themselves between sessions.

Use ideomotor signaling. Helen's question as to how she would know if a specific part of herself was listening in or trying to communicate is a common concern. The use of ideomotor signaling can be reassuring to such clients. Ideomotor signaling uses finger signals as a way to communicate with parts of self of which the CTS may not be aware. The technique originally comes from hypnotherapy, but because dissociative states have some similarities to hypnotic states, the technique works well with CTSs. To illustrate how ideomotor signaling works, I will continue the dialogue between Helen and myself from where we left off.

Heather: Other counselees have told me that they have an inner sense of what is going on inside when they just pay attention to their internal worlds. There is a kind of shortcut technique that many of my counselees have found helpful; it might give you a little better idea of how various parts of you are responding. It uses finger signals as a way for parts of you that you aren't aware of to give yes or no responses to questions without having to speak.

Helen: It sounds kind of weird, but I'd like to hear more about it.

Heather: Basically, it by-passes your cognitive processes. For instance, if I asked you right now why you have been waking up at 4:00 a.m. all week, you wouldn't be able to tell me. But we're assuming that some part of you does know. If that part of you has been hidden from your awareness for a long time, it may be easier for that part to

move your finger than to communicate the information to you through your thoughts and voice. So the idea is just to let your hand relax so that another part of you can clearly indicate the response. Sometimes the movement is very small, so you might need to exaggerate the movement so that I can see it. But it's not that I ask the question, you think of what the answer is, and then you decide to move the yes or no finger; that would defeat the whole purpose!

Any finger can be chosen, but I generally suggest that the baby finger be used for yes, the pointer finger for no, and a hand raised with palm facing outward as a stop signal, just so that I do not get confused from client to client. I go on to explain in detail what the procedure entails. I take great care to attempt to take the mystery out of it, particularly because I want to make clear that this is merely a psychological technique, that there is no New Age or Eastern spirituality involved. It is essential that clients are aware of exactly what they are consenting to and can therefore give true informed consent. I then go over the core elements again when we actually engage in the procedure. Let's assume that I have finished thoroughly describing the procedure to Helen and that she has consented to it. Following is an idea of how the conversation might go.

Heather: Okay, Helen, try to get as comfortable as you can in that chair and relax as best as you can. You don't have to close your eyes, but usually people find it easier to concentrate if they do. Remember, just as we discussed earlier, that you will be aware of everything that happens at all times. If you are uncomfortable in any way or have a question as we go along, we will pause what we're doing. If you have trouble verbalizing that you want to stop, use the stop signal. We can either continue on if your concerns have been adequately addressed, or you can decide that you don't want to go ahead with this technique, in which case we'll do something else. Ready?

Now I'd like to invite all parts of Helen to listen in. (Pause.) Helen, please wiggle the yes finger for me; now the no finger; and show me the stop signal, just to make sure that all parts of you know what they are. Okay. Are all parts of Helen listening in?

If the yes finger moves, I'll continue. If the no finger moves, I'll say, *"I'll wait a few moments to allow all parts of Helen to come."* After a pause, I'll say, *"Are all parts of Helen listening now?"* If I receive another no response, I'll ask, *"Would some part of Helen be willing to make sure that those who aren't listening in directly would still get the message?"* I've never had a no response to this question.

I'll go on to say, "My name is Heather, and I'm a counselor. Helen has asked for my help. Right now Helen is upset that she is waking up at 4:00 in the morning and feeling very scared but doesn't know why. Is the part of Helen listening that knows something about that?"

If we are still in phase one of treatment,

I do not necessarily want to know the details of what has happened, because that would prematurely plunge us into phase two, trauma processing. At this point in the process, I simply want the symptom to be contained. Therefore, if I receive a yes response, I continue on in the following way: "I assume there is a good reason that Helen is waking up at 4:00 in the morning. Am I right that there is something that needs attention?" This can be a little tricky, because I do not want to be too leading; in particular, I do not want to suggest trauma that may not be there. Therefore, I attempt to talk in general terms. If I receive a yes response, I will say, "I want you to know that Helen and I hear you. The problem is that Helen isn't ready to look at whatever is there right now. Helen needs to be able to go to work, and she needs to get as much sleep as she can. Would you be willing to wait until the time is better for Helen as long as she promises that she will look at it?"

I am assuming that Helen has experienced some type of trauma which her defense mechanism of dissociation is keeping at bay during her waking hours, but which is starting to leak through to consciousness when defenses are weaker during sleep. This strategy works well because I am merely asking her to use her ability to dissociate to compartmentalize this memory for a little longer. Of course, Helen has to agree to live up to her end of the bargain! If not, the part that has made the agreement to contain the symptom has every right to manifest the symptom again!

In a similar fashion, contracts can be made with dissociated parts of self for other intrusive symptoms, such as nightmares, flashbacks, and anxiety. These techniques also can be helpful for negotiating agreements around harmful behaviors, such as suicidal or self-destructive behavior, as well as for encouraging helpful behaviors, such as going to work or attending school. The key is to ensure that you are making these contracts with the parts of the person that have the power within the personality system to enforce the contract.

Phase Two: Processing of Traumatic Memories

Trauma processing must be handled with care. First, CTSs need to have developed good coping strategies during phase one that they can also use between memory processing sessions. Indicators that it may be appropriate to begin phase two work are (a) when you sense that the client is able to ground herself (see "Grounding Techniques" below) both within and outside of sessions with minimal help from you, and (b) when the client is able to manage posttraumatic symptoms between sessions. The final decision on whether to begin trauma processing should be a collaborative one because it is important for the client to feel that the timing is good and that she is prepared to enter a difficult process.

While helping the client to process particular traumatic memories, be cautious not to suggest or to lead with your questions. Additionally, you need to proceed in a way that minimizes the risk of retraumatizing. The strategies outlined below will be helpful with respect to these areas.

Ask the client where to begin. Dissociated parts of self generally have information that can be helpful in making a wise decision about where to start the trauma processing. Ideomotor signaling or another way of connecting with other parts of self can be helpful here. Some memories are obviously more difficult for a client to deal with than other memories. For example, sexual abuse perpetrated by an older cousin may not have quite the emotional impact of sexual abuse at the hands of the client's father or mother.

In Helen's case, the memory associated with the symptoms described above, of waking up in terror in the wee hours of the morning, was not the first traumatic incident we processed together. Because multiple perpetrators were involved, it was easier to begin elsewhere, coming back to this particular incident when her personality system as a whole indicated that the timing was right.

Invite the part of self that holds the memory to allow access to it. Accessing dissociated memories is similar to asking for a key to a locked room; once the key is available, retrieving the traumatic material is a matter of opening the door behind which it has been hiding. Having CTSs verbalize what they are seeing/experiencing helps them develop a trauma narrative. This is necessary for the integration of the emotional material that is stored in the amygdala of the brain with the cognitive content that involves the hippocampus (Schore, 2003b, 2003c Siegel, 2003, 2009).

Ask open questions. There is a big difference between asking open questions such as "What is happening now?" and "What are you seeing?" and closed questions such as "Is a man in the room?" or

"Is it your uncle?" After we agreed to look at what was behind the incidents of Helen waking up terrified, I simply asked Helen to go "inside" and to tell me what was happening. She described startling awake and hearing the door to her bedroom open. I let her continue her narrative of seeing a dark figure enter her room and approach the bed until she paused, at which point I asked, "What's happening now?" and she continued.

Keep the CTS connected to the here-and-now. Sometimes the client can get lost in the trauma memory, that is, have a full flashback in the midst of trying to process it. There is no value in reexperiencing the trauma to this extent; it merely becomes retraumatizing. The goal is to allow for various dissociated components of the memory (i.e., cognitive, affective, physical sensation, and behavior) to become reintegrated by having the CTS reexperience all of the components, at least to a minimal degree, while verbalizing what is happening. Braun's (1988) original conceptualization of the BASK model of dissociation is very helpful when it comes to understanding such dissociated components of memory. BASK is an acronym that refers to behavior (behavior that is associated in some way with the memory), affect (emotion experienced), sensation (physical aspects), and knowledge (cognitive knowledge of the incident—what we often mean when we say, "I remember"). I further elucidate how the BASK model can be used in phased work with CTSs in Gingrich (2013). Ultimately it is this ability to have one foot in the past and one foot in the present while narrating what hap-pened in the presence of a safe, compassionate individual who is able to facilitate the process that is core to the healing.

Grounding techniques are essential for this purpose. Anything that involves engaging the senses of CTSs will help keep them in the present. Asking clients to listen to your voice, open their eyes and look at various things in the room, drink cold water, suck a sour candy, or rub bare feet on a carpet are all examples of helpful grounding techniques. Anything that orients to current location is also helpful. In the Denver area where I currently live, the mountains are clearly visible. Sometimes asking CTSs to look at the mountains helps them realize that they are no longer living in the location where they were abused (providing that they did not grow up in Colorado or another mountainous state or province). Such grounding techniques are important both in the midst of the trauma processing as well as at the end of a trauma processing session so that the CTS can get home safely.

At one point, I sensed that Helen was paralyzed in a terror state during one trauma processing session. When I got no response to saying things like, "Helen, it's Heather. You're in my office. Listen to my voice," I asked her to respond through the ideomotor finger signals so that I could get information about what was happening and get her back to the present time. In rare instances, I have made use of a counting technique and some suggestion by saying, "Helen, I'm going to count to three, and when I get to three you will be back in my office. One . . . you're starting to come back. Two . . . you're almost back.

And three ... you're back in my office." Once she opened her eyes, I made use of the more common grounding techniques.

Pace the trauma processing. There is nothing gained by overwhelming CTSs by pushing through with trauma processing despite indicators that the client is in distress. The concept of pacing is applicable to how frequently trauma processing is entered into (e.g., every session, once every few months) as well as to the speed with which a particular incident is processed within a session.

Frequency. What one CTS can handle well, another may not. I have colleagues who have processed up to three memories per session over many months with some individuals. I cannot imagine moving at this kind of pace because most of my CTSs have required at least one session, if not several, between trauma processing sessions to maintain an even keel. The clients themselves likely will be the best judges of how much recuperation time is necessary.

Speed. Although I generally process an entire traumatic incident in one session, I have occasionally broken the processing down into two or three sessions. In a fashion similar to the symptom containment techniques described in the discussion on phase one, you can get agreement from all parts of the CTS to compartmentalize the rest of the trauma with respect to all components of the memory. Sometimes using visualization techniques to "lock" the memory in an internal box or imagining that the memory is stored in the filing cabinet in my office can serve as a temporary containment measure so that the CTS can function well between such sessions.

Helen found one memory in particular excruciatingly difficult to process. We went through it as though it were a recording that we were playing back frame by frame. She could only manage a few seconds of processing before she needed me to help her get back to the present, become grounded, and then go back to the memory. Although there was more time left in that initial processing session, I sensed that Helen may have had enough for one session. When I checked in with her, Helen confirmed that going further that day would potentially be destructive. We therefore stopped in the middle of that particular memory and negotiated with the part of her that had been holding the memory, asking that part to keep the rest of the memory hidden until the next opportunity to continue processing it. The contract worked; Helen did not gain access to the rest of the memory until the following session and did not experience any flashbacks or nightmares between sessions.

Process the emotions. Intense affective work is an essential aspect of phase two. Grief and loss, anger, depression, guilt, shame, hatred, self-hatred, fear, and anxiety are all common emotions experienced by CTSs. Be prepared to help your clients face and get through such strong feelings.

Christian clients in particular can experience a lot of guilt about some of these emotions. However, attempts to minimize or deny them will hinder the healing process. An analogy I use often is that of an infected wound. Unless the wound is lanced and the pus is drained out, the infection will worsen. Similarly, the feelings that are bound to arise in the midst of trauma processing are often ugly and painful, but unless they are acknowledged and worked through, healing is unlikely to happen. Letting CTSs know that their emotional reactions are normal given what was done to them, and that God already knows what is there and loves them regardless can be very freeing.

Phase Three: Consolidation and Resolution

In the third phase of counseling, the focus is on consolidating changes and helping the client live as an integrated whole. Techniques used in this final phase are not unique to work with CTSs but will encompass anything counselors use with their other clients. For this reason, I will briefly mention the areas of focus that are important in this phase without discussing specific techniques.

While emotions connected to specific trauma memories will have been processed in phase two, there is often continued work to do in phase three as CTSs are now aware of the details of the totality of the trauma that has been perpetrated against them. No longer relying on dissociation as their primary defense mechanism, CTSs also need to *develop new coping strategies*; they can no longer as easily compartmentalize an overwhelming feeling. Helen, for example, had to get comfortable with experiencing anger. For many years, these emotions had been relegated to a specific part of her, but she could no longer just store anger away until something triggered her anger and it erupted in potentially dangerous ways (e.g., resulting in physically as-

saulting someone). She had to learn not to run away from her anger, but allow herself to experience it while working out how to healthily deal with it (e.g., use relaxation techniques to calm herself down or exercise when the anger was intense, and learn to appropriately confront someone she felt had wronged her).

As CTSs heal and become healthier, their relationships will be impacted. While there is the potential for some relationships to become healthier, others will not survive. Helen, for example, recognized that the individual who had been instrumental in leading her to Christ was at this point in her life actually impeding her spiritual and psychological growth because of the strong fundamentalist leanings she had theologically. Helen needed to *grieve* this and other losses and *establish new, healthy relationships*. Counselors will often need to help facilitate these processes.

While forgiveness of the perpetrator may have been a topic of discussion earlier in counseling, it tends to take center stage in phase three. Sells and Hervey (2011) give a good summary of various approaches to dealing with the issue of forgiveness with sexual abuse survivors; I see these as being equally applicable to work with other CTSs. Whether to confront the perpetrator is often a question that arises during this phase. While Helen's primary perpetrator, her father, was already dead, Helen had to determine how forgiveness applied to her mother who also abused her and did nothing to protect her.

Many of the techniques discussed so far under the heading "Strategies, Interventions, and Techniques for Complex

Trauma" can also be helpful for survivors who do not have a complex trauma background. In the following paragraphs, I will discuss some of the overlap in techniques as well as some of the differences.

Strategies Previously Discussed

Although the PTSD literature does not generally discuss treatment phases, I believe that a phased approach can be helpful. Note that the amount of time spent in each phase will likely be truncated. Certainly those with PTSD need to know that they are safe; the difference is that developing rapport and safety within the therapeutic relationship may be established more quickly if their trauma did not involve betrayal by someone close to them, which is the case with CTSs. The length of time may vary from a session or two to a number of months for clients with PTSD, as opposed to months or years for CTSs.

Mindfulness and grounding techniques are useful to both types of clients with respect to symptom containment. I have found that techniques usually reserved for CT survivors (e.g., ideomotor signaling and parts work) at times work very well for individuals struggling with PTSD. A good illustration is a published case study (Gingrich, 2002) in which I worked with a client presenting with PTSD using many of the techniques I find helpful with CTSs.

The phase two trauma processing described earlier for CTSs is in fact a type of exposure therapy according to Briere and Scott's (2013) definition of exposure as "any activity engaged in by the therapist or the client that provokes or triggers client memories of traumatic events" (p. 143). In my opinion, the difference in the approaches is primarily theoretical in that exposure therapy, according to behavior therapists, is important in that it desensitizes survivors to the trauma (Taylor, 2006). I believe that the desensitization component is important, but that the integrative function is potentially more significant to the healing process, at least for CTSs. Other similarities are that both individuals with PTSD and CTSs need to work through the emotions and cognitions attached to the trauma, including those related to spirituality. Appropriate pacing of trauma processing is also important for both.

With respect to phase three, clients with PTSD need to consolidate the gains made as well as potentially resolve issues with the relational and other systems that impact them. If there has not been much damage done to these systems due to the post-traumatic symptoms, those with PTSD may not have as much work to do as CTSs.

Eye Movement Desensitization and Reprocessing

I would be remiss in not mentioning eye movement desensitization and reprocessing (EMDR), as it is becoming increasingly popular as a protocol for use with trauma survivors. Specific training in use of EMDR is necessary. It has some good research support for single-event traumas. See the website www.emdrnetwork.org for links to research findings and more information about EMDR in general.

However, several cautions about using EMDR with multiple-trauma PTSD and CT cases are in order. While results can be dramatic, EMDR is best used as part of your tool kit within a broader trauma treatment approach. Regular EMDR protocols should not be used with highly dissociative clients because other dissociated parts of self can become activated, creating a lot of inner confusion and turmoil. Therefore, while EMDR can be helpful with some CTSs, its use could actually be damaging to others. I encourage you to use a brief screening instrument, such as the Dissociative Experiences Scale-II (DES-II) before doing EMDR with a particular client. A copy of the DES-II along with instructions for scoring is available at the back of my book on complex trauma (Gingrich, 2013). The DES-II can also be found online using a search engine.

Use of Explicit Spiritual Resources

Explicit use of prayer, Scripture, and spiritual practices may be useful with particular trauma clients at certain points and harmful at other times. Sbanotto, Gingrich, and Gingrich (2016) in their chapter "Appreciating the Sacred" summarize what Christian authors have written with respect to the area of spirituality and counseling in general. Many of the chapters in *Treating Trauma in Christian Counseling* (Gingrich & Gingrich, 2017) and *Spiritually Oriented Psychotherapy for Trauma* (Walker, Courtois, & Aten, 2015) look specifically at treatment strategies with respect to spirituality. In Helen's case, her trauma involved severe sexual and physical

torture, often perpetrated under the guise of religion. For this reason, explicit spiritual resources were not implemented until a number of years into the therapy process, after she indicated a desire and willingness to go there.

CONCLUSION

Trauma survivors, both those with PTSD and those who have suffered complex forms of trauma, need counselors who are well trained in trauma treatment. Understanding that CT treatment requires a three-phase approach (i.e., phase one: safety and symptom stabilization; phase two: processing of traumatic memories; and phase three: consolidation and resolution), which is quite different from the cognitive behavioral approaches used to treat PTSD, is essential. Christian counselors have the advantage of being able to recognize the importance of the spiritual questions with which trauma survivors wrestle, as well as being willing to learn how to respectfully and appropriately use spiritual resources. Ultimately, though, you need to know good trauma treatment strategies and techniques.

You may be wondering what happened to Helen! Despite the horror, her story has a happy ending. While the physical and sexual abuse has left a legacy of severe medical problems that have worsened as she ages, Helen describes herself as emotionally and spiritually healed and happy. She has a vibrant relationship with Christ, has deep, healthy friendships, has reconnected with nonabusive family members, and has held a job that she loves for several decades, all of which she attributes to her experience of counseling. I trust that Helen's journey provides you with hope that healing is possible for even those who have been severely traumatized, and that this chapter whets your appetite for learning more about the treatment of both PTSD and complex trauma.

RECOMMENDED READING

Courtois, C. A., & Ford, J. D. (Eds.). (2009). *Treating complex traumatic stress disorders: An evidence-based guide.* New York, NY: Guilford Press.

Gingrich, H. D. (2013). *Restoring the shattered self: A Christian counselor's guide to complex trauma.* Downers Grove, IL: InterVarsity.

Gingrich, H. D., & Gingrich, F. C. (Eds.). (2017). *Treating trauma in Christian counseling.* Downers Grove, IL: InterVarsity.

Herman, J. (1997). *Trauma and recovery: The aftermath of violence—from domestic abuse to political terror.* New York, NY: Basic Books.

CHAPTER 23

Nonsuicidal Self-Injury-Focused Strategies

David Lawson, PsyD *

The LORD is a refuge for the oppressed,
a stronghold in times of trouble.

PSALM 9:9

Almost twenty-five years ago, as I sat in my office waiting for a referral from the dean of students, I had one of the most profound and therapeutically transformative moments of my life. The student entered the session, sat down, and relayed a story that did not fit any clinical category I had developed. As her story began unfolding and the discussion of self-injury began, I immediately panicked and began evaluating for the risk of suicide. As she discussed the pain and meticulous cutting that she performed on her arms, I kept interrupting to quickly assess for the possible and almost certain risk of suicide that I had been taught to evaluate for. As my concerns grew, particularly as she described her regular habit of cutting, she suddenly shifted gears, looked at me, and boldly declared, "I'm not suicidal. I just cut, and I can't seem to stop it or figure out why." Although I doubted her statement at first, I became more aware of the truth of her words and the chronicity of the behavior as we unpacked the history of her cutting and its progression throughout her teenage years.

Of course, the second challenge I had, once I was no longer concerned that the client was suicidal, was the evaluation for borderline personality disorder (BPD). These were the only two categories I had for cutting, and since we had "mostly" ruled out suicide, I had only the alternative of diagnosing one of our severest and most chronic pathologies in the *Diagnostic and Statistical Manual* (DSM-5; American Psychiatric Association, 2013). To be honest, I had hoped in that moment that my prospective client was suicidal; otherwise, I would be working with her, possibly for years, helping her to manage the cutting along with the borderline behavior.

---

* Special thanks to Chelsea Breiholz, MA, for her work on this chapter.

This was the dilemma of most therapists treating cutting and self-injury fifteen to twenty-five years ago. Many of us had been taught that cutting could fit into only one of two categories. Since the prevailing wisdom of that time was limited to these two categories, a number of therapists—including myself—panicked, knowing it meant the possibility of both suicidal behavior and the chronic nature of BPD, both of which can be personally and professionally taxing. Many therapists preferred to avoid these types of clients altogether because of the emotional weight of carrying their issues. I even had one supervisor during my training who immediately referred these clients or hospitalized them to help him deal with the threats of those who self-injured.

I relay this part of my training history to help create perspective on how little was understood regarding self-injury and also to explain why many who engage in self-injury feel stigmatized by the mental health community. It is no wonder that many who self-injure today still do so in silence and are often ashamed or terrified of the responses from friends, family, and, yes, even the mental health community. One of the therapeutic challenges is to enter into the life and story of the client. Unfortunately, for many therapists, however, self-injury is not well understood and can often trouble the inner world of the therapist.

This chapter will develop a framework for understanding the complexity involved when working with clients who self-injure (nonsuicidal self-injury). Specifically, this chapter examines the *Diagnostic and Sta-* *tistical Manual 5* (DSM-5; American Psychiatric Association, 2013) and its review of self-injury as a diagnosis, as well as statistics, demographics, and the emergence of online communities as a significant influential factor in self-injury. Various etiologies and conceptualization models will be discussed, as well as therapeutic treatment modalities, including creative techniques that can be appropriate when intransigent self-injury is observed. These techniques and treatment modalities will be illustrated in two case studies to facilitate deeper understanding and practical application.

THEOLOGY AND PSYCHOLOGY OF SELF-INJURY

Self-injury has a long history, both culturally and religiously. Many cultures throughout history, along with our modern cultures, have practices and have even created formal rituals that include self-harm. Since self-injury was a common practice among pagan religions (cf. 1 Kings 18:24–29), the Bible spoke directly to the issue. God commanded the Israelites not to cut themselves and, in fact, not to have tattoos, because they were "the children of the LORD your God" (Deut. 14:1; cf. Lev. 19:28). In one New Testament passage, self-injury is associated with demonic possession (Mark 5:2–5). Moreover, each person's body is God's temple, having the Spirit of God living within us as believers. Since our bodies do not belong to ourselves, we do not have the right to do whatever we want to them. Our human task, then, is to steward our bodies to glorify God with them (1 Cor. 6:19–20).

Most importantly, we serve a Savior who has borne our shame and pain in his body so that we can find freedom from our pain and eternal damnation. Because Jesus bore and bears our pain in the form of scars, the need for someone to scar her or his own body to relieve internal suffering can minimize the redemptive work of the gospel. The prophet Isaiah captured the reality of Jesus's violent death: "Surely he took up our pain and bore our suffering, yet we considered him punished by God, stricken by him, and afflicted" (Isa. 53:4). But for most who self-injure, their pain and shame often seem overwhelming. Like John the Baptist, who was incarcerated in prison and needed confirmation that Jesus was the Messiah who performs miracles (Luke 7:18–35), we, too, need affirmation and confirmation that God is real, that his work is real, and that his hope for humanity is real.

In the end, there are ways we can weave theology into the life of someone who self-injures. Such clients benefit from learning that Jesus chose to maintain his scars after his resurrection for many reasons; for cutters this can be a salve of healing. God understands pain and wounds. His Son, with whom he is well pleased (Matt. 3:17), bears scars also. These words can deepen the connection to God while also decreasing the shame that often entangles someone who self-injures. Jesus has wounds just like you. And it is even possible for someone who self-injures to begin trading their marks for his marks. As my colleague Dr. John Thomas says, "The world is full of people with wounds looking for those with scars.

We need to look no further than our Lord and Savior, Jesus Christ, who experienced the worse wounds so that he could bear our scars."

Historical Context of Self-Injury

After the black plague wiped out millions in Europe in the fourteenth century, the practice of self-flogging became a popular method of appeasing a sternly righteous God who many believed was imposing his wrath in the form of the plague on the earth. Body piercing has been a cultural or social practice and part of society dating back to Middle Eastern practices four thousand years ago. Piercings and even tattoos were signs of wealth, slavery, or bondage. Religion also has a long history with self-injury. Nearly every major religious tradition has some form of self-punitive process to help cleanse, purge, or limit the flesh's impact on spiritual and religious life. In the vast majority of these traditions, self-injury is practiced as a method to develop deeper faith or more intimate communion with God(s), as in the case of Hinduism; the devout who harm themselves desire to attain spiritual or sometimes even material gain.

Because of these cultural and spiritual factors, identifying and delineating self-injury as a unique mental health diagnosis can be somewhat controversial. I do believe that cultural and spiritual self-injury have limited the willingness of researchers to venture into the investigation of self-injury as a unique problem not affiliated with either suicidality or severe pathology like BPD. However, in the DSM-5 (American Psychiatric Association, 2013), self-injury is now listed as an area for additional study, which may bring the issue into greater awareness or discussion as a unique problem with its own diagnosis and treatment. Until then, we in the mental health community will need to continue developing appropriate methods to evaluate and treat this issue while not adding to the shame and misunderstanding associated with it. My hope is that as you work through this chapter you will become more aware of the issues involved in working with clients who self-injure and that you will learn some of the tools necessary to begin working with this population.

Phenomenology of Self-Injury

Because self-injury does not have a specific diagnostic criterion that has been universally established, many therapists working with self-injury define the issue in a way that fits their own theoretical theory and philosophy. Yet most prominent among all definitions of self-injury is the idea that the self-harm cannot be a suicide attempt. If you believe the harm is suicidal in nature, the general diagnosis of self-injury cannot be used. With that, the current outline provided by the DSM-5 (American Psychiatric Association, 2013) will be used as the foundation for diagnosing the issue. The DSM-5 also describes self-injury as nonsuicidal self-injury (NSSI) and defines NSSI in this way: over the past year, the person has for at least five days engaged in self-injury, with the anticipation that the injury will result in some bodily harm. No suicidal intent.

- The act is not socially acceptable.
- The act or its consequence can cause significant distress to the individual's daily life.
- The act is not taking place during psychotic episodes, delirium, substance intoxication, or substance withdrawal. It also cannot be explained by another medical condition.
- The individual engaged in self-injury expecting to do the following:
  - Soothe a negative emotion
  - Cope with interpersonal struggles
  - Create a positive emotion
- The self-injury is associated with one of the following:
  - The individual experienced negative feelings right before committing the act.
  - Right before self-injury, the individual was preoccupied with the planned act.
  - The individual thinks a lot about self-injury even if the act does not take place.

DSM-5's (American Psychiatric Association, 2013) definition captures much of what the research has identified as key factors in diagnosing self-injury/self-harm.

What is not described at all by the DSM-5 (American Psychiatric Association, 2013), however, are the types of behaviors associated with self-injury—this is left to the discretion of the therapist. And although most of what has been popularized or discussed within the therapeutic community has focused on cutting, other forms of injuries are becoming increasingly popular as well, such as burning, bruising, hitting, scraping, and even repetitive picking at skin or scabs (American Psychiatric Association, 2013). Although self-injury through cutting has been highlighted as being more common among females and garners the most attention in the research, it is possible that males may be more likely to use different methods. Consequently, self-injury in the male population may be underreported. For example, it is possible that males who are high risk takers, or even those who have been identified as clumsy, could potentially be engaging in a unique form of self-injury (Gratz, 2006; Gratz & Chapman, 2007).

According to relatively recent statistics, 2 to 5 percent of the population struggle with some form of self-injury (Walker, 2012). Several studies report that self-injury rates can be as high as 40.5 percent in college student populations, and that in this population, the rates do tend to cluster around that percentage (Nobakht & Dale, 2017). Part of the difficulty in identifying accurate numbers is the stigma associated with the behavior. Although as a culture we are less hostile or shaming than we used to be, there are still many individuals, groups, faiths, and agencies who struggle to understand and accept self-injury behavior for what it is. I have consulted with many churches over the last fifteen years whose youth groups had multiple girls struggling with the issue. Often, out of concern for the teen and to protect the group from a contagion effect—that is, the spread of the behavior—many have removed the young people from the youth group, threatened to report them to the authorities, or even

indicated it was a sin or some form of spiritual evil. Although these responses appeared to have some effect, often those struggling went into deeper hiding, threatening never to share this with anyone again. Threats can also often have the inverse effect of causing the self-injury behavior to increase as the shame gets internalized by the teen.

Although self-injury has been seen in very young children and is often seen in later adulthood, the greatest number of reported cases consistently occurs during the teen years (Calder, 2007). Additionally, as previously mentioned, college student populations are displaying increasingly high levels of self-injury behaviors (Nobakht & Dale, 2017). I had a small number of cases where self-injury occurred throughout the client's whole life as the client remembered it. One client told me that she had "always remembered" needing to cut herself. In this case, I believe the client had stumbled upon the behavior by accident but had discovered that cutting helped her get through the stressors of the day.

Etiological Considerations

Self-injury is a clear indication that something is deeply wrong under the person's skin that manifests itself on the skin. Why that occurs, however, is debatable. Many believe that individuals who self-injure are attention seeking or are doing it as an explicit threat of suicide, but neither of these ideas captures the actual issues of those who self-injure. That is not to say that some individuals who self-injure are not seeking attention at times, or that self-injury might not be a risk factor for suicide, but they are not the primary motivations. However, while taking all of this information about generalities into consideration, it is still important to be aware of and assess for attention-seeking and suicidal motivations.

Although the reader has been cautioned not to see self-injury as an immediate threat for suicide, a risk assessment is a therapeutic must for those who are self-injuring. One way to make this determination is to evaluate self-harming and suicide behaviors separately and differently. During the intake or formal assessment phase, make it clear that suicide assessment is a normal evaluative process. Seeing this as a common component of therapy destigmatizes it and sends the message that self-injury and suicide are two separate issues. Another technique is to educate the client on the significance of suicide assessments during the natural course of therapy, helping the client differentiate between the self-injury behaviors and suicide behaviors. Whatever option is chosen, it is imperative that you continue to assess suicidality.

Additionally, when an attention-seeking motivation is present, it is generally associated with a personality disorder, especially BPD. The client who presents with attention-seeking self-injury often initially presents with one of the other reasons for self-harm, and only through careful evaluation of the motivation for the self-injury can it be truly teased out. Sometimes it is not until the therapist realizes that maladaptive personality behaviors are present that she can then make a more accurate evaluation. Often the self-injury is deeply intertwined in the personality relational dynamic so that it is treated as part of the ongoing work with the personality disorder.

For the vast majority who self-injure, embarrassment, shame, guilt, and negative cognitions are more common. Many clients I have counseled describe hating the behavior and are horribly ashamed if or when others find out. In fact, many expend a tremendous amount of energy hiding their harm from others by wearing long sleeves despite the temperature, hiding the marks on their arms and telling stories to explain them away. Many negative thoughts and feelings can play a significant role in the life of one who self-injures. For example, Levenkron (2006) found that between 40 and 50 percent of those who have self-injured have done so while actively thinking about suicide or death. This is much higher for children and adolescents who use or abuse substances. These statistics stand in contrast to what I previously mentioned about self-injury and suicidality being unrelated, and therefore are a testament to the complexity of this issue. It is important to be aware that self-injury is not a black-and-white phenomenon and can present either with or without suicidal thoughts/intentions, even though the DSM-5 (American Psychiatric Association, 2013) differentiates this in its proposed definition of nonsuicidal self-injury.

Some research has been done on what types of internal complications are more likely to create self-injury in children and adolescents. And although this list is far from exhaustive, it highlights the types of issues that can lead to the development of self-injury (Strong, 1998). They include the following:

- developmental delay
- school failure or school problems
- communication difficulties
- low self-esteem
- parent/career conflicts
- family conflict/breakdown
- rejection
- abuse
- bullying
- parental mental illness
- alcohol/drug abuse
- poverty
- homelessness
- loss

Alone, any one of these issues could create the foundation for the development of self-injury; combined, they create a tsunami of pain and hurt that many children and adolescents struggle to deal with. In many cases, children and adolescents don't have the coping mechanisms necessary to manage all of the inner pain and torment they feel. Additionally, many families whose children and adolescents struggle with these complications have less robust support and coping ability, or have limited capacity internally to help the children and adolescents work toward a satisfactory level of emotional regulation. It is unsurprising, then, that many children who struggle with self-injury behaviors do so because of the lack of systemic coping (Gratz, 2006).

Although this list seems to potentially explain the why of the development of self-

injury, most clients who enter counseling explain their personal "why" very differently. For example, I have often had clients enter therapy dealing with self-injury issues and during the course of their therapy have discovered that they had histories or complications found on the preceding list. But not all. Many of my clients did not or could not connect their history or feelings to the list and to their current self-harm behavior. Some clients could cognitively acknowledge the significance of the events in their lives but then struggled to grasp how these issues connected to the self-injury behavior now being experienced. After years of failed attempts to connect their past to their current behaviors and discovering that my often "incredibly insightful connections" were not particularly helpful to the client, I had the brilliant idea of asking them about their own feelings and thoughts to see if they were capable of connecting them to their self-injury behavior. Not surprisingly, most could describe the feelings that often led to the behavior.

The literature frequently describes three broad categories regarding the mechanism or personal "why" many people have for engaging in self-injury: physical grounding, control, and the silent scream (Walker, 2012). Although myriad other issues can play a role, most of my clients fall into these categories—which is also consistent with research findings. I have discovered as well that clients express these categories uniquely, and some struggle connecting to the categories; however, most clients can connect with one, and sometimes more than one, reason for their self-injury. Keep your clinical mind open, however, since not all clients neatly fit into one category versus another. Finally, I have discovered that although helping clients gain insight can lead to a clearer understanding of their triggers and facilitate improved self-regulation, some clients appear to have little concern or desire for this. Many self-injuring clients are more concrete and need or desire greater pragmatic life-skill or behavioral help. I caution you about assuming that pragmatic needs are defense mechanisms, as I once did. Many individuals who self-injure have developmental delays or social issues, necessitating focusing on pragmatic work.

Clients' attachment styles may also impair the way they express themselves when discussing issues related to their self-injury. For example, avoidant styles tend to detach from feelings and internal experiences. Clients often maintain their distraction from their pain by focusing their sessions on daily life. The smoke and mirrors are not confabulated stories of frustrations or trouble. Most often those clients do hold frustrations and levels of suffering that merit attention and can be redirected back to the real issue. But to solely focus on the distractions is like an emergency room physician cleaning up abrasions, cuts, and fractured bones when the patient is in cardiac arrest.

Category one: physical grounding. When I first began working with self-injury clients, one of the more challenging experiences I had was understanding that they needed to cut to feel their bodies. I had no context for not feeling my own body. My sense of self had nearly always been distinctly grounded in my awareness

and experience of my personal body. However, for some who self-injure, there is a distinct split between their sense of self and their body. It is almost as if the body and their physical experience of the world are disconnected from their identity/self. One client described it to me like this: "I feel like I am walking through the world, and I am aware of myself with all of my hurts and pain. But as I'm walking, I become aware that I am without a body, almost like a ghost with no form. I know my body is there and is experiencing things, but it feels really disconnected from who I am."

Words like *disconnect* and *disembodied*, or phrases like "I don't feel things in my body," describe and even define the experiences of some self-injuring clients. Probably the closest thing therapeutically to this experience is dissociation, mentally escaping the physical or experiential moment. Specifically, it seems to correspond with the constructs of depersonalization and derealization, in which individuals feel like they are not "real" or that the world around them is not "real." Dissociation itself has actually been found to correlate significantly with self-injury, particularly among college students (Nobakht & Dale, 2017). For many who self-injure, this feeling of disconnection appears to be a continual experience of life, not just present for short periods of time. They become in their minds disembodied beings, no longer feeling like a whole person. Self-injury for many in this camp is the attempt to reconnect the body into the moment. Once placed into this context, the behavior of self-injury makes sense. If you are physically disconnected from life, why not try to yank the body back into connection with the self and the world through physical pain, thus allowing you to feel aware of your own body? The body can only numb so much before something breaks through the threshold of awareness, and suddenly there is an experience. I have had clients state that the moment they jolted their body back into awareness was like waking up to life. "I had been physically dead," one client explained, "and when I cut, I woke up to life."

Category two: control. The second category develops out of the need to manage or control, usually because clients' lives feel deeply out of control. This paradoxical experience often confuses clients as they begin the process of understanding their "why." What I discovered through asking questions of those who self-injure is that their lives feel completely out of control or at times overly controlled by another. I recall one client requesting help with her cutting behaviors, which had developed in adolescence. As we explored her early life and adolescent experiences, it became abundantly clear that the client's mother, who struggled with severe anxiety, tried to control her household and her children as a way of reducing her anxiety. This led my client to adopt self-injury behaviors as a way of privately exerting control and influence over her life. In many ways, her story is like others who have experienced the stress of living under dominance or high and often unrealistic expectations. High levels of control or expectations can send some children and adolescents into private behaviors that help them feel as if they do have personal control over their lives. Often self-injury behaviors develop in secrecy

so that the persons practicing them cannot be robbed from the experience of taking life into their own hands.

Self-injurious behavior can produce the sense of feeling powerful and autonomous. In reality, to be human is to desire being in control, which is linked problematically to the fall and at the same time associated with sound mental health. The marks from self-injury behaviors can be tangible evidence that self-harming persons' lives are in their own hands. Children and adolescents naturally develop the need for autonomy, and often family rules or personal pathology within the family clashes with that need. The resulting behaviors, although developed for autonomy, can become the primary way they learn to cope with the people or environments that threaten their autonomy or integrity.

Category three: the silent scream. The third category that I have discovered when working with those who self-injure is connected to the expression of pain. People struggle to effectively find words to describe what their lives have been like because their emotional distress seems to stifle their abilities to communicate. Thus, in comparison to the two previously mentioned categories, this one can be the most challenging.

For those who struggle with finding words to make sense of their pain, the use of self-injury seems to replace the need for words. The cutting or other forms of harm (e.g., burning, picking, scraping) represent both the pain they feel on the inside and the visual representation of the emotional hurt in their bodies. A client expressed this after months of therapy: "I felt so much pain inside of me, and it had no way to get out. I had no words, or maybe my words were never heard. I discovered cutting as a way to tell myself this is how I'm feeling right now. And maybe I was hoping at some point others would hear my pain and hear my voice by seeing the scars I had on my body. But ultimately my words were shameful too, and I had to hide my voice and my pain along with my scars."

Her description captured this type of self-injury better than any words I could string together. There is a tension between self-injuring individuals feeling the need to "speak" or "share" their pain and a general lack of words or lack of support. To reconcile the crucible, some individuals develop an "alternative language" that allows them a path of expression and a method to release the inner hurt. Often what follows, though, is additional shame of the physical scars they now bear. And this can lead to a shame spiral, where every pain leads to cutting or self-injury, which leads to shame about the cutting, which leads to more pain and then more shame.

Category four: self-punishment. Although this can be its own category, all three of the previously mentioned motivations can also be present here. In this type of self-injury, people typically struggle with intense negative thoughts and feelings centered around the theme of *I am bad*, with variations such as *I am worthless, I am unlovable, I am dirty, I am cursed, I am a mistake, I did something bad*, among others—therefore including both shame and guilt. These thoughts lead to beliefs such as *I need to be punished* or *I deserve to suffer*, which thus lead to engaging in

self-injury as punishment. This type of self-injury can also be engaged in as an attempt to "purify" oneself, make one's "badness" less bad, or satisfy some inner need for "justice"—that is, *I am bad or did something bad, therefore I must suffer/ be punished to make things right again*. These thought processes, while irrational to many of us, make complete sense to the one engaging in the behavior, and it is important to remember that.

With this category of motivation, as with all of the possible motivations mentioned here, considering the influence of trauma in the development of self-injury is critical, as both dissociation and trauma have been highly associated with self-injury (Nobakht & Dale, 2017). Trauma history assessments are especially important with clients who present with or later reveal self-injuring behaviors.

One more phenomenon to mention here is that I have had self-injuring clients reveal to me one of the motivations behind their self-injury was the aftercare—that is, the process of cleaning, bandaging, and caring for their wounds after self-infliction. One teenage client told me that this was the only way she felt loved and cared for; if no one else loved her enough to take care of her and tend to her pain, doing it herself through the ritual acts of cleaning and bandaging helped her feel cared for in a very tangible way. Be aware of and assess for this dynamic, especially when working with younger clients.

Online Communities

Although cutting seems to have developed from more experimental or accidental responses in the past, people who self-injure today have often discovered or experimented with self-injury after reading about it or interacting with someone online who had been harming (Boeckmann, 2008). This was shocking to me as a therapist fifteen years ago, as my clients started sharing their stories of these online groups. Individuals in these groups would emotionally support one another and share information to help each other, such as how to cover up the marks of self-injury, avoid infection, cut or burn without endangering their lives, and so on. Individuals participating in these communities can often unintentionally have a contagion effect on each other, propelling each other deeper and deeper into the self-injury cycle. The copycat effect is also present, as people will often post pictures or videos of their self-injury, which can be extremely graphic; these visuals can be very triggering for those who struggle, and lead them to self-injury in their own way or to copy the particular type of self-injury they saw in another's post.

For many who have felt crazy for wanting to injure, however, these communities have served to normalize self-injury behaviors, helping them feel less alone (Cash, Thelwall, Peck, Ferrell, & Bridge, 2013). Additionally, many who participate in these communities have stated that they feel heartbroken for their online peers who struggle, are moved by deep compassion for each other, and find strength in encouraging one another to stay strong, seek help, go to counseling, and have hope. Encouraging one another to get well and simply being present witnesses to one another's pain actually does serve as a source of personal motivation to seek help and get well themselves. Not overlooking the positive aspects reported by clients of these online communities is critical.

However, current research is still unclear about whether these online communities and the use of internet and social media sites have more beneficial or detrimental effects on those who engage in self-injury. Marchant and colleagues (Marchant et al., 2017), after conducting an extensive review of the literature, state that this is likely due to limitations in study design. Quantitative studies were associated with negative results, while qualitative studies were associated with positive results—although most of the qualitative studies appear to be low quality. Therefore, more research is needed before definitive conclusions can be drawn. Be sure to consider both the good and bad qualities of online communities when working with self-injuring clients. Assessing for a client's involvement in these types of communities, forums, or websites is important. Ask open-ended questions, and listen to what your client has to say about them.

CASE STUDY

Grace was an African American college student who came to counseling at the insistence of her roommate. Grace reported that her father had unexpectedly died of a heart attack four months earlier. As she talked, she described normal grieving experiences, but she could not verbally say she was grieving or felt sad. Most of the first session, she discussed how her body felt and how her body's experiences had changed after her father's death. I attempted to evaluate for a history of abuse or a complicated relationship with the family, but she would only describe her family as being a wonderful Christian example to their black American community.

Therapy continued with an emphasis on helping Grace grieve the loss of her father, taking the time to reflect on his life and their relationship and on the losses that had occurred since his death. In session four, Grace entered looking more somber than normal. If there was any way she could be looking at the floor more than she had been, she was. I asked what was happening, and she responded with, "*My roommate caught me.*" "*Caught you what?*" I asked. "*She caught me doing this,*" she replied, and rolled up her sleeves to show me scars and cuts on her arms. "*Wow,*" I said. "*How long have you been cutting?*" Her eyes continued to focus on the ground, and she whispered, "*A long time.*"

I asked, "*Can we talk about the scars and cutting, or is it too tough right now?*" She didn't reply with anything but silence. I took that as an opportunity to ask more questions and continued, "*Do you remember when this started?*" She shook her head no. Although very few clients ever start in childhood, I wanted to make sure she had not started early, which would increase the chances that the behavior could be chronic. We spent the rest of the session with mostly nonverbal responses to questions from me as I tried to understand the severity of the cutting and whether there was any suicidality in the behavior, which there was not. Grace left the session promising to come back next week and share any

feelings of suicidality she might have while we were working on the grieving and the cutting behavior.

STRATEGIES, INTERVENTIONS, AND TECHNIQUES FOR TREATING SELF-INJURY

Since there is no agreed on protocol, therapists have treated self-injury in various ways. As noted above, the lack of any formal diagnostic criteria has led many on the front lines of praxis without a clear process for diagnosis and treatment. Thus, some therapists have treated self-injury as a subset of other diagnoses, so considering dual diagnoses—or multiple diagnoses—with your clients is important.

In discussions with other therapists, I have learned that some practitioners treat self-injury as a part of obsessive-compulsive disorder (OCD). Although one might see the similarities in obsessive thoughts leading to the compulsion to self-injure, making some of the anxiety-based connections that are foundational to the OCD diagnosis is difficult. I have heard parenthetically that therapists who have classified it as a subset of OCD have had marginal levels of success.

Another group of therapists have diagnosed and treated self-injury as a subset of substance abuse. The idea that self-injury is addictive is not new (Bornovalova, Tull, Gratz, Levy, & Lejuez, 2011). Many addiction websites and researchers claim that self-injury is simply another addictive process (Futterman, Lorente, & Silverman, 2005). In talking to clients who self-injure, you will discover that many feel very addicted to the behavior. I had one client who came into my office to work on another issue but finally broke down crying and said she also struggled with cutting and had tried stopping multiple times but couldn't. She consistently had the impulse to cut even though she had often promised to stop. This sounds very similar to the substance abusers/addicts who also present with discussions of wanting to stop and who are trying to stop but are unable to do so. Additionally, studies have found evidence for the involvement of endogenous opioids in the perpetuation of self-injury behaviors, demonstrating that similar neurochemistry does exist in this cycle and reinforcing the addiction conceptualization (Blasco-Fontecilla et al., 2016; Sher & Stanley, 2008). One benefit of viewing self-injury through an addiction or neurobiological conceptualization is the ability to approach the issues from a psychopharmacological treatment perspective, as well as consider physical or neurochemical etiologies, which do appear to be a reality and should not be overlooked (Blasco-Fontecilla et al., 2016).

Although controversy over this issue still exists, research also supports the idea that self-injury, while similar to addiction in that both involve reinforcement dynamics and even similar neurobiological phenomena, fits more with an emotion-regulation model than with an addictions model (Sher & Stanley, 2008; Victor, Glenn, & Klonsky, 2012). Many of the ways that addiction specialists describe an addiction, if taken to an extreme, could potentially include diagnoses like depression and anxiety. Many who enter with these diagnoses also discuss wanting to stop their depression or anxiety and feel trapped in repeating behaviors, thoughts, or feelings that they wish they could stop.

For the purposes of this chapter, I will classify and treat NSSI as a separate phenomenon from either OCD or addiction, recognizing that many who self-injure also have features of both diagnostic categories or may have co-occurring disorders. For example, returning to our case study, Grace reported that she did experience a compulsion to cut, hence exhibiting a feature of OCD; she also reported not wanting to cut but feeling like she couldn't stop, also a feature of addiction. However, I did not believe that she could be diagnosed with either OCD or an addiction. For her, the cutting simply shared a similarity with one aspect of those disorders. Recognizing this, however, helped me to better understand her experience of self-injury by thinking about it in these contexts.

Of course, there are many other ways in which to conceptualize self-injury. Self-injury can be conceptualized within or as a feature of several other disorders, such as depression, anxiety, post-traumatic stress disorder (PTSD), or dissociative disorder, among others. It can often, but not always, be associated with trauma or neglect, where the self-injury could be a method of emotional regulation, grounding, self-punishment, or an attempt to regain control. Considering multiple conceptualization models when addressing this issue is always important.

Treatment Modalities

Three distinct treatment modalities—systems therapy, cognitive behavioral therapy, and psychoanalytic/relational therapy—can be effective when working with self-injury. Each modality has strengths and weaknesses, and each one has been demonstrated as effective in the clinical literature and from personal discussions with other clinicians. I have found that it is often unhelpful to hold to a particular "school" of therapy when a broader range of strategies is needed. Nearly everyone I have interacted with in the field uses multiple modalities, although they may have a primary theory from which they work. For a number of clinicians, evidence-based treatments guide their work. Some of the best therapists I have had the privilege of interacting with have seamlessly and effortlessly moved between and integrated multiple modalities and theories when working with clients.

Systems therapy. Two key elements of system therapy, sometimes known as family therapy, play a significant role in understanding self-injury clients. First, in family therapy, clients are only the representative, or as some say, "scapegoat," for the family's pathology. Family therapists recognize that most pathologies are systemic in nature, not individual. As such, any pathology observed in a client coming into therapy really is an interplay of pathology found in the system. Second, pathology often develops between other members of the family system, generally the caretakers or father and mother. As the couple or dyad (mother/father) are incapable of holding and dealing with their own problems, children and others connected to the family system start holding and managing their pathology. Thus, any time a client walks into therapy, what is observed is really the stress and anxiety or unresolved issues between other members being inadequately held by someone in the family.

The strength of family therapy when working with those who self-injure is found in the awareness of the connection to family as a participant in the pathology. Often clients who will not, or feel that they cannot, change their behaviors are unwilling or feel unable to do so because of the alignment they have with their family of origin, even if they are no longer living with them. These connections are often unconscious, and I have even had adults who continue to protect their family out of fear of what their movement toward health might do to their family. *Changing Self-Destructive Habits: Pathways to Solutions with Couples and Families* by Matthew D. Selekman and Mark Beyebach is a great resource for family therapists.

When Grace first came to therapy, she described her family as being "a perfect Christian example." As therapy progressed, however, I gained a clearer picture of her family dynamics. Her father and mother had both grown up very poor and had met in church. Her father had "dedicated his life to Jesus" at a very early age and had promised many in the church that he would enter the ministry and preach. His wife, then girlfriend, was excited that they would be pastors, and their relationship was built with that dream in mind. Somewhere in his journey, the father decided that he really didn't want to preach and instead wanted to make money. "He was tired of being forever poor," Grace said. Although the couple married, they engaged in intense fighting about his call to the ministry and the hope she had of being a pastor with her husband.

As the couple started having children, Grace's father quit going to church altogether. The family was surprised and hurt by his decision, but the mother never quit going. The father went to college, got a bachelor's degree, and entered a profession that afforded them more money than they had ever had, "but no one in the family was happy." Grace described her father as kind but moody: "You never knew who you were going to get, Jekyll or Hyde." She described her mother as being supportive of the kids, but sad. Although the client never mentioned any form of abuse in the family, I was concerned that there was something more to the moody Jekyll and Hyde and the very sad mother.

Grace described many "crazy" moments with her father, but she never described abuse. Then we discussed her father's "weird ways" of dealing with church. In session nine she described her father's encouragement that the family attend church weekly even though he never went himself. However, he would never "let" the family discuss or talk about anything that happened at church. Any time they would come home from church and mention anything about what happened, her father would "explode on them." This was the first time she had mentioned the father's negative affect, and I pursued it: "*So, any time you talked about church, he didn't want you to talk about it?*"

"*No, he said he liked us going, but then he would scream at us if we tried to share what happened or if something positive was going on. I once tried to talk to him about my friend at church, and he looked at me and screamed, 'You know my rule. I don't want to hear anything about church,'*" Grace said. "*Was that the only time he screamed at you?*" I asked. "*Well, he started screaming more at us and particularly at Mama as we got older,*" she reported.

Over the course of our sessions, I began to piece together a father who was not only hostile to church but hostile to almost anything the girls did outside of the house. Because so many of her friends were connected to her school and church, he started screaming when she would talk about anything. She stated in one session, "*I think he was really sad about not going to church. But he couldn't figure out how to deal with his sadness and took it out on us. Mama got the worst of it, but he screamed at all of us.*"

As Grace continued describing the verbal and emotional abuse she experienced, I started asking about the beginning of her cutting. Because we had processed the family pathology, she seemed readier to explore the start of the cutting behavior: "*It began one day after Daddy screamed loud at me. I remember going into my room and wanting to cry, but I just couldn't let out any tears, and I got so angry at myself for being weak or not being able to cry that I scratched my arm with my nails. For some reason the pain felt good, and I really felt relieved, like a pressure was taken off my chest.*"

Although some clients can describe the day and time the first self-injury incident occurred in detail, others cannot remember the details. They are clouded in a fog that seems dissociative in nature. Then they come back to themselves and notice they bear the marks on their wrists, arms, or other chosen body parts.

About session sixteen, I decided Grace had developed enough trust with me to ask the key question of therapy: "Would you like to reduce the cutting behavior?" I had waited a little longer than with some clients because the cutting was negatively connected to her father, and even though he had been abusive, the loss could potentially cause more cutting as a way of connecting to the deceased father. So I cautiously approached reducing the cutting behavior. This really emphasized to me the importance of having explored her family system first, as it revealed potential connections between her family and her self-injury. I use this as an illustration to help you recognize the value in using a systems approach with self-injuring clients, particularly when the client is unsure of the reasons behind why her self-injury began. I also caution you to remember that sometimes family pathology may not be connected to the self-injury at all. Regardless, understanding the client's family history and dynamics can almost always be helpful in some way.

Cognitive behavioral therapy. Although CBT is not my personal "go to" theory when working with clients, some research indicates that it is effective with self-injuring clients (Labelle, Pouliot, & Janelle, 2015). Most CBT methods begin with the premise that our thoughts create emotional responses, which then prompt behaviors. Therefore, for a self-injuring client, the behavior would be preceded by an emotion, which would be preceded by a thought. Much of the therapeutic process,

especially at the beginning of therapy, is filled with discussions around behaviors and what emotion(s) were connected to them. Then, as therapy progresses, the process moves to working on the cognitions that birthed the self-injury, although there is a bit of education involved in helping clients understand this process. CBT helps clients recognize that triggers from their environment are ultimately the beginning of a cascade effect that leads through cognition, affect, and to the self-injury response.

For many in the self-injury community, numerous triggers center around experiences of shame, control, and anything they interpret as an attack on their self or their integrity. Once these triggers are experienced, often the cognitive response is very black and white; they see it as all or nothing. For example, *I am worthless, I am powerless, I have no hope*, or *I am bad*. These internal thoughts create exceptionally strong emotional responses whether the person self-injures or not. These shame-based messages are, perhaps, even more potent for Christians who fear that being known will result in utter rejection and the belief that they are too bad for God's grace.

CBT begins changing the cascade through changing the negative thoughts. This is a key aspect for CBT as clients learn to begin replacing thoughts like *I am bad* with more positive thoughts like *I am inherently valuable*. As new thoughts are absorbed into the client's life, suddenly the trigger no longer sends the client into the cascade that led to cutting. Homework is also a significant part of CBT.

Most therapists include insight or awareness exercises related to the thinking/feeling/doing process. After clients gain insight into thinking, feeling, and doing, environmental triggers are added to the homework. The homework can be used to explore the people, places, and things that cause triggers for the client and to develop alternatives that can help them avoid or "deal with" the trigger before it happens. By anticipating and developing a plan for the trigger(s), which for many clients are predictable, therapists can help clients plan for the triggers that they currently experience and develop methods of coping for future unplanned triggers. CBT can be very useful in helping clients figure out the thoughts and feelings associated with their self; as mentioned earlier in this chapter, many clients can struggle with not knowing why they self-injure or not being able to identify the emotions surrounding it.

When Grace first told me about her self-injury in therapy, she exhibited intense shame about it but was confused about why she cut or what emotions she was feeling. Over several weeks, she and I began working on noticing when she tends to cut and what types of emotions might be triggering her. To help her learn to pay attention to what was going on with her, I assigned her simple homework of writing down observations: When did she cut? What was happening right before she cut? What was she feeling and thinking? What was she feeling and thinking while she was cutting (if anything)? What did she feel and think after cutting? This process was initially very difficult for her, as she did not have experience with noticing or identifying her feelings or thoughts. Clients can struggle with this, and it can take time to walk alongside them and help them learn these skills. Safety is paramount, as feeling safe will likely be the greatest factor in clients learning how to look at their thoughts and feelings without fear of being overwhelmed and "drowned" by them. As time went on and Grace continually experienced feeling safe, she was able to learn these CBT skills, and they helped her to see a pattern connecting the self-injury behavior back to experiences with her father.

One of the things Grace discovered was that when others expressed strong distressful and afflictive emotions, she felt so scared that she would cut herself for several reasons: she wanted to punish herself for "being weak," she could not tolerate the strong emotions she felt, and she knew that the cutting would "release" the emotions so she could "feel better." She then figured out that the thought behind her fear was, *I am in danger, and I am too weak to protect myself.* An alternative thought she chose to practice was *I am safe, and I can protect myself,* and we worked on changing her perspective—that she is not a little girl being screamed at by her father anymore, she is an adult, she has a voice, and she can make her own choices. She also discovered that almost every emotion she had was stuck inside, and she used the cutting behavior to help express herself. She found that it was the only way she felt she could "get the pain out of her." She also slowly connected feelings that were in her body with specific words to describe what those feelings meant. Recall from the case study section that Grace had spent her first counseling session discussing physical feelings in her body that had changed since her father died. She was eventually able to recognize that this was her body's way of expressing her emotions as well. She realized that she needed to find another effective way to express emotions and pain. One of the final pieces we integrated into her work to confront her fear was guided imagery of Jesus holding her hand as she walked along a beach. She specifically chose a beach scene for the image because it brought peace. And as we began the process of bringing a "safe," "loving" Jesus into her world, she found it easier to return to this image whenever she felt scared or was afraid.

Psychodynamic/relational therapy. Relational therapy is the most modern version of psychoanalysis, and it sets itself apart from the more traditional psychoanalytic therapies in a couple of key ways. First, there has been a movement away from drives, although there is an awareness of them, and a greater emphasis on the dynamic relationship occurring in the session (Andersen & Chen, 2002). This movement away from drives is grounded in the awareness that people need relationships, and relationships are as strong as or stronger than drives.

Second, history is still important in contextualizing the client's past experiences to the current set of behaviors and issues, and this helps balance the past and present. This is in stark contrast to older models that spent tremendous time only on the past. This unilateral focus on the past often left clients confused about the connections between their current behaviors or problems and their past experiences. As mentioned previously in the section on systems therapy, sometimes a client's past is not associated with current struggles. Some therapists also did not make the connection clear, thus leaving clients wondering why there was so much discussion about their relationships with their mothers.

Third, the unconscious still plays a significant role in therapy, but only in as much as the client is confused by behaviors—for example, saying, "I have no idea why I did that"—or in situations where the client expresses being "stuck"—"I feel like I am on a hamster wheel and keep repeating the exact same behaviors even though I don't want to." The emphasis on generally exploring the unconscious has been replaced with a pragmatic connection between what clients want or who they are and the inability to change or stop behaviors.

Fourth, the relationship is key to the therapy. Thus, interpersonal dynamics, attachment styles, and coping mechanisms are key markers to understanding the client's needs, both met and unmet, and helping a client explore those three elements is foundational to progress in therapy.

A key concept within this framework is that people are wounded in relationship and therefore must heal in relationship. Transference and countertransference are still important parts of relational therapy. However, there is a greater emphasis on the utility of both transference and countertransference versus the negative qualities. For example, it is natural and assumed that clients will treat us like people from their past—transference—and it is important to evaluate how we're feeling about clients—countertransference—so that we can understand them through the countertransference experience. Finally, many relational therapists want to understand what a behavior or pathology means to the client before ever working to reduce it. It is the client's meaning given to any behavior that helps us know the "why" behind it. Only then can we help clients make changes to their behaviors, because only then will we understand how the changes we are working on will affect the client.

Thus, for a relational therapist, attachment theory and therapy offer additional insight and techniques. First, set an environment that is caring, empathic, and nonjudgmental. Simply, these clients need a safe haven (Thomas & Sosin, 2011). Of course, you would want to do this regardless of your chosen therapeutic modality. This "holding," as it is regarded in relational therapy, is useful to help begin evaluating clients' responses. Their responses, either positively or negatively, will begin helping you frame their early attachment style with the family or caregivers and define how they play out their attachments in current relational dynamics. As therapy progresses, greater emphasis is placed on clients' meaning regarding a behavior—in this case, self-injury. Exploring how clients feel about the self-injury and what purpose the self-injury serves for them is essential. This is similar to what we previously discussed in the CBT section, as we help clients to understand their experiences.

It is also at this stage that therapists begin challenging ways in which their clients predict or misread interpersonal relationships. These are gentle challenges, with constant reminders that the hold is in place and will be stable throughout the course of treatment. These reminders constantly ground clients in the healthy relational dynamic and reinforce the potential of healthy connections and relationships in their lives. During the challenges and confrontations transference and countertransference will increase. Therefore, being aware of yourself as a therapist and how you are feeling personally and relationally is key during this time. Otherwise, you are likely to reenact some previous unhealthy relational dynamic. Be aware that making mistakes during therapy is normal. And in relational therapy, owning our mistakes with clients not only humanizes us and the process but builds trust with clients as we genuinely own and hold the mistakes we make.

Once safety and understanding have been established, we are able to work on finding replacement behaviors that can, in a healthy way, effectively serve the same purpose as the self-injury. This is also similar to the CBT concept discussed above of replacing negative/untrue cognitions with positive/true ones.

Grace was experiencing deep shame over her self-injury, and this was very evident in therapy by the barely audible softness of her voice, avoidance of eye contact, and struggle to find words when first discussing her cutting with me. Because of this, I knew that creating a safe "holding" environment for her would be of the greatest importance. As time passed, Grace eventually admitted to me that sometimes she felt afraid that I would "yell at her." She didn't know why she felt this way, but she said that sometimes she didn't want to talk about things because she was worried that I would yell at her. Because we had already discussed her childhood family dynamics in great detail, I asked her if she felt this way with her father growing up, afraid to talk to him because she was afraid he would yell at her. She said this was true, and suddenly she realized that she was emotionally responding to me the same way she did to him. She realized that her emotional response was about her relationship with her father, not about her relationship with me. This was an excellent illustration of transference and a great opportunity for healing for her, as her relationship with me over time helped her to emotionally learn that not all men will treat her as her father did and that she can feel safe, respected, heard, and valued as a person.

Additionally, I decided to incorporate art therapy into our work. About twenty-eight weeks into therapy, we began using nonverbal alternatives to self-injury to see if Grace connected with something other than words. As we explored what might be an alternative, I discovered that she really loved art and loved to draw. Although this played a significant role in her daily life as she doodled everywhere, she had never discussed it in therapy before. I asked her one week to find a picture that portrayed what she felt like when she wanted to cut. She came back the next week with the perfect picture to describe her pain: *The Scream* by Edvard Munch. She brought in a copy of the picture and said, "*This is how I feel*

when I want to cut." I was mesmerized by the picture. Even more so by how accurately this looked like the pain and hurt my client had described to me.

I asked her if looking at the picture helped her not to cut, and she shook her head no. "*Hmm,*" I wondered out loud, "*would it possibly help you to draw the picture when you felt overwhelmed by your emotions?*" She thought about this for some time and then said that she would try. We practiced drawing the picture in session, but replacing the screamer with her. She liked the idea of placing her face in the picture. As she drew the scream that was her, she smiled for the first time in therapy. She meticulously detailed the picture, and as she integrated her face into the art, there was a moment when she seemed to feel what her pain was like inside of her, and she teared up. When she finished, she said, "I look really scared and sad, don't I?" I agreed that in the picture she looked really scared and sad. I said, "It must have been really tough for this little girl to experience all of that pain and try to hold it inside." She nodded and for the second time teared up.

As therapy continued over the next couple of weeks, Grace tried different pencils and coloring pencils. She actually tried drawing very softly at times and then very intensely to see if that changed the way she processed her feelings. Each time she saw herself as the little girl in the scream, she would tear up and almost cry. She slowly started making the connection between her pain and the pain she saw in herself in the picture. Drawing was slowly allowing her to begin feeling her feelings. For the first time since childhood, she was able to start crying and expressing her sadness and fear. In Grace's case, art was slowly becoming the replacement behavior that was strong enough to replace cutting as a way for her to connect to and express her emotions.

Neuropsychological Techniques

While I did not use any of the following neuropsychological techniques in my work with Grace, it is important to mention them in this chapter. Many of them have been shown to be effective in helping clients who struggle with self-injury. Awareness of these techniques may be useful to you as you work with different clients, especially with clients who may not be responding well to other types of therapy. Be creative, seek consultation and/or supervision, and continually update yourself on current research, as only a few techniques will be mentioned here.

Yoga. One nontraditional and alternative treatment strategy is encouraging clients to enroll in yoga classes. In the last ten years, volumes of research have suggested that taking yoga classes or practicing the breathing and poses helps with everything from depression to anxiety (Harkess, Delfabbro, Moritmer, Hannaford, & Cohen-Woods, 2017; West, Liang, & Spinazzola, 2017). Pairing yoga with any form of therapy when working with self-injury can be an effective way for clients to feel more grounded in their bodies. Self-injuring clients who engage in yoga also report feeling less overwhelmed in general, thus potentially decreasing the need to cut.

Meridian. A second alternative method is directing a client to put pressure on the upper lip, just below the nose. This is called a "meridian point." This technique was discovered by neuropsychologists as a bodily spot that floods the brain with signals of intense pain, and it satisfies both the grounding need to express inner pain and to feel aware of one's own body (Diepold, 2000). Assigning this exercise as homework so that clients can practice using this pressure point is additive to the entire treatment process, particularly as self-injuring clients are more likely to cut while working through their issues.

Ice. Consider having a self-injuring client use ice as a method of causing bodily pain in a safer way, thus emulating the typical injurious behavior. This technique, borrowed from standard dialectical behavior therapy (DBT) protocols (Linehan, 2014), works especially well with what can be called intransigent cutting. The use of ice to emulate the cutting process not only creates the pain sensation as the cold moves over and down into the skin, but ice melts as the client is applying it to his skin. The melting ice becomes a metaphor for the bleeding that is concomitant with cutting. Again, this technique has been found to be especially helpful with cutting that seems immune to other techniques and more traditional forms of therapy.

Other similar techniques can be used toward the same effect, such as having a client wear rubber bands on her wrists and snap them against her skin when feeling the urge to self-injure, satisfying the desire for stimulation or grounding in a less harmful way. Some people also find drawing on their skin with pens or markers to be effective when they feel the urge to self-injure, especially those whose preferred method of self-injury involves cutting words or particular designs into their skin. Any of these techniques should be used in moderation and limited to situations where the client needs to stop or reduce cutting behaviors due to environmental or situational needs.

Be and Stay with Self-Harmers

Regardless of your chosen therapeutic approach, it is imperative for you to be present with your clients. Client stories are often not offered as a whole, but fragments. At first, pieces do not seem to fit. The stories don't seem to make sense. In my work with Grace, the stories didn't seem to make sense at first. I felt disoriented and wondered whether I was fully present or if the client's reality didn't make sense to her either. The bits and pieces of the story offered no more than ideas of what had happened to her when she was young. I reflected on her own confusion of what happened and assured her that together we would figure it out.

CONCLUSION

Although many therapists struggle with the idea of cutting or other forms of self-injury such as burning, hair pulling, craving, ripping skin, and impacting with objects, current research and practitioners have helped bring new hope to those who injure and feel ashamed or overwhelmed. Online communities are an important factor to consider and inquire about when working with these clients. Additionally, contrary to popular belief, the majority of those who self-injure do not commit suicide and are not diagnosed with BPD; physical grounding, control, expressions of pain, and self-punishment appear to be four of the most common motivations behind this issue, although clients can often struggle to understand or verbalize their own particular motivations.

Several conceptualization models have been presented in this chapter, as well as several different treatment modalities (CBT, psychodynamic, systems, yoga, etc.), and it is important to be aware of this variety, as every client is unique and has his or her own individual story. What works well for one person does not always work well with another, hence the importance of having a plethora of perspectives and techniques at your disposal. Other models and treatments are not listed here, as this chapter is not exhaustive, and you are encouraged to continue in your research of this topic. Our goal on this journey is to enter the world of our clients, and for those who self-injure, we can do so knowing from our experience and/or research that there is hope and that our therapy truly does bring healing into the lives of the people we serve.

RECOMMENDED READING

Bandura, A. (1986). *Social foundations of thought and action: A social cognitive perspective.* Upper Saddle River, NJ: Prentice Hall.

Calder, M. (2007). *Understanding, assessing, and engaging with young people who self-harm.* Lyme Regis, UK: Russell House.

Fox, C., & Hawton, K. (2004). *Deliberate self-harm in adolescence.* London: Jessica Kingsley.

Gratz, K. L., & Chapman, A. (2009). *Freedom from self-harm: Overcoming self-injury with skills from DBT and other treatments.* Oakland, CA: New Harbinger.

Levenkron, S. (2006). *Cutting: Understanding and overcoming self-mutilation.* New York, NY: W. W. Norton.

Pipher, M. (1994). *Reviving Ophelia: Saving the selves of adolescent girls.* New York, NY: Ballantine.

Strong, M. (1998). *A bright red scream: Self-mutilation and the language of pain.* New York, NY: Penguin.

Walker, S. (2012). *Responding to self-harm in children and adolescents: A professional's guide to identification, intervention and support.* Philadelphia, PA: Jessica Kingsley.

CHAPTER 24

Loss-Focused Strategies

ERIC SCALISE, PHD

Blessed are those who mourn,
for they shall be comforted.
MATTHEW 5:4 ESV

The phone call on a Sunday morning between church services was a bit unusual, but I could hear the distress in my friend's voice. "Can you please come to the funeral home right away? We need to talk with you." I rushed out of the church, and while driving my mind was racing as I tried to decipher his words, wondering what had happened. After pulling into the parking lot, I walked quickly into a small chapel and saw a couple sitting in the front pew. They were clutching each other, shoulders hunched in despondency, their eyes red with tears. My face begged the question, and the reply was heart-wrenching. Jenny, their precious newborn daughter, had just died of sudden infant death syndrome (SIDS). It was Mother's Day.

A wife who loses a husband is called a *widow*. A husband who loses a wife is called a *widower*. A child who loses his or her parents is called an *orphan*. There is no word for a parent who loses a child—in fact, it speaks to the very essence of grief work—a loss of words. Grief and loss issues transcend every culture, every people group, every educational and socioeconomic level, and every belief system. Countless articles pepper the research literature, along with hundreds of books and an abundance of resources. Why? Because grief is so universal, prevalent, and personal. Ironically, it can be extremely difficult to comprehend.

In the midst of grief, faith and spirituality are mysterious but real. They have offered countless people a place of refuge, solace, comfort, hope, and a deeper sense of purpose and meaning—especially in times of tragedy where grief and despair seek to rob a person of vitality and life. Although the role of faith continues to be an evolving construct among the social sciences, thus far the research literature generally affirms its profound and dynamic impact on mental health and overall well-being. An individual's religious beliefs and practice often serve as a positive source of interpersonal strength. A vibrant personal faith encounter has proven to increase resilience, coping, and successful treatment for a variety of conditions. These include chronic pain (Glover-Graf, Marini, Baker, & Buck, 2007), poly-substance abuse (Heinze, Epstein, & Preston, 2007), and comorbidity among trauma survivors (Fallot & Heckman, 2005). According to Koenig (2000), merely completing the process of a spiritual history with a client (where faith is valued) yields treatment benefits. In a large comprehensive meta-analysis, McCullough and associates (McCullough, Hoyt, Larson, Koenig, & Thoresen, 2000) reviewed and summarized forty-two study samples that evaluated a total of 126,000 people. They found that religious involvement increased life expectancy by 29 percent.

As counselors and mental health practitioners, we frequently engage others at their point of pain. Indeed, grief and loss issues are often at the forefront of a client's presenting problems. We must, therefore, be equipped with the necessary tools and strategies to assist others as they navigate the harsh journey of these significant events. Grief is a deeply personal journey, and any invitation into that private place by those who are devastated from a loss is a sacred trust.

THEOLOGY AND PSYCHOLOGY OF LOSS

From Mourning to Mourning

Grief can only be experienced when there has been the loss of an intimate relationship with a person or some other object of concern and/or affection. It is an "active, intentional, decision to face the pain of the loss" (Zonnebelt-Smeenge & DeVries, 2006, p. 20). Grief is also a discovery process and a normal human response that includes feelings of intense sorrow, anger, loneliness, depression, and possible physical symptoms. More often than not, it takes enormous courage and resolve to work "through" rather than merely attempting to work "out of" the process. The great missionary Hudson Taylor, who almost single-handedly opened up China to the gospel, lost his beloved wife to cholera a week after she gave birth to their son, who also died. In his anguish, Taylor refused to eat or even leave the gravesite for days as he wrestled within himself and with his God. While the grief was overwhelming for Taylor, by God's grace he was able to work "through" the loss rather than "out of" the loss. When bearing the weight of grief, the experience is often characterized by the very human desire to work out of, around, and over the pain, even when walking through the process can help lead to a greater sense of closure. Grieving "through" a loss is a profound challenge into a dark wilderness of the unknown. But "through" is the only way to heal.

According to grief expert H. Norman Wright (2003), there are different types of losses—some related to the normal aging process, some defined by the nature of certain events, and some that simply go unrecognized. They include the following (pp. 69–73):

- *Unspeakable losses*—for example, miscarriage, infertility issues, postabortion consequences, etc., where the issues are not identified, shared, or discussed

- **Frequent losses**—for example, the loss of mobility, energy, mental capacity, and friends later in life due to old age, or disease
- **Gradual losses**—for example, the loss of children to graduation, marriage, and other empty-nest events
- **Accumulated losses**—for example, an array of growing medical, financial, or stress-related problems and conditions
- **Final losses**—for example, those that occur when there is insufficient time for a full recovery or restoration, such as a spouse who dies after decades of marriage or losing a job late in a career
- **Identity losses**—for example, the lack of purpose or meaning in life
- **Threatened losses**—for example, awaiting the outcome of a biopsy, a possible separation and divorce, a pending lawsuit, a layoff at work

Rarely are there easy answers to events that seem so inherently tragic and untimely. The list is endless: rape, suicide, murder, abduction, children with cancer, sexual abuse, the death of a spouse, divorce, natural disasters, a mastectomy, or sudden income loss. The pain is often crushing, sleep becomes fitful, and questions constantly intrude into our waking moments. The most human of all questions is simply "Why?" *Why me? Why us? Why this? Why now?* people wonder. Unfortunately, it is difficult to find answers to these questions, much less answers that offer a measure of satisfaction or relief. Perhaps there is some comfort in knowing that Jesus himself cried out in great pain at Golgotha, pleading with his Father to answer a

why question only to be met with apparent silence (Matt. 27:46). Scripture describes our suffering Messiah as a man of sorrows and One who is acquainted with grief (Isa. 53:3). Therefore, we have a Savior who fully understands exactly where people are in every moment of their loss and lonely despair.

A crisis leading to grief can be real (e.g., an unexpected death), anticipated (e.g., notification of a pending layoff at work), or imagined (e.g., a psychotic break). However, under any of these conditions, the potential impact is essentially the same. While grief, loss, and suffering are universal, the time frame and how a person approaches them is individual and unique. C. S. Lewis (1940), the beloved British novelist and theologian, once commented that "God whispers to us in our pleasures, speaks in our conscious, but shouts in our pain. It is His megaphone to rouse a deaf world" (p. 91). In times such as these, God has ordained his body, the church, to provide a healing community for those whose burdens are too much to bear alone. The prevalence of grief and loss issues that are often associated with everyday life represent a significant priority for most helping professionals and ministry leaders. As counselors, we have powerful opportunities to see the pieces of a broken world slowly knit back together again into a tapestry that proclaims God's restorative compassion and care.

When it comes to grief work, Elizabeth Kübler-Ross, a Swiss American psychiatrist viewed as a seminal researcher in the arena of hospice care, developed an initial framework to understand what people typically experience when facing death. In her groundbreaking book, *On Death and Dying* (1969), she presented a model of distinct stages of grief, which has since been broadened to include the following (*The Seven Stages of Grief*, Social Work Tech, n.d.):

- *Shock and denial stage.* People often experience learning of the loss with stunned disbelief. The first stage is the initial emotional and psychological paralysis after becoming aware of the loss. Soon the griever will attempt to avoid the inevitable and stave off the coming pain by not allowing the reality of the loss to be experienced.

- *Pain and guilt stage.* As denial subsides, it is replaced with the suffering of excruciating pain. Although it feels unbearable, the griever must experience it fully, avoid running from it, and not seek escape. Often remorse or guilt feelings occur over what the griever did or didn't do. Life feels chaotic and scary.

- *Anger and bargaining stage.* The griever experiences frustrated outpouring of bottled-up emotion and the loss of control. He or she may lash out toward others and express unwarranted blame of someone. In an attempt to create a sense of meaning out of the chaos and seeking in vain for a way out of the "journey," the griever attempts to bargain with God and others.

- *Depression, reflection, and loneliness stage.* The griever may enter a long period of sadness in which he or she begins to realize the magnitude of the loss. The griever may reflect on the loss and focus on memories, leading to a sense of emptiness and despair.

- *The upward turn.* Eventually life becomes a little calmer and more organized. The griever notices a slightly lifted mood as physical, emotional, and spiritual symptoms lessen.

- *Accepting and hope stage.* Acceptance emerges as the griever faces the reality of the loss. The griever learns that normal is gone, and a new normal must be established and accepted. He or she seeks new alternative and realistic solutions as a means of survival and moving forward in life without wrenching pain. Much to the surprise of the griever, hope begins to slowly engender strength.

- *Reconstruction stage.* The griever becomes more functional and seeks new and realistic solutions to life and problems posed.

- Noting that Kübler-Ross's model does not address the stages of grief for survivors but for the person dying is key. Though similarities exist, avoid misapplying it.

Many of us have our own testimonies demonstrating God's faithfulness through these stages and his ability to resurrect life out of tragedy and heartbreak. The words of God recorded through Jeremiah become a new heritage: "I will turn their mourning into gladness; I will give them comfort and joy instead of sorrow" (31:13). Nevertheless, there are also times when people become "stuck" and therefore struggle to break free from the powerful grip of traumatic circumstances. Factors that help determine the intensity, severity, and duration of a grief response include the type of loss that was experienced, prior knowledge and anticipation, one's support systems or lack thereof, and one's beliefs. When grief remains unresolved and without reasonable closure over a significant period, it is known as complicated grief. It is associated with more serious problems such as clinical depression, anxiety disorders, acute hopelessness, suicidal ideation, substance abuse, post-traumatic stress disorder (PTSD), as well as major disruptions in normal routines, functionality, and relationships (Lobb, Aoun, & Monterosso, 2006). Several dynamics lead to the formation of complicated grief, including the following (Shear et al., 2007):

- The mode of the loss is considered incomprehensible, senseless, tragic, or preventable.
- The loss is considered exceptionally untimely.
- The mourner feels guilty being party to the event that caused the loss.
- The survivor had an extreme dependency on the deceased, who provided much of the mourner's sense of self-worth, self-confidence, or meaning in life.
- The mourner's work, family, or environmental circumstances disallow the expression of grief.
- The mourner has an excessive attachment and proximity to a deceased person's possessions.
- The mourner has an excessive and premature "jumping back" into normal activities without allowing time to grieve.

- The mourner's overall relationships show evidence of an insecure attachment style.
- The griever believes, contrary to biblical teaching and the example of Christ, that Christians should never grieve but only rejoice.

In their extensive meta-analysis, Lobb and colleagues (Lobb et al., 2006) examined more than seven hundred peer-reviewed articles and concluded that approximately 10 to 20 percent of the population experiences complicated grief after a significant loss and are therefore at a greater risk for adverse physical effects and somatic complaints. They said, "People who suffer from complicated grief experience a sense of persistent and disturbing disbelief regarding the loss and greater resistance to accepting the painful reality" (p. 10). Historically, researchers have maintained that complicated grief is either a type of major depressive disorder or an anxiety-based disorder that has been triggered by a death or significant loss. More recently, other scholars have concluded that grief symptoms only partially coincide with symptoms of depression and other psychopathologies such as anxiety and PTSD (Perper, 2013). Even though there may be some shared and expected variance, complicated grief reactions do demonstrate a sufficiently distinct variance to warrant separate consideration. Prigerson and Jacobs (2001), who developed the Inventory of Complicated Grief, were among the first to offer a clinical road map. They describe complicated grief as being present when there are prolonged symptoms (more than six months) with an elevated negative mood because of what they term separation and/or traumatic distress. In such cases, professional counseling is usually recommended in conjunction with other supportive interventions and resources.

According to the National Institutes of Health, approximately 25 percent of all children in the United States will experience at least one significant traumatic event before the age of sixteen, with 15 percent of girls and 6 percent of boys developing symptoms of PTSD (Cohen & Scheeringa, 2009). The *Diagnostic and Statistical Manual*, fifth edition (DSM-5; American Psychiatric Association, 2013) now includes a category for minors under the age of six. Based on the theory of developmental trauma disorder (DTD), this addition to the diagnostic classification system was endorsed because the previous descriptors for PTSD were inadequate in addressing childhood traumatization. Children and adolescents who have experienced repetitive trauma suffer greater emotional and physiological dysregulation because there is a chronic activation of certain neurobiological systems. These systems produce stronger and more immediate reactions to emotional stimuli, with the effects often lingering into adulthood (Schmid, Peterman, & Fegert, 2013).

Complex trauma results in a protracted overactivation (sensitized neural responses) of an individual's autonomic nervous system. This results in fight-flight-freeze responses to seemingly random and unrelated cues long after exposure to traumatic experiences have ended (Sherin, 2011). The amygdala and the hippocampus, both part of the limbic system and highly sensitive to stress hormones, change after exposure to a traumatic event. A person's ability to plan and think objectively is dramatically distorted, and the essence of objective thinking and judgment is significantly impaired when a triggering episode occurs. In the flight or fight process, rational and calm thinking is compromised because adrenaline signals the body to move blood out of the brain and to the major muscle groups where it may be more needed to facilitate movement.

One of the best moderators of complex trauma is the capacity for and development of resilience, also referred to as buoyancy or "bounce back" ability. Resiliency can also be defined as an emotional and/or psychological elasticity. It is important to think of this quality as necessary before, during, and after a traumatic event as part of the resilience life cycle (Dees, 2011). Research on the subject seems to indicate that most people can build a measure of resilience, as it is a skill-based dynamic involving thoughts and behaviors, which are acquired and developed over time. Still, individuals do experience the pain and emotional distress of trauma. Most move toward post-traumatic growth in a more systematic and intentional manner, however. In fact, how a person faces and works through trauma may in some cases increase suffering. Resilience-building factors, much like the protective shield of an inoculation, include the following (Dees, 2011):

- The presence of caring and supportive relationships
- A positive outlook and keeping things in perspective with realistic expectations
- Impulse control and management of strong emotions through appropriate outlets
- The ability to set reasonable goals and objectives
- A commitment to self-care, rest, time management, and a balanced life
- Meditation and integrating faith-affirming strategies
- Utilization of outside and professional resources when necessary

Throughout his life, the Old Testament's King David often needed to demonstrate a measure of resilience because over the years he experienced multiple losses. Many times he battled hopelessness and discouragement. In Psalm 42:3, 5, David lamented, "My tears have been my food day and night. . . . Why, my soul, are you downcast? Why so disturbed within me?" Sometimes he even wondered if the Lord was actually engaged in what was going on: "You have put me in the lowest pit, in the darkest depths," and again, "You have taken from me friend and neighbor—darkness is my closest friend" (Ps. 88:6, 18). Yet David also proclaimed that God "heals the brokenhearted and binds up their wounds" (Ps. 147:3).

The dark night of the soul can be overwhelming at times and consume our will to survive the emotional storm. I have had clients who described their grief and pain as feeling chained within the confines of a dungeon, engulfed by darkness. It is in that lonely and isolated place that a spirit of fear can gain a strong foothold in a person's life and do so with devastating effects. The fear of changes that may come as the result of the loss or the fear of the unknown, a common denominator with complicated grief, is a growing awareness of secondary loss, the loss of control.

This perceived loss of control frequently leads to increased control behaviors. When painful and tragic events take place, people believe they have little to no control. They may conclude that a lack of control may increase risk for more pain and suffering. They may then rationalize that the opposite must also be true. Figuring out how to maintain control of their environment and the people within it will somehow make it bearable. Unfortunately, this kind of excessive control rarely provides any relief and often exacerbates the situation. Much of this process is fueled by a prevailing fear.

I view fear as the darkroom that develops all our negatives. In other words, fear is usually a dark place where negative thoughts, emotions, and behaviors give rise to destructive forces in a person's life. There is only one thing I know of that will stop a developing photograph in its tracks—light! This is because light penetrates darkness. As counselors, it is critical that we carefully and genuinely bring the light of God's Word into the lives of those with whom we work. Indeed, it is a "lamp for [our] feet, a light on [our] path" (Ps. 119:105). When the Lord illuminates areas of the heart, it is rarely to condemn or give greater burden of guilt or shame. Rather, God is likely preparing to perform divine surgery to bring healing or restorative purpose: "Everything exposed by the light becomes visible—and everything that is illuminated becomes a light" (Eph. 5:13). Otherwise, the darkness causes fear to grow. It is only a "monster under the bed" until the light is turned on. When the light of God's Word and Spirit pierces the dark areas of the heart, fears are often rooted out along with negative thought patterns, their associated behaviors, and especially the underlying anxiety related to the perceived threat.

The presence of "light" creates an environment for release and recovery. It is much like reconstructive surgery with burn victims, people born with a cleft pallet, and other traumas. The doctors do what they can and then let the wound heal a bit; afterward they do more, building on the previous surgery. God sometimes works in the same manner. He knows what a person can handle at any given time and what that person is willing to allow him to do. Consider what happens when someone accidentally grips a live electrical wire. If the current is strong enough, the hand and wrist muscles contract, tightening the grip even more. Everything inside the person is screaming to let go, but to no avail. It is also pointless to treat the person's hand while the power is still on. Not until the electricity is cut off from the source is it possible to let go. Just releasing the wire doesn't bring healing, but at least now treating the injuries can commence.

We grieve because we love, and love often speaks of relationship—being connected to someone or something that we value and cherish. The loss of this "object of affection" can leave a person empty, tormented, and in despair. People can choose to love and risk loss or simply isolate themselves with loneliness in an attempt to avoid anything painful. "The fact remains that sometimes, love hurts. So we have to resign ourselves to being capable of love that hurts. To do otherwise would be to withdraw from life, to exist in a sort of emotional exile, not benefiting from or feeling all the joys of the human experience. Our love may be especially hurtful, but the reality of that love is a gift" (Staudacher, 1994, p. 97).

The words of the psalmist bring comfort to many who likewise have proclaimed that "weeping may stay for the night, but rejoicing comes in the morning" (Ps. 30:5).

CASE STUDY: WHEN THE QUIVER IS EMPTY—THE SILENT STRUGGLE OF INFERTILITY

They were young, in love, full of life with dreams to match, newly married, and ready to start their family. Ben and Sara were as normal as any other couple. They had a strong sense of faith and sincerely believed that having children was a sign of God's blessing in someone's life. They could quote nearly every Scripture on the subject in their sleep (Gen. 1:28; Ps. 127:3–5; Prov. 17:6; 22:6).

Yet God chose a different path for Ben and Sara, one that would challenge their faith to the core and take them on a journey of anguish and despair. Sara experienced four successive miscarriages and three times went into labor only to deliver a dead baby. One of the hardest aspects for her was the deafening silence and the utter sense of stillness after having heard a tiny heart beating within her.

As you might imagine, the questions burned deeply as Ben and Sara wrestled with God in their human weakness, examining over and over again their walk with him. "Have we displeased you in some way? Is this your judgment? Didn't you give Isaac to Sarah, Samuel to Hannah, and John to Elizabeth? We've read their stories. You answered their heart cries. Lord, why not us? Why this? Do you still love us? We don't understand!"

While any loss and resulting grief can exact a toll on multiple levels (emotionally, psychologically, physically, relationally, and spiritually), infertility is unique in a number of ways for it represents multiple losses. It rarely kills; it is usually not visible; typically it is not discussed in public or grieved by family and friends in the same manner as other losses; and it can create a crisis of faith. Although infertility is formally defined as the inability to get pregnant after one year of trying, or six months if a woman is thirty-five or older, problems associated with infertility can refer to difficulty conceiving, bearing, or carrying a child to term. The American Pregnancy Association (2017) estimates that approximately 7.3 million women in the United States between the ages of fif-

teen and forty-four experience some form of infertility. Infertility accounts for 35 to 40 percent of all cases and includes complications such as the failure to ovulate (the most prevalent cause), hormonal imbalance, polycystic ovarian disease and pelvic inflammatory disease, uterine fibroids, endometriosis, an abnormally shaped uterus, and sexually transmitted diseases, among other problems. About one-fourth of cases involve both birth parents, and another third are primarily due to male issues (deficient sperm accounts for 90 percent of these cases). In Ben and Sara's case, it was determined that Sara was suffering from an immune system disorder that compromised the viability of the pregnancy.

Miscarriage, sometimes referred to as "spontaneous abortion," is defined as the loss of a pregnancy during the first twenty weeks, or in subsequent weeks, as a preterm delivery. This can be nature's way of the body sensing fetal abnormality or nonviability (representing 50 to 70 percent of first-trimester miscarriages). When a miscarriage occurs beyond the fifth month of pregnancy, it is usually referred to as a stillbirth. Sara's third pregnancy resulted in a stillbirth. Approximately 10 to 20 percent of known pregnancies end in miscarriage, and more than 80 percent of these losses take place before twelve weeks. Some studies have found that 30 to 50 percent of fertilized eggs are lost before or during implantation, and a woman may not even realize that she was pregnant (American Pregnancy Association, 2017).

Ben and Sara have mostly suffered in silence. Like any number of grief-related issues, their infertility problems may constitute a "hidden" loss and one that carries the additional burden of shame. Individually or as a couple, they may be reluctant to seek out care, support, and counseling. The lingering mental and emotional turmoil often continues long after the physical aftermath is over. A woman's emotions may feel like a roller coaster of numbness, disbelief, and anger; and depending on when the loss occurred, some level of postpartum depression may also be evident.

The reality is that grief almost never waits for an invitation; it merely arrives, usually unannounced. Grief and loss create detours in one's life and can change focus, direction, and a sense of meaning or purpose (Zonnebelt-Smeenge & DeVries, 2006). This happened for Ben and Sara, who moved from a place of utter despair, wrestling with their faith, and then slowly allowing God to meet them in a place of raw but honest vulnerability. The end result for them was greater confidence that God was not finished with their story, something that may speak to a new narrative, which can in turn engender hope (Hedtke, 2014). Thus, remembering the following axiom is important for all counselors: everyone has a story to tell, and everyone needs that story. This is especially true for grief and loss issues and when working with this population.

STRATEGIES, INTERVENTIONS, AND TECHNIQUES FOR LOSS

How Ben and Sara "work through" their grief can, as in some cases, result in greater pain and distress than the original event.

James and Gilliland (2005) maintain that three terms coexist in the world of crisis intervention, of which counselors must know the difference: "*bereavement*, which is an objective state or condition of deprivation that is especially caused by death and is then followed or accompanied by . . . *grief*, a psychic state or condition of mental anguish or emotional suffering and a result or anticipation of the bereavement; and *mourning*, a social or cultural state or condition expressing the grief or feeling because of the bereavement" (p. 325). Ben and Sara are suffering with all three.

The couple's suffering was lessened by finding meaning in their broader family unit, community, and culture (Neimeyer, Klass, & Dennis, 2014). In these three related but distinct processes (bereavement, grief, and mourning) is where my approach (e.g., skills, techniques, cultural competency, biblical integration, the ministry of presence) intersected with their brokenness. Having a practical and effective set of therapeutic "tools" made the difference in therapeutic outcomes. However, it was my empathic and compassionate responses that truly made the difference.

Merriam-Webster's Collegiate Dictionary (2003) defines the term *compassion* as a "sympathetic consciousness of others' distress together with a desire to alleviate it." The word is derived from the Latin *pati* (to suffer) and the prefix *cum* (to bear alongside). Much of the research on this subject underscores the critical importance of the helping relationship along with caregivers who are frequently in close proximity to the emotional suffering and resulting grief of those they minister to and counsel.

Lilius and associates (Lilius et al., 2003) expanded the definition of *compassion*: an "empathetic emotional response to another person's pain or suffering that moves people to act in a way that will either ease the person's condition or make it more bearable" (p. 4). This is the essence of the therapeutic alliance and a vital factor that should not be overlooked when working with clients like Ben and Sara.

Empathy, on the other hand, is often referred to as the ability to "put oneself into another's shoes." Titchener (1909) was one of the first modern psychologists to use the term, which he defined as a "process of humanizing objects, of reading or feeling ourselves into them" (p. 417). His conceptualization of empathy was a rendering from an even earlier construct originating in German aesthetics called *Einfühlung* and described as a person's spontaneous projection of intuitive feelings toward another (Vischer, 1883, as cited in Listowel, 1934). While sympathy tends to focus on one's own thoughts and feelings (i.e., what she is experiencing on a personal level in respect to another's loss), empathy, though somewhat similar, shifts the attention more directly to the other person and what he is feeling in the moment. Pregnancy loss can certainly elicit feelings of sympathy for a client. However, a more effective response is to empathically understand Ben and Sara through their eyes, their thoughts, their perceptions, and their view of the spiritual dynamics that may be in play. In a review of Norman Levine's book, *A Passion for Compassion*, Ohrman (2002) commented that "other-centeredness" can become a meaningful guide to life, taking place through

what is described as the exchange of genuine and authentic relationships. This is at the core of the client-therapist paradigm.

Indeed, the interplay between compassion and empathy—defined by this author as a *compathic* response—has significance to the counselor. For Young-Mason (2001), compassion is "born of wisdom and courage," and to fully comprehend the construct, it "means to study the nature of suffering—the intertwining of moral, spiritual, psychological, and physical suffering" and, "like freedom, is a word whose meaning becomes clearer and finally clarified in practice" (p. 347). Ben and Sara do not need sympathy, but rather the compassionate and empathic statements that demonstrate the counselor's capacity to understand their pain and brokenness (Capretto, 2015).

Christ's compassion is one of his distinguishing characteristics, as evidenced in his relational style with all whom he came in contact with. In both the Old and New Testaments, numerous passages describe this model (cf. Ps. 103:4; 135:14; Isa. 49:13; 54:8; Jer. 42:12; Mic. 7:19; Matt. 15:32; 20:34; James 5:11). Consider the examples in which Jesus confronted the Pharisees for their dedication to traditions and rules taking precedence over people: Jesus reprimanded these legalists by saying, "I desire compassion, and not a sacrifice" (Matt. 12:7 NASB). The original Greek word, *splanchnizomai*, captures the idea of tender affection from one's innermost being. In the Hebrew text, the word *rāḥam* refers to deep mercies.

The closest analogy in understanding this phenomenon would be the principle of acoustic resonance, which occurs when two violins are in the same room. As a string is plucked on one, it causes the string tuned to the same frequency on the second violin to begin to vibrate as well. This is a beautiful picture of the Christ-centered counselor being attuned not only to Ben and Sara but to the Spirit of the living God—in unison and moving together to accomplish his will.

Cultural Considerations

As our society grows increasingly diverse and the people seeking counseling come with multiple and, at times, seemingly incongruent value systems, counselors must learn to integrate and balance both biblical principles and cultural relevancy while still adhering to ethical practice. To be effective, we must engage clients through the lens of ethnic diversity while demonstrating respect and cultural competency. McGoldrick and her colleagues (McGoldrick, Giordano, & Garcia-Preto, 2005) provide an excellent practice resource developed through her work as director of the Multicultural Family Institute in Highland Park, New Jersey.

Grief, loss, and suffering are not limited to North America or Western civilization. One can hardly pick up a newspaper today, turn on the television, or go online without hearing about a global tragedy, natural disaster, or act of terror, destructive aftermath of armed conflict, sex trafficking, or other trauma-related stories. The pain is evident, and the pain is real, often causing people to yearn for good news, for something positive, something hopeful.

The United States has a rich history of compassionate outreach and goodwill. However, in a world that continues to

shrink due to innovative technologies, instant communication, and complex integrated economies, overtly westernized counseling strategies may not be the optimal approach when it comes to the caregiving paradigm—especially in terms of assessment and treatment protocols, diagnostic categories, certain theoretical constructs, and even the definition of some psychological disorders. Though the core and principled tenets of Christian counseling should always be anchored in God's Word, the methodology and process may require periodic adjustments to remain culturally relevant with a servant-oriented focus (Scalise, 2011). Practitioners should be cognizant of the geographic, ethnic, cultural, and even political nuances that have an impact on the delivery of services and resources.

Today there is a greater global focus on mental health and well-being, including an emphasis on caregiving and counseling. During the Third Lausanne Congress (Cape Town, South Africa) on World Evangelization in 2010, there was a watershed moment for Christian counseling. The Lausanne Care and Counsel as Mission Interest Group (LCCMIG) met to draft a document that provided a much-needed framework for a growing international counseling effort. The *Cape Town Declaration on Care and Counsel as Mission* (for more information, see www.careandcounselasmission.org) outlined the Three-Circle Paradigm of Care and Counsel that focuses on missionary care and support, support for the global church, and care and counsel as mission (Smith & Gingrich, 2011).

As biblically based therapists, each of us has the distinct privilege of faithfully representing Christ in our professional work or ministry with others. To accomplish this task effectively, we must employ balance in demonstrating the grace and compassion of a loving Savior in a culturally sensitive way. One of the messages of Pentecost and the birth of the church is that people were hearing the gospel, "each . . . [in]their own language" (Acts 2:6 ESV). Likewise, the message we carry as counselors must be relevant for the culture before us and in a "language" that culture can easily comprehend and respond to. This is critical when considering grief work with a client.

Grief Pattern Inventory

Clients like Ben and Sara demonstrate different patterns of grief. Understanding their pattern can assist in formulating an appropriate course of action. There are three basic orientations (Martin, 2006):

1. *Instrumental.* The focus is on cognition and a moderated affect where feelings are less intense, brief periods of cognitive dysfunction are common, and there is a desire to "master" the environment. Thus, most grief "energy" is focused on problem solving and planned activities as an adaptive strategy. Because there is a general reluctance to talk about feelings, the person's grief is intellectualized, prompting the person to explain the circumstances of the loss rather than to affective cues. Grief can be experienced physically and takes the form of restlessness or nervousness. Instrumental grievers tend to be unaware of internal arousal, can feel disenfranchised as others may not accept their grief pat-

tern, and may be uncomfortable with strongly expressed emotions by others.

2. *Intuitive.* Here the focus is on affect over cognition, and there is longer-term cognitive impairment due to prolonged periods of confusion, the inability to concentrate, disorganization, and disorientation. Intuitive grievers are less likely than instrumental grievers to seek out potential problems and solve them. Feelings are intensely experienced, and expressions such as crying and lamenting mirror inner experience. Grief that is expressed is a grief experienced, and therefore, physical exhaustion and/or anxiety may result. Grievers often feel that people do not allow for adequate expression of their grief and may be unable or unwilling to distance themselves from feelings expressed by others.

3. *Blended.* This orientation has elements common to both instrumental and intuitive patterns even though there is usually a general preference for one or the other. Blended grievers may benefit from a variety of adaptive strategies from which to select.

Martin (2006, cited in Martin & Doka, 2000) did a pilot study on a tool to measure these primary grieving styles, resulting in a short inventory called The Grief Pattern Inventory. Ben's results indicated that he was more of an instrumental griever (wanting solutions and a prescribed step-by-step process), and Sara was more of an intuitive griever (very much focused on her intense feelings). You can gather responses by interviewing the client or by having the client simply complete the inventory.

General Considerations

For Ben and Sara, like many facing grief and loss issues, the heart usually leads the brain. Sara reported that for her, grieving felt like having to clean out an infected wound. It was messy and not particularly easy or attractive to look it. There was great tenderness surrounding the wound. If these are left unattended, it tends to spread, as in this case, to other areas of a client's life (e.g., a marriage, family members, the workplace, social relationships, one's view of God). Since grief is unique to the individual, so are the ways in which a person will cope with the loss. However, before examining specific interventions, the following are general counseling principles that are important and applicable to most kinds of grief work and would certainly apply to Ben and Sara's miscarriage and stillbirth losses:

- Create a milieu of safety and trust that can help people get through, not over, their grief. Active listening skills, both verbal and nonverbal, are important, and self-disclosure, if relevant, may be appropriate. For example, if you have personally experienced infertility issues, this may be comforting to Ben and Sara.
- Understand the value and power of your presence. Be available, but do not assume that means there needs to be constant or two-way conversation. The appropriate use of silence is a useful and necessary tool for "being in the moment" with Ben and Sara.
- A narrative orientation is excellent to give grievers space to share their story as many times as necessary.

- Help clients understand that grieving is a process that takes far longer than most people are willing to extend understanding.
- Let clients know that expressing feelings is acceptable and beneficial, but not in such a way that they feel forced to do so. Help them distinguish between the expression of feelings and cognitive statements.
- Do not be surprised at strong outbursts of tears or anger, the need to overthink or overprocess the loss, and a tendency to withdraw and isolate. Learn how to respond and not react to visceral emotions.
- Let clients know that what they are feeling is not necessarily abnormal or an indication of a lack of faith—this truth may need to be communicated directly, clearly, and more than once.
- When the timing is right, gently challenge any pathological, irrational, or unbiblical responses to the loss—sometimes a rational-emotive behavioral approach is useful when a client needs to "connect the dots" between behaviors, feelings, thoughts, and beliefs.
- Because grieving individuals can and often do feel alone, disconnected, and alienated, they need to know there are many ways to grieve; there is no timetable for grief's duration, and there are no rules, boundaries, or absolute protocols for grieving. Ensure that any treatment plan is individualized and not universally applied, even in similar kinds of losses.
- Reinforce the active and intentional decision to face the pain. Give clients permission to grieve, and encourage them to feel and show emotion.

- Give clients permission to heal, and help them understand that healing does not mean forgetting.
- If the loss is anticipated, encourage discussion before it occurs (e.g., an imminent death due to terminal illness). Ask descriptive questions and talk about the loss.
- Help clients make necessary decisions (consider smaller steps) without feeling the pressure to make major decisions right away if unnecessary (e.g., moving, selling a home, leaving a workplace). Develop an action plan (where and when appropriate) to help them regain their sense of control after a loss.
- Help facilitate support and concern toward the practical and tangible (e.g., arranging meals, running errands, watching children, etc.)—identifying family members, friends, and coworkers who can be recruited to assist in day-to-day or other responsibilities decreases the risk of withdrawal and isolation.
- Encourage grieving rituals when they can help bring closure, comfort, and support—symbolic activities (discussed further below) are powerful healing agents.
- With consent, pray for and with clients, and comfort with your words and with Scripture as appropriate. Avoid "sermonizing" or using religious clichés, and have a list of Bible verses available that are related to grief and loss.
- Explore the availability, use, and appropriateness of support groups (e.g., Grief Share, Divorce Care). Maintain a list of local groups and their accompanying contact points (be aware that some clients may be too acute or emotionally fragile).

Experiential Interventions

Cognitive behavioral interventions and techniques are empirically supported treatments, especially with complicated grief (Bhattacharya, 2015). However, for the purposes of this chapter, greater focus will be on experiential work. This orientation with grieving clients includes reconstructing a world of meaning through narrative storytelling, therapeutic writing, metaphorical language, and visualization (Neimeyer, Burke, & Mackay, 2010). Experiential therapy (first developed in the 1970s) differs from traditional "talk" therapies and can be extremely effective. This is especially true with children who often lack the developmental maturity to describe and "dialogue" what they are feeling or to gain deeper insights on a particular loss. Empirical studies (Greenberg & Watson, 1998; Jaison, 2015; Kottler & Montgomery, 2010) show that experiential methods help with psychological and emotional symptom reduction, including the following:

- A lowered intensity of perceived stress
- Fewer compulsive thoughts, impulses, and actions
- A greater orientation to the present
- A greater likelihood to express feelings and be authentic in the counseling process
- An improved capacity to develop meaningful and supportive relationships
- Practical techniques designed to face pain and loss
- Better navigation of unresolved issues with a person who has died
- Facilitation of closure and saying goodbye

- Allowing individuals to see themselves in action and "play out" relational dynamics
- A greater capacity to move beyond normal defense mechanisms
- Opportunities to have direct experience with the self (by identifying negative emotions and triggers) in a safe and structured environment versus using compulsive behaviors to avoid and isolate
- Personal relationships being examined, including how they are affecting current behaviors
- Encouragement for clients to move out of "their heads" and into a fuller experience, at which time they can experience problems and rehearse solutions in a new way with creativity and internal safety—identifying potential roadblocks and creating detours around them
- A greater understanding of how to address hidden or subconscious issues

Emotion-focused therapy (EFT). Developed by Sue Johnson and Les Greenberg, EFT, also known as process-experiential therapy, merges the core conditions of client-centered theory (Rogers), existential theory (Frankl, Yalom), Gestalt theory (Perls), and attachment theory (Bowlby). Since grief and loss issues often represent such an emotionally laden time for people, EFT is a useful approach when attempting to work on maladaptive emotions and negative patterns of interaction. Receive appropriate orientation and training before you incorporate this approach.

When incorporating experiential techniques, bear in mind that not every exercise works for every client, and that the client's personality and grieving style must also be taken into account. I thoroughly discussed options with Ben and Sara to see what would appeal to them. Explain that the focus is more on expression, affect, actions, movement, activities, and deep insight than on thinking and cognition. The "here and now" is emphasized through symbolic experiences (pivotal moments that serve as a catalyst for change), which encourage individual growth and authenticity. In other words, this approach represents a "back door" entrance into the heart of a matter. Contraindications for the use of experiential interventions include dissociative disorders, certain personality disorders, acute PTSD, and any client who is hyperaroused, suicidal, or psychotic. Therefore, a thorough assessment must first be completed and the client's consent secured before proceeding.

Specific Techniques and Therapeutic Interventions

The truth about grief and loss is that some people need to talk it out, some need to cry it out, some need to shout or write it out, and some need to work or draw it out. The bottom line is that whatever is inside will find its way out, but it should happen safely, therapeutically, and in a manner that promotes healing and restoration. The following approaches should be carefully examined for possible use when working with grief and loss cases such as Ben and Sara's.

Psychodrama. Psychodrama is an action-oriented intervention that utilizes elements of theater such as dramatization and role playing to reenact real-life and past situations in the present. Developed by J. L. Moreno (1994), it is a form of individual therapy incorporated within a group setting. A typical session is normally between ninety minutes and two hours. Components can include *doubling* (where another person attempts to verbalize thoughts and feelings for the client to spur a release), *role playing* (where the client portrays a person or object that is considered problematic), *soliloquy* (where the client speaks thoughts aloud to build self-awareness and knowledge), and *role reversal* (where the client portrays another person while a second actor portrays the client). Due to the potential for surfacing and addressing inner conflict and other "unfinished business," it should only be conducted under the supervision of a licensed mental health practitioner who is trained in the associated techniques. Psychodrama was particularly helpful for Ben and Sara because both of them were "stuck" in their grief and lacked sufficient awareness of their thoughts and feelings. Using a role reversal, I took the role of Ben. Ben was more tuned in to some of his negative thought patterns and how he was projecting blame and anger onto God for the miscarriages. A variation with technique I used was to play the role of God, which allowed the couple to work through some of their spiritual issues, providing a tangible and visceral experience of speaking out loud to another, as well as having a healthier balance when it came to understanding biblical principles.

Empty chair technique. Empty chair can be utilized for deep-rooted problems stemming from a relationship or life experience. It is a form of role playing in which the client addresses an empty chair and is given the opportunity to express thoughts and feelings that can lead to greater emotional release. I asked Ben and Sara to each have a "conversation" with God about their infertility issues and the miscarriages. This occurred as a buildup and "dress rehearsal" for the role play experience described above. In talking to the empty chair, both Ben and Sara were able to form their thoughts and feelings into words, so when it was time to look into someone else's eyes and say the same things (this time I role-played God), their awareness of their own thoughts and feelings toward God was increased, which is critical to moving forward in any grief journey. Sometimes in counseling, clients need to hear their own voices speaking God's truth to their own ears. This promotes greater ownership of the process.

Rituals. Humans are "hardwired" to incorporate and derive meaning from participating in rituals. Rituals can have cultural and spiritual significance and often provide a symbolic medium in which to celebrate, process, or bring closure to certain life events. Helping Ben and Sara construct meaningful ritual was an effective tool that gave a renewed sense of control. Together we worked to find and utilize tangible and concrete elements/acts connected to the miscarriages. One ritual we talked through, planned out, and employed was going back and having an actual memorial service for their lost children and giving names to each child.

Equine-assisted therapy and other pet therapies (canine, feline, etc.). Many animals naturally connect/bond with people in a nurturing and nonthreatening way. This can allow a grieving person some measure of control over the environment. Relaxation, trust, confidence, lower levels of anxiety and depression, and an increased sense of well-being are all potential benefits. Studies have shown that animals can increase levels of oxytocin, a hormone produced in the hypothalamus and released from the posterior lobe of the pituitary gland, which primarily acts as a neuromodulator in the brain (Grimm, 2015). Oxytocin, the "bonding" or "cuddle" hormone, has a calming effect over the fight-flight-freeze defensive network within a person. If the amygdala excites the sympathetic nerves, the arousal centers of the brain release noradrenaline, which causes the heart to pump blood to muscles and makes an individual feel anxious. Oxytocin can block this effect by dramatically increasing the number of noradrenaline's inhibitory receptors that act as off switches. In this way, oxytocin not only prevents a rise in heart rate and blood pressure but also causes both to be lowered, producing a sense of well-being. The use of animal-assisted therapies should be supervised by properly trained handlers and/or therapists and preferably involve animals that have been specifically trained to work with clients. Under supervision, I used an animal (e.g., dog, cat) during sessions with Ben and Sara and allowed them to hold and pet the animal, yielding notable positive results in them processing their pain.

Creative/expressive therapies (e.g., art therapy, play therapy, music therapy). These therapeutic orientations allow for an alternative expression of powerful emotions and thoughts for clients through structured activities, formats, and environments. For example, music is experienced in all areas of the brain and can have a profound and positive impact on neurological functioning. Mental health professionals often receive further training and/or certification as art, music, and play therapists. In working with Ben and Sara, I explored the various creative options they were willing to try. Since they were struggling to find the right words to express their inner thoughts, particularly Ben, creative techniques were beneficial to them.

Life timeline. A timeline is a chronological narrative of losses that may be experienced and can be ranked in terms of significance and impact on the client. The process helps identify secondary losses, assess transformative perceptions and life assumptions, and help formulate a theology of suffering.

Memorials. Much like rituals, memorials can help facilitate needed closure. For example, Ben and Sara arranged a memorial service after assigning the miscarried babies names. For many grievers, memorials can create healthy memories and still allow one or more grievers to grieve separately and together.

Collages. These pictorial and creative projects can be effective with almost any grief issue and allow the client to select images and concepts that are personally relevant to the loss. The focus is on the process, not on creating a piece of artwork.

Journaling. Reflective writing helps with emotional and cognitive clarity, provides a measure of concreteness by validating certain life experiences, and can open up paths to deeper meaning and understanding. This is particularly useful for nonverbal clients because the very act of writing can be therapeutic in and of itself. One of the benefits in utilizing this approach with Ben and Sara was the freedom to continue "processing" thoughts and emotions outside the office and "in the moment." They also brought their journals to the sessions to discuss the process.

Writing a letter. Sometimes saying goodbye to a deceased loved one in letter format allows a person to express thoughts that were never conveyed prior to death due to the suddenness of the event or lack of access to a loved one or friend. Have clients who have lost a child write a letter to their child—regardless of the stage of pregnancy when the miscarriage occurred. One of the hopes for Christ followers is the assurance that we will someday be united with lost loved ones who trusted in Christ for salvation. Clients can express their thoughts and feelings about this future union and the certainty of heaven for children and those who die in Christ.

Writing a psalm. The use of "lament," or the passionate expression of grief and sorrow, is frequently utilized in the book of Psalms and is an excellent format to connect both the expression of feelings and a person's faith in God. Many of the great and historic hymns of the church were penned in the throes of the writer's anguish and pain. Common elements are an opening address, which includes a vocative, such as, "O Lord . . ."; the actual lament or complaint, which provides a description of the trouble or distress; a plea or petition for God's response, often giving reasons for God to act; a profession of trust, faith, or confidence in God; and a vow of praise to God or a sacrifice. Ben and Sara individually and then later together composed letters and brought them to a session to read them out loud.

Daily examen. More than four hundred years ago, St. Ignatius of Loyola encouraged prayer-filled mindfulness by proposing what has been called the daily examen. This is a time of reflection and prayer at the end of the day to allow the Holy Spirit to give wisdom and insight in "examining" the day to detect God's presence and discern his direction. It is an opportunity for similar reflection that I used on a session-by-session basis with Ben and Sara, incorporating the following elements/questions:

- In this session, how/where did you discern the Lord's presence?
- What interactions and/or exercises were particularly meaningful to you in relation to your grief?
- What strengths and gifts has God given to you during the session that speak to your grief?
- What weaknesses, growth areas, and/or needs did the Holy Spirit reveal to you during the session that speak to your grief?
- What is your greatest insight from the session?
- What praise and/or thanksgiving comes from the session?
- In what ways is the Holy Spirit calling you to think, to be, and to act in such a manner that you can more truly follow Jesus Christ?

CONCLUSION

God and miscarriage, faith and disease, joy and sorrow, life and death—these themes may seem like paradoxical opposites, unintended for and not belonging to the same conversation. Yet they often wind their way into our hearts and minds and into our prayers. For Christians who acknowledge an omnipotent and compassionate God, there must likewise be a recognition of his divine sovereignty and the mystery of his ways. The questions invariably follow soon after the tragedy or fiery trial. "*When* can I go and meet with God? My tears have been my food day and night, while people say to me all day long, '*Where* is your God?'" (Ps. 42:2–3, emphasis added). In the case study, it would certainly be natural for Ben and Sara to express these thoughts.

Yet many believers gain great comfort and solace from the Psalms—transparent glimpses into the lives of the people of God as they journeyed through life—not always having the answers but ultimately being aware of God's gracious provision in time of need. We were created with emotions and at the same time permitted to express ourselves to the Maker—"Trust in him at all times, you people; pour out your hearts to him, for God is our refuge" (Ps. 62:8). Like others who look to God in these Gethsemane moments, Ben and Sara found themselves drawing nearer to the Lord with a strengthened faith and a renewed commitment to him. The key is how they navigate the journey, and a competent counselor can make a significant difference in the outcome.

As counselors, we are frequently trained in matters pertaining to trauma, anxiety and depression, loss, complicated grief, stress and pain management, and similar presenting problems. Our education and experience may tempt us to suggest sound clinical advice. However, we must be careful that these efforts at wise counsel are not just filtered and received as well-intentioned but hollow sound bites that fail to stem the emotional bleeding. Sometimes it is the simple power of one's presence in the act of empathetically listening to a client's story. Sometimes it means allowing the God of all comfort to function in this important role through his Word and through the agency of his Holy Spirit.

It is good for clients like Ben and Sara to remind themselves of God's lovingkindness, which brings the promise of hope, new life, restoration, good news, and a peace that passes all understanding. In his vision on the island of Patmos, the apostle John was given a small foretaste of our inheritance in Christ.

Then I saw "a new heaven and a new earth," for the first heaven and the first earth had passed away, and there was no longer any sea. I saw the Holy City, the new Jerusalem, coming down out of heaven from God, prepared as a bride beautifully dressed for her husband. And I heard a loud voice from the throne saying, "Look! God's dwelling place is now among the people, and he will dwell with them. They will be his people, and God himself will be with them and be their God. 'He will wipe every tear from their eyes. There will be no more death' or mourning or crying or pain, for the old order of things has passed away."

He who was seated on the throne said, "I am making everything new!" Then he said, "Write this down, for these words are trustworthy and true." (Rev. 21:1–5)

Jesus told his disciples there would be challenges on this side of eternity (John 16:33). Because of him, the Prince of Peace, we, too, can have great confidence: "Everyone born of God overcomes the world. This is the victory that has overcome the world, even our faith. Who is it that overcomes the world? Only the one who believes that Jesus is the Son of God" (1 John 5:4–5). Courage in the face of grief and loss is not the absence of fear but conquering that fear by God's grace.

RECOMMENDED READING

Bonanno, G. A. (2010). *The other side of sadness: What the new science of bereavement tells us about life after loss.* New York, NY: Perseus.

Brizendine, J. (2011). *Stunned by grief: Remapping your life when loss changes everything.* Lake Forest, CA: BennettKnepp.

Forrest, A. (2015). *Anchored in hope: Devotionals for infertility.* Charleston, SC: Create Space Independent.

Illse, S. (2015). *Empty arms: Coping with miscarriage, stillbirths, and infant death.* Maple Plain, MN: Wintergreen.

King, J., Prout, B., & Stuhl, A. (2016). Scrapbooking as an intervention to enhance coping in individuals experiencing grief and loss. *Therapeutic Recreation Journal, 50*(2), 181–187.

Kohn, I., & Moffitt, P. L. (2000). *Pregnancy loss: Guidance and support for you and your family.* New York, NY: Routledge.

Lewis, C. S. (1989). *A grief observed.* New York: NY: Harper Collins.

Neimeyer, R. A. (Ed.). (2012). *Techniques of grief therapy: Creative practices for counseling the bereaved.* New York, NY: Routledge.

Sittser, J. (2004). *A grace disguised: How the soul grows through loss* (Expanded ed.). Grand Rapids, MI: Zondervan.

Westberg, G. E. (2010). *Good grief: 50th anniversary edition.* Minneapolis, MN: Fortress.

Wolfelt, A. D. (2004). *Understanding your grief: Ten essential touchstones for finding hope and healing your heart.* Fort Collins, CO: Companion.

Worden, J. W. (2008). *Grief counseling and grief therapy: A handbook for the mental health practitioner* (4th ed.). New York, NY: Springer.

Zonnebelt-Smeenge, S. J., & DeVries, R. C. (2006). *Traveling through grief: Learning to live again after the death of a loved one.* Grand Rapids, MI: Baker.

WEBSITES

Elizabeth Kübler-Ross Foundation: http://www.ekrfoundation.org/five-stages-of-grief/
Grief.com: http://grief.com/group-resources/
Grief-Share: https://www.griefshare.org/

CHAPTER 25

Sexual Addiction-Focused Strategies

Mark R. Laaser, MDiv, PhD

Like a dog that returns to his vomit
is a fool who repeats his folly.

PROVERBS 26:11 ESV

The term *sexual addiction* was first conceived by a group of ten therapists in 1976. Five years later, the first book on sexual addiction was written by one of them, Pat Carnes, published under the title *The Sex Addiction* in an ugly plain green cover. Not surprisingly, sales were poor. It was wisely retitled *Out of the Shadows* (Carnes, 1983, 1992, 2001). That book has become the "bible" of the field. It also began a debate about the existence of sex addiction. Although there was hope that the current edition of the *Diagnostic and Statistical Manual*, fifth edition (DSM-5; American Psychiatric Association, 2013) would include the proposed hypersexual disorder, it was disregarded as a disorder because the concept was judged to follow moral norms and psychosocial values. I'm writing as one who, along with thousands of other professionals in both the secular and Christian communities, firmly acknowledges its existence as a disorder.

In 1987 the reality of this condition hit home when my colleagues staged an intervention after learning that I had been sexually acting out. Since age eleven, I was obsessed with sex to the point of my behavior being out of control. Because of the compassion of one colleague, I entered the first sexual addiction treatment center, which was established by Dr. Carnes in 1986. For the next thirty days, the Golden Valley Health Center was my home. That experience laid the foundation for thirty-two years (and counting) of sobriety.

The treatment not only saved my life but set a new trajectory for my personal and professional future. Eventually I began working at the treatment center (after all, what else was a "fallen" pastor and counselor to do?). From my own recovery and under the tutelage of Dr. Carnes, I learned how to treat individuals suffering with sexual addiction. For four incredible and rewarding years, I had the privilege of teaching and working alongside Dr. Carnes, which God blessed to springboard me into a nationwide speaking and teaching ministry. An early presentation was to the professional Christian counseling community at a conference called "Atlanta '88" (the forerunner of the American Association of Christian Counselors), which also led to my first book, *Healing the Wounds of Sexual Addiction* (Laaser, 1991, 1992, 1996, 2004, 2009, 2014).

Based on my thirty plus years of experience, this chapter provides the essentials of working with sex addicts, including useful and effective strategies, interventions, and techniques (SITs) to augment your clinical tool kit. Although the focus of the chapter is on males, most of the content is applicable to counseling female sex addicts, of which there are a growing number (Ferree, 2012).

THEOLOGY AND PSYCHOLOGY OF SEX ADDICTION

The evangelical community struggles with sexual addiction, particularly with internet pornography. While estimates vary, there is a wide consensus that no fewer than 50 percent and possibly as high as 66 percent of evangelical men have, at least at some time, battled pornography use (Lee, 2016). Since the church is also part of the larger society, it isn't too surprising—though tragic—that a growing number of sex addicts stand behind pulpits (Adams, 2003; Gregoire, 2004). Also particularly noteworthy is that recent speculation suggests the rate of addiction in Christian women is somewhere between 25 and 33

percent (Learn, 2010). These percentages have dramatically increased for women in the last twenty-five years (Ferree, 2012). The internet has provided a proverbial playground in which Christian men and women can access the "forbidden fruit" of pornography and sexuality in anonymity. Some have hypothesized that one factor behind the high percentages of Christians using pornography is being raised in repressive religious homes (Carnes, 1989).

Across a wide spectrum of theological flavors, the church has historically neglected teaching a biblically based healthy sexuality. By contrast, churches seem to be consumed with inculcating its congregants with the "don'ts" of sex. As Christians, we are parched for positive ideas of what to "do." Subsequently, most church members are left on their own to find answers, a practice that is dreadfully failing. Being ignorant of truth only serves to augment vulnerability to the dangers of sexual experimentation and predispose the person to addiction.

The Nature of Sexual Addiction

Numerous attempts to define sexual addiction are peppered throughout the literature. Carnes's (1983, 1992, 2001) widely accepted definition stems from an understanding of the impact of chemical addiction on the life of an addict: "When the sexual behavior becomes the most important aspect of the addict's life, the addict now has a pathological relationship with a mood-altering behavior" (2001, p. 14). Later Carnes noted a list of characteristics that were consistent in style with the format of the DSM. While a useful list, it is simpler to understand the following five basic characteristics.

Unmanageability. A culture that is sexually crazed and driven is primed for sexual mismanagement. This characteristic is best understood as feeling out of control and is based on other addiction criteria, such as that of Alcoholics Anonymous (AA), whose first step to recovery is to own powerlessness over alcohol and acknowledge that life has become unmanageable. The apostle Paul captured the concept when he wrote that he found himself doing the evil he hated and not doing the good he wanted to do (Rom. 7:15). Given the innumerable unsuccessful attempts to stop, an addict realizes, but often cannot admit, that stopping or controlling acting out is essentially impossible. The average man reports to me that he has repeatedly beseeched God for help, and most men long for freedom, which seems elusive. The addict may have tried bargaining with God or employing "surefire formulas," such as spending a certain amount of time praying, reading the Bible, and attending religious activities, all without positive results. Of course, any time we move away from centering our lives in God, we will spiral into unmanageability in some way. In truth, the most common dependence is addiction to self, in particular power and control. Making a "god" of self is easy, and this is true for sex addicts. Also common for addicts is the belief that not acting out or sinning is the answer to the problem. However, the real problem isn't the action but making life about anything other than pursuing and glorifying God.

It isn't surprising that the addict may be angry with God for not freeing him from sinful sexual activities. After all, God is supposed to do what we cannot do for ourselves. The question without any clear answer is, "Why won't he heal me?" The underbelly of this thinking process is that the addict expects God to do all the work. Profound disappointment accompanies this unmet expectation.

The original couple also came to believe that the God with whom they personally walked was holding back on them. Prompted by Satan's deception, Adam and Eve concluded that God wasn't good after all, so they decided to meet their own needs, a choice that only moved them further from him. For the sex addict, God seems neither good nor trustworthy. His rebellion toward God is fueled by frustration, disappointment, and hurt. Avoiding surrender to God and his will seems like the only way to get his longings met. The sex addict does not totally surrender his sexuality to God because it seems that God cannot meet what is perceived as the real need. Instead, the addict bolsters his resolve to control his own sexuality despite perpetual failures.

Neurochemical tolerance. Nerve cells produce a prescribed amount of neurochemicals at a determined rate for daily functioning. Substances, fantasies (thoughts), and activities can generate powerful releases of certain neurotransmitters and neuropeptides that alter the brain's homeostasis. Satinover (2004) suggests that pornography triggers chemicals in the brain that create a euphoric experience similar to that of heroin. Reisman (2004) states that the addiction is to "erototoxins," which are produced in the pornography consumer's brain. Because of the immediate cognitive processing of a pornographic image, the brain creates memories that can be recalled either intentionally or unintentionally in a microsecond.

Specifically, substances, thoughts, and behaviors release several brain biochemicals such as dopamine (pleasure), serotonin (mood), oxytocin (bonding), vasopressin (commitment and bonding), adrenaline (energy), and endorphins (calming). In response to these neurochemicals, glucose (energy) is released to generate energy, and the erotic cocktail is overwhelming. When the releases are repetitive, a tolerance develops, in part because the brain generates additional receptor sites to accommodate and receive increased chemical levels. Eventually a reinforcing cycle of use, neurochemical pleasure, tolerance, and craving is produced. Just as drug addicts strongly crave their substance, sex addicts hunger for more as well.

A few chemicals deserve special attention: adrenaline, dopamine, oxytocin, and catecholamines. Adrenaline (epinephrine), which amps up the brain, is linked with sensation seeking and the presence of an intense feeling, such as fear or sex. The dominance and authority of adrenaline is its power to override caution; it propels an individual toward a goal without consideration of physical, emotional, social, legal, or financial risks. The brain is so charged by sex that adrenaline is both released and increased with sexual thoughts such as fantasy.

Add dopamine, known as the "pleasure chemical," to adrenaline, and a formidable cocktail is created. Dopamine is primarily released in the mesolimbic pathway of the brain stem, which has been called the "reward center" of the brain. Every sexual hit rewards the person with desirous gratification, and the brain demands more of the same. Though the combined effect of adrenaline and dopamine is similar to the effect of cocaine, research has shown that very pleasurable food and sexual stimuli activate the brain's reward circuitry far more than highly addictive drugs (Milkman & Sunderwirth, 2010).

The chemical cocktail can also include oxytocin, the bonding ingredient. It is a hormone primarily manufactured in the hypothalamus to promote attachment between two people, contentment, calmness, and security. Oxytocin is therefore, in part, responsible for maintaining sexual fidelity. Simply having skin-to-skin contact, thinking of one's loved one, and anticipating a connection releases high levels of oxytocin. The lack of it, whether by purposely suppressing or unintentionally repressing its activation, lessens the creation or maintenance of the chemical bond. Often addicts unwittingly or intentionally shut down oxytocin release to avoid bonding with any sexual partner. It thus becomes easier to move on without strings attached. In these cases, rather than leading to bonding, contentment, and calmness, oxytocin acts as a natural tranquilizer, medicating the addict's stress and anxiety in an unhealthy way.

Finally, orgasm produces a group of neurochemicals called the catecholamines, which are heroin-like in their effect. Even just thinking or fantasizing about sex can produce a powerful response in the brain to which tolerance can occur. Dr. William Struthers (2009) has written a fascinating book titled *Wired for Intimacy*, which unpacks the dynamics of brain functioning and sexual addiction in far more detail.

Seeking either a high or calming from a substance or behavior, sometimes called a "fix," will unwittingly cause an insatiable desire for more. The more we sin, the easier it becomes to sin. We build up "sin tolerance" to our sexual sinful habits and hang-ups. Our whole person (e.g., soul, neurobiology) conspires together to root sexual addiction deeper into us.

Escalation. Because addicts will need more and more of their "drug," sexual acting out escalates, a progression that occurs in two ways. First, escalation occurs in frequency and gravity; that is, the addiction takes greater hold. An addict who starts out masturbating once a month, for example, will likely escalate eventually to daily masturbation. An addict who crosses the "flesh line" (i.e., has a sexual encounter with another person) will find it easier to cross that line again. The frequency of sexual encounters increases, and perhaps more partners are added. One of my clients vividly remembers the first time he had a sexual encounter and how rapidly his behavior escalated. By the time I met him, he had been with thirty different partners.

Second, the addict "graduates" to newer and more adrenaline-filled experiences. Commonly, an addict moves from basic nudity pornography to more sexually explicit material, progressing from pictures to very graphic videos. Far too many clients progressed from legal to illegal mate-rial, the prohibited or illicit nature producing more adrenaline. The most common form of escalation is to graphic underage material. The clear majority of these clients are not oriented to children or adolescents, but the allure of the forbidden fruit draws them in.

In my story, I moved from sexual encounters with single adult women to married women. The verboten boundary of violating another marriage was part of the allure. In the case of those drawn to minor pornography, it isn't that an actual person wants to be sexual with children, but the addict part within craves it and dictates the choices. Taking a detailed history of acting out will reveal an escalating pattern over long periods of time, even spanning from adolescence to and throughout adulthood.

Medication. Addicts use neurochemistry to effectively regulate or medicate painful feelings. They may be lonely, sad, tired, or bored, and the mood-elevating quality of sexual arousal lifts their frame of mind. They may be anxious, agitated, stressed, and unable to get to sleep, and the relaxing quality of oxytocin and catecholamines calms them. Addicts are continually adjusting or regulating moods on a daily basis. Nothing regulates deep distress so much as escape from it. In essence, they are practicing pharmacology without a license. Without their "drug," they would be emotionally dysregulated and out of control. This explains why many addicts sincerely believe they would not survive without their addiction; it is as necessary as air. Their addiction is how addicts "cope" with their afflicted emotions.

This ineffective coping creates associations in the memory center of the brain. These impressions, established in the first days of an addiction, will become lifelong bonds.

My mother was an admirable Christian woman who well provided for my physical needs. She was not equipped, however, at providing emotional and spiritual connection. I cannot bring into my memory the image of her smiling. When I saw my first pornographic picture in a *Playboy* magazine, the model was smiling. In addition to the neurochemistry of seeing a nude woman, my brain honed in on and locked onto the smile. My brain cross-wired nude women with the lack of emotional attunement from my mother. My arousal template formed by associating pornography with the relief of emotional and spiritual loneliness.

Another neurochemical process known as mirror neurons provides key insight into sexual addiction. The brain has cells that respond to witnessing an event the same as experiencing it. The system encodes the similarity between witnessed events and internal-generating actions that represent a link between observer and actor (Rizzolatti & Arbib, 1998). An example of this process is a person's sexual arousal and desire to engage in an activity that is being viewed on a pornographic website. Addicts' brains become neurologically and behaviorally conditioned to whatever input they receive.

Sex as a reward. Early in their acting out, addicts learned that without sex they feel like their basic needs are unmet. Addicts develop the feeling that they need sex if they are to survive or as compensation

for a period of sobriety. Doing so medicates their feelings of loneliness and isolation (Laaser, 2009). So they reward themselves with some form of sexual activity. The act of sex and its pleasure is "deserved." It is a treat, compensation for a perceived debt owed them. Simply, they are entitled to it and justified in their sexual behaviors. This thinking is reinforced when a spouse uses sex as a reward for "good husband" behavior.

Sexual Addiction Assessment

Over the years, two assessment inventories have been developed to identify sexual addiction. The first is the Sexual Addiction Screening Test (SAST), a twenty-five-question true-or-false test created by Carnes. If thirteen or more questions are answered "true," the person is considered a sex addict. Subsequently, this test has been expanded, and specialized forms have been developed for women and homosexuals. The SAST is in the public domain and can be accessed for self-assessment on Dr. Carnes's website, www.sexhelp.com.

Carnes collaborated with David Delmonico on research that resulted in a new test called the Sexual Dependence Inventory (SDI; Carnes, 1991). Even though I was involved in its development, I believe it is cumbersome. While comprehensive and in-depth (more than five hundred items), it is expensive and suffers from the ambiguities and limitations of any inventory. Even with the SDI's results, it must be reviewed with the client to verify the findings. I prefer to rely on my ability to take a detailed history of the client and his acting out. Pull from this resource and other sexual addiction materials to develop your own clinical intuition to develop your own skills in carefully taking a sexual history.

Carnes (1983, 1992, 2001) was also interested in categorizing sexual addiction into types, similar to the categories of substance use disorders. He originally conceived of categorizing sexual addiction into nonprogressive levels, which represented groupings of sexual activities. Level one included masturbation, pornography, fantasy, prostitution, and affairs. Level two involved illegal activities, including paraphilias such as exhibitionism, voyeurism, and inappropriate touching (indecent liberties). Level three comprised sexual offenses such as incest, sexual harassment, sexual activity with minors or vulnerable adults, and the use of one's professional role to gain sexual access. (Professional sexual misconduct is called "authority rape" and includes pastors being sexual with congregants.). Carnes (1991) later abandoned the levels of classification in favor of typing ten sexual behaviors to customize treatment. My strategy is to apply principles of effective treatment regardless of the type.

As part of my assessment, I have an extremely useful question that is simple to ask but profound in what it reveals: "When did you choose sex as a solution to your emotional pain?" This question accomplishes two goals. First, it directs the client to the fact that sex is not the problem but the chosen solution for the problem of emotional distress. Second, the question shifts the client's hyperfocus on sex to what is happening psychologically. Part of the assessment, as well as beginning to teach the client essential psychological information, is identifying cognitive errors, irrational thinking, and cognitive distortions. Additionally, the answer to this question helps link the client's story to four core beliefs that have been found to be part of a sex addict's deeper thinking.

Core Beliefs and Cognitive Distortions

Counselors should look beneath the client's behaviors to uncover the specific foundational cognitions. Carnes (1983, 1992, 2001) describes four core beliefs that all sex addicts hold.

I am a bad, unworthy person (p. 171). Among churchgoing people, sexual sins are often considered worse than other sins. Those in the Christian community have been quick to condemn people who sexually act out. Addicts often feel like modern-day lepers. Judgments are often passed out with such defaming labels as *perverts*, *sluts*, and *lowlives*. The addict's internal shame-based labels, such as *I am a despicable person*, are reinforced and become cauterized in the addict's heart and mind. (See chapter 21, "Shame-Focused Strategies," for more information.) Behaviors and desires are unwittingly fused together with shame and convince addicts that the messages accurately represent them. This core belief is woven into the addict's identity, contributing to a severer shame-based identity. Core beliefs have roots in early life traumas and are confirmed over the years by the addict's experience of his own behavior. Reid (2010) reports that hypersexual men, including individuals struggling with pornography use, tend to experience less positive emotion and more negative emotion compared to control participants. In other words, sexual addicts may feel greater sadness and anxiety as well as feel less joy or excitement compared to nonsexual addicts. The belief is also compounded by the fact that sexual acting out reinforces the distorted belief even more.

If you knew me, you would hate me and leave me (p. 173). This belief is also shame based and for most addicts reflects a history of being judged and criticized. In my opinion, this belief is based on anxiety of being known. It leads addicts to be liars and deceivers, covering up the secret part of their lives, creating a double life. The associated behaviors and desires of sex addicts must be feverishly guarded to maintain secrecy. It amazes me how early in development this behavior occurs, even going back to preschool. In a study with Adams (Laaser & Adams, 2002), we found that sexually addicted clergy experienced childhoods marked by physical and sexual abuse, chronic loneliness, and isolation that developed into intimacy deficits. This is consistent with Carnes's (1989) research, in which he contended that "early childhood experiences, family environment and associated emotions are critical to understanding sexual addiction" (p. 63).

No one will take care of my needs but me (p. 174). Like the previous beliefs, this one is also shame based. Occurring because of neglect or abandonment trauma, the child's attachment is impaired. Because parents or caregivers were "gone" physically, emotionally, and/or spiritually, addicts were deprived of basic needs and desires. This produces an avoidant attachment. Although self-reliance can serve a person well, avoidant attachment prohibits connecting with others.

Sex is my most important need (p. 176). This belief reflects the fact, as described above, that addicts have used the neurochemistry of sex to regulate their moods. Sex becomes "the central organizing principle of an addict's life." You will find how many decisions, even very important ones, are based on gaining greater freedom and access to sexual activity.

The four core beliefs address the addict's self-image (*I'm bad*), relationships (*No one will love me*), needs (*I must meet my own needs*), and sexuality (*Sex is my most important need*). Each belief contributes to the disconnection between the addict's intrapsychic self and his interpersonal self. Moreover, it further alienates the addict from God, who can heal them. The intense pain that haunts the addict's internal world prompts impression management activities. The problem is that the projected image is inadequate to mask the turmoil going on inside.

While the above captured convictions are most common, other distorted beliefs, such as *Nothing will help, I can stop if I really wanted to, I just need to control it better*, and *It really doesn't hurt anyone*, exist as well. Denial, minimization, compartmentalization, blame shifting, and other defensive strategies pose a challenge to even seasoned professionals. Evacuating all faulty beliefs is critical so that clients learn the roots of their acting out and treatment can be properly directed. Your job is to challenge these lies with truth.

The Sexual Addiction Cycle

One of Carnes's (1983) greatest contributions has been his description of the sex-addiction cycle. The cycle is preceded by the experience of early life trauma, either invasion or neglect. The trauma(s) gives life to shame-based core beliefs. The cycle is then birthed with what was originally called "preoccupation" or fantasy, which is being captivated by lustful thoughts and mental images of sexual experiences. Addicts can spend hours each day lost in sexual thought. Pornography contributes to the images, but most addicts are incredibly creative in concocting their own. Even without pornography, the archive of images in the brain along with customized images is sufficient.

The next stage is called rituals. Whereas the first stage involves mental preoccupation, rituals involve preparing for acting out. These are the action steps necessary to behaviorally realize the fantasy. Rituals can be short and long. For example, masturbation rituals start with fantasies and may progress to action steps to be alone. I had a short ritual that involved waiting for my wife, Debbie, to go to bed, assessing that she was asleep, and then going downstairs to watch pornography and masturbate. Fetish rituals can involve obtaining "sex toys" or looking at pornography specific to the fetish. Affair rituals can be as simple as connecting with a partner on the internet to cultivating a relationship that leads to ongoing sexual activity. Masturbation rituals, ones that involve acquiring and looking at pornography, and long affair rituals can occur simultaneously. Many addicts use several rituals at the same time.

Acting out, the third stage, is the one in which addicts engage their chosen behaviors. It is the realization of the fantasy and rituals. The fact that most addicts have ignored a desire to stop provokes feelings of guilt and shame. This brings the onset of the final or fourth stage of the cycle, despair. Depression and despondency accompany the shame and guilt. Such intolerable feelings must be quieted. Once again, the addict seeks to silence them by becoming preoccupied with sex. And around the cycle goes.

Many addicts have multiple addictions, so they may turn to an alternative form of medication. Carnes (1991) found that the greater the amount of trauma the more likely the person has multiple addictions. In an unpublished study, I surveyed a group of pastors who had self-identified as sex addicts and found that 88 percent of them struggled with work addiction. The most common coaddiction in the general population is alcoholism, about 50 percent. This dynamic has come to be called addiction interaction disorder (Carnes, Murray, & Charpentier, 2004). It occurs when an addict arrives at the stage of despair and rather than becoming preoccupied with sex, activates a preoccupation with another addiction(s). Obviously, these are more difficult to untangle.

The Role of Trauma in Sex Addiction

There are two kinds of abuse: invasion and abandonment or neglect. Invasive abuse occurs when interactions that shouldn't take place do. These destructive interactions may damage people emotionally (e.g., yelling, screaming, put-downs, name-calling), physically (e.g., hitting, slapping, shoving, spanking in rage), sexually (e.g., touching or penetrating genital area, teasing about body, sexual humor), or spiritually (e.g., judgmental and angry messages about God, self-righteousness, overly negative messages about sex). When these kinds of boundaries are crossed, victims feel afraid, alone, and ashamed. Invasive abuse is extremely stressful and traumatic for anyone to endure, particularly children. When parental responses to their children's needs and distress are unreliable and improvised and children are unable to develop self-soothing skills, they will seek relief and consolation in self-destructive ways.

The other kind of abuse is neglect and abandonment, which is often harder to identify and understand. It is one thing to be able to remember invasive traumatic experiences and designate them as harmful. It's quite another to recognize normal, healthy, positive behaviors that should have happened but never did. The challenge is, how do you recognize that something never happened? How do you know what you missed? Neglect occurs when parents consciously or unconsciously fail to provide physical and emotional needs for their children. Abandonment, a more profound form of neglect, occurs when children do not get the love, attention, nurturing, or information they need to thrive. The bottom line is that the child does not receive the necessary physical or psychological protection. When such neglect and abandonment are repetitive, the child becomes confused, self-preoccupied, and damaged.

Not receiving a sense of safety, belonging, acceptance, nurturance, healthy touch, physical affection, and intimacy, and not having any of these modeled leaves children with distorted views of themselves, others, and God. The messages the child introjects from neglect and abandonment generate paralyzing fear. Self-loathing and disgust, which create toxic shame, become deeply rooted in the brain and heart. Often overlooked is the neglect of failing to be taught healthy sexuality, in particular a biblical view of sexuality and sex. Left to their own devices, where and what will children learn about sex? In more recent years, the percentages of those addicts who were invaded has decreased. I have never known an addict, however, who hasn't experienced abandonment, whether he recognizes it or not.

In the early days of the field, it was assumed that all addicts had experienced trauma, particularly from their abusive families. Carnes's (1991) original research found that 81 percent of the patients who came to inpatient treatment had been sexually abused, and 74 percent had been physically abused. Family abuse is the damage created by one member of the family to another member of the family sexually, physically, or emotionally. Inpatient treatment counselors were charged with the responsibility of discovering abuse and encouraging the patient to confront the abusers in the context of the program's family week. Additionally, when abuse occurs, it does not necessarily come from inside the family. It can occur in such places as neighborhoods, schools, clubs, and organizations, and even our churches. It can originate from individuals close to the family, complete strangers, and anywhere and from anybody in between.

The cycle of abuse is vicious. Most people who abuse have been abused themselves (Glasser et al., 2001). This has been labeled as the "victim to victimizer cycle." In many families, the trail of abuse extends back for generations. Abuse is one vehicle whereby the "sins of the father" (or the mother) are passed down from one generation to the next (cf. Ex. 20:5).

The notion of examining family history for abuse leads some to wonder if sex addicts are just trying to blame their families or their abusers to justify their behaviors. The fact is that unrecovered sex addicts do indeed blame lots of people, including parents. However, blame for the purpose of blame is unhealthy and, in fact, violates the commandment to honor mothers and fathers. Sex addicts committed to recovery seek to understand their abuse to heal from it. The understanding doesn't negate responsibility for their own choices and behaviors. Understanding abuse allows people to recognize what happened to them and to learn how they cope through their addictions. It helps them acknowledge and appreciate how painful the abuse was, how frightened they were, how alone they felt, and how angry they are. Admitting these feelings and finding healthy ways to express and cope with them is healing.

Sex addicts must look at what happened to them, understand it, allow themselves to feel the pain rather than addictively avoid it, and then confront it as a sign that they know it was wrong. This process may take a long time, and it is vital to making healthier choices in the future. Healthier new choices break the cycle of sinful abusive behavior. Then the sins of the parents won't be passed down to subsequent generations.

As noted earlier, sex addicts believe that sexual activity is the only way to meet their needs for love and nurturing. For many of them, sex was the only way they received attention and physical touch. They made the connection between love, nurture, touch, and sex. Sex became their most important need because it was an intense experience of having their needs met. Invasive abuse may affect the type of acting out that one chooses, but abandonment is the energy that propels the search for love and nurture and creates the fourth core belief that sex is the most important need.

The Bible and Sex Addiction

Two equally problematic traps are revealed when considering biblical truth and the concept of sexual addiction. A too common snare for Christians is to believe that considering a pattern of behavior as an addiction is explaining away what God has called sin. In contrast, the second deception is using the idea of addiction to explain away the fact that the Bible calls such immoral thoughts and behaviors lust and sin. The question is whether the fact that a thought, desire, or behavior is a sin is the only way to regard sexual acting out or that psychological issues mitigate and subsequently justify the behavior as not sinful.

Theologically, any sexual activity outside the bonds of marriage is always, not sometimes, sin.* Even in marriage, sex can exploit, manipulate, or abuse the other spouse. By nature, sin is addicting, and for many a particular sin or few sins, such as sex, might prove the most problematic. Sex addicts are in bondage to sexual activities just as any sin keeps someone in bondage.

The Bible pulls back the curtain to unveil the roots of sexual immorality. Genesis 3 shines the light on original sin, which underlies every human malady. With Adam and Eve's rebellion and separation from God, shame and fear (anxiety) were born. The new primary operative system would carry shame, which ultimately leads to sexual immorality. In the garden of Eden, sexuality and sexual behavior were corrupted.

More will be said about this later, but God's grace extends to each person regardless of the sins that pose the greatest threat. Additionally, in the seven things that God hates, sexual immorality is not listed (Prov. 6:16–19). God's gaze sees beyond behavior, including sexual acting out to focus on the person's heart (1 Sam. 16:7). He sees the casualties that sin has caused to human souls, the brokenness of all hearts, and he grieves over sin's present hold on humanity. Biblical truths not only condemn the addict's sexual immorality but also provide marvelous hope for the addict to find healing.

Mental Health Issues

Accurate diagnosis of any potential co-occurring mental health issue is important. Numerous possible comorbid dis-

orders can be present, such as depression, anxiety, substance abuse, pathological gambling, and impulse control disorders. It is my experience that the most frequent comorbid disorder for sex addiction is attention-deficit/hyperactivity disorder (ADHD). Roughly 50 percent of men who come to us suffer with one form of ADHD (Blankenship & Laaser, 2004). Per the findings from brain scan studies, these symptoms primarily can be caused by lack of blood flow in the prefrontal cortex (Amen, 1998, 2015).

CASE STUDIES

It is very difficult to narrow the vast range of acting out behaviors into one case or even a few, for that matter. Two cases are described below to represent a range of acting out. The first case is more typical, and the second case involves illegal activities.

Case One

Stan is a married man in his fifties. He related a history of sexualization that began at age eleven when he discovered his father's "stash" of pornography. Stan was never invasively abused as a child. His abandonment abuse was from his mother not being emotionally or spiritually present in any meaningful way. Subsequently, he found the perceived "kindness" of the women in pornography to be very powerful.

Stan discovered masturbation one night when he had a nocturnal emission or "wet dream." The next night he chose to reproduce it by stimulating himself.

---

* Cf. Acts 15:19–20; 1 Cor. 5:1; 6:13, 18–20; 7:2, 8–9; 10:8; 2 Cor. 12:21; Gal. 5:19–21; Eph. 5:3; Col. 3:5; 1 Thess. 4:3–5; Heb. 13:4; Jude 7.

Throughout his adolescence and teenage years, he continued to regularly masturbate and look at pornography. As he got older, he graduated to more explicit forms of pornography, such as watching graphic internet videos of men and women having sex.

Stan became a Christian at a youth retreat when he was twelve. He hoped that his new faith would allow him to give up pornography and masturbation, but it never did. Throughout his teenage years, he repeatedly prayed and repented, hoping that God would simply take his lust away. To his dismay, it never happened. He thought marriage would eventually solve his problems. Although he described his marriage as "good," he quickly learned that his and his wife's ideas of sexual frequency were very different. The perpetual tension led to a deterioration of their sex life and closeness. Moreover, Stan found that his ongoing use of pornography and masturbation made it increasingly hard for him to be sexually stimulated with his wife. When he came in for treatment, he couldn't remember the last time they had had sex.

Throughout his life, Stan had achieved a number of periods of weeks and months when he refrained from acting out. Yet he always returned. Once or twice Stan had talked to a pastor, and he even met with a Christian counselor, but he never found anyone who even knew how to ask him the right questions or provide effective help.

Case Two

Bill was sent to my program by his probation officer, having been arrested for possession of underage pornography. He was now a convicted sex offender and sentenced to jail time and five years' probation. The judge also required him to get treatment.

Bill had grown up in a large metropolitan area and had experimented with pornography and masturbation. When he was sixteen, his father had an affair and eventually "ran off" with the woman, not to be seen again by Bill for many years. His mother was despondent, unable to work, and certainly not available to Bill. Eventually she decided to move in with her parents. Bill's grandparents were farmers in a rural area of another state. In one swoop, Bill was forced to leave his large urban high school to attend a very small consolidated rural school. Further, living on a farm required a new routine of rising at 4:30 a.m. to feed the livestock and do chores. Then he boarded the school bus to face rejection from classmates who didn't want anything to do with this "big city kid."

Bill was miserable and terribly lonely. No one gave him emotional support. Bill's grandfather required him to go to church on Sunday and to youth group on Wednesday, where Bill met a very attractive fifteen-year-old blonde-haired girl. Taking pity on him, she began a relationship with him. One day after school, she invited him to her home while her parents weren't home. Their pattern of "making out" escalated to their first experience of sexual intercourse. Bill was exhilarated. He found that their ongoing sexual experiences lifted him out of his loneliness and depression. Sex was the best part of his life.

When Bill's mom found a new job back in their home city, Bill returned to his old surroundings and friends. He certainly missed the regular sexual encounters with his girlfriend, but he now knew how to find relief.

Eventually Bill graduated from college, met his wife, found a job, and started having children. Although he occasionally viewed pornography and masturbated, his actions were far from being out of control. When Bill was in his forties, his job was not going so well, his family was having financial difficulties, and he and his wife had grown apart. One night, very lonely and depressed, he decided to medicate with pornography. On the internet he saw a link to underage girls. He searched the site for sixteen-year-old blonde girls. It was not hard to find. He was exhilarated again. For life to stay bearable, Bill frequented the site, occasionally finding enjoyment with other ages.

On the day of his wedding anniversary, the police knocked on Bill's door with a search warrant. They confiscated every computer and electronic device in his house and arrested him. His wife decided to divorce him. Engulfed in shame and despair, when Bill arrived at my three-day Men of Valor workshop, he wasn't sure of the future of his marriage.

STRATEGIES, INTERVENTIONS, AND TECHNIQUES FOR SEXUAL ADDICTION

Universally applicable SITs were used in both cases. Bill, labeled a sex offender and court ordered to treatment, required incorporating additional assessment, case managing, and treatment factors to satisfy the probation system. This included a psychosexual assessment such as the Abel Screen, a polygraph taken usually at the end of treatment, and a very rigorous aftercare plan.

Treatment for sexual addiction has always been multifactorial, which can be a difficult concept for traditional evangelical Christian clients to accept. Such men often search for what Alcohol Anonymous (AA) calls "an easier, softer way." That is, they expect God to do all the work while they do nothing. Unsurprisingly, the average Christian sexual addict is angry with God because he hasn't been "zapped" with healing even after repeated attempts to "give it over."

Clinical Interview

Carefully assess characteristics and experiences of a client's family of origin, early life events, and romantic/sexual history. Inquiry about a family history of any addiction, not just sexual acting out in previous and current generations, problems associated with establishing intimate relationships, family dynamics (e.g., rigid, insecure attachment styles, enmeshed or disengaged families), sexual messages overtly or covertly introjected from family and significant others, various abuses, significant losses, excessive and hyperreligiosity, and early sexualization.

A Model of Healthy Development

Years ago, my colleague Ginger Manley introduced me to a model of healthy sexuality that included five dimensions: physical, behavioral, relational, emotional, and spiritual. Unfortunately, she never published her model, but those dimensions assist in assessing, conceptualizing, and treatment planning (Laaser, 2015). Strategies and techniques are connected to the five dimensions and were applied to both Stan's and Bill's cases.

Physical dimension. This includes brain detoxification, sexual activity, and medical issues such as medications and health assessments.

The abstinence contract. A fundamental strategy is to detoxify a client's brain from the neurochemical tolerance and to provide a client with a period of sobriety. The intervention is to request that the client consider refraining from any sexual activity that can produce an orgasm for a specified period of time. I encourage the addict to sign an abstinence contract. For married addicts, the wife must consent. The apostle Paul taught in 1 Corinthians 7:5 that couples are not to deny themselves unless by mutual consent and for a period of time. Carnes originally recommended ninety days. Though neuroscience research has found that detox can happen in seven to twenty-one days (Struthers, 2009), I prefer ninety days to allow time for facilitating a couple's spiritual life. The biggest roadblock to this request is often the spouse wanting, or actually "needing," to stay connected to her husband. It is interesting to watch how this contract plays out with every couple.

Teaching yada sex. The abstinence contract also allows the couple to focus on the more important parts of marriage. The second part of 1 Corinthians 7:5 says that refraining from sex provides time for prayer. For all sex addicts, and far too

many others, sex is primarily, if not solely, one-dimensional: physicality, perhaps with a side of fantasy. Sex addicts are unfamiliar with the geographical position and with the landscape of healthy sexuality. Limiting sex to the physical dimension is not traveling far enough to reach the beautiful place of marital intimacy. I say that, rather than too far, they are not taking sex far enough.

The first mention of sexual intercourse in the Bible is described as Adam "knowing" Eve (Gen. 4:1). The Hebrew verb is *yada*, a holistic term that refers to knowing one's spouse physically, emotionally, and spiritually. David used this word repeatedly in Psalms to refer to knowing God intimately. Sadly, Christians often leave spirituality out of the bedroom, finding it difficult to connect having sex with relating to God. God is in the bedroom or in the car, whether the couple recognizes it or desires it. *Yada* sex is always used to refer to marital sex as opposed to *shekobeth*, which means to lie with someone outside of marriage. The Greek language uses different words for different types of love. *Eros* refers to erotic love or sexuality. *Agape*, committed and sacrificial love, is far more than the physical. So biblical language clearly distinguishes between *yada* and *agape* sex, which is three-dimensional (physical, emotional, and spiritual), and *shekobeth* and *eros*, which is motivated by sensuality. Healthy sex can only be found in covenant marriage, where the inclusion of emotional and spiritual intimacy transforms sex.

Most importantly, God needs to be central to the marriage. We find that couples who are spiritually intimate will find it

546   Clinical Issue–Based Strategies

much easier to include his presence in the bedroom during sex. This is certainly what Paul meant when he compared a couple's one-flesh union to the relationship of Christ to the church in Ephesians 5:25–33.

Stan and Bill and their wives need to keenly understand that sex is meant to reflect their spiritual and emotional intimacy. Sex addicts, for the most part, only know the physical dimension of sex. You must teach them about healthy sexuality. You must also encourage your couple to commit to developing a deeper spiritual connection by praying together, reading and studying Scripture together, reading devotionals and spiritually oriented books together, participating in church activities together, and practicing spiritual disciplines. What they do together isn't as important as the emotional and spiritual connection that occurs.

The couple's developing spiritual and emotional intimacy sets the stage for healthy sex. All addicts, like Stan and Bill, are encouraged to participate in sex only when they can be sure they are emotionally and spiritually connected to their wives. When their hearts are in tune with the hearts of their mates, they are completely present in the bedroom, totally focused on the other, and both seeking and giving pleasure and enjoyment. Stan's mind would drift and soon hyperfocus on the pornographic images and related fantasies. The lack of arousal he felt from his wife led to him centering his thoughts on what did stimulate him. Bill gradually trained his brain to be satisfied only with the face of his wife. I emphasize that sex that is only biological will never be satisfying.

On the other hand, sex that is spiritually oriented will transcend all the sex they've ever known. Biological sex leads to marital sexual neurochemical tolerance. Sex that is spiritually based does not.

The abstinence contract is the initial phase of establishing these deeper connections. When the contract ends, couples are directed to change their sexual practices. Bill and Stan were instructed only to have sex face-to-face with their wives with eyes wide open. This practice allows a new association to develop. The new, healthier sexual experiences will form new neural networks that will reorient the brain to healthy arousal and sex. Altering Stan and his wife's sexual focus seemed to be one of the most helpful techniques. Interestingly, couples who follow the abstinence contract most often report growing in emotional and spiritual intimacy. When the focus shifts from physical to emotion and spirituality, the real magic of sex happens.

Referral to sex therapy. It is not uncommon for sexual addicts and their spouses to have developed various sexual dysfunctions, such as erectile dysfunction, female interest/arousal disorder, orgasmic disorder, and other DSM-5 listed disorders (American Psychiatric Association, 2013). Unless you have specific training in working with sexual dysfunctions, I highly recommend that you refer these clients to a sex therapist, if at all possible a Christian sex therapist (see chapter 28 for information on working with couple sexual problems).

Many of the men, such as Stan, have been acting out with themselves (masturbation) or others and have not been active with their wives. Most wives find the lack of initiative or receptive desire from their husbands hard to understand. How can their husbands be so interested in sex yet not be interested in them? Problems of self-image are exacerbated, in particular the women's body image. Debbie and I sometimes work together in counseling, and we regularly refer couples who have sexual dysfunctions to a Christian sex therapist. In fact, a whole new field of sex therapy has developed called sexual reintegration therapy (SRT; Berkaw & Berkaw, 2010).

Medical interventions. Medical care, psychiatric care, and prescriptions are often necessary for clients with sex addictions. Related to these services is a nutritionist and a pelvic floor physical therapist. Testing for sexually transmitted diseases (STDs) is often needed. Stan really didn't need testing since his acting out did not involve other partners. The same was true for Bill. Sexually transmitted disease testing will be required for all addicts who have "crossed the flesh line," even if they are adamant that they used protection. Instruct the wife to set a boundary of no sexual activity until she and her spouse have been tested. Ensure that they request a full panel of testing since the standard test does not screen for all infections. Urological and gynecological care might also be necessary.

Behavioral dimension. Sex addicts must get sober first. My definition of sobriety is based on Christian beliefs—no sex with self (masturbation) or others outside of their own heterosexual marriage. Maintaining these goals involves aggressive participation in groups and accountability (Laaser, 2011c).

Support groups and accountability. Today a variety of secular and Christian support groups can be found across the country, ranging from twelve-step-based sex addiction groups (Sexaholics Anonymous, Sex Addicts Anonymous, and Sex and Love Addicts Anonymous) to church-based support groups (Laaser, 2015). Christ-centered groups often use materials that rely on twelve-step principles after having "translated" them into clear Christian language (Carnes, Laaser, & Laaser, 1999).

Accountability is a very poorly understood word in the Christian community. I use the book of Nehemiah to illustrate key accountability principles (Laaser, 2011c). When the king of Persia allowed Nehemiah to go back to Jerusalem, the king also sent the army and the cavalry with him (Neh. 2:9). All of us who seek to remain sexually pure in a sexually provocative culture must have a group of men who stand like an army with us. Both Stan and Bill participated in evening counseling groups that also provided accountability. Addicts cannot remain sober with only one accountability partner.

Men tend to think in terms of behavioral dimension. One way this plays out is with accountability, which is typically viewed about the things "I don't do." Such was Stan's thinking. In Nehemiah 4:16–18, when rebuilding the walls of Jerusalem, half of the men defended against attack while half built. Accountability means that I will build and defend in equal measure. Accountability must be about encouraging us not just to avoid temptation but also to build positive behaviors in our lives (Laaser, 2011c). The sex drive is about our instinctual drive to be creative, productive, and passionate. People who don't have creative, productive, and passionate activity in their lives are much more susceptible to sexual temptation.

Committed to a recovery program. A recovery program doesn't end until death. I am often asked how I have stayed sober for so long. My response has always been, "By doing today what I did in year one of my recovery." I still attend counseling, although less frequently, and I regularly meet with a group ("my wise man counsel"). The last follow-ups with Stan and Bill found that they continue to do so as well.

Relational dimension. Couples' counseling for those who are married is a must. Both Stan and Bill invited their wives into couple counseling, and they agreed to come. Support for spouses is often neglected but should be strongly encouraged (see chapter 26, "Infidelity-Focused Strategies"). Any spouse who has been sexually betrayed needs safe people to talk with and a place to work through the trauma. Ideally, that would be other spouses who have gone through similar experiences. Debbie and I find that developing and encouraging groups for spouses is necessary for effective help.

Spouses are often blamed for the infidelity. One pastor demanded that a spouse report to him how often she was having sex with her husband. He told her, "If you had been more available, your husband wouldn't have strayed." Such attitudes are completely false and, in fact, very spiritually abusive.

Managing disclosure. If trust is going to be restored, complete disclosure must take place. A spouse needs to know the full extent of the husband or wife's acting out (Laaser, 2008). The addict sinned against God and his spouse. Therefore, she needs to know. I create a timeline of the husband's acting out, paying attention to key specifics and leaving out graphic content. Debbie meets with the spouse to create a list of unanswered questions. Then all four of us have a joint session to conduct the disclosure session. We typically schedule two hours to accommodate the emotional impact of the experience. Given the sensitive subject, we have found it best to advise couples to disclose in the presence of a pastor or counselor. Stan and Bill both agreed, reluctantly at first, to do full disclosure. Today they would say that this was one of the most productive and transforming experiences they did in couple counseling. There is freedom in not having any secrets. Also, in the process of rebuilding trust, the addict must be willing to keep his spouse proactively informed about his sobriety. That is, she needs to know that he is working his recovery program, including maintaining self-care. This will gradually allow the spouse to ask fewer questions as she knows and begins to trust that he is willing to communicate and inform her of the status of his recovery.

A model that I learned from Virginia Satir called the iceberg model facilitates diving deeper below the surface of behavioral problems. Briefly, her model starts with "behavior" at the tip of the iceberg. Coping stances are partially above and more fully below the waterline. The next layer of the iceberg is feelings, which is followed by a person's feelings about feelings.

The next part of the iceberg is perceptions of reality, including beliefs and assumptions, followed by expectations of others, of self, and from others; yearnings, such as being loved, validated, and having meaning, and the bottom of the iceberg being self (I am), which Satir describes as life force, spirit, soul, and essence—based in a humanistic rather than a biblical worldview.[†] Some adaptations of the model include adding values under the level of expectations, which is a useful concept to include. I taught the iceberg model to Stan and Bill, which allowed them to talk about feelings, perceptions, core beliefs, needs, expectations, and their deepest desires with their wives. It also allowed them to speak truth to their spouses and vice versa (Laaser & Laaser, 2008). After the workshop, they were to continue to practice using the model. One primary use of the iceberg model is to help individuals and couples understand that the problem is not the problem. We help spouses work down through feelings, perceptions and core beliefs, needs, expectations, desires of the heart, the truth to who they are in Christ, and finally how they are willing to serve each other. It generally takes a lot of sessions and time for clients to grasp and learn the model.

The word *restored* does not really capture the goal of marital therapy for sexual addiction. It is likely that even without the sexual sin, the couple's marriage was not in good shape. Helping couples get to newer levels of communication and spiritual, emotional, and physical intimacy is essential (Laaser & Laaser, 2008). A couple in recovery doesn't just survive; they thrive.

Emotional dimension. The emotional dimension includes the full range of human emotions, how clients seek to regulate them, and significant life events that flood clients with intense emotions (e.g., trauma) and overwhelm their coping capacities. The healing of trauma is critical (see chapter 22, "Trauma-Focused Strategies"). Family systems therapy such as that of Virginia Satir is an excellent approach to use. Effective use of Christ-centered therapy such as Theophostic therapy (Smith, 2005) can also be very powerful.

Ultimately the healing of trauma goes through a process very similar to grieving. Stan had to grieve the emotional and spiritual absence of his mother. Bill had to grieve the complete abandonment of his father as well as the consequences of his actions. The addict must first accept and understand the nature of his trauma. He will then become angry about it. It has been taught that this is the stage in which an addict needs to confront those who harmed him. Both of us have been present at some of these very painful confrontations and have never found them particularly healing. Rather, they often lead to painful, long-lasting harm to the relationship. The addict needs to do anger work

---

[†] Many descriptions of the Satir iceberg can be found on the internet, along with opportunities to purchase posters of it. I prefer to write it on the whiteboard so that I can integrate a biblical worldview throughout the model—for example, addressing how original sin and ongoing sins fit into the model, as well as adapting the bottom of the iceberg's emphasis on self-promotion and self-actualization as opposed to spiritual formation.

through verbally expressing it, journaling it, and sometimes physically expressing it. I beat up many innocent pillows in my early days of counseling. Being able to express anger to your community of support can be very helpful as can techniques that encourage emotional expression.

At times, counselors are too quick to process the experience of trauma. Others have clients repeatedly rehash the history of the trauma, which is likely to redamage the brain in similar ways to the original event. While the benefit of retelling one's trauma history is debated, most victims want to understand what happened to them. It is very difficult to find freedom apart from truth. I attempt to move the addict to later stages of the grieving process that include acceptance of the trauma and, when possible, to make a decision to forgive the perpetrators. Later in their individual and group counseling, both Stan and Bill realized the freedom that comes from forgiving those who had hurt them. The major turning point for Bill was when his group members, which included Stan, challenged his blaming the judicial system rather than owning his own behavior.

While trauma can lead to post-traumatic stress disorder (PTSD), a new school of thought and research called post-traumatic growth (PTG; Tedeschi & Calhoun, 2004) suggests that trauma can actually lead to emotional growth. Tedeschi and Calhoun (2004) describe PTG as an increased appreciation of life, development of more meaningful relationships, increased sense of inner strength, new priorities, and spiritual growth. While this secular understanding of the potential for spiritual growth is based on new research, the Bible teaches these truths (Ps. 73:26; Isa. 43:2; Matt. 11:28; Rom. 5:3–5; 8:28–29; 2 Cor. 1:3–7; James 1:2–4; 1 Peter 5:10). God never wastes pain (Thomas & Habermas, 2008).

Post-traumatic growth "shatters" old core beliefs (Tedeschi & Calhoun, 2004). The Christian addict comes to believe that he is not worthless, rather that he is a precious child of God who is fearfully and wonderfully made. He learns that healthy community and healthy relationships love him and care about his needs. Finally, he grasps that sex is not his most important need. God is. Though they may not acknowledge God, addicts who do not identify with the Christian faith can still deepen their spiritual dimension. As a Christian, Stan now has a much deeper spirituality, and Bill has even said he is grateful for being arrested because the experience ultimately produced a deep and genuine faith.

Reclaiming thoughts and fantasy. Post-traumatic growth occurs as the addict's thought life changes. Taking control of the thought life is essential to recovery (M. Laaser, 2011b). Remember that in the addiction cycle, it is preoccupation with sex and fantasies that leads to rituals, acting out, and despair. Paul tells us in 2 Corinthians 10:5 to take every thought captive and make it obedient to Christ. Addicts certainly would love to understand that verse. If they could control their thoughts and fantasies, their cravings and pursuits would diminish and eventually disappear (Laaser, 2011b). Over the years of my sobriety and based on treating thousands of men, there is a basic approach to taking thoughts captive. Most believe that taking captive sexual fantasies means to "get rid of them," "tell them to go away," and "don't dwell on them or think about them." These approaches don't work. The fantasies ultimately return with abandon.

Fantasy inventory. When you take a captive, you don't release him (Laaser, 2011b). That would allow the "enemy" to return to harm you. Rather, you keep the captive guarded and interrogate him. The same is true for problematic sexual thoughts. Thinking must be guarded and the thoughts interrogated. Every fantasy contains a message about the pain deep inside the client's soul. The pain cries out, longing to be heard and healed. It must be listened and attended to. Christ's help is needed to heal the deep soul wounds. Rather than effectively and spiritually addressing the pain, people "invent" images that are believed to bring healing. Perhaps you have had a fantasy about some past event that was painful. Often your fantasy will create a different outcome. I have sport fantasies, for example, that create a different result for every loss and failure. Fantasies attempt to "correct" some event from the past. Yet reality is unchanged. They fool the soul into thinking that unmet emotional longings have been fulfilled. My sport fantasies bring me lots of attention and admiration. My money fantasies correct the feeling of being a poor preacher's kid along with my gaining loads of attention and respect. Some people have power or status fantasies: *If I were only president of my company, then I would be respected.* This fantasy might be correcting

years of perceived disrespect and criticism. Whatever the longing, fantasies give a sense of what has never been, and at the same time they distance one from reality.

Some fantasies repeat exciting or comforting times, such as Bill's story. Bill needed to wrestle with his father abandoning him. In his support group, he was advised to select several older men with whom he could develop deep, meaningful relationships. While no man can take the place of a father, Bill's "surrogate" fathers helped him heal. Bill's wound of abandonment by his mother fueled his ongoing obsession and search for female nurturing through pornography. Counseling facilitated Bill and his wife's emotional and spiritual intimacy through, in part, practicing Satir's iceberg model. By working down through the layers of the iceberg, they were able to get to the deeper soul issues. Additionally, Bill found a greater ability to resist the temptations of viewing pornography.

Ask clients to tell you their fantasies. Get as much detail as possible. Quiet your soul to listen to your clients' longing. Client histories hold the clues to making sense of the fantasies and what pain they are trying to heal. Then, as a soul healer, you will be able to point them to God's true healing. When you understand the messages in fantasies and when you facilitate true healing for the client's pain, fantasies are no longer necessary and fade away. Some male sex addicts, for example, fantasize about women who look like their mothers. Bill, on the other hand, fantasized about sixteen-year-old girls. He wasn't searching for the physical characteristics of his mother. Rather, he sought out the physical characteristics of the girl who he believed was the solution to his "mother wound." Perhaps the pornographic images are bringing love, nurturance, and attention that their mothers or other caregivers didn't. When I first saw a pornographic picture of a woman, she was doing something my mom never did—she was smiling. I associated that perception of warmth with nudity. My soul's combustible material of unmet needs along with this new fuel flamed a passion to find other "nurturing women" in all kinds of pornography. Today I can happily say, I truly find love and nurture in Christ and in the spiritual and emotional connection I only have with Debbie. Pornography no longer holds appeal.

Healing communities. Addicts also learn to find healing in their community. The unrealized heart desires that they were medicating with sexual fantasy now come to be met (Laaser & Laaser, 2008, 2013), and new associations start forming in the brain. Gradually these new associations will override the old ones. Due to the neuroplasticity of the brain, new connections are possible—both healthy and unhealthy connections. God and a healing community provide pathways toward health. Instead of the old arousal template, a Christ-centered and healthy arousal template supplants it. Through repetition of new healthy associations, the old ones deaden. Fantasies disappear. Stan found the fellowship he so desperately needed in his community and in the genuine love he developed with his wife. Bill understood that underage pornography was medicating the pain of his dad's abandonment.

He cultivated a network of relationships with older men, surrogate fathers, and his underage fantasies died. Stan's arrested longings found meaningful satisfaction in the acceptance, love, encouragement, and belonging he experienced from his deepening relationship with Christ, his male community, and his marriage. Bill also found a sense of fulfillment in receiving validation, particularly from older men.

Men may be attracted to other men and concoct fantasies spanning a wide assortment of sexual activity. Such men long to find the essence of manhood, probably in ways that their fathers never showed them. You see, every sinful fantasy has a meaning of what the soul longs for. Making these soul longings "obedient" to Christ is true satisfaction of longings.

Spiritual dimension. Even secular-oriented therapeutic models, particularly those that have a twelve-step foundation, emphasize that true healing is a deeply spiritual journey. Christian counseling is essential for those of us who really accept that no true healing is possible outside of a personal relationship with Christ. Often the role of a Christian counselor crosses over to that of spiritual director. Since the role of counseling limits involvement with clients' lives, encouraging clients to find sound spiritual directors to foster spiritual formation is crucial to healing. A competent spiritual director will encourage spiritual disciplines such as prayer, Bible study, meditation, worship, solitude, and fasting. First Timothy 4:7 says that we should discipline ourselves for the purpose of godliness. These new disciplines become new habits that replace the former unhealthy habits. The goal of sexual addiction recovery isn't controlling sexual impulses. It is becoming more like Christ. Here are several goals to assist your clients with spiritual formation.

First, the addict must become entirely willing. This is the goal of the right motivation. Addicts are double-minded. As noted in James 1, such people are tossed like the waves of the sea. The ambivalence is between wanting to be well and wanting to hold on to their addiction, at times being afraid to let go. They haven't completely surrendered their entire lives to Christ. They may have tried to stay sober out of fear of consequences, but they are not internally motivated to totally depend on God.

Second, determine what the addict is truly searching for in his life. From a biblical perspective, what is the addict "really" thirsty for? Addicts think that the next "drink" of lust will satisfy some deep soul longing. Like Jesus tells the woman at the well in John 4, drink will never satisfy true thirst (see Laaser, 2011a; Laaser & Clinton, 2015, for more information on this point).

The third goal is for the addict to become sacrificial. Everything about addiction is selfish, and everything about sobriety is selfless. We are biblically challenged to be sacrificial and to love as Christ loved the church (Eph. 5:1–3). Ask addicts the hard questions of who they really serve, in fact, who they would really die for (Laaser, 2011a). For example, just as Christ died for us, is the addict willing to die for his wife? And if so, is he willing to honor her with his body? Willingness to die to something or for someone is the opposite of being selfish (Laaser, 2014). Being willing to give up selfish desires and perceived needs is an area to explore.

Fourth, develop a program of daily meditation. A very old form of Benedictine meditation called lectio divina (Latin for "divine reading") promotes spiritual growth. It is a four-part process of choosing a text to read, slowing down, quieting the self, and reading Scripture. The goal is to read the biblical text slowly and reflectively to allow it to sink in. Men who meditate have a much easier time controlling their thought lives. Online sites, even Wikipedia, elaborate on the essentials of this form of meditation to teach your clients.

Fifth, develop a theology of suffering. Suffering encompasses a wide range of experiences from physical pain and injuries to such emotional disappointments as broken relationships. There is nothing virtuous about suffering in and of itself. The value of suffering is in the changes it can produce in us (Thomas & Habermas, 2008, 2011). Suffering can redirect us to trust God more than ourselves and to focus on God, or it can have the opposite effect. Utilizing the pain of suffering is what PTG is about. Finding God and losing self while in the pit of despair creates a profound means of emotional regulation. When the addict has meaning for his suffering, he is able to steward his pain in healthier ways.

Sixth, cultivate an attitude of forgiveness (see chapter 20, "Forgiveness-Focused Strategies"). Addicts are angry—angry with God, their spouses, the world, and themselves. Explore the client's history for frozen resentments and emotional cutoffs. Like all of us, clients need to learn how to forgive themselves as well as others. This is, in fact, our spiritual commandment, to love and forgive as we are loved and forgiven. Forgiveness is God's method to "get over it."

Finally, encourage clients to develop a vision for their lives—one that encompasses their unique callings, talents, and giftedness. My friend John Thomas first has clients develop a mission statement to redirect focus to a succinct positive purpose of their lives. Then he has them link the vision statement to it.

Referrals: Intensive Outpatient and Inpatient Treatment

Counselors who work with sex addiction need to know when to make referrals and what referrals to make. Several very effective outpatient centers now exist across the country that specialize in treating sex addiction. My center, for example, offers individual and marriage counseling as well as groups for men and women, intensives, and workshops. The program works collaboratively with local pastors and Christian therapists. The three-day workshops have proven to be highly effective ways to "turn people around." For example, studies of program participants indicate a significant reduction of shame as a result of the workshop (Underwood, 2014). Attendance at a weekend program significantly moves the client forward and enhances the effectiveness of outpatient counseling.

Referral to an inpatient program is warranted when the client has more significant pathology, such as depression, suicide, self-injury, and psychosis. Inpatient also merits consideration when outpatient counseling was unsuccessful.

Unfortunately, inpatient programs come with notable limitations. First, they are incredibly expensive. A thirty-day period of residential treatment for sex addiction in some programs can cost more than $37,000, with little chance of insurance coverage (Ley, 2011). Second, the programs have become longer, up to six weeks. Finally, while some treatment centers have an openness to Christian faith, a completely Christ-centered and fully clinically competent program is hard to come by.

CONCLUSION

I'm keenly aware that authors in edited volumes such as this one can only scratch the surface and offer a broad overview of conceptualizations and treatment strategies. It is vital that you become trained, because sexually addicted men and women will present for counseling whether you are aware or not. Our culture is experiencing a moral decline, the likes of which has not been seen before; it is pervasive and as damaging as a tsunami. It is killing the souls of millions of people. A day doesn't go by when I don't hear from people who are frustrated with the answers they get from their pastors and counselors. Get more training, even certification. I welcome being a resource.

There is great hope for addicts and their spouses. Marriages can be healed. The psalmist wrote, "You, LORD, have delivered me from death, my eyes from tears, my feet from stumbling, that I may walk before the LORD in the land of the living" (Ps. 116:8–9). Addicts obtain long-lasting sobriety and purity when you guide them from the land of death to the land of the living. They need the help of people like you. Working with sexual addicts may be the greatest source of fulfillment you will ever know. Even as I write, I am praying that this chapter will be a blessing and awaken a desire to redeem unhealthy sexuality. May it be so with God's help.

RECOMMENDED READING

Allender, D. (1990). *The wounded heart*. Colorado Springs: NavPress.

Bader E., & Pearson, P. (1988). *In quest of the mythical mate*. New York, NY: Bruner/Mazel.

Carnes, P. (1970). *Sexual anorexia*. Center City, MN: Hazelden.

Carnes, P. (1989). *Contrary to love: Helping the sexual addict*. Center City, MN: Hazelden.

Carnes, P., Carnes, S., & Baily, J. (2005). *Facing the shadow*. Wickensburg, AZ: Gentle Path.

Jennings, T. (2013). *The God-shaped brain*. Downers Grove, IL: InterVarsity.

Laaser, M., & Clinton, T. (2010). *The quick reference to sexuality and relationship counseling*. Grand Rapids: Baker.

Laaser, M., & Clinton, T. (2015). *The fight of your life*. Shippensburg, PA: Destiny Image.

Laaser, M., & Earle, R. (2002). *The pornography trap*. Kansas City, KS: Beacon Hill.

May, G. (1988). *Addiction and grace*. New York, NY: Harper.

CHAPTER 26

Infidelity-Focused Strategies

MICHAEL SYTSMA, PhD

DOUGLAS ROSENAU, EdD

Can you build a fire in your lap
  and not burn your pants?
Can you walk barefoot on hot coals
  and not get blisters?
It's the same when you have sex with your neighbor's wife:
  Touch her and you'll pay for it. No excuses.

PROVERBS 6:27–29 MSG

A better scheme could not have been devised for striking at the heart of marriage than infidelity. Shirley Glass (2003) states that healthy relationships are bolstered by what are considered safe assumptions: exclusive commitment, moral values of monogamy, mutual love, and safety. According to Glass, "Our basic assumptions provide a set of operation instructions for living. . . . We are traumatized when these assumptions are shattered because our safe, predictable world is no longer safe or predictable" (p. 95). Infidelity devastates companionship, destroys trust, and toxically distorts sexual intimacy. Clients presenting for help recovering from infidelity need a counselor able to guide them through their grief and healing journey. This chapter is designed to help prepare you to be just such a guide.

We will begin by defining infidelity and its prevalence, followed by a look at critical concepts in counseling infidelity. The focus of the chapter, however, is to introduce strategies for counseling couples recovering from this common wound. We have seen that affair counseling is different than other types of couple counseling given the trauma and disruptive force to the marital system.

THEOLOGY AND PSYCHOLOGY OF INFIDELITY

Infidelity by the Numbers

By listening to the radio, watching movies or television, glancing at the tabloids, or surfing the online news, we can get the idea that nearly no people are faithful in their marriages. Is everyone having affairs? Despite being the focus of multiple research studies (for a sample of reviews see Munsch, 2012; Thompson, 1983; Wiederman, 1997), this question is difficult to answer for a host of reasons, including denial, definitions of infidelity, and sample bias. Infidelity appears to be universally common and is the number one reason for divorce in 160 cultures (Betzig, 1989). Hite (1981) reported incidence as high as 66 percent for males, but newer studies seem to suggest that for decades the rate has hovered around 20 to 25 percent for men and 10 to 15 percent for women (Carr, 2010). The latest surveys suggest the gender difference is lessening. Carr (2010) found that younger women (ages eighteen to twenty-four) cheated at a rate almost equal to their male counterparts (12.9 percent for females compared to 15.9 percent for males). This appears to be more of a sociological trend than a generational effect. A 2009 study showed no significant gender differences (23 percent of men compared to 19 percent of women). However, it did show a slight but significant age difference and a significant difference in religious belief, with those who had affairs less likely to see religion as important (Mark, Janssen, & Milhausen, 2011).

Beliefs on the acceptability of infidelity also seem to be slightly shifting. A Gallup poll suggests that infidelity is increasingly morally unacceptable, with 91 percent stating that an affair is morally wrong (Newport & Himelfarb, 2013). Only 6 percent stated infidelity was acceptable—this, despite the reported popularity of online affair sites.

The cost of infidelity remains high. Infidelity is still illegal in twenty-one states (Rhode, 2016). About half of US couples who experience an extramarital affair divorce (Allen & Atkins, 2012). It has been estimated that infidelity is the event that brings 25 percent of couples to counseling, with another 30 percent of couples revealing infidelity during the course of treatment (Wagers, 2003). Daly and Wilson (1988) report that actual or suspected infidelity on the part of a wife is the leading cause of spousal battering and spousal homicide.

Clearly, counselors need to be able to address healing from an affair. About 65 to 70 percent of couples who experience infidelity stay married, with half of those reporting a stronger relationship than before the affair (Snyder, Baucom, & Gordon, 2007). Much of the time this happens with the help of a counselor.

Defining Infidelity

The *American Heritage Dictionary* (2016) defines infidelity as "unfaithfulness to a sexual partner, especially a spouse." While "an *act* of sexual unfaithfulness" (emphasis added) is one of the definitions, viewing infidelity as a broader state of "unfaithfulness" allows for more than sexual intercourse with someone other than one's spouse to qualify as infidelity. Couples will often distract from the issue of the wound and offense by arguing about whether the infidelity was an affair. This can include at what level of physical or emotional involvement an affair has occurred. "We didn't have sex; we just kissed." "This was only an emotional affair." But are emotional affairs void of any sexual component? It might be argued that emotional affairs have the capacity to damage the marital system even more than a casual encounter. When a client is minimizing an emotional affair and seeing it as nonsexual, it is fair to ask, "So, can you imagine the object of your emotional attachment being eighty years old, obese, and unattractive?"

These discussions can quickly become a trap that draws you into the couple's unhealthy dance (i.e., interactional dynamic patterns) and results in aligning with one spouse over the other. In time, the couple that heals will develop a shared narrative of what happened. Pushing for agreement on that narrative too early can stall the process. Focusing on the healing process tends to be a better choice.

In this chapter, "infidelity" is defined broadly and can include any unfaithfulness that causes a wound in the marriage, including emotional affairs that never culminate in physical sex; addictive/compulsive sexual acting out; brief or more casual sexual hookups; shorter emotional, sexual affairs growing out of a friendship; long-term love relationships; and online emotionally romantic relationships. In Matthew 5:28, Jesus expanded the definition of infidelity beyond the physical to include mind and emotions. A person can sexually adulterate (contaminate by adding a foreign substance) a marriage through thoughts and mental obsessions, not just by engaging in sexual intercourse.

Infidelity can also be defined as a fantasy. Unfortunately, fantasies are bigger than real life and, thus, very powerful. Exaggerated by the fantasy, the object of the affair will often possess something the mate doesn't have or isn't doing. The affair partner may love cuddling, kinky sex, or deep conversations, or may seem to really desire the person. The offending spouse internally exaggerates these desired characteristics that seem totally absent in the marriage. A fantasy can be so extremely inviting and deceiving. Real life with kids, fatigue, and familiarity aren't as exciting. The fact that the people in the affair are sharing secrets is also very bonding and toxic to the marital relationship and a part of maintaining the fantasy. Thus, exposing the fantasy is an important component and strategy.

Finally, since different writers label the various parties in the infidelity, we will call the spouse who was not part of the infidelity the *wounded spouse*, and the unfaithful one the *offending spouse*. The *affair partner* is the third party the offending spouse had the relationship with. You may choose different language in session, and often couples have a preferred language when referencing their roles. What is most important is agreeing on a clear language with the couple so you are not confused in who the "she" or "he" is during storytelling. We also work to elevate language. "Your affair partner" is more detached and clinical than "your mistress."

Critical Concepts in Working with Infidelity

As with any counseling issue, a few core concepts should be considered in preparing to do this work.

Self-of-the-therapist. Carlson and Sperry (2010) write, "The most effective infidelity couples therapists have achieved LTLR [long-term loving relationship] stage three experience ["stage three" means they are well differentiated] in their own lives and have worked through their own infidelity experiences and issues" (p. 28). While we don't believe this level of life experience is required to work well with infidelity, it does speak to the character of counselors who work best with infidelity. You must be able to tolerate a high level of pain in the room and keep the couple focused on healing. Hearing the stories can be very painful to highly erotic for the counselor. If you cannot manage your own emotions, this will come out in session and stifle the couple.

Educate yourself on the theory and practice of working with infidelity. Several professional texts on treating infidelity (i.e., Baucom, Snyder, & Gordon, 2009; Carlson & Sperry, 2010; Peluso, 2007; Piercy, Hertlein, & Wetchler, 2005; Weeks, Gambescia, & Jenkins, 2003) are available that will help you explore treatment models and increase your knowledge of the issues. Many counselors seem to believe some of the common myths discussed by Pittman (1989): everybody has affairs, affairs prove love is gone or never existed in a marriage, the affair partner is sexier, the affair is the fault of the one cheated on, divorce is inevitable after an affair, and there is safety in ignorance about the affair. Educating yourself on these common myths and the truths behind them can help ensure that you don't derail in guiding the couple.

You would also do well to learn the common phases of infidelity (Rosenau, 1998): inception, pre-discovery, discovery, recovery, resolution. These phases will orient you during the initial assessment. Awareness of the phases sheds light on some of the issues and tasks the couple still must work through.

Infidelity is varied and complex. The reasons given for infidelity demonstrate the complexity of this topic. Infidelity can occur in decent marriages out of curiosity or a friendship that is romanticized over time. Affairs may be mostly sexual, or they may involve trying to get nonsexual needs (e.g., affirmation, sympathetic listening, adventure) met in a romantic relationship. Infidelity can be symptomatic of midlife crisis or marital dissatisfaction; it can be used for revenge or to end a marriage; or it may be a part of personal problems like addiction. Sometimes affairs are a way of distancing from intimacy and keeping a marriage shallow or living out the patterns of the family of origin. Many have never learned monogamy in dating relationships and are ill equipped to be faithful in marriage.

Components of the infidelity can also be highly varied, including the length and intensity of the affair; intensity of the emotional attachment; relationship of the parties before the infidelity (i.e., affair with a spouse's best friend); state of the marital intimacy before, during, and after the affair; level of individual health and stability of each affected party; environmental factors (finances, children, work pressures, etc.); nature of discovery and disclosure; and each party's initial response to discovery/disclosure. Variations in each of these story components (and others) can dramatically change the assessment and counseling approach. Recognizing infidelity as varied and complex helps you approach

560 Clinical Issue–Based Strategies

each story with an open stance and adapt counseling techniques accordingly.

Infidelity as complex trauma. While understanding the meaning and context of infidelity is important, perhaps the most important core concept is the recognition of infidelity as a kind of complex trauma. Spending time focused on the "why" and details of the infidelity without attending to the trauma is treating a gunshot wound by locking up the guns and putting a Band-Aid on the entry wound. The real threat and damage is the traumatic wound caused by the bullet propelling deep into the body. You must attend to the complexity of the wound if the individuals and couple are going to heal.

The psychological impact of an affair involves multiple losses and trauma to both partners and the marital system. Steffens and Rennie (2006) found that a majority of wives (69.6 percent) responded to disclosure of infidelity with post-traumatic stress disorder (PTSD) symptoms, with 50 percent reporting moderate to severe symptoms. Spring (2006, p. 13) identifies multiple areas of possible confusion, grief, and loss with marital infidelity:

1. Loss of identity: personally and within the marriage, with views of the partner's character and healthy roles within the marriage shifting and being doubted
2. Loss of a sense of specialness
3. Loss of self-respect for debasing self to win the partner back and failing to acknowledge all the wrong that has been perpetrated
4. Loss of control over thoughts, emotions, and the stability of the marriage

5. Loss of a fundamental sense of order and justice: in the world in general and especially in the way the marriage was supposed to play out
6. Loss of religious faith: Where is God in all this trauma, and why aren't people of faith in my life coming through with the help I need?
7. Loss of true connection with others: Who has my back? and who can I confide in?
8. Loss of a sense of purpose: Can I be loved, and is all this worth it? This isn't the life and marriage I had envisioned.

Both partners, and especially the one who has been betrayed, are thrown into this complex trauma from which they must heal over time. Grieving must take place with all of the stages in grief (Kübler-Ross, 1969): denial (*I can't believe this is happening to me*); anger, with a thousand questions and "You and the whole marriage are a sham"; bargaining with trying to regain control and make sense of what has happened; depression and intense grieving; acceptance and resolution that can take years.

Grieving is not just for the wounded spouse. The offending spouse will typically experience a kind of grief. For the offending spouse, grief is often a trigger for the wounded spouse, but the counselor must create space for both to grieve. Post-affair counseling truly involves trauma work of processing the story and helping the victims begin to create a new, transformative counternarrative.

Infidelity as sin. Adultery, defined as sex with another man's wife or betrothed

(Marsh, 2016), made it to God's top ten list of "Thou shalt nots" (Ex. 20:14) in Scripture. It is an offense against God (Prov. 2:17) and against the spouse (Prov. 6:34–35), and it was a sin punishable by the death of both parties in Old Testament times (Deut. 22:22). Various Scripture passages speak to the sin and destruction adultery brings on an individual and society (i.e., Prov. 6:32–35). Christ and the New Testament reaffirm adultery as sin (cf. Matt. 19:18; 1 Cor. 6:9), and while Jesus chose not to condemn the woman caught in adultery (John 8:11), he affirmed that what she was doing was sin and also expanded the definition of adultery to include lustful desire (Matt. 5:28).

While Scripture doesn't speak directly to nonsexual infidelity in marriage, it does regularly draw comparisons between adultery and God's people turning away from him in idolatry and apostasy (Jer. 3:6–9; Hos. 1:2–3). God is serious about his covenant with us and calls us to be pure in our pursuit of him. Thus, it is reasonable to maintain the analogy and see any breach of the sacredness of the marital bed (Heb. 13:4) as missing the mark, defilement, or sin.

CASE STUDY

Geri was surprised when her close work friendship with Hank included a passionate kiss on the stairwell to the underground parking lot. After disclosing this to her best girlfriend, she realized an emotional affair had been slowly building for some time. When she confessed the relationship, Geri's husband Cam forgave her and didn't want her to quit her job. She broke off the friendship with Hank, was able to transfer to another work group, and agreed to keep any interaction with Hank totally business and would tell Cam. The marriage slowly healed though an innocent trust had been lost.

Cam was surprised at Geri's reactions when she was using his computer and discovered a sexually explicit email he forgot to erase. His affair with Jan began while on a business trip at the hotel bar. He didn't think he would get a free pass just because he was drunk and the woman had been the aggressor when they met, but he thought Geri's emotional affair four years earlier would make her more understanding. When Cam told Geri about meeting the woman and since then meeting up with her three times, Geri collapsed in tears, and then intense anger followed. "How could you? Wasn't I enough for you? Do you love her? I thought we had a good sex life. Are you planning on leaving?"

He wondered if the accusations and interrogation would ever end. He saw the affair as a sexualized friendship with no real love feelings. It began casually, remained very casual, and was easy to end. Both Cam and Geri realized they weren't going to rebuild trust on their own until they sought counseling.

Over the course of months of counseling, Geri and Cam realized that her emotional affair, though four years old, had never been entirely dealt with and healed. Both were surprised at their intense roller coaster of feelings as they worked to reconcile. Disclosure, honesty, and working on trust helped. They had good days, and then something would trigger the hurt and anger, with both wondering if this would ever end. Slowly trust was rebuilding, and lovemaking began again with deeper meaning. Though their naive innocence was lost, they were creating a sacred commitment that had never existed before.

STRATEGIES, INTERVENTIONS, AND TECHNIQUES FOR COUNSELING INFIDELITY

Working through affair recovery requires you to attend to many critical issues that are unique to affair counseling. We have found the following strategies helpful in facilitating healing in those who have been affected by infidelity.

Initial Sessions and Assessing

The first couple session is critical in setting the path for healing. Couples present for counseling at various stages of the healing process (from hours after first discovery to years in), but the initial process remains fairly constant.

Session one. The first session should be with both spouses whenever possible. Often spouses will want to schedule the first session alone, but this is often an attempt to create an unhealthy alliance with the counselor. Having the couple present allows you to assess the current state of the system better as you watch the interaction around the story. Moreover, it starts the couple on a healing journey together.

After the normal first session ritual (informed consent, introductions, etc.), ask the wounded spouse to tell the story from wherever they believe the story begins. Beginning with the wounded spouse has several advantages. One is to hear where the wounded spouse is in the process. If still raw, intensely angry, or crushed, those feelings will likely show as the story is told. You will also be able to see whether the wounded spouse is able to contain, or not be overwhelmed by, the story and emotion. Second, you will hear the story from the wounded spouse's perspective. What do they believe went on? What was their experience of the journey? Effective counseling at this point requires that you are not afraid of the pain in the room. A well-differentiated counselor will absorb a lot more pain, allowing it to be expressed. Therapists who are afraid the pain will crash the system will often not allow it to be fully expressed.

It is common for the offending spouse to want to correct or take over the story. Honor that concern, observing any patterns of where they seek to do this, but gradually shift back to the wounded spouse's perspective. Occasionally invite the offending spouse to speak up if the story gets too disparaging or if you see the offending spouse checking out of the session.

In addition to assessing the story and the state of the wounded spouse, another task in the initial session is watching how the offending spouse handles hearing the emotion of the wounded spouse telling the story. Work to be very gracious in your interpretation, but watching a spouse be visibly sorrowful is a hopeful sign. A spouse who is blaming, overly defensive, or generally unrepentant means a rougher journey, more work on the counselor's part, and poorer prognosis.

Doing all of the above will help you assess the strengths and weaknesses of the marriage at hand. One strategy I [Mike] often use is quite direct. After hearing the story, I simply ask in a very caring, curious way, "So, why are you choosing to fight for the marriage when this is what he (she) has done?" Similarly, in a caring tone I ask the offending spouse why they are choosing the marriage and not the affair partner. Questions this direct, when asked with tender tone, invite the couple to really consider why they are choosing the healing path (or dealing with other issues in the affair). Sometimes the answers are weak or uncertain, but whatever the answer, you have a better sense of the resources currently available in working toward recovery.

The final strategy of the initial session is that of providing realistic hope. Clients arrive after an affair in chaos and uncertain of their future. They need to experience a counselor who is confident and hopeful. You are not giving them an unrealistic hope, however.

Counselor: *I am truly sorry for the events that have your marriage, and each of you, in this much pain. Unfortunately, this type of wound is very familiar to me, which means we know how to treat it. If you are willing to stay on the journey, you can heal quite fully. Your marriage is forever changed, but it can grow from this point into the kind of marriage you both really want and others deeply admire.*

Part of providing realistic hope is mapping out the expected recovery path. This path is discussed below for the purpose of this chapter and shared with the couple at this point.

Next, move forward with individual sessions. Occasionally this plan needs to be disrupted to provide additional containment for a couple who are highly fragile or where the possibility of violence is suspected (see below). If these are suspected, prioritize your treatment plan and the presenting problems well and provide stabilization before progressing. Otherwise, the strategy of assessment moves forward with the next two sessions.

Session two. Assuming the tasks were adequately addressed in session one, the second session should be with the offending partner. I schedule a double session (two hours) to unpack the whole story. I do this individually for a couple of reasons. First, I am going to ask very direct, probing questions. The wounded spouse does not need to hear the questions or the discussion that follows, which will only deepen the wound. Second, I intentionally and carefully avoid asking the offending spouse to bring anything into the first session that isn't true. My focus is on the wounded spouse's story, and I rarely ask the offending spouse to verify the information. I do not want them to feel the need to lie in front of their spouse about something they may need to defend later with me. In an individual session, however, I will invite them to be totally transparent regarding where they are currently at.

The strategy here is to chronologically unpack the development of the affair relationship. For classic "one night stands," this will be a bit shorter, but every relationship has a narrative, even if the story is how they made themselves susceptible to the one night stand. Asking how the offending partner initially met the affair partner, what their first impression was, and why they pursued or allowed the relationship to continue is a start. Thoroughly explore all aspects of the relationship.

Fully unpacking the development of the relationship has three primary purposes. First, the counselor and client are able to understand how the affair developed. Later this is useful in marriage counseling to provide guardrails for preventing future infidelity. Second, the client faces the story all at once. Due to the denial and minimization that tends to be an inherent part of an affair, they likely haven't faced it all at once. Telling the story to you facilitates them viewing it as a whole and preparing for full disclosure with their spouse. Finally, it allows for a bit of a confessional experience. If you can establish a safe setting for the client to truly unpack the story without your condemnation, the confession can be healing.

Session three. The focus of the third session is to accomplish three main tasks with the wounded spouse. Since you have sorted through the details of the affair with the offending spouse, it may become clear that the wounded spouse is still largely in the dark. Learning what the wounded spouse does and doesn't know is important in charting a path forward. Sometimes the wounded spouse reveals they have inside data that discloses a much larger story than has been told. They may be holding that information to test if the offending spouse is coming clean. The next task is to assess how much resolve the spouse has toward working on the marriage. This is a continuation of the "Why are you willing to work on this?" question. Sometimes you realize they are simply gathering data to use in a divorce. Other times they are quite unhealthy, preventing them from leaving no matter what damage was done. Whatever the case, it is important to understand the setting you have before you. A final task is to allow them to express their pain. Sometimes they have been telling the world, but often profound shame prompts silence. Having a place to begin to exhale the poison is valuable.

While the above lays out strategy for the initial three sessions, there are a number of valuable strategies that may be utilized anywhere in the healing journey.

Setting Expectations

Normalizing the typical recovery process early in therapy has value. Couples often have unspoken expectations that recovery from infidelity can be a quick process. Clients have often reported that they were told by other therapists that if the wounded partner would just forgive the offending spouse, healing would automatically occur, and the infidelity would be a thing of the past. Unfortunately, this totally disrespects the sanctity of the marriage and the intensity of the trauma. Leading a couple to believe that the wound can be healed quickly is as irresponsible as leading them to believe that grief from the death of a close friend can be healed quickly with a few steps.

Somewhere early in the counseling process (often the first session) I ask the couple how long they believe it will take to heal from the infidelity. After assessing their beliefs, I let them know my experience.

Counselor: In my experience, the normal healing process takes three to five years. This doesn't mean you will be devastated for that long. The first three months tend to be very painful and chaotic—lots of anger, sadness, and hurt. Then, the next nine months look like a volatile stock market with lots of quick ups and downs but a steady trend up. The year anniversary is hard again, but the next two years are a slow growth. There will still be rough spots with an increasing number of good days versus bad days. You will also spend time during this stage addressing weak spots in the marriage and growing it strong. By year three, the infidelity is becoming part of the story of your past. It will be easy for a trigger to open it again, but it is quite containable. By year five, the infidelity should be something you are not proud of, but it is in the past. It will still be tender but will not define your spouse or your marriage. Triggers will be quickly managed by both of you.

Tell the couple that counseling will be more frequent in the beginning but will taper off as they progress. Volatile couples in the early stages may need to meet more than once a week for containment, whereas couples in the later stages may attend counseling only monthly to quarterly, if at all.

Also point out that the offending partner will heal long before the wounded partner. This gives the wounded partner permission to experience grief and encourages the offending partner to be patient and contrite. Depending on how emotionally intertwined the infidelity was, the offending partner may reach the point of rarely thinking of the affair partner within weeks. The only time they think of the infidelity is when the wounded partner brings it up. Point out that this is normal for differential healing to take place, with the offending spouse glad to be out of the sinful secrecy and wanting to move on, while the offended spouse needs time to sort through the chaos. If their physician told them they had an 85 percent blockage in their heart and needed immediate bypass surgery, they would not expect life to be "normal" for a long time—maybe never. Healing can be full and complete, but life will be very different for months while they go through the recovery process. Recovering from infidelity can be very similar.

Providing Hope

Providing hope is a strategy that sounds easier than it is. The anger and hurt that are a natural by-product of infidelity must be countered with hope. Infidelity need not end in divorce. God is in the forgiveness and redemption business, even with very destructive sins. Geri didn't understand how her Cam could ever betray her and wondered if the marriage was all a sham. Cam felt relieved to have the secret out but wondered if the damage was so great that at best he would forever be on probation as the "infidel" who cheated. In the midst all this trauma, fear, and hurt, the counselor needed to step in and provide hope that would permeate the post-affair counseling process.

In addition to the reality that they had chosen to be in the counselor's office, the counselor watched closely for any signs of affection, commitment, or caring during their sessions. Those provided hope as they became "toe holds" to begin to build on. One powerful technique was to end a session by pointing out the ways Cam and Geri cared for each other even in the midst of expressing their trauma. Presenting vision can be a powerful way to provide hope.

Counselor: You can exit this marriage any time you want, but I believe if you hang on through the trauma of this early recovery you can learn to grow strong. You [*addressing the offending spouse*] can learn a contrition, repentance, humility, and selflessness that is not typical in humans. You [*addressing the wounded spouse*] can learn a grace, mercy, forgiveness, and acceptance that is truly Christlike.

First Corinthians 13:13 says, "These three remain: faith, hope and love. But the greatest of these is love." After an affair, hope may be the greatest of these. Skilled counselors learn how to have and speak hope into the trauma.

Risk Assessment

We are listing risk assessment as a separate strategy, but it begins in the first session and continues through the entire course of healing. As stated in the introduction, infidelity is one of the leading causes of violence in marriage (Nemeth, Bonomi, Lee, & Ludwin, 2012; Rhode, 2016). Experienced therapists may ask outright if there have been any physical expressions of anger or if there is the potential of such. Getting a truthful answer can be tricky as couples will sometimes collude to keep this information from the counselor. Threatening to leave counseling or the relationship if the violence is revealed is one way this happens. While you cannot know what the couple is unwilling to reveal, it is important to ask and assess.

If you suspect the potential of violence in the home, a safety plan and agreements should be discussed. Sometimes it is prudent to work on an immediate structured separation to help ensure the safety of all parties. This especially holds true when there are children in the home, as safety plans must include plans for their safety. Depending on the level of threat suspected, you may need to consider mandated reporting.

In addition to threat to the offending or wounded spouse, sometimes the risk is to self. Either may experience urges to harm self. The offending spouse may seek to do so out of guilt, or he or she may have urges to self-harm to avoid the pain or to punish the wounded spouse. Being trained and supervised in a model of suicide prevention like the collaborative assessment and management of suicidality (CAMS) approach (Jobes & Linehan, 2016) can be important in working with couples with a high level of pain.

Structured Separation

While the experienced counselor recognizes common patterns, each couple and individual responds to trauma differently. While many couples struggle to stay together, some couples will have separated immediately after the discovery of infidelity or will separate as intensity grows. Separation may be to another bedroom, friend's home, or apartment. We have learned to accept whatever the couple has chosen but also to help bring structure to that separation. Conversely, when a couple is highly reactive and doing damage to each other or the risk of violence is present, you may need to recommend a structured separation.

While the definition of *separation* is varied and accurate data makes estimates tenuous, it is estimated that 79 percent of couples who separate divorce within three years (Tumin, Han, & Qian, 2015). With this awareness, you may push for couples to end the separation too quickly. Despite the reason for choosing the separation (i.e., management of pain, punishing, fear of violence, etc.), it may have value beyond what you can immediately see. So instead of pushing to end the separation, we recommend adding structure to it and utilizing it as a strategy (Granvold & Tarrant, 1983).

Setting up a structured, or therapeutic, separation provides enough physical distance that the reactivity can begin to settle. Spouses are not always on high alert or being regularly triggered by each other. In a structured separation, time together is planned and purposeful. This can include time for meaningful processing, interaction with children, and fun dates to rebuild. Boundaries are established, and unhealthy patterns are shifted.

Establishing the Rules

One strategy that can work very well is establishing a set of "rules" for the couple to follow. Because much of their life is in chaos, having the directive of "rules" that must be followed can be comforting. Further, it strengthens hope (*If we follow the rules, we can get better*) and provides for ongoing protection for the marriage (even if fallible). Further, the couple requires the change of marital patterns that allowed the infidelity to survive. Toward this end, ask clients to agree to a couple of core rules. Wait until after the assessment to request the following rules. The couple must be ready first. If the infidelity is continuing, there is no sense in asking for the rules to be followed.

Absolutely **no** *contact with the affair partner.* The first rule is quite straightforward but is often difficult for the offending spouse. Clarify by going back through the ways the affair partners made contact (identified in session 2) and discussing how to close these pathways of communication. This often means changing phone numbers, blocking calls, shutting down secret email accounts, blocking emails, canceling hidden phone accounts, and so forth. Then ask, "If they wanted to reach you just to make sure you were doing okay, how would they connect with you?" Work on closing those pathways also.

The reality is, contact almost always occurs after agreeing to this first rule. Hence, tell them to expect the affair partner to reach out at some point. If they truly cared for each other, they will want to make sure the other is okay. An important strategy at this point is to plan for just such an event. This includes what to do with unsolicited phone calls, texts, or emails arriving from the affair partner. My strategy includes stopping the communication, bringing the spouse into the middle of the relationship, and giving the spouse some power and control—all reversals of the pattern undermine the infidelity.

Counselor: So, Sue, how would you handle it if an unknown number calls your desk and you pick up the phone and hear his (affair partner's) voice on the other end of the call?

Wife/Sue: I'm not sure. I don't want to be rude.

Counselor: Given the choice of being rude to him or protecting your marriage, can I invite you to protect your marriage? [*Wife nods reluctantly.*] The moment you hear it is his voice, you need to say, "I need to hang up now. Please don't call again," and hang up. You may feel horrible, but know it's the right thing to do. Next, you immediately call your husband. When he answers, tell him exactly what happened. "I answered an unknown call and heard his voice. He was saying. . . . I said. . . . I hung up the phone and called you." Can you do that?

Ensure that the wounded spouse is on board, and coach them in how to be grateful without punishing their honesty. This can be done in a similar vein for emails, texts, and other types of communication.

Be truthful in all things. The next rule is to break the pattern of the infidelity by requiring total transparency. The nature of infidelity is lies, fantasy, and deception.

Living such a life requires a lack of integrity. To break these patterns, assist clients to realize the value of openness, honesty, and transparency in everything. Be aware that counselors disagree on whether complete honesty is wise. Research does suggest that keeping secrets in marriage damages the relationship. Further, there are a number of clinical advantages of truthfulness. For example, Atkins (Atkins, Eldridge, Baucom, & Christensen, 2005) found that couples who pursued truthfulness and full disclosure improved at a greater rate and showed better overall progress. This rule is consistent with biblical teaching that lauds truthfulness (cf. Zech. 8:16–17; Eph. 4:25) and sets deception as destructive and against God (cf. Ps. 101:7).

Doing "Good Therapy"

It may seem strange to list this as a strategy, but the greater the pain and damage, the more important basic skills become. In our experience, there are two "good therapy" strategies that are worth highlighting.

Modeling and teaching active listening skills. All couple counseling requires the counselor to help each partner empathize with a different reality—to objectively walk in someone else's shoes. This is especially important in counseling the trauma of an affair. You can utilize the model you are familiar with; however, modeling and teaching active listening skills are important strategies in effective infidelity counseling. Active listening during infidelity recovery involves greater self-awareness and the ability for both the offender and the wounded to understand and communicate their feelings while learning to empathize with a very different reality and experience. Empathy does not entail agreement. It is about understanding and acknowledging the other's feelings and reality.

Guiding active listening during session can also slow the process down and make it more manageable. It also short circuits much of the normal escalation. After the wounded spouse has verbally vomited their pain all over the offending spouse, the normal human response is to defend self.

Counselor: Cam, your wife is expressing a lot of pain and anger. Normal humans have difficulty hearing that level of pain, especially when it's directed at them. I'm wondering if you can tell me what you heard. What is her heart saying?

This invites him to step back, review what she said, and put it into his own words. This slows the process down and asks for empathy. In time, Cam can be coached to reflect it to her instead of the counselor. This works well with the wounded spouse also.

Counselor: Geri, your husband has just made some very important statements about his feelings for you versus his feelings for his affair partner. Those can be hard to hear at this stage of recovery. Could you tell me what you heard him say?

Systemic understanding and second-order change. Every marriage has a dance, a system; and sexual infidelity dramatically alters the system's functioning. The reader may be aware that first-order change doesn't alter the structure of a system while second-order change qualitatively alters the systemic order. Thus, only second-order change yields any forward movement toward healing. "Good therapy" works to understand the present marital dynamics and effect second-order changes.

Cam regretted his affair, or as he described it, "his stupid mistake." But he couldn't understand why Geri was so upset over a casual, meaningless hookup. He began counseling to emphasize the importance of forgiveness in a good marriage.

Counselor: Cam, I appreciate you coming in, and I can see that you love Geri and want this marriage to work. As I'm listening to Geri, there are levels of hurt and betrayal that include, but go deeper than, this one-night affair. She doesn't think you "get it" yet, but I know you want to understand. I'm looking forward to helping both of you build that intimate marriage you both want as we explore the pattern illustrated by the affair more carefully.

As therapy progressed, Cam began to experience real remorse and could see more clearly a real lack of appropriate boundaries in his flirting with women that had continually betrayed Geri beyond the "one nighter." What he thought was going to be a two- or three-session excursion turned into a year of couple counseling as he and Geri worked through many issues they had never addressed. Cam was amazed at how different his marriage was, and he had experienced what he called from his corporate background "a true paradigm shift."

Healing the Wound before Attacking the Disease

It is not uncommon for one spouse or the other to want to focus on the "why" of the infidelity or to focus on the dysfunction of the marriage. While these issues are important to know and address, dealing with them early in the journey short circuits the grief process the couple must work through. Keeping the couple focused on the current wound is a strategy that our experience has shown facilitates a more complete healing.

To assist in understanding this principle, we encourage couples to consider someone showing up to the emergency room with both a cancerous tumor and a deep cut to their leg that has severed a major artery. While the cancer needs to be treated, if they don't treat the artery first, the individual will not survive long enough to treat the cancer. Infidelity is like a cut to a major artery. Even if the ER doctor spots the cancer, her focus must be the wound that is killing the patient. As recovery proceeds, the cancer that was threatening the marriage, and often set up the infidelity, will reveal itself more in the couple's relational patterns. These cancerous causes or setups may be wounds that occurred in the mother and/or father relationship, or low self-esteem, or wanting better sexual intimacy. Keep in mind that this is not the time to treat the cancer; the couple stays in intensive care. Resist clients' attempts to redirect to "causes."

TV personality Dr. Phil McGraw once applied a common catch phrase of his to dealing with affairs: "You can't make sense out of nonsense." Translating that into our Christian perspective, none of the causes will ultimately be satisfactory reasons for infidelity—because affairs and infidelity are contrary to a covenantal marriage. Even the offending spouse will ultimately see the flimsiness of their reasons.

Acknowledge the Possibility of an STI

One of the very real risks of infidelity is contracting a sexually transmitted infection (STI). While research on risk is sparse, risk of STI is obviously higher in infidelity than in monogamous sex, but it is even higher than openly nonmonogamous individuals (Conley, Moors, Ziegler, & Karathanasis, 2012). Clearly addressing this very real risk early in the process is vital because the couple will often live in denial that STIs could be an issue. Sexually transmitted infections are often asymptomatic. They are a real threat to the health of the family and the wounded spouse who is choosing to stay in the marriage. The fear can be removed in days with a clean lab report, and if there is an STI, a plan can be made for curing or managing the infection. Testing will include at least the most common STIs: HIV, herpes, HPV, gonorrhea, chlamydia, trichomoniasis, and syphilis (Mayo Clinic, 2015). Some physicians and couples may adjust this list or test for additional STIs (i.e., hepatitis) depending on the risk factors. Testing can be anonymous and quick at most health centers, as well as by those who specialize in this testing. For clients who are uncomfortable in discussing STIs with their personal physician, this is a welcome alternative.

One strategy is to point out how STIs provide an interesting example of the infectious nature of sin and the far-reaching consequences of transgressing God's chosen plan for marital fidelity. Rarely do spouses have an affair to cause damage, but sin damages. STIs pose a legitimate risk to both spouses. Though God forgives sin, the consequences often remain, especially with viral STIs.

Rebuilding Trust

A primary task and strategy is the restoring of trust and honesty to the relationship. According to Rosenau (2002), "The process of forgiving and letting go and rebuilding trust and respect takes time. Partners don't forgive and immediately forget—they slowly let go as trust is earned" (p. 351). One strategy for helping the wounded spouse sort through trust is in drawing and sorting through the following grid (table 26.1). In this grid, the first column identifies the wounded spouse's options, and the top row identifies the offending spouse's options.

In the ideal, the truth would be told and trusted. In this ideal, there is hope for the marriage to grow through the damage. On the opposite side, if the truth isn't told and there is no trust, the marriage will eventually end. If the truth is told and the spouse doesn't trust, the marriage is stuck. Therapeutic progress will stall, and the couple will bog down without growth.

The fear is that trust will be given in spite of the offending spouse's dishonesty. In this scenario, any healing is built on lies. When the truth finally comes out, the damage will be extensive and can permanently break the relationship.

In sorting through this grid, point out that the only choice the wounded spouse has if they want to grow in the marriage is to trust. When they complain, "This isn't fair," consider quickly pointing out, "None of this is fair, but it is how it works." Give permission to withhold trust for a season knowing they are stuck until they choose to trust. The offending spouse can rarely *prove* he or she is telling the truth. Mention that if the offending spouse is continuing to lie (not following "the rules"), the truth will eventually be discovered. Their spouse is likely extending all the grace they have, and further disclosure may break the marriage at that point.

Guide a Full Disclosure (Confession)

Carter (1990) addresses the critical nature of a full disclosure: "If sin can be explained away, then it can be seen as less deadly than it is. However, true healing requires a total admission of wrong" (p. 158). Harvey (1995) lists potential questions for the wounded spouse to consider during the offending spouse's first confession: With whom did you have an affair?

Table 26.1. Offending and wounding spouses' options

Options	*Tell the Truth*	*Don't Tell the Truth*
Trust	Hope/growth	Growth until discovery
Don't Trust	Stuck	No hope

How and when did you meet? Who else knew of your relationship? How many times did you have sex? Where did you have sex? Did you ever have sex in our house or bed? Has the relationship been severed? How do you feel about him/her now? Has there ever been anyone else? Is there anything else that I should know? (pp. 113–114). Not all questions may be appropriate for all couples, while many other questions might need to be added.

Clients have often started the confession prior to counseling. You must guide from that point on. Unfortunately, the offending spouse often gives out the confession in dribbles of information (the installment plan) and keeps destroying trust with each new revelation. Trickle disclosure is the most damaging type of disclosure. You can encourage a thorough disclosure by helping the offending spouse write up a careful confession that will be shared with the wounded partner.

The questions that follow the full disclosure also need to adhere to "the rules" (see above). Questions need to be honestly answered without details that can generate constant triggers or create nightmares. Guide the couple to progress to more "process" questions and not "detail" questions. Process questions are those that discuss the marital dance/system and promote understanding and healing. For example, What can we do to become intimate companions again? How did the love for someone else grow? Where is our sex life now? How can I help build trust more? are more process questions. Detail questions that focus on when, where, how many times, and what positions tend to create vivid nightmares

and are counterproductive as the imagination runs wild.

Most wounded spouses easily bog down in detail questions that ultimately highly wound them. One helpful metaphor is that of viewing the body but not endless autopsy. Remember that when we sin, something dies (James 1:15). A major loss or death has occurred with an affair, and the dead body needs to be viewed and acknowledged through a full disclosure. At some point after viewing the body, the wounded spouse needs to be encouraged not to constantly exhume the body, doing endless autopsies. While driven by many factors, it is not healthy individually or as a couple.

Many affairs go undiscovered, with clients and counselors wrestling with what is most helpful to do. Confession and disclosure break the power of secrecy, relieve guilt, and allow the adulterous spouse no longer to feel like an *imposter* (*If my mate knew, would he or she still love me?*). These benefits are forfeited if disclosure never occurs, and the individual flaws and cancers in the marriage are never addressed. We strongly encourage confession even of past affairs and the difficult work of restoring the marital intimacy. Client and counselor can pray about this, and on rare occasions the confession may occur just between the client, God, and the counselor.

Healthy Penance vs. Punishment

Encountering a need for punishment and vengeance by the wounded partner is not unusual. Punishment is generally destructive to the relationship and to the individual punishing. Nevertheless, the wounded partner may have a desire to see the offending spouse hurt and pay a cost for their offense. Here, a strategy of *penance* can be helpful.

Penance, with intentional acts of restitution, is a scriptural idea. After his conversion, Zacchaeus stated that he would pay back four times the amount to anyone he had cheated as a tax collector, and Christ saw true penance and repentance in this act (Luke 19:8–9). Ezekiel 33:14–15 encourages that if a person will "turn away from their sin and do what is just and right . . . return what they have stolen, follow the decrees that give life, and do no evil—that person will surely live."

An adulterer has stolen intimacy and commitment from his or her partner. Restitution in kind seems appropriate. Restitution not only heals what has been damaged but also the one who has cheated. The offender can grow through penitence, making real changes in his or her life and marriage relationship. The offending spouse has incurred a great debt. Penance can mean investing time, money, and energy to rebuild the marital intimacy that has been so damaged by infidelity.

Penance is temporary to avoid it devolving into punishment. It is human to want to seek retribution and balance the scales. Often the wounded spouse will want the offending spouse to suffer as much as they have suffered. This never works because the offending spouse will never feel the same pain but will moderate the pain through the filter of their own very different reality—and usually feel abused rather than gain greater insight into their mate's suffering. Scripturally, the concept of vengeance is ineffective in

promoting systemic change. It is also a sin. "Do not take revenge, my dear friends, but leave room for God's wrath, for it is written: 'It is mine to avenge; I will repay,' says the Lord. On the contrary: 'If your enemy is hungry, feed him; if he is thirsty, give him something to drink. In doing this, you will heap burning coals on his head.' Do not be overcome by evil, but overcome evil with good" (Rom. 12:19–21).

Challenge wounded spouses to avoid being infected and sinning because their spouse engaged in sin. This is giving the infidelity too much power. The sacrament of penance versus the human tendency for punishment can make a profound difference in the recovery process by allowing a "payment" for the sin without exacting punishment.

Helping Them Choose Their Role

Another helpful strategy is understanding the roles each partner can and cannot assume for healing to take place. Both spouses have unhealthy roles they can default into and hinder the healing journey. The wounded spouse often moves into a controlling role by attempting to manage behavior (theirs or their spouse's) or understand every detail of the story. The role of detective can be especially corrosive for the wounded spouse as can being the accountability partner for the offending spouse. Instead, we encourage them to keep the focus on their tasks of healing the trauma, forgiving, leaning into the marriage (if safe), and being centered.

For the offending spouse, common roles they step into are the defensive blamer, guilt-ridden "infidel," or impatient victim

("Are you not over this yet?"). These roles do not reflect true brokenness and contriteness. They impair their mate from moving through the pain. Instead, we encourage them toward being transparent, repentant, committed spouses.

Rebuilding Sexual Intimacy

The sexual part of the marriage can be profoundly impacted by an affair and typically requires special attention in the recovery process. You can encourage a level of sexual oneness and lovemaking that exceeds anything ever experienced in their prior marriage. Following are some guidelines for the counselor that promote dialogue and healing.

Attend to the trauma. Remember that affairs are traumatic, especially to the one who has been betrayed. They are often traumatic to the offending spouse also, for they experienced a kind of sex not present in the marriage. As stated above, both must work through their own grieving process, and you can facilitate this in the sexual relationship also. Each individual and couple will respond to the trauma slightly differently. Some jump into high-frequency, intense sex, while others shut totally down and refuse any sexual contact.

We seek to normalize their reactions and help guide them toward healthy sexual connection, reminding them that either response is only temporary as we follow the best trauma model for that couple. Counselors can provide hope and guidance as they help the couple "pray for the wisdom and courage to do that which initially feels uncomfortable. Talking and being vulnerably transparent can build trust and safe surrendering. Trying things, moving forward and then backing up, processing, growing, and healing is a process for most couples" (Rosenau & Neel, 2013, p. 88).

After Geri discovered Cam's affair, she recoiled at even a hug and couldn't imagine ever wanting to make love again. At the suggestion, they went on a sixty-day sexual fast in which they would refrain from genital sexuality and focus on healing. After many difficult sessions and hours spent talking, Geri felt forgiveness creeping in and was seeing changes in Cam that were new to their nine years of marriage. As trust slowly returned, minimal physical affection was appreciated as long as it didn't go into flirting or more overt sexual approaches. She still remembers the day she asked him to kiss her on the mouth, and they started becoming lovers again. As she looks back now, their lovemaking is more intimately connecting than ever before, and she is more open and uninhibited.

Making needed changes. You have an important role in helping a couple talk through how an affair has changed their sex life. In an honest manner, confront and draw it into the open. Are there activities or places that may be off limits now that weren't before? Did the offending spouse learn something in the affair they wish to bring into the marriage? Can the wounded spouse participate without being triggered each time? Couples must explore what can be reclaimed and what to grieve the loss of. Here again, an affair can be a catalyst for change with new attitudes and some new behaviors.

Meaning making. A helpful exercise is to encourage a couple to discuss what they want to express through their lovemaking and sex life, both individually and as a couple. Playfulness? Pursuit? Seduction? Openness and lack of inhibition? What do they want their sexual relationship to look like in the future, and how can they get it to stay there? This is also an opportunity to enhance a sex life and maybe for the first time in their marriage truly make love rather than just have sex. The effects of post-affair counseling as couples learn to be transparent and communicate openly can be quite dramatic in enhancing their sex lives.

The Resolution Phase and Relapse Prevention

Couples working on recovery slowly reestablish the equilibrium and deepen the intimacy of their partnership. The primary strategy of containment is less critical as the couple settles into the marriage. Triggers are still prevalent, but the couple has learned to manage them better. Now comes the final resolution phase of an affair as the healing process merges back into the humdrum of routine existence.

Making deeper, systemic, permanent change is not easy. The continued emotional and spiritual growth is hard won, as both partners continually resist sliding back into old patterns and ruts. Encourage couples to flag warning signs that they are in danger of relapse and to self-monitor. Some key warning signs when their newly found growth and intimacy starts to lapse:

- Making love infrequently, not flirting and pursuing each other
- Avoiding conflict and stockpiling anger
- Neglecting spirituality: no prayer, poor church attendance, etc.

- Keeping secrets or tiptoeing around some issue
- Canceling date nights and lacking in time alone together

Affair prevention will notice these warning signs and make needed adjustments. Think with clients about what might be a continued chink in their armor. What type of person and situation would be most seductive? Help the couple never to allow complacency and to constantly repair marital fences, maintain close same-sex and couple friendships with those who also value fidelity, never keep secrets, discipline their sexual thought lives, and grow ever closer to Christ and his wisdom.

CONCLUSION

Petersen (1984) teaches couples to affair-proof their marriages by continuing to prioritize the intimate oneness of their covenant relationship. It is important to "focus on, and stay true to, what is at the center, and like planets around the sun of our marriage, the other elements of our life will find their right places. Be faithful, stay faithful, have faith—and happiness will happen" (p. 204). Through the counseling and recovery process, marital partners are creating a new and improved relationship that is being nurtured by transparency, trust, respect, and a bonding sexual intimacy. It's a "God thing." The amazing Trinity can always trump Satan and even work through human sin and stupidity to bring a marriage to a better place. The number one consequence of an affair on a marriage that has worked through the recovery process: a better marriage!

RECOMMENDED READING

Baucom, D. H., Snyder, D. K., & Gordon, K. C. (2009). *Helping couples get past the affair: A clinician's guide*. New York, NY: Guilford Press.

Carder, D. (2008). *Torn asunder: Recovering from an extramarital affair*. Chicago, IL: Moody.

Carlson, J., & Sperry, L. (2010). *Recovering intimacy in love relationships*. New York, NY: Taylor & Francis.

Carter, L. (1990). *The prodigal spouse*. Nashville, TN: Thomas Nelson.

Harvey, D. R. (1995). *Surviving betrayal: Counseling an adulterous marriage*. Grand Rapids, MI: Baker.

Pittman, F. (1989). *Private lies: Infidelity and the betrayal of intimacy*. New York, NY: W. W. Norton.

Rosenau, D. (2002). *A celebration of sex*. Nashville, TN: Thomas Nelson.

Rosenau, D., & Neel, D. (2013). *Total intimacy: A guide to loving by colors*. Atlanta, GA: Sexual Wholeness Resources.

Shriver M., & Shriver, G. (2009). *Unfaithful: Hope and healing after infidelity*. Colorado Springs, CO: David C. Cook.

CHAPTER 27

Betrayed Spouse–Focused Strategies

Debra Laaser, LMFT

> My most trusted friend has turned against me,
> though he ate at my table.
>
> **PSALM 41:9 CEV**

In 1987 I became a victim of relational betrayal. The information of my husband's sexual addiction rocked my world. I felt as if a tornado had blown through my life and blown everything to pieces. Everything that I thought was true about him, me, our marriage, and the future was shattered. It was truly the darkest, loneliest day of my life.

Then I became a client in a healing journey. My husband left for inpatient treatment, which included a family week, a time for me to join him. My education about addiction and my first experiences of counseling began. It was intimidating and exhilarating all at the same time. I now know that this was the beginning of my journey to finding purpose in my pain. My commitment to counseling, groups, reading, and intensives led me to be a new person. I was hooked on the process of transforming, of becoming better, not bitter, from betrayal.

Today I am trained as a licensed marriage and family therapist, having helped hundreds of spouses navigate healing and growth from the crisis of relational betrayal. My husband's willingness to be public about his story gave me the freedom to be public about mine—thus, I believe, more helpful to those I counsel.

I am grateful that there are more trained professionals and helpful resources for spouses today than there were in 1987, the year my life "crashed and burned." When wives were counseled, it was often from the twelve-step model that suggested she was a co-addict and a codependent and had just as much to "work on" as the addict. Those were difficult labels to hear when the secret world of a husband's sinful life had just been exposed.

Recently, another model to help betrayed spouses has been identified as the trauma model (Steffens & Rennic, 2006). This theory validates the trauma of being betrayed as significant enough to be called post-traumatic stress disorder (PTSD).

It suggests that all symptoms a woman experiences are related to her betrayal. The trauma model certainly helps a betrayed spouse to be heard about her pain. It does not, however, encourage "work on self" or suggest looking at potential growth from adversity. In my opinion, it can leave a woman feeling victimized and powerless over her pain. I do not believe this is a healthy or hopeful response to a betrayed spouse.

My approach in counseling betrayed women is a merging of the twelve-step model and the trauma model to look at the biblically based and clinically supported model called post-traumatic growth (PTG). Post-traumatic growth is the positive personal change that is possible after experiencing a very traumatic event in one's life. Research validated that PTG is manifested in several ways, including greater appreciation for life, richer interpersonal relationships, increased personal strength, new priorities, and spiritual growth (Tedeschi & Calhoun, 2004). In my own recovery and in my counseling practice, I see the importance of validating the pain of betrayal (the trauma model) and of encouraging a woman to "look at herself" so she can grow through this pain (the twelve-step model). How do we help a woman who is devastated from betrayal find purpose in this pain? That will be the focus of this chapter.

For the writing of this chapter, I will be referencing women who have been betrayed by a male sexual addict. While it is true that both men and women struggle with sexual addiction, my journey through recovery has been as a wife of my husband's addiction. Additionally, I work exclusively today with female betrayed spouses, making that my area of expertise. The opportunity to heal and grow from betrayal is very similar whether sexuality is identified as an addiction or was just considered a "problem." I use the same counseling strategies for a woman regardless of the extent of betrayal. I will cover various strategies, interventions, and techniques (SITs) through a session-by-session basis, working through next steps to heal and grow from broken trust and infidelity.

THEOLOGY AND PSYCHOLOGY OF BETRAYAL

Relational betrayal—either emotional betrayal, sexual betrayal, or both—is an increasing problem in committed relationships today. People involved in committed relationships most often expect to have certain needs met exclusively by their partner. A violation of an expectation of emotional and/or physical exclusivity with one's partner is called a relationship betrayal (Whisman & Wagers, 2005). As we explore the strategies for helping a betrayed spouse, realize that it may be that betrayal was created from many different behaviors, including pornography, masturbation, strip clubs, massage parlors, prostitutes, emotional affairs, sexual affairs, sexting, cybersex, internet chat rooms, or creating online profiles.

Is Relationship Betrayal Traumatic?

According to Sheikh (2008), "A trauma is an event that profoundly challenges an individual's schemas, beliefs, goals, as well as the ability to manage emotional distress, and profoundly affects that individual's life narrative" (p. 87). Whisman and Wagers (2005) state, "Women who had experienced either their husbands' infidelity or threats of marital dissolution were six times more likely to be diagnosed with a major depressive episode . . . and were also more likely to report elevated symptoms of nonspecific depression and anxiety" (p. 1389).

The trauma of betrayal is like that of individuals struggling with post-traumatic symptoms from other life crises. They may have difficulties with sleep disturbances, irritability or anger outbursts, trouble concentrating, hypervigilance, exaggerated startle response, and obsessive-compulsive thoughts of the betrayal (Whisman & Wagers, 2005).

Schneider (2003) found in her study of ninety-one women and three men that more than 60 percent of the respondents were partners of cybersex users that did not include offline sex. Open-ended questions revealed that study participants experienced "strong feelings of hurt, betrayal, rejection, abandonment, devastation, loneliness, shame, isolations, humiliation, jealousy, and anger . . . as well as loss of self-esteem. . . . Being lied to repeatedly was a major cause of distress" (p. 353).

In current research with more than two hundred betrayed women, 96 percent said that discovery of their husbands' relational betrayals was either "very traumatic," "extremely traumatic," or "the most traumatic" experience of their lives (Laaser, 2013). Research would suggest that relational betrayal is usually remarkably traumatic, producing many symptoms of post-traumatic stress disorder (Schneider, 2003; Steffens & Rennie, 2006; Whisman & Wagers, 2005).

Why Should a Betrayed Spouse Get Help When the Offender Has the Problem?

Historically greater emphasis has been placed on the loss and suffering of traumatic life events and less focus on the possibility of growth. While it is true that trauma survivors experience loss and suffering in the initial phase of a traumatic incident, current research has found that solely concentrating on the distress of trauma eliminates the potential for personal growth (Vis & Boynton, 2008). Sheikh (2008) says that there has been a shift in focus to the positive outcomes that are birthed out of trauma.

Two psychologists and researchers from the University of North Carolina, Tedeschi and Calhoun (1995), note that there is overwhelming evidence to suggest that hardship in the form of physical and psychological symptoms accompany traumatic events. They also state that new studies are finding that even the most traumatic life events are producing personal and relational growth outcomes: for example, rape, bereavement, cancer, heart attacks, disasters, and combat. The results of research by my colleagues and me (Laaser, Putney, Bundick, Delmonico, & Griffin, 2017) also indicated that with time, use of resources, and engagement in therapeutic activities, relationally betrayed women reported significant post-traumatic growth. These results did not deny that distress coexisted with growth but showed that they could coexist.

Biblically, we have been taught about the troubled life we will face: "In this world you will have trouble" (John 16:33), but we can "glory in our sufferings, because we know that suffering produces perseverance; perseverance, character; and character, hope" (Rom. 5:3–4). Jesus certainly knew the pain of betrayal too. We witness through his suffering on the cross that there are no feelings we could experience in our betrayals that he has not experienced as well. He understands us. His betrayal led to the greatest transformation anyone could hope for—a risen Christ. Hope can be found even in the darkest hour. We have also been assured that God will not waste our pain, that our troubles and trials can be transformed. For this reason, I invite all betrayed women into a journey of facing their pain—to find the growth that is available to all who explore their trials. I believe that it is our responsibility as counselors to cast this vision for betrayed women seeking help. While validating the pain in the present, we can also share biblical truths and clinical research that reminds us that there is more to experience than the trauma of this day. We can hold that hope for our clients while they join in the journey of getting well.

CASE STUDY

Betrayal can involve many possible variables. Is this the client's first discovery of her husband's betrayal? Did she find out, or did he confess? Did she know of any of his struggles prior to committing to the relationship? Is this a single act of infidelity, or were there many? Was he using pornography and masturbation and/or "crossing the flesh line"? Were his consequences insignificant or extreme? The details of being betrayed contribute to very different presentations and needs of clients. It is difficult to find a case study that represents the many women I counsel. However, herein, I share one story with you.

Beth sat limply in the waiting room where I met her for our first appointment. She was looking blankly at the wall. I invited her to join me in my office, and I asked her some basic questions about her life. Then I asked her to tell me about what brought her in and what kind of help she was looking for. She calmly started to tell me that she was aware of her husband's pornography struggle the first ten years of their marriage. She said that she didn't think he was struggling with it today, though. When she asked him about it recently, he said he had taken care of it and it was no longer a problem. They never sought help for his pornography use, even though it had created a great deal of tension in their marriage. He said their pastor was holding him accountable since he was an elder, and that was all he needed.

She continued, describing that several months earlier she had discovered her husband's text messages to another woman. "It was sexually graphic," she said, "and shocking." She confronted him, and at first he denied that it was his text. With more questions, he finally broke down and admitted that he had been texting a work colleague for the last month, but "nothing more." He also admitted to several other women he had connected with via email, but he said he had stopped communicating with them when it appeared to be getting out of hand. Beth didn't know what to believe. She said she felt "crazy" as she tried to put the facts together. Her discoveries led her to question some of the hunches and "red flags" she had experienced over the years. She wondered if her husband was a little "too friendly" with women at church or if all those nights he stayed up late were really about not being able to sleep. She shared that she had consistently talked herself out of those questioning places. She began to cry as her story poured out. Her tears flowing easily now, she reached for one tissue after another, trying to choke out her words: "I can't believe he has lied to me this way. I must not be enough for him. How could I ever trust him again? My life is ruined. I'm a mess."

I validated her pain and asked her what kind of help she needed. She hung her head, crying again, and said she had no idea what she needed: "I feel so alone. I can't talk to anyone about this. I tried telling my best friend, and she just told me I should leave him. I knew that is not what I wanted, so I stopped talking to her." She said she was not sleeping at all. She woke up with obsessive thoughts about what her husband had been doing. She couldn't stop "snooping around," she said. She confessed that she had even hit her husband and screamed at him because she was so angry and confused. "How could he serve as an elder at our church and do these things?" she asked. "I hate who I've become in my anger." As we looked at the pile of tissues beside her, I asked her if she would be will-ing to come back and let me help her use those tears for healing. "This may be some of the greatest pain you have ever experienced," I said, "and I believe that with resources and support of other people who understand betrayal, there is great hope that you can heal. You do not need to do this alone. Perhaps I can hold your hope for now while we get started."

Beth agreed to get help but clearly told me that she was not willing to live with a husband who would not be faithful to her. She said bluntly, "I am willing to work on this healing journey, as you call it, but I will need him to do the same. I am no longer going to sit back and be quiet about this. I need a faithful husband!"

STRATEGIES, INTERVENTIONS, AND TECHNIQUES FOR BETRAYED SPOUSES

The First Session

In a first counseling session with a betrayed woman, I tell her that I only want to spend a brief time with intake questions. I explain that I want to hear about the story that brings her in and to explore what she needs. We can then talk about how I might help her and decide if that seems like a "fit" for both of us. If so, I mention that we will take more time to complete intake questions on follow-up appointments. I have learned to start my sessions this way with new clients because I know they need to be heard and understood about their pain—immediately.

For the betrayed spouse, the counselor is most often the first person with whom she has had to share the details of her story.

You are often the first and safest person to talk to—one who can allow the client to be in pain without judging her decisions or giving advice. Beth already started her "pile of tissues" by the end of our first appointment and felt relieved that she could finally talk about "this" with someone.

Before a first session ends, I always want to remind my client of this truth: she did not cause her husband's betrayal. I tell her that unfortunately there are still too many professionals who do not know how to respond in a helpful way. These responses were given by betrayed women when asked what was the most unhelpful advice they received when they first sought help: (1) You need to leave him. (2) Just forgive and forget the past. (3) He will never change. (4) Pornography is not considered betrayal. (5) If you had been more sexually available, he would not have betrayed you (Laaser et al., 2017).

I remind her that if she is working at our counseling center, we will focus on each spouse taking responsibility for his or her own behavior. No one "makes" another person act the way they do. We each have our work to do to become the person God calls us to be. In our case study, Beth began weeping when I said this, sharing with me that she had tried so many things to be a better wife, but nothing had helped. And, along the way, she shared that she had lost herself in attempting to please her husband. She looked relieved at the new possibility I was suggesting. She said that she wanted to stay and see if they could work things out.

The first session with a client includes my beliefs about resources that will help her: initially a counselor just for her and a group of other women who are personally involved in this same journey. We talk about how difficult it is to be all alone, not to have anyone who "gets it" or who is safe to talk with about sexual and emotional betrayal. I tell her that the greatest enemy of sexual health for a sexual addict is silence (Laaser, 1992), and that it is just as true for her. Trying to heal from betrayal all alone or by reading books never works, in my opinion.

I ask the client if she has any safe people to share with; the usual answer is "my mother" or "my sister" or "my best friend," but that is all. It gives me a chance to discuss who usually feels safe when we share: someone who doesn't give a lot of uninvited advice or judge you, a person who won't pry for more information than what you want to share. It is someone who will keep information confidential—even from her own spouse—who won't overspiritualize your situation, and who won't just try and "fix" you so that you are not in so much pain. It is also someone who can stay impartial and still love both you and your husband. That list eliminates most people for the women I counsel, so considering the possibility of a counseling or support group is appealing. In Beth's story, she had reached out to her best friend and unfortunately was given advice to leave. This was not helpful to Beth and led her to even more isolation.

Most betrayed women have stumbled onto information about their husbands' pornography use, emotional or physical affairs, sensual massages, strip club participation, online sexting, or other acts considered unfaithful to them. When confronted with this information or asked questions, many spouses will deny or minimize the truth, leaving a woman confused and feeling "crazy." Sometimes a betrayed woman just has gut feelings, red flags, intuitions, or hunches that something isn't right. I will talk to her about what it means to trust herself—listening to the Holy Spirit within who is seeking to guide her to truth—and how difficult that can be when the person you would like to trust the most is not validating your reality. We discuss her need for full disclosure at some time so that her internal reality and external reality are congruent. I remind her that feeling "crazy" happens when the world she sees, hears, and knows does not match up with her "knowing" within. I tell her confidently that she is not crazy.

Additionally, we talk about her husband getting help if he hasn't yet. She might invite him to join her in a couple's session to talk about the vision for getting well together and creating a plan with professional help. Or if she states that he won't come, I encourage her to get started for herself. It is the only thing she can control. She can choose to heal regardless of her husband's choices. She can learn that she always has choices for her future.

Lastly, a first session will always include some words of hope and the possibility of great growth that can happen when we have people and resources with which to work through difficult situations. I tell her I wouldn't be doing what I'm doing if I hadn't experienced that for myself, and that in my work I watch many others grow through the trauma of betrayal too.

And then I invite her to come back if she is feeling safe. I want the client to feel no pressure from me—only a gentle and encouraging voice to let her know that I can help her if she is ready.

The Second and Third Sessions

In subsequent sessions, we begin to work on many things, led by the client's initiative. I want her to practice initiating what is important to her—her questions, her arguments at home, her needs, or her feelings about a situation. If I have an agenda for our time, it does not allow her to focus on what is important to her. I have created a short "check-in" that I like to use for our sessions: (1) "What are you feeling today?" (I have a feeling chart so that we avoid the usual "good" and "fine.") (2) "What is something you have done that has been good for you this week?" (3) "What is something you did not do very well for you or your relationship (something you want to change)?" (4) "What is something, big or small, that gave you passion this week?" (5) "What would you like to talk about today?"

This check-in allows me to talk further about self-care (question 2) and some small steps the client can do to feel better and more peaceful. It also leads to discussion about her behaviors that she is admitting to that lead her not to like herself (question 3). In a very gentle and slow process, this begins the client's journey of looking at herself. Beth admitted to screaming at her husband and even hitting him one time when she was so angry. She said, "I can't believe I did that; it is not who I am at all." We talk at this point about things she can work on to "like who she is"—in any and every situation—to be the best version of herself that she can be at that time, seeking to please God in every way. I remind her that while we all regularly fail to live up to God's ways, Christ will always love us and delight in our desire to be all that we can be. I suggest that this is a journey she can be on regardless of the choices her husband is making for himself. The bottom line of recovery, after all, isn't really to heal from the betrayal or the addiction, but is to put on Christ and grow in him. We want to allow God to move us forward in becoming like Christ, a goal that is impossible to achieve in this world. Regardless of where we start or where we are now, God is for us. When this is the trajectory of our lives, such living brings with it indescribable healing.

Lastly, the fourth question of the check-in gives us a chance to talk about "loss of herself"—her interests, passion, and purpose in life. What has she sacrificed along the way? What happened to her dreams? When did she stop feeling joy in her days? I tell her that I wouldn't expect her to have passion when she is experiencing so much distress. And I tell her that finding passion and joy again (or maybe for the first time) will be part of her journey of getting well.

In these next sessions, I take time to diagram the client's genogram and ask questions about earlier life experiences: educational, relational, sexual, and spiritual. I also allow time for any current issues or questions so that she leaves with practical next steps. I divide our time to focus on both. More intake allows me to start talking to her about earlier abuse or neglect, family patterns she may have been trying to change when she met her spouse, attachment style, unhealthy coping strategies she learned that helped her with pain, core beliefs, and unmet "desires of her heart." I share seven desires that I believe are common to all men and women—to be heard and understood, affirmed, blessed, safe, touched in nonsexual and safe ways, chosen or desired, and included (Laaser & Laaser, 2008, 2013). If possible, I want to help the client see the desires that are common to both her and her husband, desires that connect them rather than divide them. I do not dwell on this historical information. It does, however, provide a framework of her life to connect to when she talks about current triggers and emotions. It also starts her internal churning to bring up memories of the past and begin incorporating those in the work we do.

I believe that the timing of introducing a betrayed woman to "her work," to "looking at herself," is very critical. Oftentimes it can be introduced too quickly (almost immediately) in the counseling process, and I've seen that a woman may disengage from the counseling opportunity when this is done. Hearing labels of herself as codependent or a co-addict are not helpful, especially in the early stages of counseling a betrayed woman. These labels often lead her to believe she is being blamed for the betrayal. If we do not take sufficient time to hear a woman's anger, sorrow, and hopelessness before we help her look at things she may want to change about herself, we may destroy our chance to lead her to posttraumatic growth (PTG).

When I intersperse this intake of earlier life information, I tell the client that I do that so that we can look at her story—from the very beginning—to figure out how it served to shape and form her to be the person she is. It is not about finding blame in her family, nor to find "sickness" in her. It is about wanting to figure out what she will want to keep from that story and what she will want to change as she moves forward. I might use an example of how people in her system trusted. What did she notice about how her parents trusted each other (or did not)? Who was trustworthy, and who was not? How did they repair trust? Did they own what they did wrong? Or did they just expect forgiveness and move on when trust was broken? We can talk about and relate many things to how she has trusted today.

In the ongoing sessions, I may use any number of techniques to explore her life and what she believes about herself, others, and her world. Together we will create a genogram of her family of origin; discuss what she learned about marriage by watching her parents and other adults; explore issues of physical, sexual, emotional and/or spiritual abuse or neglect in her life; name some of the ways she began to cope when life got hard; talk about how safe she is when communicating with others; look at patterns she acquired from early life; and assess her style of attachment in relationships—to name but a few.

Counseling never looks the same for any two women, yet there are certain themes we address at one time or another. The timing of when women address these topics is not the same either. I do not try and shoe-horn women into a one-size-fits-all re-covery plan. As a therapist, I have learned to be patient and allow God's timing to be exactly what it needs to be for each woman. One woman I counseled was not willing to establish a "bottom line" for her husband's pornography use. She was terrified of his anger when she talked about it. Her early work focused on her fears, learning to have a voice about things that mattered to her, and deciding how vulnerable she would be in the relationship if her husband was not sober. Although that would not have been my choice, I let her process be "right" for her, with no judgmental statements or advice from me. I trusted that it is God's timing. One year later, this woman was ready to set boundaries for those behaviors.

I will begin to discuss the following strategies or topics of counseling, either in individual counseling or in the therapy groups I lead for women.

Physical health. Very early in the process of counseling, I want to hear about how my client is doing physically. Foundationally, is she getting enough sleep? Is she eating well? Is she struggling with extreme anxiety or panic attacks? Is she able to manage her responsibilities at home and/or at work? If she has issues with any of these areas, I strongly urge her to get medical attention. I also normalize these difficulties, reminding her that betrayal is traumatic and that it is understandable that her body would be responding to stress. We talk about first things first. If she is going to have energy to work on getting well, she must attend to her body.

When Beth told me about her many sleepless nights, I suggested that she talk to her family physician about needing help.

Visiting her doctor aided her in multiple ways: she practiced sharing her story with another caring professional, she experienced asking for help instead of trying to "go it alone," and she soon started sleeping better and was more able to engage in her life as a mom and in counseling.

We can also talk about historical physical ailments, as often the client has had other mental health issues or chronic physical conditions prior to betrayal. Having this conversation gives me a chance to share what I have experienced: when women have worked on their own emotional health in recovery, they have often found that their physical health has improved dramatically. It is a gift to the self.

Before we leave this topic, it is important to talk about the need for sexually transmitted disease (STD) testing in the event that there has been unprotected sex in the client's husband's acting out history—or if she is unsure. Some women have so much shame about this that they do not want to see a doctor for testing. I ask the client if she worries about her health, if her husband has had unprotected sex, or if she doesn't know all his acting out history. If she is choosing not to be sexual, we discuss whether she needs for her spouse and/or herself to be tested for STDs before she is willing to be sexual with him. As a caring professional, I encourage her to "choose herself" and her well-being by getting tested regardless of what her husband is willing to do. I also support her in telling him that she will not be sexual with him without him being tested as well.

Needing space/separation. Sometimes a betrayed woman needs to create distance from the husband who has caused her so much pain. Her anger may be so intense that she cannot find peace in their home. He may be blaming her and or not validating the pain he has caused. Whatever the specific situation, pain has a way of creating a fight or flight response in our bodies—a God-given autonomic response built into our brains so that we will take care of ourselves when we sense danger. If emotional or physical abuse is present in the home, the betrayed woman has an additional cause for wanting "space." If the betrayed woman asks a spouse to leave or states that she is leaving, she may be calling for a separation to begin but with no guidelines or purpose. Doing so can lead to increased tension and unresolved false perceptions of the couple's conversations and behaviors. Leaving can simply be punitive and become an easy way to walk out of the relationship.

If a woman needs distance from her husband for a time but does not necessarily want to leave the relationship, I introduce the idea of an intentional separation. In our counseling center, we call it a "redemptive separation," one that will have purpose, guidelines, and supervision by a counselor, so that time away from the marriage will be designated time for the couple to focus on their individual journeys. Our couple's counseling will focus on establishing the details of the separation with follow-up each month on its progress. This intervention usually begins with much chaos, but we find that with encouragement and guidance, individuals can more easily devote time to safety and self-reflection. If both are committed to the process, they eventually have more emotional and spiritual health to bring back to the relationship when a decision is made to end the separation. More detailed explanation of this process can be found in *The Toolkit for Individuals and Couples* (Laaser & Laaser, 2016).

Making decisions. A woman has many important decisions to make after the discovery of her husband's infidelity. She will often plead for me to make them for her because she does not know what to do. Should I stay? Should I make him leave? Do the kids need to know? Should I keep being sexual with him? These issues provide an opportunity for talking about "listening to herself" and what that means. For many of us, I tell her, life is so fast paced that it is difficult to hear God's voice, the Holy Spirit within us. And furthermore, many women may not have been encouraged to make decisions for themselves, so their decision-making "muscles" are rather undeveloped. I remind her that another part of growing will be practicing listening to that "still small voice" within for direction. Jesus taught this in John 14:16–17, when he said that we will receive "the Spirit of truth" to guide us from within.

Slowing down reactions and decisions will be another part of making wise choices. Slowing down allows for the client to listen carefully, to check out her motivations, and to sit with her decision awhile before actually following through. A decision aligned with God's path for her will feel life giving, not draining. She will feel more peace. The more she practices making decisions with the Spirit's presence, the more confidence she will gain in trusting

that she has all she needs within to walk through difficult decisions.

The roller coaster ride. A common perception is that once a woman has help, she will have a slow but smooth ride to a better future. Unfortunately, that generally is not the case. I find that it is helpful to name what is normal: the journey will seem like a scary roller coaster ride with emotions coming and going and thoughts of both hopefulness and hopelessness lacing the client's days. We talk about the fact that this can be a healthy sign of progress, because historically the client was probably finding ways to medicate negative feelings and thoughts so as not to deal with them. When she starts eliminating coping behaviors and substances in the recovery process, the whole scope of feelings and thoughts emerge. They are right there, interrupting her days. This is the beginning of becoming more authentic. It is normal. She will have a gentler, smoother ride in the future if she can hang on for now.

The ampersand—the concept of both/and. I teach betrayed women the concept of the "ampersand" as soon as possible. The Bible says it this way: "It is good to grasp the one and not let go of the other. Whoever fears God will avoid all extremes" (Eccl. 7:18). As we seek to live in the truth, we recognize that the truth is often complicated. The language of many people who are describing their thoughts or situations is very black and white—in other words, the truth is either "this" or "that." It is an "either/or" statement with no room for another possibility. Black-and-white thinking can be easier in that there are no choices. But what if we hold

588 Clinical Issue–Based Strategies

two different feelings about something or two different thoughts about a situation and both are true at the same time? That can certainly create tension in a person's mind and heart. And when something is uncomfortable, we want to go back to an easy answer—a black-and-white one—to resolve that inner tension. But reality is complex. We believe that if we are to speak truth to one another, we need to learn to look for the "both/and," the "ampersand." We need to surrender our black-and-white thinking and embrace "gray."

So, we explore a couple of examples together. A client might say, "I am staying because I love my husband and family" *and* "I hate him for what he has done." Or another might say, "I love being held and heard about my sadness" *and* "I can't stand for him to touch me." If we use "but" in place of our ampersand, then the first part of the sentence is negated—and the statements become only a partial truth. The ampersand allows for the truth to be more complicated. And it helps a hurting woman make sense of her confusion.

Managing anger. Maya Angelou (n.d., para. 7) once said, "I've learned that even when I have pains, I don't have to be one." I've always liked that quote. I want women to learn to express all their feelings, including anger and frustration. If we work on being authentic, we cannot hide away the difficult emotions and not expect them to "leak out" onto other people or "leak into" our bodies and do physical harm. The journey to living a Christlike life, however, is going to challenge us not to sin in our anger. That is a huge challenge when you have been betrayed. And

yet that is our goal: to like the person we are and how we respond to others when we are in pain. The truth is also that if we desire to be heard about this pain, yelling at someone or throwing stuff or being out of control is only going to drive the other person away. We sabotage the very thing we want. Learning what to do to slow down reactions and be intentional about talking about pain in a healthy way is an important part of building a healthy relationship.

Educating about sexual addiction. I teach that the healing journey for a betrayed woman is more than just watching her husband stop behaviors. A behavioral approach to getting well focuses on stopping behaviors. Period. I share with her that we want to understand root causes of behaviors. Root causes are very old, older than her relationship with her husband, I remind her. The "why" will help her understand how his sexual acting out has been used to medicate unwanted feelings and to serve some desire of his heart that was not getting met. Unfortunately, his choices were unhealthy ones and eventually led to more pain and distance in their relationship.

When we understand the "why" for someone else's behaviors, we can hopefully "depersonalize" those choices. This understanding is important if a wife is ever to reframe her beliefs about her trauma. It is also crucial for trusting that the future can be different. If she doesn't know why something happened, then she will struggle to trust that her husband can walk through life in a sexually saturated world, avoiding the land mines of temptation. I ask betrayed wives to read *Healing the Wounds of Sexual Addiction* (Laaser, 1991, 1992,

1996, 2004, 2009, 2014), *Out of the Shadows* (Carnes, 1983, 1992, 2001), or books by other reputable leaders in the field of sexual addiction to learn about addiction and the process of looking for causes. I also remind them that there are other authors writing about sexual addiction who will still want to make them responsible for their husbands' sobriety. They will need to discern what information fits their beliefs.

Living in truth. Most women I counsel know about infidelity because *they* found it. Their searching, policing, or detective work led them to information of their husbands' infidelity. When confronting their spouses, there may have been denial at first. Eventually there may have been some confession of at least some of the truth. What I see is that many women cannot stop being detectives. They hate that they are doing it, and yet they are driven to find the truth—the whole truth. I ask in our sessions whether a woman believes she knows the whole truth. She might say that she has gotten the "installment plan" as I have called it—little bits of the truth over several weeks or months of interrogating. Others say that if they ask questions, their husbands will answer them, but they offer no additional information. Other women report that they don't know if they have all the truth. Beth, in our case study, struggled with this. She hated herself for "snooping around" as she called it, and she could not stop herself. It is understandable. I believe that women who continue to search for information or ask many questions do not have the whole truth. Their intuitive knowing (I believe the Holy Spirit within) wants them to live in truth (1 John 1:5–7).

Our whole being longs to live in truth, and we will do whatever it takes to find it. The problem is, if we search for information or ask questions to get it, we may always wonder if we have looked thoroughly enough or asked enough questions. We will never live in truth unless we are *offered* information. At our counseling center, we lead a couple through a process of "full disclosure" that allows a husband who has lied and hidden his double life to willingly *offer* the story of his life to his wife. For more information about our process, we have created a PDF that is available in our bookstore at faithfulandtrue.com (Laaser & Laaser, 2016a).

Without truth, you can feel crazy. I validate this feeling that betrayed women have felt. Some have not only been lied to for many years, but others have also been blamed for or denied their reality when they have tried to talk about it. When women's internal reality screams, *Something is wrong!* and their external reality is denied by their spouses, a tension is created that confuses their brains and bodies. Many women begin to believe there is something wrong with them. Others carry this confusion in their bodies and struggle with physical pain of some kind. Building trust in the relationship begins here—with truth. All betrayed women need it. Any man who seeks to restore his relationship needs to provide it. It is that simple.

Rebuilding trust. This is the million-dollar question that all betrayed women ask, including Beth: Is it possible to rebuild trust, and if so, how? In my research (Laaser, 2013), I found that these behaviors by the husband created the most trust:

1. He owned that he had a problem.
2. He was broken and remorseful for what he did.
3. He entered counseling.
4. He worked at restoring safety in the relationship (this could be emotional, physical, sexual, spiritual, and/or financial).
5. He was noticeably a "different person" after he got help.
6. He was willing to disclose all information about betrayal.
7. He created boundaries for himself to resist future sexual or emotional temptations.

I would also add that the husband's offering *daily* information about his sobriety is extremely helpful in building trust. In *Shattered Vows* (Laaser, 2008, p. 185), a check-in is described for couples to stay connected that provides for this sharing. It is called "FANOS." Each letter stands for something that will be shared by spouses every day: F = feelings; A = affirmation of your spouse; N = a practical need you have; O = owning something you did, saying you are sorry; and S = a statement about sobriety for the addict (or for the wife, a check-in about something she is working to change about herself).

These behaviors and heart changes represent a man who is working on *becoming trustworthy*. They are a vital part of rebuilding the wife's trust. She also needs to work on *trusting herself*, something we discuss in counseling. All women I have counseled who experienced betrayal have said that there were "signs" from the past that things were not right. They had hunches, red flags, intuition, or some holy whispers of truth that they talked themselves out of believing and justified in some way: "I thought all men did this," or "I know he is just a really kind person, so all the attention to other women seemed like part of his personality," or "When he said he had to stay up late at night to work, I believed him." Beth talked herself out of her hunches too. She thought her husband's overly friendly nature was just who he was and that his excuses to stay up late were probably legitimate.

Once the truth about a husband's behaviors is known, it is much easier to make sense of these signs. We are learning to trust, though, that our bodies don't lie to us. Our emotions or physical reactions are usually telling us something. We are not crazy for noticing them, and we will pursue figuring out what they are saying. We betrayed ourselves in the past when we ignored important "knowings." Learning to trust ourselves is something I encourage women to practice. I encourage them also to have a community of other safe people with whom they can share these signs. As we are learning to trust ourselves, others who are further along in this journey can be voices of wisdom to present other possibilities or meanings for the inner truths we are listening to. This is a process to gain confidence in the Holy Spirit within while being open to other possibilities.

Finally, we explore what it means to trust God more completely. A betrayed woman will learn how to advocate for her needs and to have a voice about things that matter to her. She will do what she can, and then she will begin surrendering to God and his plan for her. The timing of things is often hard to understand. What we want takes much longer than we have patience for. But we learn that God's timing, whatever it is, will be perfect. We don't always know what to do, but when we decide on the next right step and turn it over to God, we wait to see where he will lead—"Whether you turn to the right or to the left, your ears will hear a voice behind you, saying, 'This is the way; walk in it'" (Isa. 30:21).

If we can't seem to get information that we need to feel at peace, we ask for God's help to provide what is important. If we have financial concerns for getting the help we need with no solution in sight, we turn to God for his help. If a spouse is not taking his recovery seriously, she learns to surrender him to God. I have witnessed in most of the women I counsel through betrayal that their dependence on God grows beyond what they have ever experienced. Their peace and trust come from a deep knowing that God is truly "in charge of it all"—their spouse, their future, and their well-being. This new kind of trust building—watching to see whether a spouse is working on being trustworthy, learning to trust self, and trusting God— is very different than the simplistic trust of earlier days.

Boundaries and bottom lines. Boundaries are simply needs or desires we have. Sometimes it is for something we need to happen. Sometimes it is for something to stop. Beth had some difficulty knowing what she needed when I first asked. I suggested (a need) that she get help with her inability to sleep. We

also landed on a need she had to have others to talk to. And then she got going with other needs: "I won't be quiet about this anymore. I need him to get help, and I need a faithful husband!" Expressing needs and desires is often a new experience for women. Most haven't thought about what they need; they take care of things by themselves. Many don't feel as if they can have needs. I encourage women to listen to their feelings because they are often the messengers of something they need. If a woman is feeling afraid, for instance, she may be worrying that her husband will not continue to provide financially for her, and she needs to know. If she is resentful, she may need help from her husband because she is doing too much for the family. If she is lonely, she might think about how to spend more time with others or find new friends. Feelings are great messengers if we will learn to identify them and then take them seriously. Women who are intentional about asking for what they need begin to feel more empowered and at peace. They realize they can be agents for change.

Bottom lines are boundaries that are absolutes. They are nonnegotiable needs. Women learn to distinguish between which of their needs/desires they are willing to wait for, get met in alternative ways, or surrender altogether, and which ones are nonnegotiable. They also learn that it will be important to be ready to *do* something about a bottom line, not just speak about it. Action is what can be difficult. So as not to make a need a threat to a spouse, it is possible for a woman to have a bottom line and not know today exactly what her action would be. She does not need to know or share that next step; she can simply know that her need is extremely important to her, and if it is not met, she will be considering what she will decide to do.

Sometimes we change our minds about how to act. Other times we get new information that leads to a different action step. Beth's bottom line was that she would not tolerate any more sexual or emotional affairs. She hadn't shared this bottom line with her husband, but she knew it in her heart. She was considering her action steps if her husband did have another affair.

I find that most women have not been attentive to their own needs and desires. In fact, I experience that most women I work with do not even know what they need or desire. In many of the stories I hear, I am told that they have been taught that they should not have needs because having needs is selfish. They are only to serve the needs of others. In one of my therapy groups this week, all eight of the women chuckled and agreed that they were experts at taking care of others' needs, but they were not good at knowing or caring for their own.

Jesus was continually taking care of the needs of people: a wedding party needed more wine; a lame man by a pool needed to be healed; five thousand hungry people needed food; Mary and Martha needed their brother to be raised from the dead; terrified disciples on a rough lake needed the waters to be calmed. Jesus himself needed to get away from the crowds. He needed some close friends. He needed meaningful conversation. The stories about needs are abundant, and many Scriptures speak to our needs: "The LORD will guide you always; he will satisfy your needs" (Isa. 58:11). "Your Father knows what you need before you ask him" (Matt. 6:8). "Do not be anxious about anything, but in every situation . . . present your requests to God" (Phil. 4:6). I find the greater problem in a woman's healing journey is figuring out what she does need and finding a voice to speak about her needs.

Accountability partners. I occasionally hear a wife declare that she is her husband's accountability partner because he doesn't have anyone else to help him. Sometimes she has been advised to be in that role. I ask her how she likes that responsibility. I have never heard a wife say that it has felt "right." This gives us an opportunity to talk about the problem (in my opinion) of having a wife serve as an accountability partner. In this role, she becomes her husband's authority figure—a "parent," really. She has power over him, as he will be reporting to her, possibly be reprimanded by her if there are issues, and be under her leadership for his sobriety. This makes him the "child" to her "parenting" role. I have never seen this arrangement work long term. It may give her some temporary relief and control; it may give him a solution when he has not found other safe men on the journey.

The ideal relationship for growth is one in which we have two partners of equal value connecting emotionally, spiritually, and physically. Something is innately unsettling about a parent and a child trying to create a one-flesh union. It creates frustration and anger. If the betrayed wife believes this is a problem, too, we work to eliminate this parent-child dilemma in the husband's accountability by having her ask him to find other men to be in that role. And then we go to work on figuring out where else she may be "parenting" in their relationship, or where she has become the "child" herself. It is a big step in changing some very unhealthy patterns in the marriage.

Safe community. I talk to all women I counsel about the need for community. Since we only know what we know, I remind them that a group provides power that is just not available in one-on-one counseling. The stories of others provide rich information to broaden their thinking, their friendships, and their arena for practicing new ways of relating. A group is a place where a woman can talk about her pain, share all her emotions and thoughts, and take off a few "layers" of her emotional energy so as not to flood her husband with all of them. It is also a place where she can share her own shame and experience grace from her new friends.

Having safe women in community is indispensable. "A safe woman would be trustworthy and able to keep a confidence. She is a good listener and doesn't try to fix your situation; she doesn't judge your decisions; she is vulnerable about adversity in her own life; she affirms your efforts; she respects your desire not to share at times and doesn't pressure you; and she doesn't use your confidences to feel prideful in her relationship with you" (Laaser, 2008). I always spend time helping a client determine who are safe women for her, as it is essential to have companionship in her journey if she is to get well. I usually suggest that support groups and therapy groups are often places where safe community can be found. At the very least, a counselor can be a safe person to begin this community.

Reframing distorted beliefs. Relational betrayal shatters core beliefs. What a woman believes about herself, about her husband, and about her future becomes very distorted. _I must not have been enough for my husband_, she may believe, or _I will never be able to trust him again_, or _My life is ruined_, or _How can I talk to anyone about this?_ Helping a betrayed woman work through her distorted core beliefs is essential to relieving her pain. In fact, the pain of betrayal is caused by her shattered thoughts (Janoff-Bulman, 1992, p. 63). Cognitive restructuring is an integral part of individual counseling and group work—learning to name the beliefs initially, looking at how she has coped with the pain birthed by distorted beliefs, exploring truths, and being intentional about changing her behaviors to support her new truths is all part of this process.

Looking back at family of origin experiences to see what distorted beliefs were birthed there is also important. I slowly connect the pain of the past with any current pain so that women can understand the "snowball effect" of piling pain on top of pain. Flashbacks may be associated with PTSD initially created in earlier life experiences and now reintroduced by current trauma. These may also be the brain's attempt to work through shattered thoughts until truth is sorted out from distorted beliefs.

In Beth's story, she could not stop thinking about the woman her husband acted out with. In her case, she needed more information about his affair and who this woman was in case she ever ran into her. She also had some repressed experiences in her early life when her father betrayed her mother and no one was willing to talk about it. She needed to work through that pain as well. I have found psychotherapy, eye movement desensitization and reprocessing (EMDR), and experiential therapy to be helpful strategies to work through trauma. Also, there may be a need for brain assessment, especially looking at the anterior cingulate gyrus, to detect if there is any issue with obsessive-compulsive disorder (OCD) that keeps a woman "stuck" on negative thoughts. Brain dysfunction caused by PTSD can create increased anxiety, anger, depression, and/or hypervigilance. A woman's brain must be working well if she wants to be well (Amen, 1998, 2015, pp. 141–142).

Neurochemistry is included in many of the workshops in the mental health field now. Mental health professionals are seeing that brain health affects emotional, physical, and spiritual health, and activities associated with the brain must be included in a treatment plan if the client is going to get well. If a client struggles with anxiety, depression, attention deficit disorder (ADD), emotional dysregulation, sleep disorders, or the like, the clinical work that you are doing to make the needed and desired changes may be thwarted. We have certainly found that to be true for many of our clients in our counseling practice, even though they have been committed and desiring of change all along.

Knowing whether to stay or leave. Reconciliation is often determined by current decisions a husband is making: Is he getting help for his infidelity, or has he returned to his secretive, sinful life? Is he still struggling with sobriety? Is there still sexual pressure or sexual anorexia (i.e., sexual avoidance) in marriage? Does he still have angry outbursts or persist in emotional abuse? Has he refused to get help for mental health issues that get in the way of "being well"? Has he switched to other addictive behaviors or substances (labeled "addiction interaction" in the field of sexual addiction)?

Of course, if I am helping a betrayed woman, I will want her to answer these questions. No marriage will change if only one person is changing in the system. If she has done her work and she perceives that her husband has not, she may be aligned with this woman's comment: "I am no longer willing to sacrifice my health, my children's health, or my sanity to stay in my marriage." One danger I see is a woman who has no bottom line for what she will tolerate in her marriage. This only contributes to a life of being a victim. I will never advise a woman about staying or leaving. That must always be her choice. We will explore the decisions she is making to understand the motivation, the fears, or the roadblocks to feeling confident about her choice. And I will always remind her that she has choices.

Forgiveness. Choosing to forgive the past is a process. In my research (Laaser et al., 2017), women stated that the worst advice they were given was to "forgive and forget" immediately. Quick forgiveness, I have found, does not give a hurting woman a chance to process her pain, and thus she ends up carrying it with her into the future. It also enables a betraying husband to avoid taking his recovery seriously. We might even call it "cheap grace," for it often contributes to future relapse when no work was done to change the root causes of acting out. I also believe that a betrayed woman needs to know *what* she is forgiving (which she does not fully know until there is a full disclosure process). She needs to have a chance to move through the emotions of the losses and to have a voice about what has happened.

Forgiveness assumes the behaviors have stopped, so the wife must know current information about the betraying husband's sobriety. For many women, clarifying that forgiveness is a different decision than that of reconciliation is important. Forgiveness is a complicated decision and needs time if it is to be heartfelt and lived out. I remind women that the decision to stay and work on betrayal pain is a first step to forgiveness (Laaser, 2008, pp. 201–212).

Overriding old associations. The hope that a betrayed woman holds is that someday things can be different, healthier. We talk about the hope of transformation, which begins when we "override" the old associations of pain and acting out with new experiences. A betrayed wife may be noticing that her husband is different—he has a heart change, his behaviors are changing, he is sober, he has healthy self-care practices—and as a couple, new experiences are slowly replacing the old ones. This is a stage of recovery in which we devote time to creating vision. What does the wife want her life to be? Where does she find purpose and passion? And in her marriage, what do she and her husband

want to be proactive about in creating the healthy life they long for? I also help the wife work on eliminating her maladaptive coping behaviors/substances, taking care of mental health issues (anxiety, depression, OCD, PTSD, sleep issues, attention-deficit/hyperactivity disorder [ADHD]), being alone and alright if necessary, and thereby choosing the relationship out of love, not need. Each small step of putting in something healthier begins to replace the memories and patterns of unhealthier days. It overrides the old and makes room for the new.

Beth's story exemplifies these beliefs. One year later, Beth's life looked quite different. Both she and her husband committed to getting regular help. They both received individual counseling and joined therapy groups. They went to couple counseling and began reading books together. Beth said one day, "My whole life seems to be revolving around getting help! It's a full-time job." I agreed that the investment can be huge on the front end of recovery—and in my opinion, well worth the time and money spent to transform their lives. She said she could feel that she was changing. Life was getting better, more peaceful, and more authentic. She found that it was getting easier to talk to her husband; in fact, they were talking about things they had never talked about before. And yet recovery was hard, she admitted: "Sometimes I just want to run away from all of it and pretend this never happened to me."

After another year of counseling and group involvement, Beth shared some of the new joy she was experiencing: "I am learning about myself every day. I know I still have work to do with the pain I have inside. I'm still building trust, slowly. I'm now realizing my relationship with my husband doesn't just happen—we work on it daily. I have chosen to forgive him, and I'm working hard to focus on the new life we are creating. I know he is sober today, because he offers me that information regularly. I see it in the changed life he is living. I am a different person—a different mom and wife and friend. I am experiencing God's grace and love in a whole new way. My relationship with God is so much deeper today than it has ever been."

CONCLUSION

Women who have been betrayed come for help from many diverse situations, which makes it difficult to create a "one right way" treatment plan. Their pain is different, their knowledge is different, and their willingness to engage in a process of healing is different. As a counselor, it is important to join a betrayed woman at *her* place of the journey, slowly offering her resources, information, and insight at the pace she can handle. We want her to "work on herself" and heal from this betrayal, but what does that mean exactly? The usual perception is that her husband is what we need to work on! His journey seems more straightforward: stop acting out.

What is most difficult for the betrayed woman, I believe, is that her end goal is unclear and confusing when she begins this journey. Is it waiting for her spouse to get well? To stop his infidelity? Will she be fine if he is fine? Explaining to her that a healing journey is much more than waiting for

a husband to be sober is difficult. Knowing that there is opportunity for her to grow through this painful circumstance is even harder to portray. Usually I find that it is a slow process of her trusting the counselor to lead her one day at a time to a new life.

There is also no "one right timetable" to the betrayed wife's journey. God's timing is amazingly different for each client. We must be patient with differences that arise in the healing journeys of women. One woman I counseled waited three years for full disclosure. One woman knowingly allowed her spouse to be in an active affair for one and a half years while getting help herself. What I would tolerate or need is often very different from what a counselee might need. I have learned to withhold my judgment and advice while helping wives explore their decisions. God has worked in many of these situations with amazing outcomes.

If we believe that God dwells in us, then my job as a counselor is to help my clients access the truth that is uniquely theirs. We can ponder choices together. We can explore the motivation of their decisions together. We can look at fears that keep them stuck or seeking others' advice for them instead of trusting their own. I teach women to trust themselves and God as they make each next right step.

Research indicates that betrayed women who over time had recovery resources and engaged in therapeutic activities experienced significant post-traumatic growth. Furthermore, women who reported symptoms of PTSD from relational betrayal experienced *greater* PTG than those who had not met the criteria of PTSD (Laaser et al., 2017). Having confirmation of the positive outcomes that are available to betrayed women is encouraging.

Foundationally, the journey of a betrayed spouse is a spiritual journey. Instead of asking, "Why me?" she learns to ask, "What would you have me learn, God? How can I find purpose in this pain?" Betrayal can be an opportunity for PTG. Trauma can transform. Despair and growth can coexist.

Sharing with a client that the healing journey is available to all betrayed women, whether their husbands get well/sober or not, is paramount. Growth happens when we look at how "*I* want to change"—to be the person God calls me to be. A woman's sanctification is not dependent on anyone else. No one can stand in the way of her becoming more Christlike. In fact, it is when we are in the greatest pain that our true character is most revealed.

Consider it pure joy, my brothers and sisters, whenever you face trials of many kinds, because you know that the testing of your faith produces perseverance. Let perseverance finish its work so that you may be mature and complete, not lacking anything. (James 1:2–4)

RECOMMENDED READING

Beattie, M. (1987). *Codependent no more.* New York, NY: Harper/Hazelden.

Beattie, M. (1990). *Codependents' guide to the twelve steps.* New York, NY: Simon & Schuster.

Beattie, M. (1990). *The language of letting go.* Center City, MN: Hazelden.

Carnes, P. (1983, 2001). *Out of the shadows.* Center City, MN: Hazelden.

Carnes, P. (1997). *The betrayal bond.* Deerfield Beach, FL: Health Communications.

Janoff-Bulman, R. (1992). *Shattered assumptions: Towards a new psychology of trauma.* New York, NY: Free Press.

Kendall, R. T. (2002). *Total forgiveness.* Lake Mary, FL: Charisma House.

Kidd, S. M. (1990). *When the heart waits.* New York, NY: HarperCollins.

Laaser, D. (2008). *Shattered vows.* Grand Rapids, MI: Zondervan.

Laaser, M., & Laaser, D. (2008). *Seven desires.* Grand Rapids, MI: Zondervan.

Langberg, D. (1999). *On the threshold of hope.* Wheaton, IL: Tyndale.

Love, P. (1990). *Emotional incest syndrome.* New York, NY: Bantam.

Mellody, P. (1989). *Facing codependence.* San Francisco, CA: HarperSanFrancisco.

Nouwen, H. (1994). *The return of the prodigal son.* New York, NY: Image.

Tedeschi, R. G., & Calhoun, L. G. (1995). *Trauma and transformation: Growing in the aftermath of suffering.* Thousand Oaks, CA: Sage.

Vernick, L. (2013). *The emotionally destructive marriage.* Colorado Springs, CO: WaterBrook.

CHAPTER 28

Couple Sexual Problems–Focused Strategies

Michael Sytsma, PhD

> Let my beloved come into his garden
> and taste its choice fruits. . . .
> Eat, friends, and drink;
> drink your fill of love.
>
> **SONG OF SONGS 4:16; 5:1**

Virtually every couple experiences some level of sexual problem at some point in their lives and marriage.[*] Actual prevalence rates of sexual problems vary depending on how "problem" is defined and the population assessed, but between 40 and 50 percent of women and up to 100 percent of men report at least one sexual dysfunction by their eighties (McCabe et al., 2016b). As high as these rates appear, they do not include sexual problems that fail to reach a clinically significant level. As many as 49 percent of couples consider seeking professional help related to sexual desire discrepancy in marriage (Sytsma, 2004), a common couple sexual problem that does not meet dysfunctional criteria.

With such a high prevalence of sexual problems, most couples who seek counseling will present with sexual issues. The issues they present with may be the primary problem bringing them to therapy (i.e., unconsummated marriage or inability to orgasm), or they may arise while the couple are working on other issues (i.e., lack of sexual desire secondary to primary depression), but they will be there. Therefore, you need skills and training for addressing sexual problems.

After a brief consideration of the theology and psychology of sexual problems, I will introduce a few illustrative case examples. I will discuss preparing yourself for working with sexual issues, identifying different types of sexual issues, and becoming knowledgeable about common

---

[*] The author offers special thanks to Hailey Whitley, MS, and Andrea Farnham, PhD candidate, for assisting with editing this chapter.

etiologies. I will also describe in detail one of the most commonly used models for counseling sexual issues, the DEC-R: dialogue, educate, coach, and refer (Rosenau, Sytsma, & Taylor, 2002), using multiple case illustrations.

THEOLOGY AND PSYCHOLOGY OF SEXUAL PROBLEMS

The church continues to develop a working theology of sexuality (Rosenau & Sytsma, 2004). If one holds to a more restrictive view that deems sex as solely about procreation, many of the issues couples bring cease to be legitimate—except for erectile dysfunction and inability to orgasm in the male since they directly prevent procreation. If, however, sex is about intimacy, oneness, and sharing pleasure with each other, a stronger, more comprehensive foundation is necessary to competently address the sexual problems with which your clients will inevitably present.

Most modern Christian authors believe sex was created by God and is intrinsically good, including its consequences (pleasure, procreation, connection, etc.). Our sexual parts, and the way they are designed to function, are part of God's perfect, reflective design. For example, the rush of oxytocin that accompanies partnered orgasm chemically binds a couple. Sex is indeed good. In fact, very good since God's response to creating man and woman was "very good" (Gen. 1:26–27, 31; Ps. 139:13–14; Eph. 2:10).

Under such a theology of sex, sexual pleasure and desire are not sinful, but sin distorts how fallen creatures treat sexual desire and function. To keep sex sacred and protect a design of monogamous bonding, God placed boundaries around sex. Honoring these boundaries can keep sex beautiful and meaningful. Still, God allows us to ignore his boundaries and pursue our ungodly desires to our own detriment (Rom. 1:18–32). Many of the sexual problems couples bring to counseling are the result of not pursuing God's ideal nor honoring God's boundaries. Others are simply the effects of living in a sin-marred world.

From this perspective, counseling for sexual problems becomes a matter of helping couples pursue God's intended design for sex. Couples are counseled in a sexuality that reflects both how God pursues us and how Scripture models sexual connection (e.g., Song of Songs). Healthy sex includes a desire for intimate connection and initiation reflective of how God desires and pursues us. It includes a receptivity and passion we are called to in responding to him. In helping couples pursue God's design for them, we assist with arousal and orgasmic problems as well as helping combat pain and unhealthy trauma pairings. We often help couples increase sexual discipline to better keep them moving forward in boundaried, honoring, playful, and passionate sexual connecting that further bonds them emotionally, physically, and spiritually.

At their core, theories of sexual response (see below) are not inconsistent with this theological integration. While various theories may disagree on the how and why, most will hold to primary concepts of desire, initiation, arousal, orgasm, resolution, and absence of unwanted pain. The primary arena for disagreement might be where, and if, to draw boundaries on sexual behavior. While the handling of atypical sexual behavior (kink), extramarital sex, and the primary goals of sex (pleasure, intimacy, connection, etc.) may be disagreed upon, decreasing subjective sexual distress is generally viewed as a worthy therapeutic goal.

Because sexual problems are so common, virtually every counseling theory speaks to sex therapy. While the most common interventions tend to follow a Masters and Johnson behavioral model (1966, 1970), sex therapy may also be addressed from psychodynamic (Scharff, 1998), systemic (Hertlein, Weeks, & Gambescia, 2015), narrative (Findlay, 2017), emotionally focused (S. M. Johnson, 2017), brief (Green, Flemons, & Flemons, 2007), and internal family systems (Schwartz, 2003), as well as other models. The recommended reading list at the end of the chapter provides useful resources to further explore the integration, theology, or psychology of sexual problems. Otherwise, this chapter will guide you in biblically consistent and evidence-based basic strategies for addressing sexual problems.

CASE STUDIES

Because sexual problems are highly varied in etiology, presentation, and methodology, it is not possible to identify a typical case for sexual problems. A few common scenarios are presented below, and additional case vignettes are scattered throughout the chapter.

Case One

Lloyd and Jenny are in their midsixties and have been married for thirty-eight years. They present for counseling due to "problems getting it up," but report a good sex life with normal frequency struggles throughout their marriage. Both deny history of sexual pain or difficulty with arousal or orgasm. Lloyd reports he is occasionally able to obtain and maintain an erection, but more recently erections have become unreliable. Jenny fears he no longer finds her aging body attractive. Both exhibit a high level of anxiety, resulting in them pulling apart and initiating physical touch less often.

Case Two

Kurt and Susan, a married couple in their late thirties, present for counseling due to growing conflict. This is the second marriage for both. Though they report an overall positive marriage, fighting over sexual frequency has become an increasing strain on their closeness. They report that sexual frequency has been declining, and Kurt's anger has been increasing. They have sought counseling after a bad fight, in which Susan agreed to come to counseling so she could be "fixed."

Case Three

Jim and Terri are a newly married couple in their midtwenties presenting for sexual counseling because Jim has been ejaculating within seconds of penetration. This is causing both spouses a high level of sexual frustration. Terri is upset at the lack of fulfillment in their sexual encounters, and Jim has become even more afraid of disappointing both of them. His feelings of inadequacy and her desire to protect his ego have left them distanced. This has dramatically decreased their desire to engage in sexual play and has exacerbated the problem.

Case Four

Carter and Kristi are in their early thirties and have been married for several years. They present for counseling because Kristi has never had an orgasm with Carter. At first, Kristi presented to have an orgasm, believing it to be important to Carter. In fact, he would pride himself on being able to please his wife every time they made love. He was shocked and devastated when he learned that Kristi had been "faking it all along." Not only had their sexual relationship been impaired by the discovery of that fact, but their entire relationship became unstable due to senses of betrayal and demandingness that each experienced.

STRATEGIES, INTERVENTIONS, AND TECHNIQUES FOR COUPLE SEXUAL PROBLEMS

The first strategy one should always employ when working with sexual issues is preparation; however, preparation alone is insufficient. Also imperative is accurately identifying the problem(s), as clients may not always be aware. Determining whether a problem is related to disease, dysfunction, or discomfort is one strategy for identifying the problem(s). Additionally, it is imperative that you and your clients work together to explore the etiology of sexu-

al problems. While etiology exploration should not necessarily be or remain the focus of counseling, it is important, and issues such as lack of knowledge or poor communication should be investigated.

Preparing Yourself for the Work

Possibly more than any other type of counseling, working with sexual problems requires you to prepare yourself for the work (Turns, Morris, & Lentz, 2013). "Self-of-the-therapist" work (Aponte, 1994; Timm & Blow, 1999) includes sorting through one's own sexual history, developing a theology of sexuality, and becoming well educated in sexual anatomy, physiology, and sex therapy (Rosenau, Sytsma, & Taylor, 2002).

Prepare yourself to experience some level of sexual attraction within the counseling relationship at some point in your career. Sexual attraction *toward* clients and *from* clients is normal (Giovazolias & Davis, 2001) and can feel especially powerful during couple counseling (Harris, 2001). It is, thus, risky and unadvisable to counsel sexual issues without the support of peers, colleagues, and/or supervisors. Luca and Boyden (2014) found that denial and avoidance are common even in experienced counselors when it comes to issues of sexual attraction. Supervision, or at least peer consult, can keep the power of sexual attraction in check (Pope & Bouhoutsos, 1986). It is not a matter of *if* you will experience sexual attraction but *when* and how to ethically navigate this common unspoken dynamic (Luca, 2014). While feeling slightly uncomfortable when talking about sacred, private issues with someone whom you are not intimate with is healthy and desensitizing, learning to center yourself is essential. A well-prepared, confident, young female counselor can work with many couples of whom the husband struggles with erectile difficulty. If the counselor is uncomfortable with her own sexuality, however, the client's discomfort will increase, and the process and progress of therapy will short circuit. Learning to handle sexual flirting, direct sexual statements, and reflexive sexual responses are important aspects of preparing yourself for working with couple sexual problems.

Additionally, prepare yourself to hear great brokenness. Individuals often carry enormous shame when it comes to their sexuality. For years, I have read or listened to more than two hundred sexual autobiographies per year. No matter the nature of the writer's personal story, shame is virtually always present. If you are unable to deeply care for the individual behind the behavior, you will only reinforce his or her shame and cause more harm rather than becoming an agent of reconciliation (2 Cor. 5:16–21).

Relatedly, some client stories may feel offensive to you. Hearing someone discuss their proclivity toward child or incest pornography could understandably raise strong emotions. Learn to see past the offensive desire or behavior to care for the intense level of shame and out-of-control feelings of the individual. Otherwise, unwittingly, you may align with the terrified, condemning spouse; affirm the spouse's fear; add to the woundedness of the individual struggling; or exacerbate the damage and distance in the relationship. If you

are able to lean in and care for the shame, understand the origination of the interest, and hang on to hope for change, the potential to rebalance the system and find a path for healing remains possible.

Finally, if you are unwilling or unable to do work with sexuality, avoid treating sexual issues. Much damage can be done toward clients through unintentional messages of shame and condemnation, even by well-meaning counselors. Clients who share their sexual problems are vulnerable. Your duty is to do no harm and be mindful and respectful of when you are not the person best equipped to help. Know when to refer, and be humble enough to do so.

Identifying the Sexual Problem

While the problem might seem obvious, couples often wrongly identify it. It may also be one of myriad problems. For example, one partner complains that his spouse lacks desire, but further investigation reveals that she experiences pain during sex, and thus treating the pain becomes primary. While Lloyd and Jenny reported erectile dysfunction (ED) as the presenting problem, a thorough evaluation revealed the need to grieve a normal aging process instead. Failure to accurately identify the problem will likely result in choosing ineffective treatment strategies.

Sexual dysfunction nosology is a debated issue (Derogatis, Sand, Balon, Rosen, & Parish, 2016; Parish et al., 2016) and defined slightly differently by the DSM-5 (American Psychiatric Association, 2013), International Classification of Diseases, tenth edition (ICD-10; World Health Organization, 2016), and International Consultation of Sexual Medicine (ICSM; Mc-Cabe et al., 2016a). Generally three broad categories remain consistent: (1) a defined dysfunction (i.e., arousal, orgasm, pain, etc.), (2) problem severity, and (3) subsequent distress. Couples also seek help for problems that don't meet clinical criteria. Disagreement over sexual practices, for example, is a common problem but does not meet diagnostic criteria.

One helpful way to conceptualize the presenting problem is to determine if it is a disease, dysfunction, or discomfort. While the problem often fits partially into all three, one of these categories is typically prominent. The nuances of each are described below.

Disease. A sexually impactful disease is outside the realm of the counselor, but the backlash of the disease can be addressed in counseling. A lack of ejaculation after removal of the prostate and seminal vesicles due to prostate surgery is one example. Other examples include erectile dysfunction caused by diabetes, inability to have intercourse due to lichen sclerosis, or changes in sexual function after surgery affecting the genital nerves. For sexual problems caused by a disease, regaining full sexual functioning is typically not a viable counseling goal. Instead, helping the couple to grieve the loss of ideal sexual functioning and pursue creative, healthy sexual connection despite the disease is a valuable goal.

Dysfunction. This category includes problems defined by clinical taxonomies as sexual dysfunctions, which have defined protocols necessitating training (e.g., Metz & McCarthy, 2004, for ED). While diagnosed as individual issues (e.g., erectile dysfunction, female orgasmic disorder), relational problems are typical and are often treated successfully in a dyadic context (Harvey, Wenzel, & Sprecher 2004). See table 28.1 for a list of the sexual dysfunctions with their ICD-10 codes.

Discomfort. A host of sexual problems do not meet criteria for a disease or dysfunction but are a significant source of distress for couples. Disagreements about sexual positions, frequency, and practices are common. A spouse pressuring the other for oral sex, for example, does not

Table 28.1 ICD-10 Nosology for sexual dysfunction

F520 Hypoactive sexual disorder	F524 Premature ejaculation
F221 Sexual aversion disorder	F525 Vaginismus not due to a substance or known physiological condition
F5221 Male erectile disorder	F526 Dyspareunia not due to substance or known physiological condition
F5222 Female sexual arousal disorder	F528 Other sexual dysfunction not due to a substance or known physiological condition
F5231 Female orgasmic disorder	F529 Unspecified sexual dysfunction not due to a substance or known physiological condition
F5231 Male orgasmic disorder	

meet criteria for sexual dysfunction and is rarely related to disease. Yet this behavior can cause significant distress that is both symptomatic of, and generalizes to, other areas in their relationship. Watch for these issues, and be well prepared with strategies to guide couples toward resolution.

ETIOLOGY OF SEXUAL PROBLEMS

The etiology for specific sexual problems is almost always complex and varied. Avoid obvious conceptualizations or oversimplifying cause and effect. The result is often blaming and pointing fingers. Kurt (case two) reported, "We are here because my wife never wants sex. She was abused as a kid, and that's caused her to not like sex." While Susan's childhood sexual abuse is certainly part of the puzzle, it is only part. Kurt's attitude toward her, as revealed by how he shared her story, may be a larger piece and more indicative of the true problem. Imagine the difference if instead of blaming Susan and her trauma, Kurt was sympathetic and desired to create a new experience of sex for her. Encourage both partners to take responsibility for their contribution to the dysfunctional pattern without blaming either of them as the "cause." Responsibility, not blame, is key for moving forward as each understands the contributions made by both without the language of causation and blame.

"Everything is something, and nothing is everything" is a good principle when sorting through the causes of sexual problems. Watch for multiple causes and contributions, and the complex interrelations among them. One important strategy is helping a couple think complexly about their sexuality. Consider the following statement said to Kurt.

It has been my experience, and I believe this is supported by the research, that low sexual desire is like a table held up by six different legs. There are likely several valid reasons (or legs) as to why Susan may not express sexual desire. A six-legged table, for example, is quite stable. Even if we can identify three of the legs and remove them, a three-legged table is still quite stable. Sometimes there is a pedestal in the middle like sexual abuse, but it is never the only support. Your wife, and her sexuality, are more than just a result of a traumatic past. She is more complex than that. Let's explore what other issues might be contributing to this lack of desire.

Whether one uses narrative (Brown & Augusta-Scott, 2007; White, 2007), internal family systems (Schwartz, 2013), cognitive reframing (LoPiccolo & Friedman, 1988), or another preferred method, guiding the couple to explore the larger picture is key to creating an effective treatment plan.

While etiology is important, avoid getting stuck trying to figure out *the* cause. Some common themes are apparent, however, in contributing to couple sexual problems.

Lack of knowledge. Become well educated on human sexuality. Myths and misinformation often cause problems for couples and include the following.

Basic anatomy and physiology. A lack of knowledge about body parts and their design is core to many sexual problems. For example, couples who seek counseling for female orgasmic disorder (American Psychiatric Association, 2013) may be treating the vagina like an inverted penis and expect vaginal penetration to be sufficient for an orgasm. Many couples believe because direct stimulation to the penis alone can be enough for a male orgasm, direct stimulation to the vagina alone should suffice. Learning that the clitoris, rather than the vagina, is the homologous organ to the penis can entirely change the approach to sex. Most women need clitoral stimulation to orgasm and physically cannot achieve orgasm through vaginal penetration alone.

Effects of aging. Significant physiological changes arise as aging occurs. The refractory period, or latency time, between male orgasms tends to increase as men age. If either spouse expects the man's body (and sexuality) to parallel that of an eighteen-year-old, sexual problems can arise (as with Lloyd and Jenny). Similarly for women, decreased vaginal elasticity and natural lubrication may mean sex becomes painful. In addition to medication or artificial lubricants, education can help with normalization and encourage the couple to creatively problem solve.

Pregnancy and childbirth. Radical changes in the female's physiology (especially her hormonal makeup), stress, fatigue, self-competency, changing roles, and a host of other issues can cause significant sexual problems throughout pregnancy and childbirth (Serati et al., 2010; Slade, 2006; Williams, Herron-Marx, & Knibb, 2007).

Adjusting to changes in body composition following childbirth can also be difficult. Women (and sometimes the husband) often experience challenges embracing their altered bodies after giving birth (Olsson, Lundqvist, Faxelid, & Nissen, 2005).

Gender differences. Couples often lack correct information on the full impact of gender differences in physiology, hormones, sexual response cycles, and sexual desire. Each of these can contribute to significant distress in couple relationships. Couples often experience challenges understanding and appreciating how gender impacts sex. For example, on average men can reach orgasm within minutes of direct penile stimulation, whereas women take much longer to climax and require longer direct clitoral stimulation.

Fatigue and stress are also important areas that impact sex for men and women differently. Hart, Weber, and Taylor (1998) reported that the number one sexual problem women identified was not having enough energy for sex. How the woman's brain is wired versus a man's makes it much more challenging for women to tune out stressors and fatigue to focus on sexual pleasure. Consequently, relational tension occurs when the husband does not understand his wife's inability to have sex when tired (Hart et al., 1998). Fatigue can, therefore, be unintentionally minimized and considered an illegitimate excuse, creating resentment between partners. Whereas a husband feels rejected because he believes his wife is making excuses, the wife feels hurt and alienated because her husband does not seem to support or understand all of her stressors.

Poor sexual communication. A second common source of couple sexual problems is simply a lack of communication around sexual issues (Byers, 2011). Research has shown a positive correlation between sexual communication and sexual satisfaction (Babin, 2013; MacNeil & Byers, 2009). Frequently couples not only exhibit poor overall communication skills but bear evidence of not having communicated effectively to fully understand each other's perspective on the sexual problem.

An effective assessment is one strategy that begins to address this issue. During assessment, you gently walk couples through their typical sexual encounter (who initiates and how, what happens next, etc.), regularly asking to understand what is and isn't working ("And do you like doing it that way?"). After guiding couples through this discussion, it is common for them to acknowledge that they learned a lot from each other during the session. Rarely do couples discuss each step of their lovemaking, and if they like what they do, with each other. With your modeling as a base, encouraging them to continue the discussion or assigning other exercises listed below can help them continue their sexual communication.

Attributional errors related to sexual issues. Attributions are beliefs regarding the causes of an event (Heider, 1958; Weiner, 1986). An attribution framework has been applied to marriage (Bradbury, Beach, Fincham, & Nelson, 1996; Davey, Fincham, Beach, & Brody, 2001) and sexual issues (Fichten, Spector, & Libman, 1988; Loos, Bridges, & Critelli, 1987; Rowland, Kostelyk, & Tempel, 2016). Research has shown

the most predictive component of distress over sexual desire discrepancy was the attributional errors made by the high-desire spouse and the low-desire spouse regarding each other (Sytsma, 2004).

Even if the original source of a sexual problem is disease related (e.g., Lloyd's ED due to normal aging and low levels of testosterone), the attributions made by the individual or their spouse (e.g., "He cannot achieve an erection because he is not physically attracted to me") can significantly exacerbate any sexual problem. Asking "How do you explain it?" and "Why do you think that is so?" often reveals attributional errors.

Trauma. Because our sexuality is central to the core of who we are, trauma will often affect sexuality (Maltz, 2001). While it is possible for general trauma to impact our sexuality, sexual or relational trauma, such as rape, incest, or sexual abuse, is most likely to cause sexual problems (Barnes, 1995; Gregory, 2014; Maltz, 2002; O'Driscoll & Flanagan, 2016; Sarwer & Durlak, 1996). Utilize a variety of techniques to address the impact of such abuse (see chapter 22, "Trauma-Focused Strategies"). Additionally, sexual traumas, including childbirth, infertility, and infidelity, can also be contributors.

Childbirth is typically considered a positive event but is often the cause of sexual problems (Serati et al., 2010; Slade, 2006; Williams et al., 2007). Childbirth does meet the criteria for trauma (Verreault et al., 2012). While it typically resolves within six months, the effects can last for years. Related shifts in hormones, fatigue, feelings of inadequacy, and changing views of one's body and sexuality can all affect sexual functioning. Oboro and Tabowei (2002) found that 77 percent of couples reported decreased coitus and 47 percent of women reported sexual dysfunction post-childbirth. Williams, Herron-Marx, and Knibb (2007) showed that 54 percent of women reported sexual problems twelve months post-childbirth. Though research is sparse on the impact to husbands, clinical reports suggest it can be significant and worth exploring.

Infertility is estimated to impact a high percentage of couples. While 48.5 million are impacted worldwide, nearly 50 million couples were unable to give birth after five years of trying in 2010 (Mascarenhas, Flaxman, Boerma, Vanderpoel, & Stevens, 2012). Between 7 and 15.5 percent of couples in the United States will experience infertility (Thoma et al., 2013), with as many as 63 percent of infertile women reporting sexual dysfunction (Rohina et al., 2016). While *treating* infertility is not a counseling goal, infertility, including past infertility, can contribute to sexual problems. Additionally, couples seeking counseling for infertility should be assessed for sexual dysfunction. Similarly, be mindful of the impact of miscarriages on sexual desire, sexual functioning, and marital closeness.

Meta-analyses spanning from 1993 to 2008 have suggested that between 11 and 16 percent of women and between 21 and 25 percent of men admitted extra-dyadic sex at least once over the course of their lives (Luo, Cartun, & Snider, 2010). Sexual problems can lay a foundation for infidelity (Fisher et al., 2010; Mark,

Janssen, & Milhausen, 2011), and infidelity can lead to sexual dysfunction (Humphrey, 1987). There does not seem to be a predictable pattern in how individuals and couples respond to the trauma of infidelity (or even if they will view it as trauma), yet it remains a common factor in sexual dysfunction.

Physiological issues. Because physiology is such a core part of sex, many physical issues can impede sexual connecting. Some diseases like diabetes and cancer have a powerful and direct impact on sexual functioning, whereas other diseases have a secondary effect on sexual functioning. Additionally, consider the deleterious effect that other physical issues, such as aging, disability, body size/shape, overall health, stress, and fatigue, have on sexual functioning.

All medications have the potential for side effects, and sexual problems are a very common negative side effect (Finger, Lund, & Slagle, 1997; Hugo, Gomes, & Lima, 2016). Antihistamines dry up more than just the mucus membranes in our sinuses. Antihypertensives, used to lower overall blood pressure, also may prevent vasocongestion and arousal. While clients often believe that natural supplements (vitamins, minerals, herbs, etc.) cannot be a source of sexual problems, a trial of not taking the supplement will show if the problems cease. If the problem returns when the supplement is continued, there is a good likelihood the supplement is problematic.

Divergent, distractive, or destructive sexual goals. Couples can also have conflict or distress surrounding differing ideas about their sexual goals or what they want out of sex. For example, if one partner thinks the goal is for both to reach orgasm and the other partner believes it is to feel close and connected, friction is likely. Another example is making sex just about procreation, while the other wants to have fun or connect. Divergence over sexual ideas, definitions, and goals for sexual intimacy are numerous. It necessitates that the counselor be attuned to areas of difference. Teaching couples how to learn from each other and allowing space for differences is key for change.

Particular goals a partner may have for sex can be very destructive. Consider a partner who has a goal of causing or obtaining a vaginal orgasm during intercourse. This is a setup for failure, as the majority of women need direct clitoral stimulation to achieve orgasm. Such a goal can lead to feelings of hurt, anger, inadequacy, and a host of other detrimental impacts to the individual and relationship. Another common problematic scenario is when one partner is adamant on including specific sexual acts or behaviors.

Attending to the Symptom or the Distress

Most accepted protocols for addressing couple sexual problems focus on treating a core symptom. If a couple is presenting for premature ejaculation, strategies tend to focus on extending the time to engage in intercourse before orgasm (Metz & McCarthy, 2003). While becoming proficient in using these protocols is important, in cases of disease and some dysfunctions, changing the core symptom may not be

feasible, especially when etiology is unclear or outside the realm of counseling. Premature ejaculation (PE), for example, has been shown to be correlated to low serum leptin levels (Atmaca, Kuloglu, Tezcan, Ustundag, & Semercioz, 2003). While PE can often be treated with a selective serotonin reuptake inhibitor (SSRI; Althof et al., 2010), the side effects can cause other sexually related problems and may not be advisable for some clients.

One valuable strategy is to attend to the distress rather than the problem itself. For a diagnosis, the DSM-5 (American Psychiatric Association, 2013) requires both a symptom (consistently ejaculating within one minute or less of vaginal penetration) and symptom distress (symptom results in clinically significant distress, sexual frustration, dissatisfaction, or tension between partners). If there is no distress, there is no diagnosis. This strategic reframing can be highly effective for many entrenched issues. Using a variety of techniques to decrease distress is a treatment success even if the symptom has not changed. Sometimes with resolution of distress the symptom will naturally decrease.

In the case of Jim and Terri above, while one strategy would be to directly work to increase the time Jim can last, an alternative strategy is to decrease their distress. Redefining Jim's quick ejaculation as being overwhelmed by Terri's beauty and sensuality might help her feel less like he was withholding. Redefining the target as intimately connecting versus satisfying intercourse might allow them to accept the early orgasm as part of their lovemaking. After Jim's orgasm, they could reengage in intense foreplay to enhance Terri's arousal and allow Jim to achieve a second erection. While he is still in the refractory period, they could engage in several minutes of intercourse before Jim orgasmed again. Finding success in achieving satisfying intercourse and feeling successful can allow them both to lean back into each other and enjoy sex. The release of pressure from Jim, combined with the increasing frequency and positive experience for both, can lead to the secondary effect of delaying his original orgasm until it is within normal range. The working strategy is decreasing the distress through redefining a narrative and sexual pattern that can lead to success despite the presence of the symptom.

A Model for Helping

Rosenau, Sytsma, and Taylor (2002) developed a model for guiding counseling with sexual issues. The model identifies four components using the acronym DEC-R mentioned earlier: dialogue, educate, coach, and refer. These components are not sequential stages but rather strategies to attend to throughout the counseling. As you become more proficient with the model, you will recognize when the skills are needed and how to navigate their interconnectedness. Referral, for example, may need to occur early in the counseling process. Encouraging dialogue, on the other hand, will never end. It is, however, helpful to present each strategy sequentially to create a foundation on which to begin counseling.

Dialogue. The first strategy is to create dialogue. While our broader culture seems increasingly comfortable with sexu-

al dialogue, the topic of sex remains a private matter, often loaded with shame and embarrassment. Helping couples to talk through sexual problems is a critical skill.

Dialogue with the counselor. The initial task is to facilitate comfortable dialogue between the couple and yourself, as well as between spouses. The dialogue phase is where you identify the cause of the problem and attend to distress. Dialogue can start with a form requesting sexual information. For some, completing a form may be less threatening than sharing verbally. Common marital assessments like the Dyadic Adjustment Scale (Spanier, 1976) or Gottman Sound Relationship House Scales (Gottman, 1999) have subscales or specific questions that assess a couple's sexual functioning.

Simply asking a soft but direct question, such as "How are things going in the sexual part of your relationship?" can open sexual dialogue. Your comfort in asking questions will help the couple share. If sexual concerns are noted in their paperwork, beginning dialogue is even easier: "I see you have marked some concern with sexual desire in your marriage. Please tell me more about this." Either way, you are taking primary responsibility for initiating dialogue on sexual issues.

Most couples address sexual problems in light of their discomfort—that is, descriptively explaining the problem as they see it. While this is always valuable, explore further. Just because the husband believes he has erectile dysfunction does not mean he meets criteria. An older male who requires more direct stimulation to become erect or who may lose and regain an erection during lovemaking is experiencing a normal age-related issue. Effective dialogue is required to further assess the problem (disease, dysfunction, or distress) and choose an appropriate intervention.

As dialogue continues, spend time with each partner individually. Individual sessions are typically ineffective or even detrimental in couple counseling (Doherty, 2002). Nevertheless, the occasional individual session is valuable, especially when facilitating early dialogue. Individual sessions allow exploration of individual sexual histories and individual narratives to the problem. Honesty is more likely when questions about pornography and masturbation history, paraphilias, extradyadic sex, personal attributions for the sexual problem, and satisfaction about sexual encounters are asked individually. Inform clients on your approach to secrets shared during individual sessions before meeting individually with clients seeking dyadic counseling (Bass & Quimby, 2006; Kuo, 2009). After meeting individually, a conjoint session allows you to synthesize the information, clarify points of confusion, and continue encouraging couple dialogue.

Couples develop a sexual routine (how they initiate and perform typical sexual behaviors) early in their sexual relationship that tends to remain fairly habitual. I call it their "sexual dance." For many couple problems, it is helpful to talk through their dance. Exploring this dance in a conjoint session sets the stage for the couple to dialogue as they hear each other discuss their sexual relationship with you. Couples often begin to problem solve quickly when they hear each other's perspective.

Counselor: [*to Kristi after establishing that her husband typically initiates sex*] So, how do you know Carter is wanting to connect sexually? How does he initiate?

Kristi: [*laughing*] He brushes his teeth and uses mouthwash, then comes and gives me a big kiss.

Counselor: And how does that work for you?

Kristi: When you are pregnant, certain smells just make you nauseous. While pregnant with our third, it was mint. Unfortunately, it hasn't gone away. Sometimes when Carter gives me a deep kiss, it takes everything in me not to throw up in his mouth.

Counselor: [*while Carter looks on with surprise*] And how old is your youngest?

Carter: Two and a half.

Counselor: Have you told Carter this before?

Kristi: No. I know he is trying and means well.

During the following session, the couple reported that on the way home Carter stopped at the drugstore to purchase orange toothpaste and mouthwash. Couples rarely dialogue about their sexual play. Getting them to discuss it with you while the other listens is a great start.

Walk through each step of the couple's sexual dance. How does she respond to his initiation? What is the first thing they do? Do they remove each other's clothing or get naked and climb in bed? Do they kiss? If so, how, and for how long? When do they know it's time to move to the next step? Who makes that decision?

At each step of the process, assess what is and is not working. How much does the couple like what they do? Would they prefer something different? Have they tried different things? Helping the couple to think through and describe what they do is a valuable strategy for most sexual problems. Couples are often hesitant to share due to fear of hurting their partner's feelings, especially when something is disliked. Dialoguing with you can ease this fear by softly opening up conversations about sexual preferences.

Dialogue within the couple. Be well versed in effective communication strategies and experienced in how best to apply these strategies to sexuality. One effective dialogue strategy is to begin initially directing their conversation through you. Model the kind of communication you would like them to have with each other. I would ask Kristi what she thinks and attend to her well by reflecting what I heard her say. Then I would shift to Carter and ask him what it's like from his side of the world and model attentive, active listening. A helpful analogy is to take on the role of switchboard operator. Communicating with each partner separately, paraphrasing and reflecting and then turning to the other partner to inquiry what they are hearing are helpful ways you can do this. Next, turn the spouses toward each other as they continue to share, and then leave the couple dialoguing.

Counselor: So, what I believe I'm hearing Kristi say is that you would like to learn to have an orgasm—that not having one causes you some concern.

Kristi: Well, I'm not sure how much concern it causes me. I would like to have one, but it's not all that important to me. I think it causes Carter more concern.

At this point, Kristi and I have been dialoguing about what appears to be female orgasmic disorder, lifelong, generalized (American Psychiatric Association, 2013). Both appear to be comfortable dialoguing with me about the problem. I turned the couple toward each other.

Counselor: Carter, did you just hear what your wife was saying? What did you hear her say?

Carter: I'm the one who wants her to have one, that maybe it's not that important to her.

Counselor: You looked a bit confused when she said that. Ask her to explain it to you.

Carter: [*to Kristi*] I thought you wanted to have an orgasm.

Kristi: I kinda do, but it's not that important to me. I enjoy sex with you even without it. It isn't that important. I'm curious but not sure it will change what I like.

At this point, Carter and Kristi have begun talking with each other about the problem. Rather than inviting them to talk to you, encourage the dialogue between the couple, coaching as needed. While you explore what is important in their sexual relationship, why not also teach the necessary skills to handle future problems on their own?

The strategy of encouraging dialogue is especially important when addressing attributional errors within the couple. Because sexual attribution errors are often tied to core fears, unhealthy parts of ourselves, and other entrenched coping strategies, they can be difficult to recognize and change at times.

Richard and Dawn presented with concerns of ED. Dawn emphatically stated that Richard's ED was due to no longer being attracted to her because she had gained weight. Richard rolled his eyes and looked away with an exasperated look on his face.

Counselor: Richard, tell me what that facial expression means. I'm not sure what you are trying to say.

Richard: I keep telling her it has nothing to do with her, but she won't believe me.

Counselor: You don't think that your ED difficulty is related to her weight gain?

Richard: I love her and find her attractive. It's not that.

Counselor: Dawn, what do you hear Richard saying?

Dawn: He has to say that. It's not true. He had erections before I gained this weight.

Dawn's resolute attribution created a barrier to partner together to resolve their sexual problem. Sometimes it is effective to invite the resistant client to attend to the core good in their spouse and then play "What if?"

Counselor: Dawn, I hear that you don't believe him, but what do you hear him saying?

Dawn: He said he is still attracted to me, and the reason he can't get hard isn't because I've gained weight.

Counselor: That's what I heard also. I wonder, does Richard typically lie to you about important issues in your marriage? [*Dawn looks up with a confused look on her face.*] Because you are calling him a liar about something that is important.

Dawn: No, he doesn't, but I know that's why.

Counselor: But your husband is saying that's not. I wonder if you could believe in what you know about him, that you didn't marry a liar, and play "what if" with me. [*Dawn looks up for an explanation.*] What if Richard is telling the truth, and your weight isn't why he can't get an erection? What if your weight is not the reason?

Some clients remain resistant for a bit and require extra coaching, but Dawn dropped her defenses enough to consider what it would mean if Richard was telling the truth.

Dawn: I guess that would mean there is another reason.

Counselor: I agree with you. Richard is saying there is another reason. Your gaining weight doesn't have that much power over his erections. I'm just getting to know you, so I'm not sure, but I'm guessing that may be the truth. What would it take to believe Richard isn't lying and accept his answer instead?

Keeping the dialogue open allowed Dawn to challenge her own attributions for the problem and to consider other explanations. Observing Richard's obesity and four different anti-hypertensives listed on his paperwork led me to suspect physical causation was more to blame. Allowing the etiology of a problem to remain outside our immediate influence can be difficult, but doing so leaves room for the true etiology to eventually reveal itself.

Additional strategies for encouraging sexual dialogue. Become well experienced using a host of strategies for encouraging couple dialogue. While the strategies themselves fit better into the "coaching" component of the DEC-R, a couple effective strategies are listed below.

Reading out loud together. Recommend a trusted book that will help the couple discuss their presenting problem. To do so requires you to keep abreast of new publications and ensure that they communicate the right content. Instruct the couple to find quiet, uninterrupted time to read the book out loud to each other. Encourage the couple to pause often and share their opinions or ask their spouse's opinion about what they are reading. A well-chosen book provides education and a shared language for talking, desensitizes words, and serves as a launching pad for understanding each other and sharing about self. I encourage couples to speak up any time they disagree with the author to express self and explore what their spouse believes. One husband paused while reading the *Secrets of Eve* (Hart, Weber, & Taylor, 1998), a study of two thousand Christian women's sexuality, to say, "That's crazy! No one is like

that." The wife said, "But I am." They reported an enlightening conversation as they learned how differently they viewed that aspect of sex.

Brakes and accelerators. I provide couples with a handout listing one of the four stages of the lovemaking cycle (Mc-Cluskey & McCluskey, 2004) to complete as homework. Couples are instructed to list brakes (behaviors that impede ongoing sexual interest and arousal) and accelerators (behaviors that energize sexual interest and arousal). In the following session, each will read one accelerator and explain what they like about it. Again, I model and coach the couple in effective communication techniques, helping them to hear and be heard. It is not uncommon for an accelerator on one's list to be a brake on the other's list. Helping the couple problem solve these discrepancies provides an opportunity to model a healthy way of resolving sexual disagreement.

Scheduling coffee time. Encourage couples *not* to critique their partner during the sexual act itself or immediately afterward. This window of time leaves partners feeling too vulnerable to be able to hear and process a complaint or criticism effectively. I encourage couples to schedule "coffee time" the day after sex. Over coffee (or tea, soda, etc.) is a great time to sort through what was and not liked. Couples can then practice the reflective or empathic communication skills taught them to keep the dialogue safe and productive.

Help couples identify sexual expectations and goals. Another common cause of couples' sexual problems is incongruent expectations and goals. A valuable strategy is to assist them in sorting through and expressing a vision for their sexuality. Please keep in mind, as with any effective dialogue, this should be modeled in session first. Throughout the assessment dialogue, you will hear stated expectations and desired goals as they discuss both their history and hopes. Examples of questions include, What defines a healthy sex life? What defines a good sexual experience? What defines a great sexual experience? What is the purpose for your sex life, and has that varied throughout your marriage? After dialogue over this topic has been sufficiently modeled, I provide a handout of similar questions for the couple to discuss at home.

Educate. You may have already noticed the strategies for DEC-R are intertwined. Many of the strategies designed to help couples dialogue require a good deal of communication coaching as well as education. Be willing to overlap strategies from each component. Because misunderstandings, myths, and misinformation significantly contribute to sexual problems, providing accurate and effective psychoeducation is essential.

Of obvious note is the importance of staying self-educated. Not only does the sexual culture continue to change, but research on sexuality is ongoing. Being an effective educator means staying current with academic journals in the field of sexuality and sex therapy.

Effective education is more than just knowing and teaching the client, however. Many inexperienced counselors begin the education process too early, sometimes solely to impart the wealth of their wisdom. Timing and tone are important parts of the education strategy. Maintain a curious stance, and always inquire about what the client knows before assuming you need to teach. This is essential in part because of the enormous amount of shame, embarrassment, and fear surrounding the topic of sexuality.

Timing. Recognizing an area where a client lacks information does not give automatic permission to teach. Bear in mind that additional dialogue comes first. Not only does listening to clients earn the counselor a greater right to be heard, but it allows the counselor to assess the extent of an information deficit. Another risk of educating too soon is inadvertently invalidating the client's problem. Fully understanding the client and earning credibility is part of the education strategy.

Tone. While you might have valuable information for a client to know, this does not imply that you are an expert on the client. Caution should be taken in the tone of approach. Proposing information tends to work better than definitively providing information. A curious, exploring tone in softly presenting the research, asking what the client thinks and how it might apply to their situation is more effective than defining the client based on research data.

Your tone will either convey acceptance or rejection of the client and issue. If you fail to see the pain or confusion an individual is experiencing first, the tone will come across as critical and demeaning. Genuinely caring for a client by getting to know them and their story first yields a more accepting tone. Often clients have experienced shame and judgment, whether from self or others, around sexuality and may be reactive to a certain perceived tone.

Topic. While you may need to teach on any sexual topic, basic sexual anatomy and physiology, effects of aging, and gender differences may be most common. An example of educating on basic anatomy and physiology might look like this.

Counselor: So, you believe your wife should be able to have an orgasm even if the only stimulation she receives is your penis moving in and out of her vagina?

Husband: That's enough for me. It was enough for my previous girlfriend. I would think it should be enough for her.

Counselor: Do you ever provide direct stimulation to her clitoris?

Wife: [*Somewhat shortly*] No. [*Husband looks a bit exposed and confused.*]

Counselor: The tissue on her body that is the equivalent to your penis is her clitoris. Stroking the tissue in her vagina is more like her stroking just the skin on your scrotal sack. While that might feel good, it may not be enough stimulation to help you achieve an orgasm. I'm guessing having your penis stimulated is rather important to you. Would you be open to learning how to provide that level of pleasure to your wife?

Many sexual problems are solved with a bit of education that normalizes the "problem" followed with coaching on how to move forward. This type of education is often central to cases like Lloyd and Jenny's where educating about the effect normal aging has on sexuality allows for a decrease in the distress.

Because of the great variance from one male to another and from one female to another, educating on gender can be difficult. While most men might appreciate their wives coming up from behind and fondling them, most wives would not appreciate the same. However, some husbands would feel offended, and some wives would fantasize about their husband being so sexually bold with them. Read regularly about common gender differences, and provide this information to normalize differences in the couple whenever possible. I commonly educate by saying, "I believe you are thinking like a female, and most husbands don't think that way. Can we ask how he views it?" Whenever possible, invite spouses to be the teacher in how their masculinity or femininity makes them different from each other. If valuable, provide additional education on the normal gendered difference their conversation presents.

An additional education topic is models of sexual response. The typical sex therapy textbook may include several models of sexual response, including Masters and Johnson (1966), Kaplan's triphasic model (1974), Schnarch's quantum model (1991), David Reed's erotic stimulus pathway model (Stayton, 1996), McCluskey's lovemaking cycle (McCluskey & McCluskey, 2004), Basson's model of female sexual response (2000), and the newer incentive-motivation model (Toates, 2009). While controversy exists for which model is best (Basson et al., 2015; Giraldi, Kristensen, & Sand, 2015a, 2015b; Sand & Fisher, 2007), to educate a client in any given model of sexual response may be of value in helping couples enrich time spent pursuing arousal versus orgasm. The circular models (i.e., Basson, 2000; McCluskey & McCluskey, 2004; Whipple & Brash-McGreer, 1997) teach clients the importance of affirming and being sensual with each other throughout the course of each day. Basson's model (2000) is excellent in encouraging the high-desire spouse to understand the low-desire spouse better.

In addition to these four topics (basic anatomy/physiology, aging, gender, models of sexual response), the serious professional will be prepared to teach on subjects such as the role of trauma in sexuality, medication effects, disease effects, typical sexual response times, sexual desire—including low desire and compulsive desire, sexual orientation, gender identity, atypical sexuality, and sexual development. Because most individuals are poorly educated in sexuality, be prepared to take that role in helping them move forward.

Coach. The third component of the DEC-R model is coaching. It refers to guiding couples into growing sexual intimacy as well as assigning exercises around specific problems (Rosenau et al., 2002). Counseling couples with sexual problems is unique in that we do not directly observe the problem. As Rosenau and colleagues (Rosenau et al., 2002) point out, we aren't on the field or sidelines with them. Rather, we are in the locker room talking, drawing on the whiteboard, and coaching them in how to be successful.

Setting. Creating the right setting before and during coaching is crucial. Couples can interpret coaching in numerous ways. They may feel a sense of failure

and, thus, threatened. They might also feel defensive and judged.

Impossible to fail. Reframe homework from negative connotations, such as grading, drudgery, ranking, failure, and so forth, to a positive idea using invitation. For example, you may say, "I would love to invite you both to consider doing an exercise at home I think would be helpful." Ensure clients that it is impossible to "fail" at any exercise they try. I look forward to hearing how the homework experience went, knowing any outcome will be useful. Consider the following dialogue between Carter and Kristi.

Carter: We failed at our homework this week.

Counselor: I'm not sure that's possible. Can you tell me what happened?

Carter: We just couldn't find the time. Whenever we thought we could, we were interrupted by something to do with the kids.

This outcome is a total success. One barrier to this couple's sexual problems has revealed itself—time. The rest of the session might then be spent discussing how the kids interfere and ways to address these interferences. Typically, I use a structural perspective (Minuchin, 1974; Minuchin & Fishman, 1981; Minuchin, Lee, & Simon, 1996), but I have used internal family systems (Schwartz, 1995), motivational interviewing (Miller & Rollnick, 2013), and other models to help the couple make time a priority and develop healthy boundaries to protect that time. If a couple can't find protected space to read a chapter together, how will they ever be able to carve out the space needed to be intimate with each other? Inform clients that whatever information they bring into session is important and is grist for the mill.

Choosing an ethical model of intervention. Another consideration in moving forward with coaching begins by attending to the type of problem the couple is experiencing. If a couple presents with a sexual problem caused by a disease (i.e., ED secondary to diabetes), coaching strategies will be different than those used with a couple in distress who argue over preferred sexual positions. With a diagnosable sexual dysfunction, the ethical counselor will begin by exploring empirically supported interventions. As noted earlier, this requires you to stay educated and up to date on the ever-evolving field of sex therapy. It is incumbent on you as the therapist to research current best practices so that you do not fail to stay current or encounter a sexual problem that you are not well educated in.

For example, many textbooks and training programs teach a Heiman and LoPiccolo (1988) approach to addressing female orgasmic disorder that involves masturbatory training. While research shows it is 70 to 90 percent effective at facilitating female orgasm, only 21 percent can experience an orgasm with their partner using this approach (Kuriansky & Sharpe, 1981). This suggests masturbatory training may not be the most effective strategy. The International Society for Sexual Medicine recommends twelve standard operating procedures to attend to when treating female orgasmic disorder (Laan, Rellini, Barnes, & International Society for Sexual Medicine, 2013). Be ethical by attending to these standards of practice before attempting to engage in specific coaching techniques for female orgasmic disorder.

The current ethical code for the American Counseling Association (2014 C,2,a) states, "Counselors practice only within the boundaries of their competence, based on their education, training, supervised experience, state and national professional credentials, and appropriate professional experience." Other codes of ethics have similar statements that put the weight of seeking appropriate training and staying current on the professional. Several peer-reviewed journals, including *The Journal of Sexual Medicine, Journal of Sex and Marital Therapy*, and *Sexual and Relationship Therapy*, are worth following, as well as graduate- or professional-level textbooks.

Coaching strategies. A selection of coaching strategies that are valuable for couple sexual problems are discussed below.

Bibliotherapy. Depending on the resource chosen, this strategy can educate, normalize, provide guidance and techniques, and assist the couple in communicating with each other. The specifics of how to use bibliotherapy are in the "Dialogue" section above.

Occasionally, bibliotherapy is sufficient alone. I have had more than one couple come in for ED who never rescheduled, only to call back after a few months and say, "Just wanted you to know that book was all we needed. Thanks for your help."

Other couples do need ongoing encouragement and coaching during bibliotherapy. The book then becomes a manual to use in walking them through the steps of recovery. Each session we explore how they did in reading the assigned section and trying the exercises in the book. Couples also feel more empowered with a manual; they realize nothing magical exists inside the counselor's office or mind.

Acceptance and grieving. Much of counseling is grief work. We regularly help clients to accept spouses, parents, children, employers or employees, careers, and so forth for what *is* and help them grieve what *isn't*. This can be especially true in sexuality.

Wife: My first husband was tall and strong. I could curl up in bed with him and feel so safe and protected. It helped me relax and be erotic with him. [*My current husband*] is a smaller man and is soft, tender, and gentle. I feel like I'm always the protector. I can't curl up in him. I don't fit. I'm the one who initiates sex, and it always seems awkward because I have to guide him in each thing.

It is unlikely that counseling will make this wife's current husband more like her first husband. In fact, she acknowledges that the strength and corresponding aggressiveness of her first husband was a big part of why the marriage ended, and that the passivity of her current husband is why she chose him. Her work is to grieve the loss of who her current husband is not. Failure to grieve "who he is not" will prevent her from accepting who he is—thus, allowing the discontent to grow into

contempt, leaving her more vulnerable to temptation when a tall, strong male starts showing her attention.

Jacobson and Christianson (1996) called their guide to integrative couple therapy, an empirically supported treatment model of couple counseling, *Acceptance and Change*. They point out that the greatest opportunity for change in a marriage comes as we change ourselves to accept what is. Effectively assisting a husband to accept that his wife finds oral sex offensive, or even sinful, requires grieving, as does the impact of chronic disease, such as being told by a doctor that prostate surgery would prevent the husband from ejaculating. Acceptance and grief work can open the door to finding alternative ways to lean in and enjoy sexuality together again.

When possible, help couples first try any new technique in session. If a technique isn't modeled, coached, and experienced in session, couples are far less likely to try it at home. Therefore, model reflective or empathic listening, coach couples in it, let them experience when it is working (by also pointing out when it isn't for comparison), and then assign it as homework.

Obviously, most techniques for treating sexual problems cannot be performed in session. You cannot observe couples in the act nor have them practice certain techniques in your office. Systemic approaches for working with couples, such as Minuchin's (Minuchin, Lee, & Simon, 2006; Minuchin et al., 2014) enactment technique, posits that couples will enact the pattern of their interactions during sessions. The observant counselor will watch for such patterns and explore how they play out in a couple's sexual relationship. An aggressive and demanding husband in session is likely similar when having sex. A wife who is stiff and critical in the office is likely the same way during sex. Facilitating change in communication, as well as the spirit and tone the couple use, allows for change in session to translate during sex.

This concept can be taken further using other counseling exercises. A favorite change strategy is to invite the couple to caress each other's hands for approximately fifteen minutes three times a week. I begin by having them enact it in session first. My primary goal is to teach mindfulness and attentiveness skills in sensuality. When performed well, couples can experience very intimate moments just through caressing each other's hands. Just sending couples home to caress each other's hands without practicing in session first would not begin to accomplish the goal. Once I have guided couples in my office and during homework, I can help them translate the skill to touching higher level erogenous zones at home.

Refer. The final component of the DEC-R model is *referral* (Rosenau et al., 2002). Because of the complexity of human sexuality, referral is an essential strategy to master in addressing couple sexual problems. Counselors often refer to physicians for physical assessments and treatment of disease, medications, and medical side effects. Physical therapists with pelvic floor certifications are important when working with problems such as sexual pain.

Referrals can be made to therapy or support groups. Group therapy is effective for treating low sexual desire (Brotto &

Basson, 2014) and anorgasmia (Kuriansky, Sharpe, & O'Connor, 1982) in women. It is also effective in addressing issues of sexual integrity or sexual compulsivity.

Also, readily refer to other specialized counselors when in the best interest of the client. A presenting issue of low desire, difficulty with arousal, or conflict over sexual practices may be related to an underlying anxiety disorder, obsessive-compulsive disorder (OCD), substance abuse, and the like. While you probably have some training in these issues, some counselors are more specialized in working with these disorders. This can be especially true in referring one spouse for trauma work or another to a sex addiction specialist. Often the specialist can address the individual issue while you continue to work with the couple.

Finally, most counselors receive little to no training in sex therapy and ethically can work only with basic sexual problems. This means there will be times when a sexual problem goes beyond the counselor's training, experience, and expertise. The first option is to refer to a counselor trained in sex therapy. The second option is to work directly with a sex therapy supervisor who can oversee the counseling. Know your limits and how to connect clients to the right professional.

CONCLUSION

Sexual problems will undoubtedly present in counseling whether the reason for therapy is sexually related or not. Unfortunately, most counseling training programs do not equip students to treat these problems

(Zeglin, Van Dam, & Hergenrather, 2017). An underlying assumption seems to exist that if couples improve their relationship, then any sexual problem will resolve itself as the relationship improves (Byers, 2011). This is simply untrue and a harmful assumption, leading to failure to address real areas of distress for couples.

First, remember to address your own discomfort with sex and sexuality and attend to your own sexual journey and sexual history—either through consultation, counseling, peer groups, or taking stock of your own beliefs and values, including messages you have learned about sex. Most people carry various amounts of shame associated with sex and sexuality. Second, learn how to assess varying types of sexual dysfunctions, diseases, or distresses so

that you can assess when to treat or refer. Third, educate yourself on basic information about sexual issues and dysfunctions. Begin by focusing on a few of the common sexual problems such as sexual desire, sexual pain, erectile dysfunction, and premature ejaculation. Compile resources such as books, websites, and articles. Locating a colleague or supervisor you can consult with is highly recommended. Fourth, learn how to conceptualize and identify possible causes of distress and dysfunction. Finally, select a framework or model, including the DEC-R, to use with sexual problems. While sex therapy may not be your area of focus, sexual problems are extremely prevalent. Thus, all counselors would benefit from familiarizing and preparing themselves for when sexual problems do present.

RECOMMENDED READING

Binik, Y. M., & Hall, K. S. K. (Eds.). (2014). *Principles and practice of sex therapy* (5th ed.). New York, NY: Guilford Press. (Note: All five editions are recommended as each addresses differing problems from different perspectives.)

Levine, S. B., Risen, C. B., & Althof, S. (Eds.). (2016). *Handbook of clinical sexuality for mental health professionals* (3rd ed.). New York, NY: Routledge.

Penner, C., & Penner, J. (2003). *The gift of sex: A guide to sexual fulfillment*. Nashville, TN: Word.

Penner, J., & Penner, C. (2005). *Counseling for sexual disorders*. N.p.: Penner Books and Tapes.

Peterson, Z. D. (2017). *The Wiley-Blackwell handbook of sex therapy*. New York, NY: Wiley.

Rosenau, D. (2002). *A celebration of sex* (Rev. and updated ed.). Nashville, TN: Thomas Nelson.

References

Abrahamson, C. E. (1998). Storytelling as a pedagogical tool in higher education. *Education, 118*(3), 440–451.

Abramowitz, J. S., Deacon, B. J., & Whiteside, S. P. H. (2012). *Exposure therapy for anxiety: Principles and practices.* New York, NY: Guilford Press.

Ackerman, S. J., & Hilsenroth, M. J. (2003). A review of therapist characteristics and techniques positively impacting the therapeutic alliance. *Clinical Psychology Review, 23*(1), 1–33. doi:10.1016/S0272-7358(02)00146-0

Adams, K. M. (2003). Clergy sex abuse: A commentary on celibacy. *Sexual Addiction & Compulsivity, 10,* 91–92.

Ahles, J. J., Mezulis, A. H., & Hudson, M. R. (2016). Religious coping as a moderator of the relationship between stress and depressive symptoms. *Psychology of Religion and Spirituality, 8*(3), 228–234. doi:10.1037/rel000003

Ainsworth, M. D. (1964). Patterns of attachment behavior shown by the infant in interaction with his mother. *Merrill-Palmer Quarterly of Behavior and Development, 10*(1), 51–58.

Ainsworth, M. D. S., Blehar, M. C., & Waters, E. (2015). *Patterns of attachment: A psychological study of the strange situation.* New York, NY: Routledge.

Ainsworth, M. D. S., Blehar, M. C., Waters, E., & Wall, S. (1978). *Patterns of attachment: A psychological study of the strange situation.* Hillsdale, NJ: Erlbaum.

Alden, R. L. (1985). Malachi. In F. E. Gaebelein (Ed.), *The expositor's Bible commentary* (Vol. 7, pp. 701–725). Grand Rapids, MI: Zondervan.

Alden, R. L. (1993). Job, vol. 11, *The new American commentary* (p. 150). Nashville, TN: Broadman & Holman.

Aldwin, C. M., Skinner, E. A., Zimmer-Gembeck, M. J., & Taylor, A. L. (2010). Coping and self-regulation across the life span. In K. L. Fingerman, C. Berg, J. Smith, & T. C. Antonucci (Eds.), *Handbook of life-span development* (pp. 561–588). New York, NY: Springer.

Allen, E. S., & Atkins, D. C. (2012). The association of divorce and extramarital sex in a representative U.S. Sample. *Journal of Family Issues, 33*(11), 1477–1493. doi:10.1177/0192513X12439692

Allen, J. G., & Fonagy, P. (2006). *Handbook of mentalization-based treatment.* Chichester, UK: Wiley.

Allen, J. G., Fonagy, P., & Bateman, A. (2008). *Mentalizing in clinical practice.* Arlington, VA: American Psychiatric Publishing.

Allen, J. P. (2008). The attachment system in adolescence. In J. Cassidy & P. R. Shaver (Eds.), *Handbook of attachment: Theory, research, and clinical applications* (2nd ed., pp. 419–435). New York, NY: Guilford Press.

Alsdurf, J., & Alsdurf, P. (1998). *Battered into submission: The tragedy of wife abuse in the Christian home.* Eugene, OR: Wipf and Stock.

Althof, S. E., Abdo, C. H. N., Dean, J., Hackett, G., McCabe, M., McMahon, C. G., & Tan, H. M. (2010). International Society for Sexual Medicine's Guidelines for the

Diagnosis and Treatment of Premature Ejaculation. *Journal of Sexual Medicine, 7*(9), 2947–2969. doi:10.1111/j.1743-6109.2010.01975.x

Amato, P., & Keith, B. (1991). Parental divorce and adult well-being: A meta-analysis. *Journal of Marriage and Family, 53*(1), 43–58. doi:10.2307/353132

Amen, D. (1998, 2015). *Change your brain, change your life.* New York, NY: Penguin.

American Counseling Association. (2005). *Code of ethics and standards of practice.* Alexandria, VA: Author.

American Counseling Association. (2011). *The effectiveness of and need for professional counseling services.* Office of Public Policy and Legislation. Alexandria, VA: Author.

American Counseling Association. (2014). *Code of ethics.* Retrieved from https://www.counseling.org/resources/aca-code-of-ethics.pdf

The American heritage dictionary of the English language. (2016). (5th ed.). Boston: Houghton Mifflin Harcourt.

American Pregnancy Association. (2017). Retrieved from http://americanpregnancy.org/

American Psychiatric Association. (2000). *Diagnostic and statistical manual of mental disorders.* (4th ed., text revision). Washington, DC: Author.

American Psychiatric Association. (2013). *Diagnostic and statistical manual of mental disorders* (5th ed.). Washington, DC: Author.

American Psychological Association. (n.d.). *Stress effects on the body.* Retrieved from http://www.apa.org/helpcenter/stress-body.aspx

American Psychological Association. (Producer). (2006). *Christian counseling.* [DVD]. Available from http://www.apa.org/videos/

American Psychological Association. (2010). *Ethical principles for psychologists and code of conduct.* Washington, DC: Author.

Andersen, S., & Chen, S. (2002). The relational self: An interpersonal social-cognitive theory. *Psychological Review, 109*(4), 619–645.

Anderson, N. T. (2000). *The bondage breaker* (2nd ed.). Eugene, OR: Harvest House.

Anderson, N. T. (2013). *Victory over the darkness: Realize the power of your identity in Christ* (3rd ed.). Eugene, OR: Harvest House.

Anderson, T., Ogles, B. M., Patterson, C. L., Lambert, M. J., & Vermeersch, D. A. (2009). Therapist effects: Facilitative interpersonal skills as a predictor of therapist success. *Journal of Clinical Psychology, 65,* 755–768.

Angelou, Maya. (n.d.). Getting there. Retrieved from https://www.politico.com/story/2014/05/getting-there-maya-angelou-107195

Aponte, H. J. (1994). How personal can training get? *Journal of Marital and Family Therapy, 20*(1), 3–15.

Aponte, H. J., & Kissil, K. (2016). *The person of the therapist training model: Mastering the use of self.* New York, NY: Routledge.

Appleby, D. W., & Ohlschlager, G. (2013). *Transformative encounters: The intervention of God in Christian counseling and pastoral care.* Downers Grove, IL: InterVarsity.

Arkowitz, H., Miller, W. R., & Rollnick, S. (Eds.). (2015). *Motivational interviewing in the treatment of psychological problems.* New York, NY: Guilford Press.

Arnold, C. E. (2002). Ephesians. In C. E. Arnold (Ed.), *Zondervan illustrated Bible backgrounds commentary* (Vol. 3, pp. 300–341). Grand Rapids, MI: Zondervan.

Arnold, C., & Fisch, R. (2011). *The impact of complex trauma on development.* Lanham, MD: Jason Aronson.

Ashby, J. S., Rice, K. G., & Martin, J. L. (2006). Perfectionism, shame, and depressive symptoms. *Journal of Counseling and Development, 84,* 148–156.

Aten, J. D., & Leach, M. M. (2009). *Spirituality and the therapeutic process: A comprehensive resource from intake to termination.* Washington, DC: American Psychological Association.

Atkins, D. C., Eldridge, K. A., Baucom, D. H., & Christensen, A. (2005). Infidelity and behavioral couple therapy: Optimism in the face of betrayal. *Journal of Consulting and Clinical Psychology, 73*(1), 144–150.

Atmaca, M., Kuloglu, M., Tezcan, E., Ustundag, B., & Semercioz, A. (2003). Serum leptin levels in patients with premature ejaculation before and after citalopram treatment. *BJU International*, *91*(3), 252–254. doi:10.1046/j.1464–410X.2003.04052.x

Axline, V. (1964). *Dibs: In search of self*. Boston, MA: Houghton Mifflin.

Ayllon, T., & Azrin, N. H. (1968). The measurement and reinforcement of behavior of psychotics. *Journal of Experiential Analysis of Behavior*, *8*(6), 357–383.

Babin, E. A. (2013). An examination of predictors of nonverbal and verbal communication of pleasure during sex and sexual satisfaction. *Journal of Social and Personal Relationships*, *30*(3), 270–292.

Backus, W., & Chapian, M. (2000). *Telling yourself the truth*. Bloomington, MN: Bethany House.

Bade, M., & Cook, S. (2008). Functions of Christian prayer in the coping process. *Journal for the Scientific Study of Religion*, *47*, 123–133.

Badenoch, B. (2008). *Being a brain-wise therapist: A practical guide to interpersonal neurobiology*. New York, NY: W. W. Norton.

Bader E., & Pearson, P. (1988). *In quest of the mythical mate*. New York, NY: Bruner/Mazel.

Baglivio, M. T., Jackowski, K., Greenwald, M. A., & Wolff, K. T. (2014). Comparison of multisystemic therapy and functional family therapy effectiveness: A multiyear statewide propensity score matching analysis of juvenile offenders. *Criminal Justice and Behavior*, *41*(9), 1033–1056.

Baker, L. M. (2010a). *Counselling Christian women on how to deal with domestic violence*. Bowen Hills, Queensland: Australian Academic Press.

Baker, L. M. (2010b). Domestic violence: Recognising spiritual abuse—its nature and impact. *Counselling Australia*, *10*(4), 6–8.

Baker, L. M. (2011). Domestic violence: Assisting women of faith. *Counselling Australia*, *11*(1), 24–28.

Bakermans-Kranenburg, M. J., & van IJzendoorn, M. H. (1993). A psychometric study of the adult attachment interview: Reliability and discriminant validity. *Developmental Psychology*, *29*(5), 870–879.

Ball, R. A., & Goodyear, R. K. (1991). Self-reported professional practices of Christian psychologists. *Journal of Psychology and Christianity*, *10*, 144–153.

Ballantine Dykes, F., Kopp, B., & Postings, T. (2014). *Counselling skills and studies*. London: Sage.

Balswick, J. O., King, P. E., & Reimer, K. S. (2005). *The reciprocating self: Human development in theological perspective*. Downers Grove, IL: IVP Academic.

Bandler, R., & Grinder, J. (2005). *The structure of magic*, vol. 1: *A book about language and therapy* (1st ed.). Palo Alto, CA: Science and Behavioral Books.

Bandura, A. (1967). Behavioral psychotherapy. *Scientific American*, *216*, 78–86.

Bandura, A. (1977). *Social learning theory*. Englewood Cliffs, NJ: Prentice Hall.

Banks, T., & Zionts, P. (2009). REBT used with children and adolescents who have emotional and behavioral disorders in educational settings: A review of the literature. *Journal of Rational-Emotive & Cognitive-Behavioral Therapy*, *27*, 51–65.

Barabas, S. (1981). Forgiveness. In M. C. Tenney (Ed.), *The Zondervan pictorial Bible dictionary* (p. 289). Grand Rapids, MI: Zondervan.

Barbour, J. D. (2004). *The value of solitude: The ethics and spirituality of aloneness in autobiography*. Charlottesville, VA: University of Virginia Press.

Barlow, D. H., Farchione, T. J., Fairholme, C. P., Ellard, K. K., Boisseau, C. L., Allen, L. B., & Ehrenreich-May, J. T. (2011). *Unified protocol for transdiagnostic treatment of treatment of emotional disorders: Therapist guide* (1st ed.). New York, NY: Oxford University Press.

Barna, G. (2011). *Maximum faith: Live like Jesus*. Ventura, CA: Metaformation.

Barnard, L. K., & Curry, J. F. (2011). The relationship of clergy burnout to self-compassion and other personality dimensions. *Pastoral Psychology*, *61*, 149–163.

Barnes, M. F. (1995). Sex therapy in the couples' context: Therapy issues of victims of sexual trauma. *American Journal of Family Therapy*, *23*(4), 351–360. doi:10.1080/01926189508251365

Bartholomew, K., & Horowitz, L. M. (1991). Attachment styles among young adults: A test of a four-category model. *Journal of Personality and Social Psychology*, *61*(2), 226–244. doi:10.1037/0022–3514.61.2.226

Barton, R. H. (2006). *Sacred rhythms: Arranging our lives for spiritual transformation*. Downers Grove, IL: InterVarsity.

Bass, B. A., & Quimby, J. L. (2006). Addressing secrets in couples counseling: An alternative approach to informed consent. *Family Journal*, *14*(1), 77–80. doi:10.1177/1066480705282060

Basson, R. (2000). The female sexual response: A different model. *Journal of Sex Marital Therapy*, *26*, 51–65.

Basson, R., Correia, S., Driscoll, M., Laan, E., Toates, F., & Tiefer, L. (2015). Problematic endorsement of models describing sexual response of men and women with a sexual partner. *Journal of Sexual Medicine*, *12*(8), 1848–1850. doi:10.1111/jsm.12947

Batten, S. V. (2011). *Essentials of acceptance and commitment therapy*. Thousand Oaks, CA: Sage.

Baucom, D. H., Snyder, D. K., & Gordon, K. C. (2009). *Helping couples get past the affair: A clinician's guide*. New York, NY: Guilford Press.

Bauer, M. J. (2013). *Arts ministry: Nurturing the creative life of God's people*. Grand Rapids, MI: Eerdmans.

Baumrind, D. (1973). The development of instrumental competence through socialization. In A. Pick (Ed.), *Minnesota Symposia on Child Psychology* (Vol. 7, pp. 3–46). Minneapolis, MN: University of Minnesota Press.

Beattie, M. (1987). *Codependent no more: How to stop controlling others and start caring for yourself*. Center City, MN: Hazelden.

Beattie, M. (1990). *The language of letting go: Daily meditations for codependents*. Center City, MN: Hazelden.

Beaulieu, D. (2003, July/August). Beyond just words: Multisensory interventions can heighten therapy's impact. *Psychotherapy Networker*, *27*(4), 69–77.

Beck, A. T. (1967a). *Depression: Clinical, experimental, and theoretical aspects*. New York, NY: Harper and Row. Republished as: Beck, A. T. (1970). *Depression: Causes and treatment*. Philadelphia, PA: University of Pennsylvania Press.

Beck, A. T. (1967b). *The diagnosis and management of depression*. Philadelphia, PA: University of Pennsylvania Press.

Beck, A. T. (1976). *Cognitive therapy and the emotional disorders*. New York, NY: Meridian.

Beck, A. T. (1995). Foreword. In D. Greenberger & C. A. Padesky (Eds.), *Change how you feel by changing the way you think*. New York, NY: Guilford Press.

Beck, A. T., Rush, A. J., Shaw, B. F., & Emery, G. (1979). *Cognitive therapy of depression*. New York, NY: Guilford Press.

Beck, A. T., Steer, R. A., Beck, J. S., & Newman, C. F. (1993). Hopelessness, depression, suicidal ideation and clinical diagnosis of depression. *Suicide and Life-Threatening Behavior*, *23*, 139–145.

Beck, J. S. (1995). *Cognitive behavioral therapy: Basic and beyond*. New York, NY: Guilford Press.

Beck, J. S. (2011). *Cognitive behavior therapy: Basics and beyond* (2nd ed.). New York, NY: Guilford Press.

Beck, T. D. (2009). The divine dis-comforter: The Holy Spirit's role in transformative suffering. *Journal of Spiritual Formation and Soul Care*, *2*(2), 199–218.

Behrendt, H., & Ben-Ari, R. (2012). The positive side of negative emotion: The role of guilt and shame in coping with interpersonal conflict. *Journal of Conflict Resolution*, *56*(6), 1116–1138.

Bender, L. (producer), & Van Sant, G. (director) (1997). *Good will hunting* [Motion picture]. United States: Be Gentlemen.

Ben-Naim, S., Hirschberger, G., Ein-Dor, T., & Mikulincer, M. (2013). An experimental study of emotion regulation during relationship conflict interactions: The moderating role of attachment orientations. *Emotion, 13*, 506–519.

Benner, D. G. (2010). *Opening to God: Lectio divina and life as prayer.* Downers Grove, IL: InterVarsity.

Bennett, B. E., Bricklin, P. M., Harris, E., Knapp, S., VandeCreek, L., & Younggren, J. N. (2006). *Assessing and managing risk in psychological practice: An individualized approach* (pp. 89–104). Rockville, MD: The Trust. doi:10.1037/14293–005

Benschoter, R. A., Eaton, M. T., & Smith, P. (1965). Use of videotape to provide individual instruction in techniques of psychotherapy. *Journal of Medical Education, 40*, 1159–1161.

Bent-Goodley, T., St. Vil, N., & Hubbert, P. (2012). A spirit unbroken: The black church's evolving response to domestic violence. *Social Work and Christianity, 39*(1), 53–65.

Berk, L. E. (2006). *Development through the life span* (4th ed.). Boston, MA: Allyn & Bacon.

Berkaw, B., & Berkaw, G. (2010). *A couples' guide to intimacy.* Pasadena, CA: California Center for Healing.

Berking, M., & Whitley, B. (2014). *Affect regulation training: A practitioners' manual.* New York, NY: Springer.

Bermond, B., Clayton, K., Luminet, O., & Wicherts, J. (2007). A cognitive and an affective dimension of alexithymia in six languages and seven populations. *Cognition and Emotion, 21*, 1125–1136.

Berry, J. W., Worthington, E. L., O'Connor, L. E., Parrott, L., III, & Wade, N. G. (2005). Forgivingness, vengeful rumination, and affective traits. *Journal of Personality, 73*, 1–43.

Betzig, L. (1989). Causes of conjugal dissolution: A cross-cultural study. *Current Anthropology, 30*(5), 654–676. doi:10.1086/203798

Bhattacharya, B. (2015). Cognitive-behavioral intervention in prolonged grief reaction. *Journal of Rational-Emotive & Cognitive-Behavior Therapy, 33*(1), 37–48.

Bickel, C. O., Ciarrocchi, J. W., Sheers, N. J., Estadt, B. K., Powell, D. A., & Pargament, K. I. (1998). Perceived stress, religious coping styles, and depressive affect. *Journal of Psychology and Christianity, 17*(1), 33–42.

Binkley, E. (2013). Creative strategies for treating victims of domestic violence. *Journal of Creativity in Mental Health, 8*, 306–213. doi:10.1080/15401383.2013.821932

Binks, E., Smith, D. L., Smith, L. J., & Joshi, R. M. (2009). Tell me your story: A reflection strategy for preservice teachers. *Teacher Education Quarterly, 36*(3), 141–156.

Blankenship, B., & Laaser, M. (2004). Sexual addiction and ADHD: Is there a connection? *Sexual Addiction & Compulsivity, 11*, 7–20. doi:10.1080/10720160490458184

Blasco-Fontecilla, H., Fernandez-Fernandez, R., Colino, L., Fajardo, L., Perteguer-Barrio, R., & de Leon, J. (2016). The addictive model of self-harming (non-suicidal and suicidal) behavior. *Frontiers in Psychiatry, 7*(8), 1–7.

Blum, A. (2008). Shame and guilt, misconceptions and controversies: A critical review of the literature. *Traumatology, 14*, 91–201. doi:10.1177/1534765608321070

Bobgan, M., & Bobgan, D. (1987). *Psychoheresy: The psychological seduction of Christianity.* Santa Barbara, CA: East Gate.

Boden, M., & Thompson, R. (2015). Facets of emotional awareness and associations with emotion regulation and depression. *Emotion, 15*, 399–410.

Boeckmann, E. L. (2008). *Self-injury knowledge and peer perceptions among members of internet self-injury groups.* Bowling Green, KY: Western Kentucky University.

Bornovalova, M. A., Tull, M. T., Gratz, K. L., Levy, R., & Lejuez, C. W. (2011). Extending models of deliberate self-harm and suicide attempts to substance users: Exploring the roles of childhood abuse, posttraumatic stress, and difficulties controlling impulsive behavior when distressed. *Psychological Trauma: Theory, Research, Practice, and Policy, 3*(4), 349–359.

Bornstein, R. F. (2004). Integrating cognitive and existential treatment strategies in psychotherapy with dependent patients. *Journal of Contemporary Psychotherapy, 34*(4), 293–309.

Bourne, E. (2016). *Coping with anxiety: Ten simple ways to relieve anxiety, fear, and worry.* Oakland, CA: New Harbinger.

Bowen, M. (1976). Theory in the practice of psychotherapy. In P. J. Guerin (Ed.), *Family therapy* (pp. 42–90). New York, NY: Gardner.

Bowen, M. (1978). *Family therapy in clinical practice.* New York, NY: Aronson.

Bowlby, J. (1969, 1982). *Attachment and loss: Vol. 1. Attachment.* New York, NY: Basic Books.

Bowlby, J. (1988). *A secure base: Clinical applications of attachment theory.* London: Routledge.

Bowlby, J. (2012a). *The making and breaking of affectional bonds.* Hoboken, NJ: Taylor and Francis.

Bowlby, J. (2012b). *A secure base: Clinical applications of attachment theory.* Hoboken, NJ: Taylor and Francis.

Bradbury, T. N., Beach, S. R. H., Fincham, F. D., & Nelson, G. M. (1996). Attributions and behavior in functional and dysfunctional marriages. *Journal of Consulting & Clinical Psychology, 64*(3), 569–576.

Bradley, L. J., Whiting, P., Hendricks, B., Parr, G., & Jones, E. G. (2008). The use of expressive techniques in counseling. *Journal of Creativity in Mental Health, 3*, 44–57. doi:10.1080/15401380802023605

Bradshaw, J. (1988). *Healing the shame that binds you.* Deerfield Beach, FL: Health Communications.

Brady, A., & Raines, D. (2009). Dynamic hierarchies: A controlled paradigm for exposure therapy. *The Cognitive Behavioural Therapist, 2,* 51–62. doi:10.1017/S1754470X0800010X

Brantley, J., McKay, M., & Wood, J. C. (2007). *The Dialectical Behavior Therapy skills workbook: Practical DBT exercises for learning mindfulness, interpersonal effectiveness, emotional regulation and distress tolerance.* Oakland, CA: New Harbinger.

Bratton, S. C., & Ferebee, K. W. (1998). The use of structured expressive art activities in group activity therapy with preadolescents. In D. S. Sweeney & L. E. Homeyer (Eds.), *The handbook of group play therapy: How to do it, how it works, whom it's best for* (pp. 192–214). Hoboken, NJ: Jossey-Bass.

Bratton, S. C., Taylor, D. D., & Akay, S. (2014). Integrating play and expressive therapy into small group counseling with preadolescents: A humanistic approach. In E. J. Green & A. A. Drewes (Eds.), *Integrating expressive arts and play therapy with children and adolescents* (pp. 253–282). Hoboken, NJ: Wiley.

Braun, B. G. (1988). The BASK model of dissociation: Clinical applications. *Dissociation, 1*(2), 16–23.

Breiding, M. J., Basile, K. C., Smith, S. G., Black, M. C., & Mahendra, R. R. (2015). *Intimate partner violence surveillance: Uniform definitions and recommended data elements, Version 2.0.* Atlanta, GA: National Center for Injury Prevention and Control, Centers for Disease Control and Prevention. Retrieved from http://www.cdc.gov/violenceprevention/pdf/intimatepartnerviolence.pdf

Bretherton, I. (1992). The origins of attachment theory: John Bowlby and Mary Ainsworth. *Developmental Psychology, 28*(5), 759–775.

Bretherton, I., & Munholland, K. A. (2008). Internal working models in attachment relationships: Elaborating a central construct in attachment theory. In. J. Cassidy & P. R. Shaver (Eds.), *Handbook of attachment: Theory, research, and clinical applications* (2nd ed., pp. 102–127). New York, NY: Guilford Press.

Briere, J. N., & Scott, C. (2013). *Principles of trauma therapy: A guide to symptoms, evaluation, and treatment* (2nd ed.). Los Angeles, CA: Sage.

Briere, J. N., & Scott, C. (2015). Complex trauma in adolescents and adults: Effects and treatment. *Psychiatric Clinics of North America, 38*(3), 515–527.

Brisch, K. H. (2002). *Treating attachment disorders: From theory to therapy.* New York, NY: Guilford Press.

Broderick, P. C., & Blewitt, P. (2010). *The life span: Human development for healing professionals.* Upper Saddle River, NJ: Pearson Education.

Brody, S. (2007). Vaginal orgasm is associated with better psychological function. *Sexual and Relationship Therapy, 22*(2), 173–191. doi:10.1080/14681990601059669

Broger, J. C. (1991). *Self-confrontation: A manual for in-depth discipleship.* Palm Desert, CA: Biblical Counseling Foundation.

Brotto, L. A., & Basson, R. (2014). Group mindfulness-based therapy significantly improves sexual desire in women. *Behaviour Research and Therapy, 57,* 43–54. doi:10.1016/j.brat.2014.04.001

Brown, C. (1968). *Philosophy and the Christian faith: A historical sketch from the Middle Ages to the present day.* Downers Grove, IL: InterVarsity.

Brown, C., & Augusta-Scott, T. (2007). *Narrative therapy: Making meaning, making lives.* Thousand Oaks, CA: Sage.

Brown, J. (2004). Shame and domestic violence: Treatment perspectives for perpetrators from self psychology and affect theory. *Sexual and Relationship Therapy, 19*(1), 39–56.

Brown, L. B. (1994). An experimental perspective as a therapeutic resource. In H. Grzymala-Moszczynska & B. Beit-Hallahmi (Eds.), *Religion, psychology and coping* (pp. 159–176). Amsterdam: Rodopi.

Brown, T. A., & Barlow, D. H. (2009). A proposal for a dimensional classification system based on the shared features of the DSM-IV anxiety and mood disorders: Implications for assessment and treatment. *Psychological Assessment, 21*(3), 256–271.

Buber, M. (2010). *I and Thou.* Mansfield Centre, CT: Martino.

Buechner, F. (2004, 2013). *Beyond words: Daily readings in the ABCs of faith.* New York, NY: HarperCollins.

Bufford, R. K. (1981). *The human reflex: Behavioral psychology in biblical perspective.* San Francisco, CA: Harper & Row.

Bunyan, J. (1678). *The pilgrims progress.* New York, NY: Payson & Clarke Ltd.

Burchard, G. A., Yarhouse, M. A., Worthington, E. L., Jr., Berry, J. W., Killian, M., & Canter, D. E. (2003). A study of two marital enrichment programs and couples' quality of life. *Journal of Psychology and Theology, 31,* 240–252.

Burdick, D. (2013). *Mindfulness skills workbook for clinicians and clients: 111 tools, techniques, activities & worksheets.* Eau Claire, WI: PESI Publishing and Media.

Burns, D. D. (1993, 1999). *Ten days to self-esteem.* New York, NY: William Morrow.

Burns, D. D. (2008). *The feeling good handbook.* New York, NY: Harper.

Burns, G. W. (2001). *101 healing stories: Using metaphors in therapy* (1st ed.). Hoboken, NJ: Wiley.

Burns, G. W. (2005). *101 healing stories for kids and teens: Using metaphors in therapy* (1st ed.). Hoboken, NJ: Wiley.

Burton-Christie, D. (1993). *The word of the desert: Scripture and the quest for holiness in early Christian monasticism.* Oxford: Oxford University Press.

Busby, D. M., Gardner, B. C., & Taniguchi, N. (2005). The family of origin parachute model: Landing safely in adult romantic relationships. *Family Relations, 54*(2), 254–264.

Busby, D. M., & Holman, T. B. (2009). Perceived match or mismatch on the Gottman conflict styles: Association with relationship outcome variables. *Family Process, 48*(4), 531–514. doi:10.1111/j.1545-5300 .2009.01300.x

Buss, D. M., & Shackelford, T. K. (1997). Susceptibility to infidelity in the first year of marriage. *Journal of Research in Personality, 31*(2), 193–221.

Butner, J., Diamond, L. M., & Hicks, A. M. (2007). Attachment style and two forms of affect coregulation between romantic partners. *Personal Relationships*, *14*(3), 431–455. doi:10.1111/j.1475–6811.2007.00164.x

Byers, E. S. (2011). Beyond the birds and the bees and was it good for you? Thirty years of research on sexual communication. *Canadian Psychology/Psychologie canadienne*, *52*(1), 20–28. doi:10.1037/a0022048

Byers, E. S., Nichols, S., & Voyer, S. D. (2013). Challenging stereotypes: Sexual functioning of single adults with high-functioning autism spectrum disorder. *Journal of Autism and Developmental Disorders*, *43*, 2617–2627.

Calder, M. (2007). *Understanding, assessing, and engaging with young people who self-harm*. London: Russell House.

Calhoun, A. A. (2005). *Spiritual disciplines handbook*. Downers Grove, IL: IVP.

Campbell, J. S., & Elison, J. (2005). Shame coping styles and psychopathic personality traits. *Journal of Personality Assessment*, *84*, 96–104.

Canary, H., & Canary, D. (2013). *Family conflict: Managing the unexpected*. New York, NY: Wiley.

Capretto, P. (2015). Empathy and silence in pastoral care for traumatic grief. *Journal of Religion and Health*, *54*(1), 339–357.

Carder, D. (2008). *Torn asunder: Recovering from an extramarital affair*. Chicago, IL: Moody.

Cares, A. C., & Cusick, G. R. (2012). Risks and opportunities of faith and culture: The case of abused Jewish women. *Journal of Family Violence*, *27*, 427–435. https://doi.org/10.1007/s10896-012-9435-3

Carich, M. S. (1989). Variations of the "as if" technique. *Individual Psychology: The Journal of Adlerian Theory, Research, & Practice*, *45*(4), 538–545.

Carlson, J., & Sperry, L. (2010). *Recovering intimacy in love relationships*. New York, NY: Taylor & Francis.

Carlson, J., Watts, R. E., & Maniacci, M. (2006). *Adlerian therapy: Theory and practice*. Washington, DC: American Psychological Association.

Carnes, P. J. (1983, 1992, 2001). *Out of the shadows*. Center City, MN: Hazelden.

Carnes, P. J. (1989). *Contrary to love: Helping the sexual addict*. Minneapolis, MN: CompCare.

Carnes, P. J. (1991). *Don't call it love*. New York, NY: Random House.

Carnes, P. J. (1997). *The betrayal bond: Breaking free of exploitative relationships*. Deerfield Beach, FL: Health Communications.

Carnes, P., Laaser, M., & Laaser, D. (1999). *Open hearts*. Wickensburg, AZ: Gentle Path.

Carnes, P. J., Murray, R. E., & Charpentier, L. (2004). Addictive interaction disorder. In R. H. Coombs (Ed.), *Handbook of addictive disorders: A practical guide to diagnosis and treatment* (pp. 31–59). New York, NY: Wiley.

Carr, A. (2014). The evidence base for family therapy and systemic interventions for child-focused problems. *Journal of Family Therapy*, *36*(2), 107–157.

Carr, D. (2010, August). Cheating hearts. *Contexts*, 58–60. doi:10.2307/41960779

Carson, D. K., Becker, K. W., Vance, K. E., & Forth, N. L. (2003). The role of creativity in marriage and family therapy practice: A national online study. *Contemporary Family Therapy*, *25*, 89–109. doi:10.1023/A:1022562122420

Carter, B., & McGoldrick, M. (1989). *The changing family life-cycle: A framework to family therapy* (2nd ed.). Boston, MA: Allyn & Bacon.

Carter, L. (1990). *The prodigal spouse*. Nashville, TN: Thomas Nelson.

Casey, K. L. (1998). Surviving abuse: Shame, anger, forgiveness. *Pastoral Psychology*, *46*(4), 223–231.

Cash, S. J., Thelwall, M., Peck, S. N., Ferrell, J. Z., & Bridge, J. A. (2013). Adolescent suicide statements on MySpace. *Cyberpsychology, Behavior, and Social Networking*, *16*(3), 166–174.

Cashwell, C. S., Bentley, P. B., & Yarborough, J. P. (2007). The only way out is through: The peril of spiritual by-pass. *Counseling and Values, 51*, 139–148.

Cashwell, C. S., & Giordano, A. L. (2014). Spiritual diversity. In D. Hays & B. Erford (Eds.), *Developing multicultural counseling competence: A systems approach* (pp. 448–474). New York, NY: Pearson.

Cassidy, J., & Shaver, P. R. (2008). *Handbook of attachment: Theory, research, and clinical applications.* New York, NY: Guilford Press.

Catherall, D. (2012). *Emotional safety: Viewing couples through the lens of affect.* New York, NY: Routledge.

Cautela, J. R. (1967). Covert sensitization. *Psychological Reports, 20*, 459–468.

Cautela, J. R., & Kearney, A. J. (1986). *The covert conditioning handbook.* New York, NY: Springer.

Chambers, O. (1935). *My utmost for His highest.* Westwood, NJ: Dodd, Mead & Co.

Chambless, D. L., & Hollom, S. D. (1998). Defining empirically supported therapies. *Journal of Consulting and Clinical Psychology, 66*(1), 7–18.

Chetty, S., Friedman, A. R., Taravosh-Lahn, K., Kirby, E. D., Mirescu, C., Guo, F., & Kaufer, D. (2014). Stress and glucocorticoids promote oligodendrogenesis in the adult hippocampus. *Molecular Psychiatry, 19*(12), 1275–1283. doi:10.1038/mp.2013.190

Christensen, A., Atkins, D. C., Baucom, B., & Yi, J. (2010). Marital status and satisfaction five years following a randomized clinical trial comparing traditional versus integrative behavioral couple therapy. *Journal of Consulting and Clinical Psychology, 78*(2), 225–235.

Chung, S. F. (2013). A review of psychodrama and group process. *International Journal of Social Work and Human Services Practice, 1*(2), 105–114.

Cicchetti, D., & Toth, S. L. (1995). A developmental psychopathology perspective on child abuse and neglect. *Journal of the American Academy of Child and Adolescent Psychiatry, 34*, 541–565.

Cipani, E., & Schock, K. M. (2008). *Functional behavioral assessment, diagnosis, and treatment: A complete system for education and mental health settings* (2nd ed.). New York, NY: Springer.

Citron, F. M. M., & Goldberg, A. E. (2014). Metaphorical sentences are more emotionally engaging than their literal counterparts. *Journal of Cognitive Neuroscience, 26*, 2585–2595. doi:10.1162/jocn_a_00654

Claesson, K., & Sohlberg, S. (2002). Internalized shame and early interactions characterized by indifference, abandonment and rejection: Replicated findings. *Clinical Psychology & Psychotherapy, 9*(4), 277–284. doi:10.1002/cpp.331

Clark, C., & Rabey, S. (2009). *When kids hurt: Help for adults navigating the adolescent maze.* Grand Rapids, MI: Baker.

Clebsch, W. A., & Jaekle, C. R. (1964). *Pastoral care in historical perspective, an essay with exhibits.* Englewood Cliffs, NJ: Prentice-Hall.

Clinton, T., & Laaser, M. (2010). *The quick reference guide to sexuality and relationship counseling.* Grand Rapids, MI: Baker.

Clinton, T., & Langberg, D. (2011). *Counseling women.* Grand Rapids, MI: Baker.

Clinton, T., & Oschlager, G. W. (2002). *Competent Christian counseling.* Colorado Springs, CO: WaterBrook.

Clinton, T., & Sibcy, G. (2002). *Attachments: Why you love, feel and act the way you do.* Nashville, TN: Thomas Nelson.

Clinton, T., & Sibcy, G. (2006). *Why you do the things you do: The secret to healthy relationships.* Nashville, TN: Thomas Nelson.

Clinton, T., & Sibcy, G. (2012). Christian counseling, interpersonal neurobiology, and the future. *Journal of Psychology & Theology, 40*(2), 141–145.

Clinton, T., & Straub, J. (2010). *God attachment: Why you believe, act, and feel the way you do about God.* New York, NY: Howard.

Clouse, B. (1985). Moral reasoning and Christian faith. *Journal of Psychology and Theology, 13*, 190–198.

Coe, J. (2016). Special issue: Suffering and the Christian life. *Journal of Spiritual Formation and Soul Care, 9*(2). Retrieved from http://journals.biola.edu/sfj/volumes/9

Cohen, J. A., & Scheeringa, M. S. (2009). Posttraumatic stress disorder diagnosis in children: Challenges and promises. *Dialogues in Clinical Neuroscience, 11*(1), 91–99.

Cole, M. A., & Caron, S. L. (2010). Exploring factors which lead to successful reunification in domestic violence cases: Interviews with caseworkers. *Journal of Family Violence, 25,* 297–310. doi:10.1007/s10896-009-9292-x

Conley, T. D., Moors, A. C., Ziegler, A., & Karathanasis, C. (2012). Unfaithful individuals are less likely to practice safer sex than openly nonmonogamous individuals. *Journal of Sexual Medicine, 9*(6), 1559–1565. doi:10.1111/j.1743-6109.2012.02712.x

Connors, M. E. (2011). Attachment theory: A "secure base" for psychotherapy integration. *Journal of Psychotherapy Integration, 21*(3), 348–362. doi:10.1037/a0025460

Conte, C. (2009). *Advanced techniques for counseling and psychotherapy.* New York, NY: Springer.

Cooley, C. H. (1902). *Human nature and the social order.* New York, NY: Charles Scribner's Sons.

Cooley, C. H. (1909). *Social organization: A study of the larger mind.* New York, NY: Charles Scribner's Sons.

Cooper, J. O., Heron, T. E., & Heward, W. L. (2007). *Applied behavior analysis* (2nd ed.). Upper Saddle River, NJ: Pearson.

Cooper-White, P. (1995). *The cry of Tamar: Violence against women and the church's response.* Minneapolis, MN: Fortress.

Corcoran, K., & Fischer, J. (2013). *Measures for clinical practice and research: A sourcebook.* New York, NY: Oxford University Press.

Corey, G. (2005). *Theory and practice of counseling and psychotherapy* (7th ed.). Belmont, CA: Thompson Learning.

Corey, G. (2017). *Theory and practice of counseling and psychotherapy* (10th ed.). Boston, MA: Cengage.

Cormier, W. H., & Cormier, L. S. (1985). *Interviewing strategies for helpers: Fundamental skills and cognitive behavioral interventions.* Belmont, CA: Brooks/Cole.

Cosgrove, M. P. (2006). *Foundations of Christian thought: Faith, learning, and the Christian worldview.* Grand Rapids, MI: Kregel Academic & Professional.

Courtois, C. A., & Ford, J. D. (Eds.). (2009). *Treating complex traumatic stress disorders: An evidence-based guide.* New York, NY: Guilford Press.

Cozolino, L. J. (2014). *The neuroscience of human relationships: Attachment and the developing social brain.* New York, NY: W. W. Norton.

Crabb, L. (1977). *Effective biblical counseling.* Grand Rapids, MI: Zondervan.

Crabb, L. (2001). *Shattered dreams: God's unexpected pathway to joy.* Colorado Springs, CO: WaterBrook.

Crane, J. M., & Baggerly, J. N. (2014). Integrating play and expressive art therapy into educational settings: A pedagogy for optimistic therapists. In E. J. Green & A. A. Drewes (Eds.), *Integrating expressive arts and play therapy with children and adolescents* (pp. 231–251). Hoboken, NJ: Wiley.

Craske, M. G., & Tsao, J. C. I. (1999). Self-monitoring with panic and anxiety disorders. *Psychological Assessment, 11,* 466–479.

Crenshaw, D., & Mordock, J. (2005). *Understanding and treating the aggression of children: Fawns in gorilla suits.* Lanham, MD: Jason Aronson.

Crippen, J. (2015). *Unholy charade: Unmasking the domestic abuser in the church.* Tillamook, OR: Justice Keepers.

Crittenden, P. M., Claussen, A. H., & Kozlowska, K. (2007). Choosing a valid assessment of attachment for clinical use: A comparative study. *Australian & New Zealand Journal of Family Therapy, 28*(2), 78–87.

Crittenden, P. M., & Landini, A. (2011). *Assessing adult attachment: A dynamic-maturational approach to discourse analysis.* New York, NY: W. W. Norton.

Cromier, W. H., & Cromier, L. S. (1985). *Interviewing strategies for helpers: Fundamental* skills and cognitive behavioral interventions. Monterey, CA: Brooks/Cole.

Cromier, W. H., Nurius, P. S., & Osborn, C. J. (2008). Interviewing strategies for helpers: Fundamental skills and cognitive behavioral interventions (6th ed.). Monterey, CA: Brooks/Cole.

Cross, F. L., & Livingstone, E. A. (Eds.). (2005). Actual sin. In The Oxford dictionary of the Christian Church (3rd rev. ed., p. 14). New York, NY: Oxford University Press.

Cummings, A. L. (1992). A model for teaching experiential counseling interventions to novice counselors. Counselor Education & Supervision, 32(1), 23–31.

Cummings, E. M., & Davies, P. T. (2002). Effects of marital conflict on children: Recent advances and emerging themes in process-oriented research. Journal of Child Psychology and Psychiatry and Allied Disciplines, 43(1), 31–63.

Cummings, E. M., & Davies, P. T. (2011). Marital conflict and children: An emotional security perspective. New York, NY: Guilford Press.

Dale, M. A., & Lyddon, W. J. (1998). Sandplay: A constructivist strategy for assessment and change. Journal of Constructivist Psychology, 13, 135–154.

Daly, M., & Wilson, M. (1988). Homicide. New York, NY: A. de Gruyter.

Danielson, T., Lucas, P., Malinowski, R., & Pittman, S. (2009). Set Free Ministries: A comprehensive model for domestic violence congregational interventions. Social Work and Christianity, 36(4), 480–494.

Davey, A., Fincham, F. D., Beach, S. R. H., & Brody, G. H. (2001). Attributions in marriage: Examining the entailment model in dyadic context. Journal of Family Psychology, 15(4), 721–734.

Davidson, R. J., Kabat-Zinn, J., Schumacher, J., Rosenkranz, M., Muller, D., Santorelli, S. F., . . . Sheridan, J. F. (2003). Alterations in brain and immune function produced by mindfulness meditation. Psychosomatic Medicine, 65(4), 564–570.

Davidson, R. M. (2011). Sexual abuse in the Old Testament. In A. J. Schmutzer (Ed.), The long journey home: Understanding and ministering to the sexually abused (pp. 126–154). Eugene, OR: Wipf and Stock.

Davies, P. T., & Cummings, E. M. (1994). Marital conflict and child adjustment: An emotional security hypothesis. Psychological Bulletin, 116(3), 387–411.

Davis, D. E., Hook, J. N., Van Tongeren, D. R., DeBlaere, C., Rice, K. G., & Worthington, E. L., Jr. (2015). Making a decision to forgive. Journal of Counseling Psychology, 62(2), 280–288.

Davis, D. E., Yang, X., DeBlaere, C., McElroy, S. E., Van Tongeren, D. R., Hook, J. N., & Worthington, E. L., Jr. (2016). The injustice gap. Psychology of Religion and Spirituality, 8(3), 175–184.

Dawson, A., Allen, J., Martson, E., Hafen, C., & Schad, M. (2014). Adolescent insecure attachment as a predictor of maladaptive coping and externalizing behaviors in emerging adulthood. Attachment & Human Development, 16, 462–478.

Dayton, T. (2005). The living stage: A step-by-step guide to psychodrama, sociometry and group psychotherapy. Deerfield Beach, FL: Health Communications.

Dearing, R. L., & Tangney, J. P. (Eds.). (2011). Shame in the therapy hour. Washington, DC: American Psychological Association.

Dees, R. F. (2011). Resilient warriors. San Diego, CA: Creative Team.

Degges-White, S., & Davis, N. L. (Eds.). (2011). Integrating the expressive arts into counseling practice: Theory-based interventions (1st ed.). New York, NY: Springer.

Dekker, J., Stauder, A., & Penedo, F. J. (2016). Defining the field of behavioral medicine: A collaborative endeavor. International Journal of Behavioral Medicine. doi:10.1007/s 12529-016-9616–1

Delitzsch, F. (1899). A system of biblical psychology. Edinburgh: T. & T. Clark. Reprinted Grand Rapids, MI: Baker, 1966.

DePrince, A. P., Brown, L. S., Cheit, R. E., Freyd, J. J., Gold, S. N., Pezdek, K., & Quina, K. (2012). Motivated forgetting and misremembering: Perspectives from betrayal trauma theory. *Nebraska Symposium on Motivation*, *58*, 193–242.

Derogatis, L. R., Sand, M., Balon, R., Rosen, R., & Parish, S. J. (2016). Toward a more evidence-based nosology and nomenclature for female sexual dysfunctions: Part 1. *Journal of Sexual Medicine*, *13*(12), 1881–1887. doi:10.1016/j.jsxm.2016.09.014

Deveaux, F., & Lubell, I. (1994). Training the supervisor: Integrating a family of origin approach. *Contemporary Family Therapy*, *16*(4), 291–299. doi:10.1007/BF02196881

DeYoung, P. (2015). *Understanding and treating chronic shame: A relational/neurobiological approach*. New York, NY: Routledge.

Diamond, T., & Muller, R. T. (2004). The relationship between witnessing parental conflict during childhood and later psychological adjustment among university students: Disentangling confounding risk factors. *Canadian Journal of Behavioural Science / Revue canadienne des sciences du comportement*, *36*(4), 295–309. http://dx.doi.org/10.1037/h0087238

DiBlasio, F. A. (in press). Self-forgiveness and personality disorders. In L. Woodyatt, E. L. Worthington, Jr., M. Wenzel, & B. J. Griffin (Eds.), *Handbook of the psychology of self-forgiveness*. New York, NY: Springer.

DiBlasio, F. A. (1998). Harry Aponte: The person behind the Person-Practice Model. *Marriage and the Family: A Christian Journal*, *1*(4), 335–340.

DiBlasio, F. A. (2000a). Decision-based forgiveness treatment in cases of marital infidelity. *Psychotherapy*, *37*, 149–158.

DiBlasio, F. A. (2000b). Systemic thinking and therapeutic intervention. *Journal of Marriage and the Family: A Christian Journal*, *3*, 281–300.

DiBlasio, F. A. (2010). Christ-like forgiveness in marital counseling: A clinical follow-up of two empirical studies. *Journal of Psychology and Christianity*, *29*, 291–300.

DiBlasio, F. A. (2013). Marital couples and forgiveness intervention. In E. L. Worthington, Jr., E. L., Johnson, J. N. Hook, & J. D. Aten (Eds.), *Evidence-based practices for Christian counseling and psychotherapy* (pp. 232–254). Downers Grove, IL: InterVarsity.

DiBlasio, F. A. (2017). Self-forgiveness and personality disorders. In L. Woodyatt, E. L. Worthington, Jr., M. Wenzel, & B. J. Griffin (Eds.), *Handbook of the psychology of self-forgiveness* (pp. 235–248). New York, NY: Springer.

DiBlasio, F. A., Hester, C. P., & Belcher, J. L. R. (2014). Emotional and interpersonal dyslexia: Thoughts toward a neurological theory of personality disorders. *Journal of Psychology and Christianity*, *33*, 374–384.

DiBlasio, F. A., Worthington, E. L., Jr., & Jennings, D. J., II (2012). Forgiveness interventions with children, adolescents, and families. In D. F. Walker, & W. L. Hathaway (Eds.), *Spiritual interventions in child and adolescent psychotherapy* (pp. 233–258). Washington, DC: American Psychological Association.

Dickerson, S. S., Gruenwald, T. L., & Kemeny, M. E. (2004). When the social self is threatened: Shame, physiology, and health. *Journal of Personality*, *72*(6), 1191–1216.

Dickie, J., Eshleman, A., Merasco, D., Shepard, A., Vander Wilt, M., & Johnson, M. (1997). Parent-child relationships and children's images of God. *Journal for the Scientific Study of Religion*, *36*. doi:10.2307/1387880

Diepold, J. (2000). Touch and breathe: An alternative treatment approach with meridian-based psychotherapies. *Traumatology: An International Journal*, *6*(2), 109–118.

Dimidjian, S., Martell, C. R., Herman-Dunn, R., & Hubley, S. (2014). Behavioral activation for depression. In D. H. Barlow (Ed.), *Clinical handbook of psychological disorders, a step-by-step treatment manual* (5th ed., pp. 353–393). New York, NY: Guilford Press.

Dinkmeyer, D. C., Dinkmeyer, D. C., Jr., & Sperry, L. (1987). *Adlerian counseling and psychotherapy* (2nd ed.). Columbus, OH: Merrill.

Dixon, D. N., & Glover, J. A. (1984). *Counseling: A problem-solving approach*. New York, NY: Wiley.

Dobson, D., & Dobson, K. (2009). *Evidence-based practice of cognitive-behavioral therapy*. New York, NY: Guilford Press.

Dobson, D., & Dobson, K. (2017). *Evidence-based practice of cognitive-behavioral therapy* (2nd ed.). New York, NY: Guilford Press.

Doherty, W. J. (2002). How therapists harm marriages and what we can do about it. *Journal of Couple & Relationship Therapy, 1*(2), 1–17.

Dozier, M., Stovall-McClough, K. C., & Albus, K. E. (2008). Attachment and psychopathology in adulthood. In. J. Cassidy & P. R. Shaver (Eds.), *Handbook of attachment: Theory, research, and clinical applications* (2nd ed., pp. 718–744). New York, NY: Guilford Press.

Drisko, J. W. (2004). Common factors in psychotherapy outcome: Meta-analytic findings and their implications for practice and research. *Families in Society, 85*(1), 81–90.

Drumm, R. D., Popescu, M., & Riggs, M. L. (2009). Gender variations in partner abuse: Findings from a conservative Christian denomination. *Affilia: Journal of Women and Social Work, 24*(1), 56–68. doi:10.1177/0886109908326737

Dryden-Edwards, R. (2018). Grief: Loss of a loved one. *MedicineNet*. Retrieved from https://www.medicinenet.com/loss_grief_and_bereavement/article.htm#what_are_the_causes_and_risk_factors_of_prolonged_grief

Duffey, T. (2006/2007). Promoting relational competencies in counselor education through creativity and relational-cultural theory. *Journal of Creativity in Mental Health, 2*(1), 47–60.

Duffey, T., Haberstroh, S., & Trepal, T. (2009). A grounded theory of relational competencies and creativity in counseling: Beginning the dialogue. *Journal of Creativity in Mental Health, 4*, 89–112. doi:10.1080/15401380902951911

Duffey, T., Somody, C., & Eckstein, D. (2009). Musical relationship metaphors: Using a musical chronology and the emerging life song with couples. *The Family Journal, 17*, 151–155. doi:10.1177/ 1066480709332714

Duker, P. C., & Seys, D. M. (1983). Long-term follow-up effects of extinction and overcorrection procedures with severely retarded individuals. *The British Journal of Subnormality, 29*, 74–80.

Duncan, B. L. (2010). *On becoming a better therapist*, Washington, DC: American Psychological Association.

Duncan, B. L., Miller, S. D., Wampold, B. E., & Hubble, M. A. (Eds.). (2010). *The heart and soul of change: Delivering what works in therapy* (2nd ed.). Washington, DC, US: American Psychological Association. doi:10.1037/12075-000

Dunning, D., Heath, C., & Suls, J. M. (2004). Flawed self-assessment. *Psychological science in the public interest, 5*(3), 69–106.

Eareckson-Tada, J., & Estes, S. (1997). *When God weeps: Why our sufferings matter to the Almighty*. Grand Rapids, MI: Zondervan.

Eck, B. E. (2002). An exploration of the therapeutic use of spiritual disciplines in clinical practice. *Journal of Psychology and Christianity, 21*(3), 266–280.

Edgar, D. (1969). *Audio-visual methods in teaching* (3rd ed.). New York, NY: Holt, Rinehart, & Winston.

Egan, G. (2014). *The skilled helper: A problem-management and opportunity development approach to helping* (10th ed.). Belmont, CA: Brooks/Cole.

Eilts, M. B. (1995). Saving the family: When is covenant broken? In C. J. Adams & M. M. Fortune (Eds.), *Violence against women and children: A Christian theological sourcebook* (pp. 444–450). New York, NY: Continuum.

Elise, D. (2008). Sex and shame: The inhibition of female desires. *Journal of American Psychoanalysis Association, 56*, 173–198.

Elison, J., Lennon, R., & Pulos, S. (2006). Investigating the Compass of Shame: The development of the Compass of Shame Scale. *Social Behavior and Personality, 34*(3), 221–238.

Elison, J., Pulos, S., & Lennon, R. (2006). Shame-focused coping: An empirical study of the Compass of Shame. *Social Behavior and Personality, 34*(2), 161–168.

Elkin, I., Shea, M., Watkins, J. T., Imber, S. D., Sotsky, S. M., Collins, J. F., . . . Parloff, M. B. (1989). National Institute of Mental Health Treatment of Depression Collaborative Research Program: General effectiveness of treatments. *Archives of General Psychiatry, 46*(11), 971–982.

Elkins, D. N. (2007). Empirically supported treatments: The deconstruction of a myth. *Journal of Humanistic Psychology, 47,* 474–500.

Elkins, D. N. (2009). The medical model in psychotherapy: Its limitations and failures. *Journal of Humanistic Psychology, 49,* 66–84.

Elliott, R., Davis, K. L., & Slatick, E. (1998). Process-experiential therapy for post-traumatic stress disorder. In L. S. Greenberg, J. C. Watson, & G. Lietaer (Eds.). *Handbook of experiential therapy* (pp. 49–271). New York, NY: Guilford Press.

Ellis, A., & Grieger, R. (1977). *Handbook of rational-emotive therapy* (Vol. 2). New York, NY: Springer.

Ellis, A., & MacLaren, C. (2005). *Rational emotive behavior therapy: A therapist's guide* (2nd ed.). Oakland, CA: Impact.

Ellison, H. L. (1985). Jonah. In F. E. Gaebelein (Ed.), *The expositor's Bible commentary* (Vol. 7, pp. 359–391). Grand Rapids, MI: Zondervan.

Emmons, R. A., Colby, P. M., & Kaiser, H. (1998). When losses lead to gains: Personal goals and the recovery of meaning. In P. T. Wong & P. S. Fry (Eds.), *The human quest for meaning* (pp. 163–178). Mahwah, NJ: Erlbaum.

Engelhard, I. M., Leer, A., Lange, E., & Olatunji, B. O. (2014). Shaking that icky feeling: Effects of extinction and counter-conditioning on learned disgust. *Behavior Therapy, 45,* 708–719.

Enright, R. D. (2001). *Forgiveness is a choice: A step-by-step process for resolving anger and resolving hope.* Washington, DC: American Psychological Press.

Enright, R. D., & Fitzgibbons, R. P. (2014). *Forgiveness therapy: An empirical guide for re-solving anger and restoring hope.* Washington, DC: American Psychological Association.

Erb, E. D., & Hooker, D. (1971). *The psychology of the emerging self: An integrated interpretation of goal-directed behavior* (2nd ed.). Philadelphia, PA: F. A. Davis.

Erikson, E. (1950, 1963). *Childhood and society.* New York, NY: W. W. Norton.

Evans, C. S. (1990). *Soren Kierkegaard's Christian psychology: Insight for counseling and pastoral care.* Vancouver, BC: Regent College.

Exline, J. J., Worthington, E. L., Jr., Hill, P., & McCullough, M. E. (2003). Forgiveness and justice: A research agenda for social and personality psychology. *Personality Social Psychology Review, 7*(4), 337–348.

Eyre, H. L. (2004). *The Shame and Guilt Inventory: Development of a new scenario-based measure of shame-and guilt-proneness* (Unpublished doctoral dissertation). University of Kentucky, Lexington.

Eysenck, H. J. (1992). *Decline and fall of the Freudian empire.* London: Penguin.

Eysenck, H. J. (1992). *The rise and fall of the Freudian empire.* New York, NY: Penguin Psychology.

Fabricius, W. V., & Luecken, L. J. (2007). Postdivorce living arrangements, parent conflict, and long-term physical health correlates for children of divorce. *Journal of Family Psychology, 21*(2), 195–205.

Fall, K. A., Holden, J. M., & Marquis, A. (2010). *Theoretical models of counseling and psychotherapy* (2nd ed.). New York, NY: Routledge.

Fallot, R. D. (2001). Spirituality and religion in psychiatric rehabilitation and recovery from mental illness. *International Review of Psychiatry, 13*(1), 110–116.

Fallot, R. D., & Heckman, J. P. (2005). Religious/spiritual coping among women trauma survivors with mental health and substance use disorders. *Journal of Behavioral Health Services & Research, 32*(2), 215–226.

Farnfield, S., & Holmes, P. (2014). *The Routledge handbook of attachment: Assessment.* New York, NY: Routledge.

Fergus, T. A., Valentiner, D. P., McGrath, P. B., & Jencius, S. (2010). Shame-and guilt-proneness: Relationships with anxiety disorder symptoms in a clinical sample. *Journal of Anxiety Disorders, 24*, 811–815.

Ferree, M. C. (Ed.). (2012). *Making advances: A comprehensive guide for treating female sex and love addicts.* Roystone, GA: SASH.

Ferrer-Chancey, M., & Fugate, M. N. (2003). Helping your child develop a healthy self-concept. *Document FCS2205, one of a series of the Family Youth and Community Sciences Department, UF/IFAS Extension.* http://citeseerx.ist.psu.edu/viewdoc/download;jsessionid=A96C1BF5552887F A79B8B24764908743?doi=10.1.1.59 8.7459&rep=rep1&type=pdfFichten

Findlay, R. (2017). A narrative therapy approach to sex therapy. In Z. Peterson (Ed.), *The Wiley handbook of sex therapy* (pp. 231–249). New York, NY: Wiley-Blackwell.

Fine, A. H. (2015). *Handbook on animal assisted therapy* (4th ed.). San Diego, CA: Academic Press.

Finger, W. W., Lund, M., & Slagle, M. A. (1997). Medications that may contribute to sexual disorders. A guide to assessment and treatment in family practice. *Journal of Family Practice, 44*(1), 33–43.

Firestone, R. W. (2001). *Voice therapy: A psychotherapeutic approach to self-destructive behavior.* Santa Barbara, CA: Glendon Association.

Fischer, M. S., Baucom, D. H., & Cohen, M. J. (2016). Cognitive-behavioral couple therapies: Review of the evidence for the treatment of relationship distress, psychopathology, and chronic health conditions. *Family Process, 55*(3), 423–442.

Fishbane, M. D. (2007). Wired to connect: Neuroscience, relationships, and therapy. *Family Process, 46*(3), 395–412.

Fisher, A. D., Corona, G., Bandini, E., Mannucci, E., Lotti, F., Boddi, V., & Maggi, M. (2010). Psychobiological correlates of extramarital affairs and differences between stable and occasional infidelity among men with sexual dysfunctions. *Journal of Sexual Medicine, 6*(3), 866–875. doi:10.1111/j.1743-6109.2008.01140.x

Fisher, J. E., & O'Donohue, W. T. (Eds.). (2006). *Practitioner's guide to evidence-based psychotherapy.* New York, NY: Springer.

Fishman, D. B., Rego, S. A., & Muller, K. L. (2011). Behavioral theories of psychotherapy. In J. C. Norcross, G. R. Vandenbos, & D. K. Freedheim (Eds.), *History of psychotherapy: Continuity and change* (2nd ed., pp. 101–140). Washington, DC: American Psychological Association.

Fitzsimmonds, F. S. (1996). Walk. In D. R. Wood, I. Howard Marshall, A. R. Millard, J. I. Packer, & D. J. Wiseman (Eds.), *New Bible dictionary* (3rd ed.). Downers Grove, IL: InterVarsity.

Fletcher, M. S. (1912). *The psychology of the New Testament.* London: Hodder & Stoughton.

Foa, E. B., Hembree, E. A., & Rothbaum, B. O. (2007). *Prolonged exposure therapy for PTSD: Therapist guide.* New York, NY: Oxford University Press.

Foa, E. B., Yadin, E., & Lichner, T. K. (2012). *Exposure and response (ritual) for obsessive-compulsive disorder: Therapist guide* (Treatments That Work). New York, NY: Oxford University Press.

Forster, J. L. (1873). *Biblical psychology: In four parts.* London: Longmans, Green, & Co.

Fosha, D., Siegel, D., & Solomon, M. (Eds.). (2009). *The healing power of emotion: Affective neuroscience, development & clinical practice.* New York, NY: W. W. Norton.

Fossum, M. A., & Mason, M. J. (1986). *Facing shame: Families in recovery.* New York, NY: W. W. Norton.

Foster, R. J. (1998). *Celebration of discipline: The path to spiritual growth* (25th anniversary ed.). San Francisco, CA: HarperCollins.

Foster, R. J. (2002). *Prayer: Finding the heart's true home.* San Francisco, CA: HarperCollins.

Foster, S. L., Laverty-Finch, C., Gizzo, D. P., & Osantowski, J. (1999). Practical issues in self-observation. *Psychological Assessment, 11*, 426–438. doi:10.1037/1040-3590.11.4.426

Fowers, B. J. (2005). Psychotherapy, character, and the good life. In B. D. Slife, J. S. Reber, & F. C. Richardson (Eds.), *Critical thinking about psychology: Hidden assumptions and plausible alternatives* (pp. 39–59). Washington, DC: American Psychological Association.

Fraley, R. C., Waller, N. G., & Brennan, K. A. (2000). An item-response theory analysis of self-report measures of adult attachment. *Journal of Personality and Social Psychology, 78,* 350–365.

Framo, J. (1992). *Family-of-origin therapy: An intergenerational approach.* New York, NY: Brunner/Mazel.

Framo, J., Weber, T., & Levine, F. (2003). *Coming home again: A family-of-origin consultation.* New York, NY: Brunner/Routledge.

Frederick, T. V. (2008). Solution-focused brief therapy and the kingdom of God: A cosmological integration. *Pastoral Psychology, 56*(4), 413–419.

Freedman, S. (1998). Forgiveness and reconciliation: The importance of understanding how they differ. *Counseling and Values, 42*(3), 155–232.

Freud, A. (1937). *The ego and the mechanisms of defense.* London: Hogarth Press and Institute of Psycho-Analysis.

Freud, S. (1927, 2010). *The future of an illusion.* Blacksburg, VA: Wilder.

Freyd, J. J., DePrince, A. P., & Gleaves, D. H. (2007). The state of betrayal trauma theory. *Memory, 15,* 295–311.

Freytag, G. (1900). *Technique of dramatic composition and art: An exposition of dramatic composition and art* (3rd ed.). Translation from the 6th German edition by E. J. MacEwan. Chicago, IL: Scott, Foresman.

Fullagar, S. (2003). Wasted lives: The social dynamics of shame and youth suicide. *Journal of Sociology, 39,* 291–307. doi:10.1177/0004869003035076

Futterman, R., Lorente, M., & Silverman, S. (2005). Beyond harm reduction: A new model of substance abuse treatment further

integrating psychological techniques. *Journal of Psychotherapy Integration, 15*(1), 3–18.

Galvin, K. M., Braitwaite, D. O., & Bylund, C. L. (2016). *Family communication: Cohesion and change* (9th ed.). New York, NY: Routledge.

Gardner, B., Busby, D., Burr, B., & Lyon, S. (2011). Getting to the root of relationship attributions: Family-of-origin perspectives on self and partner views. *Contemporary Family Therapy: An International Journal, 33*(3), 253–272.

Garfield, A. E., & Bergin, S. L. E. (1986). *Handbook of psychotherapy and behavior change.* Hoboken, NJ: Wiley.

Garland, D. E. (2002). Mark. In C. E. Arnold (Ed.), *Zondervan illustrated Bible backgrounds commentary* (Vol. 1, pp. 204–317). Grand Rapids, MI: Zondervan.

Garnefski, N., Van Den Kommer, T., Kraaij, V., Teerds, J., Legerstee, J., & Onstein, E. (2002). The relationship between cognitive emotion regulation strategies and emotional problems: Comparison between a clinical and non-clinical sample. *European Journal of Personality, 16,* 403–420.

Garner, A. M. (2014). Preparing the mind and body for performance: Conquering stage fright through effective practice. *Clavier Companion, 6*(4), 54–57.

Garrett, R. (2006). Critical storytelling as a teaching strategy in physical teacher education. *European Physical Educational Review, 12*(3), 339–360. doi:10.1177/1356336X06069277

Garzon, F. L. (2005). Interventions that apply Scripture in psychotherapy. *Journal of Psychology and Theology, 33*(2), 113–121.

Garzon, F. L. (2013). Christian devotional meditation for anxiety. In E. L. Worthington, Jr., E. L., Johnson, J. N. Hook, & J. D. Aten (Eds.), *Evidence-based practices for Christian counseling and psychotherapy* (pp. 59–76). Downers Grove, IL: IVP Academic.

Garzon, F., & Burkett, L. (2002). Healing of memories: Models, research, future directions. *Journal of Psychology and Christianity, 21*(2) 42–49.

Garzon, F., & Ford, K. (2016). Adapting mindfulness for conservative Christians. *Journal of Psychology and Christianity, 35*(3), 23–268.

Garzon, F., Worthington, E., Tan, S.-Y., & Worthington, R. (2009). Lay Christian counseling and client expectations for integration in therapy. *Journal of Psychology and Christianity, 28*, 113–120.

Gasman, D. (1992). Double-exposure therapy: Videotape homework as a psychotherapeutic adjunct. *American Journal of Psychotherapy, 46*, 91–101.

Geertsma, R., & Reivich, R. (1965). Repetitive self-observation by videotape playback. *Journal of Nervous and Mental Disorders, 141*, 29–41.

Geldard, D., & Geldard, K. (2012). *Basic personal counselling: A training manual for counsellors* (7th ed.). Frenchs Forest, NSW: Pearson Education.

Gelo, O. C. G., & Mergenthaler, E. (2012). Unconventional metaphors and emotional-cognitive regulation in a metacognitive interpersonal therapy. *Psychotherapy Research, 22*, 159–175. doi:10.1080/10503307.2011.629636

Gendlin, E. T. (1982). *Focusing*. New York, NY: Bantam.

Gendlin, E. T. (1996). *Focusing psychotherapy: A manual of the experiential method*. New York, NY: Guilford Press.

Genuchi, M. C., Hopper, B., & Morrison, C. R. (2017). Using metaphors to facilitate exploration of emotional content in counseling with college men. *Journal of Men's Studies, 25*(2), 133–149. doi:10.1177/1060826516661187

George, C., Kaplan, N., & Main, M. (1985). *The Adult Attachment Interview* (Unpublished manuscript). University of California at Berkeley. Retrieved from http://www.psychology.sunysb.edu/attachment/measures/content/aai_interview.pdf

Germer, C. K., & Neff, K. D. (2013). Self-compassion in clinical practice. *Journal of Clinical Psychology, 69*(8), 856–867. doi:10.1002/jclp.22021

Gil, E. (1996). *Treating abused adolescents*. New York, NY: Guilford Press

Gilbert, P. (2010). *Compassion focused therapy: The distinctive features*. London: Routledge.

Gilbert, P., & Procter, S. (2006). Compassionate mind training for people with high shame and self-criticism: A pilot study of a group therapy approach. *Clinical Psychology and Psychotherapy, 13*, 353–379. doi:10.1002/cpp.507

Gilman, R., & Chard, K. M. (2007). Cognitive-behavioral and behavioral approaches. In H. T. Prout & D. T. Brown (Eds.), *Counseling and psychotherapy with children and adolescents: Theory and practice for school and clinical settings* (4th ed., pp. 241–278). Hoboken, NJ: Wiley.

Gingrich, H. D. (2002). Stalked by death: Cross-cultural trauma work with a tribal missionary. *Journal of Psychology and Christianity, 21*(3), 262–265.

Gingrich, H. D. (2013). *Restoring the shattered self: A Christian counselor's guide to complex trauma*. Downers Grove, IL: IVP Academic.

Gingrich, H. D., & Gingrich, F. C. (Eds.). (2017). *Treating trauma in Christian counseling*. Downers Grove, IL: IVP Academic.

Ginot, E. (2007). Intersubjectivity and neuroscience: Understanding enactments and their therapeutic significance within emerging paradigms. *Psychoanalytic Psychology, 24*(2), 317–332. http://dx.doi.org/10.1037/0736-9735.24.2.317

Ginot, E. (2012). Self-narratives and dysregulated affective states: The neuropsychological links between self-narratives, attachment, affect and cognition. *Psychoanalytic Psychology, 29*, 59–80.

Giovazolias, T., & Davis, P. (2001). How common is sexual attraction towards clients? The experiences of sexual attraction of counselling psychologists toward their clients and its impact on the therapeutic process. *Counselling Psychology Quarterly, 14*(4), 281–286. doi:10.1080/09515070110100974

Giraldi, A., Kristensen, E., & Sand, M. (2015a). Endorsement of models describing sexual response of men and women with a sexual partner: An online survey in a population sample of Danish adults ages 20–65 years. *Journal of Sexual Medicine, 12*(1), 116–128. doi:10.1111/jsm.12720

Giraldi, A., Kristensen, E., & Sand, M. (2015b). Response and rebuttal of "endorsement of models describing sexual response of men and women with a sexual partner: An online survey in a population sample of Danish adults ages 20–65 Years." *Journal of Sexual Medicine, 12*(9), 1981–1982. doi:10.1111/jsm.12984

Gladding, S. T. (1979). The creative use of poetry in the counseling process. *Personnel & Guidance Journal, 57*(6), 57–59.

Gladding, S. T. (2005). *Counseling as an art: The creative arts in counseling* (3rd ed.). Alexandria, VA: American Counseling Association.

Gladding, S. T. (2006). *The counseling dictionary: Concise definitions of frequently used terms.* Upper Saddle River, NJ: Pearson.

Gladding, S. T., & Henderson, D. A. (2000). Creativity and family counseling: The SCAMPER model as a template for promoting creative processes. *The Family Journal, 8,* 245–249. doi:10.1177/1066480700083005

Glass, S. P. (2000). Infidelity. *AAMFT Clinical Update, 2*(1), 1–8.

Glass, S. P. (2003). *Not "just friends": Rebuilding trust and recovering your sanity after infidelity.* New York, NY: Free Press.

Glasser, M., Kolvin, I., Campbell, D., Glasser, A., Leitch, A., & Farrelly, S. (2001). Cycle of child sexual abuse: Links between being a victim and becoming a perpetrator. *British Journal of Psychiatry, 179,* 495–497.

Glover-Graf, N. M., Marini, I., Baker, J., & Buck, T. (2007). Religious and spiritual beliefs and practices of persons with chronic pain. *Rehabilitation Counseling Bulletin, 51*(1), 21–33.

Glynn, L. M., Wadhwa, P. D., & Sandman, C. A. (2000). The influence of corticotropin releasing hormone on human fetal development and parturition. *Journal of Prenatal and Perinatal Psychic Health, 14,* 243–256.

Goffman, E. (1959). *The presentation of self in everyday life.* New York, NY: Doubleday.

Gonzalez, J. E., Nelson, J. R., Gutkin, T. B., Saunders, A., Galloway, A., & Shwery, C. S. (2004). Rational emotive therapy with children and adolescents: A meta-analysis. *Journal of Emotional and Behavioral Disorders, 12,* 222–235.

Good, M. C. (2017). *Real talk: Creating space for hearts to change.* Sisters, OR: Deep River.

Gottman, J. M. (1993). A theory of marital dissolution and stability. *Journal of Family Psychology, 7*(1), 57–75. doi.org/10.1037/0893-3200.7.1.57

Gottman, J. M. (1999). *The marriage clinic: A scientifically-based marital therapy.* New York, NY: W. W. Norton.

Gottman, J. M., Coan, J., Carrere, S., & Swanson, C. (1998). Predicting marital happiness and stability from newlywed interactions. *Journal of Marriage and the Family, 60*(1), 5–22.

Gottman, J. M., & Levenson, R. W. (2002). A two-factor model for predicting when a couple will divorce: Exploratory analyses using 14-year longitudinal data. *Family Process, 41*(1), 83–96.

Gottman, J. M., & Silver, N. (2012). *What makes love last? How to build trust and avoid betrayal.* New York, NY: Simon & Schuster.

Grabhorn, R., Stenner, H., Stangier, U., & Kaufhold, J. (2006). Social anxiety in anorexia and bulimia nervosa: The mediating role of shame. *Clinical Psychology and Psychotherapy, 13*(1), 12–19.

Gräfenberg, E. (1950). The role of the urethra in female orgasm. *International Journal of Sexology, 3*(3), 145–148.

Graham, R. B. (1999). *Prodigals and those who love them.* Grand Rapids, MI: Baker.

Graham-Bermann, S. A., & Perkins, S. (2010). Effects of early exposure and lifetime exposure to intimate partner violence (IPV) on child adjustment. *Violence and Victims, 25*(4), 427–439.

Granvold, D. K. (1994). Cognitive and behavioral treatment: Methods and applications. Belmont, CA: Thomson Brooks/Cole.

Granvold, D. K., & Tarrant, R. (1983). Structured marital separation as a marital treatment method. *Journal of Marital and Family Therapy, 9*(2), 189–198. doi:10.1111/j.1752-0606.1983.tb01499.x

Gratz, K. L. (2006). Risk factors for deliberate self-harm among female college students: The role and interaction of childhood maltreatment, emotional inexpressivity, and affect intensity/reactivity. *American Journal of Orthopsychiatry, 76*(2), 238–250.

Gratz, K. L., & Chapman, A. (2007). The role of emotional responding and childhood maltreatment in the development and maintenance of deliberate self-harm among male undergraduates. *Psychology of Men & Masculinity, 8*(1), 1–14.

Grecucci, A., Pappaianni, E., Siugzdaite, R., Theuninck, A., & Job, R. (2015). Mindful emotion regulation: Exploring the neurocognitive mechanisms behind mindfulness. *BioMed Research International*, Article ID: 670742.

Green, S., Flemons, D., & Flemons, D. G. (2007). *Quickies: The handbook of brief sex therapy.* New York, NY: W. W. Norton.

Greenberg, L. J., Warwar, S. H., & Malcolm, W. M. (2008). Differential effects of emotion-focused therapy and psychoeducation in facilitating forgiveness and letting go of emotional injuries. *Journal of Counseling Psychology, 55*, 185–196.

Greenberg, L. S. (2002). *Emotion-focused therapy.* Washington, DC: American Psychological Association.

Greenberg, L. S., Rice, L. N., & Elliott, R. (1993). *Facilitating emotional change: The moment by moment process.* New York, NY: Guilford Press.

Greenberg, L. S., & Van Balen, R. (1998). The theory of experience-centered therapies. In L. S. Greenberg, J. C. Watson, & G.

Lietaer (Eds.), *Handbook of experiential psychotherapy* (pp. 28–57). New York, NY: Guilford Press.

Greenberg, L. S., & Watson, J. C. (2010). Experiential therapy of depression: Differential effects of client-centered relationship conditions and process experiential interventions. *Psychotherapy Research, 8*(2), 210–224.

Greenberg, L. S., & Watson, J. (1998). Experiential therapy of depression: Differential effects of client-centered relationship conditions and process experiential interventions. *Psychotherapy Research, 8*, 210–224.

Greenberg, L. S., Watson, J. C., & Lietaer, G. O. (1998). *Handbook of experiential psychotherapy* (1st ed.). New York, NY: Guilford Press.

Greenberg, M. T., Cicchetti, D., & Cummings, E. M. (1990). *Attachment in the preschool years: Theory, research, & intervention.* Chicago, IL: University of Chicago Press.

Greer, C. L., Worthington, E. L., Van Tongeren, D. R., Gartner, A. L., Jennings, D. J., Lin, Y., . . . Ho, M. Y. (2014). Forgiveness of ingroup offenders in Christian congregations. *Psychology of Religion and Spirituality, 6*(2), 150–161.

Greggo, S. P. (2008). *Trekking toward wholeness: A resource for care group leaders.* Downers Grove, IL: InterVarsity.

Greggo, S. P. (2016). Counselor identity and Christian imagination: Striving for professional case conceptualization and artistic contextualization. *Journal of Psychology and Christianity, 35*(1), 22–35.

Greggo, S. P. (2017). *Assessment in Christian perspective: Craftsmanship and connection.* Downers Grove, IL: InterVarsity.

Greggo, S. P., & Lawrence, K. (2012). Clinical appraisal of spirituality: In search of rapid assessment instruments (RAIs) for Christian counseling. *Journal of Psychology and Christianity, 31*(3), 253–266.

Gregoire, J. (2004). Sexual addiction and compulsivity among clergy: How spiritual directors can help in the context of seminary formation. *Sexual Addiction & Compulsivity, 11*(1/2), 71–81.

Gregory, A. (2014). The impact of trauma on sexual functioning. *International Journal of Urological Nursing, 8*(1), 44–48. doi:10.1111/ijun.12031

Grice, H. P. (1975). Logic and conversation. In D. Davidson & G. Harman (Eds.), *The logic of grammar* (pp. 64–153). Encino, CA: Dickinson.

Griffin, B. J., Worthington, E. L., Jr., Lavelock, C. R., Greer, C. L., Lin, Y., Davis, D. E., & Hook, J. N. (2015). Efficacy of a self-forgiveness workbook: A randomized controlled trial with interpersonal offenders. *Journal of Counseling Psychology, 62*(2), 124–136.

Grimm, D. (2015, April 16). How dogs stole our hearts. Retrieved from http://www.sciencemag.org/news/2015/04/how-dogs-stole-our-hearts

Grinder, J., & Bandler, R. (1976). *The structure of magic II: A book about communication and change* (1st ed.). Palo Alto, CA: Science and Behavioral Books.

Gross, A. M. (1985). Self-control therapy. In A. S. Bellack & M. Hersen (Eds.), *Dictionary of behavioral therapy techniques* (pp. 192–194). Elmsford, NY: Pergamon.

Gross, J., & John, O. (2003). Individual differences in two emotion regulation processes: Implications for affect, relationships and well-being. *Journal of Personality and Social Psychology, 85*, 348–362.

Grossman, K. E., Grossman, K., & Waters, E. (2005). *Attachment from infancy to adulthood: The major longitudinal studies.* New York, NY: Guilford Press.

Grych, J. H. (1998). Children's appraisals of interparental conflict: Situational and contextual influences. *Journal of Family Psychology, 12*, 437–453.

Grych, J. H., & Fincham, F. D. (1990). Marital conflict and children's adjustment: A cognitive-contextual framework. *Psychology Bulletin, 108*(2), 267–290.

Gurman, A. S., & Kniskern, D. P. (1981). *Handbook of family therapy* (Vol. 1). New York, NY: Brunner/Mazel.

Gurman, A. S., Lebow, J. L., & Snyder, D. K. (Eds.). (2015). *Clinical handbook of couple therapy* (5th ed.). New York, NY: Guilford Press.

Haber, R., & Hawley, L. (2004). Family of origin as a supervisory consultative resource. *Family Process, 43*(3), 373–390.

Hahn, D. (Producer), Allers, R., & Minkoff, R. (Directors). (1994). *The Lion King* [Motion Picture]. United States: Disney.

Haley, J. (1984). *Ordeal therapy: Unusual ways to change behavior.* San Francisco, CA: Jossey-Bass.

Haley, J. (1991). *Problem-solving therapy.* San Francisco. CA: Jossey-Bass.

Haley, J., & Hoffman, L. (1967). *Techniques of family therapy: Five leading therapists reveal their working styles, strategies, and approaches.* New York, NY: Basic Books.

Hall, E. (2006). *Guided imagery: Creative interventions in counselling & psychotherapy.* Thousand Oaks, CA: Sage.

Hall, E., Hall, C., Stradling, P., & Young, D. (2006). *Guided imagery: Creative interventions in counseling and psychotherapy.* Thousand Oaks, CA: Sage.

Hall, M. E. (2016). Suffering in God's presence: The role of lament in transformation. *Journal of Spiritual Formation and Soul Care, 9*(2), 219–232.

Halpenny, E. A., & Linzmayer, C. D. (2013). "It was fun": An evaluation of sand tray pictures, an innovative visually expressive method for researching children's experiences with nature. *International Journal of Qualitative Methods, 12*, 310–337. Retrieved from http://ejournals.library.ualberta.ca/index.php/IJQM/article/view/17085/15435

Haltzman, S. (2013). *The secrets of surviving infidelity.* Baltimore, MD: Johns Hopkins University Press.

Hamilton, M., & Weiss, M. (2007). *Why use storytelling as a teacher too?* Retrieved from www.beautyandthebeaststorytellers.com/Handouts/WhyUseStorytelling.pdf

Harder, D. W., Cutler, L., & Rockart, L. (1992). Assessment of shame and guilt and their relationships to psychopathology. *Journal of Personality Assessment, 59*(3), 584–604.

Harkess, K., Delfabbro, P., Mortimer, J., Hannaford, Z., & Cohen-Woods, S. (2017). Brief report on the psychophysiological effects of a yoga intervention for chronic stress: Preliminary findings. *Journal of Psychophysiology, 31*, 38–48.

Harmon, R., & Lee, D. (2010). The role of shame and self-critical thinking in the development and maintenance of current threat in post-traumatic stress disorder. *Clinical Psychology & Psychotherapy, 17*, 13–24. doi:10/1002/cpp.636

Harper, A. F. (1967). Ecclesiastes. In A. F. Harper, W. M. Greathouse, R. Earle, & W. T. Purkiser (Eds.), *Beacon Bible commentary* (Vol. 3, pp. 545–597). Kansas City, MO: Beacon Hill.

Harper, J. M., & Hoopes, M. H. (1990). *Uncovering shame: An approach integrating individuals and their family systems.* New York, NY: W. W. Norton.

Harper, Q., Worthington, E. L., Jr., Griffin, B. J., Lavelock, C. R., Hook, J. N., Vrana, S. R., & Greer, C. L. (2014). Efficacy of a workbook to promote forgiveness: A randomized controlled trial with university students. *Journal of Clinical Psychology, 70*(12), 1158–1169.

Harris, S. M. (2001). Teaching family therapists about sexual attraction in therapy. *Journal of Marital and Family Therapy, 27*(1), 123–128. doi:10.1111/j.1752-0606.2001.tb01145.x

Hart, A. D., Weber, C. H., & Taylor, D. (1998). *Secrets of Eve: Understand the mystery of female sexuality.* Nashville, TN: Word.

Hart, T. (2000). Through the arts: Hearing, seeing, and touching the truth. In J. S. Begbie (Ed.), *Beholding the glory: Incarnation through the arts* (pp. 1–26). Grand Rapids, MI: Baker.

Harter, S. (2012a). *The construction of the self* (2nd ed.). New York, NY: Guilford Press.

Harter, S. (2012b). Emerging self-processes during childhood and adolescence. In M. R.

Leary & J. P. Tangney (Eds.), *Handbook of self and identity* (pp. 680–715). New York, NY: Guilford Press.

Harvey, D. R. (1995). *Surviving betrayal: Counseling an adulterous marriage.* Grand Rapids, MI: Baker.

Harvey, J. H., Wenzel, A., & Sprecher, S. (Eds.). (2004). *The handbook of sexuality in close relationships.* New York, NY: Psychology Press.

Haynes, S. C., Strosahl, K. D., & Wilson, K. G. (1999). *Acceptance and commitment therapy: An experiential approach to behavior change.* New York, NY: Guilford Press.

Heath, W., & Darley, S. (2008). *The expressive arts activity book: A resource for professionals.* Philadelphia, PA: Jessica Kingsley.

Hedtke, L. (2013). Creating stories of hope: A narrative approach to illness, death, and grief. *International Journal of Narrative Therapy & Community Work, 1*, 1–10.

Hegstrom, P. (2004). *Angry men and the women who love them: Breaking the cycle of physical and emotional abuse* (Rev. ed.). Kansas City, MO: Beacon Hill.

Heider, F. (1958). *The psychology of interpersonal relations.* New York, NY: Wiley.

Heiman, J., & LoPiccolo, J. (1988). *Becoming orgasmic: A sexual and personal growth program for women* (Rev. and expanded ed.). New York, NY: Prentice Hall.

Heinz, A., Epstein, D. H., & Preston, K. L. (2007). Spiritual/religious experiences and in-treatment outcome in an inner-city program for heroin and cocaine dependence. *Journal of Psychoactive Drugs, 39*(1), 41–49.

Henderson, D. A., & Thompson, C. L. (2011). *Counseling children* (8th ed.). Belmont, CA: Brooks/Cole.

Hendricks, C. B., & Bradley, L. J. (2005). Interpersonal theory and music techniques: A case study for a family with a depressed adolescent. *The Family Journal, 13*, 400–405. doi:10.1177/1066480705278469

Henslee, A. M., & Coffey, S. F. (2010). Exposure therapy for post-traumatic stress disorder in a residential substance use treatment facility. *Professional Psychology:*

Research and Practice, 41, 34–40. doi:10.1037/a0018235

Herbers, J. E., Cutuli, J. J., Supkoff, L. M., Narayan, A. J., & Masten, A. S. (2014). Parenting and coregulation: Adaptive systems for competence in children experiencing homelessness. American Journal of Orthopsychiatry, 84(4), 420–430. doi:10.1037/h0099843

Herman, J. (1997). Trauma and recovery: The aftermath of violence-from domestic abuse to political terror. New York, NY: Basic Books.

Hermann, A., Beiber, A., Keck, T., Vaitl, D., & Stark, R. (2014). Brain structural basis of cognitive reappraisal and excessive suppression. SCAN, 9, 1435–1442.

Hertlein, K. M., Weeks, G. R., & Gambescia, N. (2015). Systemic sex therapy. New York, NY: Taylor & Francis.

Herzberg, K. N., Sheppard, S. C., Forsyth, J. P., Credé, M., Earleywine, M., & Eifert, G. H. (2012). The believability of anxious feelings and thoughts questionnaire (BAFT): A psychometric evaluation of cognitive fusion in a nonclinical and highly anxious community sample. Psychological Assessment, 24(4), 877–891. doi:10.1037/a0027782

Hesse, E. (2008). The adult attachment interview: Protocol, method of analysis, and empirical studies. In J. Cassidy & P. R. Shaver (Eds.), Handbook of attachment: Theory, research, and clinical applications (2nd ed., pp. 552–598). New York, NY: Guilford Press.

Higgins, S. T., & Petry, N. M. (1990). Contingency management: Incentives for sobriety. Alcohol Research & Health, 23(2), 122–127.

Hill, P., Pargament, K., Hood, R., Jr., McCullough, M., Swyers, J., Larson, D., & Zinnbauer, B. (2000). Conceptualizing religion and spirituality: Points of commonality, points of departure. Journal for the Theory of Social Behavior, 30, 51–77.

Hite, S. (1981). The Hite report on male sexuality (1st ed.). New York, NY: Knopf.

Hogan, S., & Coulter, A. M. (2014). The introductory guide to art therapy: Experiential teaching for students and practitioners (1st ed.). New York, NY: Routledge.

Hogg, M. A., Adelman, J. R., & Blagg, R. D. (2010). Religion in the face of uncertainty: An uncertainty-identity theory account of religiousness. Personality and Social Psychology Review, 14, 72–38.

Homan, K. (2012). Attachment to God mitigates negative effect of media exposure on women's body image. Psychology of Spirituality and Religion, 4, 324–331.

Homeyer, L. E. (2016). Sandtray/sandplay therapy. In K. J. O'Conner, C. Schaefer, & L. D. Braverman (Eds.), Handbook of play therapy (2nd ed., pp. 243–257). Hoboken, NJ: Wiley.

Hook, J. N., Worthington, E. L., Jr., Aten, J. D., & Johnson, E. (2013). Conducting clinical outcome studies in Christian counseling and psychotherapy. In E. L. Worthington, Jr., E. L. Johnson, J. N. Hook, & J. D. Aten (Eds.), Evidence-based practices for Christian counseling and psychotherapy (pp. 303–324). Downers Grove, IL: InterVarsity.

Howell, E. F. (2005). The dissociative mind. Hillsdale, NJ: Analytic Press.

Howell, K. H., Miller, L. E., & Graham-Bermann, S. A. (2012). Evaluating preschool children's attitudes and beliefs about intimate partner violence. Violence and Victims, 27(6). Retrieved from http://journals.sagepub.com/doi/abs/10.1177/0886260511421675?journalCode=jiva

Hughes, D. (2007). Attachment-focused family therapy. New York, NY: W. W. Norton.

Hugo, A., Gomes, J., & Lima, G. (2016). Sexual dysfunction as a side effect of psychopharmacology: What to do now? European Psychiatry, 33, S739. https://www.europsy-journal.com/article/S0924-9338(16)02211-2/pdf

Hull, K. (2009). Computer/video games as a play therapy tool in reducing emotional disturbances in children. Dissertation Abstracts International: Section B: The Sciences and Engineering, Vol. 70 (12-B), 7854.

Hull, K. (2011). Play therapy and Asperger's Syndrome: Helping children and adolescents grow, connect, and heal through the art of play. Lanham, MD: Jason Aronson.

Hull, K. (2014). *Group therapy techniques with children, adolescents, and adults on the autism spectrum*. Lanham, MD: Jason Aronson.

Hull, K. (2015). Technology in the playroom. In K. J. O'Conner, C. Schaefer, & L. D. Braverman (Eds.), *Handbook of play therapy* (2nd ed., pp. 613–627). Hoboken, NJ: Wiley.

Hull, K. (2016). *Where there is despair, hope*. Lynchburg, VA: Liberty Mountain.

Hulstrand, K. L. (2015). *Shame—the good, the bad and the ugly: Therapist perspectives* (Unpublished master's thesis). St. Catherine University and the University of St. Thomas, St. Paul, MN.

Humphrey, R. (1987). Treating extramarital sexual relationships in sex and couples therapy. In G. R. Weeks & L. Hof (Eds.), *Integrating sex and marital therapy: A clinical guide* (pp. 149–170). New York, NY: Brunner/Mazel.

Hunt, D., & McMahon, T. (1985). *The seduction of Christianity: Spiritual discernment in the last days*. Eugene, OR: Harvest House.

Hunt, J. (2014). *The biblical counseling reference guide*. Eugene, OR: Harvest House.

Hunter, L. A., & Yarhouse, M. A. (2009). Considerations and recommendations for use of religiously based interventions in a licensed setting. *Journal of Psychology and Christianity, 28*(2), 159-166.

Hutchby, I. (2005). "Active listening": Formulations and the elicitation of feelings-talk in child counselling. *Research on Language and Social Interaction, 38*(3), 303–329. doi:http://dx.doi.org/10.1207/s15327973rlsi3803_4

Ivey, A. E., Ivey, M. B., & Zalaquett, C. P. (2018). *Intentional interviewing and counseling* (9th ed.). Boston, MA: Cengage.

Jacobs, E. (1992). *Creative counseling techniques: An illustrated guide*. Odessa, FL: PAR.

Jacobs, E. (1994). *Impact therapy*. Odessa, FL: PAR.

Jacobson, N. S., & Christensen, A. (1996). *Acceptance and change in couple therapy: A therapist's guide to transforming relationships*. New York, NY: W. W. Norton.

Jaison, B. (2015). *How to do deep therapy—briefly and how to do brief therapy—deeply* (2nd ed.). Amazon Digital Services: Focusing for Creative Living.

James, R. K., & Gilliland, B. E. (2005). *Crisis intervention strategies* (5th ed.). Belmont, CA: Brooks/Cole.

James, W. (1890). *The principles of psychology*. New York, NY: Henry Holt & Company.

Janoff-Bulman, R. (1992). *Shattered assumptions: Towards a new psychology of trauma*. New York, NY: Free Press.

Jobes, D. A., & Linehan, M. M. (2016). *Managing suicidal risk: A collaborative approach* (2nd ed.). New York, NY: Guilford Press.

Johnson, E. L. (2007). *Foundations for soul care: A Christian psychology proposal*. Downers Grove, IL: IVP Academic.

Johnson, E. L. (2009). *Foundations of soul care: A Christian psychology*. Downers Grove, IL: IVP Academic.

Johnson, E. L. (2017). *God and soul care: The therapeutic resources of the Christian faith*. Downers Grove, IL: InterVarsity.

Johnson, E. L., & Jones, I. F. (2009). The use of Scripture in counseling. *Christian counseling today, 16*(4), 47–50.

Johnson, P. E. (1995). *Reason in the balance: The case against naturalism in science, law & education*. Downers Grove, IL: InterVarsity.

Johnson, S. M. (1996). *Creating connection: The practice of emotionally focused marital therapy*. New York, NY: Brunner/Mazel.

Johnson, S. M. (2003). Couples therapy research: Status and directions. In G. P. Shovelar (Ed.). *Textbook of family and couples therapy: Clinical application* (pp. 797–814). Washington, DC: American Psychiatric Association.

Johnson, S. M. (2004). *The practice of emotionally focused couple therapy* (2nd ed.). New York, NY: Brunner-Routledge.

Johnson, S. M. (2008). *Hold me tight: Seven conversations for a lifetime of love.* New York, NY: Little, Brown & Co.

Johnson, S. M. (2017). An emotionally focused approach to sex therapy. In Z. Peterson (Ed.), *The Wiley handbook of sex therapy* (pp. 250–266). New York, NY: Wiley-Blackwell.

Johnson, S. M., & Denton, W. (2002). Emotionally focused couples therapy: Creating connection. In A. S. Gurman (Ed.), *The clinical handbook of couple therapy* (3rd ed., pp. 221–250). New York, NY: Guilford Press.

Johnson, S. M., & Lee, A. (2000). Emotionally focused family therapy: Restructuring attachment. In E. Bailey (Ed.), *Working with children in family therapy.* New York, NY: Brunner/Mazel.

Johnson, S. M., Maddeaux, C., & Blouin, J. (1998). Emotionally focused family therapy for bulimia: Changing attachment patterns. *Psychotherapy: Theory, Research, Practice, Training, 35*(2), 238–247.

Jones, C. D., Lowe, L. A., & Risler, E. A. (2004). The effectiveness of wilderness adventure therapy programs for young people involved in the Juvenile Justice System. *Residential Treatment for Children and Youth, 22*(2), 53–67. doi:10.1300/J007v22n02_04

Jones, I. F. (2006). *The counsel of heaven on earth: Foundations for biblical Christian counseling.* Nashville, TN: Broadman & Holman.

Jones, I. F. (2007). Inner healing and therapeutic prayer: The parameters and power of prayer in counseling, *Christian Counseling Today, 15*(2), 25–27.

Jones, L. G. (1995). *Embodying forgiveness: A theological analysis.* Grand Rapids, MI: Eerdmans.

Jones, M. K., & Menzies, R. G. (1997). Danger ideation reduction therapy (DIRT): Preliminary findings with three obsessive-compulsive washers. *Behavior, Research, and Therapy, 35*(10), 955–960. doi:10.110016/S0005-7967(97)00042–9

Jones, M. K., & Menzies, R. G. (1998). Danger ideation reduction therapy (DIRT) for obsessive-compulsive washers: A controlled trial. *Behavior Research and Therapy, 36,* 959–970.

Jones, S. L., & Butman, R. E. (2011). *Modern psychotherapies: A comprehensive Christian appraisal* (2nd ed.). Downers Grove, IL: InterVarsity.

Jones, S. L., Watson, E., & Wolfram, T. (1992). Results of the Rech Conference Survey on religious faith and professional psychology. *Journal of Psychology and Theology, 20,* 147–158.

Jorgensen, M. M., Zachariae, R., Skytthe, A., & Kyvik, K. (2007). Genetic and environmental factors in alexithymia: A population-based study of Danish twin pairs. *Psychotherapy and Psychosomatics, 76,* 369–375.

Josefson, D. (2001). Rebirthing therapy banned after girl died in 70-minute struggle. *The BMJ, 322*(7293), 1014.

Joseph, R. (1992). *The right brain and the unconscious.* New York, NY: Plenum.

Joy, D. M. (1986). *Rebonding: Preventing and restoring damaged relationships.* Dallas, TX: Word.

Jung, C. G. (1957). *The undiscovered self.* New York, NY: American Library.

Kallay, E. (2015). Physical and psychological benefits of written emotional expression: Review of meta-analyses and recommendations. *European Psychologist, 20,* 242–251.

Kandel, E. R., Schwartz, J. H., Jessell, T. M., Siegelbaum, S. A., & Hudspeth, A. J. (2012). *Principles of neural science* (5th ed.). New York, NY: McGraw-Hill.

Kaplan, H. S. (1974). *The new sex therapy.* New York, NY: Brunner/Mazel.

Karen, R. (1998). *Becoming attached: First relationships and how they shape our capacity to love.* New York, NY: Oxford University Press.

Katehakis, A. (2009). Affective neuroscience and the treatment of sexual addiction. *Journal of Sexual Addiction and Compulsivity, 16,* 1–31.

Kaufman, G. (1992). *Shame, the power of caring* (3rd ed.). Rochester VT: Schenkman.

Kazdin, A. E. (1982). The token economy: A decade later. *Journal of Applied Behavior Analysis, 15*(3), 431–445.

Keim, J. P. (1997). Strategic family therapy of oppositional behavior. In F. M. Dattilio (Ed.), *Integrative cases in marriage and family therapy: A cognitive-behavioral approach.* New York, NY: Guilford Press.

Kellemen, R. W. (2007). *Spiritual friends: A methodology of soul care and spiritual direction* (Rev. ed.). Winona Lake, IN: BMH Books.

Keller, P. S., Cummings, E. M., Davies, P. T., & Mitchell, P. M. (2008). Longitudinal relations between parental drinking problems, family functioning, and child adjustment. *Developmental Psychopathology, 20*(1), 195–212. doi:10.1017/S0954 579408000096

Kendall, P. C. (Ed.). (2011). *Child and adolescent therapy: Cognitive-behavioral procedures* (4th ed.). New York, NY: Guilford Press.

Kendall, R. T. (2002). *Total forgiveness.* Lake Mary, FL: Charisma House.

Kerkhof, I., Vansteenwegen, D., Baeyens, F., & Hermans, D. (2001). Counterconditioning: An effective technique for changing conditioned preferences. *Experimental Psychology, 58*, 31–38. doi:10.1027/1618-3169/a000063; 10.1027/1618-3169/a000063

Kerr, M. E., & Bowen, M. (1988). *Multigenerational emotional process.* In M. E. Kerr & M. Bowen (Eds.), *Family evaluation: An approach based on Bowen theory* (pp. 221–255). New York, NY: W. W. Norton.

Kestly, T. A. (2014). *The interpersonal neurobiology of play: Brain-building interventions for emotional well-being.* New York, NY: W. W. Norton.

Kiecolt-Glaser, J. K., & Newton, T. L. (2001). Marriage and health: His and hers. *Psychological Bulletin, 127*(1), 472–503. doi:10.1037/0033-2909.127.4.472

Kilchevsky, A., Vardi, Y., Lowenstein, L., & Gruenwald, I. (2012). Is the female G-spot truly a distinct anatomic entity? *Journal of Sexual Medicine, 9*(3), 719–726.

Killingsworth, M. A., & Gilbert, D. T. (2010). A wandering mind is an unhappy mind. *Science, 330*, 932–932. doi:10.1126/science.1192439

Kilpatrick, L. A. (1992). *The international journal for the psychology of religion, 2*(1), 3–28.

King, C. M. (1998). Changing women's lives: The primary prevention of violence against women. In J. Campbell (Ed.), *Empowering survivors of abuse: Health care for battered women and their children* (pp. 177–189). Thousand Oaks, CA: Sage.

Kirby, J. S., & Baucom, D. H. (2007). Treating emotion dysregulation in a couple's context: A pilot study of a couple's skills group intervention. *Journal of Marital and Family Therapy, 33*(3), 375–391.

Klontz, B. T., Garos, S., & Klontz, P. T. (2005). The effectiveness of Brief Multimodal Experiential Therapy in the treatment of sexual addiction. *Sexual Addiction & Compulsivity, 12*(4), 275–294.

Klontz, B. T., Wolf, E. M., & Bivens, A. (2000). The effectiveness of multimodal brief group experiential psychotherapy approach. *The International Journal of Action Methods; Washington, 53*(3/4), 119–135.

Knapp, D. J., Sandberg, J. G., Novak, J., & Larson, J. H. (2015). The mediating role of attachment behaviors on the relationship between family-of-origin and couple communication: Implications for couples' therapy. *Journal of Couple & Relationship Therapy, 14*(1), 17–38.

Koenig, H. G. (2000). Religion, spirituality and medicine: Application to spiritual practice. *Journal of the American Medical Association, 284*, 1708.

Koenig, H., King, D., & Carson, V. (Eds.). (2012). *Handbook of religion and health.* New York, NY: Oxford University Press.

Koerner, A. F., & Fitzpatrick, M. A. (2009). Family type and conflict: The impact of conversation orientation and conformity orientation on conflict in the family. *Communication Studies, 48*(1), 59–75. doi:10.1080/10510979709368491

Kohlberg, L. (1976). Moral stages and moralization: The cognitive developmental approach. In T. Lickona (Ed.), *Moral development and behavior: Theory, research, and social issues* (pp. 31–53). New York, NY: Hold, Rinehart, & Winston.

Kohlenberg, R. J., & Tsai, M. (1994). Functional analytic psychotherapy: A radical behavioral approach to treatment and integration. *Journal of Psychotherapy Integration, 4*, 175–201.

Koocher, G. P., & D'Angelo E. J. (1992). Evolution of practice in child psychotherapy. In D. K. Freedheim, H. J. Freudenberger, J. W. Kessler, S. B. Messer, & D. R. Peterson (Eds.), *History of psychotherapy: A century of change* (pp. 457–492). Washington DC: American Psychological Association.

Korotitsch, W. J., & Nelson-Gray, R. O. (1999). An overview of self-monitoring research in assessment and treatment. *Psychological Assessment, 11*, 415–425.

Kottler, J. (2017). *On being a therapist* (5th ed.). New York, NY: Oxford University Press.

Kottler, J. A., & Montgomery, M. J. (2010). *Theories of counseling and therapy: An experiential approach* (2nd ed.). Thousand Oaks, CA: Sage.

Kottman, T. (2003). *Partners in play: An Adlerian approach to play therapy.* Alexandria, VA: American Counseling Association.

Kottman, T. (2009). Adlerian play therapy. In K. J. O'Connor & L. D. Braverman (Eds.), *Play therapy and practice: Comparing theories and techniques* (2nd ed., pp. 237–282). Hoboken, NJ: Wiley.

Kozlowska, K. (2007). Intergenerational processes, attachment and unexplained medical symptoms. *Australian & New Zealand Journal of Family Therapy, 28*(2), 88–99.

Kramer, B. J., Boelk, A. Z., & Auer, C. (2006). Family conflict at the end of life: Lessons learned in a model program for vulnerable older adults. *Journal of Palliative Medicine, 9*(3), 791–801.

Kring, A. M., & Solan, D. M. (2010). *Emotion regulation and psychopathology: A transdiagnostic approach to etiology and treatment.* New York, NY: Guilford Press.

Kübler-Ross, E. (1969). *On death and dying: What the dying have to teach doctors, nurses, clergy and their own families.* New York, NY: Scribner.

Kuchinskas, S. (2009). *The chemistry of connection: How the oxytocin response can help you find trust, intimacy and love.* Oakland, CA: New Harbinger.

Kuhlman, K. R., Howell, K. H., & Graham-Bermann, S. A. (2012). Physical health in preschool children exposed to intimate partner violence. *Journal of Family Violence, 27*, 499–510. doi:10.1007/s10896-012-9444-2

Kuo, F. C. (2009). Secrets or no secrets: Confidentiality in couple therapy. *American Journal of Family Therapy, 37*(5), 351–354. doi:10.1080/01926180701862970

Kuriansky, J. B., & Sharpe, L. (1981). Clinical and research implications of the evaluation of women's group therapy for anorgasmia: A review. *Journal of Sex and Marital Therapy, 7*(4), 268–277. doi:10.1080/00926238108405428

Kuriansky, J. B., Sharpe, L., & O'Connor, D. (1982). The treatment of anorgasmia: Long-term effectiveness of a short-term behavioral group therapy. *Journal of Sex and Marital Therapy, 8*(1), 29–43.

Laan, E., Rellini, A. H., Barnes, T., & International Society for Sexual Medicine (2013). Standard operating procedures for female orgasmic disorder: Consensus of the International Society for Sexual Medicine. *Journal of Sexual Medication, 10*(1), 74–82. doi:10.1111/j.1743-6109.2012.02880.x

Laaser, D. (2008). *Shattered vows: Hope and healing for women who have been sexually betrayed.* Grand Rapids, MI: Zondervan.

Laaser, D. (2013). *Exploring posttraumatic growth in relationally betrayed women.* Unpublished manuscript.

Laaser, D., Putney, H., Bundick, M., Delmonico, D. L., & Griffin, E. J. (2017). Posttraumatic growth in relationally betrayed women. *Journal of Marital and Family Therapy, 43*(3), 435–447.

Laaser, M. (1991, 1992, 1996, 2004, 2009, 2014). *Healing the wounds of sexual addiction*. Grand Rapids, MI: Zondervan.

Laaser, M. (1992). *Teaching at monthly Men of Valor Men's intensive workshops*. Eden Prairie, MN: Faithful and True.

Laaser, M. (2002). *The L.I.F.E. guide for men*. Orlando, FL: L.I.F.E. Recovery International.

Laaser, M. (2011a). *Becoming a man of valor*. Kansas City, KS: Beacon Hill.

Laaser, M. (2011b). *Taking every thought captive*. Kansas City, KS: Beacon Hill.

Laaser, M. (2011c). *The seven principles of highly accountable men*. Kansas City, KS: Beacon Hill.

Laaser, M. (2015). *Faithful and true workbook*. Eden Prairie, MN: Faithful and True.

Laaser, M., & Adams, K. M. (2002). Pastors and sexual addiction. In P. Carnes (Ed.), *Clinical management of sexual addiction* (pp. 285–297). New York, NY: Brunner-Routledge.

Laaser, M., & Clinton, T. (2015). *The fight of your life: Manning up to the challenges of sexual integrity*. Shippensburg, PA: Destiny Image.

Laaser, M., & Laaser, D. (2008, 2013). *The seven desires of the heart*. Grand Rapids, MI: Zondervan.

Laaser, M., & Laaser, D. (2016a). *Full disclosure*. Available at Eden Prairie, MN: Faithful & True.

Laaser, M., & Laaser, D. (2016b). *Toolkit for individuals and couples*. Eden Prairie, MN: Faithful & True.

Labelle, R., Pouliot, L., & Janelle, A. (2015). A systematic review and meta-analysis of cognitive behavioural treatments for suicidal and self-harm behaviours in adolescents. *Canadian Psychology/Psychologie Canadienne, 56*(4), 368–378.

Ladas, A. K., Whipple, B., & Perry, J. D. (2005). *The G spot: And other discoveries about human sexuality*. New York, NY: Macmillan.

Lake, D. M. (1975). Woman. In M. C. Tenney (Ed.), *The Zondervan pictorial encyclopedia of the Bible* (Vol. 5, pp. 950–955). Grand Rapids, MI: Zondervan.

Lambert, M. J. (2013). Outcome in psychotherapy: The past and important advances. *Psychotherapy, 50*, 42–51. https://doi.org/10.1037/a0030682

Lampton, C., Oliver, G., Worthington, E. L., Jr., & Berry, J. W. (2005). Helping Christian college students become more forgiving: An intervention study to promote forgiveness as part of a program to shape Christian character. *Journal of Psychology and Theology, 33*, 278–290.

Landgarten, H. B. (1987). *Family art psychotherapy: A clinical guide and casebook*. New York, NY: Brunner Mazel.

Landgarten, H. B. (2013). *Clinical art therapy: A comprehensive guide*. New York, NY: Brunner-Mazel.

Landreth, G. L. (2012). *Play therapy: The art of the relationship* (3rd ed.). New York, NY: Routledge.

Landreth, G. L., & Bratton, S. C. (2006). *Child-parent relationship therapy (CPRT): A 10-session filial therapy model*. New York, NY: Routledge.

Langberg, D. (1999). *On the threshold of hope*. Wheaton, IL: Tyndale.

Langberg, D. (2015). *Suffering and the heart of God: How trauma destroys and Christ restores*. Greensboro, NC: New Growth.

LaVigna, G. W., & Donnellan, A. M. (1986). *Alternative to punishment: Solving behavior problems with non-aversive strategies*. New York, NY: Irvington.

Lawler, K., Younger, J., Piferi, R., Jobe, R., Edmondson, K., & Jones, W. (2005). The unique effects of forgiveness on health: An exploration of pathways. *Journal of Behavioral Medicine, 28*(2), 157–167.

Lazarus, R. S. (2000). Toward better research on stress and coping. *American Psychologist, 55*(6), 665–673. http://dx.doi.org/10.1037/0003-066X.55.6.665

Lazarus, R. S., & Cohen, J. B. (1977). Environmental stress. In I. Altman & J. F. Wohlwill (Eds.), *Human Behavior and Environment*

(Vol. 2, pp. 89–127). New York, NY: Plenum.

Lazarus, R. S., & Folkman, S. (1984). *Stress, appraisal, and coping.* New York, NY: Springer.

Lea, T. D., & Griffin, H. P. (1992). *The new American commentary: Volume 34: 1, 2 Timothy, Titus.* Nashville, TN: B&H.

Leaf, C. (2013). *Switch on your brain: The key to peak happiness, thinking, and health.* Grand Rapids, MI: Baker.

Leahy, R. L. (2003). *Cognitive therapy techniques: A practitioner's guide.* New York, NY: Guilford Press.

Leahy, R. L. (2015). *Emotional schema therapy.* New York, NY: Guilford Press.

Leahy, R. L. (2017). *Cognitive therapy techniques: A practitioner's guide* (2nd ed.). New York, NY: Guilford Press

Learn, L. (2010, February). Women and porn. *Today's Christian Woman.* Retrieved from http://www.todayschristianwoman.com/articles/2010/february/women-and-porn.html

Leblanc, M., & Ritchie, M. (2001). A meta-analysis of play therapy outcomes. *Counselling Psychology Quarterly, 14*(2), 149–163.

Lebow, J. L., Chambers, A. L., Christensen, A., & Johnson, S. M. (2012). Research on the treatment of couple distress. *Journal of Marital and Family Therapy, 38*(1), 145–168.

Lee, M. (2016, January 26). Here's how 770 pastors describe their struggle with porn. *Christianity Today.* Retrieved from http://www.christianitytoday.com/news/2016/january/how-pastors-struggle-porn-phenomenon-josh-mcdowell-barna.html

Lehman, K. (2016). *The Immanuel approach for emotional healing and for life.* Chicago, IL: Immanuel.

Lei, Y., Yaroslavsky, I., & Tejani-Butt, S. M. (2009). Strain differences in the distribution of N-Methyl-D-Aspartate and Gamma (γ)–aminobutyric acid-A receptors in rat brain. *Life Sciences, 85*(23–26), 794–799. doi:10.1016/j.lfs.2009.10.010

Leibert, T. W., Smith, J. B., & Agaskar, V. R. (2011). Relationship between the working alliance and social support on counseling outcome. *Journal of Clinical Psychology, 67*(7), 709–719.

Leitenberg, H., Yorst, L. W., & Carroll-Wilson, M. (1986). Negative cognitive errors in children: Questionnaire development, normative data, and comparisons between children with and without self-reported symptoms of depression, low self-esteem, and evaluation anxiety. *Journal of Consulting & Clinical Psychology, 54*(4), 528–536.

Leitner, L. M. (2007). Theory, technique, and person: Technical integration in experiential constructivist psychotherapy. *Journal of Psychotherapy Integration, 17*(1), 33–49.

Lenzenweger, M. F., Lane, M. C., Loranger, A. W., & Kessler, R. C. (2007). DSM-IV personality disorders in the national comorbidity survey replication. *Biological Psychiatry, 62,* 553–564.

Levenkron, S. (2006). *Cutting: Understanding and overcoming self-mutilation.* New York, NY: W. W. Norton.

Levinson, D. (1978). *The seasons of a man's life.* New York, NY: Ballantine.

Lewis, C. S. (1940). *The problem of pain.* San Francisco, CA: HarperOne.

Lewis, C. S. (1977). *Mere Christianity: A revised and enlarged edition, with a new introduction of the three books, The Case for Christianity, Christian Behavior, and Beyond Personality.* New York, NY: Macmillan.

Lewis, C. S. (1989). *A grief observed.* New York, NY: HarperCollins.

Lewis, H. B. (1971). *Shame and guilt in neurosis.* New York, NY: International University Press.

Ley, D. J. (2011, November 16). The profit in sex addiction. *Psychology Today.* Retrieved from https://www.psychologytoday.com/blog/women-who-stray/201111/the-profit-in-sex-addiction

Liefeld, W. L. (1984). Luke. In F. E. Gaebelein (Ed.), *The expositor's Bible commentary* (Vol. 8, pp. 797–1059). Grand Rapids, MI: Zondervan.

Lilius, J. M., Worline, M. C., Dutton, J. E., Kanov, J., Frost, P. J., & Maitlis, S. (2003, August). *What good is compassion at work?* Paper presented at the meeting of the National Academy of Management Meetings, Seattle.

Lin, Y., Worthington, E. L., Jr., Griffin, B. J., Greer, C. L., Opare-Henaku, A., Lavelock, C., . . . Muller, H. (2014). Efficacy of REACH Forgiveness across cultures. *Journal of Clinical Psychology, 70*(9), 781–793.

Linehan, M. M. (1993). *Skills training manual for treating Borderline Personality Disorder*. New York, NY: Guilford Press.

Linehan, M. M. (2014). *DBT skills training manual* (2nd ed.). New York, NY: Guilford Press.

Linehan, M. M. (2015). *DBT skills training handouts and worksheets*. New York, NY: Guilford Press.

Lin-Roark, I. H., Church, A. T., & McCubbin, L. D. (2015). Battered women's evaluations of their intimate partners as a possible mediator between abuse and self-esteem. *Journal of Family Violence, 30*, 201–214. Retrieved from https://rd.springer.com/content/pdf/10.1007/s10896-014-9661-y.pdf

Listowel, E. (1934). *Critical history of aesthetics*. London: G. Allen & Unwin.

Liu, J. (2004). Childhood externalizing behavior: Theory and implications. *Journal of Child and Adolescent Psychiatric Nursing, 17*, 93–103.

Lobb, K. L., Aoun, S., & Monterosso, L. (2006). *A systematic review of the literature on complicated grief*. Prepared by the WA Centre for Cancer & Palliative Care. Joondalup WA. Australia: Edith Cowan University.

Lock J., Agras W. S., Bryson S., & Kraemer H. C. A (2005). Comparison of short- and long-term family therapy for adolescent anorexia nervosa. *Journal of the American Academy Child Adolescent Psychiatry, 44*(7), 632–639.

Lock, J., Le Grange, D., Agras, W. S., & Dare, C. (2001). *Treatment manual for anorexia nervosa: A family-based approach*. New York, NY: Guilford Press.

Lombardi, R. (2014). Art therapy. In E. J. Green & A. A. Drewes (Eds.), *Integrating*

expressive arts and play therapy with children and adolescents (pp. 41–66). Hoboken, NJ: Wiley.

Loos, V. E., Bridges, C. F., & Critelli, J. W. (1987). Weiner's attribution theory and female orgasmic consistency. *Journal of Sex Research, 23*(3), 348–361.

Lopez, F., Gover, M., Leskela, J., Sauer, E., Schirmer, L., & Wyssmann, J. (1997). Attachment styles, shame, guilt and collaborative problem-solving orientation. *Personal Relationships, 4*, 187–199.

LoPiccolo, J. (1993). *Becoming orgasmic*. Chapel Hill, NC: The Sinclair Institute.

LoPiccolo, J., & Friedman, J. M. (1988). *Broad-spectrum treatment of low sexual desire: Integration of cognitive, behavioral, and systemic therapy*. New York, NY: Guilford Press.

Loue, S. (2008). *The transformative power of metaphor in therapy* (1st ed.). New York, NY: Springer.

Lougheed, J., Hollenstein, T., Lichtwarck-Aschoff, A., & Granic, I. (2015). Maternal regulation of child affect in externalizing and typically-developing children. *Journal of Family Psychology, 29*(1), 10–19. doi:10.1037/a0038429

Lougheed, J., Koval, P., & Hollenstein, T. (2016). Sharing the burden: The interpersonal regulation of emotional arousal in mother-daughter dyads. *Emotion, 16*, 83–93.

Love, P., & Stosny, S. (2008). *How to improve your marriage without talking about it*. New York, NY: Broadway.

Luborsky, L., Diguer, L., Seligman, D. A., Rosenthal, R., Krause, E. D., & Johnson, S. (1999). The researcher's own therapy allegiances: A wildcard in comparisons of treatment efficacy. *Clinical Psychology: Science and Practice, 6*(1), 96–106.

Luca, M. (2014). *Sexual attraction in therapy: Clinical perspectives on moving beyond the taboo: A guide for training and practice*. New York, NY: Wiley.

Luca, M., & Boyden, M. (2014). An elephant in the room: A grounded theory of experienced psychotherapists' reactions and attitudes to sexual attraction. In M. Luca (Ed.), *Sexual attraction in therapy* (pp. 193–208). Hoboken, NJ: Wiley.

Luo, S., Cartun, M. A., & Snider, A. G. (2010). Assessing extradyadic behavior: A review, a new measure, and two new models. *Personality and Individual Differences, 49*(3), 155–163. doi:10.1016/j.paid.2010.03.033

Lutjen, L. J., Stilton, N. R., & Flannelly, K. J. (2012). Religion, forgiveness, hostility and health: A structural equation analysis. *Journal of Religion and Health, 2,* 468–478.

Luyten, P., Fonagy, P., Lemma, A., & Target, M. (2012). Depression. In A. W. Bateman & P. Fonagy (Eds.), *Handbook of mentalizing in mental health practice* (pp. 385–417). Arlington, VA: American Psychiatric Association.

Lyons-Ruth, K., & Jacobvitz, D. (2008). Attachment disorganization: Genetic factors, parenting contexts, and developmental transformation from infancy to adulthood. In. J. Cassidy & P. R. Shaver (Eds.), *Handbook of attachment: Theory, research, and clinical applications* (2nd ed., pp. 666–697). New York, NY: Guilford Press.

MacBeth, A., & Gumley, A. (2012). Exploring compassion: A meta-analysis of the association between self-compassion and psychotherapy. *Clinical Psychology Review, 32*(6), 545–552.

Maccoby, E. E., & Martin, J. A. (1983). Socialization in the context of the family: Parent-child interaction. In P. Mussen (Ed.) *Handbook of child psychology* (Vol. 4). New York, NY: Wiley.

Mackewn, J. (1997). *Developing gestalt counselling: A field theoretical and relational model of contemporary gestalt counselling and psychotherapy.* London: Sage.

MacNeil, S., & Byers, E. S. (2009). Role of sexual self-disclosure in the sexual satisfaction of long-term heterosexual couples. *Journal of Sex Research, 46,* 3–14. doi:10.1080/00224490802398399

Madanes, C. (1981). *Strategic family therapy.* San Francisco, CA: Jossey-Bass.

Magai, C. (2008). Attachment in middle and later life. In J. Cassidy & P. R. Shaver (Eds.), *Handbook of attachment: Theory, research, and clinical applications* (2nd ed., pp. 532–551). New York, NY: Guilford Press.

Mahrer, A. R. (2004). *The complete guide to experiential psychotherapy.* Boulder, CO: Bull.

Main, M. (1995). Recent studies in attachment: Overview, with selected implications for clinical work. In S. Goldberg, R. Muir, & J. Kerr (Eds.), *Attachment theory: Social, developmental, and clinical perspectives* (pp. 407–474). New York, NY: Routledge.

Main, M., & Hesse, E. (1990). Parents' unresolved traumatic experiences are related to infant disorganized attachment status: Is frightened and/or frightening parental behavior the linking mechanism? In M. T. Greenberg, D. Cicchetti, & E. M. Cummings (Eds.), *The John D. and Catherine T. MacArthur Foundation series on mental health and development. Attachment in the preschool years: Theory, research, and intervention* (pp. 161–182). Chicago, IL: University of Chicago Press.

Main, M., & Solomon, J. (1986). Discovery of an insecure-disorganized/disoriented attachment pattern. In T. B. Brazelton & M. W. Yogman (Eds.), *Affective development in infancy* (pp. 95–124). Westport, CT: Ablex.

Malchiodi, C. A. (2007). *The art therapy sourcebook.* New York, NY: McGraw-Hill.

Maloney, P. (2013). *The therapy industry: The irresistible rise of the talking cure, and why it doesn't work.* Chicago, IL: Pluto.

Maltz, W. (2001). *The sexual healing journey: A guide for survivors of sexual abuse.* New York, NY: HarperCollins.

Maltz, W. (2002). Treating the sexual intimacy concerns of sexual abuse survivors. *Sexual and Relationship Therapy, 17*(4), 321–327. doi:10.1080/1468199021000017173

Mancini, K. J., Luebbe, A. M., & Bell, D. J. (2016). Valence-specific emotion transmission: Potential influences on parent-adolescent emotion coregulation. *Emotion, 16*(5), 567–574. doi:10.1037/emo0000160

Mandolfo, C. (2014). Language of lament in the Psalms. In W. P. Brown (Ed.), *The Oxford Handbook of the Psalms* (p. 114). Oxford: Oxford University Press.

Mann, D. (2010). *Gestalt therapy: 100 key points & techniques*. New York, NY: Routledge.

Maraniss, D. (1999). *When pride still mattered: A life of Vince Lombardi*. New York, NY: Simon & Schuster.

Marchant, A., Hawton, K., Stewart, A., Montgomery, P. S., Singaravelu, V., Lloyd, K., . . . John, A. (2017). A systematic review of the relationship between internet use, self-harm and suicidal behavior in young people: The good, the bad and the unknown. *PLOS One, 13*(3), e0193937. https://doi.org/10.1371/journal.pone.0193937

Marfe, E. (2003). Assessing risk following deliberate self-harm. *Pediatric Nursing 15*(8), 32–34.

Marganska, A., Gallagher, M., & Miranda, R. (2013). Adult attachment, emotion dysregulation and symptoms of depression and generalized anxiety disorder. *American Journal of Orthopsychiatry, 83*, 131–141.

Mark, K. P., Janssen, E., & Milhausen, R. R. (2011). Infidelity in heterosexual couples: Demographic, interpersonal, and personality-related predictors of extradyadic sex. *Archives of Sexual Behavior, 40*(5), 971–982. doi:10.1007/s10508-011-9771-z

Marsh, N. M. (2016). Adultery in the Bible. In J. D. Barry, D. Bomar, D. R. Brown, R. Klippenstein, D. Mangum, C. Sinclair Wolcott, . . . W. Widder (Eds.), *The Lexham Bible dictionary*. Bellingham, WA: Lexham.

Martin, J. (1999). Communication and interpersonal effectiveness: Skills training for older adults. *Educational Gerontology, 25*, 269–284.

Martin, M. M., & Rubin, R. B. (1994). A new measure of cognitive flexibility. *Psychological Reports, 76*(2), 623-626.

Martin, J., & Sugarman, J. (2003). *Psychology and the question of agency*. Albany, NY: State of University of New York Press.

Martin, T. L. (2006). A pilot study of a tool to measure instrumental and intuitive styles of grieving. *Omega, 53*(4), 263–278.

Martin, T. L., & Doka, K. J. (2000). *Men don't cry . . . women do: Transcending gender stereotypes of grief*. Philadelphia, PA: Brunner/Mazel.

Mascarenhas, M. N., Flaxman, S. R., Boerma, T., Vanderpoel, S., & Stevens, G. A. (2012). National, regional, and global trends in infertility prevalence since 1990: A systematic analysis of 277 health surveys. *PLOS Medicine, 9*(12), e1001356.

Maslow, A. (1964). *Religions, values, and peak experiences*. New York, NY: Penguin.

Maslow, A. (1970). *Motivation and personality* (2nd ed.). New York, NY: Harper & Row.

Masson, J. M. (1984). *The assault on truth: Freud's suppression of the seduction theory*. New York, NY: Farrar, Straus & Giroux.

Masters, J. C., Burish, T. G., Hollon, S. D., & Rimm, D. C. (1987). *Behavior therapy: Techniques and empirical findings*. New York, NY: Carcourt College.

Masters, W. H., & Johnson, V. E. (1966). *Human sexual response*. Boston, MA: Little, Brown.

Masters, W. H., & Johnson, V. E. (1970). *Human sexual inadequacy*. New York, NY: Little, Brown.

Mathews, K. A. (1996). *The new American commentary. Volume 1A: Genesis 1–11:26*. Nashville, TN: Broadman & Holman.

Matos, M., & Pinto-Gouveia, J. (2014). Shamed by a parent or by others: The role of attachment in shame memories relation to depression. *International Journal of Psychology and Psychological Therapy, 14*, 217–244.

May, G. (1988). *Addiction and grace*. New York, NY: Harper.

Maynard, E. A., Gorsuch, R. L., & Bjorck, J. P. (2001). Religious coping style, concept of God, and personal religious variables in threat, loss, and challenge situations. *Journal for the Scientific Study of Religion, 40*, 65–74.

Mayo Clinic Staff. (2015). STD symptoms: Common STDs and their symptoms. Retrieved from http://www.mayoclinic.org/diseases-conditions/sexually-transmitted-diseases-stds/in-depth/std-symptoms/art-20047081

McAllister, J. M., & Roberts-Lewis, A. (2010). Social worker's role in helping the church address intimate partner violence: An invisible problem. *Social Work and Christianity, 37*(2), 161–187.

McCabe, M. P., Sharlip, I. D., Atalla, E., Balon, R., Fisher, A. D., Laumann, E., & Segraves, R. T. (2016a). Definitions of sexual dysfunctions in women and men: A consensus statement from the Fourth International Consultation on Sexual Medicine 2015. *Journal of Sexual Medicine, 13*(2), 135–143. doi:10.1016/j.jsxm.2015.12.019

McCabe, M. P., Sharlip, I. D., Lewis, R., Atalla, E., Balon, R., Fisher, A. D., & Segraves, R. T. (2016b). Incidence and prevalence of sexual dysfunction in women and men: A consensus statement from the Fourth International Consultation on Sexual Medicine 2015. *Journal of Sexual Medicine, 13*(2), 144–152. doi:10.1016/j.jsxm.2015.12.034

McCluskey, C., & McCluskey, R. (2004). *When two become one: Achieving sexual intimacy in marriage*. Grand Rapids, MI: Revell.

McCoy, K. P., George, M. R. W., Cummings, E. M., & Davies, P. T. (2013). Constructive and destructive marital conflict, parenting, and children's school and social adjustment. *Social Development, 22*(4), doi:10.1111/sode.12015

McCullough, J. P. (2000). *Treatment for chronic depression: Cognitive Behavioral Analysis System of Psychotherapy (CBASP)*. New York, NY: Guilford Press.

McCullough, J. P. (2006). *Distinctive treatment for persistent depressive disorder: Distinctive feature series*. New York, NY: Routledge.

McCullough, J. P. (2010). *Treating chronic depression with disciplined personal involvement*. Cognitive Behavioral Analysis System of Psychotherapy (CBASP). New York, NY: Springer.

McCullough, J. P., Jr., Lord, B. D., Conley, K. A. & Martin, A .M. (2010). A method for conducting intensive psychological studies with early-onset chronically depressed patients. *American Journal of Psychotherapy, 64*, 317–338.

McCullough, M. E., Hoyt, W. T., Larson, D. B., Koenig, H. G., & Thoresen, C. (2000). Religious involvement and mortality: A meta-analytic review. *Health Psychology, 19*(3), 211–222.

McCullough, M. E., Rachal, K. C., Sandage, S. J., Worthington, E. L., Jr., Brown, S. W., & Hight, T. L. (1998). Interpersonal forgiving in close relationships II: Theoretical elaboration and measurement. *Journal of Personality and Social Psychology, 75*, 1586–1603.

McGilchrist, I. (2009). *The master and his emissary: The divided brain and the making of the Western world*. New Haven, CT: Yale University Press.

McGoldrick, M. (2011). *The Genogram journey: Reconnecting with your family*. New York, NY: W. W. Norton.

McGoldrick, M., Giordano, J., & Garcia-Preto, N. (Eds.). (2005). *Ethnicity and family therapy* (3rd ed.). New York, NY: Guilford Press.

McKay, M., Wood, J. C., & Brantley, J. (2010). *The dialectical behavior therapy skills workbook*. Oakland, CA: New Harbinger.

McMahon, C. G., Jannini, E., Waldinger, M., & Rowland, D. (2013). Standard operating procedures in the disorders of orgasm and ejaculation. *Journal of Sexual Medicine, 10*, 204–229. doi:10.1111/j.1743-6109.2012.02824.x

McMinn, M. R. (2007). *Cognitive therapy techniques in Christian counseling*. Eugene, OR: Wipf and Stock.

McMinn, M. R. (2008). *Sin and grace in Christian counseling: An integrative paradigm*. Downers Grove, IL: InterVarsity.

McMullin, R. A. (1986). *Handbook of cognitive behavioral techniques*. New York, NY: Norton.

McNeill, J. (1951). *A history of the cure of souls*. New York, NY: Harper & Row.

McQuiggan, S. W., Robinson, J. L., & Lester, J. C. (2010). Affective transitions in narrative-centered learning environments. *Educational Technology & Society, 13*(1), 40–43.

Mead, G. H. (1934). *Mind, self, and society: From the standpoint of a social behaviorist*. Chicago, IL: University of Chicago Press.

Meichenbaum, D. (1985). *Stress inoculation training.* London: Pergamon.

Menninger, K. (1973). *Whatever became of sin?* New York, NY: Hawthorn.

Merriam-Webster's Collegiate Dictionary. (2003). 11th ed. Springfield, MA: Merriam-Webster.

Metz, M. E., & McCarthy, B. W. (2003). *Coping with premature ejaculation: How to overcome PE, please your partner & have great sex.* Oakland, CA: New Harbinger.

Metz, M. E., & McCarthy, B. W. (2004). *Coping with erectile dysfunction: How to regain confidence and enjoy great sex.* Oakland, CA: New Harbinger.

Miguel-Hidalgo, J. J. (2013). Adolescents with psychiatric disorders: Brain structural and functional changes. In L. Sher & J. Merrick (Eds.), *Adolescent psychiatry: A contemporary perspective for health professionals.* Boston: De Gruyter.

Mikulincer, M., & Shaver, P. R. (2007). *Attachment in adulthood: Structure, dynamics, and change.* New York, NY: Guilford Press.

Miles, A. (2000). *Domestic violence: What every pastor needs to know.* Minneapolis, MN: Augsburg Fortress.

Miles, A. (2002). *Violence in families: What every Christian needs to know.* Minneapolis, MN: Augsburg.

Milkman, H. B., & Sunderwirth, S. G. (2010). *Craving for ecstasy.* Thousand Oaks, CA: Sage.

Miller, A. (2012). *Healing the unimaginable: Treating ritual abuse and mind control.* London: Karnac.

Miller, S. D., Duncan, D. B., & Hubble, M. A. (2004). Beyond integration: The triumph of outcome over process in clinical practice. *Psychotherapy in Australia, 10*(2), 2–19.

Miller, W. R., & Rollnick, S. (2013). *Motivational interviewing: Helping people change* (3rd ed.). New York, NY: Guilford Press.

Miller, W. R., & Rollnick, S. (2014). *Applications of motivational interviewing: Motivational interviewing, helping people change* (3rd ed.). New York, NY: Guilford Press.

Miltenberger, R. (2012). *Behavioral modification, principles and procedures* (5th ed.). Belmont, CA: Wadsworth.

Milton, J. (2002). *The road to malpsychia: Humanistic psychology and our discontents.* San Francisco, CA: Encounter.

Mintle, L. (2015). *We need to talk: How to successfully navigate conflict.* Grand Rapids, MI: Baker.

Minuchin, S. (1974). *Families and family therapy.* Cambridge, MA: Harvard University Press.

Minuchin, S., & Fishman, H. C. (1981). *Family therapy techniques.* Cambridge, MA: Harvard University Press.

Minuchin, S., Lee, W. Y., & Simon, G. M. (1996). *Mastering family therapy: Journeys of growth and transformation.* New York, NY: Wiley.

Minuchin, S., Lee, W. Y., & Simon, G. M. (2006). *Mastering family therapy: Journeys of growth and transformation.* New York, NY: Wiley.

Minuchin, S., Reiter, M. D., Borda, C., Walker, S. A., Pascale, R., & Reynolds, H. T. M. (2014). *The craft of family therapy: Challenging certainties.* New York, NY: Routledge.

Mojang. (2012). *MineCraft* (Personal Computer Version). Stockholm, Sweden: Mojang.

Moreno, J. L. (1994). *Psychodrama and group psychotherapy* (4th ed.). New York, NY: Mental Health Resources.

Moriarty, G., & Hoffman, L. (Eds.). (2013). *The God image handbook for spiritual counseling and psychotherapy: Research, theory, and practice.* New York, NY: Routledge.

Mosak, H. H., & Maniacci, M. P. (1998). *Tactics in counseling and psychotherapy.* Itasca, IL: F. E. Peacock.

Mosak, H. H., & Maniacci, M. P. (2008). Adlerian psychotherapy. In R. J. Corsini & D. Wedding (Eds.), *Current psychotherapies* (8th ed., pp. 328–367). Belmont, CA: Thompson.

Mounce, William D. (Ed.). (2006). *Mounce's complete expository dictionary of Old and New Testament words.* Grand Rapids: Zondervan.

Moutsiana, C., Fearon, P., Murray, L., Cooper, P., Goodyear, I. Johnstone, T., & Halligan, S. (2014). Making an effort to feel positive: Insecure attachment in infancy predicts the neural underpinnings of emotional regulation in adulthood. *Journal of Child Psychology and Psychiatry, 55*, 999–1008.

Mozdzierz, G. J., & Greenblatt, R. (1994). Technique in psychotherapy: Cautions and concerns. *Individual Psychology, 50*(2), 232–249.

Mozdzierz, G. J., Peluso, P. R., & Lisiecki, J. (2011). Evidence-based psychological practices and therapist training: At the crossroads. *Journal of Humanistic Psychology, 51*(4), 439–464. Retrieved from http://journals.sagepub.com/doi/abs/10.1177/0022167810386959

Munsch, C. (2012). The science of two-timing: The state of infidelity research. *Sociology Compass, 6*, 46–59.

Murray, M. (1991). *Prisoner of another war: A remarkable journey of healing from childhood*. Bradenton, FL: Page Mill.

Murray, P. E., & Rotter, J. C. (2002). Creative counseling techniques for family therapists. *Family Journal, 10*(2), 203–206.

Myerbroker, K., & Emmelkamp, P. M. G. (2010). Virtual reality exposure therapy in anxiety disorders & systematic review of process-and-outcomes studies. *Depression & Anxiety, 27*, 933–944. doi:10.1002/da.20734

Naar-King, S., & Suarez, M. (2010). *Motivational interviewing with adolescents and young adults*. New York, NY: Guilford Press.

Nason-Clark, N. (2009). Christianity and the experience of domestic violence: What does faith have to do with it? *Social Work and Christianity, 36*(4), 379–393.

Nathan, P. E., & Gorman, J. M. (2002). *Treatments that work* (2nd ed.). New York, NY: Oxford University Press.

Nation, J. A., Wertheim, E. H., & Worthington, E. L., Jr. (2017). *Outcomes, predictors of outcomes, program adherence, and mechanisms of change for an online self-help REACH forgiveness program*. Manuscript under editorial consideration, Latrobe University, Melbourne, Victoria, Australia.

National Center for PTSD. (2016, Oct. 3). *How common is PTSD?* Retrieved from http://www.ptsd.va.gov/public/PTSD-overview/basics/how-common-is-ptsd.asp

Neff, K. D. (2011). Self-compassion, self-esteem, and well-being. *Social and Personality Psychology Compass, 5*(1), 1–12. doi:10.1111/j.1751-9004.2010.00330.x

Neff, K. D., & McGehee, P. (2010). Self-compassion and psychological resilience among adolescents and young adults. *Self & Identity, 9*(3), 225–240. doi:10.1080/15298860902979307

Neimeyer, R. A. (2009). *Constructivist psychotherapy: Distinctive features*. London: Routledge.

Neimeyer, R. A. (Ed.). (2012). *Techniques of grief therapy: Creative practices for counseling the bereaved*. New York, NY: Routledge.

Neimeyer, R. A., Burke, L. A., & Mackay, M. M. (2010). Grief therapy and the reconstruction of meaning: From principles to practice. *Journal of Contemporary Psychotherapy, 40*(2), 73–92.

Neimeyer, R. A., Klass, D., & Dennis, M. R. (2014). A social constructionist account of grief: Loss and the narration of meaning. *Death Studies, 38*, 485–498.

Nelson, J. M. (2009). *Psychology, religion, and spirituality*. New York, NY: Springer.

Nemeth, J. M., Bonomi, A. E., Lee, M. A., & Ludwin, J. M. (2012). Sexual infidelity as trigger for intimate partner violence. *Journal of Women's Health (Larchmt), 21*(9), 942–949.

Newport, F., & Himelfarb, I. (2013). In U.S., record-high say gay, lesbian relations morally OK. Retrieved from http://www.gallup.com/poll/162689/record-high-say-gay-lesbian-relations-morally.aspx

Nichols, M. P., & Davis, S. D. (2017). *Family therapy: Concepts and methods* (11th ed.). New York, NY: Pearson.

Nickerson, E. T., & O'Laughlin, K. S. (1982). *Helping through action: Action-oriented therapies*. Amherst, MA: Human Resource Development Press.

Nielson, J. B. (1965). The epistle to the Colossians. In A. F. Harper, W. M. Greathouse, R. Earle, & W. T. Purkiser (Eds.), *Beacon Bible commentary* (Vol. 9, pp. 357–430). Kansas City, MO: Beacon Hill.

Nims, D. R. (2011). Solution-focused play therapy: Helping children and families find solutions. In C. E. Schaefer (Ed.), *Foundations of play therapy* (pp. 297–312). Hoboken, NJ: Wiley.

Nobakht, H. N., & Dale, K. Y. (2017). The prevalence of deliberate self-harm and its relationships to trauma and dissociation among Iranian young adults. *Journal of Trauma and Dissociation, 18*(4), 610–623.

Norcross, J. C. (Ed.). (2011). *Psychotherapy relationships that work: Evidence-based responsiveness* (2nd ed.). New York, NY: Oxford University Press.

Noricks, J. (2011). *Parts psychology: A trauma-based, self-state therapy for emotional healing*. Los Angeles, CA: New University Press.

Nouwen, H. (1996). *The inner voice of love*. New York, NY: Doubleday.

Oaklander, V. (1988). *Windows to our children: A Gestalt therapy approach to children and adolescents*. Highland, NY: Gestalt Journal Press.

Oboro, V. O., & Tabowei, T. O. (2002). Sexual function after childbirth in Nigerian women. *International Journal of Gynecology & Obstetrics, 78*(3), 249–250.

O'Brien, K. L., Cohen, L., Pooley, J. A., & Taylor, M. F. (2012). Lifting the domestic violence cloak of silence: Resilient Australian women's reflected memories of their childhood experiences of witnessing domestic violence. *Journal of Family Violence, 28*, 95–108. doi:101007/s10896-012-9484-7

O'Connor, K. J., & Braverman, L. D. (Eds.). (2016). *Play therapy and practice: Comparing theories and techniques*. Hoboken, NJ: Wiley.

Oden, T. C. (1987). *Classical pastoral care* (Vols. 1–4). Grand Rapids, MI: Baker.

Oden, T. C. (1994). *Classical pastoral care: Pastoral counsel* (Vol. 3). Grand Rapids, MI: Baker.

O'Driscoll, C., & Flanagan, E. (2016). Sexual problems and post-traumatic stress disorder following sexual trauma: A meta-analytic review. *Psychology and Psychotherapy: Theory, Research and Practice, 89*(3), 351–367. doi:10.1111/papt.12077

O'Hanlon, W. H., & Hexum, A. L. (1991). *An uncommon casebook: The complete clinical work of Milton H. Erickson, M.D.* New York, NY: W. W. Norton.

Ohlschlager, G. (2006). God and you: Embracing the relationship that transcends all others. In T. Clinton & G. Sibcy (Eds.), *Why you do the things you do: The secret to healthy relationships* (pp. 127–151). Nashville, TN: Thomas Nelson.

Ohrman, K. J. (2002). A passion for compassion. *Advisor Today, 97*, 72–75.

Olsson, A., Lundqvist, M., Faxelid, E., & Nissen, E. (2005). Women's thoughts about sexual life after childbirth: Focus group discussions with women after childbirth. *Scandinavian Journal of Caring Sciences, 19*(4), 381–387. doi:10.1111/j.1471-6712.2005.00357.x

O'Neill, A., D'Souza, A., Carballedo, A., Joseph, S., Kerskens C., & Frodl, T. (2013). Magnetic resonance imaging in patients with borderline personality disorder: A study of volumetric abnormalities. *Psychiatry Research, 213*, 1–10.

Opialla, S., Lutz, J., Scherpiet, S., Hittmeyer, A., Jancke, L., Rufer, M., . . . Bruhl, A. (2015). Neural circuits of emotion regulation: A comparison of mindfulness-based and cognitive reappraisal strategies. *European Archive of Psychiatry & Clinical Neuroscience, 265*(1), 45–55. doi:10.1007/s00406-014-0510-z

Orlinsky, D. E. (2010). Foreword. In B. L. Duncan, S. D. Miller, B. E. Wampold, & M. A. Hubble (Eds.). *The heart and soul of change: Delivering what works in therapy* (2nd ed.). Washington, DC: American Psychological Association.

Ortberg, J. (2002). *The life you've always wanted: Spiritual disciplines for ordinary people.* Grand Rapids, MI: Zondervan.

Osborn, A. F. (1963). *Applied imagination: Principles and procedures of creative problem-solving.* New York, NY: Scribner.

Packer, J. I. (1993). *Concise theology: A guide to historic Christian beliefs.* Wheaton, IL: Tyndale.

Padesky, C. A. (1993). *Socratic questioning: Changing minds or guiding discovery?* Key note address delivered at the European Congress of Behavioural and Cognitive Therapies, London.

Panksepp, J. (2009). Core consciousness. In T. Bayne, A. Cleeremans, & P. Wilken (Eds.), *The Oxford companion to consciousness* (pp. 198–200). Oxford: Oxford University Press.

Pargament, K. I. (1997). *The psychology of religion and coping: Theory, research, practice.* New York, NY: Guilford Press.

Pargament, K. I. (2002). The bitter and the sweet: An evaluation of the costs and benefits of religiousness. *Psychological Inquiry, 13*(3), 168–181.

Pargament, K. I. (2007). *Spiritually integrated psychotherapy: Understanding and addressing the sacred.* New York, NY: Guilford Press.

Pargament, K. I., & Brant, C. R. (1998). Religion and coping. In H. G. Koenig (Ed.), *Handbook of religion and mental health* (pp. 111–128). San Diego: Academic Press.

Pargament, K. I., Falb, M. D., Ano, G. G., & Wachholtz, A. B. (2013). The religious dimension of coping: Advances in theory, research, and practice. In R. F. Paloutzian & C. L. Park (Eds.), *Handbook of the psychology of religion and spirituality* (2nd ed., pp. 560–579). New York, NY: Guilford Press.

Pargament, K. I., Smith, B. W., Koenig, H. G., & Perez, L. (1998). Patterns of positive and negative religious coping with major life stressors. *Journal for the Scientific Study of Religion, 37*(4), 710–724.

Parish, S. J., Goldstein, A. T., Goldstein, S. W., Goldstein, I., Pfaus, J., Clayton, A. H., & Whipple, B. (2016). Toward a more evidence-based nosology and nomenclature for female sexual dysfunction; Part II. *Journal of Sexual Medicine, 13*(12), 1888–1906. doi:10.1016/j.jsxm.2016.09.020

Park, C. L. (2005). Religion and meaning. In R. F. Paloutzian & C. L. Park (Eds.). *Handbook of theology of religion and spirituality* (2nd ed., pp. 357–379). New York, NY: Guilford Press.

Park, C. L., Smith, P. H., Lee, S. Y., Mazure, C. M., McKee, S. A., & Hoff, R. (2016). Positive and negative religious/spiritual coping and combat exposure as predictors of posttraumatic stress and perceived growth in Iraq and Afghanistan veterans. *Psychology of Religion and Spirituality.* Advance online publication. http://dx.doi.org/10.1037/rel0000086

Parker, S., & Thomas, R. (2009). Psychological differences in shame vs. guilt: Implications for mental health counselors. *Journal of Mental Health Counseling, 31,* 213–224.

Pascual, A., Conejero, S., & Etxebarria, I. (2016). Coping strategies and emotion regulation in adolescents: Adequacy and gender differences. *Ansiedad y Estres, 22,* 1–4.

Pattakos, A. (2010). *Prisoners of our thoughts: Viktor Frankl's principles for discovering meaning in life and work* (2nd ed.). Oakland, CA: Berret-Koehler.

Paul, G. L. (1967). Strategy of outcome research in psychotherapy. *Journal of Consulting Psychology, 31*(2), 109–118.

Pearce, M. (2016). *Cognitive therapy for Christians with depression: A practical tool-based primer.* West Conshohocken, PA: Templeton.

Peisker, A. D. (1966). The book of Jonah. In A. F. Harper, W. M. Greathouse, R. Earle,

& W. T. Purkiser (Eds.), *Beacon Bible commentary* (Vol. 5, pp. 159–187). Kansas City, MO: Beacon Hill.

Peluso, P. R. (2007). *Infidelity: A practitioner's guide to working with couples in crisis.* New York, NY: Routledge.

Pennebaker, J. W. (2010). Expressive writing in a clinical setting. *The Independent Practitioner, 30,* 23–25.

Pennebaker, J., & Beall, S. (1986). Confronting a traumatic event: Toward an understanding of inhibition and disease. *Journal of Abnormal Psychology, 95,* 274–281.

Perkinson, R. R., Jongsma, A. E., & Bruce, T. J. (2009). *The addiction treatment planner* (4th ed.). Hoboken, NJ: Wiley.

Perper, R. (2013). Grief, depression, and the DSM-5. *San Diego Psychologist, 28*(4), 1–8.

Peterman, G. W., & Schmutzer, A. J. (2016). *Between pain and grace: A biblical theology of suffering.* Chicago, IL: Moody.

Petersen, J. A. (1984). *The myth of the greener grass.* Carol Stream, IL: Tyndale.

Piaget, J., & Inhelder, B. (1969). *The psychology of the child.* New York, NY: Basic Books.

Piercy, F. P., Hertlein, K. M., & Wetchler, J. L. (2005). *Handbook of the clinical treatment of infidelity.* New York, NY: Haworth.

Pineles, S. L., Street, A. E., & Koenen, K. C. (2006). The differential relationship of shame-proneness and guilt-proneness to psychological and somatization symptoms. *Journal of Social and Clinical Psychology, 25*(6), 688–704.

Pinto-Gouveia, J., & Matos, M. (2011). Can shame memories become a key to identity? The centrality of shame memories predicts psychopathology. *Applied Cognitive Psychology, 25,* 281–290.

Piper, J., & Taylor, J. (Eds.). (2006). *Suffering and the sovereignty of God.* Wheaton, IL: Crossway.

Pistole, M. C., & Arricale, F. (2003). Understanding attachment: Beliefs about conflict. *Journal of Counseling & Development, 81*(3), 318–328.

Pittman, F. (1989). *Private lies: Infidelity and the betrayal of intimacy.* New York, NY: W. W. Norton.

Plante, T. G. (2009). *Spiritual practices in psychotherapy: Thirteen tools for enhancing psychological health.* Washington, DC: American Psychological Association.

Plutchik, R. (2001). The nature of emotions. *American Scientist, 89*(4), 344–350.

Poling, A., Schlinger, H., Starin, S., & Blakely, E. (2013). *Psychology: A behavioral overview.* New York, NY: Springer.

Pope, A. (1711). *An essay on criticism.* London. Printed for W. Lewis in Russel Street, Covent Garden, and sold by W. Taylor at the Ship in Pater-Noster Row, T. Osborn near the Walks, and J. Graves in St. James Street. Retrieved May 21, 2015, via Google Books.

Pope, K. S., & Bouhoutsos, J. C. (1986). *Sexual intimacy between therapists and patients.* Santa Barbara, CA: Praeger.

Popescu, M., & Drumm, R. (2009). Religion, faith communities, and intimate partner violence. *Social Work and Christianity, 36*(4), 375–378.

Popescu, M., Drumm, R., Mayer, S., Cooper, L., Foster, T., Seifert, M., . . . Dewan, S. (2009). "Because of my beliefs that I had acquired from the church . . .": Religious belief-based barriers for Adventist women in domestic violence relationships. *Social Work and Christianity, 36*(4), 394–414.

Potter-Efron, R. (2007). *Rage.* Oakland, CA: New Harbinger.

Powell, B., Cooper, G., Hoffman, K., & Marvin, B. (2016). *The circle of security intervention.* New York, NY: Guilford Press.

Powlison, D. (2003). *Seeing with new eyes: Counseling and the human condition through the lens of Scripture.* Phillipsburg, NJ: P&R.

Powlison, D., & Lowe, J. (2012, February 22). *A picture of shame and guilt.* Podcast retrieved from: http://ccef.libsyn.com/a-picture-of-shame-and-guilt-

Premack, D., & Woodruff, G. (1978a). Does the chimpanzee have a "theory of mind"? *Behavioral and Brain Sciences, 4*, 515–526.

Premack, D., & Woodruff, G. (1978b). Chimpanzee problem comprehension: Insufficient evidence. *Science, 206*, 1202.

Pressley, J., & Spinazzola, J. (2015). *Journal of Psychology and Theology, 43*, 8–22.

Prigerson, H., & Jacobs, S. (2001). Caring for bereaved patients: All the doctors just suddenly go. *Journal of the American Medical Association, 286*(11), 1369–1376.

Prochaska, J., & DiClemente, C. (1982). Transtheoretical therapy: Toward a more integrative model of change. *Psychotherapy: Theory, Research and Practice, 19*(3), 276–288.

Puentedura, E. J., & Flynn, T. (2016). Combining manual therapy with pain neuroscience education in the treatment of chronic low back pain: A narrative review of the literature. *Physiotherapy Theory and Practice, 32*(5), 408–414.

Purkiser, W. T. (1965). The book of Samuel. In A. F. Harper, W. M. Greathouse, R. Earle & W. T. Purkiser (Eds.), *Beacon Bible commentary* (Vol. 2, pp. 205–334). Kansas City, MO: Beacon Hill.

Purkiser, W. T. (1967). The book of Psalms. In A. F. Harper, W. M. Greathouse, R. Earle, & W. T. Purkiser (Eds.), *Beacon Bible commentary* (Vol. 3, pp. 125–452). Kansas City, MO: Beacon Hill.

Purves, A. (2001). *Pastoral theology in the classical tradition*. Louisville, KY: Westminster John Knox.

Putnam, F. W. (1997). *Dissociation in children and adolescents: A developmental perspective*. New York, NY: Guilford Press.

Pyne, R. J. (2003). Humanity and Sin. In C. R. Swindoll & R. B. Zuck (Eds.), *Understanding Christian theology* (pp. 643–784). Nashville, TN: Thomas Nelson.

Raines, C. (1996). Self-disclosure in clinical social work. *Clinical Social Work Journal, 24*(4), 357–375.

Ramnerö, J., & Törneke, N. (2008). *The ABCs of human behavior: Behavioral principles for the practicing clinician*. Oakland, CA: New Harbinger.

Ray, D. (2011). *Advanced play therapy: Essential conditions, knowledge, and skills for child practice*. New York, NY: Routledge.

Reid, R. C. (2010). Differentiating emotions in a sample of men in treatment for hypersexual behavior. *Journal of Social Work Practice in the Addictions, 10*, 197–213. doi:10.1080/15332561003769369

Reid, R., Bramen, J., Anderson, A., & Cohen, M. (2014). Mindfulness, emotion dysregulation, impulsivity, and stress proneness among hypersexual patients. *Journal of Clinical Psychology, 70*, 313–321.

Reinherz, H. Z., Giaconia, R. M., Hauf, A. M., Wasserman, M. S., & Paradis, A. D. (2000). General and specific childhood risk factors for depression and drug disorders by early adulthood. *Journal of the American Academy of Child and Adolescent Psychiatry, 39*(2), 223–231.

Reisman, J. A. (2004). The sex industrial complex: Big sexology, big pornography, and big pharmacology. Retrieved from http://www.drjudithreisman.com/archives/2005/12/the_sex-industr.html

Rhode, D. L. (2016). *Adultery: Infidelity and the law*. Cambridge, MA: Harvard University Press.

Ricciardi, E., Rota, G., Sani, L., Gentili, C., Gaglianese, A., Guazzelli, M., & Pietrini, P. (2013). How the brain heals emotional wounds: The functional neuroanatomy of forgiveness. *Frontiers in Human Neuroscience, 7*, 1–9.

Richards, P. S., & Bergin, A. E. (2005). *A spiritual strategy for counseling and psychotherapy* (2nd ed.). Washington, DC: American Psychological Association.

Richards, P. S., Smith, T. B., Schowalter, M., Richard, M., Berrett, M. E., & Hardman, R. K. (2005). Development and validation of the Theistic Spiritual Outcome Survey. *Psychotherapy Research, 15*(4), 457–469.

Richardson, J. F. (2012). The world of the sand tray and the child on the autism spectrum.

In L. Gallo-Lopez & L. C. Rubin (Eds.), *Play-based interventions for children and adolescents with autism spectrum disorders* (pp. 209–227). New York, NY: Routledge/Taylor & Francis Group.

Richeport-Haley, M. (1998). Ethnicity in family therapy: A comparison of brief strategic therapy and culture-focused therapy. *American Journal of Family Therapy, 26,* 77–90.

Rieff, P. (1966). *The triumph of the therapeutic: Uses of faith after Freud.* New York, NY: Harper & Row.

Rinck, M. J. (1998). Christian men who hate women. In C. C. Kroeger & J. R. Beck (Eds.), *Healing the hurting: Giving hope and help to abused women* (pp. 83–98). Grand Rapids, MI: Baker.

Ripley, J. S., Leon, C., Worthington, E. J., Berry, J. W., Davis, E. B., Smith, A., . . . Sierra, T. (2014). Efficacy of religion-accommodative strategic hope-focused theory applied to couples therapy. *Couple and Family Psychology: Research and Practice, 3,* 83–98. doi:10.1037/cfp0000019

Ripley, J. S., & Worthington, E. L., Jr. (2002). Hope-focused and forgiveness group interventions to promote marital enrichment. *Journal of Counseling and Development, 80,* 452–463. doi:10.1002/j.1556-6678.2002.tb00212.x

Ripley, J. S., & Worthington, E. L., Jr. (2014). *Couple therapy: A new hope-focused approach.* Downers Grove, IL: InterVarsity.

Rizzolatti, G., & Arbib, M. A. (1998). Language within our grasp. *Trends in Neurosciences, 21,* 188–194.

Robbins, M. S., Alexander, J. F., Turner, C. W., & Hollimon, A. (2016). Evolution of functional family therapy as an evidence-based practice for adolescents with disruptive behavior problems. *Family Process, 55*(3), 543–557.

Roberts, R. C. (1987). Therapeutic virtues and the grammar of faith. *Journal of Psychology and Theology, 15*(3), 191–204.

Roberts, R. C. (2001). Outline of Pauline psychotherapy. In M. R. McMinn & T. R. Phillips (Eds.), *Care for the soul: Exploring the intersection of psychology & theology* (pp. 134–163). Downers Grove, IL: IVP Academic.

Roberts, R. C. (2007). *Spiritual emotions: A psychology of Christian virtues.* Grand Rapids, MI: Eerdmans.

Roberts, T., & Koval, J. (2003). Applying brain research to couple therapy: Emotional restructuring. *Journal of Couple and Relationship Therapy, 2,* 1–13.

Roberts-Lewis, A., & Armstrong, T. D. (2010). Moving the church to social action. *Social Work and Christianity, 37*(2), 115–127.

Robinson, G. (2009). *Adventure and the way of Jesus: An experiential approach to spiritual formation.* Bethany, OK: Woods N. Barnes.

Rochester, K. M. (2016). Integrated suffering: Healing disconnections between the emotional, the rational, and the spiritual thought through lament. *Journal of Spiritual Formation and Soul Care, 9*(2), 270–281.

Rodrigo, M. J., León, I., González, I. Q., Castellanos, A. L., Byrne, S., & Bobes, M. A. (2011). Brain and personality bases of insensitivity to infant cues in neglectful mothers: An event-related potential study. *Development and Psychopathology, 23,* 163–176.

Roemer, L., & Orsillo, S. M. (2014). An acceptance-based behavioral therapy for generalized anxiety disorder. In D. H. Barlow (Ed.), *Clinical handbook of psychological disorders: A step-by-step treatment manual* (5th ed., pp. 206–236). New York, NY: Guilford Press.

Rogers, C. R. (1951). *Client-centered therapy, its current practice, implications, and theory.* Boston, MA: Houghton Mifflin.

Rogers, C. R. (1959). *A theory of therapy, personality, and interpersonal relationships, as developed in the client-centered framework.* New York, NY: McGraw-Hill.

Rogers, C. R. (1961). *On becoming a person: A therapist's view of psychotherapy.* Boston, MA: Houghton Mifflin.

Rogers, C. R. (1992). The necessary and sufficient conditions of therapeutic personality change. *Journal of Consulting and Clinical Psychology, 60*(6), 827–832.

Rogers, C. R. (2004). *On becoming a person: A therapist's view of psychotherapy* (2nd ed.). Boston, MA: Houghton Mifflin.

Rohina, S. A., Vineet, V. M., Navin, A. P., Nital, H. P., Vrushali, V. D., & Anil, F. J. (2016). Incidence and prevalence of sexual dysfunction in infertile females. *Bangladesh Journal of Obstetrics & Gynecology, 28*, 26–30.

Rolider, A., & Van Houten, R. (1984). Training parents to use extinction to eliminate nighttime crying by gradually increasing the criteria for ignoring crying. *Education and Treatment of Children, 7*(2), 119–124.

Romig, C. A., & Gruenke, C. (1991). The use of metaphor to overcome inmate resistance to mental health counseling. *Journal of Counseling & Development, 69*, 414–418.

Ronan, K. R., Kendall, P. C., & Rowe, M. (1994). Negative affectivity in children: Development and validation of a self-statement questionnaire. *Cognitive Therapy and Research, 18*(6), 509–528.

Rosen, C. M., & Atkins, S. S. (2014). Am I doing expressive arts therapy or creativity in counseling? *Journal of Creativity in Mental Health, 9*, 292–303. doi:10.1080/15401383.2014.906874

Rosenau, D. (1998). Extramarital affairs: Therapeutic understanding and clinical interventions. *Marriage & Family: A Christian Journal, 1*, 355–368.

Rosenau, D. (2002). *A celebration of sex.* Nashville, TN: Thomas Nelson.

Rosenau, D., & Neel, D. (2013). *Total intimacy: A guide to loving by colors.* Atlanta, GA: Sexual Wholeness Resources.

Rosenau, D., & Sytsma, M. (2004). A theology of sexual intimacy: Insights into the Creator. *Journal of Psychology and Christianity, 23*(3), 261–270.

Rosenau, D., Sytsma, M., & Taylor, D. L. (2002). Sexuality and sexual therapy: Learning and practicing the DEC-R model. In T. Clinton & G. Ohlschlager (Eds.), *Competent Christian Counseling* (Vol. 1, pp. 490–516). Colorado Springs, CO: WaterBrook.

Rosenthal, H. G. (Ed.). (1998). *Favorite counseling and therapy techniques: 51 therapists share their most creative strategies.* New York, NY: Brunner-Routledge.

Ross, A. P. (1991). Proverbs. In F. E. Gaebelein (Ed.), *The expositor's Bible commentary* (Vol. 6, pp. 881–1134). Grand Rapids, MI: Zondervan.

Ross, T. (2012). *A survival guide for health research methods.* Berkshire, UK: Open University Press.

Rowland, D. L., Kostelyk, K. A., & Tempel, A. R. (2016). Attribution patterns in men with sexual problems: Analysis and implications for treatment. *Sexual and Relationship Therapy, 31*(2), 148–158. doi:10.1080/14681994.2015.1126669

Rubin, J. A. (2005). *Child art therapy* (Deluxe ed.). Hoboken, NJ: Wiley.

Rubin, J. A. (2011). *The art of art therapy: What every therapist needs to know.* New York, NY: Routledge.

Rude, S. S., & Bates, D. (2005). The use of cognitive and experiential techniques to treat depression. *Clinical Case Studies, 4*(4), 363–379. doi:10.1177/1534650103259749

Runko, M. A., & Jaeger, G. J. (2012). The standard definition of creativity. *Creativity Research Journal, 24*(1), 92–96. doi:10.1080/10400419.2012.650092

Rüsch, N., Bracht, T., Kreher, B. W., Schnell, S., Glauche, V., Il'yasov, K. A., & Tebartz van Elst, L. (2010). Reduced interhemispheric structural connectivity between anterior cingulate cortices in borderline personality disorder. *Psychiatry Research: Neuroimaging, 181*, 151–154.

Russell, R. L., Jones, M. E., & Miller, S. A. (2007). Core process components in psychotherapy: A synthetic review of P-technique studies. *Psychotherapy Research, 17*(3), 273–291.

Rye, M. S., & Pargament, K. I. (2002). Forgiveness and romantic relationships in college: Can it heal the wounded heart? *Journal of Clinical Psychology, 54*, 419–441.

Rye, M. S., Pargament, K. I., Pan, W., Yingling, D. W., Shogren, K. A., & Ito, M. (2005).

5

Can group interventions facilitate forgiveness of an ex-spouse? A randomized clinical trial. *Journal of Consulting and Clinical Psychology, 73*, 880–892.

Ryrie, C. C. (1999). *Basic theology: A popular systematic guide to understanding biblical truth* (2nd ed.). Chicago, IL: Moody.

Sackett, D. L., Rosenburg, W. M. C., Muir-Gray, J. A., Haynes, R. B., & Richardson, W. S. (1996). Evidence-based medicine, what it is and what it isn't. *British Medical Journal, 312*, 71–72.

Sadeghi, A., Sirati-Nir, M., Ebadi, A., Aliasgari, M., & Hajiamini, Z. (2015). The effect of progressive muscle relaxation on pregnant women's general health. *Iranian Journal of Nursing & Midwifery Research, 20*(6), 655–660. doi:10.4103/1735-9066.170005

Sala, M. N., Testa, S., Pons, F., & Molina, P. (2015). Emotion regulation and defense mechanisms. *Journal of Individual Differences, 36*, 19–29. doi:10.1027/1614-0001/a000151

Salavert, J., Gasol, M., Vieta, E., Cervantes, A., Trampal, C., & Gispert, J. D. (2011). Fronto-limbic dysfunction in borderline personality disorder: A 18F-FDG positron emission tomography study. *Journal of Affective Disorders, 131*, 260–267.

Salend, S. J., & Meddaugh, D. (1985). Using a peer-mediated extinction procedure to decrease obscene language. *The Pointer, 30*, 811.

Salvatore, J. E., Kuo, S., Steele, R. D., Simpson, J. A., & Collins, W. A. (2011). Recovering from conflict in romantic relationships: A developmental perspective. *Psychological Science, 22*(3), 376–383. doi:10.1177/0956797610397055

Samur, D., Lai, T., Hagoort, P., & Willems, R. M. (2015). Emotional context modulates embodied metaphor comprehension. *Neuropsychologia, 78*, 108–114. doi:10.1016/j.neuropsychologia.2015.10.003

Sand, M., & Fisher, W. A. (2007). Women's endorsement of models of female sexual response: The nurses' sexuality study. *Journal of Sexual Medicine, 4*(3), 708–719. doi:10.1111/j.1743-6109.2007.00496.x

Sandage, S. J., Jankowski, P. J., Bissonette, C. D., & Paine, D. R. (2017). Vulnerable narcissism, forgiveness, humility, and depression: Mediator effects for differentiation of self. *Psychoanalytic Psychology, 34*(3), 300–310. doi:10.1037/pap0000042

Sandage, S. J., Long, B., Moen, R., Jankowski, P. J., Worthington, E. L., Jr., Rye, M. S., & Wade, N. G. (2015). Forgiveness in the treatment of Borderline Personality Disorder: A quasi-experimental pilot study. *Journal of Clinical Psychology, 71*(7), 625–640.

Sanders, R. K. (2013). *Christian counseling ethics: A handbook for therapists, pastors, & counselors* (2nd ed.). Downers Grove, IL: IVP Academic.

Sanderson, C. (2015). *Counselling skills for working with shame.* London: Jessica Kingsley.

Sanner, A. E. (1964). The gospel according to Mark. In A. F. Harper, W. M. Greathouse, R. Earle, & W. T. Purkiser (Eds.), *Beacon Bible commentary* (Vol. 6, pp. 261–416). Kansas City, MO: Beacon Hill.

Santrock, J. W. (2015). *Life-span development* (15th ed.). New York, NY: McGraw-Hill.

Sarwer, D. B., & Durlak, J. A. (1996). Childhood sexual abuse as a predictor of adult female sexual dysfunction: A study of couples seeking sex therapy. *Child Abuse & Neglect, 20*(10), 963–972.

Satinover, J. (2004). A written testimony presented before the United States Senate Subcommittee on Science, Technology, and Space of the Committee on Commerce, Science, and Transportation. Washington, DC.

Satir, V. (1983). *Conjoint family therapy* (3rd revision). Palo Alto, CA: Science and Behavioral Books.

Satir, V. (1987). The therapist story. *Journal of Psychotherapy and the Family, 3*, 17–25.

Satir, V., & Baldwin, M. (1984). *Satir step-by-step: A guide to creating change in families.* Palo Alto, CA: Science and Behavioral Books.

Saunders, S. M. (2001). Pretreatment correlates of the therapeutic bond. *Journal of Clinical Psychology, 57*(12), 1339–1352.

Saxbe, D., & Repetti, R. L. (2010). For better or worse? Coregulation of couples' cortisol levels and mood states. *Journal of Personality and Social Psychology, 98*, 92–103. doi:10.1037/a0016959

Sayegh, L., Locke, K. D., Pistilli, D., Penberthy, J. K., Chachamovich, E., McCullough, J. P., Jr., & Turecki, G. (2012). Cognitive behavioural analysis system of psychotherapy for treatment-resistant depression: Adaptation to a group modality. *Behavior Change Journal, 29*, 97–108.

Sbanotto, E. A. N., Gingrich, H. D., & Gingrich, F. C. (2016). *Skills for effective counseling: A faith-based integration.* Downers Grove, IL: InterVarsity.

Scalise, E. T. (2011). Counseling the whole person throughout the whole world. *Christian Counseling Today, 18*(3), 1–2.

Scazzero, P. (2014). *Emotionally healthy spirituality.* Grand Rapids, MI: Zondervan.

Schaefer, C. E. (2001). Prescriptive play therapy. *International Journal of Play Therapy, 10*(2), 57–73. doi:10.1037/h0089480

Schaefer, K. (2001). *Psalms.* Collegeville, MN: Liturgical Press.

Schaeffer, F. (1968). *The God who is there.* Downers Grove, IL: InterVarsity.

Schaeffer, F. (1971). *True spirituality/He is there and he is not silent.* Carol Streams, IL: Tyndale.

Scharff, D. E. (1998). *The sexual relationship: An object relations view of sex and the family.* Northvale, NJ: Jason Aronson.

Scharff, D. E., & Scharff, J. S. (1987). *Object relations family therapy.* Lanham, MD: Jason Aronson.

Schimmel, C. J. (2007). Seeing is remembering: The impact of using creative props with children in schools and community agencies. *Journal of Creativity in Mental Health, 2*(2), 59–74.

Schirda, B., Valentine, T., Aldao, A., & Shaurya Prakash, R. (2016). Age-related differences in emotion regulation strategies: Examining the role of contextual factors. *Developmental Psychology, 52*, 1370–1380.

Schmader, T., & Lickel, B. (2006). The approach and avoidance function of personal and vicarious shame and guilt. *Motivation and Emotion, 30*, 43–56. doi:10.1007/s11031-006-9006-0

Schmid, M., Peterman, F., & Fegert, J. (2013). Developmental trauma disorder: Pros and cons of including formal criteria in the psychiatric diagnostic systems. *BMC Psychiatry, 13*(3). Retrieved from ncbi.nlm.nih.gov/pmc/articles/PMC3541245/

Schmutzer, A. J. (2011). A theology of sexuality and its abuse: Creation, evil, and the relational ecosystem. In A. J. Schmutzer (Ed.), *The long journey home: Understanding and ministering to the sexually abused* (pp. 105–135). Eugene, OR: Wipf and Stock.

Schmutzer, A. J. (2016). Introduction to the special issue: Suffering and the Christian life. *Journal of Spiritual Formation and Soul Care, 9*(2), 147–150.

Schnarch, D. (1991). *Constructing the sexual crucible: An integration of sexual and marital therapy.* New York, NY: W. W. Norton.

Schneider, J. P. (2003). The impact of compulsive cybersex behaviors on the family. *Sexual and Relationship Therapy, 18*(3), 329–353.

Schneider, K. J., & Krug, O. T. (2010). *Existential-humanistic therapy* (1st ed.). Washington, DC: American Psychological Association.

Schniering, C. A., & Rapee, R. M. (2002). Development and validation of a measure of children's automatic thoughts: The children's automatic thoughts scale. *Behaviour Research and Therapy, 40*(9), 1091–1109. doi:10.1016/S005-7967(02)00022-0

Schoenleber, M., & Berenbaum, H. (2012). Shame regulation in personality pathology. *Journal of Abnormal Psychology, 121*(2), 433–446.

Scholz, M., Neumann, C., Wild, K., Garreis, F., Hammer, C., Ropohl, A., . . . Burger, P. (2016). Teaching to relax: Development of a program to potentiate stress. Results of a feasibility study with medical undergraduate students. *Applied Psychophysiology & Biofeedback, 40*(3), 275–281. doi:10.1007/s10484-015-9327-4

Schore, A. N. (1994). *Affect regulation and origins of the self.* Mahwah, NJ: Erlbaum.

Schore, A. N. (2000). Attachment and the regulation of the right brain. *Attachment and Human Development, 2*(1), 23–47.

Schore, A. N. (2001). The effects of early relational trauma on right brain development, affect regulation, and infant mental health. *Infant Mental Health Journal, 22*, 201–269.

Schore, A. N. (2003a). *Affect dysregulation and disorders of the self.* New York, NY: W. W. Norton.

Schore, A. N. (2003b). *Affect regulation and the repair of the self.* New York, NY: W. W. Norton.

Schore, A. N. (2003c). Early relational trauma, disorganized attachment, and the development of a predisposition to violence. In M. F. Solomon & D. J. Siegel (Eds.), *Healing trauma: Attachment, mind, body, and brain* (pp. 107–167). New York, NY: W. W. Norton.

Schore, A. N. (2005). A neuropsychoanalytic viewpoint. Commentary on paper by Steven H. Knoblauch, *Psychoanalytic dialogue, 17*, 753–767.

Schore, A. N. (2012). *The science of the art of psychotherapy.* New York, NY: W. W. Norton.

Schore, J., & Schore, A. (2008). Modern attachment theory: The central role of affect regulation in development and treatment. *Clinical Social Work Journal, 36*, 9–20.

Schuster, M. A., Stein, B. D., Jaycox, L. H., Collins, R. L., Marshall, G. N., Elliott, M. N., & Berry, S. H. (2001). A national survey of stress reactions after the September 11, 2001, terrorist attacks. *New England Journal of Medicine, 345*, 1507–1512.

Schwartz, R. C. (1995). *Internal family systems therapy.* New York, NY: Guilford Press.

Schwartz, R. C. (2001). *Introduction to the internal family systems model.* Oak Park, CA: Trailheads.

Schwartz, R. C. (2003). Pathways to sexual intimacy. *Psychotherapy Networker, 27*(3), 36–43.

Schwartz, R. C. (2013). Internal family systems. In A. Rambo, C. West, A. Schooley, & T. V. Boyd (Eds.), *Family therapy review: Contrasting contemporary models* (pp. 196–198). New York, NY: Routledge/Taylor & Francis Group.

Seabury, J. B. (Ed.). (1900). *Pope's essay on man and essay on criticism.* New York, NY: Silver, Burdett & Company.

Segal, Z. V., Bieling, P., Young, T., MacQueen, G., Cooke, R., Martin, L., & Levitan, R. D. (2010). Antidepressant monotherapy vs. sequential pharmacotherapy and mindfulness-based cognitive therapy, or placebo, for relapse prophylaxis in recurrent depression. *Archives of General Psychiatry, 67*(12), 1256–1264. doi:10.1001/archgenpsychiatry.2010.168

Segal, Z. V., Williams, J. M. G., & Teasdale, J. D. (2013). *Mindfulness-based cognitive therapy for depression* (2nd ed.). New York, NY: Guilford Press.

Seigler, R. S., Deloache, J. S., & Eisenberg, N. (2006). *How children develop* (3rd ed.). New York, NY: Worth.

Selby, A. & Smith-Osborne, A. (2013). A systematic review of effectiveness of complementary and adjunct therapies and interventions involving equines. *Health Psychology, 32*(4), 418–432. doi:10.1037/a0029188

Selcuk, E., Zayas, V., Gunaydin, G., Hazan, C., & Kross, E. (2012). Mental representations of attachment figures facilitate recovery following upsetting autobiographical memory recall. *Journal of Personality and Social Psychology, 103*, 362–378.

Selekman, M., & Beyebach, M. (2013). *Changing self-destructive habits: Pathways to solutions with couples and families.* New York, NY: Routledge.

Sells, J., & Hervey, E. G. (2011). Forgiveness in sexual abuse: Defining our identity in the journey toward wholeness. In A. J. Schmutzer (Ed.), *The long journey home: Understanding and ministering to the sexually abused* (pp. 169–185). Eugene, OR: Wipf and Stock.

Sells, S. P. (2004). *Treating the tough adolescent: A family based, step-by-step guide* (1st ed.). New York, NY: Guilford Press.

Serati, M., Salvatore, S., Siesto, G., Cattoni, E., Zanirato, M., Khullar, V., & Bolis, P. (2010). Female sexual function during pregnancy and after childbirth. *Journal of Sexual Medicine, 7*(8), 2782–2790. doi:10.1111/j.1743-6109.2010.01893.x

Sexton, T. L., Datachi-Phillips, C., Evans, L. E., LaFollette, J., & Wright, L. (2013). The effectiveness of couple and family therapy interventions. In M. Lambert (Ed.), *Bergin and Garfield's handbook of psychotherapy and behaviour change* (6th ed., pp. 587–640). New York, NY: Wiley.

Shadbolt, C. (2009). Sexuality and shame. *Transactional Analysis Journal, 39*(2), 163–172.

Shallcross, L. (2012). The recipe for truly great counseling. *Counseling Today.* Retrieved from https://ct.counseling.org/2012/12/the-recipe-for-truly-great-counseling/

Shapiro, S. (2016). *Easy ego-state interventions: Strategies for working with parts.* New York, NY: W. W. Norton.

Sharp, S. (2010). How does prayer help manage emotions? *Social Psychology Quarterly, 73*(4), 417–437.

Shear, K., Monk, T., Houck, P., Melhem, N., Frank, E., Reynolds, C., & Sillowash, R. (2007). An attachment-based model of complicated grief including the role of avoidance. *European Archives of Psychiatry and Clinical Neuroscience, 257*(8), 453–461.

Shedler, J. (2015). Where is evidence for evidence based therapies? *Journal of Psychological Therapies in Primary Care, 4*, 47–59.

Sheikh, A. I. (2008). Theory and practice. *Counseling Psychology Quarterly, 21*(1), 85–97.

Sheperis, D. S., Henning, S. L., & Kocet, M. M. (2016). *Ethical decision making for the 21st century counselor.* Los Angeles, CA: Sage.

Sher, L., & Stanley, B. H. (2008). The role of endogenous opioids in the pathophysiology of self-injurious and suicidal behavior. *Archives of Suicide Research, 12*(4), 299–308.

Sherin, J. E. (2011). Post-traumatic stress disorder: The neurobiological impact of psychological trauma. *Dialogues in Clinical Neuroscience, 13*(3), 263–278.

Shoenfelt, J. L., & Weston, C. G. (2007). Managing obsessive compulsive disorder in children and adolescents. *Psychiatry, 4*(5), 47–53.

Shriver M., & Shriver, G. (2009). *Unfaithful: Hope and healing after infidelity.* Colorado Springs, CO: David C. Cook.

Shults, F. L., & Sandage, S. J. (2003). *The faces of forgiveness: Searching for wholeness and salvation.* Grand Rapids, MI: Baker Academic.

Sibcy, G. (2007). Attachment therapy for complex trauma. *Christian Counseling Today, 15*(3), 24–27.

Sibcy, G. (2017). Interpersonal neurobiology 2.0. [Presentation].

Siegel, D. J. (2001). Toward an interpersonal neurobiology of the developing mind: Attachment relationships, "mindsight," and neural integration. *Infant Mental Health Journal, 22*(1–2), 68–94.

Siegel, D. J. (2003). An interpersonal neurobiology of psychotherapy: The developing mind and the resolution of trauma. In M. F. Solomon & D. J. Siegel (Eds.), *Healing trauma: Attachment, mind, body, and brain* (pp. 1–56). New York, NY: W. W. Norton.

Siegel, D. J. (2009). Emotion as integration: A possible answer to the question, what is emotion? In D. Fosha, D. J. Siegel, & M. Solomon (Eds.), *The healing power of emotion: Affective neuroscience, development, and clinical practice* (pp. 145–171). New York, NY: W. W. Norton.

Siegel, D. J. (2012). *The developing mind: How relationships and the brain interact to shape who we are.* New York, NY: Guilford Press.

Siegel, D. J. (2013). *Brainstorm: The power and purpose of the teenage brain.* New York, NY: Penguin.

Siegel, D. J., & Payne Bryson, T. (2011). *The whole-brain child: 12 revolutionary strategies to nurture your child's developing mind.* New York, NY: Delacorte.

Simon, G. M. (1995). A revisionist rendering of structural family therapy. *Journal of Marital and Family Therapy, 21*, 17–26.

Simons, J. C., & Gaher, R. M. (2005). The Distress Tolerance Scale: Development and validation of the self-report measure. *Motivation and Emotion, 29*(2), 83–102. doi:10.1007/s11031-005-7955-3

Sire, J. W. (2009). *The universe next door: A basic worldview catalog* (5th ed.) Downers Grove, IL: InterVarsity.

Sisemore, T. A. (2015). *The psychology of religion and spirituality: From the inside out.* Hoboken, NJ: Wiley.

Sittser, J. L. (2003). *When God doesn't answer your prayer.* Grand Rapids, MI: Zondervan.

Sittser, J. L. (2004). *A grace disguised: How the soul grows through loss* (Expanded ed.). Grand Rapids, MI: Zondervan.

Skinner, B. F. (1953). *Science and human behavior.* New York, NY: Macmillan.

Skinner, B. F. (1972). *Beyond freedom and dignity.* New York, NY: Bantam.

Sklare, G. (2005). *Brief counseling that works: A solution-focused approach for school counselors and administrations* (2nd ed.). Thousand Oaks, CA: Corwin.

Slade, P. (2006). Towards a conceptual framework for understanding post-traumatic stress symptoms following childbirth and implications for further research. *Journal of Psychosomatic Obstetrics & Gynecology, 27*(2), 99–105.

Slee, N., Garnefski, N., van der Leeden, R., Arensman, E., & Spinhoven, P. (2008). Cognitive-behavioral intervention for self-harm: Randomized control trial. *British Journal of Psychiatry, 192,* 202–211.

Slife, B. D., & Whoolery, M. (2006). Are psychology's main methods biased against the worldview of many religious people? *Journal of Psychology and Theology, 34*(3), 217–231.

Smith, B. M., & Gingrich, F. C. (2011). The Cape Town Declaration: A bolder vision for counseling as mission worldwide. *Christian Counseling Today, 18*(3), 12–16.

Smith, E. (2005). *Healing life's hurts through Theophostic prayer.* Royal Oak, MI: New Creation.

Smith, P., James, T., Lorentzon, M., & Pope, R. (2004). *Evidence-based nursing and health care.* London: Churchill Livingstone.

Snyder, C. R., & Dinoff, B. L. (1999). *Coping: The psychology of what works.* New York, NY: Oxford University Press.

Snyder, D. K., Baucom, D. H., & Gordon, K. C. (2007). *Getting past the affair: A program to help you cope, heal, and move on—together or apart.* New York, NY: Guilford Press.

Sobell, L. C., & Sobell, M. C. (2008). *Motivational interviewing strategies and techniques: Rationales and examples.* Retrieved from http://www.ncjfcj.org/sites/default/files/MI%20Strategies%20%26%20Techniques%20-%20Rationales%20and%20examples.pdf

Social Work Tech. (n.d.). The seven stages of grief. Retrieved from http://socialworktech.com/wp-content/uploads/2012/11/Social-Work-Tech-Seven-Stages-of-Grief.pdf

Solomon, J., & George, C. (2008). The measurement of attachment security and related constructs in infancy and early childhood. In J. Cassidy & P. R. Shaver (Eds.), *Handbook of attachment: Theory, research, and clinical applications* (2nd ed., pp. 383–418). New York, NY: Guilford Press.

Solomon, M. F., & Siegel, D. J. (2003). *Healing trauma: Attachment, mind, body, and brain.* New York, NY: W. W. Norton.

Somerfield, M. R., & McCrae, R. R. (2000). Stress and coping research: Methodological challenges, theoretical advances, and clinical applications. *American Psychologist, 55*(6), 620–625.

Spanier, G. B. (1976). Measuring dyadic adjustment: New scales for assessing the quality of marriage and similar dyads. *Journal of Marriage and Family, 38,* 15–38.

Spector, I., & Libman, E. (1988). Client attributions for sexual dysfunction. *Journal of Sex Marital Therapy, 14*(3), 208–224. doi:10.1080/00926238808403919

Spiegler M. D., & Guevremont, D. C. (2010). *Contemporary behavior* (5th ed.). Belmont, CA: Wadsworth.

Sprenkle, D. (2012). Intervention research in couple and family therapy: A methodological and substantive review and an introduction to the special issue. *Journal of Marital and Family Therapy, 38,* 3–29.

Spring, J. A. (2006). *After the affair: Healing the pain and rebuilding trust when a partner has been unfaithful.* New York, NY: Harper.

Sprinkle, J. (1997). Old Testament perspectives on divorce and remarriage. *Journal of the Evangelical Theological Society, 40*(4), 529–550.

Stadter, M. (2015). The inner world of shaming and ashamed: An object relations perspective and therapeutic approach. In R. L. Dearing & J. P. Tangney (Eds.), *Shame in the therapy hour* (pp. 45–68). Washington, DC: American Psychological Association.

Stallard, P., & Rayner, H. (2005). The development and preliminary evaluation of a schema questionnaire for children. *Behavioural and Cognitive Psychotherapy, 33*(2), 217–224.

Star, K. L., & Cox, J. A. (2008). The use of phototherapy in couples and family counseling. *Journal of Creativity in Mental Health, 3,* 373–382. doi:10.1080/15401380802527472

Staudacher, C. (1994). *A time to grieve: Meditations for healing.* San Francisco, CA: HarperCollins.

Stavlund, M. (2013). *A force of will: The reshaping of faith in a year of grief.* Grand Rapids, MI: Baker.

Stayton, W. (1996). A theology of sexual pleasure. In E. Stuart & A. Thatcher (Eds.), *Christian perspectives on sexuality and gender* (pp. 332–346). Herefordshire, UK: Gracewing.

Steele, H., Steele, M., Sroufe, J., & Jacobvitz, D. (2008). *Clinical applications of the adult attachment interview.* New York, NY: Guilford Press.

Steele, K., Boon, S., & van der Hart, O. (2017). *Treating trauma-related dissociation: A practical, integrative approach.* New York, NY: W. W. Norton.

Steffens, B. A., & Rennie, R. L. (2006). The traumatic nature of disclosure for wives of sexual addicts. *Sexual Addiction & Compulsivity, 13*(2–3), 247–267. doi:10.1080/10720160600870802

Stein, M. I. (1953). Creativity and culture. *Journal of Psychology, 36,* 311–322. doi.org/10.1080/00223980.1953.9712897

Stone, C., & Isaacs, M. L. (2003). Confidentiality with minors: The need for policy to promote and protect. *Journal of Educational Research, 96,* 140–150. doi:10.1080/00220670309598802

Strassel, J. K., Cherkin, D. C., Steuten, L., Sherman, K. J., & Vrijhoef, H. J. (2011). A systematic review of the evidence for the effectiveness of dance therapy. *Alternative Therapies in Health and Medicine, 17*(3), 50–59.

Stratton, P., Silver, E., Nascimento, N., McDonnell, L., Powell, G., & Nowotny, E. (2015). Couple and family therapy outcome research in the previous decade: What does the evidence tell us? *Contemporary Family Therapy: An International Journal, 37*(1), 1–12.

Strauss, M. (2002). Luke. In C. E. Arnold (Ed.), *Zondervan illustrated Bible backgrounds commentary* (Vol. 1, pp. 318–515). Grand Rapids, MI: Zondervan.

Strelan, P., & Covic, T. (2006). A review of forgiveness process models and a coping framework to guide future research. *Journal of Social and Clinical Psychology, 25*(10), 1059–1085.

Strong, M. (1998). *A bright red scream: Self-mutilation and the language of pain.* New York, NY: Penguin.

Strunk, D. R., Hollars, S. N., Adler, A. D., Goldstein, L. A., & Braun, J. D. (2014). Assessing patients' cognitive therapy skills: Initial evaluation of the competencies of cognitive therapy scale. *Cognitive Therapy Research, 38*(5), 559–569.

Struthers, W. (2009). *Wired for intimacy.* Downers Grove, IL: InterVarsity.

Struthers, W. M., Ansell, K., & Wilson, A. (2017). The neurobiology of stress and trauma. In H. D. Gingrich & F. C. Gingrich (Eds.), *Treating trauma in Christian counseling* (pp. 55–77). Downers Grove, IL: InterVarsity.

Stuart, A. J., Levy, R. A., & Katzenstein, T. (2006). Beyond brand names of psychotherapy: Identifying empirically supported change processes. *Psychotherapy, 43*(22), 216–231.

Suárez, L., Bennett, S., Goldstein, C., & Barlow, D. H. (2009). Understanding anxiety disorders from a "triple vulnerabilities" framework. In M. M. Antony & M. B. Stein (Eds.), *Oxford handbook of anxiety and related disorders* (pp. 153–172). New York, NY: Oxford University Press.

Subby, R. (1987). *Lost in the shuffle*. Deerfield Beach, FL: Health Communication.

Subic-Wrana, C., Beutel, M., Brahler, E., Stobel-Richter, Y., Knebel, A., Lane, R., & Wiltink, J. (2014). How is emotional awareness related to emotion regulation strategies and self-reported negative affect in the general population? *PLOS One, 9*(3), e91846. doi:10.1371/journal.pone.0091846

Sue, D. W., & Sue, D. (2013). *Counseling the culturally diverse: Theory and practice* (6th ed.). New York, NY: Wiley.

Sulzer-Azaroff, B., & Mayer, R. G. (1991). *Behavior analysis for lasting change* (2nd ed.). Belmont, CA Wadsworth.

Sutherland, O., Perakyla, A., & Elliott, R. (2014). Conversation analysis of the two-chair self-soothing task in emotion-focused therapy. *Psychotherapy Research, 24*(6), 738–751. doi:10.1080/10503307.2014.885146

Swales, M. A., & Heard, H. L. (2009). *Dialectical behavior therapy: Distinctive features*. New York, NY: Routledge.

Swan, J. S., MacVicar, R., Christmas, D., Durham, R., Rauchhaus, P., McCullough, J. P., Jr., & Matthews, K. (2014). Cognitive Behavioral Analysis System of Psychotherapy (CBASP) for chronic depression: Clinical characteristics and six-month clinical outcomes in an open case series. *Journal of Affective Disorders, 162*, 268–276.

Sweeney, D. S., Baggerly, J. N., & Ray, D. C. (2014). *Group play therapy: A dynamic approach*. New York, NY: Taylor & Francis.

Swenson, R. (2006). Limbic system. In *Review of clinical and functional neuroscience* (chapter 9). Retrieved from https://www.dartmouth.edu/~rswenson/NeuroSci/chapter_9.html

Sytsma, M. (2004). *Sexual desire discrepancy in married couples* (Unpublished doctoral dissertation). University of Georgia, Athens.

Takeuchi, M. M., & Takeuchi, S. A. (2008). Authoritarian versus authoritative parenting styles: Application of the cost equalization principle. *Marriage & Family Review, 44*(4), 489–510.

Tan, S.-Y. (1987). Training lay Christian counselors: A basic program and some preliminary data. *Journal of Psychology and Christianity, 6*(2), 57–61.

Tan, S.-Y. (2003). Integrating spiritual direction into psychotherapy: Ethical issues and guidelines. *Journal of Psychology and Theology, 31*, 14–23.

Tan, S.-Y. (2011a). *Counseling and psychotherapy: A Christian perspective*. Grand Rapids, MI: Baker Academic.

Tan, S.-Y. (2011b). Mindfulness and acceptance-based cognitive therapies: Empirical evidence and clinical applications from a Christian perspective. *Journal of Psychology and Christianity, 30*, 243–49.

Tangney, J. P., & Dearing, R. L. (2002). *Shame and guilt*. New York, NY: Guilford Press.

Tangney, J. P., & Dearing, R. L. (2011). Working with shame in the therapy hour: Summary and integration. In R. L. Dearing & J. P. Tangney (Eds.), *Shame in the therapy hour* (pp. 375–404). Washington, DC: American Psychological Association.

Tangney, J. P., Wagner, P. E., & Gramzow, R. (1992). Proneness to shame, proneness to guilt, and psychopathology. *Journal of Abnormal Psychology, 101*, 469–478. doi:10.1037/0021-843X.101.3.469

Tay, D. (2012). Applying the notion of metaphor types to enhance counseling protocols. *Journal of Counseling & Development, 90*, 142–149.

Taylor, S. (2006). *Clinician's guide to PTSD: A cognitive-behavioral approach*. New York, NY: Guilford Press.

Taylor, W. H. (1965). The epistle to the Ephesians. In A. F. Harper, W. M. Greathouse, R. Earle, & W. T. Purkiser (Eds.), *Beacon*

Bible commentary (Vol. 9, pp. 129–276). Kansas City, MO: Beacon Hill.

Tedeschi, R. G., & Calhoun, L. G. (1995). *Trauma & transformation: Growing in the aftermath of suffering.* Thousand Oaks, CA: Sage.

Tedeschi, R. G., & Calhoun, L. G. (2004). Post-traumatic growth: Conceptual foundations and empirical evidence. *Psychological Inquiry, 15,* 1–18.

Therrien, S., & Brotto, L. A. (2016). A critical examination of the relationship between vaginal orgasm consistency and measures of psychological and sexual functioning and sexual concordance in women with sexual dysfunction. *Canadian Journal of Human Sexuality, 25*(2), 109–118. doi:10.3138/cjhs.252-A2

Thoma, M. E., McLain, A. C., Louis, J. F., King, R. B., Trumble, A. C., Sundaram, R., & Louis, G. M. B. (2013). Prevalence of infertility in the United States as estimated by the current duration approach and a traditional constructed approach. *Fertility and Sterility, 99*(5), 1324–1331.

Thomas, G. (2000). *Sacred marriage.* Grand Rapids, MI: Zondervan.

Thomas, G. (2004). *Scared parenting: How raising children shapes our souls.* Grand Rapids, MI: Zondervan.

Thomas, G., & Pring, R. (Eds.). (2004). *Evidence-based practice in education.* New York, NY: McGraw-Hill Education.

Thomas, J. C., & Habermas, G. (2008). *What's good about feeling bad: Finding purpose and a path through your pain.* Carol Stream, IL: Tyndale.

Thomas, J. C., & Habermas, G. (2011). *Enduring your season of suffering.* Lynchburg, VA: Liberty University Press.

Thomas, J. C., & Sosin, L. (2011). *Therapeutic expeditions: Equipping the Christian counselor for the journey.* Nashville, TN: B&H Academic.

Thomas, K. W. (1992). Conflict and negotiation processes in organizations. In M. D. Dunnette & L. M. Hough (Eds.). *Handbook of industrial and organizational psychology.* Palo Alto, CA: Consulting Psychological Press.

Thomas, K. W., & Kilmann, R. H. (1974). *The Thomas-Kilmann conflict mode instrument.* Mountain View, CA: Consulting Psychological Press.

Thomas, R. M., Hotsenpiller, G., & Peterson, D. A. (2007). Acute psychosocial stress reduces cell survival in adult hippocampal neurogenesis without altering proliferation. *Journal of Neuroscience, 27*(11), 2734-2743. doi:10.1523/J-NEUROSCI.3849-06.2007

Thomas, V. (2000). Discovering creativity in family therapy: A theoretical analysis. *Journal of Systemic Therapies, 19,* 4–17.

Thomason, T. C. (2010). The trend toward evidence-based practice and the future of psychotherapy. *American Journal of Psychotherapy, 64,* 29–38.

Thompson, A. P. (1983). Extramarital sex: A review of the research literature. *Journal of Sex Research, 19,* 1–22.

Thompson, C. (2010). *Anatomy of the soul: Surprising connections between neuroscience and spiritual practices that can transform your life and relationships.* Carol Stream, IL: Tyndale.

Thompson, C. (2015). *Anatomy of shame: Retelling the stories we believe about ourselves.* Downers Grove, IL: InterVarsity.

Thompson, R. A. (1994). Emotion regulation: A theme in search of definition. *Monographs of the Society for Research in Child Development, 59,* 25–52.

Thompson, R. A. (2003). *Counseling techniques: Improving relationships with others, ourselves, our families, and our environment* (2nd ed.). New York, NY: Routledge.

Thorpe, G. L., & Olson, S. L. (1997). *Behavior therapy: Concepts procedures and applications.* Boston, MA: Allyn and Bacon.

Timm, T. M., & Blow, A. J. (1999). Self-of-the-therapist work: A balance between removing restraints and identifying resources. *Contemporary Family Therapy: An International Journal, 21*(3), 331–351.

Titchener, E. (1909). *Experimental psychology of the thought processes.* New York, NY: Macmillan.

Toates, F. (2009). An integrative theoretical framework for understanding sexual motivation, arousal, and behavior. *Journal of Sex Research, 46*(2–3), 168–193. doi:10.1080/00224490902747768

Todhunter, R. G., & Deaton, J. (2010). The relationship between religious and spiritual factors and the perpetration of intimate partner violence. *Journal of Family Violence, 25*, 745–753. doi:10.1007/s10896-010-9332-6

Topham, G. L., Larson, J. H., & Holman, T. B. (2005). Family-of-origin predictors of hostile conflict in early marriage. *Contemporary Family Therapy, 27*, 101–121.

Tracy, S. R. (2011). Definitions and prevalence rates of sexual abuse: Quantifying, explaining, and facing a dark reality. In A. J. Schmutzer (Ed.), *The long journey home: Understanding and ministering to the sexually abused* (pp. 3–12). Eugene, OR: Wipf and Stock.

Trakhtenberg, E. (2008). The effects of guided imagery on the immune system: A critical review. *International Journal of Neuroscience, 118*, 839–855.

Tronick, E. Z., Als, H., Adamson, L., Wise, S., & Brazelton, T. B. (1978). The infant's response to entrapment between contradictory massages in face-to-face interaction. *Journal of the American Academy of Child Psychiatry, 17*, 1–13.

Trotter, A. H., Jr. (1996). Grace. In W. A. Elwell (Ed.), *Baker's evangelical dictionary of evangelical theology*. Grand Rapids, MI: Baker.

Tshifhumulo, R., & Mudhovozi, P. (2013). Behind closed doors: Listening to the voices of women enduring battering. *Gender and Behaviour, 11*(1), 5080–5088.

Tumin, D., Han, S., & Qian, Z. (2015). Estimates and meanings of marital separation. *Journal of Marriage and Family, 77*(1), 312–322. doi:10.1111/jomf.12149

Turner, B. (2005). *Handbook of sandplay therapy*. Cloverdale, CA: Temenos.

Turns, B. A., Morris, S. J., & Lentz, N. A. (2013). The self of the Christian therapist doing sex therapy: A model for training Christian sex therapists. *Sexual and Relationship Therapy, 28*(3), 186–200. doi:10.1080/14681994.2013.765557

Underwood, R. T. (2014). *Evaluation of an intensive workshop for men with compulsive sexual behaviors: Changes in shame, hopelessness, and readiness to change* (Order No. 10185807). Available from ProQuest Dissertations & Theses Global. (1862197245).

US Department of Justice. (n.d.). *Raising awareness about sexual abuse: Facts and statistics.* Retrieved from https://www.nsopw.gov/en-US/Education/FactsStatistics?Aspx Auto DetectCookieSupport=1#sexualabuse

Vail, K. E., III, Rothschild, Z. K., Weise, D. R., Solomon, S., Pyszczynski, T., & Greenberg, J. (2010). A terror management analysis of the psychological functions of religion. *Personality and Social Psychology Review, 14*, 84–94.

Vaisvaser, S., Lin, T., Admon, R., Podlipsky, I., Greenman, Y., Stern, N., & Hendler, T. (2013). Neural traces of stress: Cortisol-related sustained enhancement of amygdala-hippocampal functional connectivity. *Frontiers in Human Neuroscience, 7*, 313. doi:10.3389/fnhum.2013.00313

Vande Kemp, H. (1984). *Psychology and theology in Western thought, 1672–1965: A historical and annotated bibliography*. White Plains, NY: Kraus International.

Vandenberg, B., & O'Connor, S. P. (2005). Developmental psychology and the death of God. In B. D. Slife, J. S. Reber, & F. C. Richardson (Eds.), *Critical thinking about psychology: Hidden assumptions and plausible alternatives* (pp. 189–206). Washington, DC: American Psychological Association.

Van der Kolk, B. (2003). The neurobiology of childhood trauma and abuse. *Child and Adolescent Psychiatric Clinics of North America, 12*, 293–317.

Van der Kolk, B. (2015). *The body keeps the score: Brain, mind, and body in the healing of trauma*. New York, NY: Penguin.

Van der Kooij, M. A., Fantin, M., Rejmak, E., Grosse, J., Zanoletti, O., Fournier, C., & Sandi, C. (2014). Role for MMP-9 in stress-induced downregulation of nectin-3 in hippocampal CA1 and associated behavioural alterations. *Nature Communications*, 54995. doi:10.1038/ncomms5995

VanGemeren, W. A. (1991). Psalms. In F. E. Gaebelein (Ed.), *The expositor's Bible commentary* (Vol. 5, pp. 1–880). Grand Rapids, MI: Zondervan.

Vanhuele, S., Verhaeghe, P., & Desmet, M. (2011). In search of a framework for the treatment of alexithymia. *Psychology and Psychotherapy: Theory Research and Practice*, *84*, 84–97.

Van IJzendoorn, M. H. (1995). Adult attachment representations, parental responsiveness, and infant attachment: A meta-analysis on the predictive validity of the adult attachment interview. *Psychological Bulletin*, *117*(3), 387–403.

Vaughan, C. (1978). Colossians. In F. E. Gaebelein (Ed.), *The expositor's Bible commentary* (Vol. 11, pp. 161–226). Grand Rapids, MI: Zondervan.

Vaughan, D. (2007). *A divine light: The spiritual leadership of Jonathan Edwards*. Nashville, TN: Cumberland House.

Verreault, N., Da Costa, D., Marchand, A., Ireland, K., Banack, H., Dritsa, M., & Khalifé, S. (2012). PTSD following childbirth: A prospective study of incidence and risk factors in Canadian women. *Journal of Psychosomatic Research*, *73*(4), 257–263. doi:10.1016/j.jpsychores.2012.07.010

Victor, S. E., Glenn, C. R., & Klonsky, E. D. (2012). Is non-suicidal self-injury an "addiction"? A comparison of craving in substance use and non-suicidal self-injury. *Psychiatry Research*, *197*, 73–77.

Vine, W. E. (1989). *Vine's expository dictionary of New Testament words: A comprehensive dictionary of the original Greek words with their precise meanings for English readers*. McLean, VA: MacDonald.

Vis, J., & Boynton, H. M. (2008). Spirituality and transcendent meaning making: Possibilities for enhancing posttraumatic growth. *Journal of Religion & Spirituality in Social Work: Social Thought*, *27*(1–2), 69–86.

Vitz, P. C. (1977, 1994). *Psychology as religion: The cult of self-worship* (2nd ed.). Grand Rapids, MI: Eerdmans.

Volf, M. (2005). *Free of charge: Giving and forgiving in a culture stripped of grace*. Grand Rapids, MI: Zondervan.

Wachtel, P. L. (2011). *Therapeutic communication: Knowing what to say when*. New York, NY: Guilford Press.

Wade, N. G., Cornish, M. A., Tucker, J. R., Worthington, E. L., Jr., Sandage, S. J., & Rye, M. S. (2017). *Understanding group interventions to promote forgiveness: Characteristics of the treatment, the process, and the client*. Unpublished manuscript, Iowa State University.

Wade, N. G., Hoyt, W. T., Kidwell, J. E., & Worthington, E. L. (2014). Efficacy of psychotherapeutic interventions to promote forgiveness: A meta-analysis. *Journal of Consulting and Clinical Psychology*, *82*(1), 154–170.

Wagener, A. E. (2017). Metaphor in professional counseling. *The Professional Counselor*, *7*(2), 144–154. doi:10.15241/aew.7.2.144

Wagers, T. P. (2003). Assessment of infidelity. In K. Jordan & K. Jordan (Eds.), *Handbook of couple and family assessment* (pp. 129–145). Hauppauge, NY: Nova Science.

Walker, D. F., Courtois, C. A., & Aten, J. D. (Eds.). (2015). *Spiritually oriented psychotherapy for trauma* (pp. 15–28). Washington, DC: American Psychological Association. doi:10.1037/14500–002

Walker, L. (1979). *The battered woman*. New York, NY: Harper Row.

Walker, L. (1994). *Abused women and survivor therapy: A practical guide for the psychotherapist*. Washington, DC: American Psychological Association.

Walker, S. (2012). *Responding to self-harm in children and adolescents: A professional's guide to identification, intervention and support*. Philadelphia, PA: Jessica Kingsley.

Wallin, D. J. (2007). *Attachment in psychotherapy*. New York, NY: Guilford Press.

Walsh, A. (2002). Returning to normalcy. *Religion in the News*, 5, 26–28.

Waltz, T. J., & Hayes, S. C. (2010). Acceptance and commitment therapy. In N. Kazantzis & M. A. Reineckes (Eds.), *Cognitive and behavioral theories in clinical practice* (pp. 148–192). New York, NY: Guilford Press.

Wampold, B. E. (2001). *The great psychotherapy debate. Models, methods, and findings.* Mahwah, NJ: Erlbaum.

Wampold, B. E. (2006). What should be validated? The psychotherapist. In J. C. Norcross, L. E. Beutler, & R. F. Levant (Eds.), *Evidence-based practices in mental health: Debate and dialogue on the fundamental questions* (pp. 200–208). Washington, DC: American Psychological Association.

Wang, D. C., & Tan, S.-Y. (2016). Dialectical Behavior Therapy (DBT): Empirical evidence and clinical applications from a Christian perspective. *Journal of Psychology and Christianity, 35*(1), 68–76.

Ware, J. N., & Dillman-Taylor, D. (2014). Concerns about confidentiality: The application of ethical decision making within group play therapy. *International Journal of Play Therapy, 23*(3), 173–186. doi:10.1037/a0036667

Warren, T. H. (2016). *Liturgy of the ordinary: Sacred practices in everyday life.* Downers Grove, IL: InterVarsity.

Watford, T., & Stafford, J. (2015). The impact of mindfulness on emotional dysregulation and psychophysiological reactivity under emotional provocation. *Psychology of Consciousness: Theory, Research and Practice, 2*, 90–109.

Watson, T. S. (2017). Assessment and treatment of intimate partner violence: Integrating psychological and spiritual approaches. In H. D. Gingrich & F. C. Gingrich (Eds.), *Treating trauma in Christian counseling.* Downers Grove, IL: InterVarsity.

Watzlawick, P., Bavelas, J. B., & Jackson, D. D. (1967). *Pragmatics of human communication.* New York, NY: W. W. Norton.

Webb-Mitchell, B. (2001). Leaving development behind and beginning our pilgrimage. In M. R. McMinn & T. R. Phillips (Eds.), *Care for the soul: Exploring the intersection of psychology and theology* (pp. 78–101). Downers Grove, IL: IVP Academic.

Weeks, G. R., & Fife, S. T. (2014). *Couples in treatment: Techniques and approaches for effective practice* (3rd ed.). New York, NY: Taylor and Francis.

Weeks, G. R., Gambescia, N., & Jenkins, R. E. (2003). *Treating infidelity. Therapeutic dilemmas and effective strategies* (1st ed.). New York, NY: W. W. Norton & Company.

Weiner, B. (1986). *An attributional theory of motivation and emotion.* New York, NY: Springer-Verlag.

Weinstein, N., Brown, K., & Ryan, R. M. (2008). A multi-method examination of the effects of mindfulness on stress attribution, coping, and emotional well-being. *Journal of Research in Personality, 43*, 284–295. doi:10.1016/j.jrp.2008.12.008

Weiser, J. (2004). PhotoTherapy techniques in counselling and therapy: Using ordinary snapshots and photo-interactions to help clients heal their lives. *Canadian Art Therapy Association Journal, 17*(2), 23–53.

Welch, E. T. (1997). *When people are big and God is small: Overcoming peer pressure, codependency, and the fear of man.* Phillipsburg, NJ: P&R.

Weller, C. (May 20, 2016). *The 10 most inspiring inventors under 18.* Retrieved from http://www.businessinsider.com/the-greatest-inventors-under-18-2016-5

Wendt, S., & Hornosty, J. (2010). Understanding contexts of family violence in rural, farming communities: Implications for rural women's health. *Rural Society, 20*, 51–63.

West, J., Liang, B., & Spinazzola, J. (2017). Trauma-sensitive yoga as a complementary treatment for posttraumatic stress disorder: A qualitative descriptive analysis. *International Journal of Stress Management, 24*(2), 173–195.

Westra, H. A. (2012). *Motivational interviewing in the treatment of anxiety.* New York, NY: Guilford Press.

Wetterneck, C. T., Singh, S., & Hart, J. (2014). Shame proneness in symptom dimensions of obsessive-compulsive disorder. *Bulletin of the Menninger Clinic, 78*(2), 177–190.

Wheat, E., & Perkins, G. O. (1980). *Love life for every married couple: How to fall in love and stay in love.* Grand Rapids, MI: Zondervan.

Whipple, B., & Brash-McGreer, K. (1997). Management of female sexual dysfunction. In M. Sipski & C. Alexander (Eds.), *Sexual function in people with disability and chronic illness. A health professional's guide* (pp. 509–534). Gaithersburg, MD: Aspen.

Whisman, M. A., & Wagers, T. P. (2005). Assessing relationship betrayals. *Journal of Clinical Psychology, 61*(11), 1383–1391.

White, M. (2007). *Maps of narrative practice* (1st ed.). New York, NY: W. W. Norton.

Wiederman, M. W. (1997). Extramarital sex: Prevalence and correlates in a national survey. *Journal of Sex Research, 34*(2), 167–174.

Wilder, J., Khouri, E., Coursey, C., & Sutton, S. (2013). *Joy starts here: The transformation zone.* Chicago IL: Shepherd's House.

Wilkins, M. J. (2002). Matthew. In C. E. Arnold (Ed.), *Zondervan illustrated Bible backgrounds commentary* (Vol. 1, pp. 2–203). Grand Rapids, MI: Zondervan.

Willard, D. (1998). *The divine conspiracy: Rediscovering our hidden life in God.* New York, NY: HarperCollins.

Williams, A., Herron-Marx, S., & Knibb, R. (2007). The prevalence of enduring postnatal perineal morbidity and its relationship to type of birth and birth risk factors. *Journal of Clinical Nursing, 16*(3), 549–561. doi:10.1111/j.13652702.2006.01593.x

Wilmot, W., & Hocker, J. (2014). *Interpersonal conflict* (8th ed.). New York, NY: McGraw-Hill.

Wilson, B. (2013). *Alcoholics anonymous: Big book* [E-book]. Retrieved from eBookit.com

Wilson, G. (2014). *Your brain on porn: Internet pornography and the emerging science of addiction* [E-book]. Kent, UK: Commonwealth.

Wilson, G. T., & Vitousek, K. M. (1999). Self-monitoring in the assessment of eating disorders. *Psychological Assessment, 11*, 480–489.

Wilson, S. J., Jaremka, L. M., Fagundes, C. P., Andridge, R., Peng, J., Malarkey, W. B., &

Kiecolt-Glaser, J. K. (2017). Shortened sleep fuels inflammatory responses to marital conflict: Emotion regulation matters. *Psychoneuroendocrinology, 7,* 974–983.

Winter, J., & Aponte, H. J. (1987). The person and practice of the therapist. *Journal of Psychotherapy and the Family, 3,* 85–111.

Winters, A. F. (2008). Emotion, embodiment, and mirror neurons in dance/movement therapy: A connection across disciplines. *American Journal of Dance Therapy, 30*(2), 84–105.

Wittenborn, A. K., Faber, A. J., Harvey, A. M., & Thomas, V. K. (2006). Emotionally focused family therapy and play therapy techniques. *American Journal of Family Therapy, 34*(4), 333–342. doi:10.1080/01926180600553472

Wolpe, J. (1982). *The practice of behavior therapy* (2nd ed.). New York, NY: Pergamon.

Wolpe, J. (1985). Systematic desensitization. In A. S. Bellack & M. Hersen's (Eds.), *Dictionary of behavioral therapy techniques* (pp. 215–219). Elmsford, NY: Pergamon.

Wood, A. S. (1978). Ephesians. In F. E. Gaebelein (Ed.), *The expositor's Bible commentary* (Vol. 11, pp. 3–92). Grand Rapids, MI: Zondervan.

Worden, J. W. (2008). *Grief counseling and grief therapy: A handbook for the mental health practitioner* (4th ed.). New York, NY: Springer.

World Health Organization. (2016). *International statistical classification of diseases and related health problems* (10th rev. ed.). Geneva: World Health Organization.

Worthington, E. L., Jr. (2003). Hope-focused marriage: Recommendations for researchers and church workers. *Journal of Psychology and Theology, 31,* 231–239.

Worthington, E. L., Jr. (2005). *Hope-focused marriage counseling: A guide to brief therapy.* Downers Grove, IL: InterVarsity.

Worthington, E. L., Jr. (2006). The development of forgiveness. In E. M. Dowling & W. G. Scarlette (Eds.), *Encyclopedia of religious and spiritual development in children and adolescents* (pp. 165–167). Thousand Oaks, CA: Sage.

Worthington, E. L., Jr. (2009). *A just forgiveness: Responsible healing without excusing injustice.* Downers Grove, IL: IVP Academic.

Worthington, E. L., Jr. (2013). *Moving forward: Six steps to forgiving yourself and breaking free from the past.* Colorado Springs, CO: Waterbrook.

Worthington, E. L., Jr. (2010). *Coming to peace with psychology: What Christians can learn from psychological science.* Downers Grove, IL: InterVarsity.

Worthington, E. L., Jr., Berry, J. W., Hook, J. N., Davis, D. E., Scherer, M., Griffin, B. J., . . . Campana, K. L. (2015). Forgiveness-reconciliation and communication-conflict-resolution interventions versus rested controls in early married couples. *Journal of Counseling Psychology, 62*(1), 14–27.

Worthington, E. L., Jr., Hunter, J. L., Sharp, C. B., Hook, J. N., Van Tongeren, D. R., Davis, D. E., . . . Monforte-Milton, M. M. (2010). A psychoeducational intervention to promote forgiveness in Christians in the Philippines. *Journal of Mental Health Counseling, 32*(1), 75–93.

Worthington, E. L., Jr., Jennings, D. J., & DiBlasio, F. A. (2010). Interventions to promote forgiveness in couple and family context: Conceptualization, review, and analysis. *Journal of Psychology and Theology, 38,* 231–245.

Worthington, E. L., Jr., Johnson, E. L., Hook, J. N., & Aten, J. D. (Eds.). (2013). *Evidence-based practices for Christian counseling and psychotherapy.* Downers Grove, IL: InterVarsity.

Worthington, E. L., Jr., Mazzeo, S. E., & Canter, D. E. (2005). Forgiveness-promoting approach: Helping clients REACH forgiveness through using a longer model that teaches reconciliation. In Len Sperry and Edward P. Shafranske (Eds.), *Spiritually-oriented psychotherapy* (pp. 235–257). Washington, DC: American Psychological Association.

Worthington, E. L., Jr., & Sandage, S. J. (2015). *Forgiveness and spirituality in psychotherapy: A relational approach.* Washington, DC: American Psychological Association.

Worthington, E. L., Jr., Wade, N. G., Hight, T. L., Ripley, J. S., McCullough, M. E.,

Berry, J. W., . . . O'Connor, L. (2003). The Religious Commitment Inventory–10: Development, refinement, and validation of a brief scale for research and counseling. *Journal of Counseling Psychology, 50*(1), 84–96.

Wright, H. N. (2003). *Crisis and trauma counseling: A practical guide for ministers, counselors, and lay counselors.* Ventura, CA: Regal.

Wright, N. T. (2006). *Evil and the justice of God.* Downers Grove, IL: InterVarsity.

Wyrick, S. (2003). Self-control and self-willed. In C. Brand, C. Draper, & A. England (Eds.), *Holman illustrated Bible dictionary.* Nashville, TN: Holman Bible.

Yalom, I. D. (2002). *Supervision in the helping professions* (4th ed.). New York, NY: McGraw-Hill.

Yalom, I. D. (2003). *The gift of therapy—An open letter to a new generation of therapists and their patients.* New York, NY: HarperCollins.

Yalom, I. D., & Leszcz, M. (2005). *The theory and practice of group psychotherapy* (5th ed.). New York, NY: Basic Books.

Yancey, P. (1992). *Disappointment with God: Three questions no one asks aloud.* Grand Rapids, MI: Zondervan.

Yancey, P. (1997). *Where is God when it hurts?* Grand Rapids, MI: Zondervan.

Yarhouse, M. A., Butman, R. E., & McRay, B. W. (2005). *Modern psychopathologies: A comprehensive Christian appraisal.* Downers Grove, IL: InterVarsity.

Yarhouse, M. A., & Hill, W. (2013). *Understanding sexual identity: A resource for youth ministry.* Grand Rapids, MI: Zondervan.

Yontef, G. M. (1993a). *Awareness, dialogue, and process: Essays on Gestalt therapy.* Highland, NY: Gestalt Journal Press.

Yontef, G. M. (1993b). Dialogic gestalt therapy. In L. S. Greenberg, J. C. Watson, & G. Lietaer (Eds.), *Handbook of experiential psychotherapy* (pp. 82–102). New York, NY: Guilford Press.

Yontef, G., & Jacobs, L. (2008). Gestalt therapy. In R. J. Corsini & D. Wedding

(Eds.), *Current psychotherapies* (8th ed., pp. 328–367). Belmont, CA: Thompson.

Young, J. E. (1998). *The Young Schema Questionnaire: Short Form*. Accessed online at: http://home.sprynet.com/sprynet/schema/ysqs1.htm

Young-Mason, J. (2001). Understanding suffering and compassion. *Cross Currents, 51*(3), 347–356.

Yuen, E. Y., Wei, J., Liu, W., Zhong, P., Li, X., & Yan, Z. (2012). Repeated stress causes cognitive impairment by suppressing glutamate receptor expression and function in prefrontal cortex. *Neuron, 73*(5), 962–977. doi:10.1016/j.neuron.2011.12.033

Zaeri, S., & Zaeri, N. (2015). The effect of progressive muscle relaxation training on perceived stress of working women having psychosomatic symptoms. *Avicenna Journal of Phytomedicine, 5*, 150.

Zaslav, M. R. (1998). Shame-related states of mind in psychotherapy. *Journal of Psychotherapy Practice and Research, 7*(2), 154–166.

Zeglin, R., Van Dam, D., & Hergenrather, K. C. (2017, Oct. 2). An introduction to proposed human sexuality counseling competencies. *International Journal for the Advancement of Counselling*, https://link.springer.com/article/10.1007/s10447-017-9314-y

Zhang, J. (2007). A cultural look at information and communication technologies in Eastern education. *Education Technology Research Development, 55*, 301–314. doi:10/1007/s11423-007-9040-y

Zimet, D. M., & Jacob, T. (2001). Influences of marital conflict on child adjustment: Review of theory and research. *Clinical Child and Family Psychology Review, 4*(4), 319–335.

Zimmerman, M., Rothschild, L., & Chelminski, I. (2005). The prevalence of DSM-IV personality disorder in psychiatric patients. *American Journal of Psychiatry, 162*, 1911–1918.

Zodhiates, S. (1984). *May I divorce and remarry?* Chattanooga, TN: AMG.

Zonnebelt-Smeenge, S. J., & De Vries, R. C. (2006). *Traveling through grief: Learning to live again after the death of a loved one*. Grand Rapids: Baker.v

About the Contributors

Lynne M. Baker, PhD, (The University of Queensland) is a confident and accomplished speaker, skilled in working with small interactive groups and also larger audiences. Over a period of more than three decades, she has acquired an extensive range of teaching and lecturing experience at primary, college, and university levels. As a counselor, Dr. Baker spent some years with Salvo Care Line assisting clients in a variety of areas including domestic violence. She provides supervision and conducts domestic violence training seminars. Dr. Baker expresses a deep concern for those women whose commitment to their Christian faith may present a challenge in finding release from the trauma of domestic violence. Her book *Counselling Christian Women on How to Deal with Domestic Violence* confronts the reality of domestic violence and has the capacity to engender hope within women whose lives have been shattered by the impact of that violence. She is also the winner of the Caleb Prize (nonfiction) for her thought-provoking book *Counselling Christian Women*.

Amanda M. Blackburn, PsyD, is the Dean of Students and Associate Professor of Counseling at Richmont University in Atlanta. She is also a Licensed Professional Counselor and Licensed Psychologist. She received her PsyD and MA from Wheaton College and her BA from Asbury College. Her specializations include adolescent and adult women's development, interpersonal relationships, marriage, infertility and adoption, grief, spiritual issues, depression, and anxiety. She is a member of ACA, LP-CAGA, APA, and CAPS.

Todd Bowman, PhD, is currently serving as an Associate Professor of Counseling at Indiana Wesleyan University in addition to working as the Director of the SATP Institute. Dr. Bowman received his doctorate in Counseling Psychology from Oklahoma State University in 2008 and has been practicing professional counseling since that time. During his time at OSU, he served as the Director of the Nazarene Student Center. Dr. Bowman developed the SATP program in 2011 at MidAmerica Nazarene University, and it remains the only Higher Learning Commission accredited and United States Department of Education recognized sexual addiction training for mental health professionals. He continues to write and present locally, nationally, and internationally on topics related to sexual health and sexually addictive behavior, including the publication of his first book, *Angry Birds*

& Killer Bees: Talking to Your Kids about Sex (Beacon Hill Press, 2013). In addition to his specialized work assessing, diagnosing, and treating adults and adolescents with sexual addictions and attachment related concerns, Dr. Bowman has specialized training is in stress management, anxiety reduction, and other affective regulation methods, as well as psychological assessment. He operates from a relational-existential perspective in his work and regularly incorporates attachment, developmental, and neurobiological perspectives as appropriate.

Fredrick A. DiBlasio, PhD, LCSW-C, is an author, professor, researcher, and social worker/therapist. Recognized for his pioneering work in the clinical use of forgiveness, he has published early articles on forgiveness that present some of the first empirical research and conceptual clinical formulations. He serves on the board of the International Forgiveness Institute and the Foundation of Spirituality and Medicine. He was awarded major research grants for an experimental study on forgiveness between marital partners. His work in forgiveness treatment has received attention in many national newspapers, such as the *New York Times*, the *Chicago Tribune*, the *Washington Post*, and magazines, such as *Psychology Today*, and featured on ABCs *20/20* program (twice), the *Good Morning America Show*, and other televised programs. In addition to his work in forgiveness, he has published in well-respected journals and presented nationally on issues involving Christianity, family therapy, personality disorders,

and adolescent behavior. He is currently full professor at the School of Social Work, University of Maryland.

Fernando Garzon, PsyD, is a professor in the School of Psychology and Counseling at Regent University. His research and writing interests focus on investigating spiritual interventions in clinical practice and lay Christian counseling approaches in the church (e.g., Freedom in Christ, Transformation Prayer Ministry) and evaluating counselor education practices in spirituality. His professional experiences encompasses outpatient practice, managed care, hospital, pastoral care, and church settings. Dr. Garzon has written in the areas of Christian interventions research, inner healing prayer, multicultural issues, the teaching of Christian spirituality in counseling, and lay counseling models of ministry.

Heather Davediuk Gingrich, PhD, is a counselor, scholar, teacher, and former missionary. She is professor of counseling at Denver Seminary and maintains a small private practice working with complex trauma survivors. She is the author of *Restoring the Shattered Self*, coauthor of *Skills for Effective Counseling*, and coeditor and contributor to *Treating Trauma in Christian Counseling*. Dr. Gingrich began counseling over thirty-five years ago in Canada and continued in the Philippines where she counseled, taught, and completed her doctoral studies on complex trauma. Dr. Gingrich continues her international involvements with the Institute for International Care and

Counsel at Belhaven University, as well as adjunct teaching at the Asia Graduate School of Theology in the Philippines and seminaries in Guatemala, Sri Lanka, and Singapore. She also conducts mental health assessments for missionary candidates. Dr. Gingrich is a member of the International Society for the Study of Trauma and Dissociation, the Trauma Psychology Division of the American Psychological Association, the Christian Association for Psychological Studies, and the American Association for Marriage and Family Therapy. Her scholarly work focuses on understanding and working with those who have histories of child abuse and other forms of relational trauma, particularly as they relate to issues of Christian faith and spirituality. She and her husband, Fred, have two adult sons and are raising their grandson.

Rev. Stephen P. Greggo, PsyD, is Professor of Counseling at Trinity Evangelical Divinity School (Deerfield, IL) and Director of Professional Practice for CCAHope (www.ccahope.com). He is a counselor educator, ordained minister, and licensed psychologist. Dr. Greggo has published with InterVarsity Press as the coeditor of *Counseling and Christianity: Five Approaches* (2012), author of *Trekking toward Wholeness: A Resource for Care Group Leaders* (2008), and the forthcoming *Assessment in Christian Perspective: Craftsmanship and Connection.* He has been blessed to teach internationally in Kiev, Manila, and São Paulo. For play, he enjoys hiking, traveling, the outdoors, and his lively Labrador retrievers.

Kevin Hull, PhD, owns and operates Hull and Associates, P.A., a multidisciplinary counseling practice in Lakeland, Florida. He has been in practice for the past sixteen years as a Licensed Mental Health Counselor. Dr. Hull specializes in using play therapy with Autism Spectrum Disorder, in addition to working with families and young adults. Dr. Hull has written several professional books, a novel, and numerous chapters related to play therapy and the Autism Spectrum Disorder. Dr. Hull received his PhD from Liberty University. He enjoys spending time with his wife, Wendy, their four children, and one grandchild. Additionally, he enjoys biking, swimming, golf, and going to the beach.

Ian F. Jones, PhD, PhD, is Professor of Counseling at New Orleans Baptist Theological Seminary, where he is chairman of the Division of Church and Community Ministries and holds the Baptist Community Ministries' Chair of Pastoral Counseling. His previous positions include Assistant Dean of the Division of Psychology and Counseling at Southwestern Baptist Theological Seminary and Director of the Baptist Marriage and Family Counseling Center, in Fort Worth, Texas. He serves as the Executive Director of the Board of Christian Professional and Pastoral Counselors (BCPPC), International Board of Christian Care (IBCC). He has contributed numerous articles to the field of Christian counseling and has authored *The Counsel of Heaven on Earth: Foundations for Biblical Christian Counseling* (B&H, 2006). He has taught, counseled and done family conferences in the U.S.A., Mexico, Costa Rica, Malaysia, Taiwan, Korea, and Australia. In 2009, he received the Gary R. Collins Award for Academic Excellence in Christian Counseling.

Debbie Laaser, MA, is a licensed marriage and family therapist and cofounder of Faithful & True. She has been involved in recovery with her husband, Mark, for over twenty-nine years. She is committed to helping couples find healing and transforming the pain of sexual addiction and relational betrayal. Debbie counsels women individually and leads therapy groups for women and couples. She is the author of the highly-acclaimed book *Shattered Vows* and together with Mark authored the book *The Seven Desires of Every Heart.*

Mark Laaser, MDiv, PhD, is Founder and President of Faithful and True and the host of *The Men of Valor Program*, Faithful and True's online radio show. He is nationally recognized as the leading authority in the field of sexual addiction and healthy sexuality with more than thirty years of recovery experience. Dr. Laaser lectures around the world and teaches at religious organizations, colleges, universities, and treatment centers. Dr. Laaser has written fifteen books including numerous articles and book chapters. He holds a PhD from the University of Iowa and a divinity degree from Princeton Theological Seminary.

David Lawson, PsyD, is Professor of Professor of Psychology and Counseling, Director of the Psychology and Counselor Education Programs, Orlando Campus.

Dr. Lawson is a graduate of Biola University, where he received his doctorate in clinical psychology. He returned to his home state of Virginia and finished his clinical internship in psychology at the University of Virginia; he was subsequently hired by Liberty University, where he taught for ten years in their counseling program. Dr. Lawson has written articles for the *Journal of Psychology and Christianity*, covering issues of interest related to families, sexuality, and the integration of faith and science. He has worked with the Virginia Psychological Association and has served as a board member of the Christian Association for Psychological Studies (CAPS) and the Lifeline of Central Florida, a suicide prevention hotline. Dr. Lawson has also served as the president of the marriage and family counseling chapter of the Florida Counseling Association. He has reviewed articles for *Communiqué*, the journal of the National Association of School Psychologists, and *The Journal of Counseling and Development,* the journal of the American Counseling Association; he also has served as editor of the online journal *Counseling Connections.* Dr. Lawson has spoken at numerous family conferences and was hired by the Department of Defense to provide marriage enrichment training to their staff. Dr. Lawson has presented numerous times at national conferences such as the American Psychological Association (APA), the American Association for Sex Educators Counselors and Therapists (AASECT), and CAPS. He is married to Amy Lawson, and they have four children. They currently reside in Apopka and attend Renew Church.

Linda Mintle, PhD, is an author, speaker, professor, media personality, and a licensed marriage and family therapist, a licensed clinical social worker, and a national expert on relationships and the psychology of food, weight, and body image. She is host of the *Dr. Linda Mintle Radio Show*. Dr. Mintle has over thirty years of clinical experience with couples, families, and individuals. She is a best-selling author with nineteen book titles to her credit, winner of the Mom's Choice Award, a national news consultant, and featured writer for Beliefnet, and she hosts her own website. Dr. Mintle is a professor with Liberty University's College of Osteopathic Medicine.

Jennifer Ripley, PhD, is a licensed clinical psychologist in the state of Virginia, where she is a professor of psychology and the Director of Clinical Research at the Marriage and Ministry Assessment Training and Empowerment Center at Regent University. She has sat on the board for the Christian Association for Psychological Studies (CAPS) and has served as program chair for the Psychology of Religion division of the American Psychological Association.

Doug Rosenau, EdD, was born to missionary parents in French Equatorial Africa. Dr. Rosenau has passionately been a sexual ambassador, therapist, professor, theologian, and author in evangelical Christianity for the past thirty years. Dr. Rosenau is a licensed psychologist, marriage and family therapist, certified sex therapist, and the author of many books and teaching videos on sexuality from

a Christian worldview including a best seller *A Celebration of Sex*, first published in 1994 and again in 2001. After graduating from Dallas Theological Seminary (ThM), Dr. Rosenau received his doctorate (EdD) from Northern Illinois University and teaches Human Sexuality and Sex Therapy nationally as a popular conference speaker and as a professor at Richmont Graduate University in Atlanta, Georgia. As cofounder of the Christian organization Sexual Wholeness, he has helped to create the Institute for Sexual Wholeness, which trains Christian sex therapists and educators. Dr. Rosenau and his wife, Catherine, live in Atlanta, Georgia.

Steven J. Sandage, PhD, is the Albert and Jessie Danielsen Professor of Psychology of Religion and Theology at Boston University School of Theology and Director of Research at the Danielsen Institute, with a joint appointment in the Department of Psychological and Brain Sciences. He also serves as research director and senior staff psychologist at the Danielsen Institute at Boston University. He has authored many books, including *To Forgive Is Human*, *The Faces of Forgiveness: Searching for Wholeness and Salvation*, *Transforming Spirituality: Integrating Theology and Psychology*, *Forgiveness and Spirituality: A Relational Approach* (APA), and *The Skillful Soul of the Psychotherapist*. Dr. Sandage has authored articles and chapters in areas such as forgiveness and related virtues (e.g., hope, humility, gratitude, and justice), spiritual development, marriage and family therapy, attachment, differentiation of self, intercultural competence, suicidology, and borderline personality treatment. Dr. Sandage is a licensed psychologist with over twenty years of clinical experience in a variety of settings (e.g., private practice, prisons, community mental health, university counseling centers, and inpatient treatment).

E. Nicole Saylor, PsyD, obtained her master's degree and doctorate of psychology at Wheaton College (Illinois). She is an Associate Professor of Human Services at Johnson University in Knoxville. Her practice as a clinical psychologist focuses on therapy, supervision, and preparation and assessment for adoptive parents.

Eric Scalise, PhD, is an author, speak, and former Vice President for Professional Development at AACC and former Department Chair for Counseling Programs at Regent University. Dr. Scalise is also President of Beacon Counseling & Consulting in Tidewater, Virginia. He is an adjunct professor and Senior Editor for both AACC and the Congressional Prayer Caucus Foundation. He is a licensed professional counselor and is a licensed marriage and family therapist with over thirty-seven years of clinical experience. Dr. Scalise specializes in grief and loss, professional and pastoral burnout, compassion fatigue, mood disorders, marriage and family issues, combat trauma and PTSD, addictions and recovery, crisis response, leadership development, life coaching, and lay counselor training. He is a published author with Zondervan, Baker Books, and Harvest House, and a national and international conference speaker. He frequently works with organizations, clinicians, ministry leaders, and churches on a variety of issues. Dr. Scalise and his wife, Donna, have been married for thirty-six years and have twin sons, who are combat veterans, and three grandchildren.

Gary Sibcy II, PhD, is a professor of counselor education and supervision and a Licensed Clinical Psychologist who has educated, trained, and supervised counselors for over fifteen years. Dr. Sibcy has a broad range of research and clinical interests, including the assessment and treatment of childhood disorders, anxiety and trauma disorders, and personality disorders. He also has an interest in the integration of religious beliefs in clinical practice. His current research interests focus on developing and disseminating empirically supported treatments for both children and adults. Dr. Sibcy writes, speaks, and consults nationally and internationally.

Michael Sytsma, PhD, is a Licensed Professional Counselor in the state of Georgia, a Certified Sex Therapist, and a Certified Sexual Addictions Specialist (Trainer level). He is also an ordained minister with the Wesleyan Church and has served as a staff pastor for churches with attendances from thirty to over a thousand. He is currently appointed to Building Intimate Marriages, Inc. by the Wesleyan Church. Michael received his BS in Christian Ministry from Indiana Wesleyan University, an MS in Community Counseling from Georgia State University, and a diploma in Christian counseling from Psychological Studies Institute. Michael also has a

PhD from the University of Georgia in Child and Family Development/Marriage and Family Therapy where he specialized in marital sexual therapy. His dissertation was titled "Sexual Desire Discrepancy in Married Couples." Michael is a cofounder of Sexual Wholeness, Inc.

Andi J. Thacker, PhD, has a Master of Arts in Biblical Counseling from Dallas Theological Seminary and PhD in counselor education and supervision from the University of North Texas. In addition to her teaching responsibilities at DTS, Dr. Thacker maintains a small private practice in which she specializes with children and adolescents and supervises LPC Interns. Dr. Thacker's clinical experience includes working as an inpatient program therapist for the Minirth Christian Program, serving on a mobile crisis outreach team conducting suicide risk assessments, working as a church counselor, and conducting child and adolescent psychoeducational assessments. Dr. Thacker is a Licensed Professional Counselor, a Board Approved Supervisor, a Registered Play Therapist, and a Nationally Certified Counselor. She is married to Chad, and they have two children, Emerson and Will.

Amanda G. Turnquist, MSW, LGSW, is a Licensed Graduate Social Worker (LGSW) in the state of Maryland. Amanda received her undergraduate degree in social work at Eastern University.

She went on to graduate with a master's degree in social work with a clinical concentration and a specialization in health at the School of Social Work, University of Maryland. While at the University, she served as a graduate research assistant for Dr. DiBlasio. After completing her training, she returned home to the Annapolis area. She currently works as an Oncology Social Worker at the Tate Cancer Center in Glen Burnie, Maryland.

Everett Worthington Jr., PhD, received his PhD from the University of Missouri and is a professor at Virginia Commonwealth University. He is a licensed clinical psychologist and former executive director of the Templeton Foundation's Campaign for Forgiveness Research. Worthington has studied forgiveness since the 1980s and has published more than two hundred articles and papers on forgiveness, marriage and family, psychotherapy, and virtue in a wide variety of journals and magazines. He was the founding editor of *Marriage and Family: A Christian Journal* and sits on the editorial boards of several professional journals. He has appeared on *Good Morning America*, CNN, and *The 700 Club* and been featured in award-winning documentary movies on forgiveness such as *The Power of Forgiveness* and *The Big Question*. Dr. Worthington is the author of seventeen books, including *Handbook of Forgiveness, Hope-Focused Marriage Counseling,* and *Forgiving and Reconciling.*

Name Index

Subject Index

Notes

Notes

Notes

Notes

Notes

Notes

Notes

Notes